EDEXCEL
AS/A LEVEL
HISTORY

*Active*Book included

Cobb

## Paper 1&2:

# Democracies in change: Britain and the USA in the 20th century

Stuart Clayton | Derrick Murphy | Jane Barnard | Oliver Bullock |
Series editor: Rosemary Rees

ALWAYS LEARNING

PEARSON

Published by Pearson Education Limited, 80 Strand, London, WC2R 0RL.

www.pearsonschoolsandfecolleges.co.uk

Copies of official specifications for all Edexcel qualifications may be found on the website: www.edexcel.com



Designed by Elizabeth Arnoux for Pearson

Typeset and illustrated by Phoenix Photosetting, Chatham, Kent

Produced by Out of House Publishing



Cover design by Malena Wilson-Max for Pearson

Cover photo/illustration © Getty Images: Peter Skingley/AFP

The rights of Jane Barnard, Oliver Bullock, Stuart Clayton and Derrick Murphy to be identified as authors of this work have been asserted by them in accordance with the Copyright, Designs and Patents Act 1988.

First published 2015

20

10 9 8 7

**British Library Cataloguing in Publication Data**

A catalogue record for this book is available from the British Library

ISBN 978 1 447 985297



Printed in Great Britain by Bell and Bain Ltd, Glasgow

**Websites**

Pearson Education Limited is not responsible for the content of any external internet sites. It is essential for tutors to preview each website before using it in class so as to ensure that the URL is still accurate, relevant and appropriate. We suggest that tutors bookmark useful websites and consider enabling students to access them through the school/college intranet.

**A note from the publisher**

In order to ensure that this resource offers high-quality support for the associated Pearson qualification, it has been through a review process by the awarding body. This process confirms that; this resource fully covers the teaching and learning content of the specification or part of a specification at which it is aimed. It also confirms that it demonstrates an appropriate balance between the development of subject skills, knowledge and understanding, in addition to preparation for assessment.

Endorsement does not cover any guidance on assessment activities or processes (e.g. practice questions or advice on how to answer assessment questions), included in the resource nor does it prescribe any particular approach to the teaching or delivery of a related course.

While the publishers have made every attempt to ensure that advice on the qualification and its assessment is accurate, the official specification and associated assessment guidance materials are the only authoritative source of information and should always be referred to for definitive guidance.

Pearson examiners have not contributed to any sections in this resource relevant to examination papers for which they have responsibility.

Examiners will not use endorsed resources as a source of material for any assessment set by Pearson.

Endorsement of a resource does not mean that the resource is required to achieve this Pearson qualification, nor does it mean that it is the only suitable material available to support the qualification, and any resource lists produced by the awarding body shall include this and other appropriate resources.

# Contents

# How to use this book

## STRUCTURE

This book covers Route H of the Edexcel A Level and AS Level History qualifications. Route H consists of three papers which are linked by the theme '**Democracies in change: Britain and the USA in the 20th century**'.

- Britain transformed, 1918–97
- The USA, c1920–55: boom, bust and recovery
- The USA, 1955–92: conformity and challenge

To take Route H, you must study Paper 1, plus **one** of the two Paper 2 options. You do not need to study the other Paper 2 topic for your exam, but you might like to read it for interest – it deals with similar themes to the topics you are studying.

If you are studying for A Level History, you will also need to study a Paper 3 option and produce coursework in order to complete your qualification. All Paper 3 options are covered by other textbooks in this series.

## AS LEVEL OR A LEVEL?

This book is designed to support students studying both the Edexcel AS Level and A Level qualifications. The content required for both qualifications is identical, so all the material in the papers you are studying is relevant, whichever qualification you are aiming for.

The questions you will be asked in the exam differ for the two different qualifications, so we have included separate exam-style questions and exam preparation sections. If you are studying for an AS Level, you should use the exam-style questions and exam sections highlighted in blue. If you are studying for an A Level, you should use the exam-style questions and exam sections highlighted in green.

**AS Level Exam-Style Question Section A**

Was the Second World War the main reason for changes in social welfare provision between 1918 and 1979? Explain your answer. (20 marks)

**Tip**

*This question covers a broad time period, so be selective in the arguments you deploy and ensure you include material from the beginning and the end of the period.*

**A Level Exam-Style Question Section B**

'The economic boom of the 1920s was due more to a consumer boom than to technological advances.' How far do you agree with this statement? (20 marks)

**Tip**

*You need to compare and assess the two factors in the question rather than merely describe the boom with a concluding assessment.*

The 'Preparing for your exams' section at the end of each paper contains sample answers of different standards, with comments on how weaker answers could be improved. Make sure you look at the right section for the exam you are planning to take.

## FEATURES

### Extend your knowledge

These features contain additional information that will help you gain a deeper understanding of the topic. This could be a short biography of an important person, extra background information about an event, an alternative interpretation, or even a research idea that you could follow up. Information in these boxes is not essential to your exam success, but still provides insights of value.

**EXTEND YOUR KNOWLEDGE**

**The Wall Street Crash**

On 28-29 October 1929, the American stock market saw $30 billion wiped off the value of stocks and shares, almost a quarter of the total value of all assets. The crash was due to fears that shares were over-priced: owners tried to sell them before they lost any more value. The price of shares had risen steadily throughout the 1920s but a slowdown in sales in important industries such as cars and houses, together with concern about the extent of borrowing to pay for shares, led to a loss of confidence in the market. The collapse in share prices meant many borrowers could not repay loans to banks. American banks recalled international loans in an often unsuccessful bid to avoid going bust. The banking crisis, together with a sharp fall in demand for imports, meant the economic depression spread throughout the world.

## Knowledge check activities

These activities are designed to check that you have understood the material that you have just studied. They might also ask you questions about the sources and extracts in the section to check that you have studied and analysed them thoroughly.

**ACTIVITY**
**KNOWLEDGE CHECK**

**The impact of the New Deal on ethnic minorities**

1 Identify the ways the New Deal affected the lives of:

a Black Americans

b Native Americans

c Hispanic Americans.

2 On balance, do you think the New Deal improved the lives of different ethnic minorities within the USA? Explain your answer.

## Summary activities

At the end of each chapter, you will find summary activities. These are tasks designed to help you think about the key topic you have just studied as a whole. They may involve selecting and organising key information or analysing how things changed over time. You might want to keep your answers to these questions safe – they are handy for revision.

**ACTIVITY**
**SUMMARY**

**Society in transition, 1918–79**

1 For each decade between 1920 and 1979, give a school report-style grade (with A the best down to E the worst) to Britain for the following categories: liberalisation; progress for women; race relations. Briefly explain your grades, but pay particular attention to the A and E grades: what made them so good or so bad?

2 How could links be drawn between the changes in class, liberalism, female progress and race relations? Links could be considered in terms of shared causes or interrelations between the different changes.

3 Which would you argue was the most significant change in Britain between 1918 and 1979: changes in class relations, liberalisation, female progress or improved race relations?

## Thinking Historically activities

These activities are found throughout the book and are designed to develop your understanding of history, especially around the key concepts of evidence, interpretations, causation and change. Each activity is designed to challenge a conceptual barrier that might be holding you back. This is linked to a map of conceptual barriers developed by experts. You can look up the map and find out which barrier each activity challenges by downloading the conceptual map from this website: www.pearsonschools.co.uk/historyprogressionapproach.

conceptual map reference

**Cause and consequence (6a)**

**Seeing things differently**

Different times and places have different beliefs about how the world works, how human societies should be governed and the best way to achieve economic prosperity. Other people's ideas can be radically different from our own. It is important for the historian to take this into account when considering past attitudes and be aware of the dangers of judging them against our personal beliefs and ideas from our own time.

Reread Source 2 and answer the following questions.

1 What do you think gave rise to the notion of Black Power as put forward by Stokely Carmichael?

2 If Carmichael had known how events would progress to the present day, do you think he would have changed his attitude?

3 Carmichael's attitudes to civil rights and the place of black people in the world are different from those held by other black leaders in United States, like Malcolm X. Why do you think that they are different?

4 How important is it for historians to deal with events in the context of the beliefs and values people held at the time, as well as seeing them as part of a greater pattern? Explain your answer.

## Getting the most from your online ActiveBook

This book comes with three years' access to ActiveBook* – an online, digital version of your textbook. Follow the instructions printed on the inside front cover to start using your ActiveBook.

Your ActiveBook is the perfect way to personalise your learning as you progress through your AS/A Level History course. You can:

- access your content online, anytime, anywhere
- use the inbuilt highlighting and annotation tools to personalise the content and make it really relevant to you.

Highlight tool – use this to pick out key terms or topics so you are ready and prepared for revision.

Annotations tool – use this to add your own notes, for example links to your wider reading, such as websites or other files. Or, make a note to remind yourself about work that you need to do.

*For new purchases only. If the access code has already been revealed, it may no longer be valid. If you have bought this textbook secondhand, the code may already have been used by the first owner of the book.

# Introduction AS/A Level History

## WHY HISTORY MATTERS

History is about people and people are complex, fascinating, frustrating and a whole lot of other things besides. This is why history is probably the most comprehensive and certainly one of the most intriguing subjects there is. History can also be inspiring and alarming, heartening and disturbing, a story of progress and civilisation and of catastrophe and inhumanity.

History's importance goes beyond the subject's intrinsic interest and appeal. Our beliefs and actions, our cultures, institutions and ways of living, our languages and means of making sense of ourselves are all shaped by the past. If we want to fully understand ourselves now, and to understand our possible futures, we have no alternative but to think about history.

History is a discipline as well as a subject matter. Making sense of the past develops qualities of mind that are valuable to anyone who wants to seek the truth and think clearly and intelligently about the most interesting and challenging intellectual problem of all: other people. Learning history is learning a powerful way of knowing.

## WHAT IS HISTORY?

**Figure 1** Fragment of a black granite statue possibly portraying the Roman politician Mark Antony.

History is a way of constructing knowledge about the world through research, interpretation, argument and debate.

Building historical knowledge involves identifying the traces of the past that exist in the present – in people's memories, in old documents, photographs and other remains, and in objects and artefacts ranging from bullets and lipsticks, to field systems and cities. Historians interrogate these traces and *ask questions* that transform traces into *sources of evidence* for knowledge claims about the past.

Historians aim to understand what happened in the past by *explaining why* things happened as they did. Explaining why involves trying to understand past people and their beliefs, intentions and actions. It also involves explaining the causes and evaluating the effects of large-scale changes in the past and exploring relationships between what people aimed to do, the contexts that shaped what was possible and the outcomes and consequences of actions.

Historians also aim to *understand change* in the past. People, states of affairs, ideas, movements and civilisations come into being in time, grow, develop, and ultimately decline and disappear. Historians aim to identify and compare change and continuity in the past, to measure the rate at which things change and to identify the types of change that take place. Change can be slow or sudden. It can also be understood as progressive or regressive – leading to the improvement or worsening of a situation or state of affairs. How things change and whether changes are changes for the better are two key issues that historians frequently debate.

Debate is the essence of history. Historians write arguments to support their knowledge claims and historians argue with each other to test and evaluate interpretations of the past. Historical knowledge itself changes and develops. On the one hand, new sources of knowledge and new methods of research cause *historical interpretations* to change. On the other hand, the questions that historians ask change with time and new questions produce new answers. Although the past is dead and gone, the interpretation of the past has a past, present and future.

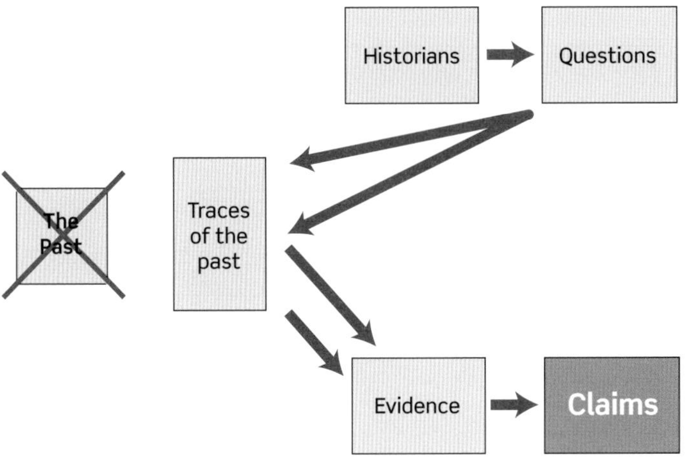


**Figure 2** Constructing knowledge about the past.

## THE CHALLENGES OF LEARNING HISTORY

Like all other Advanced Level subjects, A Level and AS Level history are difficult – that is why they are called 'advanced'. Your advanced level studies will build on knowledge and understanding of history that you developed at GCSE and at Key Stage 3 – ideas like 'historical sources', 'historical evidence' and 'cause', for example. You will need to do a lot of reading and writing to progress in history. Most importantly, you will need to do a lot of thinking, and thinking about your thinking. This book aims to support you in developing both your knowledge and your understanding.

### QUOTES ABOUT HISTORY

'Historians are dangerous people. They are capable of upsetting everything. They must be directed.'

Nikita Khrushchev

'To be ignorant of what occurred before you were born is to remain forever a child. For what is the worth of human life, unless it is woven into the life of our ancestors by the records of history?'

Marcus Tullius Cicero

History is challenging in many ways. On the one hand, it is challenging to build up the range and depth of knowledge that you need to understand the past at an advanced level. Learning about the past involves mastering new and unfamiliar concepts arising from the past itself (such as the Inquisition, Laudianism, *Volksgemeinschaft*) and building up levels of knowledge that are both detailed and well organised. This book covers the key content of the topics that you are studying for your examination and provides a number of features to help you build and organise what you know – for example, diagrams, timelines and definitions of key terms. You will need to help yourself too, of course, adding to your knowledge through further reading, building on the foundations provided by this book.

Another challenge is to develop understandings of the discipline of history. You will have to learn to think historically about evidence, cause, change and interpretations and also to write historically, in a way that develops clear and supported argument.

Historians think with evidence in ways that differ from how we often think in everyday life. In history, as Figure 2 shows, we cannot go and 'see for ourselves' because the past no longer exists. Neither can we normally rely on 'credible witnesses' to tell us 'the truth' about 'what happened'. People in the past did not write down 'the truth' for our benefit. They often had clear agendas when creating the traces that remain and, as often as not, did not themselves know 'the truth' about complex historical events.

A root of the word 'history' is the Latin word *historia*, one of whose meanings is 'enquiry' or 'finding out'. Learning history means learning to ask questions and interrogate traces, and then to reason about what the new knowledge you have gained means. This book draws on historical scholarship for its narrative and contents. It also draws on research on the nature of historical thinking and on the challenges that learning history can present for students. Throughout the book you will find 'Thinking Historically' activities designed to support the development of your thinking.

You will also find – as you would expect given the nature of history – that the book is full of questions. This book aims to help you build your understandings of the content, contexts and concepts that you will need to advance both your historical knowledge and your historical understanding, and to lay strong foundations for the future development of both.

Dr Arthur Chapman, UCL Institute of Education

# Britain transformed, 1918–97

Since around 1750, change in Britain has largely been driven by technological innovation. Steam-powered machines led to the creation of large factories near the source of the raw materials needed for production. Rural textile workers, unable to compete with cheap factory-made cloth, moved from their cottages to the new urban areas that sprang up around industrial centres. The growth of a large, urban working class greatly disrupted the old order and created new problems for the ruling class to deal with, from sanitation to mass political protest. Aristocrats, who had dominated rural societies for generations, increasingly found they were unable to control an urban society; they either had to fight to preserve their exclusive power and privilege or reform the way they ruled. In most of Europe, aristocrats successfully fought to maintain their power until they were brought down by the cataclysmic First World War. The lack of experience of **democracy** before 1918 was an important reason why non-democratic **fascism** and **communism** became so influential in continental Europe after this date.

In Britain, and in the USA, only a tiny minority of people advocated fascism or communism; at no stage between 1918 and 1979 was democracy in either country in any danger. There are many reasons why democracy was so strong in Britain compared to the rest of Europe; one key reason is that the ruling classes were quicker (though far from quick!) to respond constructively to industrial problems and pressures.

## KEY TERMS

**Democracy**
Literally 'rule by the people'. Britain and the USA are 'representative democracies' because the people elect representatives (MPs in Britain) to rule on their behalf.

**Fascism**
An ideology in which the needs and wishes of individuals are subservient to those of the state. This prioritisation justifies censorship, glorification of leaders and repression of the people. In practice, many 20th-century 'communist' states were essentially fascist.

**Communism**
A socio-economic system prophesied by German philosopher Karl Marx (1818-83). He predicted a worldwide revolution where the workers would seize power and the means of production. After the revolution, everything would be owned by the people, who would work for the common good rather than for profit. Marx predicted that the central government would wither away in such a society. There has never been a genuinely communist state.

**1918** - British victory in First World War
Representation of the People Act increases the electorate by seven million and includes women for the first time

**1926** - General Strike takes place in May

**1931** - 'National Government' coalition is formed to deal with the Great Depression

**1947** - India and Pakistan gain independence from the British Empire

**1953** - Coronation of Queen Elizabeth II

**1966** - England host and win football World Cup

**1979** - Margaret Thatcher becomes first female prime minister after Conservatives win election

1908-1911

**1908–1911** - Series of important Liberal reforms including Pensions Act and National Insurance Act

1921

**1921** - Irish Free State gains independence from the UK

1928

**1928** - Reform Act grants women the vote on the same terms as men

1939–45

**1939–45** - Second World War: Britain fights and defeats Nazi Germany with help from the USSR and USA

1948

**1948** - Launch of the National Health Service

1956

**1956** - Suez Crisis

1973

**1973** - Britain joins the European Economic Community (EEC)

1989

**1989** - Cold War ends

The **Whigs**, and more grudgingly the **Tories**, introduced a wide range of Acts in the 19th century to improve living and working conditions. Just before the First World War, parliament passed a series of Acts that together provided a safety net for the sick and injured, the poor, and the vulnerable old and young. The aristocrats and super-rich in both parties also shared more of their power more widely: whereas in 1830 only two percent of men could vote for MPs, by 1884 a series of Reform Acts had increased this to 66 percent. These reforms were not entirely altruistic: they were passed, often in the face of stiff resistance, for short-term political gain or to prevent the sort of revolution that swept away the ruling classes in France in 1789 and Russia in 1917.

The pace of technological change increased in the 20th century. New products and processes changed the sorts of jobs people did, increased their productivity at work (allowing for higher wages and more free time), improved life expectancy and promoted globalisation.

To aid historical analysis, these changes have been divided into four themes: political and economic change; changes in welfare provision; social change; and changes in the standard of living. The first two are primarily concerned with governmental attempts to cope with change, while the latter two assess the extent and impact of change on the British people.

- Now that working-class men (and some women after 1918) had the vote, what could prevent the democratic demise of privileged power? Would **capitalism**, which most benefited the rich, be swept away by **socialism**, which put the needs of the working man first? How would the major parties respond to this new political environment?
- Now that the government had begun to directly intervene in people's lives, how far should this process go? How far should the government be responsible for the welfare of the people? How would Britain afford the new costs of pensions, housing and health insurance, *and* maintain its global role in charge of the largest empire in history?
- How far would the British people change their thoughts, habits and customs in this new, increasingly democratic era? In what ways did women and ethnic minorities contribute and respond to these changes?
- How would the British use their increased amount of wealth and free time? How did this affect British popular culture?

The divisions between themes are inevitably somewhat artificial. As you study this unit, be aware that each theme strongly interacted with and affected the others.

## KEY TERMS

**Whigs**
A group of MPs who rejected James II's right to succeed to the throne and supported the rival claim of his Protestant son-in-law, William of Orange. They sympathised with the gradual reform of exclusive privilege in politics and with tolerance of religious non-conformism. They were renamed the Liberal Party in 1859.

**Tories**
A group of MPs who supported James II's right to succeed to the throne in 1685 despite his open Catholicism. The Tories became closely identified with the rights and privileges of the Crown, the aristocracy and the Church of England. They were renamed the Conservative Party in 1834.

**Capitalism**
An economic system where the allocation of resources is decided more by a free market than by government planning. Resources tend to be owned by individuals and private companies rather than by the government.

**Socialism**
A political and economic system that puts the needs of society as a whole above the needs of a particular group of individuals.

# A changing political and economic environment, 1918–79

**KEY QUESTIONS**

- To what extent did the political landscape change between 1918 and 1979?
- In what ways and with what success did governments deal with economic change between 1918 and 1979?
- How effectively did governments respond to changes in the workplace between 1918 and 1979?

## INTRODUCTION

The political and economic climate in Britain changed dramatically between 1918 and 1979. For over 200 years, the Conservative and Liberal parties (formerly known as the Tories and Whigs) had dominated British politics. As the gap between rich and poor continued to widen, this dominance was rapidly brought to an end in the first half of the 20th century by the rise of the Labour Party, which appealed to the working classes.

It was changes in the economic environment that altered the traditional political map of Britain so much. With industrialisation in the 19th century came an increase in **trade union** membership, and in 1900 the Labour Party was founded to represent union interests in parliament. The huge numbers of votes that could be guaranteed from the working classes and trade union members meant that the Labour Party became a serious political force in a short space of time, and Ramsay MacDonald became the first Labour prime minister in 1924. The link between economic and political change continued until 1979.

**KEY TERM**

**Trade union**
An organisation formed to protect the rights of workers in a particular trade, industry or profession.

Perhaps the biggest challenge to any government in the period was the aftermath of the Second World War. Massive reconstruction and the demobilisation of soldiers was required. In 1945, the British people rejected the wartime leadership of the Conservative leader Winston Churchill in favour of Labour's Clement Attlee. This marked another change in the political landscape, as Attlee pursued moderate socialist policies with the aim of creating full employment and a welfare state with free healthcare for all.

Successive Labour and Conservative governments attempted to manage the economy between 1945 and 1979 with varied success. These years became known as the 'consensus' years because both parties broadly agreed with each other on economic policy. The prevailing belief in both parties that full employment was more important than tackling rising prices (inflation) was shattered in 1979 when Margaret Thatcher was elected prime minister.

**1918** – Representation of the People Act increases electorate by seven million

David Lloyd George's coalition wins the December 'Coupon Election'

**1921** – Irish Free State gains independence from the UK

**1922** – Lloyd George coalition breaks up

Bonar Law's Conservatives win November election

**1923** – Baldwin replaces Bonar Law as PM and leader of Conservatives

Conservatives win December election, Labour gain more seats than Liberals for first time

**1924** – January: MacDonald becomes first Labour PM, leading minority government for nine months

Conservatives win October election, Baldwin becomes PM for second time

**1926** – May: General Strike

**1928** – Reform Act grants women vote on same terms as men

**1929** – Labour win May election, MacDonald becomes PM for second time

**1931** – MacDonald forms 'National Government' coalition to deal with Great Depression

National Government wins two-thirds of vote in October election

**1935** – National Government wins election with 53.7 percent of vote, Baldwin becomes PM for third time

**1937** – Baldwin steps down, Chamberlain becomes PM

**1939–45** – Second World War

**1940** – Chamberlain resigns, Churchill becomes PM

**1945** – Labour win July election with 47.8 percent of vote, Attlee becomes PM

1915 | 1920 | 1925 | 1930 | 1935 | 1940 | 1945

# TO WHAT EXTENT DID THE POLITICAL LANDSCAPE CHANGE BETWEEN 1918 AND 1979?

At the start of 1918, women could not vote in general elections and the Labour Party had yet to make a dent in the traditional tussle between the Conservative and Liberal parties. By the end of 1979, Britain had a female prime minister and the Liberals had less than two percent of seats in parliament compared to Labour's 42 percent. However, Britain remained a parliamentary democracy dominated by two parties, with the Conservatives performing consistently well in the polls. Before the Great War, and after 1979, the two major parties significantly opposed one another on many issues; yet, for a good deal of this period, they largely agreed on policy direction and between 1915–22 and 1931–45 formed coalition governments (something not repeated until 2010–15). A good deal of the change, and the uniqueness of the political landscape during this period, must be attributed to the momentous impact of two world wars and the hard economic circumstances of the 1930s and the years after the Second World War.

## Changing party fortunes, 1918-31

As demonstrated by the tables below, the major political change between 1918 and 1931 was the replacement of the Liberals by the Labour Party as the main rival to the Conservatives. This was a major change of long-lasting importance: the Liberals were doomed to third place for the rest of the century.

| Period in office | Prime Minister | Party/parties in office | Reason for fall |
|---|---|---|---|
| December 1918 - October 1922 | David Lloyd George | Liberal-Conservative coalition | Conservatives ended coalition |
| October 1922 - May 1923 | Andrew Bonar Law | Conservative | Ill health |
| May 1923 - January 1924 | Stanley Baldwin | Conservative | Lost vote of confidence |
| January 1924 - November 1924 | Ramsay MacDonald | Labour | Lost election |
| November 1924 - June 1929 | Stanley Baldwin | Conservative | Lost election |
| June 1929 - August 1931 | Ramsay MacDonald | Labour | Party division over policies to cope with the Great Depression |

**Figure 1.1** British governments 1918-1931.

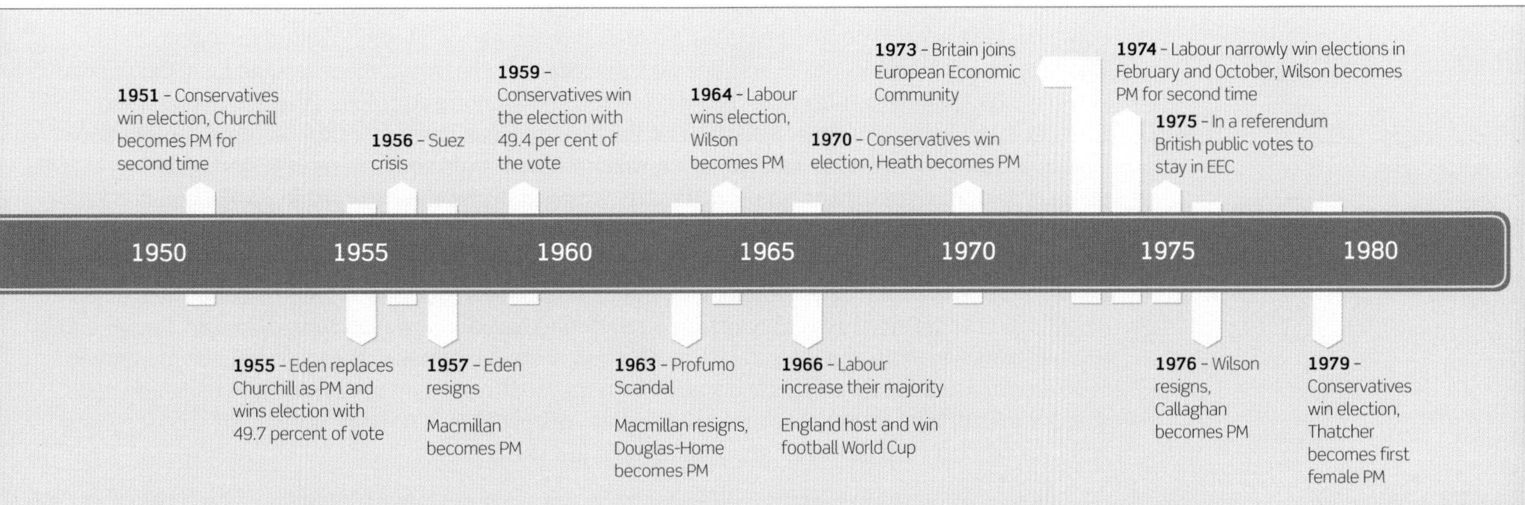

| Election year | Seats (% of votes) | | |
|---|---|---|---|
| | Conservatives | Liberals | Labour |
| December 1910 | 272 (46.3) | 272 (43.9) | 42 (7.1) |
| December 1923 | 258 (38.1) | 159 (29.6) | 191 (30.5) |
| October 1924 | 419 (48.3) | 40 (17.6) | 151 (33.0) |
| May 1929 | 260 (38.2) | 59 (23.4) | 288 (37.1) |

**Figure 1.2** Results of a selection of general elections between 1910 and 1929, chosen to demonstrate major changes in the political landscape. Results of other elections in the period are included in tables below.

## The decline and fall of the Liberal Party: democracy and division

Historians have put forward a range of arguments to explain this change in the political landscape. In 1936, George Dangerfield argued that the Liberal Party was doomed even before the First World War due to the failure of liberalism to cope with the threat of trade union strikes, suffragette militancy and problems in Northern Ireland. In 1986, George Bernstein drew attention to the failures of the party to adapt to more class-based voting habits (for example, working-class men were overwhelmingly rejected as parliamentary candidates by the Liberals). However, most historians reject these views and argue that the Liberals would have been able to adapt and survive had it not been for events after 1914. The rise of 'New Liberalism', with direct state intervention to support the vulnerable poor, sick, young and old, could have maintained working-class support and kept Labour in third place.

Writing in 1966, Trevor Wilson argued that the Liberal Party was healthy in 1914, but was run over by 'a rampant omnibus' (the war). Liberals had traditionally disliked excessive government interference in the economy and in people's lives, yet the war forced Liberals to take illiberal measures, such as economic controls, conscription and rationing, to avoid defeat. David Lloyd George, in favour of such measures, ousted the more traditional Liberal Henry Asquith as prime minister of a coalition government in December 1916. Many Liberals saw Lloyd George as a traitor to the party and continued to support Asquith as Liberal leader: the party was split and failed to reunite in time for the 1918 election.

The 'Maurice debate' in 1918 cemented the personal bitterness between Asquith and Lloyd George. General Maurice wrote a public letter that accused Lloyd George of lying to parliament about the numbers of British troops on the Western Front; Asquith led the attack on Lloyd George when the issue was discussed in parliament, but failed to oust him as prime minister.

Lloyd George was forced into the curious position of reliance on Conservative support in what became known as the 'Coupon Election'. The Coupon was a letter issued by Lloyd George and Conservative leader Andrew Bonar Law to parliamentary candidates who stood for the coalition. The Conservatives, who had not won an election since 1900, felt they needed the prestige of the 'man who won the war' to boost their votes, while Lloyd George needed Conservative support because so many Liberal Members of Parliament (MPs) stayed loyal to Asquith. The Liberals therefore emerged from the war divided into two camps, a situation they struggled to recover from.

Historians are divided on the significance of the 1918 Representation of the People Act: for some it paved the way for the rise of the Labour Party at the expense of the Liberals, while others argue it had only a limited impact. The Act meant that all men over the age of 21 were allowed to vote, with no wealth or property restrictions (it was deemed unacceptable that many men who had fought in the war would not be allowed to vote under the terms of the 1884 Reform Act). The 1918 Act also allowed some women to vote in a general election for the first time as a reward for their wartime contribution. Until 1928, there were several restrictions on which women could vote, the most important being that they had to be aged 30 or over. Despite these restrictions, women now made up 43 percent of an electorate that had trebled in size, from 7.7 million in 1910 to 21.4 million in 1918. The industrial working classes now made up 80 percent of the electorate. In the 1960s, Henry Pelling argued that the Labour Party was bound to benefit from the franchise extension due to a growing tribal working-class identification with Party issues, something he referred to as 'Labourism'. However, Duncan Tanner and Michael Hart's analysis of the electorate reveals only a small increase in the working-class majority in 1918, from 76 to 80 percent. This is because the removal of residency restrictions for voting affected younger men of all classes rather than just manual workers. They also point out that the working-class vote was split between all three parties throughout the 1920s.

Lastly, working-class women were more likely to vote Conservative, perhaps due to a perception that they stood more for stability and family values.

| Election year December 1918 | Seats (% of votes) | | | |
|---|---|---|---|---|
| | Conservative | Liberal | Labour | Total |
| Coalition | 335 (32.6) | 133 (13.5) | 10 (1.5) | 478 (47.6) |
| Non-coalition | 23 (3.4) | 28 (12.1) | 63 (22.2) | 114 (37.7) |

| Election year November 1922 | Seats (% of votes) | | | |
|---|---|---|---|---|
| | Conservatives | Lloyd George Liberal | Asquith Liberal | Labour |
| | 345 (38.2) | 62 (11.6) | 54 (17.5) | 142 (29.2) |

**Figure 1.3** Results of the 1918 and 1922 general elections.

Historians such as Paul Adelman have explained the fall of the Liberals with a focus on mistakes made and problems that faced the party after 1918. The Asquith–Lloyd George split was never healed and had a disastrous impact on the party: in May 1920, Asquith Liberals voted to eject Lloyd George supporters from the Leamington party conference, partly because Lloyd George had made serious but unsuccessful efforts to convert the temporary Liberal–Conservative coalition into a permanent anti-Labour 'Centre Party'. Rumours of corruption ('**cash for honours**') and blame for warmongering against Turkey in September 1922 (the '**Chanak incident**') led most Tories to eventually reject the coalition. Lloyd George was forced to resign as prime minister the following month and led a much smaller group of Liberal MPs after the general election.

Lloyd George had amassed a huge political fund through the sale of honours (a knighthood could be bought for £10,000) but refused to share barely any of it with the Liberal Party until they started to follow his ideas and gave his supporters top party jobs in place of Asquith's men. Without this money, the Liberals could not maintain an effective local party machine; nor could they afford to field enough candidates at general elections in 1922, 1923 and 1924. Only when Asquith stepped down as leader in 1926 did Lloyd George finally agree to hand over substantial sums of money to the party. The party then put forward some impressive, innovative policies in a series of coloured booklets but, by this point, it was too late: even though the Liberals could afford to field as many candidates as their two rivals at the 1929 election, Labour had replaced them as the preferred party of opposition to the Conservatives.

The **first past the post** (FPTP) system favoured a two-party contest; despite sizeable electoral support, the Liberals failed to convert this into parliamentary seats and remained a small third party in the 1930s and beyond. The failure of the Liberals to explore a revision of the FPTP system in 1917–18 made life very difficult for them in the 1920s: a system of **proportional representation** would certainly have helped the party avoid such catastrophic decline.

### The rise of the Labour Party: trade unions and moderate leadership

The Labour Party (known as the Labour Representation Committee until 1906) had only been formed in 1900. It had done modestly well in the pre-war general elections, but it was very much the junior party to the Liberals before 1918. Yet, in the 1923 election, Labour gained more votes than the Liberals for the first time and, in 1924, Ramsay MacDonald became the first Labour prime minister. Labour became the largest parliamentary party in May 1929 and MacDonald became prime minister for the second time.

There are several reasons for this incredible rise. Unlike the Liberals, Labour emerged united at the end of the war: there had been splits in 1914 over whether to support the war, but in 1917 Labour ministers in the wartime coalition resigned and the party was reunited. The war also led to a huge growth in trade union membership. This was significant as the unions funded the party from membership fees and provided the vast bulk of party membership. Thanks to union backing, Labour, unlike the Liberals, ran a successful local political machine and fielded similar numbers of candidates to the Conservatives in the 1922, 1923 and 1924 elections.

Historian Ross McKibbin has argued that Labour's ability to represent a growing sense of working-class identity (as opposed to regional or religious identity) helped to win supporters from the Liberals. Other historians have pointed to the significance of the Liberal split: Asquith backed a minority

#### KEY TERMS

**Cash for honours**
When honours (usually titles) are granted in exchange for political donations or direct cash payments to politicians.

**Chanak incident**
The Turks wanted to force Greek, British and French troops out of occupied positions in Turkey. When Turkish troops marched on British positions Lloyd George (and Churchill) wanted war. Army generals and the public opposed war and a negotiated settlement was agreed.

**First past the post (FPTP)**
An electoral system in which the candidate receiving the highest number of votes in a constituency is returned to parliament. None of the other votes cast in that constituency count for anything at all.

**Proportional representation**
An electoral system in which the percentage of seats allocated to a party in parliament matches the percentage of votes gained in an election. Only votes for parties who gain too small a percentage to claim a seat are wasted.

Labour government after the 1923 election because he thought it would do a bad job and would be forced to rely on Liberal support (Lloyd George feared losing a separate Liberal identity as the party of opposition to the Conservatives and attacked Labour). Asquith's gamble was a huge mistake. MacDonald ruled with economic caution and impressed everyone with his conduct of foreign affairs.

Although MacDonald made it clear that the country was safe in Labour hands, he was compelled to resign. A left-wing journalist, J. R. Campbell, had written an article in the Communist newspaper *Workers' Weekly*, calling on working-class soldiers not to shoot at fellow workers on the other side in any future war. When Campbell was threatened with prosecution for inciting mutiny, MacDonald used his political influence to have the case dropped. MacDonald now faced – and lost – a vote of no confidence. His resignation resulted in a general election. Four days before the election, the *Daily Mail* printed a letter supposedly written by Gregory Zinoviev (a leading Soviet politician) to the British Communist Party, which said that Labour had promoted Communism by recognising the Soviet Union. The Campbell case and Zinoviev letter clearly helped boost Conservative votes in 1924, but Labour won the 1929 election in part because of MacDonald's earlier economic prudence.

### Conservative success: Stanley Baldwin and 'Safety First'

Given that around 80 percent of the British electorate were working class and that the Conservatives are often seen as the party of wealth and privilege, Conservative success is an interesting historical problem that requires some explanation.

Conservative success between the wars was in part due to a successful rebranding of the party, which began in 1872 under the leadership of Benjamin Disraeli. He promoted the Conservatives as a 'one-nation' party of empire, national defence and patriotism, things that appealed to many working-class voters. Stanley Baldwin was able to build upon this rebranding after he became prime minister and leader of the party in 1923. Despite inheriting a fortune from his family's steel company, he successfully presented himself as an ordinary man of the people. He pioneered the use of radio to talk directly to the people and had a reputation for calling a spade a spade. He ran his factories fairly and was keen to promote harmony between workers and employers in the British economy (see pages 30–31 on the General Strike). At the same time, he had a clear goal to promote class-based politics and destroy the Liberal Party. Baldwin was a key speaker against Lloyd George at the October 1922 Carlton Club meeting at which the Conservatives abandoned the coalition. He won over Lloyd George's remaining supporters by adopting **protectionism** in 1923 then dropping it after it was rejected by voters in the 1924 election; in doing so, Baldwin removed the one issue that had briefly reunited the Liberals: **free trade**. Although Baldwin was accused of being dull (for example, his lacklustre 1929 election slogan: 'Safety First'), many working-class people respected his apparent financial competence. His aim to attract the remaining wealthy, middle-class Liberals to the Conservatives as the best defence against Labour socialism succeeded brilliantly.

#### KEY TERMS

**Protectionism**
The use of import taxes (tariffs) to make foreign goods more expensive than domestic ones. This protects domestic producers from foreign competition but increases the cost of imports, including food items.

**Free trade**
The rejection of tariffs. This was opposed by British arable landowners, who suffered from cheaper imports of grain from abroad, but promoted by industrialists who wanted to sell their products abroad cheaply.

#### EXTEND YOUR KNOWLEDGE

**Carlton Club meeting**
The Carlton Club meeting was a meeting of Conservative Party MPs, held on 19 October 1922. The meeting was held in order to discuss whether the Conservatives should stay in coalition with Lloyd George's Liberals. Stanley Baldwin and Andrew Bonar Law spearheaded the opposition to the coalition and, when the MPs voted on whether to remain part of the government, the opposition won by 187 votes to 87.

When the meeting ended, Conservative ministers who had served in the coalition and voted against it resigned from government, triggering Lloyd George's resignation. Bonar Law was declared the new Conservative leader and, in the subsequent general election held in November, he became prime minister when his party secured a majority.

The Conservatives also benefited electorally in the interwar period from the following:

- Until the 1948 Representation of the People Act, the 'plural vote' allowed Oxford and Cambridge Universities and the City of London to return 14 MPs, almost always Tory, between them. Because of a loophole, graduates who resided for part of the time in a university town were able to vote in more than one constituency, and some landowners were able to vote in three. Those who resided in these places were more likely to have connections with the establishment and vote Conservative.
- In 1921, the Irish Free State gained independence from the UK. While the Liberals lost the support of around 80 Irish Nationalist MPs, the Conservatives continued to receive the support of around ten Northern Irish MPs.

- The FPTP system, together with the uneven distribution of votes in different constituencies, benefited the Conservatives. In 1918, it took an average of 15,943 votes to return each Conservative MP, 29,868 for a Labour MP and 36,116 for a Liberal MP.

**SOURCE 1** A poster produced by Ern Shaw for the Labour Party in 1929. The 'Old Dears' are Lloyd George and Baldwin, while the man of the moment in the foreground is MacDonald.

**ACTIVITY**
**KNOWLEDGE CHECK**

**Changing political landscape, 1918–31**

1 How useful are general election statistics in exploring the changing political landscape between 1918 and 1931? Explain your answer with reference to the electoral data given in Figures 1.1–1.3.

2 How fair is the representation of the three party leaders in Source 1? Explain your answer.

3 a) For each of the following periods, summarise the key reasons why some historians have argued that this was when the Liberal Party began its unavoidable decline as the main rival to the Conservatives: 1914–18, 1918–22, 1922–29.

b) Which of these periods would you consider to have been the most important in changing the political fortunes of the Liberal Party? Explain why.

**AS Level Exam-Style Question Section A**

Was the 1918 Representation of the People Act the main reason for the decline of the Liberals and rise of the Labour Party in the years 1918–29? Explain your answer. (20 marks)

**Tip**

*Always start with an analysis of the stated factor (in this case the Representation of the People Act) before analysing a further two to three factors. Aim to explain why one factor was more important than the others.*

THINKING HISTORICALLY Causation (3c&d)

**Causation and intention**

1 Work on your own or with a partner to identify as many causes of the decline of the Liberal Party as you can. Write each cause on a separate card or piece of paper.

2 Divide your cards into those which represent:

a) the actions or intentions of people
b) the beliefs held by people at the time
c) contextual factors or events (i.e. political, social or economic events)
d) states of affairs (long- or short-term situations that have developed in particular ways).

3 Focus on the intentions and actions of the key people during the period 1918–29. For each person, draw on your knowledge to fill in the table below, identifying:

a) their intentions
b) the actions they took to achieve these
c) the consequences of their actions (both intended and unintended)
d) the extent to which their intentions were achieved.

| Key figure | Intentions in 1914 | Actions taken | Consequences | How far intention achieved |
|---|---|---|---|---|
| David Lloyd George | • Keep hold of power as prime minister<br>• Regain control over the whole Liberal Party<br>• Defeat the threat of Labour | • Use of the 'Coupon' and Conservative support in 1918 election<br>• Refusal to donate funds to the party until his ideas and men were accepted by all Liberals<br>• Raise fear of 'Bolshevism' against Labour in run up to 1924 election | • Retained power but clear reliance on Conservatives (intended)<br>• Party remained divided until 1926 despite temporary reunion in 1923 (unintended?)<br>• Labour formed a minority government with support of Asquith Liberals (unintended) | • Short-term – remained prime minister until November 1922, but failed to create a longer-lasting 'Centre Party'<br>• Long-term – regained overall leadership of the Liberals but failed to prevent the rise of the Labour Party |
| Henry Asquith | | | | |
| Ramsay MacDonald | | | | |
| Stanley Baldwin | | | | |

4 Discuss the following questions with a partner:

a) Who had the greatest intention of bringing about the decline of the Liberal Party?
b) How important are people's intentions in explaining Labour's replacement of the Liberals as the Conservative's main opponents.

## The National government, 1931–45

| Period in office | Prime Minister | Party/parties in office | Reason for fall |
|---|---|---|---|
| August 1931 – June 1935 | Ramsay MacDonald | National Labour-Conservative-National Liberal coalition | Ill health |
| June 1935 – May 1937 | Stanley Baldwin | Conservative-National Labour-National Liberal coalition | Retirement |
| May 1937 – May 1940 | Neville Chamberlain | Conservative-National Labour-National Liberal coalition | Resigned having failed to form coalition |
| May 1940 – July 1945 | Winston Churchill | Conservative-Labour-Liberal coalition | Lost general election |

**Figure 1.4** Prime ministers and their parties 1931–45.

### Why was a National government formed in 1931?

In October 1929, the Wall Street stock exchange in New York collapsed, leading to a global decline in trade and production. Almost all Labour ministers and MPs disagreed with making cuts in spending (especially a proposed cut of ten percent on unemployment benefits), which were thought necessary to avoid economic catastrophe. But, in 1931, MacDonald and his Chancellor of the Exchequer, Philip Snowden, saw no option but to press ahead with the cuts.

#### EXTEND YOUR KNOWLEDGE

**The Wall Street Crash**

On 28–29 October 1929, the American stock market saw $30 billion wiped off the value of stocks and shares, almost a quarter of the total value of all assets. The crash was due to fears that shares were over-priced: owners tried to sell them before they lost any more value. The price of shares had risen steadily throughout the 1920s but a slowdown in sales in important industries such as cars and houses, together with concern about the extent of borrowing to pay for shares, led to a loss of confidence in the market. The collapse in share prices meant many borrowers could not repay loans to banks. American banks recalled international loans in an often unsuccessful bid to avoid going bust. The banking crisis, together with a sharp fall in demand for imports, meant the economic depression spread throughout the world.

MacDonald and his supporting ministers were expelled from the Labour Party and a popular radical, George Lansbury, became the new party leader. MacDonald, like Lloyd George, had become a prime minister without a party and was ready to resign. However, on 24 August, MacDonald announced that he would continue to serve as the prime minister of a 'National government' to face the emergency. He had been persuaded to stay on by King George V, largely due to his sense of patriotic duty: to have governmental instability at such a time could only make things worse for Britain. The Conservatives could have formed a separate government, yet chose to support MacDonald: Baldwin saw that MacDonald would bear the blame for unpopular economic measures, leaving the way clear for a Conservative triumph when the situation improved. The British public overwhelmingly backed calls for national unity in the face of the economic crisis and voted for the National government in huge numbers.

| Election year October 1931 | Seats (% of votes) | | | |
|---|---|---|---|---|
| | **Conservative** | **Liberal** | **Labour** | **Total** |
| Coalition | 473 (55.2) | 33 (6.5) | 13 (1.6) | 554 (67.0) |
| Non-coalition | – | 4 (0.5) | 52 (30.6) | 56 (33.0) |
| **Election year November 1935** | | | | |
| Coalition | 386 (47.8) | 21 (3.7) | 8 (1.5) | 432 (53.3) |
| Non-coalition | – | 6 (0.5) | 154 (37.9) | 56 (33.0) |

**Figure 1.5** A table showing general election results during the 1930s.

As MacDonald's health began to fail Baldwin effectively served as prime minister from 1931. When MacDonald finally resigned in 1935, Baldwin was elected for a third time. His premiership got off to a rocky start: a plan to appease fascist Italy by giving them two-thirds of Abyssinia (modern Ethiopia) was hugely unpopular when leaked to the press. Baldwin, and Foreign Secretary Samuel Hoare, had to abandon the plan and pledge to work with the League of Nations (a forerunner of the United Nations) to achieve peace in Abyssinia. Baldwin was also under attack from all sides over rearmament: some wanted rapid rearmament to face the growing threat of Nazi Germany; others wanted disarmament and clear co-operation with the League of Nations. In 1935, Baldwin offered the electorate a clever, if unpopular, fudge: Britain would increase spending on rearmament to fulfil any military requests from the League. No one in 1935 (Churchill aside) could have predicted the course of events that culminated in the outbreak of the Second World War in September 1939, yet Baldwin was attacked in the 1940s and 1950s as one of the 'Guilty Men' who had appeased Hitler.

Baldwin was fortunate to recover his popular reputation before he stepped down in May 1937. He advised the popular playboy King Edward VIII (who had reigned since the death of his father, George V, in January 1936) to abdicate the throne rather than attempt to marry Mrs Wallace Simpson, an American divorcée, while king.

The monarch was still head of the Church of England (which frowned upon divorce) and divorce was a source of social stigma into the 1960s. Baldwin gained popular credit for the calm, dignified way in which he managed a potential crisis.

Baldwin was also fortunate to hand over the reins to Neville Chamberlain at an exceptionally difficult time. Chamberlain was well-liked for his successful creation of new homes and for his assured, personable performances on cinema newsreels as Chancellor of the Exchequer. His attempts to find 'peace in our time' were also hugely popular with the British public. In September 1938, he flew three times (in an age where air travel was still rare) to meet Adolf Hitler to resolve a crisis brought on by Hitler's expansionism. Chamberlain thought he had been successful but was unfortunate to have to deal with an utterly ruthless, lying megalomaniac. Churchill was critical of Chamberlain's appeasement of Hitler from the start; many others poured scorn on his timidity once war had broken out. Yet there were many solid reasons for Chamberlain's policy, not least the vivid memories of the last war and the fear of modern weapons, especially bombing raids.

Nevertheless, once the war began in earnest (after the so-called 'Phoney War', where nothing much happened in Western Europe until April 1940), it was clear that Chamberlain did not have the confidence of parliament to wage a victorious struggle. Having waited so long to be prime minister, he was forced from office after a vote of no confidence and replaced with the man who had consistently urged armed vigilance against Hitler: Winston Churchill. Churchill was appointed thanks to his backing among Labour and Liberal MPs; the king would have preferred Lord Halifax (who almost certainly would have led Britain to a negotiated peace with Germany).

### *The failure of extremism*

The National government was meant to be a temporary solution to the national crisis of economic depression but continued through the Second World War until 1945. One reason why the National government lasted for 14 years was that it held the centre ground while extreme political parties failed to attract support.

Oswald Mosley had been a promising Labour MP before he became disillusioned with the lack of innovation in tackling the economic crisis. He founded the New Party to promote his own ideas at the 1931 election, but only gained 0.2 percent of the vote. After this abysmal result, he became disillusioned with democracy itself. In 1932, he formed the British Union of Fascists (BUF), with the aim of emulating the Italian dictatorship of Benito Mussolini. The BUF was racist and anti-Semitic; in October 1936, a BUF march through East London, an area home to many Jewish and Irish immigrants, turned into a violent clash that became known as 'the Battle of Cable Street'. The struggle against fascism in the Second World War made Mosley and the BUF even more unpopular. Mosley was imprisoned for three years and the BUF was banned. He was released in 1943, when he was deemed not to be a threat to the war effort. The BUF was not the last far-right political group in Britain, but it did set a precedent in terms of its lack of success.

The far left was marginally more successful. The Communist Party of Great Britain (CPGB) gained one MP in 1924 and 1935, and two in 1945. However, with a maximum 0.4 percent of the vote, it is clear that British voters rejected communism. This was largely due to the traditions and strength of the trade union and Labour movements. This home-grown socialism was far more practical than the ideological, revolutionary socialism advocated by communists. The CPGB gained some support due to the role of Soviet Russia (the only communist state) in defeating Nazi Germany. However, the CPGB had clearly placed the needs of Moscow ahead of Britain: until Hitler attacked Russia in June 1941, the party had followed Soviet orders to oppose the war (a cynical Nazi–Soviet pact for peace had been agreed in August 1939). The only way forward for the CPGB was in a few inner-city councils, and through 'entryism' into the Labour Party: communists would conceal their true loyalties and infiltrate the Labour Party to try and steer national politics further to the radical left. This became problematic for Labour later in the century.

**ACTIVITY**
**KNOWLEDGE CHECK**

**Changing political landscape, 1931–45**

1 Summarise the reasons for the formation of the National government.

2 Explain why the National government lasted far longer than its creators expected.

## How far did the Second World War affect British democracy?

As with the First World War, there were some temporary changes in government and legislation designed to facilitate the waging of 'total war'.

- A War Cabinet of just five men (Churchill, plus two Conservative and two Labour ministers) was set up to make quick decisions about the war.
- New ministries were created: Lord Beaverbrook, a newspaper magnate with no prior political experience, became Minister for Aircraft Production. Churchill approved of men with a proven track record of getting things done rather than slavishly following procedure.
- The Emergency Powers Act (May 1940) gave wide-ranging powers over the British people to the government.
- Churchill took the post of Minister for Defence as well as prime minister. In this role, he oversaw not only the home front but also played a leading role in military strategy. His most significant success was in the maintenance of domestic morale and purposefulness: his speeches were inspirational, as were his will to win and his dynamic leadership. He was careful to maintain the support and prestige of parliament in a way that Lloyd George had not done; there was no question of these expedient wartime changes outliving the war. However, there were some political changes that Churchill, despite his popular and essential role as a war leader, was powerless to counteract.

SOURCE 2 A speech made by Winston Churchill to the House of Commons, 13 May 1940.

I would say to the House, as I said to those who have joined the government: 'I have nothing to offer but blood, toil, tears and sweat.' We have before us many, many long months of struggle and of suffering. You ask, what is our policy? I will say: It is to wage war, by sea, land and air, with all our might and with all the strength that God can give us; to wage war against a monstrous tyranny, never surpassed in the dark and lamentable catalogue of human crime. That is our policy. You ask, what is our aim? I can answer in one word: victory. Victory at all costs, victory in spite of all terror, victory, however long and hard the road may be; for without victory, there is no survival... But I take up my task with buoyancy and hope. I feel sure that our cause will not be suffered to fail among men. At this time I feel entitled to claim the aid of all, and I say, 'Come then, let us go forward together with our united strength.'

## The rise of consensus politics and political challenge, 1945–79

| Period in office | Prime Minister | Party/parties in office | Reason for fall |
|---|---|---|---|
| July 1945 - October 1951 | Clement Attlee | Labour | Lost election |
| October 1951 - April 1955 | Winston Churchill | Conservative | Retired as Prime Minister |
| April 1955 - January 1957 | Anthony Eden | Conservative | Retired due to ill health |
| January 1957 - October 1963 | Harold Macmillan | Conservative | Resigned due to ill health |
| October 1963 - October 1964 | Alec Douglas-Home | Conservative | Lost election |
| October 1964 - June 1970 | Harold Wilson | Labour | Lost election |
| June 1970 - March 1974 | Edward Heath | Conservative | Lost election |
| March 1974 - April 1976 | Harold Wilson | Labour | Resigned due to ill health |
| April 1976 - May 1979 | James Callaghan | Labour | Lost election |
| May 1979 - November 1990 | Margaret Thatcher | Conservative | Resigned as Prime Minister after leadership challenge |

**Figure 1.6** Prime ministers and their parties 1945–79.

### Why did Labour win the 1945 election by such a large margin?

Many people, Labour leader Clement Attlee included, were shocked by the results of the first election since 1935. The British voters decided that, although Churchill had won the war, he was not the best man to lead the nation in peacetime.

| Election year | Seats (% of votes) | | |
|---|---|---|---|
| | Conservatives | Labour | Liberal |
| July 1945 | 213 (39.8) | 393 (47.8) | 12 (9.0) |
| February 1950 | 298 (43.5) | 315 (46.1) | 9 (9.1) |
| October 1951 | 321 (48.0) | 295 (48.8) | 6 (2.5) |

**Figure 1.7** A table showing general election results between 1945 and 1951.

Conservative defeat was due, in part, to voters' memories of the failure to build a 'home fit for heroes' after the First World War and of the failure to solve the Depression in the 1930s. It was also due to a lacklustre election campaign by Churchill, who assumed victory was assured; he was criticised for besmirching Labour as a dangerous party who, if elected, might use secret police to enforce radical change. Given the excellent service given by a range of Labour ministers during the war (see below), this claim rang false.

However, the votes did not just fall into Attlee's lap: he worked hard to secure them. After victory in Europe in May 1945, he broke off the coalition to fight the election as a separate party. Labour was far more in tune with the demands and expectations of the British people after six years of suffering and sacrifice: unlike the Conservatives, Labour promised to implement the recommendations of the 1942 **Beveridge Report** in its 1945 manifesto, 'Let Us Face the Future'.

**KEY TERM**

**Beveridge Report**
Officially called *Social Insurance and Allied Services*, this 500-page report called for the creation of a welfare state to tackle the five 'Giant Evils' of disease, idleness, ignorance, squalor and want. It became a bestseller and six million summary leaflets were dropped as propaganda over Germany.

Despite Churchill's claims, Labour was seen as a responsible party of government thanks to the wartime contributions of its leading figures:

- Attlee had served with distinction as deputy prime minister, often acting as prime minister in the Commons while Churchill was busy with war business.
- Ernest Bevin, with his trade union roots, successfully minimised strikes and maximised output as Minister for Labour. He became Foreign Secretary after the war.
- Herbert Morrison served as Home Secretary; his finest work was the coordination of efforts to cope with the effects of the Blitz. He became deputy prime minister after the war.
- Hugh Dalton was respected for his economic competence as Minister for War Economy and then President of the Board of Trade. He became Chancellor of the Exchequer after the war.

### Why was there a post-war consensus?

The Second World War clearly contributed to short-term Labour success; however, it shaped British politics in a more profound sense for a generation. Most obviously it brought Conservative and Labour ministers together in a successful National government. This was an important foundation for the 'post-war consensus', a seemingly overwhelming agreement on a range of important policies between the rival parties. More significantly, the war not only represented the victory of democracy over fascism but also the success of **collectivism**. The common experience of a successful state-led struggle to overcome difficult challenges caused the British public, and even the bulk of Conservative MPs, to accept economic and social policies that would previously have been branded 'socialist' or 'radical'. The most important of these were the **nationalisation** of some major industries (including coal-mining) and the creation of a National Health Service (see below).

Although the Conservatives were in power for 17 years between 1945 and 1979, they did remarkably little to roll back Labour's extension of state management and provision. One reason for this is that the Labour reforms were not as radical or socialist as they might have been. Labour had a huge majority in 1945 and could have implemented a thoroughgoing socialist shake-up of the economy and society. Yet Attlee and his colleagues never attempted this. Instead, they wanted to create a 'mixed economy' or 'middle way' to prevent the failures and curb the excesses of capitalism that had led to misery for many in the 1930s. This was a compromise that many Conservatives could accept.

Another reason is that several leading Conservatives were genuinely progressive (they wanted to improve life for the average person) as a result of their experiences during the war and the Depression.

- Aged 77 in 1951, Churchill was too old to change his ways, yet, mindful of defeat in 1945, he was keen to make himself electable as a peacetime prime minister.
- Anthony Eden (prime minister 1955–57) was a **'one-nation' Tory** who was anxious for social cohesion to ensure Britain was taken seriously in foreign affairs.
- Harold Macmillan (prime minister 1957–63) was shocked at the suffering of his Stockton constituents in the 1930s. In 1938, he wrote a book called *The Middle Way* in which he set out his sympathy with more radical solutions.
- Richard A. Butler (Chancellor of the Exchequer 1951–55) was a leading reformer who was the driving force behind the 1944 Education Act (see page 56).

#### KEY TERMS

**Collectivism**
A political approach to problems whereby individuals give up some rights to work with the state for a common purpose. This is different to fascism, where the will of the state is imposed on individuals.

**Nationalisation**
The process by which governments take over the ownership and running of private firms.

**'One-nation' Tory**
Benjamin Disraeli coined this term in the 1840s and called for Conservatives to care for the poorer sections of society as a father cares for his children. He also called for them to build positive relations with the poor based on shared identities such as national greatness. Later Conservative politicians who agreed with Disraeli used his term to describe their views.

| Election year | Seats (% of votes) | | |
|---|---|---|---|
| | Conservatives | Labour | Liberal |
| May 1955 | 344 (49.7) | 277 (46.4) | 6 (2.7) |
| October 1959 | 365 (49.4) | 258 (44.8) | 6 (5.9) |
| October 1964 | 304 (43.4) | 295 (44.1) | 6 (11.2) |
| March 1966 | 253 (41.9) | 363 (47.9) | 12 (8.5) |
| June 1970 | 330 (46.4) | 287 (43.0) | 6 (7.5) |
| February 1974 | 297 (37.9) | 301 (37.1) | 14 (19.3) |
| October 1974 | 277 (35.8) | 319 (39.2) | 13 (18.3) |
| May 1979 | 339 (43.9) | 269 (36.9) | 11 (13.8) |

**Figure 1.8** General election results, 1955-79.

## Building the 'middle way': Attlee's post-war government

Although Attlee's government shied away from a genuine socialist revolution, they built on the experience of wartime planning with an array of economic initiatives:

**Nationalisation:** Bank of England (1946); air transport (1946); cable and wireless (1947); coal-mining (the National Coal Board took over 1,500 collieries in 1947); public transport (under the British Transport Commission in 1948); electricity generation (1948); gas (1949); iron and steel (after bitter Tory opposition, in 1951).

The government's aim in taking ownership of these industries was:

- to improve the efficiency of failing industries and save jobs
- to improve worker–employer relations in industries with a poor track-record such as coal mining
- to put the needs of the community above profit (for example, through the creation of a national transport system that provided a service even for remote settlements).

**Planning:** The Economic Planning Council was established in July 1947 with several committees to check on issues such as levels of production and imports. The National Agricultural Advisory Service gave advice to farmers on how best to use subsidies to improve efficiency. Many Labour MPs felt planning should have been far more ambitious in scope and scale.

**Control measures:** A period of **austerity** was enforced by Chancellor Stafford Cripps (1947–50) to aid Britain's economic recovery: wartime rationing on several foods was extended until 1951 (tea, sugar, butter, bacon); even some staple foods (bread 1946–48, potatoes 1947–48), which had not been rationed during the war, were included in the 'fair shares' scheme. Coal was rationed during the harsh winter of 1947–48, and building materials were only allocated to essential reconstruction projects and industrial recovery. Controls were also placed on maximum levels of rent, profits and interest rates. Cripps did not cap wage increases as such, but he did successfully negotiate with trade unions to voluntarily waive pay rises.

The government received criticism from the right (for too much interference and spending), the left (who thought there was not enough planning or real change) and, by 1950–51, from the people who had tired of austerity. Yet these policies, together with a loan of $2.7 billion as part of the United States' European Recovery Programme (usually called Marshall Aid), enabled some remarkable reforms in welfare provision at a time of severe economic difficulty.

**KEY TERM**

**Austerity**
A hard and disciplined approach. The word summed up the tough times the British public went through in order to restore economic stability after the Second World War.

**ACTIVITY**
**KNOWLEDGE CHECK**

**Post-war consensus**

1 Explain what is meant by the term 'post-war consensus'.

2 In your view, was the Second World War responsible for the emergence of consensus politics? What other factors were involved?

## How much political consensus was there by 1979?

In 1979, the British voted overwhelmingly for an end to the post-war consensus. Margaret Thatcher became Britain's first female prime minister. She wanted to kill off what she saw as creeping socialism in the Conservative Party and in Britain at large.

There are several reasons why many Britons, despite all the social advances that had been made since 1945, rejected the post-war consensus. The **Keynesian** economic policies followed by governments since the war were felt to be failing by the early 1970s. Leading Conservatives began to call for a return to more free-market solutions to problems such as inflation and unemployment. Efforts to implement such solutions inflamed already tense relations between workers and employers. Conservatives increasingly felt that trade unions had gained too much power and that something must be done to stop them using strike action to hold a democratically elected government to ransom for higher wages.

Edward Heath (Conservative prime minister 1970–74) had tried but failed to break the post-war political consensus. Labour prime ministers Harold Wilson (1964–70 and 1974–76) and James Callaghan (1976–79) were too dependent on trade union support to effectively tackle the growing problems.

**KEY TERM**

**Keynesianism**
An economic theory named after renowned economist John Maynard Keynes. He argued that governments should borrow in a time of recession to spend and stimulate demand and growth in the economy. This went against the classic view that governments should aim to balance the books and not interfere too much in the economy. (See also the Extend Your Knowledge box on page 26.)

The lack of success or choice on offer from both sides allowed for a remarkable resurgence of support for the Liberal Party under the dynamic leadership of Jeremy Thorpe. Unfortunately for him, just as in 1929, the FPTP system prevented the recovery of the Liberals in parliament.

It took a 'Winter of Discontent' in 1978–79 (see page 34), where rubbish piled up on city streets and the dead went unburied in Liverpool, before the British electorate opted for Thatcher's tough solutions.

**SOURCE 3** Rubbish piled up in the West End of London in February 1979.

**A Level Exam-Style Question Section A**

How far do you agree that the landslide victory of the Labour Party in the 1945 general election was only possible because of Britain's experience in the Second World War? (20 marks)

**Tip**

*A number of factors can be compared to the one given in the question, and content can go as far back as 1918 and the early successes of the Labour Party.*

## IN WHAT WAYS AND WITH WHAT SUCCESS DID GOVERNMENTS DEAL WITH ECONOMIC CHANGE BETWEEN 1918 AND 1979?

While the seriousness of certain economic problems changed over time, the range of issues remained roughly the same:

- the level of government debt (and extent to which government spending exceeded revenue)
- the balance of payments (the extent to which the value of imports exceeded that of exports)
- the value of the pound against other currencies
- the rate of inflation (the increase in average prices over time – a little is healthy but a lot is dangerous)
- the level of unemployment
- the competitiveness of British industry against international rivals
- the stability of worker–employer relations.

Britain experienced an extremely tough economic situation between 1918 and 1979 due to growing industrial competition, the impact of two world wars, the Great Depression in the 1930s and an oil crisis in 1973. However, ineffective solutions offered by politicians were also part of the problem. When trying to understand why certain solutions were pursued, it is helpful to consider the following factors:

- the extent to which solutions were considered practically achievable and politically acceptable
- the level of understanding of the root causes of the problem
- the existence of received wisdom (or an ideology) that shaped and informed decision-making
- the prioritisation of the problem.

The Chancellors' solutions were ineffective until 1931, largely because they prioritised the strength of the pound over dealing with unemployment; they inherited the traditional wisdom that a debt-free balanced budget was crucial to economic stability. Chancellors exacerbated problems in the 1950s onwards because they prioritised the balance of payments (and political gain) over investment and growth. Although post-war governments attempted greater management of the economy, this proved to be more difficult than anticipated. However, it was not all doom and gloom: the economy grew steadily until the mid-1970s and many people enjoyed greater affluence.

## TIMELINE: THE BRITISH ECONOMY IN THE 20TH CENTURY

**1920**
Brief post-war boom comes to an end, economic slump begins

**1921**
Safeguarding of Industries Act gives preference to imperial products

**1925**
Pound rejoins Gold Standard

Reduced duties on goods from the Empire

**1926**
May: General Strike, miners' strike continues until defeat in November

**1929**
Value of stocks and shares listed on American stock exchange (Wall Street) collapses

**1931**
Pound leaves Gold Standard

**1932**
Import Duties Act places ten percent duty on most manufactured goods

Government offers 'Cheap Money', reducing rate of interest from six percent to two percent

**1934**
Special Areas Act channels investment into areas hit badly by slump

**1935**
Baldwin commits to rearmament

**1939–45**
Government direction of economy vastly increases under National government

**1946–50**
Attlee's government nationalises several industries and implements austerity measures

**1952**
ROBOT, a plan to float the pound against other currencies, is dropped

**1962**
National Economic Development Council is set up but proves to be ineffective

**1967**
Pound devalued from $2.80 to $2.40

Britain goes to International Monetary Fund for second bailout loan in three years

**1971**
Decimal currency replaces pounds, shillings and pence

First auction of North Sea Oil

**1972**
Pound allowed to float freely against other currencies

**1973**
Yom Kippur War sparks oil crisis, bringing inflation and unemployment

**1976**
Britain applies to International Monetary Fund for $3.9 billion bailout

## Boom, crisis and recovery: the response to economic problems, 1918–31

### The economic legacy of the First World War

- **Loss of trade:** Before 1914, Britain had been the world's leading trading nation. The war led to a collapse in trade largely because all available shipping had been used to import essential war supplies (20 percent of all merchant ships were sunk in the process). Economic rivals like the USA and Japan filled the gap left by the decline in British exports. Britain was unable to recover its previous domination of that market after the war.
- **Debt:** The war was expensive. Once Britain had spent its reserves of gold and sold its overseas assets it was forced to borrow £850 million (£35.1 billion in 2014 values) to fight the last two years of the war. Contemporary economists thought that large government spending and debt was bad for the economy because it reduced confidence in the stability of the state.
- **The value of the pound:** Before the war, the value of the pound, like many other currencies, was fixed to the price of gold. This guarded against inflation as governments could not simply print money if they did not have sufficient gold reserves to back up the paper money. The cost of the war meant Britain had to abandon the Gold Standard in 1914 and no longer circulated gold coins. The government instead printed more paper money.
- **Inflation:** Inflation increased to 25 percent by 1918 and was a major cause of concern to the coalition government.
- **Technological development:** This was accelerated by the war, with major advances in the aircraft industry, radio communications, the car industry and medical science. There was a wider use of machine tools and assembly-line techniques, which encouraged the employment of semi-skilled labour.

SOURCE

A graph showing the rate of inflation between 1918 and 1979. The line shows the percentage change from one year to the next. From www.parliament.uk/briefing-papers/RP99-111.pdf, section XI.

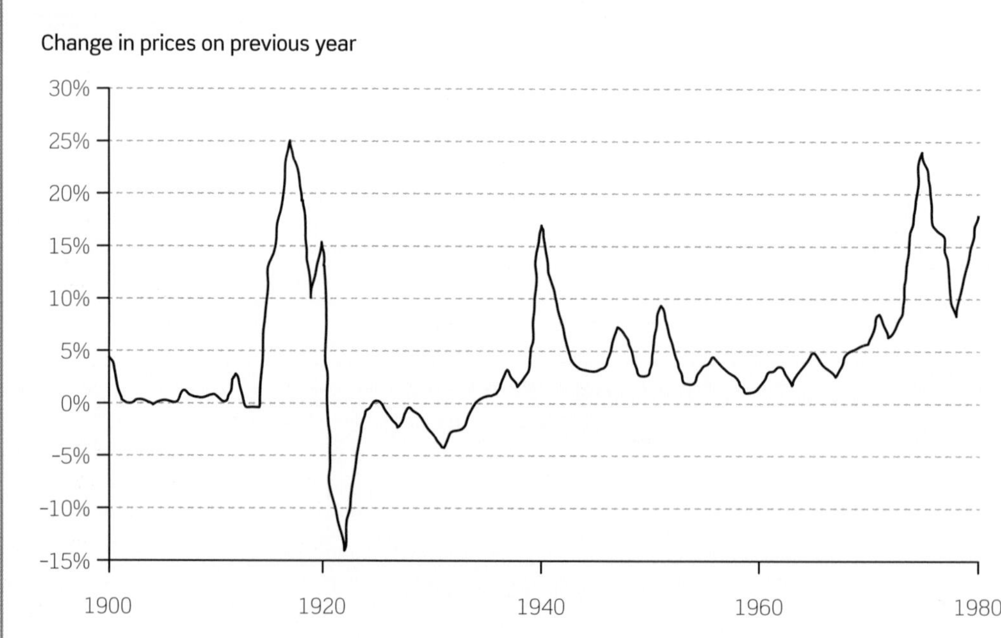

### The poverty of post-war economic solutions: the 1920s

The war cannot be blamed for all of Britain's economic problems in the 1920s: other nations, such as France and Germany, had more serious economic problems in 1918, yet were able to recover more effectively. Several British industries (shipping, mining, steel, iron and textiles) were old and struggled to compete with new international rivals. British investors were slow to back new industries and continued to seek overseas opportunities for investment, as they had done before the war. British trade unions had never been larger or more powerful (up from four million members in 1913 to 6.5 million in 1918 and a high of 8.3 million in 1920). They were able to secure reduced working hours (54 to 47 per week) without pay cuts; this further reduced competitiveness and caused redundancies.

A number of ineffective solutions were put forward:

- **Tax, spending and balancing the budget:** To try and reduce inflation, and repay war debts as quickly as possible, taxes were raised each year after 1918 from £18 per capita (person) in 1919 to £24 per capita in 1922. Government spending was also cut dramatically. In 1921, Lloyd George appointed a Commission on National Expenditure under Sir Eric Geddes to find out where savings could be made. The 1922 'Geddes Axe' led to cuts in spending on education, pensions, unemployment benefit, housing and health from £206 million to £182 million. It also prompted cuts in defence from £190 million to £111 million. Although spending began to creep back up after 1924, these cuts, like the extra taxation, contributed to growing unemployment.
- **Interest rates and the value of the pound:** The government set a high rate of interest to cut inflation, but also to encourage foreigners to buy pounds. This increased the value of the pound against other currencies, which was desired as a sign of stability and economic strength. The goal was to restore the pound to its pre-war value of $4.86 (the market valued £1 at $3.81 in 1919). Parliament's suspension of the Gold Standard was due to expire in 1925 and Chancellor Winston Churchill announced a return to the Gold Standard in April that year. However, high interest rates made it more expensive for businesses to borrow and invest and made people more likely to save than spend. The high exchange rate made British exports more expensive and therefore uncompetitive. All of this contributed to the end of a brief post-war boom (1919–20) that was based on the expectation of increased peacetime trade.
- **Protectionism:** The serious threat to British industry led the largely Conservative coalition to introduce duties to protect 'key industries' in 1921. The old industries were hit particularly hard by new competition abroad and campaigned hard for protection. Baldwin tried to go further in 1923, with a more general programme of tariffs and protection, but this was rejected by an electorate who feared more expensive food imports. More limited tariffs were added in 1925 and at the British Empire Economic Conference held in Ottawa in 1932. While this helped in the short term, it meant that these industries avoided introducing the changes needed to become competitive in the longer-term. It also meant that investment was not redirected into newer industries, such as chemicals or cars, in which Britain could have developed an advantage. Other nations also erected their own 'tariff walls', which limited international trade.

Unemployment became a huge problem: it never fell below ten percent (about one million workers) between the wars, and rose as high as 23 percent during the worst years of the slump, 1932–33. These are average figures for the UK and mask some huge regional variations (for example, 60 percent unemployment in shipbuilding areas, 49 percent in iron and steel, and 41 percent in coal mining). Although the government thought employment was not their responsibility, the soaring cost of unemployment insurance was a major cause for concern.

## Response to economic problems of the Great Depression and Second World War

### The 1930s: recovery through better solutions or pure luck?

The Wall Street Crash led to a collapse of global trade and meant many European nations were unable to repay debts to Britain. British bankers especially began to panic about the loss of money loaned to Germany; they demanded further spending cuts to boost economic confidence before they would lend any money to the UK government. Although Ramsay MacDonald imposed a fresh round of spending cuts in 1931, a loan of £80 million was fast being used up. The trigger for a change in economic policy was the mutiny of 12,000 sailors in opposition to pay cuts at Invergordon, Scotland, on 14 September. It was clear that the cuts could not continue; five days later, Britain left the Gold Standard. The pound was allowed to 'float' against other currencies and it quickly depreciated in value from $4.80 (set by Churchill during the return to the Gold Standard in 1925) to $3.40.

Although the government had been driven to this difficult decision, it was clear by the mid-1930s that the change in priorities had led to greater economic success. British exports quickly became 25 percent cheaper and far more competitive. Interest rates, which had been kept high to prop up the value of the pound, could now be cut from six to two percent. The rate on long-term government borrowing (bond yields) was cut from five to 3.5 percent. This slashed the cost of government debt repayment and allowed for increased spending in other areas, such as a restoration of unemployment benefits in 1934. This 'cheap money' also allowed businesses to borrow and invest more. Most importantly, the availability of cheaper mortgages fuelled a boom in house construction; this created almost one in three of all new jobs between 1931 and 1934. Employment was also boosted by the huge expansion of rearmament in 1935: a further 15 percent of the unemployed found work in old industries such as steel, iron and shipbuilding. All of this meant that the impact of America's Great Depression was not as hard on Britain as on continental Europe.

SOURCE 5

A graph showing levels of unemployment as a percentage of the working-age population between 1900 and 1979. From www.parliament.uk/briefing-papers/RP99-111.pdf, section XI.

## The economic legacy of the Second World War: the managed economy 1939–51

Unlike the Liberal government in 1914, the National government of 1939 had no reservations about interfering in people's lives as far as was necessary to wage 'total war'. Rationing and conscription were introduced almost immediately. Registration for employment was made compulsory in 1941; the government issued around 8.5 million Essential Work Orders, which forced people to do particular jobs. By 1945, 3.2 million people had worked in munitions, four million in other war work and 5.5 million had been conscripted to the armed forces. Although there were some strikes, these were to boost wages rather than attack government planning; people accepted the need to give up certain freedoms in order to defeat fascism.

A longer-term impact of this collective struggle was increased acceptance of government management of the economy. In 1944, the government declared its long-term responsibility for the maintenance of high employment. The war also lent weight to the theories of leading Cambridge economist John Maynard Keynes: before 1939, he had argued that, rather than aim to balance the budgets in hard times, the government should borrow and spend more money to stimulate a recovery. This had been rejected by the traditional 'treasury view' in the 1930s, but now such thinking came to dominate economic policy until the 1970s.

### EXTEND YOUR KNOWLEDGE

**John Maynard Keynes (1883–1946)**

In 1999 Keynes was voted one of the 100 most important and influential individuals of the 20th century by *Time* magazine. This was in recognition of the huge impact his economic ideas have had on government policy across the world since the 1930s.

Keynes rejected some of the key assumptions that had underpinned economic thought since Adam Smith wrote the *Wealth of Nations* in 1776; in particular, he argued that 'the invisible hand' (Smith's phrase to describe the process by which the free market will allocate goods and services in a way beneficial to all) could not solve all economic problems. Keynes argued that, during a bad recession, there was not enough money or confidence for businesses to spend or invest; the economy therefore remained trapped in the doldrums with lots of persistent unemployment.

At times like this, the government, rather than cutting spending and increasing taxation to balance the books, should spend more money to generate a 'multiplier effect': if the state spent £1,000 on roads, the workers employed as a result would have money to spend on other goods and services, which would create more jobs and lead to further demand.

The idea of borrowing money to intervene in the economy was so radical that it was ignored by almost every government. One notable exception was Nazi Germany, where the idea was used to great effect in the short term. The severity of the Great Depression discredited older notions of *laissez-faire* ('let things be') economics. Successful government borrowing during the Second World War lent weight to Keynes's arguments.

Although he died in 1946 (partly due to working so hard on negotiating better terms for a huge post-war loan from the USA), his ideas profoundly shaped the approach of all British governments to the economy until the rise of Margaret Thatcher. Keynesian solutions lost support in the 1970s because of the existence of high unemployment and inflation at the same time: Keynes's theories suggested that should not have been possible and this undermined their credibility. However, after almost three decades of a free market approach, the financial crisis of 2008 led many governments, including the UK and the USA, to revisit Keynesian solutions.

### ACTIVITY
KNOWLEDGE CHECK

**The First and Second World Wars and the economy**

1 Why do you think the British economy struggled to recover after the First World War? Try to think of at least five factors.

2 Look at the solutions put forward in the 1920s for economic problems. Create a table with the headings 'Tax', 'Interest rates and the value of the pound', and 'Protectionism'. Under each heading explain what the government was hoping to achieve with each policy and why they ultimately failed.

3 Why did the economy begin to recover in the 1930s?

## The response to economic challenges, 1951–79

### Butskellism and 'stop-go' policies: the Conservatives in power, 1951–64

The *Economist* magazine coined the phrase 'Butskellism' to sum up the almost identical economic policies of Labour and the Conservatives in the 1950s: R. A. Butler was the Tory Chancellor (1951–55), while Hugh Gaitskell was leader of the Labour Party (1955–63). Apart from the reprivatisation of steel and road haulage, the Conservatives accepted Labour's post-war reforms and subscribed to the same Keynesian approach to managing the economy. However, a range of problems began to develop that this approach was seemingly unable to solve:

- **Inflation:** A major priority was to maintain inflation at a healthy, low level. If prices began to rise, steps were taken to 'stop' the economy (for example, raising tax or limiting pay increases). Although such policies worked in the short-term, they were unable to prevent the build-up of inflationary pressure.
- **Unemployment:** The Conservatives also pledged to maintain full employment. If the economy began to dip then expansionary measures were taken (for example, cutting taxes and interest rates). The Conservatives were accused of using these more popular 'go' policies just before elections, putting political gain ahead of economic stability.
- **Slow growth:** The British economy grew at a slower rate than its competitors (2.3 percent per year compared to 5.6 percent in Italy and 5.1 percent in Germany). A key reason for this was a lack of investment in research and development in areas other than defence.

Overall, the Conservatives were criticised for responding to short-term problems rather than effectively managing the British economy. The 'stop-go' approach papered over problems rather than solving them. By the mid-1960s, the spectre of 'stagflation' (economic stagnation and inflation) hung over Britain.

SOURCE

From an article by Norman Macrae in the *Economist*, published in February 1954.

Mr Butskell is already a well-known figure in dinner table conversations in both Westminster and Whitehall and the time has come to introduce him to a wider audience. He is a composite of the present Chancellor [R. A. Butler] and the previous one [H. Gaitskell]. Whenever there is a tendency to excess Conservatism – such as... a little more unemployment to teach the workers a lesson – Mr Butskell speaks up for the cause of moderation; when there is clamour from the Government side of the House for even graver irresponsibilities from the Labour benches, Mr Butskell has so far spoken up from the other.

### The failure to cope with stagflation: 1964–79

The Labour governments of Harold Wilson and James Callaghan failed to improve on the Conservative track record. Attempts were made to improve planning and increase investment in the 'white heat' of new technology, but these failed to make a substantial impact due to continuing inflation, unemployment and slow growth. The Department of Economic Affairs was launched in 1964 under the leadership of the abrasive (and often inebriated) deputy leader George Brown. He devised a 'National Plan' to stimulate growth, but this never got off the ground due to a lack of departmental resources, defined authority or decent working relations with the Treasury. A Ministry of Technology was created, but suffered from the same lack of funding and authority.

Instead of planning, Labour responded to problems with the same 'stop-go' measures as the Conservatives before them. However, the most damaging lack of consistency was over the value of the pound: Wilson made it clear that he was determined to avoid a further devaluation by a Labour government, after the previous one in 1949. Yet, in November 1967, having attempted (and apparently failed) to borrow his way out of economic trouble, he was forced to cut the value of the pound from $2.80 to $2.40. Although Wilson went on television to explain that the 'pound in your pocket' was worth the same within the UK, he suffered a huge loss of credibility.

SOURCE

This cartoon appeared in the *Daily Mirror* on 12 October 1954.

DEAR OLD PALS . . .

This was exacerbated the same year when his application for Britain to join the European Economic Community (seen as a possible miracle cure for the economy) was vetoed by French President Charles De Gaulle.

Unemployment and inflation were boosted in the UK by events in the Middle East. On 16 October 1973, the Organization of Petroleum Exporting Countries (**OPEC**) raised oil prices by 70 percent in retaliation for American support of Israel during the Yom Kippur War (fought by a coalition of Arab states led by Syria and Egypt against Israel, 6–25 October 1973). By 1974, oil prices had risen by 400 percent; this contributed strongly to more general inflation (as high as 25 percent in 1976), due to the increased cost of energy and fuel for transport. The increased cost of imports forced the Labour government to try and cap prices and wages, and to cut spending. Neither of these measures was popular with voters and especially not with their trade union backers. Unemployment doubled between 1974 and 1976 to just below 1.5 million. These economic issues, together with mounting trade union anger, led to the 'Winter of Discontent' (1978–79), which finally blew consensus politics apart. Thatcher blamed irresponsible trade unions for most of the problems and set out to destroy them.

**KEY TERM**

OPEC
The Organization of Petroleum Exporting Countries was founded in 1960. Members co-ordinate their production of oil to ensure stable prices.

**AS Level Exam-Style Question Section B**

To what extent were Labour and Conservative governments successful in tackling the economic problems faced by Britain in the years 1945–79? (20 marks)

**Tip**

*Ensure you set out clearly what the economic problems were and use these to measure the success of the various governments of the period.*

**ACTIVITY**
**KNOWLEDGE CHECK**

**Responses to economic problems**

1 For each of the following periods, summarise the key economic problems that faced British governments: 1918-31; 1931-51; 1951-79.

2 For the same periods, summarise the key ways in which British governments sought to tackle these problems.

3 During which period would you argue that economic problems were the most severe? Explain your answer by comparing your chosen period with the others.

4 During which period do you consider that British governments were most successful in dealing with economic problems? Explain your answer by comparing your chosen period with the others.

## HOW EFFECTIVELY DID GOVERNMENTS RESPOND TO CHANGES IN THE WORKPLACE BETWEEN 1918 AND 1979?

Industrial change was the result of changing technologies and the growth of international competition. It benefited parts of the country where money was invested in the development and manufacture of new technologies, but caused a great deal of suffering for ordinary workers in the 'old industries' such as shipbuilding, steel, textiles and, above all, coal. While governments wanted to maintain a healthy and competitive economy, trade unions existed to defend the pay, jobs and working conditions of its members. This made poor industrial relations difficult to avoid, especially when the government sought to use wage caps to reduce inflation and make exports more competitive. While several approaches were used to try and improve industrial relations, anger sometimes led to widespread strike action, with especially severe strikes in 1926 and in the early 1970s. The unions saw it as their hard-won, democratic right to protect the interests of vulnerable workers against the might of employers. The government generally saw strike action as undemocratic blackmail: an unelected body disrupting the peace and prosperity of the nation to achieve selfish ends against the wishes of an elected government. The key question was whether the trade unions or the government were more to blame for the periods of miserable disruption. A further question was how far women should benefit from improvements in pay and working conditions: it is arguable that the government did more for female workers than the unions that were meant to represent them.

## TIMELINE: CHANGES IN THE WORKPLACE

**1920**
Unemployment Insurance Act

**1921**
Miners' strike defeated due to lack of support from rail and transport unions

Mines, taken over by government during the war, are returned to private owners

**1926**
May: General Strike

Miners continue to strike until their defeat in November

**1930**
Coal Mines Act attempts to improve productivity of coal mining and cuts miners' working hours

**1931**
Some unemployment benefits cut

Family Means Test introduced

**1934**
Unemployment Act undoes 1931 benefits cut and leads to the creation of the Unemployment Assistance Board two years later

Special Areas Act channels investment into areas worst-affected by slump

**1937**
Factory Act

**1939–45**
Ernest Bevin, Minister for Labour, uses negotiation and orders to restrict strikes

**1946**
Trades Disputes and Trade Union Act is repealed

**1955**
R. A. Butler announces gradual introduction of equal pay for women in the civil service

**1965**
Prices and Incomes Board is set up

**1966**
Prices and Incomes Act in 1966

**1969**
Government White Paper 'In Place of Strife' recommends new controls on ability to strike

**1970**
Equal Pay Act promotes same pay for work of equal value done by men and women on a voluntary basis

Prices and Incomes Board abolished

**1971**
Industrial Relations Act is passed; sets up ineffective National Industrial Relations Court

**1972**
Miners' strike provokes government to declare State of Emergency and a 'three-day week'

**1973**
London Stock Exchange allows first female members

**1974**
Miners strike again; 'three-day week' enforced from 1 January to 7 March

'Social Contract' agreed between new Labour government and trade unions

Pay Board and all attempts to use laws to control wage growth abolished

**1975**
Employment Protection Act sets up the Advisory, Conciliation and Arbitration Service (ACAS)

**1978–79**
Strikes by council workers, hospital staff and lorry drivers become known as 'Winter of Discontent'

## Industrial change and changing industrial relations, 1918–39

Those parts of the country heavily reliant on traditional industries fared worse than those with a growing service sector or where newer industries (such as chemicals, electrical engineering or car production) took off. Clydeside, Northumberland, Durham, Lancashire and South Wales were key areas of traditional industry, while London and the West Midlands did much better, even during the 'hungry' 1930s. Traditional industries were heavily reliant on exports and during the Great War lost their share of the market as rivals were able to fill the gaps left in the global market when British cotton and steel products were not available. Traditional industries also became less competitive compared to their European counterparts whose factories had been damaged or destroyed and so owners were forced to invest in newer machinery. More efficient American and German steel production undercut British domestic sales due to the retention of free trade (until 1932). The Great Depression led to a further contraction in demand for ships, steel, coal and textiles. Unemployment, which never fell below a million between 1921 and 1940, rose to almost three million in 1932 and 1933. Although unemployment had existed before 1918, what surprised contemporaries was the extent of long-term unemployment: in 1929, five percent of those in need of relief had been jobless for over a year; by 1932 this had risen to 16.4 percent – over 400,000 people. Against this tough economic backdrop it was unsurprising that workers in traditional industries fought to maintain jobs and pay while employers sought to cut costs and improve productivity. The government increasingly sought to provide help for the unemployed, but generally sided with employers in industrial disputes during this period. The most important example of this general pattern came during the 1926 General Strike.

### The causes and impact of the General Strike

Coal mining was dangerous: between1922 and 1924, 3,603 miners were killed and 597,158 were injured. Despite the fact that their wages had improved during the wartime nationalisation of mining, miners felt underpaid for their vital work. The Miners Federation of Great Britain (MFGB) was a formidable union, representing the interests of over a million miners. In recognition of the poor state of mining before the war, and the potential threat posed by the MFGB, the 1919 **Sankey Commission** recommended that government ownership be continued; yet the mines were handed back to private owners in 1921. Pay soon failed to keep up with prices, especially in unprofitable mines: unlike their German and Polish rivals, many owners had not invested in mechanisation and 80 percent of British coal was still mined with a pickaxe. Mine owners initially agreed to maintain wages throughout 1925, but broke this promise after a surge in German coal production and the return to the Gold Standard led to a further fall in exports. Despite a campaign to enforce a six-hour working day, mine owners increased the working day by one hour to eight hours. The miners were understandably furious. The government subsidised miners' wages for nine months (at a cost of £23 million) to avoid a general strike; this only served to give mine owners and the government time to prepare for the unavoidable clash.

**EXTRACT 1** From *The Riches Beneath our Feet: How Mining Shaped Britain*, written by Geoff Coyle in 2010.

> The men were paid by the piece: so much per ton of coal... at the end of the week, measurers came round to calculate what was due, but with inevitable attempts to avoid payment. However, anyone making too much fuss might be dismissed on the spot, losing his company housing at the same time... A major dispute occurred early in 1921 when the owners, having stocked coal, locked the men out. The men had no money and depended upon parish relief... After 9 months the dispute ended with the men returning to work with longer hours and less pay.

In March 1926, the **Samuel Commission** recommended radical restructuring of the coal industry, but also a pay cut for miners. Miners rejected this with the slogan 'Not a minute on the day, not a penny off the pay' and called for **TUC** support in a strike. Although the miners and the mine owners were highly inflexible, the TUC was prepared to negotiate with the government. However, Baldwin used a strike by printers at the *Daily Mail* on 2 May as a pretext to end the talks and declare a state of emergency. Churchill and Home Secretary William Joynson-Hicks had urged such action because they agreed that the strike would be a 'revolutionary movement, intended to inflict suffering upon the great mass of innocent persons in the community'. The TUC then followed through with its threat of a general strike on 3 May. Three million industrial workers went on strike in sympathy with the miners. Yet, just nine days later, it was all over and the miners were left to strike by themselves for another six months without success.

The General Strike failed for several reasons:

- Not all workers went on strike in sympathy with the miners, only those in printing, heavy industry, energy, textiles and transport. These workers were not ready for a strike and did not coordinate their efforts.
- The government had been preparing for a strike since July 1925: they had created the Organisation for the Maintenance of Supplies, a network of volunteers who could step in to do essential jobs (such as unloading and delivering food) not done by striking workers.

#### KEY TERMS

**Sankey Commission**
A group set up by the government to investigate wages, working hours and nationalisation in the coal industry. It was led by a judge, Sir John Sankey. Three mine owners and three miners also sat on the commission, which reported in 1919.

**Samuel Commission**
A group set up in light of the tense stand-off between mine owners and the MFGB. It was led by Liberal politician Sir Herbert Samuel, with a banker, an industrialist and Sir William Beveridge (see pages 40–41).

**TUC**
The Trades Union Congress was founded in Manchester in 1868 as a 'union of unions'. There were many small unions which, while weak by themselves, were stronger when they worked together.

- Churchill was put in charge of a government newspaper, *The British Gazette*, which turned public opinion against the strike with its hostile propaganda. It was made clear to the TUC that the government would not be held hostage to strike action.
- The TUC did as much as it could to limit violence. There were some clashes between volunteers and those on strike but no one was killed. This made the strike easier to handle for the government.
- The strike was hugely expensive for the TUC: it spent £4 million of its £12.5 million total strike fund.
- Herbert Samuel, a respected Liberal politician invited to look into the mining industry by Baldwin, offered an unofficial settlement (the Samuel Memorandum), which the TUC hoped would be enacted by the government: a National Wage Board to be set up, wage subsidies and no pay cuts before the restructuring of mining. The TUC accepted this proposal and called off the strike on 12 May. Miners, left to struggle on alone, gradually went back to an eight-hour day and reduced pay in late 1926.

The failure of the strike had a number of important consequences. Baldwin pleased the right-wing of the Conservatives by passing the Trades Dispute Act in 1927. This made sympathetic strikes illegal, exposed unions to financial damages during strikes, and scrapped 'contracting out' (union members would now have to opt in to payment of a 'political levy' for the Labour Party rather than pay this automatically). The TUC abandoned general strikes as a hopeless method. Many men became disillusioned with trade unions, in particular the TUC: membership sank to a low in 1932, before recovering. Working-class men began to look to the Labour Party to deliver political solutions in parliament rather than direct action. The strike was a powerful memory for many industrialists and politicians who sought better industrial relations in the decades after 1926.

**SOURCE 8** A table showing trade union membership and strike action between 1918 and 1979.

| Year | Number of trade unions | Number of trade union members in millions (number affiliated to TUC) | Number of strikes launched | Total number of working days lost through strikes (millions) |
|---|---|---|---|---|
| 1918 | 1,264 | 6.53 (5.23) | 1,165 | 5.88 |
| 1920 | 1,384 | 8.35 (6.42) | 1,607 | 26.57 |
| 1926 | 1,164 | 5.22 (4.16) | 323 | 162.23 |
| 1927 | 1,159 | 4.92 (3.87) | 308 | 1.17 |
| 1932 | 1,081 | 4.44 (3.37) | 389 | 6.49 |
| 1939 | 1,019 | 6.23 (4.87) | 940 | 1.36 |
| 1945 | 781 | 7.88 (6.67) | 2,293 | 2.84 |
| 1972 | 479 | 11.35 (10.00) | 2,497 | 23.91 |
| 1974 | 507 | 11.76 (10.36) | 2,922 | 14.75 |
| 1979 | 454 | 13.50 (12.17) | 2,080 | 29.47 |

**ACTIVITY**
**KNOWLEDGE CHECK**

**The General Strike**

1. Who or what was most to blame for the General Strike?
2. 'The TUC was chiefly to blame for the defeat of the General Strike.' How far do you agree with this statement?

## Changing working opportunities and conditions, 1939–79

### Key changes in the workplace

The changes in the British economy discussed above had a major impact on the nature and extent of work available in different sectors.

**SOURCE**

A table showing changing numbers of people employed in different occupational groups between 1921 and 1981.

| | Number of workers (thousands) | | | | | |
|---|---|---|---|---|---|---|
| **Occupational group** | **1921** | **1931** | **1951** | **1961** | **1971** | **1981** |
| Agriculture and fishing | 1,373 | 1,180 | 1,126 | 855 | 635 | 352 |
| Mining | 1,469 | 1,040 | 841 | 722 | 391 | 336 |
| Manufacturing | 6,723 | 5,981 | 7,902 | 8,383 | 8,136 | 5,974 |
| Construction | 826 | 970 | 1,430 | 1,705 | 1,673 | 1,564 |
| Gas, electricity and water | 180 | 224 | 358 | 377 | 362 | 338 |
| Banking and insurance | 328 | 388 | 489 | 722 | 952 | 1,295 |
| Local public service | 457 | 541 | 602 | 629 | 760 | 931 |
| National public service (inc. defence) | 480 | 368 | 1,036 | 798 | 812 | 589 |
| Transport and communications | 1,359 | 1,430 | 1,705 | 1,673 | 1,564 | 1,422 |
| Distribution and delivery | n.a. | 2,697 | 2,742 | 3,189 | 3,016 | 2,715 |
| Professional scientific | 868 | 1,018 | 1,536 | 2,120 | 2,901 | 3,649 |
| Services | n.a. | 2,713 | 2,393 | 2,270 | 2,534 | 2,522 |
| Domestic service | 1,390 | 1,509 | 499 | 362 | 239 | n.a. |

The total number of people working increased despite rises in the school-leaving age and a fall in the average age of retirement. There were huge falls in the numbers of miners and shipwrights despite government efforts to protect these traditional industries. Although the number of manufacturing workers increased until the 1980s, there was particularly marked growth in the **'white-collar'** sectors. There were several reasons for the growth of white-collar work:

- Higher disposable income fuelled an increased demand for goods and services, such as meals out at restaurants, which had previously been seen as unaffordable luxuries. This created more jobs.
- Governments increased spending on services such as health and education, creating lots more public sector jobs.
- It is far more difficult to mechanise white-collar jobs than manufacturing jobs. Fewer white-collar than **blue-collar** jobs were lost through automation.
- This shift in the balance of employment had some impact on industrial relations. First, managerial structures in white collar firms were far less distant than in industry; mutual understanding and communication were much better as a result. Second, white collar firms were less likely to be unionised and less likely to strike than industrial or manufacturing employees. Third, the decline in the overall importance of 'masculine' blue-collar employment gave more work opportunities to women.

**KEY TERM**

**White-collar/blue-collar**
A 'white-collar' worker performs administrative, managerial or professional work, often in an office. A 'blue-collar' worker performs manual labour. The terms were first coined in 1924 and referred to the typical colour of office workers' shirts and manual labourers' overalls.

## The changing role of women in the workplace

Women had made some gains in terms of the opportunities for work open to them during the First World War, but quickly returned to traditional 'women's work' (such as domestic service) after 1918. Trade unions were hostile to more permanent change and men returning from the armed forces expected employment. While single women could expect to do a certain range of non-professional jobs, the 'marriage bar' meant most married women stopped work to look after the home and children. This situation only began to change gradually after the Second World War. There was a range of reasons for the persistence of limited opportunities for women. Until the 1980s, most jobs were still in traditionally male 'blue-collar' areas of industry and manufacturing. Educational opportunities limited possible career options: until 1972, most working-class girls left school at 15; those who stayed on another year overwhelmingly took classes in secretarial skills, childcare or hairdressing. Very few women went to university and even fewer studied science, engineering, medicine or law: only 15 percent of doctors and five percent of lawyers were women in the 1960s. Throughout that decade, almost a third of all women were still teenagers when they got married; nine times as many women as men were married before the age of 19. Most women gave birth to their first child in the first three years of marriage and employers were not prepared to hire mothers. No legislation was passed to promote equal opportunities for women until 1970.

Yet, gradually, the number of women, especially married women, did increase in the workplace.

**SOURCE**

From A. Myrdal and V. Klein's *Women's Two Roles: Home and Work*, published in 1956.

...the dilemma is still with us and will remain so until society has so adjusted itself, mentally and materially, to the new conditions that it will be possible for women satisfactorily to combine the pursuit of a chosen career with marriage and family life. Only then will the emotional factors - the appeal of a traditional role, maternal example, hopes of marriage - cease to be in acute conflict with other more rational considerations.

**SOURCE 11**
A table showing changes in female employment between 1951 and 1981.

| | 1951 | 1961 | 1971 | 1981 |
|---|---|---|---|---|
| Percentage of workforce that are women | 31 | 33 | 37 | 40 |
| Percentage of 20-64-year-old women in workforce | 36 | 42 | 52 | 61 |
| Percentage of 20-64-year-old women employed part-time | 12 | 26 | 35 | 42 |
| Percentage of married women in the workforce | 26 | 35 | 49 | 62 |

The situation began to change even before changes in legislation in the 1970s. Again, there are several factors that combined to promote female working opportunities:

- The Second World War fuelled female desire to work: many women made new friends and found a new sense of fulfilment outside the home, even though some jobs were tedious or dangerous.
- Changes in education (see pages 53–60) increasingly provided a more level playing field for girls.
- The number of white-collar jobs, which were deemed 'more suitable' for women, increased throughout the century.
- Some women became more assertive because of a range of social changes in the 1960s and 1970s (see pages 73–79). An important example of this was a successful strike by female sewing machinists at Ford car plants in Halewood (Liverpool) and Dagenham (East London) in 1968. Having closed the factories for three weeks, and gained a lot of popular support, the women won a pay deal of just over 90 percent of the men's rate for similar work.

The Ford strikes, together with the need to mirror EEC laws in order to join in 1973, were a catalyst for the passage of three Acts in the 1970s designed to stop discrimination against women at work:

- The Equal Pay Act in 1970 called for 'equal pay for equal work'. It remained voluntary for businesses until 1975. Many employers (in 80 percent of cases) successfully claimed that the work men and women did was different, so the law did not apply. This loophole was removed in 1983 by replacing 'equal work' with 'work of comparable value'.
- The Sex Discrimination Act in 1975 made it illegal to treat workers of one gender less favourably than those of the other gender. While this helped in theory, in practice it was difficult and expensive for women to bring their discrimination claims to court.
- The Employment Protection Act in 1975 made it illegal to sack women because they were pregnant; it gave women the right to maternity pay and to return to their jobs if they wished.

Although there were clearly problems with the legislation, the Acts contributed to a general understanding that it was not acceptable to treat women unfairly if they wanted to work. Despite this, women were still disproportionately employed in lower-paid, lower-skilled and part-time jobs. Women were also under-represented in senior management positions. This 'glass ceiling', an upper limit to women's promotion, still limits female equality with men in the workplace today.

## Industrial relations 1939–79 and the reasons for their breakdown in 1960s and 1970s

### Industrial relations during and after the Second World War

The war led to several important developments in British industrial relations. Perhaps the most important was the shift from boom and bust with high unemployment to wartime full employment and a post-war commitment by Labour and the Conservatives to maintain it. Over time, this strengthened the bargaining position of trade unions, something that contributed to increasingly assertive action in the 1960s and 1970s. The war also led to the inclusion of trade unionists in many government decision-making bodies; the most famous example of this was the appointment of Ernest Bevin (then General Secretary of the Transport and General Workers Union) as Minister for Labour and National Service in 1940. Although wartime direction of labour and restrictions on the right to strike did not survive beyond 1945, trade unionist inclusion continued after the war, for example on the board of the nationalised Bank of England. Working with the unions, and an effort not to make industrial relations a party political dispute, were clear signs of consensus about minimising industrial disputes. Governments hoped that unions would voluntarily restrict wage demands; the spirit of wartime co-operation persisted until a spike of inflation in the early 1950s. Thereafter, governments were faced with the dilemma of whether to keep the unions happy and risk inflation, or impose controls on wages and prices and risk souring industrial relations. Governments tried a range of more or less forceful methods to limit pay demands, but none of them were particularly effective.

### Industrial relations before 1972: simmering tension

Although the British economy continued to grow throughout this period, it failed to grow as rapidly as rival economies abroad. British industry struggled to compete and jobs were lost as a result. This, together with government efforts to limit inflation through price and wage controls, led to a great deal of simmering tension. There were sporadic, serious strikes throughout the period, including a national seamen's strike in 1966. Consensus-era governments used appeasement and ineffective sanctions to deal with industrial unrest. Labour's reliance on trade union funding (since the repeal of the Trades Dispute Act in 1946) and party membership made it impossible for them to resist union demands. Barbara Castle's 1969 **White Paper** 'In Place of Strife' would have undermined union strength, but it was never implemented due to its unpopularity. Conservatives also tended to shy away from confrontation because they valued civic order and electability over a long-term solution to industrial issues. Heath (prime minister 1970–74) tried but failed to tackle the root causes of industrial unrest: the Industrial Relations Act failed to curtail union power because unions were not forced to sign up to the National Industrial Relations Court, which would have judged the legality of strike action.

**KEY TERM**

**White Paper**
A document produced by the government that sets out details of a proposed future policy. Discussion of the White Paper allows the government to form a bill to put before parliament.

### Industrial relations, 1972–79: boiling point

Industrial relations became far worse in the 1970s, when wages failed to keep up with prices for the first time since the Second World War. The escalation of industrial action was largely due to the failure of government efforts to resist increased pay demands:

- In 1971, the National Union of Miners (NUM) demanded a 43 percent pay increase. The government offered eight percent in order to try and stick to inflation targets. The NUM called for all 280,000 miners to strike on 9 January 1972. The government was forced to declare a state of emergency and a 'three-day week' in February, after flying pickets (groups of striking workers who travelled to other places of work and formed lines to stop anyone getting in) were used to shut down coal distribution depots and power stations. The strike was only called off on 19 February after the government meekly offered a 27 percent pay rise.
- The miners' victory merely encouraged other sectors to press for pay rises. Despite the creation of a Pay Board to examine wage deals that affected more than 1,000 workers and a Price Commission to limit price increases for some companies, teachers, hospital staff, train drivers, Ford car workers and gasmen went on strike in February 1973.
- The 1973 oil crisis led to even higher wage demands: the NUM demanded a further 35 percent pay increase. A further 'three-day week' was introduced on 1 January 1974. On 4 February, 81 percent of miners voted to go on strike. Heath's attempt to use a general election, campaigning on the slogan 'Who governs Britain?', to defeat the miners failed.

- Callaghan was determined to stick to a five percent limit to pay increases in 1978, yet only had a vague 'Social Contract' of agreement with the unions to enforce this policy. In November, a strike at Ford car factories led to a 17 percent pay rise and embarrassment for the government.
- On 3 January 1979, oil tanker and lorry drivers went on strike. The tanker drivers quickly won a pay rise and returned to work. The lorry drivers held out for six weeks. In that time they not only refused to deliver goods but also picketed ports to stop supplies reaching industry, shops and even hospitals. People began to panic-buy in case the shops ran out of food.
- On 22 January, 1.5 million public sector workers went on strike: almost all schools shut, as did museums, libraries and other public buildings. With no porters, cooks or cleaners, hospitals were only able to treat emergency cases. With dustmen on strike, huge piles of rubbish began to build up in parts of towns and cities across the UK. In Liverpool, the gravediggers went on strike; by the end of January, there were 225 corpses stored in a factory awaiting burial. The government accepted defeat on 14 February and allowed pay increases of 10–15 percent. By mid-March, all those who had been on strike were back at work.

By this stage, the public had been frightened and disgusted by the impact of the strikes; a vast majority now believed that the unions were too powerful and that something had to be done to limit their power. Conservative leader Margaret Thatcher promised to do just that; and it came as little surprise that she won the May 1979 general election.

## Change (5b)

### Impetus and disruption

**Developments in industrial relations**

| | | |
|---|---|---|
| General strike, 1926 | Labour landslide victory, 1945 | Barbara Castle writes White Paper, 'In Place of Strife', 1969 |
| Edward Heath's government passes the Industrial Relations Act, 1971 | Miners' strikes of 1972 and 1974 | Winter of Discontent, 1978-79 |

Patterns of development consist of changes which, at given times, converge and have a bearing on one another and, at other times, diverge and have little in common. In the above example, the changes come together to form a pattern of development that tends towards Thatcher's victory in 1979.

Working in a small group, write each change on a small piece of paper. Arrange these small pieces on an A3 sheet as you think best. Then link them with lines and write along the line what links those changes. Try to make sure that you think about how those links may have changed over time.

Answer the following questions individually or in pairs:

1 Why was 1969 an important year in industrial relations in Britain?

2 Which changes were significant in ensuring that the Labour Party attempted union reform legislation?

3 What changes were important in bringing down the Heath government?

## ACTIVITY
KNOWLEDGE CHECK

### The workplace, 1918-79

1 How did changes in employment patterns impact on industrial relations between 1918 and 1979?

2 Between 1918 and 1979, why did the role of women in the workplace not change significantly?

3 Why did Wilson, Heath and Callaghan fail to tackle the problem of poor industrial relations?

### A Level Exam-Style Question Section B

How accurate is it to say that the General Strike of 1926 marked the lowest point in industrial relations in the years 1918–79? (20 marks)

**Tip**

*Compare the General Strike to other important turning points in relations between unions and government, such as 'In Place of Strife' as well as unrest under Heath and Callaghan.*

ACTIVITY
SUMMARY

**A changing political and economic environment, 1918–79**

1. Create a graph with 'time: 1918–79' on the horizontal axis projecting midway from a vertical axis labelled 'left-wing' above and 'right-wing' below the midpoint. Aim to plot where British governments lay on the vertical axis, paying particular attention to turning points such as changes of government. Give each turning point a number and use this as a key to explain why a particular government was more or less right-wing than its predecessor.
2. Plot a similar graph but with 'economic success' and 'economic failure' on the vertical axis. Again, pay careful attention to particular changes in British economic fortunes. Give each turning point a number and use this as a key to explain the changes below the graph.
3. Draw a diagram with three boxes labelled 'changes in government', 'changes in economic policy' and 'changes in industrial relations'. Draw arrows between all three boxes and label these arrows with explanations of how each one relates to and affects the others (the direction of the arrow should indicate the flow of the effect). Which box has the most arrows coming out of it? What can you conclude from this?

## WIDER READING

**Books**

Harrison, B. *Seeking a Role: the United Kingdom 1951–1970* and *Finding a Role? The United Kingdom 1970–1990*, OUP (2010)

Lowe, N. *Mastering Modern British History*, Palgrave Macmillan (2009)

Lynch, M. *Britain 1900–51* and *Britain 1945–2007*, Hodder Education (2008)

Pearce, M. and Stewart, G. *British Political History 1867–2001: Democracy and Decline*, Routledge (2002)

**Websites**

*National Archives themed document collections*

The 1930s: www.nationalarchives.gov.uk/education/topics/thirties-britain.htm

The 1950s: www.nationalarchives.gov.uk/education/topics/fifties-britain.htm

The 1960s: www.nationalarchives.gov.uk/education/topics/sixties-britain.htm

Attlee's Britain: www.nationalarchives.gov.uk/education/topics/attlees-britain.htm

British Cabinet papers 1915–84: www.nationalarchives.gov.uk/cabinetpapers

# 1.2 Creating a welfare state, 1918–79

**KEY QUESTIONS**

- How successfully did British governments provide welfare support in the years 1918–79?
- Why, and with what impact, was the National Health Service created in 1948?
- To what extent has educational reform led to widening opportunities?

## INTRODUCTION

Welfare is aid given in the form of money or necessities to those in need, usually the old, the young, the sick and the poor. The first three groups were viewed as 'deserving' poor, rightly cared for by relatives, the Church, private organisations and increasingly the state. However, until the end of the 19th century, healthy people of working age who fell into destitution were often seen as morally at fault and, therefore, 'undeserving' poor. The process of having to prove that you 'deserved' welfare was a hated, humiliating experience.

From 1908, the Liberal government inaugurated a huge expansion of state-provided welfare. These new support mechanisms were open to all who qualified, with no distinction between 'deserving' and 'undeserving' poor. However, the new Liberal reforms were far from universal: pensions were only offered to the poorest people and unemployment insurance was only available for 15 weeks a year to workers in six industries. For those without insurance, the only option was to fall back on older forms of welfare provision.

The situation in 1918 at the close of the First World War cannot be described as a 'welfare state', one where universal support is available to anyone who needs it from cradle to grave. At best, it has been described as a 'social service state', one where a minimum of support was offered to those without independent means of survival. Although the First World War generated a desire and opportunity to create something approaching a welfare state (best shown by the creation of a **Ministry of Reconstruction** in 1917), the onset of economic problems after 1920 undermined such hopes and plans.

The adoption of Keynesian economic theories (see page 21), and a determination to avoid the broken promises made after the Great War, meant that the Second World War caused a comprehensive and sustained shift in welfare provision. The Attlee government spearheaded a welfare revolution, with the National Health Service as the jewel in the crown. However, even as the welfare state was being forged, there were concerns over the cost of such an ambitious undertaking and the effect that such universal provision would have on people's moral fibre and independence. By 1979, with an increasingly

**KEY TERM**

**Ministry of Reconstruction (1917–19)**
The Ministry of Reconstruction was established in 1917, under the leadership of Liberal MP and medical doctor Christopher Addison: 'not so much to rebuild society as it was before the war, but to mould a better world out of the social and economic conditions which have come into being during the war'. The Ministry worked in collaboration with other ministries to deal with pressing issues raised by the First World War, such as demobilisation, healthcare, housing, education and unemployment.

**1920** - Unemployment Insurance Act extends numbers of workers eligible for unemployment insurance

**1921** - Pensions raised to 10 shillings per week

**1925** - Widows', Orphans' and Contributory Old Age Pensions Act provides pension scheme for low-paid workers and sets retirement age at 65

**1929** - Local Government Act transfers welfare powers from Boards of Guardians to county councils and county boroughs

**1930** - Poor Law Act renames 'Poor Law' as 'Public Assistance'

**1931** - 'Means test' introduced for unemployment benefits as a money-saving measure

**1934** - Unemployment Assistance Act reverses 1931 benefits cut and sets up Unemployment Assistance Board to manage benefits payments

**1942** - Beveridge Report calls for universal welfare provision

**1944** - Two government White Papers, 'Employment Policy' and 'Social Insurance', accept the need to safeguard full employment and provide a universal system of welfare support

**1946** - National Insurance Act enforces compulsory insurance for pensions, sickness, maternity and unemployment

1915 | 1920 | 1925 | 1930 | 1935 | 1940 | 1945

large and expensive system, these concerns had developed into sustained criticisms. While the welfare state continued to have many supporters (not least the huge numbers of people who gained employment or effective support from it), these criticisms only grew as Britain headed into the 21st century.

# HOW SUCCESSFULLY DID BRITISH GOVERNMENTS PROVIDE WELFARE SUPPORT IN THE YEARS 1918–79?

## The extent and nature of welfare provision, 1918–39

### Unemployment

The most pressing problem for interwar governments was unemployment: this was never below one million (about 10 percent of the workforce) between the end of 1920 and mid-1940, and peaked at over three million in the early 1930s. Interwar governments wanted to support the unemployed, but also wanted to balance the books. A self-funding National Insurance scheme, with benefits paid from a fund generated by members' contributions whilst employed, was seen as the ideal solution and was implemented by the 1911 National Insurance Act. However, the war undermined this scheme because many of the 3.5 million returning troops were not eligible for the benefits it provided, either because they had not worked in one of the specified industries or they had not made sufficient contributions. The wartime coalition realised that a difficult situation was developing: it would take time to redesign the National Insurance scheme but, in the meantime, men who had fought for king and country could not be left to rely on the old Poor Law. The only alternative was to hand out dole money. As this would be paid out of general taxation (or worse still, borrowing) with no link to individual contributions, it was feared that this would upset the budget, divert funds from more productive use and encourage reliance on unearned income.

**EXTEND YOUR KNOWLEDGE**

**The Poor Laws (1500s-1948)**

The Poor Laws were a system of relief for the poor set up during the rule of the Tudor dynasty in the 16th century. The Poor Laws made a clear distinction between the 'deserving' or 'impotent' poor and the 'undeserving' able-bodied poor: the former were given food, clothing, and sometimes housing or money paid for by local rates, while the latter were often punished as criminal 'vagrants' (beggars).

In the 18th century, a large number of workhouses were built to house the poor and put them to work; this became known as 'indoor relief' and existed alongside earlier forms of 'outdoor relief' (in which people were helped in their own homes). A new Poor Law amendment was passed in 1834; this sought to encourage the able-bodied to work by making conditions in workhouses worse than in the poorest homes. It did not work well and was seen as an expensive and inhumane approach by critics. Workhouses came to be used in a more humane way to accommodate the sick and elderly and some developed decent medical facilities.

In order to qualify for outdoor relief the poor had to prove to Poor Law Guardians (local officials) that they were morally upstanding. This was a hated and humiliating process. Liberal reforms before 1914 removed this stigma for those who were eligible: pensions were received as a right and collected from post offices. However, although workhouses and the Guardians were abolished in 1929, and uninsured unemployed received assistance from the Unemployment Assistance Board (UAB) after 1934, the Poor Law system still existed as a safety net for people who were not covered under the new legislation.

The Poor Law was finally abolished as part of the 1948 National Assistance Act; people who fell through cracks in the welfare system would now have the National Assistance Board to help them.

**SOURCE**

From a report made by the Ministry of Reconstruction in February 1918.

So far as hardship due to unemployment is not met by insurance the Government of the day will inevitably be driven back on... a system of doles. It will be impossible in the middle of a great crisis to improvise any satisfactory machinery for administration and large sums will be spent in the least effective and most demoralising way. Unless a scheme of general insurance is devised and launched at the earliest possible date it may be impossible to avoid the disastrous chaos of unorganised and improvised methods of relieving distress.

**1948** – National Assistance Act provides a financial safety net for the destitute and formally abolishes Poor Law

**1973** – Manpower Services Commission created to provide employment and training services to unemployed

**1978** – Youth Opportunities Programme created for 16–18-year-olds continuously unemployed for six weeks or more

1950 1955 1960 1965 1970 1975 1980

**1971** – Family Income Supplement introduced to provide a financial safety net for poor families with children

**1975–78** – Job Creation Programme aimed at cutting levels of unemployment

The short-term solution was to issue dole money but under a different name: the 'out-of-work donation' (1918–20) was issued to returning troops and then civilian unemployed until they found work. Although it was meant to be temporary, it set two important precedents: the government accepted a duty to adequately support the unemployed, regardless of insurance contributions; and it provided more money for family dependants.

At the same time, a new Unemployment Insurance Act was developed to offer a longer-term solution. The idea was that increasing the number of workers covered by insurance would make the scheme self-funding. Unfortunately, the Act was passed in 1920, just as the effects of the post-war slump were beginning to bite: rather than create a self-funding scheme, the greater number of eligible claimants (around two-thirds of all workers) quickly drained the accumulated funds. By 1921, the government was forced to make 'extended' or 'uncovenanted' payments; these were meant to be paid for through worker contributions from future employment but were, in reality, dole payments disguised as insurance. The government chose to make these payments because the Poor Law could not cope with the scale of the problem and ministers feared a revolution if the unemployed were not adequately supported. The government was already feeling pressured as 2.4 million workers had taken part in strikes over pay and conditions in 1919. However, attempts were made to limit the expense of the new system: a 'seeking work test' was implemented in March 1921; by March 1930, three million claims had been rejected because of the test.

Major changes in the provision of welfare for the unemployed were enforced through the 1929 Local Government Act and the 1934 Unemployment Act. The Local Government Act said that county and borough councils had to set up Public Assistance Committees (PACs). These were centrally funded and replaced the Poor Law Guardians who had administered funds under the old Poor Law. In response to the financial crisis of 1931, the PACs were given the power to means-test claimants: their combined household income was thoroughly investigated to judge eligibility for dole payments. The means test was hated: not only was it an invasion of privacy, it was also unfair, as some PACs were less stringent with their tests than others. By the end of 1931, 400,000 people had suffered rejected or reduced claims because of the test.

The Unemployment Act separated the treatment of 'insurable' from long-term unemployment. Part I of the Act provided 26 weeks of benefit payments to the 14.5 million workers who paid into the scheme. Part II created a national Unemployment Assistance Board (UAB) to help those with no entitlement to insurance benefits. By 1937, the UAB had assisted one million people on a national means-tested basis. By this point, Poor Law provision had shrunk to just a few groups not covered by the UAB; these included widows, who could not yet claim a pension, and deserted wives. The government had not been able to solve unemployment, largely because the prevailing wisdom of retrenchment (spending cuts and tax rises) could not stimulate economic growth. It was only when huge state spending was poured into rearmament after 1936 that persistent unemployment was finally tackled.

Although the focus here has been on government efforts to create a level of unemployment welfare acceptable to both the treasury and those without work, the human impact of mass unemployment should not be forgotten. As historian Derek Fraser has written, 'Unemployment ... had poisoned millions of homes; it had blighted whole industrial regions; it had disinherited a generation; and it had laid low an elected government'. (Chapter 1 covers the political impact of the depression, while Chapter 4 goes into more depth about the regional differences in the impact of unemployment on the British population.)

### Pensions

State pensions had been introduced by the 1908 Pensions Act. Although they were hugely popular with the eligible over-70s (poor men and women who had worked throughout their lives and lived in the UK for 20 years), there were criticisms that they were means-tested and did not support the widows and children of the deceased. Minister for Health Neville Chamberlain addressed these concerns with his 1925 Widows', Orphans' and Old Age Contributory Pensions Act. This provided a pension of ten shillings a week for those aged 65 to 70, and provided for widows, their children and orphans. It was funded by a compulsory contribution (individuals, employers and the state paid into the scheme) rather than by taxation. This was initially unpopular with the Labour Party, who felt it unfairly penalised the poor but the tough economic conditions, together with an ageing population, led to its general acceptance. Self-employed workers of both sexes were allowed to join the scheme in 1937. The lack of tinkering with pension provision compared to unemployment payments could suggest what a good job Chamberlain did in drafting the 1925 Pensions Act. It is more likely that this reflects the enormous pressure placed on interwar governments by unemployment and the limited options they saw available to deal with the problem.

### Housing

Local and national government had made efforts to improve housing since the mid-Victorian era. There was a concern that slums promoted crime and disease and a lot of slum clearance had been undertaken before 1918. A major improvement in urban living standards was achieved by the introduction of mains water and sewerage to homes: as late as 1899, only a quarter of houses in Manchester had flushing toilets compared to 98 percent by 1914. The government had promised returning soldiers 'a home fit for heroes' and the 1919 Housing and Town Planning Act aimed to empower local authorities to use central government funds to meet housing needs. Although it was estimated that over 600,000 houses would have to be built to meet demand, only 213,000 were constructed before the onset of recession led to the 'Geddes Axe' (see page 25). The housing shortage grew worse as a result, with an estimated shortfall of 822,000 houses in 1923. One consequence of this was that young married couples had to carry on living with their parents. Nevertheless, according to historian A. J. P. Taylor, the Act 'established the principle that housing was a social service'. Conservative and Labour Housing Acts in 1923 and 1924 respectively sought to use subsidies to encourage the construction of private and state-owned housing. These Acts, together with a further Labour Housing Act in 1930, promoted a great deal of housebuilding. Between 1919 and 1940, four million homes were built in total, with one million built by the public sector (the private sector had a greater capacity for construction and was suitably incentivised by state subsidies). As historian Helen Meller has noted, 'By 1940, one-third of all houses had been built since 1918'. The 1930 Act used state funds to rehouse people living in overcrowded areas; most of the public sector houses were built in large cities such as Birmingham, Manchester, Sheffield and Liverpool. Between 1924 and 1939, 20 'cottage estates' were created on the outskirts of London: these were new suburbs connected to the centre by rail.

While the quality of housing was much improved (largely thanks to generous state subsidies for each house), some projects were not properly thought through. At the huge Becontree estate (25,800 houses and flats) a lack of local jobs nearly led to disaster, which was only avoided thanks to the construction of a new Ford car factory nearby in 1931. With the new homes came not only indoor plumbing and gardens but also increased demand for domestic goods such as new furniture, which further stimulated the economy and helped to raise the average standard of living.

## EXTEND YOUR KNOWLEDGE

### Key developments in British housing, 1930–79

The 1930s saw the extension of slum clearance with further Housing Acts in 1933 and 1935 designed to promote new housebuilding and force local authorities to end overcrowding in old housing areas.

The key challenge in the 1940s was to overcome the damage inflicted on residential property by German bombing. The New Town Act of 1946 set up local corporations to build towns such as Corby in Northamptonshire, Milton Keynes in Buckinghamshire, Skelmersdale in Lancashire, Runcorn in Cheshire and Cwmbran in Monmouthshire. The Town and Country Planning Act of 1947 laid down rules to prevent towns and cities sprawling into one another.

Most housing in the new towns replicated earlier suburban homes with gardens; high rises continued to be built nearer town and city centres. A gas explosion in May1968 led to the partial collapse of Ronan Point tower block in east London and the death of four residents. This sparked concern about high-rise accommodation and led to new building regulations in 1970 to avoid a recurrence of similar tragedies. The block was demolished in 1984 to make room for two-storey houses with gardens.

A number of laws were also passed concerning rent. Post-war Conservative governments wanted to remove legislation that controlled rent increases; they justified this by saying landlords would invest more money in the upkeep of their properties if they were allowed to charge a 'fair' market rate. The 1957 Rent Act scrapped rent control on 810,000 homes and allowed an increase on a further 4,300,000. A further Rent Act passed by the Labour government reintroduced rent controls in 1965. The Conservatives struck back with the 1972 Housing Finance Act: this forced local councils to charge a 'fair rent' to tenants in council houses. This was clearly a political move aimed at stopping Labour councils effectively buying support with subsidised rent. Margaret Thatcher went one stage further in 1980: the Housing Act allowed council house tenants to buy their homes, securing a great deal of working-class support for the Conservatives.

## ACTIVITY
## KNOWLEDGE CHECK

**Unemployment and pensions**

1 What options were available to governments to deal with unemployment between 1918 and 1939?

2 Why was there so much tinkering with unemployment welfare provision between 1918 and 1939?

3 Which had the greater success, pensions or housing provision, between 1918 and 1939?

# The impact of the Second World War, the Labour Government and consensus, 1939–64

## The impact of 'total war' on social welfare provision

The Second World War led to a wide consensus that welfare provision needed a radical overhaul: a political will developed to iron out the unfairness and inconsistency of a system that had evolved piecemeal in reaction to a series of difficult problems rather than planning to meet them. There were several reasons for this important shift in attitude among politicians and the general public.

- A 'total war', which affected rich and poor alike, had prompted 'total solutions' such as universal rationing and the provision of communal bomb shelters; the success of such policies gave a boost to **universalist**, as opposed to selective, solutions. The sacrifices endured by the whole population led to public expectation of a just reward; there was a good deal of discussion of the **fair shares** that should continue into peacetime. The evacuation of city children to the countryside opened affluent eyes to the scale of poverty still found in 'black spots' of Britain; this served as a mirror held up to the country and contributed to acceptance of the need for change.

## KEY TERMS

**Universalist**
Concerned with all people rather than a particular group.

**Fair shares**
Equal distribution of resources, which had been the philosophy underlying the system of rationing that existed during the Second World War.

- The success of a state-directed war economy increased political and popular belief in the potential of state intervention to improve peoples' lives after the war. The war had forced the British government to borrow and spend huge sums of money in pursuit of victory; why, it was argued, could similar borrowing and spending not be used in pursuit of public well-being? Keynes's economic views had been proved robust and his ideas used to fund an expansion of the welfare state.
- The war forced a coalition government; the inclusion of Labour ministers such as Attlee and Bevin led to a great deal of co-operation over wartime policy. The all-party development of a number of White Papers in 1944 cemented this generally harmonious outlook: 'Social Insurance', published in September 1944, which was the basis of the 1946 National Insurance Act, helped promote Conservative acceptance of that Act.

SOURCE 2

From the editorial of *The Times*, published on 1 July 1940.

If we speak of democracy, we do not mean a democracy which maintains the right to vote but forgets the right to work and the right to live. If we speak of freedom, we do not mean a rugged individualism which excludes social organisation and economic planning. If we speak of equality, we do not mean a political equality nullified by social and economic privilege. If we speak of economic reconstruction, we think less of maximum production… than of equitable distribution… The European house cannot be put in order unless we put our own house in order first. The new order cannot be based on the preservation of privilege whether the privilege be that of a country, of a class, or of an individual.

### The Beveridge Report (December 1942)

William Beveridge was a Liberal politician who took a great interest in social reform. In June 1941, he was appointed to head a government committee to investigate welfare provision and recommend improvements. The committee was set up at Churchill's request, in part because it had become possible to contemplate the future now that the worst of the Blitz was over, but also because of the painful failure to deliver 'homes fit for heroes' after the First World War. There was a clear feeling that the war was being fought to deliver a better world and that a more inclusive, systematic welfare system was a fundamental part of such a world. By November 1942, Beveridge was ready to deliver his report to parliament. His key recommendations were:

- for the state to tackle the 'five giants' of want (through national insurance), disease (through a national health service), ignorance (through better education), squalor (through rehousing) and idleness (through the maintenance of full employment)
- for the provision of state welfare to be centralised, regulated and systematically organised
- for state welfare to be funded entirely by a compulsory single insurance payment; he did not anticipate extra government spending on welfare under his scheme. He wanted to avoid any 'means-tested' assistance payments and the rise of a 'Santa Claus state' that gave people something for nothing. As a Liberal, he did not want the system to incentivise dependence on the state.

While Beveridge's recommendations were not new, his report drew together several developments that had taken place in a piecemeal fashion and presented them as a coherent, consolidated programme for post-war reconstruction. The popularity of the report (it sold 635,000 copies) is also explained by its timing: winning the war made state-led solutions to difficult problems seem like a realistic prospect. Copies of the report were even dropped over Germany to encourage the civilian population to demand peace.

### How far did Labour deliver on its promise to implement the Beveridge Report?

While the central thrust of the report was accepted by Attlee's government, there were some important differences between Beveridge's plan and its implementation in practice. Labour rejected his call for welfare payments to be met solely by universal insurance. As contributions were compulsory, they had to be set at a level affordable by the lowest paid; it was felt that a higher rate would penalise the poor as it took a greater proportion of their earnings.

SOURCE

The front page of the *Daily Mirror*, published on 2 December 1942.

DAILY MIRROR, Wed., December 2, 1942.

No. 12,159 ONE PENNY
Registered at the G.P.O. as a Newspaper.

# Beveridge tells how to BANISH WANT

## Cradle to grave plan | All pay—all benefit

**SIR WILLIAM BEVERIDGE'S Report, aimed at abolishing Want in Britain, is published today.**

**He calls his Plan for Social Security a revolution under which "every citizen willing to serve according to his powers has at all times an income sufficient to meet his responsibilities."**

**Here are his chief proposals:**

**All social insurance—unemployment, health, pensions—lumped into one weekly contribution for all citizens without income limit—from duke to dustman.**

**These payments, in the case of employees, would be:**

**Men 4s. 3d. Employer 3s. 3d.**
**Women 3s. 6d. Employer 2s. 6d.**

**Cradle to the grave benefits for all, including:**

**Free medical, dental, eyesight and hospital treatment;**

**Children's allowances of 8s. a week each, after the first child.**

**Increases in unemployment benefit (40s. for a couple) and abolition of the means test; industrial pension in place of workmen's compensation.**

**A charter for housewives, including marriage grant up to £10; maternity grant of £4 (and 36s. for 13 weeks for a paid worker); widow's benefit; separation and divorce provision; free domestic help in time of sickness.**

**Old age pensions rising to 40s. for a married couple on retirement.**

**Funeral grants up to £20.**

**To work the scheme a new Ministry of Social Security would open Security Offices within reach of every Citizen.**

**The 1d.-a-week-collected-at-the-door insurance schemes of the big companies would be taken over by the State.**

**Sir William says the Plan depends on a prosperous Britain, but claims that it can begin by July 1, 1944, if planning begins at once.**

[See pages 4, 5 and 7]

## Allies separate Axis armies in Africa

AMERICAN and French forces were reported last night to have driven a wedge between the two Axis armies in North Africa—between Nehring, fighting to hold Bizerta and Tunis, and Rommel, at bay at El Aghella.

**Messages from North Africa and New York stated that the Allies have reached the Tunisian coast between Gabes and Sfax.**

Nehring's land communications with Tripolitania—where the Afrika Korps is preparing for the next big attack by General Montgomery's Eighth Army—have thus been cut off.

The Americans and French are believed to have pushed to the coast through desert-like country from Gafsa, in Central Tunisia.

**In the Bizerta-Tunis triangle, Morocco radio reported, the British First Army has crossed the Axis minefields to come to grips with the main defences.**

The French are reported to have captured Pont du Fahs, a railway town 35 miles south of Tunis.

### Quit Bizerta 'Drome?

The air battle over Tunisia is being fought with an intensity believed to be unequalled since the Battle of Britain.

As the struggle grows fiercer the Germans throw in planes rushed to North Africa from Western Europe and Russia.

**One Nazi pilot shot down in Tunisia was flying over Stalingrad less than a fortnight ago.**

Bizerta airfield has been so devastated that it was believed at Allied H.Q. last night that most of the Luftwaffe bombers and fighters have been driven back to Sicily.

**Flying Fortresses have also pounded Tunis, Sfax and Gabes.**

RAF bombers rained explosives on Bizerta without a pause during Monday night, and daylight had scarcely appeared yesterday when other Allied aircraft took up the attack.

## El Agheila spearhead

Patrol activity by the advanced spearhead of the Eighth Army on the El Agheila front yesterday means that the battle for this vital position may be looming.

Indications of our growing strength in this advanced area are our constant air attacks on enemy communications on the road between El Agheila and Tripoli, and on the two enemy bases of Misurata and Tripoli.

German radio last night admitted that the spearhead of the Eighth Army had pushed closer to Axis lines, and yesterday's Italian communique also reported activity between advanced units.

### FDR AND DE GAULLE

President Roosevelt said yesterday that he would be glad to give General de Gaulle, but had not invited him to visit United States.

## Darlan is 'Chief of State'

ADMIRAL DARLAN has created an Imperial Council at Algiers and has assumed the powers of Chief of State in French Africa, Morocco radio announced last night.

**The radio said Darlan has assumed the power of Chief of State "as representative of Marshal Petain, who is at present a prisoner."**

"French Africa has resumed an official status which will enable it, pending the liberation of Metropolitan France, to defend the general interests of the Empire, to resume effectively the fight at the side of her Allies, and to represent France in the world.

The Imperial Council has already held its two first sittings.

Admiral Darlan presided over the sittings, which were attended by General Nogues, Governor-General Boisson, Governor-General Chatel, General Giraud, and General Bergeret.

### STATEMENT ON DARLAN IN SECRET

The position of Admiral Darlan and the military developments in North Africa are to be subjects of a statement in secret session in the Commons.

When Mr. Eden announced this yesterday he added that an opportunity would be provided for a debate if desired.

## NO COMMONS DEBATE BEFORE NEW YEAR

FIRST Commons comments on Sir William Beveridge's plan will be made at the next sitting, as the I.L.P. amendment to the Address is so broadly phrased that it will embrace any reconstruction proposals of this kind.

Mr. James Griffiths, from the Labour Front Bench, may indicate some of his party's reactions, but, as Sir William Jowitt indicated yesterday, the report will not be fully debated until the New Year.

The people of Occupied Europe are being told by radio of the report and its implications.

From dawn, in twenty-two languages, they will be shown how Britain, even in the midst of war, has grappled with social problems, just as in the past she took a lead on questions of social security.

Sir William will explain his report on the radio at 9.25 tonight.

## Govt. give hint of post-war planning

CHOOSING the eve of the publication of Sir William Beveridge's long-awaited report on Social Security, the Government yesterday gave the country its first indication of their own plans for post-war Britain.

These include the continuance of rationing for some time and control of industry (some industries being taken over as public corporations); the development of agriculture, forestry and public utilities like electricity.

The Government also announced the immediate setting up of a new Ministry of Town and Country Planning, and the rejection of the Scott and Uthwatt Committees' proposals for placing main responsibility for planning in the hands of a permanent commission.

### Victory First

Sir William Jowitt, Paymaster-General, answering a debate on reconstruction in the House of Commons, said:

**"We must not allow ourselves to be distracted by talk of reconstruction from the stern task of securing victory.**

"Talk of reconstruction is a mockery if the world is to remain hereafter under the constant fear of aggression."

Sir William referred to the Beveridge Report and said:

"The ideal of Social Security is one to which all thinking men and women can subscribe. We must survey his work as part of our reconstruction work as a whole.

**"I hope that early in the New Year members will be in a position to discuss the main questions raised in the Report."**

Sir William said it seemed obvious that the immediate

Continued on Back Page

## Demobilisation fixed by age and length of service

**Government plans for demobilisation after the war were outlined in the Commons yesterday by Sir William Jowitt, Paymaster-General. He said:—**

**No fighting man can expect to be demobilised at all if and so long as his services are required for some definite military purpose.**

**SUBJECT TO THAT THE BROAD PRINCIPLE ON WHICH WE HAVE DRAWN UP PLANS IS THIS: A DISCHARGE WILL BE BASED IN THE MAIN ON AGE PLUS LENGTH OF SERVICE.**

**I don't want to say any more about this at this time because it is probably undesirable to get into a demobilisation discussion at this stage of the war. To use a golfing metaphor, it would be a glaring case of taking our eyes off the ball.**

**In good time and in due course we may disclose to the House the plans that we suggest so that they may be debated.**

**In our plans we have not overlooked the question of education and training for the young whose educational careers were interrupted by the war.**

**Neither have we forgotten the disabled. We all owe it to them to see that special provisions are made for them.**

**We have passed all those matters under detailed review.**

Social security was therefore not introduced on a self-funding basis: higher taxation was used to supplement higher pension and unemployment benefits than those advocated by Beveridge. He was critical of the development of a 'pay-as-you-go' welfare system where tax payers subsidised those in receipt of benefits, rather than benefits being paid from a fund generated by contributions.

Apart from the method of funding welfare provision, Labour clearly implemented Beveridge's key ideas on social insurance:

- The Family Allowances Act of 1945 provided mothers with a non-means-tested payment of five shillings a week for each child apart from her first. MP Eleanor Rathbone successfully challenged the original plan to give the money to fathers. Mothers received their first family allowance payment in August 1946, although the final amount given was less than Beveridge had recommended.
- The National Insurance Act of 1946 created a compulsory universal contributory system to help pay for pensions (for women aged 60 and over, 65 for men), and benefits for unemployment, sickness, funeral expenses and maternity benefits.
- The Industrial Accidents Act of 1948 gave additional cover for workplace injuries.
- The National Assistance Act of 1948 established the National Assistance Board (NAB) to provide financial help to the most vulnerable poor, such as single mothers, the blind and deaf, who had not been covered by the 1946 Insurance Act. It also led local authorities to provide services for such groups. The NAB was far more popular than the old UAB because it used a less rigorous form of means-testing: 250,000 more people were able to claim a higher rate of benefits after 1948. The NAB was renamed the Benefits Commission in 1966.

The government expended a lot of time and energy in promoting public awareness of the new welfare system: the 'Family Guide to National Insurance' was a free pamphlet sent to 14 million homes – 50 million leaflets had been distributed by 1949. Uptake of the new benefits was impressive: 88 percent of those entitled to family allowance had applied for it by 1949. The removal of moral judgements and the stigma attached to 'outdoor relief' meant a much higher proportion of the poor were adequately supported through benefits. Real hardship of the kind seen in parts of the country in the 1930s became increasingly rare. Although **absolute poverty** had been comprehensively tackled, arguments began to build over levels of **relative poverty**, on the one hand, and the increased lack of incentive to find work on the other.

**KEY TERMS**

**Absolute poverty**
Someone living in absolute poverty does not have the fundamentals needed for survival, such as food, safe drinking water, decent shelter, health and sanitation.

**Relative poverty**
Somebody living in relative poverty does not have enough money to enjoy ordinary living patterns, customs and activities. Relative poverty is defined by the average standards of society and so can change over time as the average living standard rises or falls.

**ACTIVITY**
**KNOWLEDGE CHECK**

**The impact of the First and Second World Wars on welfare**

1. Explain why the Second World War changed popular and government attitudes to welfare provision.
2. Why was the Beveridge Report so popular?
3. How far did Labour successfully implement the Beveridge Report between 1945 and 1951?

## Reasons for increasing challenges to welfare state provision, 1964–79

### Why was welfare provision being challenged by 1979?

Although there was a good deal of continuity and consensus over the provision of social welfare, criticisms grew on the right wing over the cost and impact of more generous benefits, while on the left wing there was still resentment that not enough was being done to help the poorest. The cost of unemployment benefits rose from 0.6 percent of **Gross National Product** in 1939 to 5.6 percent in 1950 and 8.8 percent in 1970. Some efforts were made to improve welfare financing, especially for pensions: the 1959 National Insurance Act introduced a top-up scheme based on earnings known as the graduated pension. The 1975 Social Security Act set up the State Earnings-Related Pension Scheme (Serps); this allowed workers to opt out of all or part of the state pension in return for lower National Insurance payments.

**KEY TERM**

**Gross National Product**
The value of all exports, minus the value of all imports, added to the total value of all goods and services produced by a nation in one year.

However, the level of spending rose just as much under Conservative governments as under Labour, a fact that indicates the degree of common ground over the broad shape of welfare. It was a Conservative government that finally provided family allowance for a first child under the 1971 Family Income Support programme. Costs increased for a range of reasons:

- baby booms in the late 1940s and 1960s meant more care and education costs for children
- an increase in average life expectancy between 1941 and 1970, from 64 to 74 for women and 59 to 69 for men, meant more care for the elderly
- new social groups in need of support emerged who had not been considered in the initial plans for welfare reform: low wage-earning families and one-parent families were the most significant of these groups
- higher standards of living in general prompted demands for a higher minimum standard of life for the poorest
- the growing size of the welfare state required ever more bureaucracy to make it work.

Margaret Thatcher was a key critic of the seemingly unstoppable growth of social welfare provision. She opposed increases in benefits payments because they encouraged a culture of dependence (through the creation of a '**poverty trap**') and diverted funds away from wealth generation.

### KEY TERM

**Poverty trap**
This is a situation where an increase in earned income leads to a loss of state benefits. If the ratio of benefit loss to income gain is too high then there is no incentive to work harder, or to get a job in the first place.

**SOURCE 4** From 'This is Your Choice' by Margaret Thatcher, published in *Signpost* magazine on 1 September 1959.

When I have been canvassing... people have told me that there seems to be no point in trying to be responsible citizens. You may work harder, build up savings, pay more taxes—and then you see the people, who don't take the trouble to do any of these things, getting more out of the State than you do. Now, this criticism isn't entirely fair. One of the most welcome things this Government has done is to lower the rate of taxation. For example, earned income relief has been greatly increased, which is a direct incentive to those who are prepared to help themselves... Now let us see how these ideas compare with the principles of Socialism. In the first place, Socialism demands that all should be alike—that the unequal should be artificially made equal. It starts by dividing up the nation's total income, without giving a thought to how, or by whom, that money is to be created. What they don't, or won't, understand is that if you are to help those who need help—the weaker or older members of the community—you must encourage those who are able to make money to do so. Otherwise, where is the money coming from to help those who, through no fault of their own, are unable to help themselves? Five of the sayings of Abraham Lincoln put, more forcibly and succinctly than I can, some of the fundamental principles which Conservatives uphold:

1 You cannot strengthen the weak by weakening the strong.
2 You cannot build character and courage by taking away man's initiative and independence.
3 You cannot bring about prosperity by discouraging thrift.
4 You cannot help men permanently by doing for them what they could, and should, do for themselves.
5 You cannot further the brotherhood of man by encouraging class hatred.

Critics on the left were angry about the persistence of privilege in healthcare and education (see below). Several studies in the 1960s and 1970s also attacked the inadequacy of welfare provision at a time when relative poverty replaced absolute poverty as the key way of considering the condition of the poor. They argued that the state had to do more to ensure that people received a fair level of support to enable them to live decent lives.

**SOURCE 5** From Peter Townsend's *Poverty, Socialism and Labour in Power* (1967). Townsend was a sociologist who wrote several studies on poverty and was the co-founder of the Child Poverty Action Group.

Measures to raise low standards of living are required. The most urgent action is required to greatly increase family allowances (by at least threefold) and extend them to the first children in the family. General pensions and allowances must be introduced for the long-term sick and those disabled in civil life as well as in industry and war. Some form of regular State maintenance allowances for all fatherless families must also be introduced. A major repairs and modernisation programme is badly needed, particularly for housing but also for schools and hospitals. A variety of measures to strengthen the threadbare sections of our social services are also required. Examples of these are under-doctored areas and under-developed community-care services, under-staffed schools and under-staffed hospitals.

**SOURCE 6** A photo of two young girls at home in November 1968. Their mother had been waiting to receive better social housing for nine years.

EXTRACT 1

From *Poverty, Social Policy and Welfare* by Mark Walsh, Paul Stephens and Stephen Moore, published in 2000.

All British governments in the postwar period accepted that they had a responsibility to maintain the 'welfare state'. Arguments against the public funding of universal welfare provision held little sway, but gradually increased in influence as the 'welfare state' ran into practical and funding problems. In the late 1960s, adverse economic conditions led to questions first being asked about the assumptions on which the 'welfare state' was based. Collective and universal state provision of social welfare services were based on the belief that full employment could sustain the public funding of services, because enough money could be collected through income taxation to pay for services. Both Conservative and Labour governments had operated 'tax and spend' policies to fund welfare during the postwar years.

THINKING HISTORICALLY **Evidence (3b)**

**It depends on the question**

When considering the usefulness of a piece of evidence people often think about authenticity in the case of artefacts, reliability in the case of witness statements or methodology and structure in the case of secondary accounts. A better historical approach to the usefulness of a piece of evidence is to think about the statements that we can make about the past based on it. Different statements can be made with different degrees of certainty, depending on the evidence.

Work in small groups and answer the following:

**1** Look at Source 6.

**a)** Write three statements that you can reasonably make about the state of welfare in the 1960s based solely on Source 6.

**b)** Which of the statements can be made with the greatest degree of certainty? Why is this? Which statement can be made with the smallest degree of certainty?

**c)** What else might you need to increase your confidence in your statements?

**2** Source 6 is an artefact and Source 5 is a contemporary assessment. Which is more useful to the historian studying the state of welfare in the 1960s?

**3** Look at Extract 1. How would the historian have gone about constructing this piece? What kinds of evidence would they have needed?

Although there were criticisms of social welfare provision on the left and right, there was enough consensus in the broad middle ground between Labour and the Conservatives to ensure that there were no major overhauls of the system until the 1980s. Financial pressure limited Labour generosity while the electoral popularity of welfare provision limited Conservative cuts: Aneurin Bevan and Harold Wilson resigned over Labour's introduction of charges for spectacles and dentures in1951, while Conservative Chancellor Peter Thorneycroft resigned in 1958 when his calls for savage cuts in welfare spending were rejected.

ACTIVITY
KNOWLEDGE CHECK

**Providing social welfare**

**1** Make two parallel timelines showing the key developments in welfare provision for the unemployed and the elderly from 1918 to 1979.

**2** Explain the key ways in which social welfare provision in 1979 differed from the social welfare provision on offer in 1918.

**3** Summarise the key reasons why social welfare provision was increasingly challenged in post-war Britain.

**AS Level Exam-Style Question Section A**

Was the Second World War the main reason for changes in social welfare provision between 1918 and 1979? Explain your answer. (20 marks)

**Tip**

*This question covers a broad time period, so be selective in the arguments you deploy and ensure you include material from the beginning and the end of the period.*

**A Level Exam-Style Question Section A**

How far do you agree that the welfare state was increasingly challenged in the years 1964–79 because the post-war system of welfare provision was not fit for purpose? (20 marks)

**Tip**

*This question requires a significant discussion of the qualities of the post-war welfare state, which should be compared to other factors such as the changing social makeup of society and changing attitudes of the main political parties. You might want to return to this question having studied Chapters 3 and 4.*

## WHY, AND WITH WHAT IMPACT, WAS THE NATIONAL HEALTH SERVICE CREATED IN 1948?

Before 1911, the extent and quality of medical treatment depended almost entirely upon the wealth of the individual. While the wealthy could pay for medical treatment in private hospitals and for doctors to treat illness in the comfort of their homes, the poorest often suffered and died after ineffective self-medication. There were health insurance schemes and these were made affordable for most by local **Friendly Societies**. However, these were unregulated and non-compulsory. In areas where there was no workhouse infirmary to provide a safety net for the sick or injured, the collapse of a local Friendly Society could leave members unable to secure any treatment at all.

KEY TERM

**Friendly Society**
Members of a Friendly Society make a small regular payment. When they need financial help (e.g. for illness, unemployment or a funeral) the Friendly Society pays out a lump sum.

The National Insurance Act of 1911 improved the solution for many by providing free medical care and 13 weeks' sick pay for members. Just as with unemployment benefits, the Act only applied to certain workers and did not cover workers' families. The Labour Party argued particularly strongly in favour of greater state provision for healthcare. The Liberal government was partly persuaded by warnings about 'national efficiency': Britain's ability to compete economically and militarily with rival powers. But, despite the scale of ill-health uncovered by recruitment for the First World War, there was still a lack of political will to take on the complexity of the healthcare problem or the vested interests of doctors and Friendly Societies, some of which had developed into rich, powerful organisations.

As with social welfare provision, the Second World War fundamentally shifted political attitudes and people's expectations about healthcare. Within three years of the end of the war, a National Health Service (NHS) had been established. The founders of the NHS had a monumental task on their hands, not only in overcoming vested interests, but in attempting to impose order on the confusing muddle they had inherited. Despite this, they succeeded in creating not only a national institution with universal free treatment at the point of service but a prized national treasure that successive post-war governments dared not undermine. Criticisms did emerge over the persistence of private healthcare and over the management and cost of the NHS. While there were limited NHS reforms in the 1970s, no major overhaul of the system was undertaken until the 1990s.

## TIMELINE: BRITISH HEALTH PROVISION 1918–79

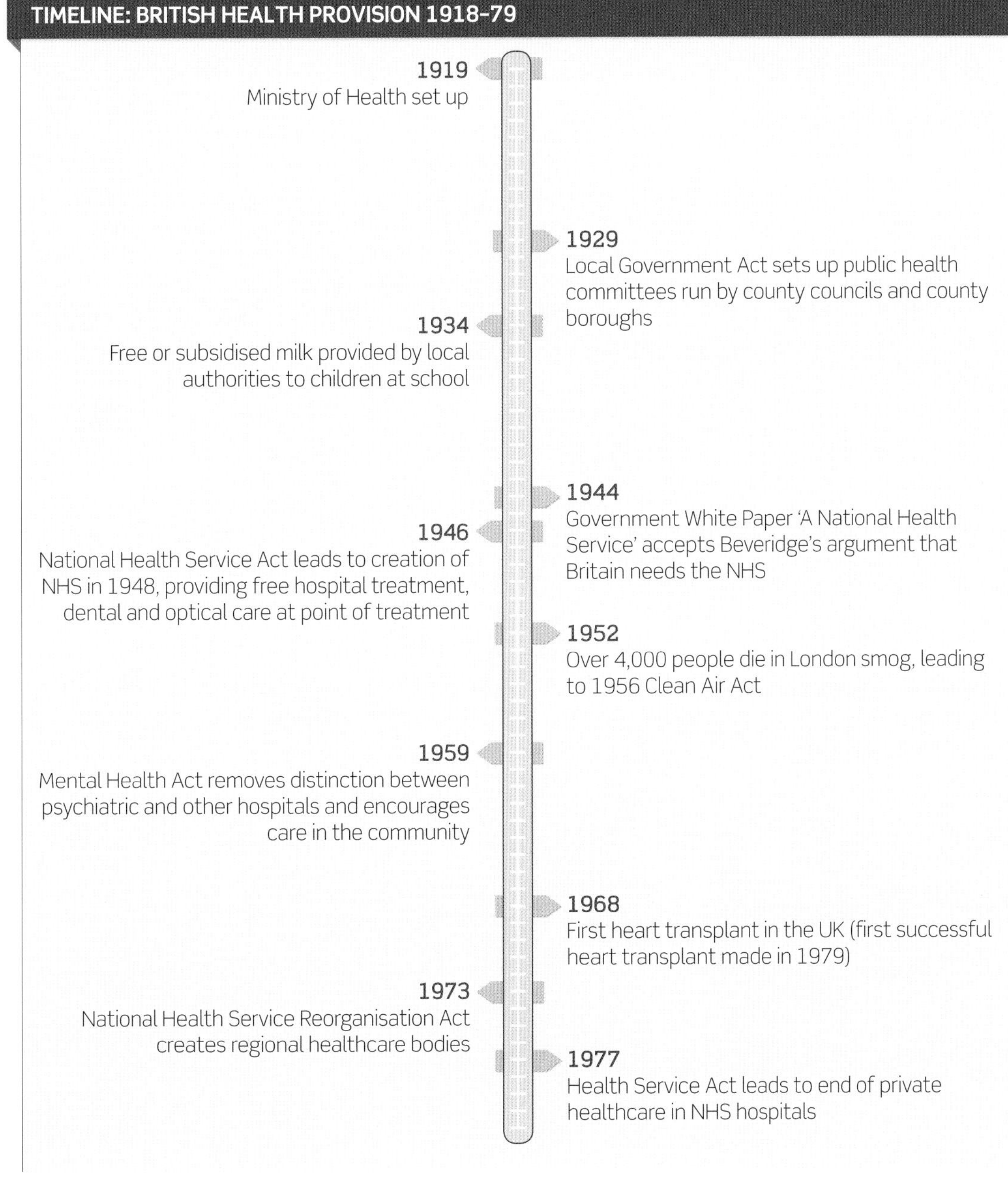

**1919**
Ministry of Health set up

**1929**
Local Government Act sets up public health committees run by county councils and county boroughs

**1934**
Free or subsidised milk provided by local authorities to children at school

**1944**
Government White Paper 'A National Health Service' accepts Beveridge's argument that Britain needs the NHS

**1946**
National Health Service Act leads to creation of NHS in 1948, providing free hospital treatment, dental and optical care at point of treatment

**1952**
Over 4,000 people die in London smog, leading to 1956 Clean Air Act

**1959**
Mental Health Act removes distinction between psychiatric and other hospitals and encourages care in the community

**1968**
First heart transplant in the UK (first successful heart transplant made in 1979)

**1973**
National Health Service Reorganisation Act creates regional healthcare bodies

**1977**
Health Service Act leads to end of private healthcare in NHS hospitals

## Health provision, 1918–45

### A lack of change

Rather like education, healthcare emerged as an odd hybrid of state and private provision in the 19th century; state healthcare was provided by a range of different agencies, including the Poor Law, public health authorities and even education authorities. The Labour Party had called for a nationally organised health system even before the First World War, but vested interests in the state and private sector meant this remained a distant hope. The First World War exposed the inadequacies of British healthcare: 41 percent of men were rated as unfit for combat roles in their medical inspection, while ten percent were judged unusable in any military capacity. The treatment of those disabled by the war was a further spur to action.

However, although a Ministry of Health was finally set up in 1919, it lacked the statutory authority and political will required to radically change the system: a range of medical services still lay within the remit of other authorities, such as the School Medical Service and the Factory Health Inspectorate. A key example of the reluctance to change the system was displayed in 1926 when the Conservative government failed to act on a Royal Commission recommendation to either scrap or reform the health insurance system: Minister for Health Neville Chamberlain advised that the insurance companies were too powerful a group to take on at a time of financial instability.

A few big insurance companies, such as the Prudential, dealt with around 75 percent of health insurance, while a large number of much smaller Friendly Societies, set up to help the poor afford basic medical treatment, handled the rest. While people could take out private health insurance, a good deal of their business came from the state thanks to Part I of the 1911 National Insurance Act: the government relied on 'Approved Societies' to collect subscriptions and pay medical costs. By 1937, around 18 million workers were covered by state health insurance.

There were problems, not only with the insurance system, but also with the medical system itself. Some of the Friendly Societies were so small that they could not afford to pay for members' hospital treatment; some went bankrupt and left their members with no insurance whatsoever. There was also a lot of duplication of roles due to the large number of societies operating in each region. The 1911 Act only insured workers: the wives, widows and children of poor workers remained without a safety net and relied on family, the local community or a sympathetic general practitioner (GP) for treatment without charge.

GPs were the first option for most medical care; it is for this reason that they are an important part of what is referred to as primary healthcare. Local authorities also provided a range of care services (see Figure 2.1). However, patients would not only have to pay for a consultation, they usually had to pay for the medicines too. In rich areas, GPs could earn a good living with not too many patients. In poor areas, people would only go to the doctor as a last resort and sometimes could not pay for their treatment; GPs could struggle to get by and sometimes had to hire debt collectors to get paid. When the NHS was finally launched in 1948, doctors were staggered by the sorts of medical issues that poor people had put up with rather than pay for treatment. These included untreated hernias and skin diseases, but more commonly toothache, dental abscesses and rotting teeth, due to the expense of dental treatment.

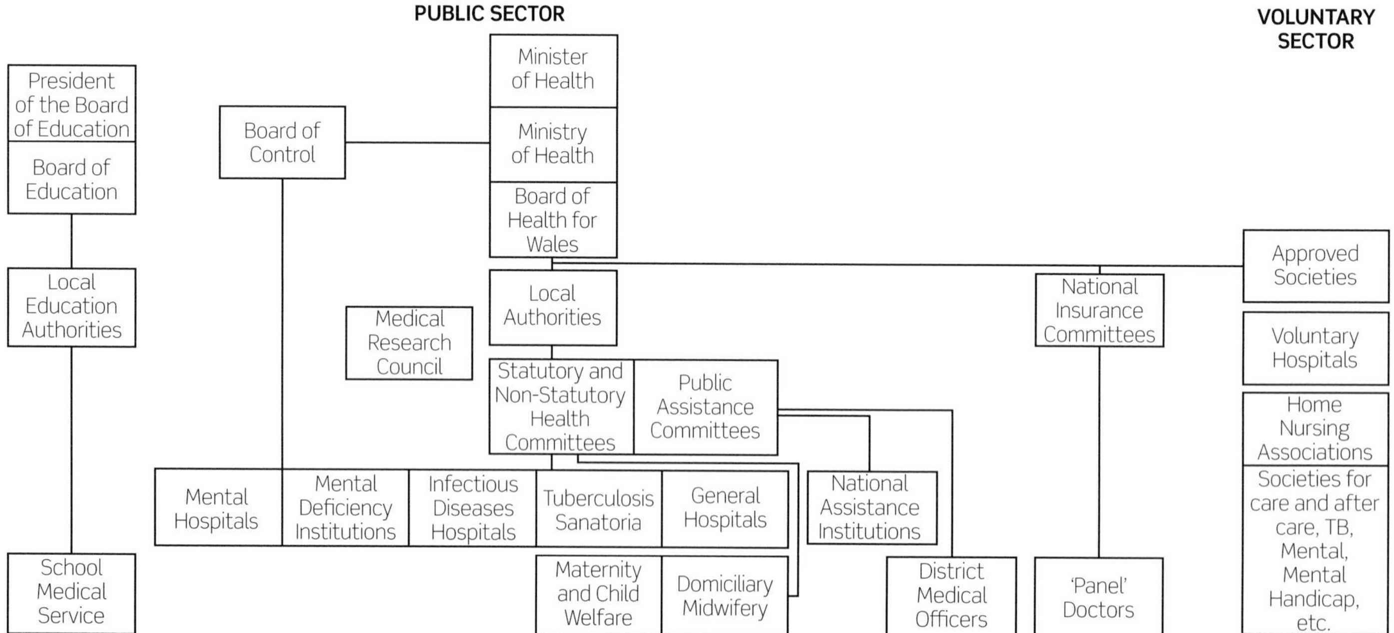


*Source:* C. Webster, *The Health Services since the War, ii, Government and Health Care. The British National Health Service 1958–1979* (London, The Stationery Office, 1996, p786).

**Figure 2.1**: A diagram illustrating the rather confusing state of healthcare in England and Wales in 1939.

A further problem was the lack of adequate hospital provision. The very best hospitals were the teaching hospitals. There were 12 of these prestigious **voluntary hospitals** in London and ten in the provinces. Hospitals such as Guy's in London had a long independent history and trained top specialists and consultants. These attracted generous donations from wealthy donors. The majority of the other 1,100 voluntary hospitals were smaller, staffed by visiting consultants or GPs, and less financially secure: when charity, fees and local authority grants did not cover costs, the hospital could declare itself bankrupt; this 'shroud waving' was usually enough to encourage further local donations to avoid closure. As the cost of more advanced medical treatment increased, it was clear that many voluntary hospitals would struggle to stay financially viable. As fees were an important part of their income, they needed a quick turnover of patients; for this reason, they did not admit the elderly or those with chronic (persistent or recurrent) illness. Such patients were forced to rely on public hospitals.

State-provided hospitals had emerged out of workhouse infirmaries. In some cases, these had become good medical centres, but all too often they were overcrowded with elderly and chronically ill patients. The 1929 Local Government Act empowered PACs (see page 38) to take over and develop these infirmaries into proper hospitals. However, there was no timetable or compulsion for action and, with a few exceptions, uptake was slow outside of London: in 1939, half of all public hospitals were still Poor Law infirmaries. A succession of governments, with their attention fixed on the economy, lacked the political will to enforce change: a national survey of hospitals conducted in 1938 revealed a shortage of beds, buildings, equipment, trained consultants, and poor patient accessibility due to the poor distribution of good hospitals. As with other welfare developments, the Second World War changed all this.

### The impact of the Second World War on healthcare

While historians such as Daniel Fox have emphasised the growing consensus over what should be done about healthcare before 1939, and others such as Paul Addison and Kenneth Morgan have focused on the pioneering role of the post-war Labour government, there is no doubt that the impact of war served as a catalyst for profound change. The prospect of war led to the creation of nationally funded organisations to deal with expected casualties: a national system of blood transfusion depots was established in 1938 near hospitals, but far enough away to avoid bombing; this continued after 1946 as the National Blood Transfusion Service. More significantly, an Emergency Medical Service was set up in 1939 to treat military personnel and, as the war progressed, a wider range of civilian casualties. National funding for the service led to an impressive growth in the number of beds, operating theatres and specialist treatments available. Examples of particular specialisms that emerged included the treatment of severe burns by plastic surgery, of kidney trauma due to the number of crush injuries and of the mending of broken bones. This successful state response to adversity inspired Beveridge to call for a National Health Service as a vital component of a 'satisfactory scheme of social security'. His report heavily influenced the 1944 White Paper, 'A National Health Service', which in turn formed a significant part of the 1946 National Health Service Act. Ironically, despite the deaths and injuries from fighting and bombing, the health of the average Briton improved during the war thanks to rationing (the rich ate less and the poor ate more) and increased government propaganda to educate people about healthy habits. Beveridge was keen that the NHS should serve as a *preventative* as well as a *curative* service; this was one aspect of his recommendations that was largely overlooked.

**ACTIVITY**
**KNOWLEDGE CHECK**

**Healthcare before the Second World War**

1. What were the shortcomings of healthcare provision in 1918? Make a list of the problems and who they affected.
2. What changes came about in the provision of healthcare before the Second World War?
3. Explain the ways in which the Second World War affected health provision.

**KEY TERM**

**Voluntary hospital**
A hospital funded by charitable (voluntary) donations.

## The creation and impact of the NHS, 1945–79

### 'Stuffing their mouths with gold': getting the doctors onside

Despite the positive experiences of state-funded national health projects during the war, there were still some significant obstacles to overcome and difficult choices to be made in the formation of the NHS. Attlee chose Aneurin Bevan as his Minister for Health to get the job done. Bevan was determined from the start to create a centrally rather than locally run system, funded by taxation rather than insurance. That he succeeded is testament to his political skill and determination, as well as the pressure of public support for change. The 1946 National Health Service Act established a much more coordinated, centralised system (see Figure 2.2). The Approved Societies were forced to rely on private clients for business and the voluntary hospitals, apart from the teaching hospitals, were nationalised. The problem that proved to be most difficult to overcome was doctors' resistance to working as state employees.

In February 1948, 90 percent of the British Medical Association voted against working within the NHS. They argued that working directly for the state would undermine their clinical independence. In reality, most doctors were more concerned about losing income. Bevan overcame their opposition by granting doctors a fee for each patient on their books, rather than paying them a direct salary, and by allowing consultants to retain private patients; on 5 July 1948, 90 percent of doctors (18,000) joined the NHS, just one month before the launch date. Bevan, a former miner, was angry that he had only gained doctors' support by 'stuffing their mouths with gold'.

SOURCE

A cartoon by Ernest H. Shepard published in *Punch* magazine on 21 January 1948. In Charles Dickens's *Nicholas Nickleby*, Dotheboys Hall is a boys' boarding school where the pupils are poorly treated to keep their spirits down.

**DOTHEBOYS HALL**

"It still tastes awful."

Minister of Health
Ministry of Health
Board of Health for Wales

- Local Health Authorities (146)
  - Health Centres
  - Ambulance Service
  - Health Visitors, Home Nurses, Domiciliary Midwives
  - Maternity and Child Welfare
  - Home Helps
  - Care and After Care
  - Vaccination and Immunisation
- Regional Hospital Boards (14)
  - Hospital Management Committees (377)
    - Hospitals and Specialists
- Boards of Governors (36)
  - Teaching Hospitals
- Boards of Governors (36)
  - General Medical Services
  - General Dental Service
  - General Pharmaceutical Service
  - Supplementary Ophthalmic Service

*Source:* C. Webster, *The National Health Service, A Political History* (Oxford, Oxford University Press, 1998), p21.

**Figure 2.2**: A diagram showing the structure of healthcare in England and Wales following the launch of the NHS.

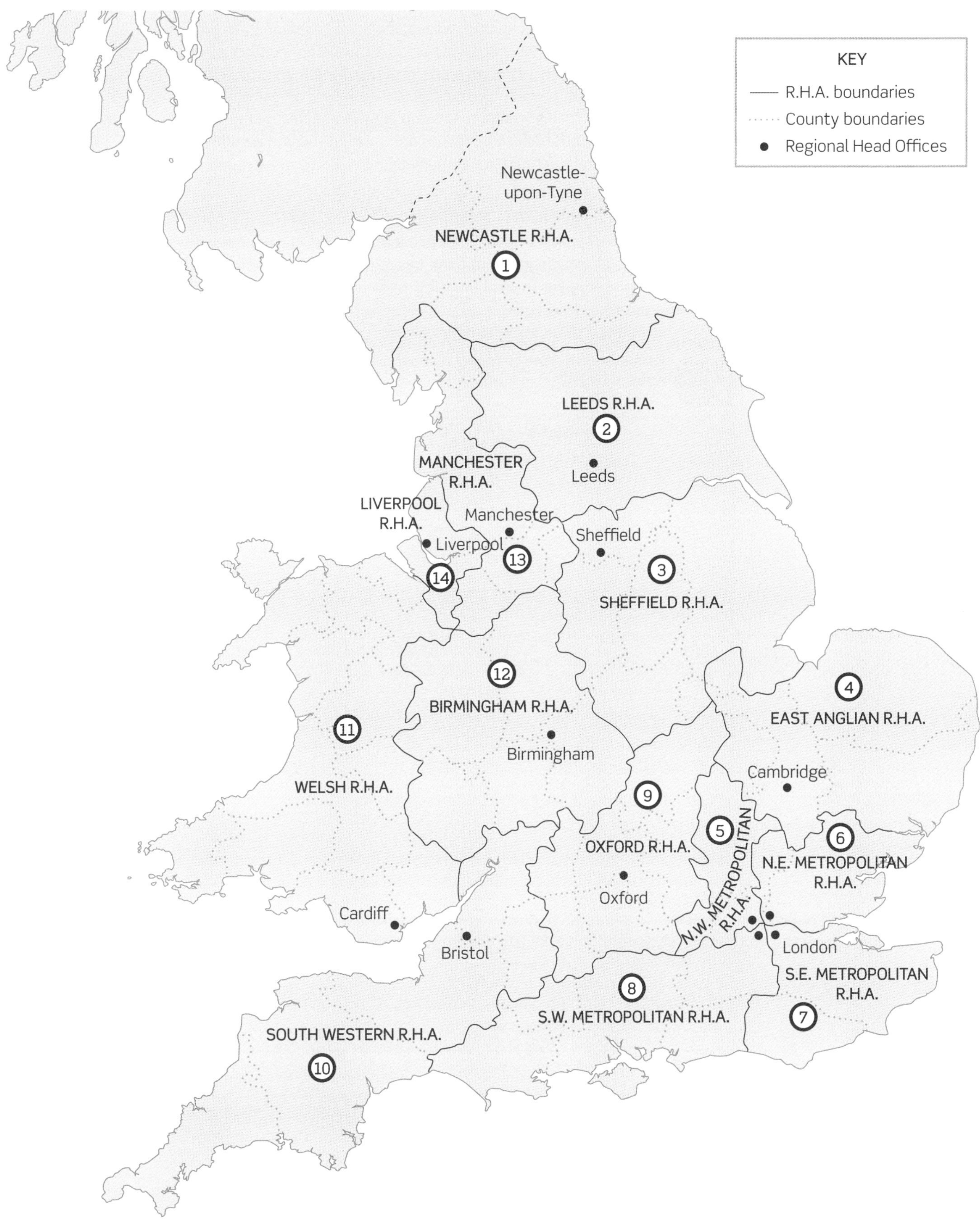


**Figure 2.3**: A map showing the boundaries of the Regional Hospital Boards (known as Regional Health Associations after 1974).

## A healthy change?

The NHS allowed many Britons to take advantage of global improvements in combating disease through research into new techniques, vaccinations and medicines. In the first ten years of the NHS, new antibiotic drugs developed in the USA caused the number of deaths from tuberculosis to fall from 25,000 to 5,000 per year. A programme of mass immunisation led to a huge drop in cases of polio and diphtheria in the mid-1950s. There was a 90 percent drop in cases of whooping cough by 1970 and syphilis was almost completely eradicated by the early 1990s. As well as these developments, the MMR (measles, mumps and rubella) vaccine was developed in 1971, again in the USA. The NHS began offering the MMR vaccine free of charge in 1988.

Improved midwifery led maternal death in childbirth to fall from one per 1,000 births in 1949 to 0.18 in 1970, which compared well with most of Europe and was lower than in the USA. Increased funding for healthcare also helped. Over 300 inadequate cottage hospitals were closed in the 1960s and new centres of excellence, with close ties to universities, were founded, along with district general hospitals for larger towns. These changes contributed to increased life expectancy: for men it increased from 66 in 1950 to 70 in 1979 and for women from 71 to 75 in the same period.

**SOURCE**

A table showing the changing number of cases of notifiable infectious diseases in England and Wales, 1948–67.

| | Tuberculosis | Diphtheria | Whooping cough | Measles |
|---|---|---|---|---|
| 1948 | 23,175 | 156 | 748 | 327 |
| 1957 | 4,784 | 4 | 87 | 94 |
| 1958 | 4,480 | 8 | 27 | 49 |
| 1959 | 3,854 | 0 | 25 | 98 |
| 1960 | 3,435 | 5 | 37 | 31 |
| 1961 | 3,334 | 10 | 27 | 152 |
| 1962 | 3,088 | 2 | 24 | 39 |
| 1963 | 2,962 | 2 | 36 | 127 |
| 1964 | 2,484 | 0 | 44 | 73 |
| 1965 | 2,282 | 0 | 21 | 115 |
| 1966 | 2,354 | 5 | 23 | 80 |
| 1967 | 2,043 | 0 | 27 | 99 |

However, a range of diseases associated with old age increased in prevalence due to the greater number of people surviving into their eighth and ninth decade. Heart disease and cancer increased throughout the 1950s and 1960s, before dipping in the 1970s due to better diets, more exercise and fewer smokers. Arthritis continued to be the largest health problem, affecting 200,000 men and 700,000 women in 1970.

### EXTEND YOUR KNOWLEDGE

**Aneurin Bevan (1897–1960)**

Aneurin Bevan is one of the most celebrated figures in Labour Party history. Born in South Wales in 1897, Bevan was from a mining family and left school at 13 to work in a colliery. He soon became a trade union activist, and was able to study in London with sponsorship from the South Wales Miners' Federation.

When Bevan returned to Wales in 1921 he found work as a union official. In 1926, he became one of the leaders of the General Strike in South Wales, and he was elected MP for Ebbw Vale in 1929. After Attlee's victory in the 1945 election, Bevan was appointed Minister of Health and oversaw the foundation of the National Health Service. After a short stint as Minister of Labour in 1951, Bevan resigned from the government in protest at the then Chancellor Hugh Gaitskell's decision to introduce charges for prescriptions, dental treatment and spectacles.

The 1950s were marked by division and in-fighting within the Labour Party, and Bevan became the figurehead for the left of the party, known as the 'Bevanites' (in contrast to the 'Gaitskellites'). Despite their rivalry, Gaitskell, now party leader, appointed Bevan shadow foreign secretary in 1956, and deputy leader in 1959. Bevan died in 1960.

## The challenge of medical advances, 1945–79

### Dentures and spectacles: the unexpected expense of the NHS

Bevan, like Beveridge, had expected the cost of healthcare to fall after 1948. People appeared to be getting healthier and it was also hoped that better access to preventative medicine would reduce the cost of more serious health problems. As the NHS would be so large, it would be able to take advantage of economies of scale (buying things more cheaply in bulk).

However, while the NHS cost 4.1 percent of GNP in 1950, by 1970 this had increased to 4.8 percent and 14 percent by 1990. There were several reasons for this increased expense:

- Advances in medical science meant there was an increase in treatments available, sometimes for illnesses that were incurable or had not even been recognised in 1948. In 1948, only one antibiotic was available; by 1968 there were 33.
- These advances fed higher public expectations and demands of healthcare. People came to depend on the NHS in a way Beveridge hoped to avoid. He had hoped that voluntary help by families and communities would support the work of medical professionals. Instead, to Bevan's dismay, a 'dandruff syndrome' rapidly emerged: people took up valuable time and resources with complaints about the most trivial problems, like dandruff.
- There was such a backlog of cases to deal with in 1948 that it was difficult to dedicate the necessary time and funds to planning and the full reorganisation of the old system. The division of healthcare within regions between general practitioner (GP), hospital specialist and public health authority made the cost-effective coordination of healthcare difficult to achieve.
- The number of staff employed by the NHS doubled from 500,000 in 1948 to over one million in 1979.

The soaring cost of the NHS (and the expense of an ongoing war in Korea between 1950 and 1953) caused an argument that led to Bevan's resignation and contributed to an acrimonious split in the Labour Party. In 1951, charges were introduced for dentures and spectacles. Bevan, and his 'Bevanite' supporters, felt this undermined the key principle that care should be free for all at the point of service. As the charge was a fixed sum, it penalised the poor more than the rich. Arguments over the cost and management of the NHS were remarkably persistent after 1951.

### Medical advances in the 1960s and 1970s

As medical advances were made in the 1960s, the public began to expect more from the NHS. This contributed towards increased costs, but also led to great improvements in healthcare.

The first kidney transplant took place at Edinburgh Royal Infirmary in 1960. The demand for kidney transplants quickly outstripped supply, and kidney failure services reached two percent of the NHS budget in the 1970s, rising to three percent in the 1990s.

The NHS had an impact on changes in wider society with the introduction of the contraceptive pill in 1961. The Pill, which suppressed fertility in women, contributed to female sexual freedom in the 1960s and 1970s (although until 1967 it was only available to married women). Between 1962 and 1969, the number of women taking the Pill on the NHS increased from fewer than 100,000 to over one million. Women now had fewer children, resulting in smaller families. The Abortion Act was passed in 1967, making abortion legal up to 28 weeks into pregnancy, if carried out by a registered doctor and if two doctors testified that it was in the best interests of the woman concerned. The post-war 'baby boom' was well and truly over.

The first full hip replacement was carried out in 1962, and Britain's first heart transplant took place at the National Heart Hospital in London in 1968. As the first patient died of complications, only six transplants were carried out between 1968 and 1978, but medical advances made the procedure much safer in the 1980s.

The CT (computerised tomography) scanner was invented in 1972 and became standard equipment for NHS hospitals, thereby contributing to improved patient care but also to increasing costs.

EXTRACT

From 'Health and Healthcare', an essay by Ray Fitzpatrick, Rebecca Surender and Tarani Chandola, in *Britain Since 1945*, edited by J. Hollowell and published in 2003.

It is quite striking how perpetual have been concerns about unsustainable costs of the NHS whilst in reality Britain has... remained behind almost all other Western European and North American countries in the percentage of national wealth that has been devoted to health care... In 1983, a review was commissioned of the management of the NHS, headed by Sir Roy Griffiths, who diagnosed a state of 'institutionalised stagnation' in the NHS... Despite suspicion that the proposed reforms were the 'thin end of the wedge' of privitisation, the changes which were implemented in 1991 did not alter the financial underpinnings of the NHS... universal coverage and relative cost control while overcoming its perceived failings - low consumer choice and [inefficiency]... More than at any stage of its history, the value and effectiveness of services in the NHS are scrutinised. Nevertheless, because access to a wide range of modern health care facilities has been provided via public funding for so long, the NHS has remained a strikingly popular institution in public opinion, despite its many upheavals.

ACTIVITY
WRITING

**The National Health Service**

Analyse Extract 2.

**1** Identify words and phrases used to describe the extent of NHS success. Write them out in order of most to least emphasis on success.

**2** Identify words and phrases used to present the views of other commentators cited by the historian.

**3** Identify words and phrases that show the historian's own attitude towards the NHS. Write a short paragraph explaining the historian's views, using quotes from the extract to back up your points.

ACTIVITY
KNOWLEDGE CHECK

**The National Health Service**

**1** What initial problems were faced by the Labour government when they introduced the NHS?

**2** Why was the NHS more expensive than its founders had expected?

### AS Level Exam-Style Question Section B

To what extent was the National Health Service a complete success in the years 1946–79? (20 marks)

**Tip**

*Pay close attention to the dates given in the question. In this case, you are expected to include the period 1946–48, when negotiations between doctors and the government were taking place.*

### A Level Exam-Style Question Section B

How accurate is it to say that the role of Aneurin Bevan was the most important reason why the provision of healthcare changed so drastically in the years 1918–79? (20 marks)

**Tip**

*Compare the role and actions of Bevan with other important turning points in the period.*

Change (4b&c)

The bird's-eye view

| Development | Medium-term consequences | Long-term consequences |
|---|---|---|
| Foundation of the NHS, 1948 | • Improvements in life expectancy and healthcare<br>• Reduction in infectious diseases<br>• Lower infant mortality<br>• Better dental health | • Medical advances led to unexpected expense<br>• People came to depend on the NHS in a way that Beveridge hoped to avoid<br>• The number of people employed by the NHS doubled between 1948 and 1979 |

Imagine you are looking at the whole of history using an interactive map like Google Maps. If you zoom out you have a general view of the sweep of developments and their consequences but you cannot see much detail. If you zoom in to the time of the foundation of the NHS, you can see the event in detail but will know nothing of its consequences in the medium or long term. If you zoom in to look at the medium- or long-term consequences, you will know about them in detail but will know very little about the event that caused them.

Look at the table above and answer the following:

1 What were the immediate consequences of the foundation of the NHS? Are there more than in the table above?

2 In what ways are the medium-term consequences different from the long-term consequences?

Work in groups of three.

Each student takes the role of the teacher for one of the above (the development, medium-term consequences or long-term consequences) and gives a short presentation to the other two, who can comment and ask questions. After each presentation, the other two members write a 100-word paragraph showing how the presentation links to their own.

Answer the following individually:

3 What happens to the detail when you zoom out to look at the whole sweep of history?

4 What are the advantages and disadvantages of zooming in to look at a specific time in detail?

5 How could you use the map in order to get a good understanding of history as a whole?

# TO WHAT EXTENT HAS EDUCATIONAL REFORM LED TO WIDENING OPPORTUNITY?

## Education in the early 20th century

Provision of formal education was very patchy before it became compulsory – in 1872 in Scotland and 1880 in England and Wales. Parents were happy for their children to learn from family and the local community before they started paid work. Where schools existed, they were provided by churches, charities and private foundations rather than the state in England and Wales (the state played a larger role in Scotland). This situation changed from the 1870s when the state plugged gaps in education with new 'board schools' and provided funding for older, failing grammar and Church schools. This was partly because the newly enfranchised workers needed some education to use their vote responsibly and because of increasing concerns over 'national efficiency'.

While private grammar schools and prestigious public schools prepared boys for university entrance, the vast majority of schools provided only an 'elementary' education to the age of 11 (or 12 after 1902): children left school with the basic tools of reading, writing, arithmetic and religious instruction, but nothing more. The 1902 Education Act increased the chances of a grammar school education for able working-class children: in return for state funding, over 1,000 grammar schools offered a quarter of their places to non-fee-paying children who did sufficiently well in entrance exams. Yet, in 1914, only 56 out of every 1,000 elementary school students gained such places. Secondary education remained the preserve of the upper and middle classes.

Reform-minded politicians felt it was unfair that the quality and duration of education was so dependent on wealth and class background. The question was how to provide the most appropriate education for the great mass of working-class children. How far should educational issues be decided locally or at the centre? Should schools aim to copy the classical syllabus of the grammar schools or provide more vocational, skills-based lessons? At what age should elementary and secondary education end? After the Second World War, further questions began to emerge: should schools promote discipline and the acquisition of knowledge or should they be more progressive and promote key skills like group work and self-motivated learning? Should schools promote competition and maximise individual progress or should they promote co-operation and greater social equality? R. A. Butler thought he had tackled most of these questions with his 1944 Education Act; almost immediately his system came under attack for a range of reasons (see page 56). These arguments persisted until 1979 and into the 21st century.

### The gender divide before 1918

In the early 20th century, there was a marked difference between the curriculums for girls and boys. In 1904, the Board of Education decided that, within elementary schools, all pupils would study three strands: humanistic and scientific skills along with domestic skills for girls and manual skills for boys. The idea that boys and girls needed different spheres of education had emerged with the industrial revolution. Prior to this, when much skilled work took place in the home in 'cottage industries' such as weaving, all family members worked and no distinction was made between boys and girls. With the advent of factory-based work, men were more likely to leave home in order to find employment, whereas women would perform unpaid domestic work or, if they did need to earn a wage, domestic work for other people as servants.

### University education before 1918

A number of universities had existed for hundreds of years. The University of Oxford was probably teaching students from the early 11th century and Cambridge was founded in 1209. In Scotland, the Universities of St Andrew's, Glasgow and Aberdeen had been in existence since the 15th century. Other than the handful of older institutions, no new universities were founded until the 19th century. Between 1880 and 1909, six new 'red-brick' universities were founded in industrial cities, including Sheffield, Leeds, Liverpool and Manchester. Their focus was on providing men with skills they could use in the workplace, especially in the field of engineering. In 1918, access to university education was limited to those, with the exception of some bursaries or scholarships, from privileged backgrounds, as government funding was still low and widening participation was not a priority.

### TIMELINE: EDUCATION IN ENGLAND AND WALES 1918–79

**1918** Fisher Education Act raises school-leaving age to 14 and abolishes remaining elementary school fees

**1919** University Grants Committee set up to administer public funding of universities

**1926** Hadow Report recommends division of students at 11 into primary and secondary schools

**1936** Education Act raises school-leaving age to 15 (not enforced until 1944)

**1944** Butler Education Act introduces 11-plus, tripartite system and division of primary schools into infant and junior schools

**1951** General Certificate of Education (GCE) replaces School Certificate for those applying to university

**1960** Robbins Committee on higher education set up; final report recommends doubling university places and expanding technological colleges and business schools

**1963** The Crowther Report calls for school-leaving age of 16 and part-time education for over-16s

**1964** Labour election victory after manifesto pledge to expand comprehensive education

**1965** Certificate of Secondary Education (CSE) is set up alongside GCE

**1967** Plowden Report recommends 'child-centred' approach to education, with particular focus on primary schools

**1969** Open University established

**1973** School-leaving age raised to 16

**1976** Education Act compels local authorities to submit plans for extension of comprehensive education

## Education policy, 1918–43

### The impact of H. A. L. Fisher and Sir Henry Hadow

Education reform, like healthcare, suffered due to a lack of funding and a lack of political will to act upon sensible ideas. The 1918 'Fisher' Education Act, named for the President of the Board of Education, H. A. L. Fisher, aimed to help with the construction of a 'home fit for heroes'. Fisher wanted to widen access to education in three ways: increasing the school-leaving age to 14, providing nursery schools for toddlers and 'continuation schools' for new workers aged over 14 to continue their studies for one day a week, and scrapping all fees for elementary education. Although basic elementary education was made free in 1891, there were loopholes that meant that parents could be made to pay for some elements of their child's education. The Act also made provisions for punishing those who employed school-age children, and provided free, compulsory health checks for secondary school pupils. Unfortunately, few nursery or 'continuation schools' were provided due to a lack of funds following the 1922 'Geddes Axe' cuts to government spending.

In 1924, the Labour Minister for Education, C. P. Trevelyan, commissioned Sir Henry Hadow to compile a report on how to improve education. The 1926 Hadow Report recommended that elementary schools be replaced with primary schools for pupils aged 5 to 11 and three types of secondary school for those aged 11–15: grammar schools for the most academically able students, 'technical schools' for those who wished to learn a practical trade; and 'modern schools' for the rest. This three-pronged structure was known as the 'tripartite system'. While the suggestions were widely accepted, almost nothing was done to act upon the Report: education was simply not a priority compared to unemployment or, later on, rearmament.

Trevelyan tried once again to increase the school-leaving age to 15 under the second Labour government in 1930. This was rejected by the House of Lords on grounds of cost and practicality, but was also opposed by Catholic MPs who spoke for members of their faith who resented having to pay taxes for state schools while also paying fees for educating their children in Catholic schools. While a minority of **Local Education Authorities** (LEAs) followed the Board of Education recommendations to set up 'modern schools', the proportion of working-class children in secondary education remained fairly static between 1918 and 1943. As a school leaving age of 15 was not enforced until 1944, children were often found in work in their early teens.

**KEY TERM**

**Local Education Authorities**
The Local Education Authorities were set up in 1902 to replace the old School Boards. They oversaw education within a county or borough. Schools were able to choose whether to receive funding from the LEAs or directly from central government.

**SOURCE**

A table showing the percentage of children in education at different ages. From C. Cook and J. Stevenson, *The Longman Handbook of Modern British History* (2001).

| Year | Percentage of 2-4-year-olds in school | Percentage of 5-10-year-olds in school | Percentage of 11-14-year-olds in school | Percentage of 15-18-year-olds in school |
|---|---|---|---|---|
| 1921 | - | - | 65.8 | 3.2 |
| 1931 | 8.8 | 91.7 | 73.0 | 6.0 |
| 1938 | 10.0 | 92.4 | 74.5 | 6.6 |
| 1951 | 7.7 | 97.2 | 93.1 | 12.5 |
| 1961 | 10.8 | 99.9 | 99.1 | 19.6 |
| 1968 | 10.7 | 99.3 | 100.0 | 30.0 |
| 1976 | 23.7 | 100.0 | 100.0 | 36.0 |

SOURCE 10 A table showing government expenditure on education between 1920 and 1980. From C. Cook and J. Stevenson, *The Longman Handbook of Modern British History* (2001).

| Year | Amount spent on education (£ millions) |
|---|---|
| 1920 | 43.2 |
| 1930 | 50.1 |
| 1940 | 65.0 |
| 1950 | 272.0 |
| 1955 | 410.6 |
| 1960 | 917.3 |
| 1965 | 1,114.9 |
| 1970 | 2,592.0 |
| 1975 | 5,348.3 |
| 1980 | 13,049.0 |

ACTIVITY
KNOWLEDGE CHECK

**Education before the Second World War**

1 What problems were there with education provision in the early 20th century?

2 What was the impact of the Fisher Act and the Hadow Report on education?

## The impact of the Butler Education Act and the Crosland Circular, 1944–79

### The tripartite system and 'parity of esteem'

One of the earliest responses to the Beveridge Report was President of the Board of Education R. A. Butler's 1944 Education Act. He aimed to tackle the 'giant' of ignorance by building upon Hadow's report. The school-leaving age was finally increased to 15 in 1947 and secondary education was to be made free and universally available. To ensure suitable secondary education was provided for all, the LEAs were to be directed and controlled by a new Ministry of Education. LEAs were still left to interpret what 'suitable' education meant; most thought Butler was referring to the tripartite model in the Hadow Report.

At the heart of the 1944 Act was the 11-plus exam, so-called because pupils took it at the end of junior school aged 11. The exam decided which type of secondary school was 'most suitable' for each pupil.

- Secondary Technical Schools: these specialised in mechanical and technical education. Very few were established because of the cost of such an education: only around five percent of students, all in towns and cities, attended such schools before 1965.
- Secondary Modern Schools: these aimed to give a general education to prepare pupils for life and work. 70 percent of pupils went to such schools in the 1950s. Pupils left with a Certificate of Education at the age of 15 and went to work; some also went to Technical College for further vocational education. These schools were sometimes single-sex but more than half took both boys and girls.
- Grammar Schools: these provided a highly academic education focused on English literature, 'classics' (Latin and ancient Greek) and pure maths. 20 percent of pupils went to grammar schools in the 1950s. At 15, most pupils stayed on for an extra, non-compulsory year and then took exams called O-Levels at 16. Many went on to take A-Levels and some then went on to university. These schools were usually single-sex.

The authors of the 1944 Act hoped that a 'parity of esteem' would exist between pupils leaving the different types of school. In reality, the extra funding enjoyed by grammar schools (ironically this extra funding was in place to help pupils from poorer backgrounds), together with the shortage of technical schools, meant that the 11-plus came to be seen as a pass/fail test, with those who failed the test condemned to what was regarded as an inferior education at a secondary modern school.

For both boys and girls at junior schools, morning lessons focused on literacy and numeracy, with a broader range of subjects later in the day. Boys and girls continued to do similar core subjects at grammar or secondary modern schools, although there were some differences: girls took subjects such as needlework, home economics and sometimes 'mothercraft' at secondary modern schools, while boys did woodwork and metalwork. These differences clearly reflected the different expectations of boys' and girls' paths upon leaving school: boys would find a career, while girls would soon settle down to marriage and motherhood. At grammar schools too, there were different expectations and there were variations in the subjects taught. Although all grammar schools had an academic focus, girls were usually encouraged to focus on the arts and languages rather than sciences and mathematics.

### The Crosland Circular (1965)

Between 1960 and 1979, the debate centred on whether comprehensive schools should replace the tripartite system that divided students based on their ability. Some LEAs, especially in Coventry, London and Leicestershire, enjoying a great deal of autonomy from central government, had rejected the tripartite system from as early as 1954. By 1964, ten percent of pupils went to comprehensive schools; these accepted pupils of all abilities. In 1965, the Labour Education Secretary, Anthony Crosland, issued a document known as Circular 10/65, calling for universal comprehensive education. In it he stated, 'It is the Government's aim to end selection at eleven plus and to eliminate separatism in secondary education… The Secretary of State requests LEAs, if they have not already done so, to prepare plans for reorganising secondary education in their areas on comprehensive lines.'

There were arguments for and against such reform and many LEAs looked as if they might ignore Circular 10/65. In 1966, the government issued another document that said funding for new schools or school refurbishment would only go to LEAs that adopted comprehensive reform; this financial pressure led many LEAs to feel coerced into adopting the new system.

| Arguments for comprehensive education | Arguments against comprehensive education |
|---|---|
| Grammar schools on average had three times the resources of secondary modern schools. This did not promote 'parity' as promised in the 1944 Education Act. | Many grammar schools were excellent and produced highly successful students. |
| In the 1960s many secondary modern schools were already run-down. Comprehensive reform would help many children to avoid these poor schools. | Grammar schools were seen as a precious opportunity for social advancement by many working-class families with bright children. |
| Pupils who failed the 11-plus were condemned to a life of fewer opportunities: only two percent of those who failed the exam were still in school at the age of 17. | In 1975, the government forced direct grant grammar schools to go comprehensive. Many went independent instead; free places were removed and poorer local parents could not afford the fees. |
| The 11-plus favoured middle-class over working-class children: very few children from working-class areas passed the exam. | The rise of more private schools in place of grammar schools led to a system that promoted less social equality. |
| The majority of the public wanted to scrap the 11-plus. | The majority of the public wanted to keep grammar schools. |

**Figure 2.4**: Arguments for and against closing grammar schools and introducing a comprehensive education system.

Momentum for comprehensive education built throughout the 1960s and 1970s. Teachers' unions and middle-class parents (who feared their children going to secondary moderns if they failed the 11-plus) were especially vocal in their support for comprehensive reform. The Conservative government (1970–74) removed the Crosland Circular, but did little to stop ongoing reform. Labour's 1976 Education Act not only reintroduced comprehensive reorganisation but removed funding from direct grant schools. Many such schools chose to become independent schools. By 1979, there were only 150 grammar schools left; whereas only 33 percent of students were educated at comprehensive schools in 1970, this figure had increased to 62 percent by 1974 and 90 percent by 1979. Such rapid change caused much debate at the time and has continued to do so into the 21st century.

Although they enjoyed their autonomy, some LEAs found it difficult to manage the conflicting aims of different head teachers and teachers in their areas. As head teachers had been given a certain amount of autonomy based on trust by the LEAs, they were able to decide how their own curriculum should be taught, particularly in primary schools. As a result, there were sometimes large variations in the way pupils were taught at different schools. Many teachers began to introduce the progressive reforms championed in the 1967 Plowden Report on primary schools. Lady Plowden reported that, 'A school is not merely a teaching shop. It must transmit values and attitudes. It is a community in which children learn to live first and foremost as children and not as future adults. The school sets out deliberately to devise the right environment for children, to allow them to be themselves and to develop in the way and at the pace appropriate to them.' The ideas contained in the Report were nothing new, as around ten percent of primary schools had already adopted more progressive methods. The progressive reforms referred to in the Report included the following:

- There was a large programme of nursery school building.
- More project-based work was carried out at primary schools, rather than teacher-led activities.
- There was a focus on learning through play in early years teaching, because of the acceptance that all children learn at a different pace.
- The teaching of punctuation and grammar was seen as a hindrance to creativity and a threat to progress.

At some schools, especially in the Inner London Education Authority (ILEA), some liberal teachers and head teachers took such reforms to an extreme: they introduced relaxed discipline, teachers were called by their first name and there was no school uniform. In one school, the William Tyndale Junior School in north London, pupils could choose which classes to attend and watch television or play table tennis if they did not feel like studying. Many parents became concerned about 'trendy teachers' and about the lack of discipline and learning in many schools, as teachers in some secondary schools also introduced reforms from the Plowden Report, such as lessons focused on learning through exploration with little teacher direction. Some genuine fears were made worse by a stream of sensationalist stories in the press and by the harsh depiction of comprehensive schools in the hit television show *Grange Hill* (first screened in 1978).

Pupils' educational opportunities were more affected by other educational reforms than the change to comprehensive education itself.

- Only the top 20 percent of students took O-Levels; the rest left with no qualifications until a new exam called the CSE was introduced in 1965. Pupils at comprehensives were streamed into CSE or O-Level classes. The numbers taking O-Levels remained at 20 percent, but many more students now left with some qualifications. While there was a greater range of subjects for CSE, they were seen as a second-class qualification by employers.
- The 1973 Education (Work Experience) Act raised the compulsory school leaving age from 15 to 16. It also allowed LEAs to set up work experience in place of lessons for final-year students. This helped school leavers find work in the tough economic climate of the mid-1970s.
- More pupils went to university, but this was a result of government funding to boost the number of places available at new universities such as Sussex and Kent. Some universities dropped a requirement for applicants to have O-Level Latin, thereby increasing applications from comprehensive schools where the subject was often not taught.

SOURCE 11 A cartoon by Michael Cummings published in the *Daily Express* on 17 April 1977.

**THINKING HISTORICALLY** Cause and consequence (3a&b)

**The might of human agency**

1 'Our lack of control'. Work in pairs. Describe to your partner a situation where things did not work out as you had intended. Then explain how you would have done things differently to make the situation work out as you would have wanted. Your partner then tells the wider group about your situation and whether they think that your alternative course of action would have had the desired effect.

2 'The tyranny of failed actions'. Work individually. Think about the role of Lady Plowden, author of the Plowden Report.

   a) Write down three ways that Lady Plowden could have reached different conclusions about the future of education.

   b) Now imagine that you are Lady Plowden. Write a defence of your actions. Try to think about the things that you would have known about at the time and make sure that you do not use the benefit of hindsight.

3 'Arguments'.

   Work in groups of between four and six.

   In turn, each group member will read out their defence of Lady Plowden's actions from question 2. Other group members suggest ways to reassure the reader that they were not a failure and that, in some ways, what happened was a good outcome.

4 Think about the influence of William Beveridge and the Beveridge Report on social reform.

   a) In what ways were the consequences of the report not anticipated by Beveridge?

   b) In what ways did levels of social reform turn out better than Beveridge intended?

5 Think about Anthony Crosland and the advent of comprehensive education. Answer the following:

   a) In what ways were the consequences of the Crosland Circular not anticipated by Crosland?

   b) In what ways did the consequences of the Circular turn out differently to the intended consequences?

6 To what extent are historical individuals in control of the history they helped to create? Explain your answer with reference to specific historical examples from this topic and others you have studied.

## The growth and social impact of university education, 1918–79

### Universities before the Robbins Committee Report

The rising number of secondary school pupils, together with growing government recognition of the economic value of higher education, enabled the growth of university education in Britain. Government funding for universities had increased from £1 million in 1919 to over £80 million in 1962. Between 1920 and 1950, the proportion of university costs met by student fees fell from a third to under an eighth, as bursaries from universities and local councils became more common. In 1962, local authorities were compelled to give an allowance or 'grant' to enable students to concentrate on their studies without worrying about paid work. The increase in student numbers began slowly before the Second World War, but received a major boost in the post-war years. In 1900 there were around 20,000 students in Britain; this had risen to 38,000 in 1938 and 113,000 in 1962.

Oxford and Cambridge had dominated university education before the 20th century and continued to play an important role after 1900: together they still educated 22 percent of all students in 1939. There was a large emphasis on classics and history at Oxford, while Cambridge began to cater more for science students. The University of London was a conglomerate of different colleges and grew hugely in the 19th century: it had 13,000 students in 1939 and grew to 23,000 by 1963. Unlike Oxbridge, it was largely non-residential and allowed external students to sit final examinations. London increasingly specialised in science, engineering and medicine. A number of smaller university colleges that had been founded under the guidance of older universities became fully independent, mostly after the Second World War. These included Reading (1926), and Nottingham, Southampton and Exeter (1948–57).

While this expansion represented progress, it should be noted that the proportion of 18–21-year-olds in university education only increased from 0.8 to four percent between 1900 and 1962; in the USA, by contrast, 50 percent of that age group went to university. The figures are far smaller when one considers the working class or women separately: in 1961, only 13 percent of Oxbridge students were female and the number of working-class students there was tiny.

### The impact of the 1960 Robbins Report

The large numbers of returning troops, together with a sense of optimism brought by peace in 1945, produced a large post-war 'baby boom' generation. By the early 1960s, this large cohort was approaching the end of secondary education. The government asked Lord Robbins to lead a Commission on Higher Education to investigate the situation and make recommendations. Robbins identified the key areas for concern as funding and the number of places available for prospective students. His highly influential 1963 report recommended that a universal national grant be provided to all students with a university place, and that there should be a large increase in state funding to enable the growth of university places. The advice was acted upon, with some impressive results.

Between 1962 and 1970, the number of universities increased from 22 to 46. Many of these, such as York and Lancaster, were known as 'plate-glass universities' because of their unique architectural style. In 1964, the Labour government further increased access to degree-level education through the creation of the Council for National Academic Awards (CNAA). This enabled non-university institutions to award degrees: 34 technology colleges elevated their status to polytechnics, which were meant to have the same status as universities. As the polytechnics continued to focus on vocational skills and offered degrees that were seen as inferior, their status was never truly as high as other universities. The CNAA also enabled the launch of the Open University in 1969 (in conjunction with Harold Wilson's Labour government). This was aimed primarily at adults and made use of radio and television to facilitate remote learning by correspondence.

The Robbins Report led to an impressive boom in university education: between 1970 and 1983, the number of full-time students increased from 185,000 (31 percent female) to 237,000 (42 percent female). Despite this, the number of students in higher education remained far lower than in other advanced industrial nations. The social impact of increased university education was also significant. With a more highly educated workforce, the number of people who could demand high salaries for skilled jobs increased. As well as this, a recurring theme of governments after 1945 was equality of opportunity and universities helped to ensure this was possible. A university degree was no longer the preserve of the rich and was, instead, for working-class people the ultimate sign of increased social mobility. Expectations of young people also began to change: the pressure to leave school (and home) at a young age was not as strong as it had been before the war.

**ACTIVITY**
**KNOWLEDGE CHECK**

**Educational reform**

1. Why did the 1944 Education Act not deal with all issues surrounding education?
2. What were the arguments for and against increased comprehensive education in the 1960s and 1970s?
3. Why was increased university education seen as necessary after the Second World War?

**AS Level Exam-Style Question Section B**

Was the Crosland Circular the most important development in education policy in the years 1945–79? (20 marks)

**Tip**

*Ensure you include primary, secondary and university education in your answer in order to reach a balanced judgement.*

**A Level Exam-Style Question Section B**

How accurate is it to say that the Education Act of 1944 transformed the provision of education in Britain in the years 1945–79? (20 marks)

**Tip**

*Your answer needs to provide a balanced assessment. Remember to include the limits to the impact of the Act.*

**ACTIVITY**
**SUMMARY**

**Creating a welfare state, 1918–79**

1 Create a graph labelled 'Time: 1918-79' on the horizontal axis and 'Rate of change in welfare' on the vertical axis. Plot three lines on the graph, for welfare provision, healthcare and education. Use the lines to show when there was a lot of change (with points plotted at the top of the vertical axis) and more continuity (lower down the vertical axis). Label turning points such as key pieces of legislation.

2 Use the graph to list the decades between 1918 and 1979 which saw most and least change in welfare provision, healthcare and education. Are there any similarities or differences between the periods that saw the most or least change in each of the three areas? If so, how might you explain them?

3 Which government would you argue had the most success with regard to welfare provision, healthcare and education? Before you answer, consider the criteria that should be used to decide the level of success. You might wish to debate these criteria, and the whole issue of governmental success or failure with regards to welfare in class.

**WIDER READING**

**Books**

Fraser, D. *The Evolution of the British Welfare State*, Palgrave Macmillan (2003)

Jones, M. and Lowe, R. (eds) *From Beveridge to Blair: the First Fifty Years of Britain's Welfare State*, Manchester (2003)

Lowe, R. *The British Welfare State Since 1945*, Palgrave Macmillan (2004)

Rees, R. *Poverty and Public Health 1890-1939*, Heinemann (2003)

Timmins, N. *The Five Giants: A Biography of the Welfare State*, HarperCollins (2001)

**Websites**

Changes in British healthcare: www.nhshistory.net

The development of education in the 20th century: www.educationengland.org.uk

Document collection on Attlee's Britain including the welfare state and NHS: www.nationalarchives.gov.uk/education/topics/attlees-britain.htm

# 1.3 Society in transition, 1918–79

**KEY QUESTIONS**

- To what extent did British class structure and social values change between 1918 and 1979?
- In what ways, for what reasons and to what extent did life change for British women, 1918–79?
- How far did relations between Britons and immigrants to Britain change between 1918 and 1979?

## INTRODUCTION

Class is at once a familiar and a complex issue: you might be able to state which class you belong to but it would take a lot longer to explain why you feel part of this class. Self-classification was more straightforward in pre-industrial Britain: although they had little notion of being part of a geographically broader class, most people were highly aware of their 'rank' within their locality, based on a vertical comparison of wealth, power, lifestyle and occupation with their neighbours. The aristocracy, thanks to their greater geographical mobility and shared experience of wielding power, developed a strong class identity beyond their locality before industrialisation. With industrialisation came the growth of mass communication, newspapers, education, trade unions and political parties; these enabled those lower down the social scale to think about and identify with a wider community of people of their rank. Popular 'class consciousness' emerged as a cultural phenomenon that built on earlier notions of rank: a self-employed shopkeeper in 1918 might have no more wealth or power than a skilled worker, but his aspirations, education, dress, leisure pursuits, church attendance and choice of newspaper could all mark him out as the middle rather than of the working class. It is important to be aware of this socio-cultural self-definition as well as the broader economic and structural determinants of class.

Since 1918, a number of factors have affected class structure and the self-identification of British people within that structure. By 1979, far more people identified themselves as middle class due to the growth in average wealth and income, and the rise of 'white-collar' jobs. Technological change, the availability of cheaper consumer goods and the growth of disposable income have enabled a wider range of people to enjoy similar fashions or leisure pursuits, things that would have been clear class identifiers in 1918. The rise of mass education and welfare promoted social mobility and blurred class boundaries before 1979. Mass media further **democratised** British society through its promotion of 'ordinary' celebrities and **satire** aimed at traditional elite figures.

While many people benefited from these changes, people in some sections of society feared this rapid change and saw the apparent breakdown of old certainties as a symptom of moral decline. Some commentators in the 1950s and 1960s deplored the way in which British youth in particular seemed to copy the 'consumer society' values of the USA. They feared for a society that abandoned

**KEY TERMS**

**Democratisation**
Change that promotes democracy. This is most obvious in relation to electoral systems but the term can also be applied more generally to popular access to power or influence.

**Satire**
A form of humour used to expose and criticise people's behaviour. It is most often used to ridicule politicians.

1954 | 1955 | 1956 | 1957 | 1958 | 1959 | 1960 | 1961 | 1962

**1955** - Ruth Ellis hanged - last woman to be executed in Britain

**1956** - John Osborne's play *Look Back in Anger* first performed

**1958** - Last debutante ball hosted by Elizabeth II

**1959** - Obscene Publications Act allows serious works of art to use 'obscene' words and images

**1960** - *Lady Chatterley's Lover* trial allows publication of this 'pornographic' novel

**1961** - Suicide Act changes law so those who fail to kill themselves will no longer be prosecuted supposed pre-war values of decorum, respect and solid tradition for novelty, liberality and instant gratification; many blamed mass media for forcing change. However, middle-aged commentators have deplored the waywardness of youth from time immemorial. In reality, changes in British values and attitudes were not as rapid as these commentators suggested, neither were they primarily driven by mass media. Large sections of British society had become more '**permissive**' by 1979, but this was more due to increased wealth, new technology and legislation than to rock'n'roll.

KEY TERMS

**Permissive**
Tolerant of a broad range of different lifestyle choices, behaviours and attitudes.

**Old Etonian**
A former student of Eton College, a public school for boys in Berkshire. Old Etonians have been perceived to dominate positions of influence in Britain.

**Death duties**
A tax paid by the inheritors of property over a certain value. The tax is a percentage of the value of the property.

# TO WHAT EXTENT DID BRITISH CLASS STRUCTURE AND SOCIAL VALUES CHANGE BETWEEN 1918 AND 1979?

## Class, social change and the impact of wars, 1918–51

### The upper class

The average Briton read about upper-class 'society' in newspapers like the *Express* and *Daily Mail*. They were distinguished from the rest of the population, not only by their huge wealth, largely tied up in landownership, but by their dress, education and exciting social calendar, called 'the Season'. The Season was divided between country pursuits such as hunting and shooting from autumn through to spring and a series of sporting and cultural events largely based in London during the summer months. The London Season began with the presentation of aristocratic daughters of marriageable age to the monarch at the 'debutantes' ball'; this ceremony continued until Elizabeth II ended it in 1958. Badminton horse trials, horse-racing at Royal Ascot, rowing at Henley, sailing at Cowes and polo matches were a must for the upper classes because they were also attended by members of the royal family. Such events gave a clear identity and social glue to the upper classes, which enabled them to survive some major challenges to their power and, to a lesser degree, their wealth. The events also made it easier for rich members of the middle class to affect an upper-class identity; this was particularly true after 1918, as more events were held in public venues rather than private London mansions, which many aristocrats were forced to sell off after the First World War. It was this dilution of the older, aristocratic element of the upper classes that led Queen Elizabeth to cancel the debutantes' ball in 1958: as her sister, Princess Margaret, said: 'We had to put a stop to it. Every tart in London was getting in.'

The First World War contributed to the decline of the landed elite in two key ways. First, it took a disproportionately heavy toll on their lives: while 12.9 percent of men in the army died, 19 percent of all peers and their sons, and 20.7 percent of **Old Etonians**, died. This was largely because they served as officers who, as they were expected to lead from the front, had a higher mortality rate. Second, the cost of the war prompted a huge increase in income tax and **death duties**: estates worth over £2 million were subject to a 40 percent duty and tax on incomes over £2,500 rose from two percent in 1914 to 57 percent in 1925. Death duties were increased in 1929, 1946 and 1949, and were not reduced at any time up to 1979. Wartime restrictions on raising rents, and the reduction in available labour due to conscription, made running country estates far harder to pay for.

**1962–63** - Beatles rise to fame with hits such as 'Love Me Do' and 'Please Please Me'

**1964** - Country House Act encourages the opening of stately homes to the public

**1965** - Murder (Abolition of the Death Penalty) Act passed

**1967** - Sexual Offences Act legalises homosexual acts between men over the age of 21, in private, in England and Wales (Scotland1980, Northern Ireland 1982)

**1968** - Theatres Act abolishes censorship of plays on stage in the UK

**1969** - Divorce Act allows divorce after two years' separation if both parties want it and five years if one party wants it

**1970** - First meeting of Gay Liberation Front

1963 1964 1965 1966 1967 1968 1969 1970 1971

All of these changes contributed to the **gentry** selling off almost a quarter of all land in England between 1918 and 1920; to put this in context, a survey of land ownership in 1883 found that the wealthiest 0.6 percent of the population owned 98.5 percent of agricultural land. An increasing number of them sold all their land: in 1937, one-third of the 4,000 gentry listed in Burke's *Landed Gentry* were landless; this had increased to half by 1951. Only the largest landowners were able to maintain their vast estates: of the 124 aristocratic families who owned over 10,000 acres in 1910, 65 percent still had over 1,000 acres in 1979. The 1979 Royal Commission on the Distribution of Income and Wealth found that a quarter of all farmland in England (six million acres) was owned by just 1,200 landowners. The increased willingness of the gentry to work for a living, rather than receive rent, and the ability of wealthy businessmen and professionals to purchase the trappings (and even titles) of aristocratic life, led to the emergence of a new upper class that was only partly based on ancestry, and overwhelmingly based on wealth.

**KEY TERM**

**Gentry**
Wealthy and often powerful individuals, often landowners but not peers (nobility with titles like Duke, Marquess, Earl, Viscount and Baron).

While the older element of the upper classes retained their land, they lost their exclusive grip on political power. Due to the middle-class (if not genuinely working-class) nature of its MPs, the rise of the Labour Party accelerated the decline of landed-elite power in the House of Commons, which had begun in the mid-Victorian era. While wealthy landowners made up 40 percent of MPs in 1910, this had fallen to around five percent by 1945.

The House of Lords no longer functioned as a bastion of aristocratic power: the Parliament Act of 1911 meant the Lords could only delay rather than block legislation; from 1958 onwards, hereditary peers were increasingly replaced by politically nominated 'life-peers'. In 1910, 39 out of the 43 Lord Lieutenants (Crown representatives in each county) had been aristocrats, a figure that had fallen to 15 out of 46 by 1970. Yet the rise of the new upper classes meant there was no real decline in elite dominance of politics before 1951. Harold MacMillan's Conservative government (1957–63) contained no fewer than 40 Old Etonian cabinet members.

The rise of satire (see Chapter 4) and greater social mobility after the Second World War undermined deference (unquestioned respect for the authority of '**Establishment**' figures) in the 1960s and 1970s. This social mobility was made possible because there was a rise in the number of middle-class jobs and educational opportunities improved with the implementation of the 1944 Education Act. Real wages for all workers improved in the 1950s, when the growth of affordable consumer goods and cars blurred

**KEY TERM**

**Establishment**
A group of privileged people who are perceived to exercise a firm grip on power through official and unofficial channels, to the exclusion of all outsiders.

**SOURCE 1** Three working class boys look on with amusement as two boys from Harrow School wait to be picked up from the Eton vs Harrow cricket match, held at Lord's Cricket Ground, 1937.

class boundaries. Yet, while Establishment figures bore the brunt of the satire boom of the 1960s, the landed elites retained widespread affection by losing political power and opening their homes to the people. A significant number of country houses, whose upkeep became unaffordable after 1918, were bought by or donated to the **National Trust**. The 1937 Country Houses Scheme allowed families to live in their stately homes rent-free for two generations if they transferred ownership to the National Trust and opened the house to the public for at least 60 days a year. The scheme also enabled the owners of stately homes to avoid paying hefty death duties when passing property on within the family. Popular admiration of country estate style and refinement, reinforced by television series such as *Brideshead Revisited* (1981) and *Upstairs Downstairs* (1971), led millions to pay entry fees and helped preserve the landed elite. The country house lifestyle remains the ultimate goal for most rich Britons and, in this way, the old upper class continues to exercise cultural, if not political, influence.

**KEY TERM**

**National Trust**
An organisation established in 1895 to preserve and protect historic houses and landscapes for the benefit of the nation.

### The middle class

The middle class is most easily defined by what it is not: they are neither the 'ruling class' at one end nor manual workers at the other. There remained a great deal of variety in the wealth, attitudes and leisure pursuits of the upper and lower middle class throughout the 20th century. The traditional divide between the middle and upper class had been based on land ownership as a means of income and aristocratic title. Although this barrier became increasingly porous, participation in 'the Season' events continued to mark some distinction between the upper class and the merely rich. The lower middle classes worked hard to differentiate themselves from the working class, not only in their jobs, but in their cultural and leisure pursuits as well (see Chapter 4). They saw themselves as upright, moral people who set the standards of the community and therefore tended to look down on the working classes. There were periods, such as the years immediately after the First World War, when the middle class feared an erosion of the material privileges that distinguished them from the working class. In particular, there was the (false) perception that working-class wages were increasing while middle-class incomes from salaries, rent or investment stagnated. In the years after the First World War, a £250 annual salary was considered a prerequisite of middle-class status, so rising working-class wages were especially troubling.

Wartime inflation contributed to this fear due to its impact on middle-class savings and incomes: something that cost £100 in 1914 would cost £276 in November 1920. Middle-class contemporaries unfairly blamed the increased strength of trade unions for pushing up wages and prices, but the inflation had more to do with the strains of a wartime economy. This helps to explain the enthusiasm of the 'strike-breakers' during the 1926 General Strike (see pages 30–31): the middle classes saw themselves as defenders of order and 'the constitution'. In the same year, middle-class residents of Bromley, Kent went as far as erecting a 2m high wall topped with broken glass across a private road to prevent working-class residents of the Downham council estate passing through the wealthier area on their way into central Bromley (the wall was finally removed by the council in 1950 to allow fire engines to use the route). Such concerns also explain why the majority of the middle class solidly backed robust Conservative policies on law and order.

However, far from suffering from working-class encroachment, the middle class went from strength to strength, recruiting more members from below whilst cementing their distinct advantages over the working class. The war gave a spur to middle-class employment, with a 34 percent growth in commercial and financial jobs in London between 1911 and 1921. The growth of respectable jobs in science, technology and engineering, the rise of salaried jobs in management and administration (from 700,000 in 1931 to 1.25 million in 1951), and the expansion of clerking jobs for women (from 170,000 in 1911 to 1.4 million in 1951) drove middle-class expansion. Workers in such jobs saw themselves as modern, progressive and financially responsible compared to the 'feckless' working classes, who earned irregular wages.

Home ownership became a defining characteristic of middle-class status. Interwar contemporaries spoke of a 'new middle class' who had bought homes since 1920. By 1939, 60 percent of the middle class were home-owners compared to 20 percent of the working class. New homes had been constructed on 'spec built' estates, largely in the south of England and especially the commuter belt around Greater London. The geographical separation of men from their place of work, and the difference between suburban life and the more sociable way of life in densely populated urban housing areas, also differentiated middle-class from working-class culture.

The middle classes led the way in the domestication of leisure time (see Chapter 4). When the greater prosperity of the 1950s and 1960s enabled the working class to assume elements of a middle-class lifestyle, privilege was partly retained through exclusive membership of certain clubs and societies, such as the Rotary Club or local golf club.

### The working class

Historians have disputed the impact of the two world wars on the working classes more than any other class. Arthur Marwick has argued that war, especially the Second World War, led to profound and lasting change. He cites the disruption of pre-war relationships, the greater inclusion of previously excluded social groups for the benefit of the war effort, and the psychological impact of increased sympathy for the underprivileged (through evacuation or press attention) as factors that contributed to a social and economic revolution. Paul Addison has rejected this view and concludes that war led 'only to a very modest change in society itself'. He argues that the key changes were an upsurge in patriotism common to all classes rather than a genuine shift in the way the working classes were perceived by 'superiors' or how they saw themselves. The general consensus is that the Second World War brought about greater change than the First and that this was largely a product of sustained and effective government intervention after 1945, compared to the 'broken promises' of a 'land fit for heroes' after 1918.

The working class was highly varied, with skilled workers in construction or engineering as the working-class aristocracy, unskilled labourers in the middle and a destitute or criminal underclass (referred to by contemporary commentators as the 'residuum') at the bottom. Full employment during both wars helped to absorb the 'residuum' into the respectable working class; trade union membership increased by 90 percent between 1914 and 1918, and unions were necessarily more inclusive after 1918.

It was the trade union movement as a whole rather than one sector of the working class that suffered from the effects of the slump after the First World War. However, the diverse regional impacts of the economic slump and Great Depression make it difficult to generalise about the experience of the working class as a whole: the major division was between those with and without work, rather than between various grades of manual labour. Those in work enjoyed rising wages and lower working hours, and began to take advantage of mass leisure activities (see Chapter 4). The writer George Orwell, a keen-eyed social commentator, blamed the passivity of the working class on the growth of consumerism between the wars (Source 3).

**SOURCE**

From Robert Roberts's book *The Classic Slum*, published in 1971. Roberts was born in 1905 to parents who ran a corner shop in Salford.

Some of the poorest in the land started to prosper as never before. In spite of war, slum grocers managed to get hold of different and better varieties of foodstuffs of a kind sold before only in middle-class shops, and the once deprived began to savour strange delights. This brought the usual charge of 'extravagance' from their social superiors. 'But why shouldn't folk eat their fancy?' my mother said. 'They work for what they get.' One of our customers, wife of a former foundry labourer, both making big money now on munitions, airily inquired one Christmas time as to when we were going to stock 'summat worth chewin''. 'Such as what?' asked my father, sour-faced. 'Tins o'lobster!' she suggested. Furious, the old man damned her from the shop. 'Before the war,' he fumed, 'that one was grateful for a bit o'bread and scrape!' He, like thousands of skilled engineers throughout the country, was filled with rage... Socially, the barriers of caste (class) that had previously existed between the skilled worker and his family and the lower grades were permanently lowered; the artisan felt less superiority, the labourer and semi-skilled man more self-assurance.

**SOURCE**

From George Orwell's book *The Road to Wigan Pier*, written in 1937. Although he was from a privileged background, Orwell was a socialist.

It is quite likely that fish and chips, art-silk stockings, tinned salmon, cut-price chocolates, the movies, the radio, strong tea and the Football Pools have between them averted revolution. The working class are submissive where they used to be openly hostile.

## THINKING HISTORICALLY Evidence (4a&b)

### The weight of evidence

Sources 2 and 3 could be used by the historian to build up a picture of the changing fortunes of the working class. Answer the following:

1 What point is the author of Source 2 making about the changing fortunes of the working class?

2 What does Source 3 suggest is the result of improved conditions for the working class?

3 Explain why Sources 2 and 3 offer different views on the condition of the working class. How might this affect their value as pieces of evidence in appraising the changing role of the working class? Explain your answer.

Discuss the following in groups.

4 Suppose the historian had ten more accounts that agreed broadly with Source 2 and only four that agreed with Source 3. What would that tell them about the event?

5 How far should the balance of the evidence play a role in constructing written history? What else must the historian consider about the evidence being used before drawing conclusions?

Yet, there were other reasons for the lack of more serious working-class protest. Trade union membership fell 40 percent during the 1920–22 recession and failed to recover in the aftermath of the General Strike. Areas of industrial growth, such as car production, tended to be non-unionised and in parts of the country that had historically seen fewer strikes (the south-east and the West Midlands, as opposed to Lancashire or South Wales). Around half the working class voted for the Conservative Party between the wars, something that also helped to preserve the remarkable stability of the British political system.

The welfare reforms introduced by the pre-1914 Liberal government, and built upon by interwar governments (see Chapter 2), helped reduce the social stigma of state assistance for those at the bottom. Those nearer the top prided themselves on responsible use of their weekly wage and aspired to middle-class standards in the community. Compared to their social superiors, a smaller percentage of the working class had fought in the First World War. This was partly due to the number of 'reserved occupations', such as coal miners, whose labour was deemed essential to the war effort and also due to the number of conscripts who were turned away on grounds of ill health or poor physique: in 1918, 10.3 percent of urban working-class men were rejected as unfit for any kind of service and 31.3 percent were classed as too sickly for combat. Rationing helped promote working-class health: life expectancy rose from 49 to 56 years for men and 53 to 60 years for women between 1911 and 1921.

In many ways, the gains expected by the working class failed to materialise. Although the state now provided a basic safety net, many people continued to live in squalid houses with poor diets. Slum clearances did not start properly until the 1950s and exploitative landlords took advantage of tenants while providing inadequate accommodation. The housing programme of many British cities from the late 1940s centred on the construction of blocks of flats. Although some working-class families were happy with the 'mod-cons' of new flats, such as more rooms and hot running water, others felt isolated due to the lack of local amenities or the day-to day interaction with neighbours in a residential street or over a garden fence. Housing schemes such as Pollok in Glasgow or Quarry Hill Flats in Leeds were felt to be dreary places to live. Despite this, there were no mass protests about the inequality of wealth in Britain (the top 0.1 percent of the population owned 33 percent of the wealth, while the bottom 75 percent had less than £100 each).

However, as one historian discusses in Extract 1, the Second World War effected some important and long-lasting changes in the working classes.

**EXTRACT 1**

From *Classes and Cultures: England 1918–51*, written by Ross McKibbin in 1998.

What then did the war do? The first and most important thing was to renew the 'traditional' working class. The war restored the staple industries [coal, steel, textiles] to full employment and thus restored the integrity of those great working class communities which had half-collapsed during the interwar years. It also universalised a working class political culture: it allowed the Labour Party to recruit large numbers of working class men and women who in the 1930s had stood outside that culture. Both wartime policy and rhetoric, by emphasizing equality of sacrifice and provision as ideologically good in themselves, and not simply as instruments to winning the war, further redistributed social esteem. The second consequence of the war was the widely noted 'rudeness' of working men and women, and particularly working class servicemen, an abandonment of traditional courtesy (or deference). This was accompanied by an obvious lurch to the left in working class opinion. For many it was simply a willingness to talk about politics. The remarkable reaction to the Beveridge Report is probably the best-known example of this.

**ACTIVITY**
**KNOWLEDGE CHECK**

**Class and the impact of war**

1 Place Sources 1-3 and Extract 1 in order of their usefulness to someone who wants to understand class in Britain between 1918 and 1951. Explain why you have chosen this order. Does the order change if the question is shifted to understanding *change* in class relations 1918-51? If so, explain why.

2 In what ways did the First and Second World Wars affect the different classes?

3 In your opinion, upon which class did the wars have the greatest impact?

**AS Level Exam-Style Question Section B**

To what extent was the impact of the Second World War the main reason for the changing class system between 1918 and 1979? (20 marks)

**Tip**

*Select approximately three other factors, apart from the Second World War, to discuss so you can develop a balanced judgement.*

## The emergence of a 'liberal society' and its opponents, 1951-79

### KEY TERMS

**Liberal values**
In a social context, people with liberal values tolerate or embrace greater individual choice and freedom with regards to sexuality, family structures, religious belief and fashion.

**Mass Observation**
An academic research organisation founded in 1937, which studied the everyday lives of British people. Volunteers were asked to keep diaries or complete questionnaires and researchers were paid to record everyday conversations and behaviour.

### Sexuality and the Sixties

Although the title of this section refers to the years 1951–79, the Sixties are often seen as the pivotal decade when legal, medical and social changes led to a profound growth in **liberal values** in Britain. Historian Arthur Marwick has argued that the 1960s marked the end of Victorianism and the rise of a more permissive society. Many right-wing politicians have agreed with this interpretation and blame the Sixties for lots of current social problems. Other historians, including Joanna Burke, have more recently argued that the liberal values we so often associate with the Sixties were only really held by a small minority of the population, and that actually many were still reserved and cautious. In order to assess the extent to which the Sixties did witness a substantial change in British values, the nature and extent of liberal views in the 1950s and 1970s must be analysed. The extent to which the values enshrined in legal reforms during this period reflected those of the British public must also be considered.

Liberal values with regards to sex and sexuality did not suddenly emerge out of thin air on 1 January 1960. Marie Stopes's *Married Love*, published in 1918, was a bestseller that challenged the general reluctance to discuss sex in public. Stopes argued that women, as well as men, should enjoy sex within marriage.

**SOURCE 4**

From Marie Stopes, *Married Love*, published in 1918.

The only secure basis for a present-day State is the welding of its units in marriage... It is never easy to make marriage a lovely thing. Knowledge is needed and, as things are at present, knowledge is almost unobtainable by those who are most in want of it... I have some things to say about sex, which, so far as I am aware, have not yet been said, things which seem to be of profound importance to men and women who wish to make marriages beautiful... Is not instinct enough? No. Instinct is not enough. In every other human activity it has been realised that training, the handing on of tradition are essential... The same is true in the subtle realm of sex.

There were widespread concerns that the Second World War had undermined traditional values by separating husbands and wives, promoting sex outside marriage and encouraging divorce. While the numbers of divorces did increase to a peak in 1947, they rapidly fell after this. **Mass Observation** reports suggest that women who had wartime affairs saw them as the product of difficult circumstances and were happy to go back to stable relationships with their husbands once the war ended. A number of popular post-war books helped to promote a more open attitude towards sexuality. The most important of these were by the American sexologist, Alfred Kinsey. His thoroughly researched 1953 book, *Sexual Behaviour in the Human Female*, did much to undermine moral condemnation of sex before marriage. The 1959 Obscene Publications Act recognised greater public openness to sexual images and discussion, but only at an elite level: while 'serious works of art' could use 'obscene' words and images, it was not until 1977 that the law was extended to include films. The further relaxation of censorship in the 1968 Theatres Act had, in practice, led the British Board of Film Directors to allow the screening of films with some sexual content before 1977: the soft porn film *Emmanuelle* was the fourth most popular film in 1974. Although public discussion of sex was no longer entirely taboo by the end the 1950s, it is clear that there was a significant change in what was deemed acceptable to read, see and discuss by the mid-1970s. Dr Alex Comfort's 1972 book, *The Joy of Sex*, became a bestseller. It was not only sexually explicit but fully illustrated; most significantly in terms of liberal values, it dealt with sex as a pleasure in its own right, rather than as part of married, family life.

**SOURCE 5**

From Dr Alex Comfort, *The Joy of Sex*, published in 1972.

We've deliberately not gone into the ethics of lifestyle. The facts are that very few of us go through life with sexual experience confined to one partner only... The real problem arises from the fact that sexual relations can be anything for different people and on different occasions, from a game to a total fusion of identities; the heartache arises when each partner sees things differently.

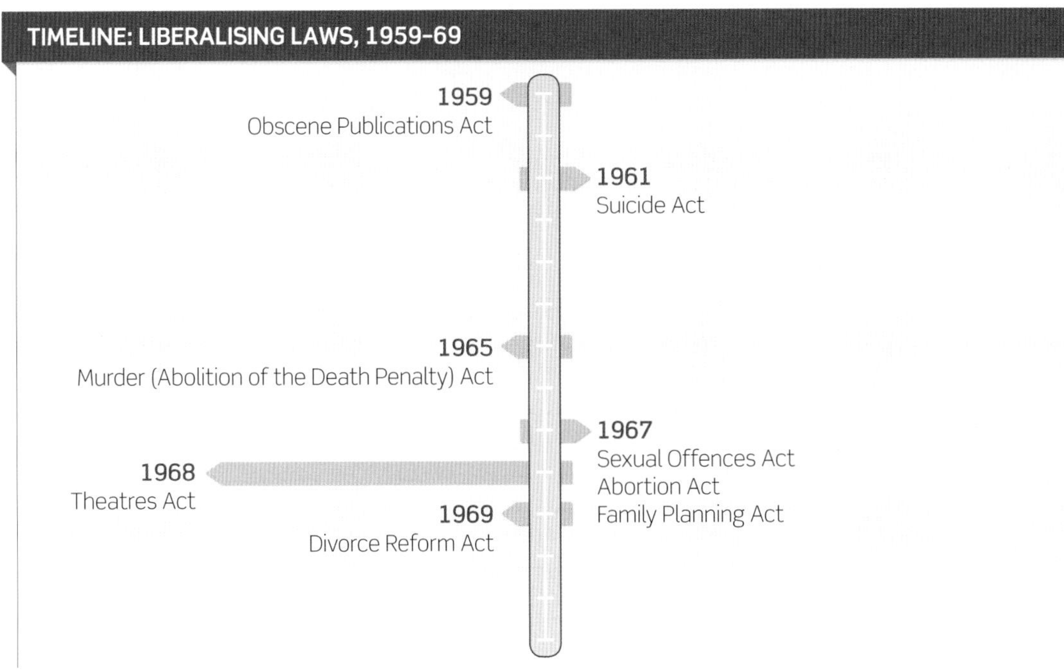


A series of liberalising laws were passed by British governments between 1959 and 1969. These laws decriminalised certain acts and relaxed the laws on other crimes relating to sex. However, just because the laws relating to divorce or homosexuality changed, it does not necessarily follow that people's attitudes towards these things changed. Demand for these liberal laws came, not from the people, but from certain backbench MPs who based their private members' bills on campaigns that had gone back several decades. Pressure for reform of the laws on homosexuality went back to the 1890s, for divorce laws to the 1910s, for birth control to the 1920s and abortion to the 1930s. David Steel's Abortion Act, or Leo Abse's Sexual Offences Act, were not the result of pressure from their constituents, but were issues that they had felt strongly about for a long time before the Sixties. Whereas previous governments had been too conservative in outlook to support liberalisation, many MPs came to agree with Steel, Abse and others that laws should be based on the practical consequences of the legislation, rather than on ethical considerations. In part, this was due to increasing evidence about the negative impact of existing legislation on many people's lives. For example, rather than debate whether abortion was morally right or wrong, Steel asked the House to consider the high number of deaths and injuries that resulted from dangerous 'back street' abortions: about 40 deaths and 100,000 injuries in 1966. Although the governing Labour Party did not want to be seen as driving forward liberal legislation for fear of alienating traditional voters, Roy Jenkins, Home Secretary in 1965–67, saw these changes as the measure of a 'civilised society' and unofficially encouraged Labour support for liberal laws. In his 1975 book, *Permissive Britain: Social Change in the Sixties and Seventies*, Christie Davies argued that the MPs failed to consider the long-term consequences of more liberal laws; they assumed, in his view incorrectly, that moral values in society would be unaffected by these Acts of Parliament. Davies believes that it is the removal of strict, clearly defined boundaries of decent behaviour that have contributed most significantly to the decline of traditional morality and a commonly held sense of respectability since the 1970s. Brian Harrison rejects this position by arguing that the legislative reform merely caught up with changes in behaviour, which had begun after the end of the Victorian era.

Two major surveys, Michael Schofield's *The Sexual Behaviour of Young People* (1965) and Geoffrey Gorer's *Sex and Marriage in England Today* (1971), suggest that notions of a 'sexual revolution' in the Sixties are hugely exaggerated and greatly misleading. Schofield found that only 18 percent of girls and ten percent of boys in his sample of 2,000 teenagers had had sex with more than three people, and that 17 percent of girls and 33 percent of boys had had sex by the age of 19. He concluded that, while promiscuity existed among teenagers, this was far from normal behaviour. Gorer's study revealed that 96 percent of women and 95 percent of men were married by the age of 45, and that the average age of marriage for women fell below 23 in 1970, down from 25 in 1946. One significant change found in the study was that young people were more tolerant of sex before marriage than their parents' generation had been. By 1990, less than one percent of first sexual intercourse took place after marriage. This statistic hints at the decline in the importance attached to marriage, a fact further confirmed by the rise of divorce and of single-parent families from the late 1960s onwards.

### Homosexuality

Homosexuality was a poorly understood and taboo topic before the 1970s. At the start of the 1950s, there was a great deal of popular fear and hatred towards homosexual men, who were thought to be predatory. Such negative views were not helped by the defection of spies Guy Burgess (homosexual) and Donald Maclean (bisexual) to Russia in 1950. A poll in 1963 revealed that 93 percent of people thought that homosexuals were ill and needed medical treatment; although this sounds illiberal to modern ears, the growing perception that homosexuality was an illness undermined the view that it ought to be punished as a crime. Before 1967 in England and Wales (1980 in Scotland and 1982 in Northern Ireland), homosexual men ran the risk of arrest and imprisonment if they wished to have sexual relations; lesbian relationships had never been illegal in Britain. Over a thousand men were in prison in the mid-1950s purely because of their sexuality; there were several cases of blackmail of high-profile homosexuals and some were even driven to suicide. The high-profile trial of Lord Montagu of Beaulieu and *Daily Mail* journalist Peter Wildeblood in 1954 also led to a growing public perception that the state should not be able to regulate what consenting adults do in their own homes. Montagu was sentenced to a year and Wildeblood to 18 months in prison, terms that were thought, even by conservative newspapers, to be excessively harsh.

**SOURCE**

From the editorial of the *Sunday Times* 'Moral Reform and the Law' published on 28 March 1954.

> The law... is not in accord with a large mass of public opinion... The case for a reform of the law as to acts committed in private between two adults is very strong... the case for an authoritative inquiry into it is overwhelming.

The arguments raised by the trial and sentence were a key reason for the formation of the government-appointed Wolfenden Committee (1957). The Committee's Report recommended that private, consenting homosexual acts should be decriminalised for men aged 21 or above. However, there was a lot of resistance in parliament to such change and it was not until the 1967 Sexual Offences Act that this advice was acted upon. Even then, it remained illegal to 'solicit' homosexual relations (i.e. to seek them in a public place). The number of men arrested for 'public indecency' trebled between 1967 and 1972 (due to increased police attention), a clear sign of the limited impact of the law. A more assertive form of gay rights activism emerged in the 1970s in response to these arrests: the Gay Liberation Front was founded in the USA, and a British branch was set up in October 1970. The group encouraged gay people to be open about their sexuality to help people see homosexuality as a normal part of life. Although there were some cultural signs that homosexuality was becoming more acceptable in the 1970s, it was not until the early 2000s that most British people felt it was not wrong to be gay. A number of pioneering men began to make camp behaviour, if not homosexual relationships, acceptable in the 1970s. Television stars such as Larry Grayson, presenter of popular shows *Shut That Door!* (ITV 1972–77) and *The Generation Game* (BBC 1978–82), and John Inman, who played the popular character Mr Humphries in the sitcom *Are You Being Served?* (BBC 1972–85), were camp but publicly denied being gay. Although Grayson had catchphrases such as 'What a gay day' and 'Seems like a nice boy', he told the *Daily Mirror* in 1972 that he just pretended to be gay. ITV screened *The Naked Civil Servant* in 1975; this was a highly successful television film about the life and times of Quentin Crisp, a flamboyant homosexual writer and life-class model who became a gay icon after he published memoirs of his early life in 1968. Also in the 1970s, some leading pop stars, such as David Bowie and Elton John, publicly admitted to being bisexual. The first ever gay pride march was held in London in 1971. In 1976, Tom Robinson released 'Glad to be Gay', which reached 18 in the singles chart.

**ACTIVITY**
**KNOWLEDGE CHECK**

**Sexuality and the Sixties**

1 In what ways did attitudes towards male and female sexuality change after 1945?

2 Why did attitudes towards homosexuality change?

## New moralism and Mary Whitehouse

More serious and sustained challenges to the permissive society came from religious leaders, public figures with a firm Christian faith, and from some Conservative politicians. Despite voting for the Abortion Act and the Sexual Offences Act, Margaret Thatcher became increasingly outspoken about her fears for public standards of decency. In January 1970, she told the *Finchley Press* that she would like to see 'a reversal of the permissive society' in the decade ahead.

SOURCE

From an interview with Margaret Thatcher in the *Finchley Press* (a local newspaper in her constituency), printed on 2 January 1970.

I should like to see a reversal of the permissive society. It is commonplace to say that behaviour is freer now than it used to be. I question whether a person who gives in to his every instinct and whim is free. It seems more likely that he is a slave to his own appetites. Surely an educated society should consist of people capable of self-disciplines; capable also of appreciating the necessity for law and order. And I should like to see the divorce rate fall, greater understanding between the generations, and more emphasis on the family as a unit.

Thatcher's attacks on permissiveness increased as the 1970s progressed; she complained in 1977 that 'basic Christian values… are under attack'. Some people reacted even more strongly against the liberal changes that unfolded in the media. Mary Whitehouse first became concerned about modern morality after talking to pupils in her first job as an art teacher. She joined a group called Moral Rearmament, originally an American evangelical movement whose aim was to 'remake the world'. In 1963, she decided to focus specifically on the damage done to British morals by mass media, in particular by Hugh Carleton-Greene, Director General of the BBC from 1960–69, whom she blamed for the growth of liberal, permissive values on television. She managed to secure 500,000 signatures for her Clean-Up TV petition in 1964, which she sent to the queen. In 1965, this campaign was merged into the National Viewers' and Listeners' Association (NVALA). In 1977, she launched a legal case against the magazine *Gay News* for publishing a 'blasphemous' poem about a Roman soldier having sex with Jesus. She won the case and magazine owner Denis Lemon was fined and given a suspended prison sentence. In her 1977 book, *Whatever Happened to Sex?* Whitehouse said that 'being gay was like having acne'. She campaigned against pornography and her letters to government officials may have played some part in the passage of a law in 1981 to force sex shops to have blacked-out windows. Her reputation still divides people, with many supporting her strong moral stand, and others seeing her as interfering, reactionary and out of touch with the real world.

### THINKING HISTORICALLY Evidence (3a)

#### The value of evidence

Look at Sources 7 and 8 then work through the tasks that follow.

1 Write down at least three ways in which the *Sunday Telegraph* cartoon is useful for establishing attitudes towards social change in the 1960s.

2 Write down two ways in which the interview with Margaret Thatcher is useful to the historian.

3 Compare your answers with a partner, then try to come up with at least two limitations of each source for establishing attitudes towards social change.

4 Discuss with a partner whether you think the cartoon or the interview is more useful for establishing attitudes towards social change and the permissive society.

5 What if the sources were used to answer the question 'Did society change for the better in the years 1951–70?' List the usefulness and limitations of the two sources for this question and for two questions of your own.

The Nationwide Festival of Light was staged in Hyde Park in September 1971 to promote Christian morality and prevent what the organisers saw as the spread of 'moral pollution'. The rally was supported by famous figures, including journalist Malcolm Muggeridge and pop star Cliff Richard; the build-up to the event inspired over 70 regional rallies. Although the events attracted combined crowds of over 100,000 people, it had little impact on permissive trends in the media or society as a whole, largely because of the declining influence of Christianity. In his book, *The Death of Christian Britain*, Callum Brown sees the 1960s as the key decade when Britain became 'secularised' (non-religious). He particularly notes the impact of girls and women's magazines on female church attendance. There was no scandal when anthropologist Desmond Morris said in his book, *The Naked Ape* (1967), that 'Religion has given rise to a great deal of unnecessary suffering and misery'; sales of the *Daily Mirror* were boosted when it serialised the book. However, many historians have criticised this view as it ignores the pre-1960s decline: numbers attending church once a week had already fallen from 35 to 13 percent of the population before 1945. 'Puzzled People', a Mass Observation report in 1947, concluded that 'most people nowadays don't think much about religion, don't set much conscious store by it and have decidedly confused ideas about it'. This shift helps to explain the overall lack of success of those who wished to restore British public morality back to a perceived golden age of the late 1940s and early 1950s.

While Carnaby Street sold itself as the heart of Swinging London in the mid-1960s, a large majority of the population experienced the so-called 'social revolution' second-hand through mass media. A poll published by the *Sunday Times* in 1966 suggested that most people were bored of hearing about new fashions and pop music. There was a regional divide in addition to the generational divide in the diffusion of liberal ideas. Many Britons would have found the following cartoon an entertaining snipe at the fashionable crowd.

**SOURCE 8** 'The Two Cultures', a cartoon published in the *Sunday Telegraph* in May 1966.

**AS Level Exam-Style Question Section A**

Was liberal legislation the main reason for the rise of more permissive values in British society between 1951 and 1979? Explain your answer. (20 marks)

**Tip**

*A significant section of the essay should be dedicated to the liberal legislation passed, particularly in the 1960s. This could include the Abortion Act and the legalisation of homosexuality.*

**ACTIVITY**
**KNOWLEDGE CHECK**

**Permissive society**

1 Explain what was meant by the term 'permissive society'.

2 In what ways could British society be said to have become more permissive between 1951 and 1979? (Revisit this question once you have read about women and family life below.)

# IN WHAT WAYS, FOR WHAT REASONS AND TO WHAT EXTENT DID LIFE CHANGE FOR BRITISH WOMEN, 1918–79?

Women were excluded from a range of opportunities open to men at the start of 1918. The hope of female suffrage campaigners was that the vote would enable further reform in a range of areas that affected women, from healthcare and education to family life and employment. Although women in 1979 enjoyed far more choice and independence than their mothers and grandmothers, progress towards a parity of opportunity with men was limited. Girls and boys had equal access to primary and secondary education, but women continued to face 'glass ceilings' in employment once they left school. Changes in the economy and the impact of two world wars promoted greater female employment, although much of this was part-time or lower paid than male work. As financial security is key to effective independence these issues served as a brake on the advancement of female freedoms. Governments passed a range of laws that sought to help women in various ways, but only began to address unequal pay and sexual discrimination in the workplace in the 1970s.

## TIMELINE: WOMEN'S LIVES 1918–79

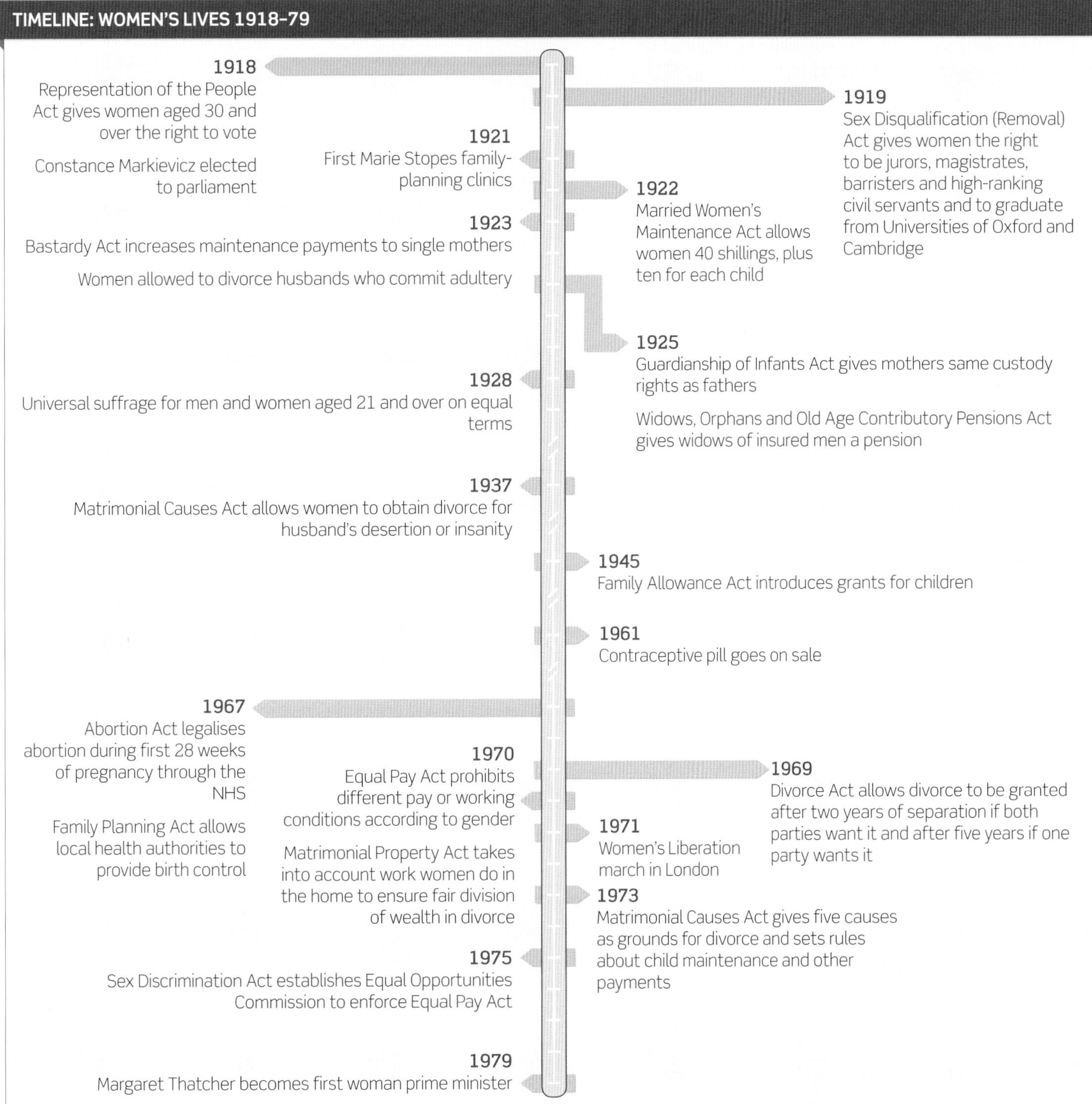

## The right to vote and political advancement, 1918–79

### Franchise reform, 1918–28

Women had campaigned for the right to vote since the 19th century. The right to vote was seen by campaigners as a fundamental right and an essential stepping stone to further progress in the quality of women's lives. In several respects the drawn-out path to the 1928 Representation of the People (Equal Franchise) Act mirrored the hard-won extension of the franchise to some women in 1918. Campaign groups were faced with apathetic or even hostile MPs who were worried that women under the age of 30 (referred to as 'the flapper vote' in unsympathetic newspapers) were too emotional and irresponsible to use the right to vote with due caution. The National Union of Women Suffrage Societies changed its name to the National Union of Societies for Equal Citizenship (NUSEC) to reflect the new focus of their campaign. Together with a range of other societies, they put pressure on MPs to support a fair franchise settlement; in 1926, they launched a sustained canvassing campaign and organised regular meetings in Hyde Park. On 3 July 1926, 3,500 women gathered there for an equal rights procession and demonstration. Although these groups were ultimately dependent upon the goodwill of male MPs (who undoubtedly looked to gain some electoral advantage through franchise reform), such sustained and peaceful pressure secured an equal franchise far more quickly than if things had been left entirely in the hands of men. From 2 July 1928, women over the age of 21 could vote on exactly the same basis as their brothers and fathers.

### Political advancement between the wars?

There was no clear correlation between the right to vote and political advancement more generally. Although 8.5 million women over the age of 30 gained the right to vote in 1918, only 17 women stood as parliamentary candidates and only one, Countess Constance Markievicz, was elected (although as an Irish Republican she refused to take her seat in the Commons). The numbers of female MPs remained low throughout the interwar years.

**SOURCE 9** A table showing the number of female MPs between 1922 and 1935.

| Year | Number of female MPs |
|---|---|
| 1922 | 5 |
| 1923 | 8 |
| 1924 | 4 |
| 1931 | 15 |
| 1935 | 9 |

There were a number of reasons for this failure to translate female majority in voting after 1928 (there tend to be slightly more women than men in the UK population, so women held 52.7 percent of total votes) into political advancement. Perhaps the most important was the structure and attitudes of the main parties. While organisations like the NUSEC were large and well-run, they lacked the sort of expertise and local party machinery to help launch an effective 'Women's Party'. The NUSEC split in 1928 largely over the issue of whether women should push for gender equality with men on men's terms, or for the equal valuation of different gender roles. Eleanor Rathbone argued for the latter and dismissed calls for equal roles and responsibilities with men as 'me too' feminism; she led the formation of the National Council for Equal Citizenship, while her opponents formed the National Union of Townswomen's Guilds. Membership of both organisations fell throughout the 1930s. Although the main parties recognised the need to try to cultivate female participation, they were unwilling to risk losing a safe seat by selecting a female candidate. This reflected the ingrained male bias against female politicians, which they had to face at every stage of their careers. One pioneering female MP, Edith Summerskill, reflected that the House of Commons was 'like a boys' school which had decided to take a few girls'. With the exception of the 1928 franchise reform, both the Conservative and Labour parties failed to promote specifically female issues. Female groups were incorporated into national organisations, where they were outnumbered by men: two Conservative women's groups joined the National Union of Conservative Associations, while Labour allowed four female representatives of the Women's Sections to sit on the main policy-making committee, the National Executive. Socialist women, in particular, faced a difficult choice between mainstream class campaigns, often favouring working men over women, and fighting for female issues; in practice, many sacrificed the latter in favour of the former. Women made important contributions to social and welfare reforms, such as the 1922 Criminal Law (Amendment) Act (which raised the age of legally acceptable consent from 13 to 16) and the 1923 Bastardy Act (which allowed children born before marriage to be recognised as legitimate after their parents' marriage), but seemed to accept the male-dominated agenda of national politics.

Female politicians tended to focus on local, rather than national, politics. There was a longer tradition of women serving on various local boards, where they helped with social issues, such as health and education, which were seen as an extension of their domestic sphere of expertise. More practically, it was difficult for women to balance family life with the pressure for national politicians to be in Westminster. Despite this tradition and expertise, women only made up around five or six percent of local councillors between 1918 and 1939. This average percentage fell slightly after 1929, when elections for Poor Law Guardians were replaced by the (usually male) invitation to join Public Assistance Committees.

### The impact of the Second World War on female political life

By 1939, there were more women, such as Nancy Astor and Eleanor Rathbone, with a good deal of parliamentary experience, who were able to address specifically female issues than had been the case in the years immediately after 1918. In recognition of the impact that the war had on women, female politicians abandoned strict party loyalty in favour of cross-party co-operation. In 1940, Astor set up the Women Power Committee to investigate and promote female-specific issues. In March 1941, Minister for Labour Ernest Bevin set up the Women's Consultative Committee to manage female participation in the war economy more effectively.

This body contributed to the registration and then conscription of women for work in March and December 1941. The intervention of female MPs such as Maud Tate in debates about compensation for wartime injuries led to the introduction of equal compensation for men and women in April 1943 (women had previously received 35p a week less than men). However, despite similar interventions in debates over work and pay, female MPs were unable to secure legislation that would have rewarded equal work between the genders with equal pay. Nevertheless, by 1945, male MPs were finally growing used to considering female issues more seriously; this undoubtedly influenced the range of social legislation passed by post-war governments.

## EXTEND YOUR KNOWLEDGE

### Pioneering women in politics

Nancy Astor (1879–1964) was the first woman to take her seat in parliament and represented the Conservatives until 1945. She is seen by some as a controversial heroine because she gained her seat thanks to her wealthy husband, who held the seat until he was elevated to the House of Lords.

Eleanor Rathbone (1872–1946) had been a suffragist. Like the suffragettes, suffragists wanted women to have the vote; the key difference was that suffragists did not believe in the use of disruptive or violent protests to force the issue. Rathbone's arguments in the House of Commons were crucial in ensuring that Family Allowance payments went to mothers rather than fathers in 1945.

Ellen Wilkinson (1891–1947) was an inspirational MP for Jarrow. She organised the 1936 Jarrow March, which delivered a petition to parliament to highlight the suffering caused by unemployment in this shipbuilding community. She also introduced the 1938 Hire Purchase Act, which gave protection to people who bought goods on credit. Wilkinson served as Minister for Education in Attlee's first post-war government, raising the school leaving age from 14 to 15.

Edith Summerskill (1901–80) was one of the first women to be trained as a doctor, before becoming a Labour MP. She was a founder of the Socialist Health Association, which put forward arguments for a National Health Service.

Barbara Castle (1910–2002) was a leading figure in Harold Wilson's Labour governments in the 1960s and 1970s. As Secretary of State for Transport (1965–68, Britain's first female Secretary of State), she made seatbelts compulsory in new cars and introduced breathalysers to combat drink-driving.

## Women in post-war politics

Having asserted themselves effectively during the war, women were unable to press home possible gains in terms of female representation in parliament. In 1945 and 1955, there were just 24 females out of 630 MPs in the House of Commons; in 1974, the figure remained a lowly 23 out of 635 MPs. The same issues that had served as barriers before 1939 continued to apply, with the candidate selection committees the most formidable. Women were rarely risked in safe seats and so had to overcome large opposition majorities to gain their seat. This meant that those women who did win a seat tended to have exceptional qualities; once in parliament, they stood a far higher chance of promotion to ministerial office (Harold Wilson's 1964 government contained seven of the 18 female Labour MPs). The post-war generation of female MPs were more determined to be seen as well-rounded politicians rather than simply as advocates for women's issues. While a few women, such as Barbara Castle as Minister for Transport, gained national prominence, the loss of cross-party cohesion weakened the advocacy of female rights in parliament after 1945. It took the growth of an extra-parliamentary women's movement in the 1970s to put female-specific issues back on the agenda. As Secretary of State for Employment, and later Secretary of State for Social Services, Castle herself was responsible for a range of significant legislation that affected women, including the 1970 Equal Pay Act, pension reform and the introduction of child benefits.

## The Women's Liberation Movement

A number of developments outside parliament contributed to the broader political advancement of women. Feminist authors drew attention to the inequalities of a profoundly patriarchal society. Betty Friedan's *The Feminine Mystique* (1963) and Germaine Greer's *The Female Eunuch* (1970) are examples of feminist literature that became bestsellers in Britain. They argued that women would remain unfulfilled, second-class citizens unless they actively stood up to the male-dominated state of affairs. The success of the 1968 strike by the female employees at the Ford car factory in Dagenham (see page 77) attracted national attention and helped galvanise female activism.

The National Women's Liberation Conference first met in Oxford in February 1970. Socialist and historian Sheila Rowbotham organised the meeting to help set an agenda for 'women's lib': equal education and opportunities, equal pay, free contraception and abortions on demand, and the universal provision of childcare for working women became the four key goals. Although disagreements over aims and tactics led to a fragmentation of the women's movement by the 1980s, a range of significant legislation had been achieved by then (see below); this success owed a great deal to the sustained pressure of feminist activists in the 1970s.

### Other forms of political advancement: trade unions and local politics

The demand for female industrial labour during the First World War meant many women joined trade unions for the first time between 1914 and 1918. Although many unions rejected female membership, or only accepted women on a temporary basis, the need for female help enabled some political progress at a national level: Margaret Bondfield, who had already been a suffrage (right to vote) and trade union activist before the war, served as part of the wartime Central Committee for Women's Employment. She was elected to the General Council of the TUC in November 1918 and this national profile paved the way for her to become a Labour MP in 1923.

Despite the breakthrough of exceptional women like Bondfield, most unions remained highly masculine environments until the 1980s, when several leading unions, such as UNISON, took deliberate steps to increase female representation at the highest decision-making levels. This was a reflection of a large increase in female trade union membership: between 1970 and 1979, this increased from 2.6 to 3.8 million (or 24 to 30 percent of total membership). It was not until the early 2000s that women began to lead trade unions (the first female leader of the TUC was appointed in 2012).

Women had a longer history of participation in local than national politics, with widows and spinsters allowed to vote in local elections from 1869 (and married women who met the property qualification after 1894). Women had served on local education boards and as Poor Law Guardians in the late 19th century and as councillors after the 1907 Qualification of Women Act. However, despite this head start, women remained under-represented in local politics. The Women's Local Government Society published leaflets in 1921 such as 'Why are Women Wanted on Town Councils?' and 'Rural Districts: Need for Women Councillors'; in 1949, the Ninth Conference of the Women Members of Local Government Authorities in England and Wales discussed how to achieve 'fair representation' of women on local councils. In 2007, the Women's Local Government Association still aimed to 'secure a greater representation of elected women in local government'. The reasons for this are disputed, but historians such as Wendy Stokes cite a focus on women's issues within councils, rather than pressing for more women in office, as more significant than the barriers to entry that have hindered female political advancement at the national level.

**ACTIVITY**
**KNOWLEDGE CHECK**

**Women and politics**

1 Why were the initial advances made by women in politics disappointing?

2 Was the Second World War politically and socially beneficial to women?

## Changes in family life and the quest for personal freedoms, 1918–79

### Family life and work

Women were far more likely to work in 1979 than in 1918 and this was especially true for married women. This was partly due to the impact of war, especially the Second World War. The number of working women in industry increased from 3.3 million in 1914 to 4.8 million in 1918, yet trade unions were quick to assert the reappointment of men at the expense of women after the war. The 1919 Restoration of Pre-War Practices Act meant women who had been employed in munitions factories were forced to return to pre-war employment or stop working if this was not possible. The 'marriage bar' (an expectation that women would stop work once married) was also quickly re-established as a social convention.

The loss of manpower during the Second World War meant women were conscripted in huge numbers to do traditionally male work after 1941: the percentage of women who worked as engineers, in transport or the chemical industry rose from 14 percent in 1939 to 33 percent in 1945. This was in addition to the thousands of women who served as farm workers in the Women's Land Army, or in non-combat roles in the armed forces. As a result, and despite government propaganda campaigns to maintain distinct gender roles, there was wider male acceptance of women as workers outside of their traditional roles between the wars: in domestic service, education, or as typists and telephonists.

Perhaps more significantly, wartime experiences of the extra money, independence and sociability that came with work, led to a permanent shift in female aspirations beyond the home. The 'flappers' of the 1920s flaunted their independence by smoking in public and dressing in far less restrictive clothing. By the late 1950s, a *Manchester Guardian* survey revealed that while 40 percent of housewives were content in this role, 50 percent were bored a lot of the time. In 1951, a quarter of married women worked; by 1961, this had risen to a third; in 1971, a half and, by 1990, two-thirds. In the 1950s, the majority of women who had a child did not return to work for ten years; by the 1970s, this period had fallen to four years.

War was not the only factor in cementing the greater participation of British women in the workplace. Labour-saving devices such as vacuum cleaners and washing machines enabled women to devote less time (in theory if not always in practice, due to heightened expectations of cleanliness put forward in women's magazines) to domestic chores. Shifts in the labour market meant there were more part-time and semi-skilled or unskilled jobs, which made up the majority of female employment. In her extensive 1965 survey sociologist Viola Klein found that 60 percent of working women did unskilled jobs. Government legislation also promoted female employment, albeit in a sluggish and ineffective fashion. The Equal Pay Act was finally passed in 1970, despite criticisms dating back to the 1940s that women took home just over half the wage of a man for similar work. A key reason for the timing of the Act was the success of the 1968 Ford Dagenham strike: a three-week strike by 300 female sewing machinists led Ford to accept equal pay for women doing similar jobs to men (although they were still only awarded 95 percent of men's pay in the final settlement). The action inspired the creation of the National Joint Action Committee for Women's Rights (NJACWR), which put pressure on leading unions to adopt equal rights targets. Union pressure led to Labour support; in 1975, the Labour government passed two important pieces of legislation. The 1975 Employment Protection Act meant women could not be sacked for getting pregnant and gave six weeks' paid maternity leave to those who qualified through two years' service. The 1975 Sex Discrimination Act made it illegal to discriminate against women in employment, training, housing and education; it also set up the Equal Opportunities Commission to help enforce the recent legislation. Women continued to experience a 'glass ceiling' in certain professions and unequal pay more generally, largely due to the impact of motherhood on career progression. Women also continued to take up unskilled and part-time work, again due to the pressures of family life.

### Family life: children and marriage

Marriage was seen as the main life goal for women before feminists began to challenge this notion in the 1960s and 1970s. The roles of dutiful wife, mother and homemaker were glamorised in a range of women's magazines, yet the reality became increasingly dull and isolating for many women. The shift from 'slum' neighbourhoods to new suburban estates or tower blocks reduced the regular social contact for women that men continued to enjoy in pubs. Higher expectations were placed on women to be ideal mothers, not just taking care of children's material well-being but nurturing them with 'mother love'. A lack of nurseries meant mothers could only aspire to part-time work and, outside of work, were further isolated by time-consuming childcare. Marriage also brought dependency on the husband in several respects: the 1946 National Insurance Act classed non-working wives as dependants who could not claim unemployment benefits; this built upon the 1920 Unemployment Insurance Act, which stated married women had to prove they were actively seeking work to claim benefits, and the 1931 Anomalies Regulation, which added the further restriction that they had to prove they were able to do insurable work. This situation was not changed until 1978, when married women began to pay full National Insurance contributions and could claim full benefits when unemployed. Women's work in the home was hardly recognised in divorce proceedings; husbands kept such a high share of the couple's wealth that some women were effectively trapped in loveless or even abusive marriages.

A number of factors began to change this dependent status of women in the home, especially after the 1960s. The 1969 Divorce Reform Act meant couples could end their marriage due to 'irreconcilable differences' after two years (or five years if only one party wanted the divorce). Before this, one party had to prove some fault or blame existed in the other to win a divorce through the courts. This was very difficult and expensive to achieve before the 1969 Act. The 1970 Matrimonial Proceedings and Property Act awarded a far higher share of the couple's wealth to the woman in divorce settlements. Rates of divorce increased from less than three in 1,000 marriages in 1965 to almost ten in 1,000 by 1976.

**SOURCE 10** A table based on figures from the Office for National Statistics, showing numbers of divorces in the UK and which party requested the divorce from 1945 to 1995.

| Year | Total number of divorces | Divorce granted on petition of husband | Divorce granted on petition of wife | Divorce granted on petition of both |
|---|---|---|---|---|
| 1945 | 15,634 | | | |
| 1955 | 26,816 | 12,034 | 14,782 | |
| 1965 | 37,785 | 15,993 | 21,633 | 159 |
| 1975 | 120,522 | 38,477 | 81,693 | 352 |
| 1985 | 160,300 | 44,574 | 115,144 | 582 |
| 1995 | 155,499 | 45,985 | 109,023 | 491 |

Women also gained greater sexual equality with men thanks to the wider availability of birth control, especially the Pill. Before this, while men could enjoy sexual pleasure in a fairly risk-free fashion, women were conscious of the consequences of pregnancy, especially before the passage of the 1967 Abortion Act. Until then, women who wished to terminate a pregnancy had to seek an illegal 'backstreet' abortion. These were carried out by untrained people, usually in their own homes; the lack of hygiene and training led to 40 maternal deaths and over 100,000 injuries in 1966 alone. MP Dr David Steel used statistics like this when he persuaded parliament to legalise abortion during the first 28 weeks of pregnancy, a measure approved of by 70 percent of the British public. Feminists were keen to promote female empowerment and enjoyment of sex and helped advocate a more equal partnership within relationships as opposed to male dominance.

**EXTEND YOUR KNOWLEDGE**

**Birth control and the Pill**

The Pill had been developed in America in the 1950s, but experts feared its introduction in Britain could promote promiscuity among unmarried women. This helps to explain its slow rise to importance. The Family Planning Association had been set up in 1930, but only offered contraception and advice to married couples. The number of such clinics increased from 65 in 1948 to 400 by 1963.

Brook clinics offered the same service to unmarried girls as young as 16; the first was set up in 1964, but there was often opposition to the opening of new clinics. The contraceptive pill was made 'available to all' in December 1961 at a subsidised price of two shillings a month; in reality, it was only given to older married women until 1967and only became available for free to all women on the NHS in 1974.

Historians Akhtar and Humphries have argued that 'the years between 1965 and 1969 were when the sexual revolution began in Britain. The pace of change was astonishing - and the Pill made it all possible'. Numbers of women using the Pill increased from 50,000 in 1961 to one million in 1970. However, it was not until the late 1970s that the Pill rivalled the condom as the contraceptive choice for most Britons.

## Role models for greater personal freedom

Radio and television were almost the exclusive preserve of men until the 1950s. The growth of women in popular culture as anything other than fragile damsels or objects of masculine desire was slow before the 1980s and this helped to reinforce a stereotyped, second-class status. Barbara Mandell (ITV, 1955) and Nan Winton (BBC, 1960) were early television newsreaders. The first permanent female news anchor was Angela Rippon, in 1975. Joyce Grenfell and Jill Day were early comedy writers and performers on radio and television, with shows in the 1950s.

A few female-dominated sitcoms were broadcast from the 1960s, including *The Rag Trade* (BBC 1961–63), *The Liver Birds* (BBC 1969–79) and *Butterflies* (BBC 1978–83), the last two written by a woman, Carla Lane. The growth of soap operas, such as *Coronation Street* (1960 onwards), has also offered more assertive female role models, which have contributed to women's desire for greater personal freedom.

**EXTRACT 2**

From Sonia M. Livingstone, *Making Sense of Television*, published in 1998.

As regards gender, the conventions of soap opera, developed for a largely female audience, require strong, active women, in direct contradiction to conventional gender roles, as shown in most other television programmes. Indeed soap operas have been thought of as countering or undermining the 'masculine' ethos of most popular culture, especially prime-time television with its certainties, consistencies and plot linearity, by providing a female voice and a feminine form... Women's pleasure in soap operas derives in part from the centrality of images of the powerful mother and also from the dominant role of the villainess, an expression of that part of themselves which women must usually suppress.

**ACTIVITY**
**KNOWLEDGE CHECK**

**Political advances and the growth of personal freedoms for women**

1 Make a detailed chronology with examples of political advancement and increased personal freedoms for women.

2 In which area would you argue that women made greater progress: political advancement or increased personal freedoms? Justify your answer.

3 In what ways and to what extent would you argue that political advancement and increased personal freedoms for women were linked between 1918 and 1979?

**A Level Exam-Style Question Section B**

How far did women succeed in attaining greater personal freedoms between 1918 and 1979? (20 marks)

**Tip**

*This is a broad question, and can include the role of women in political life, personal freedoms and employment.*

## HOW FAR DID RELATIONS BETWEEN BRITONS AND IMMIGRANTS TO BRITAIN CHANGE BETWEEN 1918 AND 1979?

Britain has been multi-ethnic and multicultural for hundreds of years: the four major national groups have periodically been joined by waves of migrants who have sought to escape persecution and make a better life for themselves. The major difference in 20th-century Britain has been the growth of a multi*racial* society. Whites made up 99.8 percent of the population until 1945; by 1979, this figure was 96 percent and is likely to fall to nearer 90 percent in the next few years. The vast majority of non-white immigration took place between the late 1950s and 1960s, with further growth of racial minority populations driven by native UK births. A key reason for this development was the existence, and decline of, the British Empire (restyled the Commonwealth in 1949). Colonial residents were legally British citizens until the 1962 Commonwealth Immigrants Act redefined their status (see below). Despite this, very few people from the '**New Commonwealth**' came to Britain until a range of UK organisations advertised for labour in those colonies during the post-war economic recovery. Although the British government did not particularly welcome this development, it was reluctant to take any action to prevent it for fear that it might antagonise increasingly strained relations with colonial leaders.

The failure of local efforts to integrate racial minorities and the eruption of violence in a few areas in 1958 eventually did force government legislation to curtail unrestricted immigration. Before restrictions were imposed people from a wide range of cultural, religious, social and educational backgrounds arrived and settled in Britain. These diverse groups have had to overcome a range of problems to establish themselves in Britain. Earlier waves of white immigrants, such as Irish or Jewish settlers, faced a good deal of prejudice, but racism added a further barrier to harmonious relations. In post-war Britain, the government and white people in general have had to adapt to this change; it has not been a straightforward process for many, especially in areas with comparatively high levels of non-white settlement. By 1979, while it was clear that newly arrived racial minorities had a lot to offer British society, there was still a good deal of casual, if not politically organised, prejudice against them.

**KEY TERM**

**New Commonwealth**
Newly independent Commonwealth countries, mostly in non-white areas in Africa and Asia, as opposed to the Old Commonwealth countries such as New Zealand, Australia and Canada, which had mostly white populations.

**EXTEND YOUR KNOWLEDGE**

**Immigration legislation before 1914**

Wartime aside, any enterprising individual who made it to Britain from around the world was allowed to settle here before the 1905 Aliens Act. Apart from 500,000 Irish workers (classed as internal migrants as Ireland was part of the UK from 1800 to 1922), very few arrived until a wave of anti-Semitic attacks in the 1880s and 1890s drove around 50,000 Jews from Eastern Europe to settle in poor areas of London. It was popular concern about this influx of 'aliens' that prompted the first restrictions on immigration. After 1905, only those who could demonstrate an ability to make a living, who had £5 to tide them over until they found work and who were genuine religious or political refugees were allowed in by immigration officers.

**TIMELINE: RACIAL MINORITIES IN BRITAIN 1948–79**

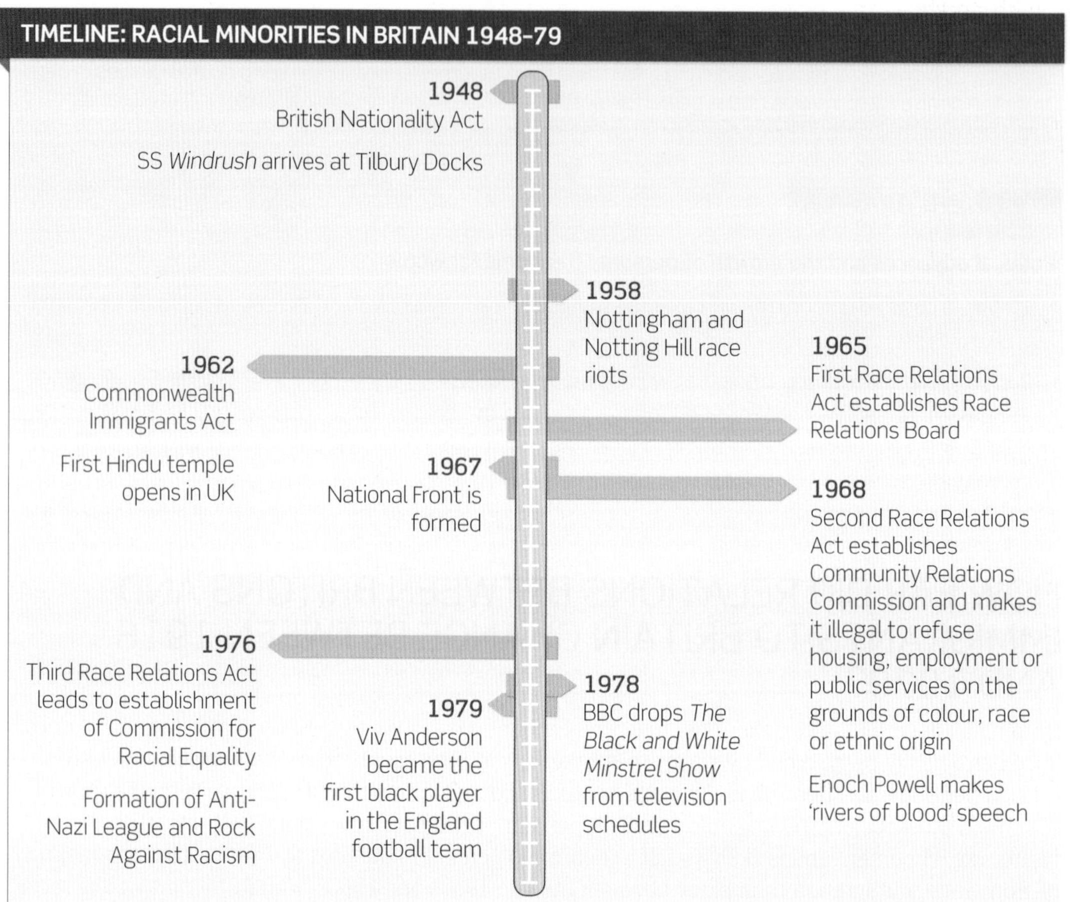


## Immigration policies and attitudes towards ethnic minorities, 1918–39

### Anti-Semitism

The 1914 British Nationality and Status Aliens Act introduced the first modern passports. They had not been required for international travel before this and were only made compulsory to prevent wartime espionage. A further Aliens Act in 1919 meant immigrants had to gain a work permit before arrival, had to register with the police upon arrival and maintain lawful behaviour to avoid immediate deportation.

Many Jews, seeking to escape Nazi persecution in Germany, emigrated and settled in Britain between 1933 and 1939; by the outbreak of the war, there were 300,000 Jews in the country. Although these settlers had been selected for their wealth and skills, there was still a lot of anti-Semitic (anti-Jewish) hostility based on widely held notions that they forced up rent and unemployment for native residents. While Oswald Mosley's British Union of Fascists (see page 18) was never very popular, it did provide a vehicle for racist, and specifically anti-Semitic, hatred. In October 1936, the BUF organised a march through the East End of London, home to significant Jewish and Irish communities; violence erupted at Cable Street, where local residents had erected barricades to divert the march. While anti-Semitism was widespread in interwar Britain, there was never any threat of the kind of persecution faced by continental European Jewish communities.

**EXTEND YOUR KNOWLEDGE**

Kindertransport (1938–40)
On the evening of 8–9 November 1938, the Nazis unleashed a wave of destruction of Jewish shops and synagogues in Germany; around 90 Jews were murdered. In response, British Jews and Quakers asked Prime Minister Neville Chamberlain if Britain would accept unaccompanied children up to the age of 17. The government agreed and, between late November 1938 and May 1940, around 10,000 German, Austrian, Czech and Dutch Jewish children were allowed to settle with British families for the duration of the war. One British stockbroker, Nicholas Winton, personally secured the safe transport of 669 Czech Jewish children to British families.

### The 'colour problem' and different solutions

There were very few non-whites in Britain before the 1950s; the only contact that the vast majority of white Britons had with racial minorities was through their depiction in photographs, illustrations and stories about the British Empire in the popular press. As a result, most white Britons, if they thought about race at all, tended to feel comfortably superior to blacks and Asians. It also meant there was no 'colour problem' in Britain outside of the few areas (London and port cities such as Cardiff, Newcastle, Hull and Liverpool) where around 74,000 black and Asian people, mostly born in the UK to earlier migrants, lived. The First World War led to a comparatively larger influx of 'coloured' sailors and workers in such cities; these people faced popular and official racial prejudice. There were race riots in several ports in 1919, largely fuelled by resentful unemployed demobilised men. The 1920 and 1925 Special Restriction (Coloured Alien Seamen) Orders forced 'coloured' seamen to register as aliens in Britain if they could not produce documentary proof of their British citizenship; the police were to arrest those who failed to produce such documents upon disembarkation. As 'aliens', they had to check in regularly with the police and ran the risk of deportation if they failed to do so. There were cases where even non-sailors were subjected to the same orders: 63 Indian labourers were registered in Glasgow. The Indian Seamen's Union was founded by N. J. Upadhyaya in 1926 to protest at the treatment of Indians and a public rally was held in support in Liverpool. As a result of such action, and official criticism from the India Office, Indian residents were allowed to apply to the Home Office for a Special Certificate of Identity and Nationality to revoke their alien status.

Not all white Britons were ignorant of or hostile towards racial minorities. The Joint Council to Promote Understanding between White and Coloured People in Britain, and the League of Coloured Peoples were both founded in 1931 to tackle what they saw as the growing 'colour problem'. These middle-class liberals sought to help individuals fight instances of racial discrimination and to raise financial aid for struggling black and Asian families in Britain. Their efforts were not always appreciated: a growing radical pan-African movement judged that only black people could resolve black 'problems'. The American-born singer and actor, Paul Robeson (who lived on and off in London between 1925 and 1939), was perhaps the most iconic supporter of anti-colonial black empowerment in interwar Britain. He was a member of the West African Students' Union (WASU), set up in London in 1925 and led for almost 30 years by Nigerian Ladipo Solanke. WASU was one of several black organisations that united in 1934 to protest against the Italian invasion of Ethiopia; the International African Service Bureau emerged from this unity and became a key influence on many post-colonial African leaders.

## The impact of the Second World War and new Commonwealth immigration

### The impact of war and post-war recovery

The fight against racist Nazi Germany had a limited impact on immigration and on British racial attitudes. Perhaps the most important shift was in the view of the colonies, which, for a while at least, changed from racial inferiors to valued wartime allies. A small number of black workers were invited to work in crucial industries during the war, for example the 1,000 West Indians invited to work at munition factories in Lancashire and Merseyside, and the further 10,000 employed as ground crew by the Royal Air Force. These men did experience some racial prejudice but this was largely driven by white American servicemen rather than British natives. These wartime experiences, coupled with severe post-war unemployment in the West Indies, encouraged the first waves of West Indian male workers to seek employment in Britain. The wartime contribution of the colonies also led to the revocation of the Alien Orders in 1942; many black people, mostly sailors but also some stowaways, took advantage of this and were able to enter Britain.

The post-war economic recovery had a more profound impact on immigration and British race relations than the war itself. Full employment and the demand for cheap labour led the British government to try to recruit workers in Europe. As many as 100,000 Poles, mostly ex-servicemen and their dependants, were recruited as part of the Polish Resettlement Corps. They had been based in Britain during the war and felt unable to return home now Poland was ruled by a Communist government. They were joined on a temporary basis by 85,000 European Voluntary Workers, mainly displaced citizens from Eastern Europe, but also many Italians. Even this was not enough to meet British demand for workers. The National Health Service, textile firms in northern England and London Transport all advertised vacant positions throughout the New Commonwealth. London Transport, who provided hostels for newly recruited workers, even sent representatives to the Caribbean to search for staff: 140 men were recruited in Barbados in 1956 alone. Black men from the Caribbean became a familiar sight on London buses as drivers and conductors in the 1950s. These overwhelmingly young, male immigrants were allowed to settle in the UK thanks to the 1948 British Nationality Act, which made all people living in the Commonwealth British citizens. Amongst the first to take advantage of this law were the 492 West Indian passengers who disembarked at Tilbury Docks, London from the SS *Empire Windrush* on 22 June 1948. They were followed by a further 108 Jamaican immigrants, who arrived on the SS *Orbita* in September that year. In the following five years, around 3,000 black immigrants were settling each year in Britain. Unofficial chains of migration were set up so that people from a particular Caribbean island settled in the same part of the UK, for example the community of Nevisians in Leicester.

**SOURCE 11** A photograph of passengers on board the SS *Empire Windrush* catching up on the latest news from Jamaica in *The Daily Gleaner* shortly before their arrival at Tilbury Docks in London on 22 June 1948.

SOURCE

A table showing the rise in numbers and percentage of the ethnic minority population in the UK between 1951 and 2001. Figures from the National Office for Statistics.

| Year | Total ethnic minority population of UK | As a percentage of total population of UK |
|---|---|---|
| 1951 | 80,000 | 0.2 |
| 1961 | 500,000 | 0.8 |
| 1971 | 1,500,000 | 3.3 |
| 1981 | 2,200,000 | 4.1 |
| 1991 | 3,000,000 | 6.4 |
| 1997 | 4,000,000 | 7.3 |

### The government response

While MPs who represented constituencies with growing 'coloured' populations were keen to secure limits to Commonwealth immigration, many leading Conservative ministers, such as Colonial Secretary Alan Lennox-Boyd, were keen to uphold the international prestige of British liberalism, especially during a period of increased nationalist agitation in the colonies. The numbers of immigrants involved were deemed to be too small to necessitate immediate action; instead, the Inter-Departmental Committee on Colonial People in the UK was set up to investigate ways to promote racial integration on a local, informal basis. The committee aimed to 'disperse' black immigrants around the country and to offer industrial training courses to facilitate their employment. While most immigrants found work, they were drawn in large numbers to a few cheap areas of cities with a booming industrial recovery, such as London and Birmingham. Councils and social services did not have the expertise to effectively promote integration, especially when popular views of black people were heavily influenced by stories of violence in Africa (for example during the Mau Mau uprising in Kenya between 1952 and 1960) and gangsters from the Harlem district of New York. So-called 'friendship councils' were set up in some affected areas, but these were more of a discussion forum for black and white residents rather than bodies that took effective action.

A few British universities directed some of their sociological research to the 'colour problem' in the 1950s: a team led by Dr Kenneth Little at Edinburgh University made clear for the first time the range of religious, class and cultural divides within racial minority groups. Little concluded that it would be unlikely for a co-ordinated black party to emerge in Britain, along the lines of the National Association for the Advancement of Coloured People in America. In 1953, he pressed Labour to adopt a policy against racial discrimination in employment. His recommendations largely fell on deaf ears until the disturbing events of 1958.

ACTIVITY
KNOWLEDGE CHECK

**Immigration**

1 What tensions existed before the outbreak of the Second World War as a result of immigration?

2 What were the main causes of immigration to Britain before 1958?

3 What initial problems existed in Britain as a result of post-war immigration?

## Government policies and racial controversy: immigration and race relations 1958–79

### Race riots

In areas of higher black settlement, such as St Ann's in Nottingham, Toxteth in Liverpool, Handsworth in Birmingham and Brixton in London, the original white population began to move out to other parts of the city. By 1957, the government became increasingly concerned about what was described as 'white flight' and 'segregation'. There were specific fears that British cities would come to resemble American ones, with poor black ghettos as seedbeds of vice and crime. The failure of local efforts to promote integration became apparent in a range of respects: trade unions complained about immigrants (both white and black) taking jobs from whites by accepting work for lower wages; some young men, especially those in working-class '**Teddy Boy**' gangs, sought to intimidate black men who were 'taking their women'; there was racial discrimination in housing with 'No coloureds' and 'No blacks' signs in some areas and overcrowded, poor quality housing for blacks in others, something that helped to reinforce negative racial stereotypes. As the black immigrants were overwhelmingly young men, they did like to drink, dance and flirt. However, sensationalised reports in newspapers about the supposed lack of cleanliness, criminal activities and sexual practices of recent immigrants further heightened racial tensions.

KEY TERM

**Teddy Boy**
Teddy, short for Edward, from the Edwardian style of the boys' long coats and drainpipe trousers. Most just liked the fashion and separate identity but some formed violent and racist gangs.

Such tensions, coupled with government unwillingness to take decisive action, led to the outbreak of race riots in 1958. In the St Ann's area of Nottingham almost 1,000 white and black youths fought each other on the night of 23 August 1958; a number of stabbings occurred. These were followed by riots in Notting Hill, London. The riot was sparked by an attack by a Teddy Boy gang on a white woman with a black partner. Over a period of almost two weeks in August and September, the riot in London escalated, with hundreds of young, white men armed with chains, knives, iron bars and petrol bombs attacking groups of black immigrants and their homes with chants such as 'Niggers out'. More than 100 white men were arrested, as well as some black men who had armed themselves in self-defence. The riots received widespread news coverage both within Britain and internationally. The Notting Hill Carnival was founded the following year to promote racial harmony.

### The consequences of the riots

Overall, British public opinion was shocked by the events at Notting Hill. Much of the British public had seen television news coverage of the police trying to keep black and white groups apart, and firefighters putting out petrol bomb fires. The riots exposed the failings of local councils and led to a re-evaluation of race relations on both sides of the divide. More than 4,000 immigrants were so angry and disillusioned with life in Britain that they returned to the Caribbean.

The Caribbean governments made a joint complaint to the British government about prejudiced policing and the impact of poor housing on their countrymen. Immigrant groups in Britain became more organised: the Organisation for the Protection of Coloured People was set up in 1958; it helped to organise rent strikes in Notting Hill until repairs were carried out on their housing. There were demands for greater expertise in race relations: the Institute of Race Relations in London was set up in 1958, under the leadership of Philip Mason. The riots also led to renewed calls for immigration legislation: it was argued by many Conservative MPs that integration could only be achieved if numbers of immigrants were limited to their current numbers. Finally, in the autumn of 1961, the Conservative government introduced a bill to restrict immigration.

### Immigration legislation

Ironically, the most significant cause of mass immigration from the New Commonwealth was the initial legislation that was meant to curtail it. In 1956, 47,000 people entered Britain from the New Commonwealth; by 1961, this had increased to 136,000, with a further 94,900 in the first six months of 1962. The cause of this huge increase was the fear among potential black and Asian migrants that Britain would close its doors to further immigration in the near future.

The 1962 Commonwealth Immigrants Act allowed immigrants to settle provided they had been awarded a voucher proving that they had a job lined up. The Act also allowed the dependants (usually wives and children) of pre-1962 immigrants to join them in Britain. Rather than slowing New Commonwealth immigration, the Act enabled existing Asian and black UK residents to organise vouchers and establish unofficial chains of migration from their original homes. The vast majority of Indians came from the Punjab and Gujarat, while most Pakistanis came from a handful of places in Sylhet (which later became part of Bangladesh). Fear of not being able to return to the UK if they went home encouraged more immigrants to settle and bring their families to Britain. Between 1962 and 1968, while 77,966 vouchers were issued, 257,220 dependants settled in the UK. Between 1968 and 1971, 318,521 people from the New Commonwealth arrived; of these, only 58,875 were male workers. Despite the surge in numbers caused by the 1962 Act, opinion polls claimed that nearly three-quarters of the British public supported these new controls on immigration.

The 1968 Commonwealth Immigrants Act sought to close these unintended chains of migration from India, Pakistan and the West Indies through a 'grandfather clause': would-be immigrants needed, in addition to an employment voucher, a British-born, adopted or naturalised parent or grandparent in order to allow them to enter the country. This was criticised as a racist measure as it would allow far more immigration from Canada, Australia and New Zealand than from the New Commonwealth. The 1971 Immigration Act meant that 12-month work permits replaced employment vouchers by the end of 1972; from 1973 onwards, immigrants could only remain in Britain for a limited period of time. Politicians in the main political parties had passed these laws due to their fear that white British alienation and anger would lead to votes for fascist parties such as the National Front (founded in 1967). By the early 1970s, Britain had some of the toughest immigration laws in the world, and virtually all black and Asian primary immigration had stopped: in 1972, just 2,290 immigrants were admitted under the voucher scheme. One notable exception to this blanket restriction was the admission of 27,000 Ugandan Asians who were forcibly expelled from their homeland by dictator Idi Amin. A further 10,000 Greek Cypriots and 15,000 Vietnamese were allowed to settle in Britain to escape violence in their home countries.

**SOURCE 13** Ugandan Asian refugees who were temporarily housed at RAF Stradishall airbase in Suffolk, 1972.

Harold Wilson's Labour government sought to tackle discrimination as well as restrict non-white immigration. The 1965 and 1968 Race Relations Acts banned incitement to racial hatred and racial discrimination in public places. This made illegal the use of restrictions such as 'no coloureds' and 'Europeans only' used by some landlords and employers. The 1968 Act extended the ban on racial discrimination to housing and employment. The Race Relations Board was set up in 1966 to deal with complaints about racial discrimination. However, many saw it as a waste of time to use it: complaints could not be made about the police and only about ten percent of complaints to the Board were ever upheld. The 1976 Race Relations Act toughened laws against racial discrimination and victimisation. It also set up the Commission for Racial Equality in September 1976 to help fight injustice and create a fairer society.

## Enoch Powell and the far right

Contemporary media suggests that many British people still held racist views by the end of the 1970s. Racial minorities were often shown in patronising or confrontational ways and there were far fewer sports or media personalities showing racial minorities in a positive, empowered fashion than in later decades. Despite this ease with the portrayal of racism in popular culture however, there were only a few cases of public support for openly racist groups or politicians. In the 1959 general election, the founder of the British Union of Fascists, Oswald Mosley, campaigned against immigration; he gained only eight percent of the constituency vote. In the 1964 general election, the Conservative candidate for Smethwick in Birmingham, Peter Griffiths, used the slogan 'If you want a nigger for a neighbour, vote Labour' as part of a successful campaign. Labour Prime Minister Harold Wilson said he should be seen as a 'parliamentary leper'.

The National Front Party was formed in 1967. It firmly opposed immigration, as well as any measures to improve race relations and multiculturalism, with noisy demonstrations and marches. It had 20,000 members by the mid-1970s, but this support had collapsed by the end of the decade. It failed to gain a single parliamentary seat, but caused widespread media reaction by gaining 16 percent of the vote in the 1973 West Bromwich by-election. In 1968, Conservative MP Enoch Powell made what became known as the 'rivers of blood' speech. He warned of a violent future for British multiracial society if the numbers of immigrants continued unchecked. Conservative leader Edward Heath sacked Powell from the Shadow Cabinet the next day; he never held a senior government position again. A petition to stop Powell being sacked gathered over 30,000 signatures. Opinion polls suggested that 75 percent of the British public agreed with his speech.

**SOURCE**

An extract from Enoch Powell's 'Rivers of Blood' speech, made on 20 April 1968.

> A week ago I had a conversation with a constituent. After a sentence or two about the weather he suddenly said: 'If I had the money to go, I wouldn't stay in this country... I have three children and two of them married now, with family. I shan't be satisfied till I have seen them all settled overseas. In this country in 15 or 20 years' time the black man will have the whip hand over the white man.' I can already hear the chorus of execration [curses]. How dare I say such a horrible thing? How dare I stir up trouble and inflame feelings by repeating such a conversation? What he is saying, thousands and hundreds of thousands are saying and thinking... Those whom the gods wish to destroy, they first make mad. We must be mad, literally mad, as a nation to be permitting the annual inflow of some 50,000 dependants. It is like watching a nation busily heaping up its own funeral pyre... As I look ahead, I am filled with foreboding: like the Roman, I seem to see 'the River Tiber foaming with much blood.'

## Conclusion

By 1979, it was unclear how far the recently arrived racial minorities would integrate into British society. However, there were already indications as to the ways in which a new multiracial society might develop. On the one hand, there was a clear lack of integration in housing. Certain areas of a few towns became magnets for chain migration and replaced the majority of whites in those areas. There were also fairly low levels of interracial marriage, although this was far more likely for black Caribbean men and Chinese women than other minority groups. The range of new religions introduced by immigrants won hardly any white British converts; Hindu temples and Islamic mosques exclusively served immigrant communities, just as synagogues had served the Jewish migrants of the 1880s and 1890s. However, British cuisine became increasingly influenced by the culinary tastes of immigrants: foods from South Asia, Italy and China became more familiar to British consumers in restaurants and on supermarket shelves by the end of the 1970s. Although still in its infancy compared to later developments, racial minorities had also begun to make an impact on British sport and popular culture.

**EXTRACT**

From 'Race Relations', an essay by Shamit Saggar in *Britain Since 1945*, edited by J. Hollowell and published in 2003.

> In the... 1997 general election, Labour's shadow Home Secretary, Jack Straw, declared that 'we should not allow... a cigarette [paper] to come between the Labour Party and the Tory government over immigration'... [This] unintentionally feed[s] public sentiment that is not only hostile to immigration, however modest and feasible to absorb, but continues to see many of the social issues raised by immigration as deeply problematic and exacerbating, possibly with a radical twist, the politics of distribution... If race... serves to divide, or at least distinguish, political behaviour, the conclusion we must draw is that political integration remains a long way off, at least in respect to some minority communities rather than others.

**ACTIVITY**
**WRITING**

**Integration: widen your vocabulary**

1. Read Extract 3 and make a note of any words that are unfamiliar to you.
2. Look them up in a dictionary and note down their definitions.
3. Aim to use as many words as possible in your own paragraph about what patterns of speech can tell us about the integration of racial minorities in post-war Britain.

## Cause and consequence (5a)

### Connections

Causes never simply come one after another. They are often present simultaneously and have an effect on one another. Sometimes new causes develop and interact with existing ones.

**Causes of social change between 1918 and 1979**

| Women gaining the vote (1918 and 1928) | Immigration | Impact of world wars on the class system | More liberal attitudes develop | Race relations legislation | Race riots (1958) |
|---|---|---|---|---|---|

Work in groups to produce a diagram of causes and the links between them:

1 On an A3 piece of paper, write all the causes of social change between 1918 and 1979. Write these in boxes, the size of which will reflect how long they were a relevant factor. For example, if you argue that 'immigration' had been an important factor since 1918, then this will be quite a big box, whereas the 'more liberal attitudes develop' may be a lot smaller. Spread these boxes over the page.

2 Then make links between all the causes. Draw lines between the boxes and annotate them to explain how the causes are connected, and in what ways each affected and altered the other. For example, between 'immigration' and 'race relations legislation', you could write something like, 'without immigration, race relations legislation would not have been implemented'.

Answer the following questions:

3 How do the causes differ in their nature? (Think in terms of events, developments, beliefs, states of affairs, etc.)

4 How do the causes differ in the roles they played in causing social change? (Think about whether each cause created the right conditions, was a trigger for events or acted in some other way.)

5 Write a 200-word paragraph explaining how important it is to recognise the relationships between causes. Give examples from your diagram. Try to include connective phrases such as: 'this created conditions conducive to...', 'this triggered an immediate reaction...' and 'this made the development of that situation more/less likely'.

## ACTIVITY
KNOWLEDGE CHECK

### Immigration and race relations

1 Why did the 1962 Commonwealth Immigrants Act not produce the results the government expected?

2 What measures were taken by governments to promote harmony in race relations?

### AS Level Exam-Style Question Section B

How far was government legislation effective in improving race relations in the years 1945–79? (20 marks)

**Tip**

*Legislation that can be discussed could include the Commonwealth Immigrants Acts of 1962 and 1968, as well as the Race Relations Act.*

### A Level Exam-Style Question Section B

How far do you agree that attitudes towards immigrants changed in the years 1945–79? (20 marks)

**Tip**

*This is an open-ended question that could include material related to social attitudes, government legislation and integration.*

ACTIVITY
SUMMARY

**Society in transition, 1918-79**

1 For each decade between 1920 and 1979, give a school report-style grade (with A the best down to E the worst) to Britain for the following categories: liberalisation; progress for women; race relations. Briefly explain your grades, but pay particular attention to the A and E grades: what made them so good or so bad?

2 How could links be drawn between the changes in class, liberalism, female progress and race relations? Links could be considered in terms of shared causes or interrelations between the different changes.

3 Which would you argue was the most significant change in Britain between 1918 and 1979: changes in class relations, liberalisation, female progress or improved race relations?

## WIDER READING

**Books**

Addison, P. and Jones, H. (eds) *A Companion to Contemporary Britain*, Blackwell (2005)

Bruley, S. *Women in Britain Since 1900*, Palgrave (1999)

Goodheart, D. *The British Dream: Successes and Failures and Failures of Post-War Immigration*, Atlantic Books (2014)

Harrrison, B. *Seeking a Role: The United Kingdom 1951–70* and *Finding a Role? The United Kingdom 1970–1990*, Oxford (2009 and 2010)

Holdsworth, A. *Out of the Doll's House: the Story of Women in the Twentieth Century*, BBC Books (1988)

Philips, M. and Philips, T. *Windrush: the Irresistible Rise of Multicultural Britain*, HarperCollins (2009)

**Websites**

*National Archives themed document collections*

The 1930s: www.nationalarchives.gov.uk/education/topics/thirties-britain.htm

The 1950s: www.nationalarchives.gov.uk/education/topics/fifties-britain.htm

The 1960s: www.nationalarchives.gov.uk/education/topics/sixties-britain.htm

Attlee's Britain: www.nationalarchives.gov.uk/education/topics/attlees-britain.htm

# 1.4 Changing quality of life, 1918–79

**KEY QUESTIONS**

- How far did living standards change in Britain between 1918 and 1979?
- In what ways and to what extent did mass popular culture affect British society between 1918 and 1979?
- To what extent did the British experience of travel and leisure pursuits change between 1918 and 1979?

## INTRODUCTION

A person's standard of living is determined by a range of variables. The most important are those that contribute to a person's physical well-being: access to clean water, adequate sanitation, quality of diet, standard of housing and availability of healthcare. In addition to such primary needs, some measures of standard of living also include less tangible variables: work–life balance, levels of **social capital** and the impact of relative rather than absolute poverty on levels of satisfaction. A number of factors affected standards of living in 20th-century Britain; variations in these factors help to explain the range of living standards found in different regions and social classes. Income levels have been the key determinant of living standards: the fivefold growth of average **real income** between 1918 and 1979 goes a long way to explaining improved diets, housing and health in this period. State intervention, through legislation, targeted spending or propaganda, also played a large role in the improving quality of life, especially during the strongly interventionist post-war consensus years. Technological advances, including those in communications, transport and domestic life, contributed to changes in living standards, though they did not always lead to straightforward improvements.

**KEY TERMS**

**Social capital**
The value gained from social networks in terms of trust, co-operation, mutual aid and a sense of connectedness.

**Real income**
This measure of income takes into account the effect of inflation on what can be bought with money earned at a particular time; it is therefore more useful when looking at changes in the standard of living over a period of time than nominal wages, which do not take inflation into account.

## HOW FAR DID LIVING STANDARDS CHANGE IN BRITAIN BETWEEN 1918 AND 1979?

### The impact of boom, crisis and recovery, 1918–39

#### Real income

A short post-war boom collapsed into a severe recession in 1921. Wages fell for the poorest in society until 1934 and many families had to get by on less than £5 a week. Yet for most Britons, living standards improved between the wars, largely because prices, especially for food, fell faster than wages: the real cost of living fell by more than a third between 1920 and 1938. Social investigator

1915 | 1920 | 1925 | 1930 | 1935 | 1940 | 1945

**1919** – Housing and Town Planning Act

**1922** – BBC established

**1923** – First FA Cup final played at new Wembley Stadium

**1926** – Electrical (Supply) Act

**1937** – First Butlins holiday camp opens at Skegness, Lincolnshire

Physical Training and Recreation Act

**1946** – Television licences introduced

BBC television broadcasts resume

Bread rationed for first time since 1918

**1947** – League football restarts after wartime suspension

Seebohm Rowntree estimated that the quality of life in York improved by 30 percent between 1899 and 1936, largely due to increases in real wages. An increase in the use of contraception, especially condoms, also meant that family sizes shrank during this period: by the late 1920s, British women had 2.19 children on average (compared to 4.6 children in the 1880s). This meant that family incomes were shared between fewer people and therefore went further.

SOURCE

A comparison of incomes and prices from D. H. Aldcroft's *The Inter-war Economy: Britain 1919–1939*, published in 1970.

| Year | Weekly (nominal) wage rate | Retail prices | Average annual real wage |
|---|---|---|---|
| 1920 | 143.7 | 157.6 | 92.2 |
| 1925 | 102.2 | 111.4 | 91.7 |
| 1930 | 100.0 | 100.0 | 100.0 |
| 1935 | 98.0 | 90.5 | 108.3 |
| 1938 | 106.3 | 98.7 | 107.7 |

## Health and diet

The war had a disastrous, permanent impact on many: 702,000 people died and a further 1,670,000 were wounded as a result of the fighting. In 1921, 1,187,450 men were in receipt of disability pensions, either for physical injuries or due to the poorly understood impact of shell shock. However, as historian Jay Winter argued in his 1986 book, *The Great War and the British People*, the war 'was the occasion of a completely unanticipated improvement in the life of the civilian population… primarily on account of the demands of the war economy'.

Certain wartime trends persisted: a decline in alcohol consumption had been forced on the people by the 1914 Defence of the Realm Act. Continued peacetime restrictions on pub opening hours, together with the rising popularity of other forms of entertainment (see below), caused the amount spent on alcohol to fall throughout the interwar period. Rationing in the last years of the war promoted a healthier diet, as did the rolling out of the 1914 Education (Provision of Meals) Act to all needy schoolchildren. Those families who hosted evacuee children during the Second World War were still shocked at the diet of the poorest children, who often refused to eat any vegetables and preferred to eat just chips or even biscuits for dinner. However, even a critical 1936 study, *Food, Health and Income* led by nutritionist Boyd Orr's Rowett Institute and funded by private donors including the Carnegie Trust, concluded that the average diet was better than before 1914. Unfortunately, such averages masked a large variation in nutritional standards between different classes.

EXTRACT

From Sue Bowden's chapter 'Consumption and Consumer Behaviour' in *A Companion to Early Twentieth-Century Britain*, published in 2003. Bowden discusses the findings of the 1936 study *Food, Health and Income.*

There was a world of difference between the nutritional intake of those at the top and those at the bottom of the income scale. The top 10 per cent of the population consumed over 3lbs of meat, nearly 2.5lbs of fruit and 2.25lbs of vegetables each a week, the bottom 10 per cent, 1.5lbs of meat, 1lb of vegetables and less than 1lb of fruit each a week. A professional man consumed 3.04lbs of meat, 1.26lbs of fish and game, 3.17lbs of fruit and 4.39lbs of vegetables a week. An unemployed man consumed 1.25lbs of meat, 0.44lbs of fish and game, 0.30lbs of fruit and 2.68lbs of vegetables... Large numbers of people were suffering from malnutrition, with serious nutritional deficiencies in a range of minerals and vitamins as well as in basic protein, fats and calories.

Healthcare improved between the wars. By 1922, infant mortality had halved from 1900 levels; tuberculosis and typhoid killed far fewer people than before the war, thanks to advances in medicine and sanitation; more people survived to the age of 65, although poor geriatric care meant life expectation beyond this age was no higher than in the 19th century. Large variations remained between different regions. Different qualities of diet were the key reason for infant mortality rates, which varied from 5.17 deaths per 1,000 live births in Wales to 0.86 in the wealthy district of Kensington in London. As well as this, because there was no national system of healthcare, hospital care was a 'postcode lottery', with varying levels of charity and local authority support for hospitals in different areas across the country.

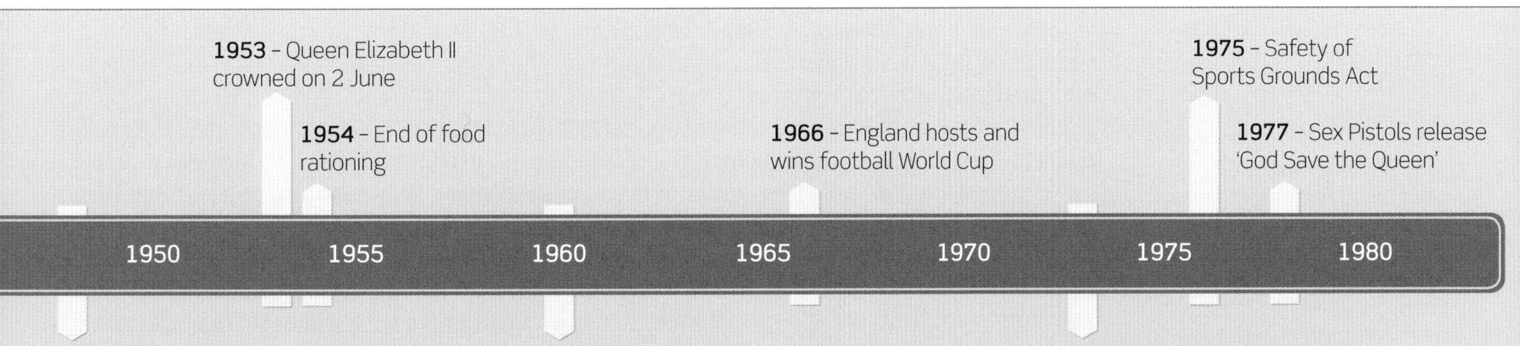

## Regional variations

Regional variations in quality of life were intimately related to the fortunes of major employers in each area. Parts of the country heavily reliant on traditional industries, such as shipbuilding or coal, steel and textile production, fared less well than those with a larger service sector or where newer industries, such as chemicals, electrical engineering or car production, took off. Clydeside, Northumberland, Durham, Lancashire and South Wales were key areas of traditional industry, while London and the West Midlands did much better, even during the 'hungry' 1930s. Traditional industries were heavily reliant on exports. The dislocation in trade during the First World War had allowed rivals to fill the gap left in the global market by the absence of British cotton or steel manufacture. Continental rivals also acquired a competitive edge thanks to the new machinery they were forced to buy to refurbish war-damaged factories. British factories did not suffer war damage to anything like the same extent and as a result continued to use outdated machinery. More efficient American and German steel production undercut British domestic sales due to the retention of free trade (until 1932). The Great Depression led to a further contraction in demand for ships, steel, coal and textiles.

Unemployment, which never fell below a million between 1921 and 1940, rose to almost three million in 1932 and 1933. Although unemployment had existed before 1918, what surprised contemporaries was the extent of long-term unemployment: in 1929, five percent of those in need of relief had been jobless for over a year; by 1932, this had risen to 16.4 percent: over 400,000 people. In 1944, William Beveridge calculated that 85 percent of all long-term unemployment was located in the north of England, South Wales and Scotland. The impact on affected local areas was terrible: 62 percent of all shipbuilders were unemployed in 1932 compared to 20 percent in car manufacture, for example. In 1936, the closure of major employer Palmer's shipyard led the unemployed shipbuilders of Jarrow to march to London. Although they failed to gain any state action to help the local economy, they did draw national sympathy to their plight and powerlessness. Regional variations in the 'means test' to determine the amount of dole money persisted until the creation of the Unemployment Assistance Board in 1937. However, even before 1937, it was family circumstance rather than region that determined how far the dole stretched: those with working-age children were more comfortably off than those with younger dependants.

**SOURCE 2**

From Helen Forrester, *Twopence to Cross the Mersey* (1974), an autobiographical account of growing up in Liverpool.

One morning, however, the wait at the unemployment exchange was particularly long and chilly, the ragged queue of weary men began to mutter rebelliously, and Father was drawn into sympathetic conversation with his fellow sufferers. They were, for the most part, respectable working men, many of whose jobs were dependent upon the ships which went in and out of Liverpool in normal times. They were curious about my father, because he spoke like an educated man. They were friendly and, as Father met them again and again, they began to fill him in on how to stay alive under almost impossible circumstances... There were agencies in the town that would provide the odd pair of shoes or a blanket for a child... An open fire, he was assured, could be kept going all day from the refuse of the streets, old shoes, scraps of paper, twigs, wooden boxes, potato peelings.

### Consumption

Regional variations in wealth and employment were reflected in patterns of consumption. Car ownership was far more widespread in the south-east (20 percent of households) than the north (with just 12 percent). An important cause of growth in consumption was the rapid electrification of the country. The number of electricity consumers increased from 730,000 in 1920 to nine million in 1938; the share of homes with electricity increased from 32 percent in 1932 to 66 percent in 1938 (and 96 percent by 1961). This expansion was encouraged by the 1926 Electrical (Supply) Act, which replaced a diverse range of voltages and networks with a Central Electricity Board and a National Grid; by 1934, the grid covered most parts of the country. However, use of electricity differed across the UK: whereas homes in the south-east consumed an average of 861 kilowatt-hours in 1938, those in the north-east used only 386 kilowatt-hours. People in the north used a higher share of electricity for lighting rather than for labour-saving devices.

SOURCE 3 A table showing regional variations of the weekly expenditure of the working class in 1937–38 from the *Ministry of Labour Gazette*, published in 1940.

| Region | Total average expenditure on all non-food items (£) | Total average expenditure on food (£) |
|---|---|---|
| South-east | 2.88 | 1.78 |
| South-west | 2.74 | 1.99 |
| North | 2.95 | 1.46 |
| North-west | 2.23 | 1.64 |
| London | 2.85 | 2.03 |
| North-east | 2.57 | 2.29 |
| Midlands | 1.97 | 1.60 |

Although consumerism spread to the middle class before 1939, it is not possible to talk of a mass consumer market in Britain before the late 1940s. Families on lower incomes could not take part in the growth in consumerism until purchase prices and running costs had fallen to an affordable level or wages had risen. Working-class households struggled to afford radios, irons and vacuum cleaners; even with the growth of hire-purchase, ownership of electric fridges, cookers, heaters and washing machines remained a middle-class phenomenon in the interwar period.

ACTIVITY
KNOWLEDGE CHECK

**Changing living standards, 1918–39**

1. Explain what is meant by 'standard of living'.
2. Make notes or create a spider diagram on ways in which the standard of living improved in Britain between 1918 and 1939. Compile examples for the following categories: diet, housing, consumption.
3. Give examples and reasons why increases in the standard of living were not shared evenly among the British people.

## The effects of 'total war' and austerity, 1939–51

### Total war

The Second World War was 'total' for Britain in that no one could escape its demands or impact. Everyone was affected to different degrees, either through rationing, restrictions on the right to travel, conscription and the stress of fearing for loved ones, damage to homes and loss of life. The 'Home Front' was more like a frontline than during the First World War as Nazi bombs sought to destroy the industry and morale needed to maintain the war effort. 60,000 civilians were killed by German bombs, most of them in London during 'the Blitz'. Many other towns and cities similarly suffered: the centre of Coventry was utterly destroyed, while Birmingham, Liverpool, Plymouth, Bristol, Glasgow, Southampton, Portsmouth and Hull also suffered severe damage. Two out of every seven houses (3.5 million) were destroyed and there were 60 million changes of address during the war. Out of 15.9 million males aged 14–64, 14.9 million were registered for war service; of the 16 million females aged 14–58, 7.1 million were engaged in the war effort. The government issued 8.5 million Essential Work Orders, which forced workers to take and remain in certain jobs. The National Service Act (September 1939) meant all men aged 18–41 (except those doing jobs essential to the war effort) were conscripted for armed service. By 1945, 5.5 million had been called up and 4.5 million had seen active service. Of these 287,859 were killed, with 274,148 seriously wounded and 184,102 prisoners of war. Over a million children were evacuated from towns and cities to the countryside, something that helped to heighten the social concern of the wealthier hosts of slum children.

### Diet and consumption

Although a potential German invasion was held off after victory in the Battle of Britain (summer 1940), Britain struggled to import enough food due to the loss of shipping to German submarines in the Battle of the Atlantic. As during the latter stages of the First World War, rationing helped to level out food consumption between classes and, in many cases, meant that the working class enjoyed a healthier diet. Government price controls meant a wide range of goods became more affordable for the poorest families, especially as average wages almost doubled during the war. Ration coupons could be exchanged for food in shops (when it was available) but also for a filling, hot meal at a 'British Restaurant'. The Ministry of Food encouraged people to 'dig for victory' by converting gardens and public parks into allotments; it also provided recipes to make the most of vegetables, such as 'carrot tart with a lemon glaze' for pudding. Clothing rationing (with coupons to the value of one complete outfit per year) also led to a levelling of fashions across previous social divides: people were encouraged to 'make do and mend' and life became increasingly drab. To help lift people's spirits, the government formed the Council for the Encouragement of Music and the Arts in 1940. It financially supported theatrical and musical tours of the country by groups who were usually London-based. The government also funded the British film industry and many morale-boosting films, for example *In Which We Serve* (1942), were produced. The government initially closed all cinemas, but a wave of complaints led to them all being reopened within a month. Historian Arthur Marwick has argued forcefully for the large scale and permanence of the impact of the Second World War (see Extract 2).

**EXTRACT 2**

From Arthur Marwick, 'Great Britain, 1939–45', a chapter in A. J. P. Taylor and J. M. Roberts, *The Twentieth Century XIV* (1979).

The war, in three ways, brought about a social and economic revolution: it involved a challenge to existing institutions, provoking, where they proved inadequate to the needs of war, their transformation; it required the participation of the underprivileged classes in the community, who correspondingly benefitted from the new need the community had for their services; and third, it aroused a strong moral feeling that post-war society must be a better one than that of the unemployed marches and the means test.

### Austerity

The noun austerity can be used with reference to individuals or whole economies. For individuals, it means a preference for a plain, disciplined existence; for an economy, it means tough conditions imposed by the government when it needs to cut spending. During and after the Second World War, Britain experienced austerity at the personal and the national level. Almost every Briton was forced to adopt an austere lifestyle during the Second World War and for six years after due to the financial sacrifices needed to wage total war. In 1946, roughly a quarter of all consumer expenditure was controlled by rationing; this rose to 30 percent in 1948, before being cut back to around 12 percent in 1949. Even bread, which had escaped rationing during the war, was rationed between 1946 and 1948. Rationing was gradually rolled back until it was finally abandoned in 1954.

**EXTRACT**

From David Kynaston, *Austerity Britain 1945–51* (2007), a social history of post-war Britain.

Britain in 1945. No supermarkets, no motorways, no teabags, no sliced bread, no frozen food, no flavoured crisps, no lager, no microwaves, no dishwashers, no Formica, no vinyl, no CDs, no computers, no mobiles, no duvets, no Pill, no trainers, no hoodies, no Starbucks. Four Indian restaurants. Shops on every corner, pubs on every corner, cinemas in every high street, red telephone boxes, Lyons Corner Houses, trams, trolley-buses, steam trains... No laundrettes, no automatic washing machines, wash day every Monday, clothes boiled in a tub, scrubbed on the draining board, rinsed in the sink, put through a mangle, hung out to dry. Central heating rare, chilblains common. Abortion illegal, homosexual relationships illegal, suicide illegal, capital punishment legal. White faces everywhere... A Bakelite wireless in the home, *Housewives' Choice* or *ITMA* on the air, televisions almost unknown, no programmes to watch, the family eating together... Suits and hats, dresses and hats ... no leisurewear, no 'teenagers'... Meat rationed, butter rationed, lard rationed, margarine rationed, sugar rationed, tea rationed, cheese rationed, jam rationed, eggs rationed, sweets rationed, soap rationed, clothes rationed. Make do and mend... A land of orderly queues, hat-doffing men walking on the outside, seats given up to the elderly, no swearing in front of children, censored books, censored films, censored plays, infinite repression of desires. Divorce almost an unthinkable social disgrace, marriage too often a lifetime sentence. Children in the street ticked off by strangers, children in the street kept an eye on by strangers, children at home rarely consulted, children stopped being children when they left school at 14 and got a job. A land of hierarchical assumptions, of accent and dress as giveaway to class, of Irish jokes and casually derogatory references to Jews and niggers... A land of domestic hobbies and domestic pets... A deeply conservative land.

[Formica was the brand name of a heat-resistant plastic work surface common in many kitchens after the 1950s. Trolley-buses were powered by electricity drawn from overhead wires via poles connected to the top of the bus used between 1911 and 1972. Bakelite is a synthetic plastic widely used for telephones and radio (known as 'the wireless' before the Second World War). ITMA stood for *It's That Man Again*, a popular comedy show.]

**ACTIVITY**
**KNOWLEDGE CHECK**

**Total War and post-war austerity**

1. Define 'total war' and 'austerity'.
2. 'The impact of the Second World War and post-war austerity was entirely negative for the British standard of living.' How far do you agree with this statement? Explain your answer with as much specific detail as possible.

# The growth of a consumer society, 1951–79

## Incomes

Historian Eric Hobsbawm called the period between the 1950s and the early 1970s the 'golden era' of western capitalism. Even more so than before 1945, a rapid increase in real incomes fuelled higher material standards of living. Real disposable income rose 30 percent in the 1950s, 22 percent in the 1960s and 30 percent in the 1970s. The period is unique in British history in that profits, interest and rent declined as a share of national income, while average wages rose. Higher wages meant people spent a smaller portion of their income on food, clothes and cigarettes, and more on housing, motoring, consumer durables and entertainment. Home-ownership increased from 29 percent of the population in 1950 to over 50 percent in 1970. Car ownership in the same period rose from 16 to 52 percent. By the early 1950s, consumer spending was back to what it was by the late 1930s; in 1957, Prime Minister Harold Macmillan was able to boast that 'most of our people have never had it so good'.

## Consumerism and the consumer society

Consumerism is best understood as a series of attitudes and behaviours associated with the consumption of goods and services. It is generally used in a negative sense: people in a consumerist society are encouraged by clever marketing to spend more and more money on things they are told will bring them happiness. As a result, people begin to define themselves and others by what they buy and place more value on the ownership of material objects than on almost anything else. The extent, growth and impact of consumerist values are disputed by historians; it is possible to argue, as James Obelkevich has done, that Britain became a 'consumer society' without becoming consumerist in outlook.

**EXTRACT 4**

From James Obelkevich, *Understanding Post-war Britain* (1994).

> A more general claim about consumption is that it is the dominant concern in contemporary life and that Britain, like other Western countries, has become a 'consumer society'. In such a society the priority is on the production of consumer goods rather than on capital equipment or military hardware; most people are no longer poor or 'sustenance driven' but have money for 'wants' as well as 'needs'; they are catered for by user-friendly shops with self-service, long opening hours, easily available credit, and price competition; and they are protected by organisations like the Consumers' Association. On these criteria, we could agree that Britain has moved some way towards becoming a consumer society. The notion of 'consumerism', however, is more ambiguous... What is lacking is any evidence that consumerism in this negative sense was either new or particularly widespread. In fact, there have always been people who spend and overspend for show and effect: conspicuous consumption was not invented in the 1980s, nor the 1950s. For the working class, it was probably more significant before the war than it is today.

## Wants and needs

Increased disposable income enabled a growing list of 'wants' and 'needs' after 1951 that would have amazed pre-war generations. Many of these were centred on the home: increased domestic energy consumption is a clear indicator of this trend. Gas sales more than doubled between 1951 and 1970, while electricity sales quadrupled. Homes became more comfortable, warmer, cleaner and nicer-smelling places in which to spend increasing amounts of free time. The shift away from open fires to central heating was key to this: fires involved a lot of effort and surfaces were covered with ash and dust. As a result most households only kept a fire going in one room. People stayed together in the room with the fire before retreating to bed. Central heating (up from five percent of homes in 1960 to 50 percent in 1977 and 84 percent in 1991) and insulation freed up the whole house for living and leisure. This change, together with increased television ownership, fuelled demand for other domestic goods. In Britain, almost every household had a television by 1970. Source 4 gives a broad overview of the expansion in consumer acquisition of luxuries.

SOURCE 4

A table showing the percentage of British homes that had a range of consumer durable products in 1955, 1975 and 1995.

| | 1955 | 1975 | 1995 |
|---|---|---|---|
| Vacuum cleaner | 51 | 90 | 96 |
| Washing machine | 18 | 70 | 91 |
| Refrigerator | 8 | 85 | 98 |
| Freezer | n/a (not available) | 15 | 79 |
| Television | 35 | 96 | 98 |
| Telephone | 19 | 52 | 92 |
| Central heating | 5 | 47 | 85 |
| Dishwasher | 1 | 2 | 12 |
| Microwave oven | n/a | n/a | 47 |
| Video recorder | n/a | n/a | 70 |
| CD-player | n/a | n/a | 63 |
| Home computer | n/a | n/a | 20 |

Personal appearance and hygiene also became more important; the role of advertising in this development at least should not be underestimated. The money spent on advertising rose threefold between 1947 and 1970 and the growth of commercial television and radio made invasive advertising a commonplace part of British life. The advertisement of Old Spice after 1957 contributed to a dramatic shift in male use of deodorant. Before 1957, only 32 percent of women aged 16 to 64 used deodorant and hardly any men used a product widely regarded as effeminate. However, by 1969, over half of all men and women regularly used scented deodorants, perfumes or aftershaves.

New fashions, such as 'the Look', meant that from the mid-1960s it was almost impossible to tell a young woman's class from the way she dressed. Designers like Mary Quant pioneered such fashions in their boutiques clustered around London's King's Road and Carnaby Street; the looks were made accessible to many by the mass production and sale of similar designs in high streets across the country. Barbara Hulanicki's fashion company, Biba, sold cheap clothes from her shops in London and across the country via mail order. The most famous model of the 1960s, Twiggy, said that whereas Mary Quant's clothes were for 'rich girls', Biba 'was for anyone'. The clothes were given a good deal of publicity in newspapers, in part because of the launch of colour sections after February 1962, and in part because of the work of a new breed of dashing photographer, including David Bailey, Brian Duffy and Terence Donovan. Mary Quant thought fashion attracted so much attention in the newspapers because it 'reflects what is really in the air': the growth of affluence and consumerism, the new confidence of youth and the changing role of women.

SOURCE 5

A photograph of Lesley Hornby, better known as Twiggy (1949– ), which helped to establish her as 'the face of 1966'.

## Shops

The first (short-lived) supermarket opened in St Albans in 1947, but it was the 1950 opening of Sainsbury's in Croydon that marked the permanent start of the supermarket era. The end of food rationing between 1951 and 1954 gave a boost to food sales. The rolling back of **Retail Price Maintenance** on groceries in 1956, and more generally in 1964, allowed supermarkets to flourish: they could take advantage of the size of their sales to slash prices and undercut smaller local shops. By 1959, there were 286 supermarkets, a figure that increased to 572 in 1961 and over 3,500 by 1971. They could be found in most town centres, and the first out-of-town supermarket opened in Nottingham in 1964. The competition generated by this huge expansion led to the closure of 60,000 (or two-thirds) of local specialist grocers' shops between 1960 and 1990. There was also a loss of range and variety of local stores with the greater standardisation of chain stores. The growth of car ownership led to the growth of even larger supermarkets on the outskirts of towns and cities. While small-scale grocers and producers lost out, the consumer gained in terms of the average cost, quality and convenience of shopping in larger stores. To help make sense of the incredible choice (and decline of personal service), the Consumer Association was founded in 1957 and launched its influential magazine *Which?* in the same year. A Ministry for Consumer Affairs, which aimed to protect consumers, existed (with slightly different official titles) from 1972 until 1983.

### KEY TERM

**Retail Price Maintenance (RPM)**
This was an agreement between producers and vendors to set a minimum price for products. This was good for both parties as it avoided price competition and a loss of profit. At its height in the mid-1950s, it covered 44 percent of consumer spending on goods. The Restrictive Trade Practices Act (1956) undermined its use on grocery products; the Resale Prices Act (1964) virtually abolished RPM, except in cases where it was thought to be in the best interests of the public.

## Consumer credit

The difficulty and social unacceptability of obtaining credit had been a major reason for the growth of hire-purchase (paying for goods in instalments). The local moneylenders used by poor people were not well-regulated and caused a good deal of harm in some cases: the interest rates they charged could be extortionate and physical force was sometimes used to intimidate borrowers into paying up.

The major breakthrough in ease of consumer access to credit began with the 1974 Consumer Credit Act. This was largely based on the recommendations of the 1971 Crowther Report, which called for the repeal and replacement of all earlier legislation on moneylending and bank loans. The Act clarified the rights and responsibilities of lenders and borrowers, and paved the way for an explosion of consumer borrowing in the 1980s and 1990s.

Credit cards were first used in Britain in 1966; although debit cards had existed for a few years prior to this, Barclaycard remained unique until the launch of the Access card in 1972.

### Cause and consequence (4a&b)

**Fragile history**

Nothing that happens is inevitable. There are causes of change that did not have to develop as they did. Something could have altered or someone could have chosen differently. What actually occurred in the past did happen, but it did not have to be like that.

Working on your own, answer the questions then discuss your answers in groups.

This table suggests reasons for changing living standards in the years 1918–79:

| Development | Event | State of affairs | Development | Event |
|---|---|---|---|---|
| Increase in availability of consumer goods | Impact of Second World War and resulting austerity | Regional variations in health and diet | Emergence of consumer credit | Opening of the first supermarkets |

1 Consider the impact of the Second World War and the availability of consumer goods.

   a) How did the Second World War affect the availability of consumer goods?

   b) Had there been no war, would things have turned out differently?

   c) What other aspects of the situation in the 1940s and 1950s would have been different if there was no war?

2 Consider regional variations in health and diet and the opening of the first supermarkets.

   a) How important was the opening of supermarkets in changes to health and diet?

   b) What might have happened if the first supermarkets had not opened?

3 What other consequences came about as a result of the information in the table? Try to identify at least one consequence for each entry.

4 Choose one factor. How might living standards have developed differently if this factor did not exist?

ACTIVITY
KNOWLEDGE CHECK

**The growth of a consumer society**

1 Explain the term 'consumer society'.

2 How accurate is it to describe Britain as a 'consumer society' in 1949, 1959, 1969 and 1979? Explain your answer for each year.

**AS Level Exam-Style Question Section A**

Was higher real income the main reason for the growth of a 'consumer society' in Britain between 1951 and 1979? Explain your answer. (20 marks)

**Tip**

*The factor of higher real income should be compared to other factors, such as the impact of the Second World War and the wider availability of consumer goods.*

**A Level Exam-Style Question Section A**

How far do you agree that living standards were in a state of crisis in the years 1918–45? (20 marks)

**Tip**

*You should include and discuss issues such as health, housing and consumption in order to come to a balanced judgement.*

# IN WHAT WAYS AND TO WHAT EXTENT DID MASS POPULAR CULTURE AFFECT BRITISH SOCIETY BETWEEN 1918 AND 1979?

## The role of cinema, radio and music, 1918–79

### Cinema

A number of factors have affected the impact of cinema on British society. The first is the shift in its overall popularity: the greater the total audience for a film, the more likely it is to affect popular views. Cinema exploded in popularity during the First World War. *The Battle of the Somme* (1916) was seen by 20 million people in its first six weeks and remains one of the most viewed films in British cinema history. *The King Visits his Armies in the Great Advance* (1916) and especially *Hearts of the World – the Story of a Village* (1917) helped to cement the popularity of going to the cinema. The introduction of 'talkies' in 1928 further increased the popularity of going to the pictures and cinema remained the most popular and important medium of popular culture in interwar Britain. The number of cinemas rose from 3,000 in 1914 to almost 5,000 in the 1930s. The nature of cinemas changed, too, from small venues that seated 200–400 people to national chains of glamorous theatres that could seat up to 2,000.

In 1950, four years after peak cinema attendance, the average person went to the cinema 28 times a year. This was more than in any other nation, including the United States. The demand for escapism and restrictions on other forms of entertainment led to a boom in cinema attendance during the Second World War. The most popular British films included *In Which We Serve* (1942) and *The Way Ahead* (1944), which showed the supreme fighting spirit of the navy and army respectively, and *The Gentle Sex* (1943) and *Millions Like Us* (1943), which explored wartime problems for women and workers respectively. Popular American films about Britain included *Mrs Miniver* (1942) and *The White Cliffs of Dover* (1943). However, after record high ticket sales of 1.635 billion in 1946, attendance fell steadily until the late 1980s. Shrinking audiences meant that over half the cinemas in the country were forced to close between 1955 and 1963. The most important reason for this decline was the rise of television (see below). It was not until the opening of state-of-the-art multiplexes (the first in 1985 in Milton Keynes) that attendances began to recover.

SOURCE 6

A table showing total cinema admissions between 1946 and 1994.

| Year | Total cinema admissions (millions) |
|---|---|
| 1946 | 1,635 |
| 1954 | 1,276 |
| 1964 | 343 |
| 1974 | 138 |
| 1984 | 53 |
| 1994 | 106 |

The impact of cinema was also affected by the make-up of the audience. There were large variations in cinema attendance. The typical profile of a regular cinemagoer was young, urban, working class and, for those over the age of 19, female. In 1946, 69 percent of 16–19-year-olds went once a week compared to 11 percent of over-60s. People in the north of England went on average almost twice as often as those in the south; this is probably because of income differences that enabled southerners to undertake alternative, more expensive, activities such as participatory sport. Despite these differences, British audiences enjoyed remarkably similar films: comedy, musical romances, drama, tragedy, history, crime, nature and reality. In all parts of the country, Saturday mornings were set aside for children with age-specific films and cheap seats. These shows were hugely popular with children in the late 1940s and early 1950s, and with their parents too.

The content of films also affected the impact of cinema. There were (rather patronising) concerns about the potential impact of films on 'impressionable' audiences, led by the conservative upper middle-class men who dominated the British Board of Film Censors (BBFC, established in 1912). However, the vast majority of cinemagoers saw films as a form of escapism: they appreciated the difference between real life and that depicted on screen and were unlikely to absorb moral values from films. The men at the BBFC did not see things this way and saw it as their duty to protect Britons from bad language, sex and subversive ideas. The '43 rules' set out in 1917 had no official legal status, and yet were accepted by most local authorities as the test of which films were acceptable to show. Between 1928 and 1939, the BBFC banned 140 films and forced thousands more to edit their content. The 1959 Obscenity Act and 1968 Theatres Act led to greater permissiveness at the BBFC. By the early 1970s, the BBFC classified films with much stronger violent or sexual content for release. Films such as *Get Carter*, *A Clockwork Orange* and *Straw Dogs* (all 1971) contained scenes of extreme violence, while *Last Tango In Paris* (1972), *Confessions of a Window Cleaner* (1974) and the *Emmanuelle* films (1974, 1975) contained nudity and sex. Some local authorities banned these films from their cinemas regardless of the BBFC classification.

The BBFC and the government were also concerned about the 'Americanisation' of cinemagoers. The First World War led to a collapse of the British film industry due to uncertainty over funding, disruption of production and the use of studios for government propaganda; by 1925, only five percent of films shown in British cinemas were British. The 1927 Quota Act ensured that British-made films made up 20 percent of those shown by 1936. The British preferred the higher production values of American films and women in particular enjoyed the glamour of American heroes and heroines. Even before the Second World War, writers and journalists had noted youths dressing like gangsters and factory girls looking like actresses, using American slang such as 'Oh yeah?' and 'Sez you!' Improved production and acting, and the toning down of elite manners and accents, made British films more popular after the war. The 1950 'Eady Levy', a small charge on ticket sales, which created a fund to subsidise film-making in Britain, gave a further boost to British film-making. The 'New Wave' films of the late 1950s and 1960s, such as *Look Back in Anger* (1959) and *Saturday Night and Sunday Morning* (1960), about gritty working-class lives received critical acclaim, but most people preferred James Bond films and comedies such as the *Carry On* series. British film production collapsed in the 1970s, which saw the re-emergence of American dominance: the number of British films made each year fell from 49 in 1968 to 31 in 1980. The key reasons for this were cuts in American funding of British films and Conservative government cuts to the National Film Finance Corporation, one of the major British sources of investment.

## Radio

Radio had a wider reach than cinema: between 1922 and 1939 the percentage of households with a receiver increased from one to 71 percent. By 1951, this figure had increased to 90 percent. The British Broadcasting Corporation (BBC), founded as a **quango** in 1927, had a **monopoly** on radio broadcasting in the UK until 1973. Two radio services were established: the National Programme and the Regional Programme. The latter was broadcast from six regions: (in order of when the first transmitter was set up) Midlands, London, North, Scottish, West, Northern Ireland, Welsh. The National Service was also carried by regional transmitters, as well as being broadcast from London by a longwave transmitter. Both programmes were aimed at a general audience, without the divisions that characterised post-war radio. In Source 7 Lord Reith, the first Director General of the BBC, explains how he saw the Corporation's role as a **public service broadcaster**.

### KEY TERMS

**Quango**
Short for 'quasi-autonomous non-governmental organisation' – an administrative body that is not part of the government but whose members are appointed by the government.

**Monopoly**
The position of having no competition in a given trade or market.

**Public service broadcaster**
A radio or television company run to serve the public interest rather than for profit.

SOURCE

From Lord Reith's autobiography, *Into the Wind*, published in 1949.

So the responsibility at the outset was conceived to carry into the greatest number of homes everything that was best in every department of human knowledge, endeavour and achievement; and to avoid whatever was or might be hurtful. In the earliest years, accused of setting out to give the public not what it wanted but what the BBC thought it should have, the answer was that few knew what they wanted, fewer what they needed. In any event, it was better to overestimate than underestimate. If another policy had been adopted - that of the lowest common denominator - what then?

KEY TERM

**Empire Day**
From 1901, this was a celebration of the British Empire held on 24 May, Queen Victoria's birthday. In 1958 it was renamed Commonwealth Day; since 1973 it has been held on the second Monday in March.

Historians David Cardiff and Paddy Scannell have argued that the BBC 'functioned as an instrument of social control' that provided 'reassuring symbols of national community'. They argue that programmes such as the monarch's Christmas message (broadcast since 1932) and anniversary programmes for New Year and **Empire Day**, acted as 'social cement that reinforced the sense of belonging to our country'. Radio certainly had an impact on British culture. At the start of the Second World War, the National and Regional Programmes were replaced with a single service, the Home Service. This was done to prevent enemy aircraft using different regional broadcasts to aid navigation; as the war went on, more programming was restored to the regions due to the fear of concentrating all production in bomb-prone London. During the war, many radio programmes, such as *Workers' Playtime*, had been aimed at groups in factories to boost morale. After the war, radio programmes were targeted at listeners at home. In this way radio promoted the domestication of leisure time. It also enhanced the existing feeling of national identity through its ability to give immediacy to an event and to reach out to the most remote parts of the country. Radio also broadened horizons: the working classes, rather than 'listening in' for a particular programme, usually had the radio on all the time and so heard the full range of programming.

The Light Programme, which replaced the wartime Forces' Programme in July 1945, with its mix of comedies and soaps such as *Mrs Dale's Diary* and *The Archers*, variety shows and famous personalities, remained by far the most popular channel, with around two-thirds of the 11 million daily listeners. Many of the daytime shows were aimed at women (a reflection of the clearly divided roles for men and women), with the most popular ones including *Housewives' Choice* and *Woman's Hour*. On Sundays, when the Light Programme broadcast shows dedicated to religious services, many of these listeners abandoned the BBC and tuned in to 'pirate radio' stations. Stations such as Radio Luxembourg and Radio Normandy had broadcast into Britain from beyond its shores since the 1930s. The 1967 Marine Broadcasting Offences Act banned pirate radio (although Radio Caroline ignored the ban). The BBC filled the gap for a pop radio station in 1967 when it split the Light Programme into Radio 2 and Radio 1, its first channel specifically dedicated to pop music and a younger audience.

After the 1973 Independent Broadcasting Authority Act, BBC radio had to compete with a range of UK-based commercial stations. Despite this, audiences for Radio 1 rose throughout the 1970s, with DJ Tony Blackburn's *Breakfast Show* attracting 20 million listeners. In 1967, the Third Programme (first launched in September 1946) became Radio 3, while the Home Service became Radio 4. The Home Service catered for 'middlebrow' tastes with news, plays and lectures, while the Third Programme was 'highbrow' with modern classical music and 'difficult' culture for the most highly educated listeners; it attracted less than two percent of the radio audience.

## Music

Although Reith and the BBC tried their hardest to promote 'serious' music, the British remained stubbornly attached to 'middlebrow' and 'popular' music. Middlebrow music refers to the range of popular classical pieces that are still played today on Classic FM. Popular music, and the dance crazes that often accompanied new styles, cut across all classes. There were several waves of American influence on popular music, the most important being the arrival of ragtime and jazz during and after the First World War, the rise of swing and bop in the late 1930s, country and western and rhythm and blues in the late 1940s, and rock'n'roll in the mid-1950s.

Dance halls became very popular after the arrival of the foxtrot dance shortly before the First World War; they remained popular thanks to other American dances such as the Charleston, swing, jive, the lindy hop and the jitterbug. As with the super-cinemas, the 'palais de danse' dance halls enabled working-class men and women to enjoy a degree of luxury not found at home. Girls in particular enjoyed dancing, partly because it gave them a socially acceptable way to meet boys, but also just for the fun of it.

As far as most people in Britain were concerned, rock'n'roll began in March 1955 with the release of the film *Blackboard Jungle* at cinemas across the country. While the origins and first popular examples of rock'n'roll were American, the popularity of such music in the 1960s does not necessarily mean that British popular music had become totally Americanised. Record companies found British 'heart-throb' performers, such as Tommy Steele, Adam Faith and Cliff Richard, to imitate Elvis Presley. They led their artists to release safer, more respectable songs in a bid to appeal to the teenage girls who bought records and went to dance halls. By the early 1960s, these once exuberant performers were releasing lightweight pop tunes to appeal to a mass audience (use YouTube to compare Cliff Richard's hit singles 'Move It!' (1958) and 'Summer Holiday' (1963) to get an idea!). Rock'n'roll almost died out and many contemporary music journalists thought that traditional jazz would be the sound of the 1960s.

The Beatles remain one of the most famous icons of the 1960s. They started out in Liverpool in 1957 as a **skiffle** band called the Quarry Men. In 1960, after a lack of success in Liverpool, they changed their name to The Beatles and went to Hamburg, where they were assured of regular gigs for American servicemen and German audiences. In Hamburg they developed into a loud, exuberant band and became more popular than the other expatriate bands. After their return to Britain, they secured a regular slot at the Cavern Club in Liverpool from February 1961. There were over 400 similar bands in Liverpool at this time, and the Mersey Beat scene was far from unique, with similar bands playing in similar clubs across the country. It was two meetings, one in November 1961 with businessman and entrepreneur Brian Epstein and another in June 1962 with record producer George Martin, that caused The Beatles to triumph over contemporary rivals. Epstein, who became the band's manager, secured a record deal with Parlophone Records, while Martin gave lots of advice that greatly influenced The Beatles' music. The band, with John Lennon on vocals and rhythm guitar, Paul McCartney on vocals and bass guitar, George Harrison on lead guitar, and Ringo Starr (who only joined the band on Martin's insistence in June 1961) on drums, first entered the charts in October 1962 with 'Love Me Do', a song written by Paul McCartney when he was only 16. From then on, Lennon and McCartney worked extremely hard to write and release their own songs; they went on to have 17 number one hits in Britain between 1963 and 1969. The quality of their songs, together with their smart, iconic look, ensured that 'Beatlemania' had spread across the country by mid-1963. In 1964, they led the 'British Invasion' of the American charts: in April 1964, The Beatles had no less than 12 records in *Billboard* magazine's Hot 100. In 1965, they were awarded MBEs for their services to British exports. They remained in the vanguard of popular music for the remainder of the 1960s, until the band finally broke up in 1970. In his 1981 book *Shout! The True Story of the Beatles*, Philip Norman estimates that, by 1970, in addition to the huge sales of singles and albums, Beatles merchandise, including hats, bags, badges, shirts, jackets, socks, handkerchiefs, tea towels, mugs, ashtrays and jigsaw puzzles, had sold for more than £100 million.

### KEY TERM

**Skiffle**
A type of music influenced by folk, blues and jazz, usually played using homemade or improvised instruments like jugs and washboards.

In the 1970s there were a number of different trends in popular music that can either be seen as escapist, or reflective of the troubling times. In the early 1970s, 'glam rock' rose to the fore with artists such as Slade, Marc Bolan and Gary Glitter. By the mid-1970s, this was going out of fashion and performers like David Bowie had to contend with the rise of New York-inspired disco. Its smooth style was rivalled by the rise of the home-made, anarchistic style of punk. The Sex Pistols rose to fame in the late 1970s with the raw anger of their music and the ripped and safety-pinned clothes of designer Vivienne Westwood. Punk did more than just give rise to provocative new fashions: it could also be seen as further promoting female independence and confidence. Bands such as The Slits were among the first all-female bands to write and perform their own music, while bands such as X-Ray Spex and The Banshees were fronted by formidable female singers like Poly Styrene and Siouxsie Sioux. One ex-punk, Adam Ant, reflected that punk empowered women to drive and front the creative process on an equal footing with men, rather than serving as attractive extras in bands.

ACTIVITY
KNOWLEDGE CHECK

**The impact of mass popular culture, 1918–79**

1 What factors have affected the extent to which mass popular culture has had an impact on British society?

2 In what ways did cinema, radio and music affect British society?

3 Could you argue that there were limits to the impact of mass popular culture on British society? What were they?

## The impact of television from the 1950s

### The rise of television ownership

Of all mass media, television had the largest impact on British behaviour (before the rise of the internet). This was not only because of the programmes it brought to the masses, but also because the existence of the television set itself profoundly affected the home dynamic and use of leisure time; as Canadian academic Marshall McLuhan argued in 1964, 'the medium is the message'.

SOURCE

From Doris Lessing's autobiography, *Walking in the Shade*, published in 1997. Lessing was a writer who here recounts her experiences of London in the early 1950s.

Before, when the men came back from work, the tea was already on the table, a fire was roaring, the radio emitted words or music softly in a corner, they washed and sat down at their places, with the woman, the child... They all talked... And then... television had arrived and sat like a toad in the corner of the kitchen. Soon the big kitchen table had been pushed along the wall, chairs were installed in a semi-circle and, on their chair arms, the swivelling supper trays. It was the end of an exuberant verbal culture.

Television cannot really be considered a *mass* medium in Britain until after the Second World War. Moving pictures were not broadcast to televisions in British homes until 1929; before 1939, the BBC only broadcast television signals to around 12,500 television sets in London. Television broadcasts were suspended during the Second World War and not resumed until June 1946. Sales of television licences did not really take off until the coronation of Queen Elizabeth II seven years later: Four percent of households had a television set in 1950, rising to 40 percent in 1955, 80 percent in 1960 and 95 percent in 1969. Following the launch of BBC2 in 1964, there were only three television channels; given the scale of ownership, the potential audience for a popular programme was very large. Between 1977 and 1979, people on average watched 16 hours of television per week in the summer and 20 hours in the winter; children and the elderly watched the most television, while women saw more than men. The Central Statistical Office recorded that watching television was one of the most popular leisure activities among all social groups: men and women spent around 23 percent of their free time in front of the small screen, twice as much as people in Belgium, Italy or Sweden. The domestication of spare time that had begun with the radio blurred class divisions that had been reinforced by more public leisure pursuits, such as dog racing (working class) or playing tennis (middle class). Now anyone could watch similar programmes from their own homes. As so many people saw the same programmes, the content of these shows formed an important part of the next day's conversations at school, at work or in the home. The impact of television was further enhanced by the spread of broadcasts and reception in colour: BBC2 began colour broadcasts in 1967, with BBC1 following in November 1969. The percentage of colour television sets increased from 1.7 in 1970 to 70 in 1979. Some authorities were worried about the impact of gory colour reports on **the Troubles** in Northern Ireland, or the Vietnam War in 1975, but this did not stop the rise of colour television as the norm.

KEY TERM

**The Troubles**
This term is commonly used to refer to the tension and violence that existed between Catholics and Protestants in Northern Ireland in its worst phase between 1968 and 1998. Catholic activists wanted Northern Ireland to join the Republic of Ireland while Protestant organisations wanted it to remain part of the UK.

SOURCE 9

Table showing sales of television licences from 1947 to 1985.

| Year | 1947 | 1955 | 1960 | 1965 | 1975 | 1985 |
|---|---|---|---|---|---|---|
| TV licences (thousands) | 15 | 344 | 10,470 | 13,253 | 17,701 | 18,716 |

## The cultural impact of television

In 1955, the BBC monopoly on television was ended when 14 independent companies were allowed to begin broadcasting, funded by advertising. As with cinema, there were concerns among cultural critics that commercial television would promote vulgar materialism and the Americanisation of British culture. One such critic, Richard Hoggart, strongly influenced the 1962 Pilkington Report on the impact of television. A good deal of the report's recommendations were ignored by the government, but the 1964 Television Act did force the ITV companies to screen two plays and two current affairs programmes in addition to the news each week, to fulfil their public service obligation. The report also led to the creation of BBC2 in April 1964 to further increase public service broadcasting. The remit of the new channel was to screen documentaries, comedy, drama and arts programmes.

The report's emphasis on the need for quality drama on television led to a demand for new plays from British playwrights. The *Wednesday Play* (BBC 1964–70) helped launch the career of influential writers Dennis Potter and Nell Dunn, and director Ken Loach. They created hard-hitting, **social realist** plays such as *Up the Junction* (1965), with a powerful home abortion scene, and *Cathy Come Home* (1966), about homelessness. While these plays had a tremendous impact on the six to ten million people who saw them, they did not directly change things very much. The passage of the 1967 Abortion Act was possibly eased by the popular reaction to *Up the Junction*, but clearly had far more to do with David Steel's campaign. Similarly, the launch of Shelter, a charity for homeless people, on 1 December 1966, had been planned for a long time; it was sheer coincidence that *Cathy Come Home* had only been screened two weeks before this. The charity was fortunate in the timing of its launch, as homelessness had been brought to the forefront of public attention.

While the *Wednesday Plays* discussed controversial topics, they did not portray or inspire a rebellion of working-class opinion against their social superiors. On the contrary, the working classes generally held the most conservative opinions about liberal reforms. The programme that working-class viewers identified with the most was the soap opera *Coronation Street*. Launched in December 1960, it had a twice-weekly audience of 20 million within its first year. Northern viewers in particular identified with the ordinary backdrop to the drama and the strong female characters, such as Elsie Tanner, who evoked a feeling of nostalgia for wartime community. The show was popular with both working-class and middle-class viewers.

A programme that did genuinely challenge social superiors and figures of authority was *That Was The Week That Was* (TW3), launched in November 1962. It represented the pinnacle of the 'satire boom' that had begun in the late 1950s with comedians such as Peter Cook and Dudley Moore, and evolved in the early 1960s through their contribution to the highly successful *Beyond the Fringe* stage show. TW3 combined current affairs with stand-up comedy; at its peak it had 12 million viewers a week and was said to empty many pubs late on Saturday night when it was screened.

**KEY TERM**

**Social realism**
An artistic style that portrays ordinary people going about their everyday lives. It often focuses on the working classes with stories of hardship and struggle.

**SOURCE 10** *Coronation Street* became hugely popular after its launch in 1960. Viewers related to the strong female characters, such as Elsie Tanner (pictured).

The most popular dramas were either based on the past, such as ITV's *Upstairs Downstairs*, set in England between 1903 and 1930, or on contemporary policing. *The Professionals*, and especially *The Sweeney*, depicted tough policemen who did whatever it took to get an arrest. At a time when suspicions were raised about corruption within the police force, Detectives Jack Reagan and George Carter were shown as hard but honest men. *The Sweeney* reflected the reality exposed by a 1969 report by *The Times*, one in which police might bend the rules to get results, but its overwhelmingly positive presentation of tough policing was very popular, with audiences of around 19 million between 1975 and 1978. A poll in 1977 revealed that 75 percent of British people thought the police were honest, a high figure that was surely influenced by such a popular programme.

The 1970s saw the production of some extremely popular sitcoms, some attracting audiences as high as 20 million for each episode. The quality of the programmes was partly fuelled by competition between the BBC and ITV for audience share: ITV invested more of its advertising revenue into programming to avoid paying government tax on profits; this forced the BBC to compete to justify its funding by the licence fee. Figure 4.1 gives an overview of some of the post popular sitcoms and suggests ways in which their main characters and typical plot lines might have influenced British attitudes.

## The influence of mass media on youth culture, 1955–79

### The influence of mass media on youth culture

The word 'teenage' was not coined until 1921, and 'teenager' only came into regular use in Britain after 1945. The interwar growth of the disposable income of young workers was a crucial prerequisite for the rise of 'youth culture'. Without the need to buy food or pay rent, teenage workers had a good deal of money to spend on entertainment and luxuries. Young people increasingly began to define and differentiate themselves from their parents through their purchases and leisure pursuits. Mass media widened the gulf in fashion and musical taste between generations even before mass television ownership. Pirate radio helped to shape the popular forms of youth culture. There was a reciprocal relationship between the advertisers who sponsored shows, the record companies and the DJs, who all wanted to tap into the lucrative youth market.

In addition to the cinema and dance hall that were familiar to their parents, teenagers in the 1950s often went to the coffee bar or milk bar to 'hang out', 'see and be seen' and listen to music. The first coffee bars were opened by Italian immigrants in London in 1952; by 1957, there were over 1,000 such bars across the country. In most coffee bars, especially in provincial towns and cities, the music was not provided by a live band, but by a jukebox. The jukebox was invented in America in 1927, but the real breakthrough came in 1948, with the invention of the 7-inch extra-play (EP) vinyl record. EPs were far thinner than the old gramophone records, and smaller than the long-play (LP) records, so up to 500 of them could be loaded into a jukebox. By 1958, there were more than 7,000 jukeboxes in Britain.

According to historian Bill Osgerby, the first popular music programmes on the BBC, such as *Hit Parade* (1952), 'were low-key in the youth appeal'; even later programmes, such as *Six-Five Special* (1957) and *Jukebox Jury* (1959) 'made concessions to an adult audience through the inclusion of variety performers and dinner-jacketed compères'. However, *Six-Five Special* was clearly designed to appeal to a teenage audience, with presenter Pete Murray, who had been a DJ on Radio Luxembourg, opening the first show. It soon attracted audiences of up to ten million and introduced many new pop acts to the nation. ITV responded with *Oh Boy!* (1958), which focused even more heavily on rock'n'roll, to the exclusion of skiffle, folk, jazz and blues, which all featured on the BBC programmes. Such shows popularised later pop trends, such as the Mod or Rocker look, at a quicker rate than the spread of earlier styles such as the Teddy Boy look. Whereas the Rockers followed the American style for jeans, white T-shirts, leather jackets and motorbikes, the Mods (short for modern) drew their inspiration from Italian fashion, with tight, smart trousers, elongated 'winkle-picker' shoes, Ben Sherman shirts and Vespa mopeds.

Youth culture was most clearly defined by music and fashion. Some of the most popular styles or identities in the 1960s and 1970s included Mods, Rockers, Beatniks, Hippies, Skinheads, Glam Rockers and Punks. For the vast majority of young people, such styles were purely about a sense of fun and identity. However, many adults, especially older generations, felt that British youth was out of control in a way that had never happened 'in their day'. In truth, while there was a slight rise in youth crime in the 1950s and 1960s, and a sharp rise in arrests for possession of marijuana (up from 235 in 1960 to 11,000 by 1973), young people were no more violent, drunk or disrespectful than they had been in previous generations.

**ACTIVITY**
**KNOWLEDGE CHECK**

**The influence of television and youth culture**

1 Explain the phrase 'the medium is the message' with regard to television. Is there any evidence in post-war Britain that supports this idea?

2 For each of the following decades, give examples of popular television shows and explain their influence on British attitudes: 1950s, 1960s, 1970s.

3 Why might changes in pop music have had more of an influence on young people than other Britons?

**AS Level Exam-Style Question Section B**

To what extent did popular culture change British society in the years 1945–79? (20 marks)

**Tip**

*As this question only covers the period after the Second World War, be careful to only include earlier material to add context and set up the debate in the question.*

| Name of sitcom | Peak audience | Main characters | Main setting | Typical plot | Potential to influence? |
|---|---|---|---|---|---|
| *Steptoe and Son*<br>BBC<br>1962–65 and 1970–74 | 28 million | Harold (in his 30s) and his father Albert (in his 60s). They are rag and bone men. | Harold's flat in Shepherd's Bush, London, crammed with old bits and pieces. | Harold wants to make something of his life but Albert prevents him through a mixture of reliance on his care, bullying, and being disgusting (hence Harold's catchphrase, 'You dirty old man!'). | Attitudes to authority (in this case elders). |
| *Porridge*<br>BBC<br>1974–77 | 16.8 million | Fletch, habitual criminal in his 40s, and his cellmate Godber, in his early 20s, in prison for the first time, and who wants to go straight | The fictional Slade Prison, mostly in Fletch and Godber's cell. | Fletch knows everything there is to know about prison and is usually involved in a scam to help Godber, often at the expense of the prison guards. | Attitudes to authority (police and prison wardens). |
| *Rising Damp*<br>ITV (Yorkshire)<br>1974–78 | 18.6 million | Rigsby, the right-wing landlord, and his tenants: Alan, a trendy left-wing student, Philip, a sophisticated black student from Croydon and Miss Jones, a middle-class spinster. | The flats. | Rigsby, trying to show how intelligent he is, has arguments about important issues with Alan and Philip. He invariably ends up looking pompous and prejudiced. Rigsby also tries, almost always unsuccessfully, to woo Miss Jones. | Attitudes to racial minorities and class. |
| *The Good Life*<br>BBC<br>1975–78 | 15.7 million | Husband and wife Tom and Barbara Good, who decide to give up their jobs and live off the land in their back garden in Surbiton, and their nouveau riche neighbours, Margot and Jerry Leadbetter. | The Goods' house and garden. | Although they fundamentally get on very well, the Leadbetters look down upon the Goods' attempts to grow vegetables and rear livestock in their garden, and the Goods criticise the Leadbetters' materialism. | Attitudes towards class and consumerism. |
| *Fawlty Towers*<br>BBC2<br>1975 and 1979, repeated 1985 | 12.5 million | Hotel manager Basil Fawlty, his wife Sybil and a Spanish waiter, Manuel. | Fawlty Towers Hotel in Torquay, Devon. | Basil is at the centre of a stressful situation. Manuel makes things worse before Sybil sorts everything out. | Attitudes towards women. |
| *Likely Lads/ Whatever Happened to the Likely Lads?*<br>BBC 1964–66 and 1973–74 | 27 million | Bob Ferris and Terry Collier, both from working-class backgrounds in Newcastle. Terry is happy with his working-class life, but Bob wants to become part of the middle class. | Bob and Terry's homes, the pub and locations around the north-east. | Bob and Terry get into various scrapes and are generally hen-pecked by the various women in their lives. | Attitudes towards women and the family. |
| *Till Death Us Do Part*<br>BBC<br>1965–68 and 1972–75 | 12 million | Alf Garnett, a right-wing, racist docker from the East End of London, his wife Else, daughter Rita and his socialist son-in-law Mike from Liverpool. | The Garnett home, generally the dining table or the lounge. | Alf rants and raves about his prejudices, often calling his wife a 'silly moo' and arguing with Mike. | Attitudes towards women and the family, racial minorities and class. |
| *Are You Being Served?*<br>BBC<br>1972–85 | 22 million | Shop assistants Captain Peacock, a pompous city gent, the camp Mr Humphries, snobby Mrs Slocombe, and attractive working-class girl Miss Brahms. | Grace Brothers, a department store in London. | Some project is being worked towards or some disaster coped with, with lots of innuendo and slapstick humour. | Attitudes towards homosexuals, class and consumerism. |

**Figure 4.1**: A table giving an overview of the most popular sitcoms in the 1970s.

**A Level Exam-Style Question Section B**

How far do you agree that popular culture reflected changing attitudes in British society in the years 1918–79? (20 marks)

**Tip**

*A key debate in this question is about whether popular culture reflected changing attitudes or whether changing attitudes were informed by popular culture.*

Change (5a)

**The strands of complex change**

This table describes how some developments in popular culture led to changes in British society:

| Strand | How the strand links to changes in British society |
|---|---|
| The popularity of cinema and music | *The Battle of the Somme* seen by 20 million people (1916). Average person attends the cinema 28 times a year (1950). 90 percent of households own a radio (1951). 'Beatlemania' (1960s). Decline in censorship (1968). Re-emergence of American dominance in the film industry (1970s). |
| The impact of television | The BBC begins broadcasting again after the Second World War (1946). *Coronation Street* begins broadcasting (1960). The satire boom is brought to television (1962). 95 percent of households own a television (1969). |
| Development of a distinct youth culture | The jukebox is invented (1927). The first coffee bars open in London (1952). The BBC broadcasts the first music programme aimed at teenage audiences (1957). |

Draw two blank graphs. On the first, plot the individual strands against the *y*-axis, with the *x*-axis providing the timeline from 1918 to 1979. Use a different colour for each - you don't need to label it with the events. On the second graph, plot a single line that is a combination of all three strands (for example, if on your first graph at a certain point, two of the three strands are plotted high up on the *y*-axis while one is plotted lower, on the second graph the line will be somewhere just above the middle of the *y*-axis).

Answer the following:

1 How have the strands combined to make change less or more likely?

2 Why did most change take place in the 1960s?

## TO WHAT EXTENT DID THE BRITISH EXPERIENCE OF TRANSPORT AND LEISURE PURSUITS CHANGE BETWEEN 1918 AND 1979?

Before the 1980s, leisure was seen as an unimportant area for historical study. However, more recent generations of historians have appreciated that British people spent an increasing amount of time outside of work and became increasingly defined by leisure pursuits rather than employment after the First World War. Time away from work, if not leisure time itself (a distinction particularly significant for housewives), began to increase in the late 19th century for a range of reasons. Rising incomes and reduced working hours were key enabling factors, but legislation such as the 1871 Bank Holiday Act, together with improvements in health, communications and technology, all made leisure more possible for those outside of the traditional 'leisured class' (upper class). Trade unions also fought hard to gain paid holidays, something that eventually bore fruit with the 1938 Holidays with Pay Act. The middle class had looked down upon traditional working-class use of free time for drinking and gambling and sought to promote leisure activities that contributed to self-improvement, such as choirs, brass bands and organised sports. This led to the growth of virtuous pursuits that promoted cultural skills and knowledge, which intensified from the 1870s. This may have had some impact, as spending on entertainment and leisure rose from £195 million in 1920 to £263 million in 1938 (at 1938 prices), while the amount spent on alcohol fell from £423 million to £306 million in the same period. However, it was not so much middle-class influence as the growth of mass commercialised leisure that predominantly shaped working-class enjoyment of free time; this centred on the music hall, football, trips to the seaside and the pub.

## The growth of spectator sports from the 1920s

The growth of spectator sports can be divided into two phases, before and after the rise of television. Radio and the national press had created a national community of interest in sports, especially in the 'national sports' of football and cricket, before the rise of television. Although there were regular cricket and football commentaries, early BBC radio sports coverage was unduly weighted in favour of events popular with the social elite: the Grand National, the Oxford–Cambridge Boat Race and other sporting contests between the universities, the golf Open and tennis at Wimbledon all became part of an established cycle of programmes. Attendance for both cricket and football increased between the wars and some of the largest crowds for regular football league fixtures were seen just before television took off in the early 1950s.

The power of television to capture the intense emotions of sporting events was noted when the 1948 London Olympics became the first to be televised. The impact of the spectacle was limited however, due to low sales of television sets and a broadcast radius of only 25 miles around the Alexandra Palace transmission station in north London. As television began to broadcast more sport, fans began to move from the terraces to their sofas. Television also injected a lot of media and advertising revenue into the sports; the extra money was a large incentive for professional players to assert their worth and reject earlier financial limits (or other forms of discrimination such as separate dressing rooms for professional and amateur players in the case of cricket).

### Football: the growth of live spectatorship

It is important to note that the growth of spectator sports, and active participation in them, affected men far more than women throughout the period. A number of different sports could be explored to chart the changes in spectator sport since 1918; football has been chosen here due to the scale of its popularity in Britain.

Although the majority of spectators at sporting events were men, women also followed live football in large numbers from the start of the Football League in 1888: Preston North End FC had to withdraw its offer of free tickets for women after 2,000 turned up to watch a match.

Britain was the global leader in the transformation of local games into established national sports with clearly defined rules or laws. There are several reasons for this, but they are all underpinned by the fact that Britain was also the first industrial nation; even within Britain, Lancashire, as the first industrial region, led the way in the growth of commercialised sport. The growth of factories made it easier to organise workers into teams and to set up local matches or leagues. The rise of mass transport and communications made

SOURCE

11 Two extracts from the *Leicester Mercury* newspaper, the first published in 1922 and the second in 1927.

(1) [At Leicester City's match against Clapton there was] a good sprinkling of women. Quite a number of women, in fact, faced the cup-tie crush without a male escort. If Leicester is any criterion, then the lure of the English Cup is rapidly infecting the female mind.

(2) A remarkable feature was the number of women who had accompanied their husbands and sweethearts. Many mothers carried babies in their arms and confessed they had brought them to see the cup-tie.

national leagues possible: the Football Association was founded in 1888, with the Scottish and Irish equivalents following in 1890. Between 1920 and 1922, three national divisions (with a Northern and Southern third division) were created, with the possibility of promotion or relegation between them. Clubs became a powerful source of local pride and loyalty. Regular working hours and the Saturday half-day enabled men to take part in competitive sport; this was encouraged by bosses and the clergy as a healthy, virtuous use of free time. The growth of national newspapers, radio broadcasts and cinema newsreels accelerated interest and participation in sport. Football was by far the most popular sport: the number of clubs affiliated to the FA increased from 12,000 in 1910 to 17,973 by 1948, 30,862 by 1967 and 41,069 by 1985. Average attendances at top-flight football matches increased from 23,000 in 1914 to almost 31,000 in 1938. Large crowds were drawn to matches by low ticket prices: a ticket cost sixpence (2.5p) in 1914, a shilling (5p) between the wars, two half-crowns (25p) in 1968 and £1 in 1981. Yet, despite this degree of popular engagement in the sport, football, like other sports, became increasingly dominated by the interests of big business rather than ordinary fans from the 1960s onwards. The reason for this was the rise of television as a medium for spectator sport.

### Football: the decline of live spectatorship

The rise of television largely helps to explain the decline in ticket sales: *Sportsview* (BBC 1954), *Grandstand* (BBC 1958), *Match of the Day* (BBC 1964) and *World of Sport* (ITV 1965) all pulled fans in front of television screens. From a peak of 41.2 million ticket sales in the 1948–49 season, attendance fell to 29.6 million in 1969–70 and 24.6 million in 1979–80. It should be noted that the rise of hooliganism also contributed to this downward trend. The increase in violence was largely due to the increased numbers of fans who could afford to go to away matches and the tendency for older, married men to stay home: where young fans had once been restrained by older relatives or work colleagues, there was increasingly nobody to stop them getting out of control. Things got so bad that many clubs built steel cage fences to keep fans off the pitch; British Rail cancelled their 'Soccer Specials', which had provided fans with cheap travel to away games, after several train carriages were totally destroyed. At the same time, it became more attractive to watch football, and other sports, on television: the rise of colour television, multiple camera angles and slow-motion replays in the 1960s all greatly enhanced viewer enjoyment; 32 million people saw England win the 1966 World

Cup final on television. In 1983, the FA finally agreed to live screening of matches in return for huge sponsorship revenue from shirt advertisements.

### The wider impact of changes in viewing habits

Growing television audiences were reflected in higher fees paid to screen sporting events and the huge increase in advertising money channelled into sport, from £1 million in 1966 to £16 million in 1976 and £100 million by 1983. Before 1963, professional footballers' wages were capped at a weekly maximum of £4 in 1914, £8 in 1919–1939, and £20 in 1961. Although this was unfair on the most talented players, it did mean ticket prices remained affordably low; it also meant the biggest clubs could not simply buy success by outspending their rivals. The threat of a strike by the Professional Footballers' Association (formed in 1961) led wage caps to be scrapped. In 1978, the *Sunday Times* reported that footballer Kevin Keegan earned £250,000, half of this from advertising and endorsements. All of this money undermined 'amateurism' which, despite its defence by old, elite sports governing bodies, was largely stamped out in cricket in the 1960s and athletics in the 1980s. The fact that top-flight teams and athletes gained the bulk of the new money undermined the financial viability of lower-league spectator sports.

**EXTRACT 5**

From Garry Whannel, *Television and the Transformation of Sport* (2009). Professor Whannel is one of the world's leading experts on the cultural analysis of media sport.

Clearly, television has transformed sport beyond all recognition. The major events, sports and organisations now command extremely high revenues. This income has enabled sport to be organised on a more elaborate and spectator basis. Top sport performers have become major global celebrities with matching earning power. The new revenue sources challenged and then usurped the traditional authority of sport governing bodies... These bodies reigned without major challenge until the rise of television. The new revenues available from television advertising endorsement and sponsorship placed amateurism under growing strain... Traditionalists fought a long, losing battle against modernisers. By the mid-1980s, amateurism was all but dead, and most governing bodies had been forced to come to terms with the new world of sport agents, sponsorship brokers, and television deals. Sport was reshaped to meet the needs of television and the promotional industry.

**THINKING HISTORICALLY** Change and continuity (4a)

**Significance**

1 Look at the accounts of the changing nature of football audiences in Source 11 and Extract 5.

2 In what ways do the extracts from the *Leicester Mercury* (Source 11) present football audiences as changing?

3 How significant do the authors of Source 11 think this is?

4 Compare this to Garry Whannel's assessment in Extract 5. What significance does Whannel ascribe to the development of television audiences?

5 Why do you think these views might differ so greatly?

### Sport and gender

Women participated far less in sport than men. Men made up 60–70 percent of viewing audiences from the 1960s and male participation in sport increased from nine percent of men in 1961 to just under 30 percent in 1979. The equivalent female figures were six and 17 percent respectively. The figures were even lower for women in lower classes and for married women of all classes. Sport helped to reinforce traditional gender images and gender divides: women were not allowed to join leading golf clubs or sport governing bodies. The one challenge to this division was cycling, where women, appropriately dressed, were able to forge a new association between sport and womanliness. It became increasingly common for women to keep fit as a healthy body became seen as part of being the ideal mother and housewife.

Participation in sport by both genders was encouraged with the construction of sport centres. In 1970, there were only 27 in England; this had increased to 167 by 1974 and to over 500 by 1979.

Access to swimming pools and health and fitness equipment was particularly important for female participation in sport, as girls and women tended to be excluded from team sports like football (one girl went to the High Court in 1978 to successfully overturn her ban from playing for Muskham United Under 11s).

ACTIVITY
KNOWLEDGE CHECK

**Spectator sports**

1 What kinds of sports were popular before rise of television? Why do you think this was?

2 Explain why the rise of television had such an impact on spectator sports in Britain.

3 'The history of spectator sports in Britain tells us nothing about British women.' How far do you agree with this statement? Explain your answer.

## The growth of leisure time and the development of mass tourism from the 1930s

### The rise of free time

The most important impact of increased free time was that leisure ceased to be a symbol of social dominance in Britain. Leisure had been the preserve of the elite, but was extended to the masses in the 20th century through greater affluence and a series of legislative changes. Workers had been allowed to take a holiday, but this was usually unpaid: in 1935, only 1.5 million out of 18.5 million workers received any paid holiday. Before 1938, less than half the population left home for even a single night during the year. With the 1938 Holidays with Pay Act, Britain became the 17th country to make paid holidays a right rather than a privilege. The Act strongly suggested that three consecutive days of holiday should be paid for by employers; by March 1938, 7.75 million workers enjoyed this benefit. This was still too short a period of time to substantially affect British holidaymaking; most holidays were still a couple of days at a local seaside resort (although this was an improvement on the day trip of previous generations). In 1937, only around a third of Britons took a holiday of a week or more away from home. The amount of leisure time for the average worker steadily increased in the 1960s and 1970s. For full-time manual workers, this increased from two weeks' paid holiday in 1960, to three in 1975 and four in 1979; the number of people who went away for four or more consecutive nights doubled between 1951 and 1990. Increases in free time and wealth afforded Britons a range of holiday choices that would have astounded previous generations.

### Holidays between the wars

The seaside visit, which comprised the vast majority of holidays undertaken by Britons between the wars, would have been highly familiar to their parents' and grandparents' generations; only the length of the trip and the numbers who went might have surprised them. As historian Edward Royle has highlighted, 'holiday locations within the UK were class-based': the better-off went to Tynemouth rather than Whitley Bay, Llandudno rather than Rhyl, Bournemouth not Margate. The holiday industry grew rapidly in the interwar period: by the 1930s, Blackpool drew seven million working-class visitors each year.

There had been signs before 1937 that more Britons wanted time away from home and work in the fresh air of the countryside: the Youth Hostel Association (founded 1929) and the Ramblers Association (1935) both saw rapid increases in membership in the 1930s. However, it was the launch of the commercial holiday camp in 1937 that witnessed a major shift in British holidaymaking. That year, William Butlin launched his first camp in Skegness; by 1939, there were 200 holiday camps in Britain, which could cater for 30,000 visitors per week. Many poorer families (those on less than £4 per week) were able to go away for the first time. The camps remained popular throughout the Second World War and into the 1950s.

### The impact of the Second World War on tourism

During the war the government used a number of methods to prevent travel for pleasure to free up the roads and railway for military and supply purposes. Petrol rationing reduced, but did not entirely prevent, the use of cars for holidays. A range of posters aimed to dissuade potential holidaymakers (see Source 13 on page 109), and orders were given to prevent railway companies putting on additional trains at peak holiday times. The latter two measures were largely ineffective. As writer Vera Brittain observed in 1941, 'the British determination to celebrate a holiday somehow was obvious to the most casual observer'. 'Wakes Week', when most factory workers in Lancashire went to Blackpool, and 'Trip Week', when workers from Swindon went to Weston-super-Mare, continued throughout the war. The government tried, with some success, to promote 'Holidays at Home' in 1941–42, but largely accepted holidays near home as the best way to maintain worker morale and productivity. Some wartime developments inadvertently promoted the spread of holiday camps after 1945: the creation of prisoner of war camps, military barracks and workers' hostels provided the infrastructure for this post-war expansion.

**EXTRACT 6**

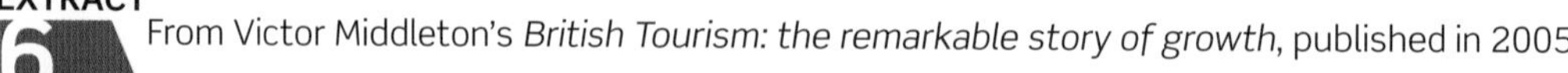

From Victor Middleton's *British Tourism: the remarkable story of growth*, published in 2005.

> Holiday camps flourished after the war... In a far-sighted deal when the war started, Butlin not only leased his existing two camps to the Navy for wartime purposes, but arranged for other sites to be built for wartime use. These sites were designed to his overall specification, so that they were suitable for conversion to future holiday use and he leased them on the understanding that he could buy them back after the war at 60 per cent of cost price... As a result he was in business very soon after the war with fully built operational holiday centres.

### Post-war holidays: home or away?

With more disposable income, more people could afford foreign holidays and caravan holidays. By the end of the 1970s, almost half the UK population had been on a caravan holiday. The caravan opened up parts of Britain like Devon, Cornwall and Carmarthenshire, which had previously been restricted to the wealthy few with second homes.

**SOURCE 12**

A table showing changes in the share of holiday transport between 1951 and 1981.

| Mode of transport | 1951 | 1961 | 1971 | 1981 |
|---|---|---|---|---|
| Car | 28 | 49 | 63 | 72 |
| Train | 48 | 28 | 10 | 12 |
| Bus or coach | 24 | 23 | 17 | 12 |

In 1951, 25 million Britons went on holiday in the UK and two million went abroad. 20 years later, the figures were 34 million and seven million respectively. Numbers heading abroad increased rapidly after the mid-1970s due to the availability of cheap overseas package-tour holidays and the end of currency restrictions (Britons had only been allowed to take £50 on foreign holidays between 1966 and 1970). The number of passengers on international flights from the UK increased from 887,000 in 1951 to just under 15 million in 1979; around 60 percent of those who took foreign holidays used package tour operators like Thomas Cook. Whereas in 1971 only a third of Britons had been on a foreign holiday, by 1979 just over a third had not. Resorts like Benidorm and Torremolinos in Spain became the most popular foreign destinations; British people were nervous of foreign travel and such resorts offered the familiar foods and comforts of home with far better weather. As a result of caravanning and foreign holidays, the traditional seaside holiday declined in popularity and holiday camps began to suffer by the mid-1960s.

Experience of foreign travel had some important effects on the British. In part, it might help to explain a decisive 'yes' vote in the 1975 referendum to stay in the European Economic Community. It also changed culinary tastes dramatically. Wine consumption doubled in the 1960s and again in the 1970s (up from 2.3 bottles per person per year to 12.6 bottles). Continental lager made up only three percent of the British beer market in 1960; by 1970, almost all pubs offered lagers like Skol and Carling Black Label. Greek and Italian restaurants, where food included exotic ingredients such as garlic, aubergine and fresh pasta became popular. It would have been impossible to fool a British audience in 1977 that spaghetti grew on trees as an April Fool's report on *Panorama* did in 1957.

SOURCE 13 A poster produced by the Railway Executive Committee in 1942. The artist was Bert Thomas.

## The impact of car ownership and travel developments, 1918–79

### Cars

The rise of car ownership in Britain has profoundly changed the life of its citizens. It has not only affected where they live and work, but it has moulded their leisure pursuits and, some historians claim, even the way they perceive themselves. Car ownership followed the trend of other consumer durables in gradually trickling down from the upper to the middle class between the wars and then exploding into a mass market in the 25 years after the end of austerity in the early 1950s. In 1904, there were only 9,000 private cars registered in Britain; at that time they were prohibitively expensive and mechanically unreliable. Car ownership increased at a rapid rate after the First World War, from 100,000 in 1919 to two million in 1939. Cheaper, smaller cars such as the Austin Seven (launched in 1922) meant motoring became affordable for the middle class: the average price of cars, adjusted for inflation, fell from £259 in 1924 to £130 in 1938. By 1939, around 1.4 million jobs were dependent on the motor industry. Motorists also benefited from large state subsidies for road transport: the Ministry of Transport (established 1919) spent far more on road improvements than was collected in road tax until the mid-1930s. There were few restrictions on early motorists and this also helped to popularise cars: before the introduction of driving tests in 1934, anyone physically fit over the age of 17 was allowed to drive. A speed limit of 20mph was abolished in 1930. While a limit of 30mph was introduced in built up areas in 1934, some country roads had no speed limits until 1965. The trend for increased car ownership accelerated after the Second World War: the end of petrol rationing, more efficient production techniques and greater average incomes led car ownership to double between 1960 and 1970 from 5,650,000 to 11,802,000.

Private motorists were not the only road users to benefit from improvements. Commuting to work by car was still quite rare; far more people got to work on a bicycle. Between 1929 and 1935, sales of bicycles increased from six to ten million, far outstripping the rise in car sales. Before the Second World War, buses were more important to the working class: they enabled people to commute from suburbs to their place of work and to enjoy day trips to the seaside. The number of passenger miles travelled by bus increased from 3.5 million in 1920 to 19 million in 1938. Buses overtook trams in passenger miles in 1932.

The replacement of rail and tram track with buses and cars led to a shift in settlement: houses and factories began to stretch out along roads (**ribbon development**) rather than clustering around the urban nucleus of the train station. More people were able to live further out in suburbs rather than the centre. The divide between town and country reduced as more people took advantage of improvements in transport to move from town centres to outlying areas: the populations of London, Blackburn, Bolton, Gateshead, Halifax, Manchester, Oldham, Salford, South Shields and Wigan all declined between 1911 and 1951. Motoring also made weekend excursions to the surrounding countryside possible and opened up more remote parts of the UK to holidaymakers.

Car ownership also impacted upon consumer habits as people could load up on greater quantities of groceries and other items in one big weekly shop. The rise of refrigerator ownership and the greater proportion of female employment also accelerated this trend. The first purpose-built multistorey car park opened in Blackpool in 1939; the rise of urban congestion in the 1960s led to the growth of out-of-town supermarkets, the first, an Asda, opening in Nottinghamshire in 1964 with 1,000 car-parking spaces. It became highly successful and spawned hundreds of imitators across the country.

**KEY TERM**

**Ribbon development**
The construction of houses and communities along transport routes, such as railway lines or roads, between existing towns and cities.

Motoring was overwhelmingly a male activity: in 1933, women only held 12 percent of all private driving licences. By 1975–76, only 29 percent of women, compared to 69 percent of men, held driving licences.

### Planes

The First World War saw a rapid improvement in the design of aircraft and, by 1918, flight became a commercially viable option for travel. It remained expensive throughout the interwar years and was only affordable for wealthy businessmen; as a result, flight remained unprofitable and four pioneering private companies had to be financially supported by the state. Imperial Airways was formed out of these companies in 1924; it was subsidised by the government to promote an image of British power and modernity rather than to make a profit. British Airways was set up as a private company in 1935, but this too had to be rescued with state financial assistance; in 1939, it merged with Imperial Airways to form the British Overseas Airways Corporation (BOAC). Civil aviation was nationalised in 1946, and was not privatised again until 1987 (see Chapter 5). Scheduled internal flights began in the early 1930s, but were slow to grow in popularity. Improvements in design, safety and economy led to a rapid growth in air transport after the Second World War. This was a key reason why so many Britons were able to enjoy holidays in Greece and Spain from the 1960s onwards.

### Trains

The First World War saw the state take control of railway operations from 120 different local companies. It became clear that the rail network ran more smoothly with fewer operators; the 1921 Railway Act forced all rail companies to merge into just four: Great Western Railway; London, Midland and Scottish Railway; London and North Eastern Railway and Southern Railway. The growth of railways encouraged ribbon development before the impact of cars and buses. The most famous example of this was the growth of 'Metro-land', a series of suburbs north of London linked to the city centre by the Metropolitan Railway. Metro-land was promoted by the company (from 1915 until its absorption by the London Passenger Transport Board in 1933) as an ideal rural retreat from the congested, polluted centre.

SOURCE **14** A poster advertising Butlin's holiday camps.

Holidays at Butlin's are *always* bright and gay whatever tricks our fickle weather chooses to play.

On a Butlin Holiday there's such a variety of fun, sport and entertainment for *everyone*—both outdoors in the glorious seaside air or under cover in magnificent heated swimming pools, palatial ballrooms, theatres, games rooms, cafés and bars.

Butlin Holidays are tremendous fun for the kiddies, exciting for young people, gay and carefree for Mum and Dad (who know the children are well looked after), restful and interesting to those who sometimes prefer to sit back and watch other people enjoying themselves.

Find out more about the holiday which makes you independent of weather—the modern Butlin Holiday.

*Swimming is a real joy at Butlin s—in luxurious heated open-air pools—in warmed indoor pools or in the bracing sea.*

*Kiddies of all ages find Butlin's a wonderland of exciting rides, slides, boats, games and entertainments—and they are all FREE.*

*Young people make new friends, and revel in the wealth of sport and gay amusement on a Butlin holiday.*

*In the gay, carefree atmosphere of colourful cafés and bars like this, you'll meet friendly people of all ages.*

*Parents too can choose their own entertainments, knowing the older children are enjoying themselves in safety and the kiddies are watched over by our special staff.*

THERE'S NOWHERE QUITE LIKE Butlin's

TRAVEL BY RAIL

Butlin's HOLIDAY BROCHURE FREE!

NAME.................................................

Block capitals please

ADDRESS.................................................

.................................................

W.D.5

from BUTLIN'S LTD., DEPT. H.B., 439 OXFORD STREET, LONDON, W.1.

(Postage in unsealed envelope, 2d.)

POST THIS COUPON NOW

Butlin's FOR YOUR HOLIDAY where you make new friends

Poet Sir John Betjeman wrote a series of poems to celebrate the spirit of Metroland (he dropped the hyphen) and even created a Metroland documentary for the BBC in 1973. Other observers of the suburbs were less kind: historian A. N. Wilson said that the Metropolitan Railway 'merely ended up creating an endless ribbon… not perhaps… town or country'.

The 'big four' struggled to compete with the growth of road transport; in 1948, they were nationalised to create British Rail, an entity that survived until its privatisation in 1994–97. The major change in train transport came as a result of two reports written by Dr Richard Beeching in 1963 and 1965. In these reports, Beeching recommended the closure of over half of all stations and almost a third of all track miles (around 5,000 miles in total) to make British Rail profitable. Track closures had begun before 1963, but dramatically accelerated in the mid-1960s. Many communities were cut off from the rail network as a result of the closures and left with no form of public transport. This furthered the demand for car ownership in the 1960s and beyond.

**ACTIVITY**
**KNOWLEDGE CHECK**

**The growth of leisure and mass tourism**

1 How did government legislation impact on leisure time and tourism?

2 Why did the traditional seaside holiday go into decline after the Second World War?

3 What impact did increased car ownership have on people's lives?

**AS Level Exam-Style Question Section A**

Was the increase in car ownership the main reason for changing leisure pursuits in the years 1945–79? Explain your answer. (20 marks)

**Tip**

*Issues that can be covered in this question include holidays, sport and television. Remember to discuss other reasons for changing leisure pursuits and directly compare them with car ownership.*

**A Level Exam-Style Question Section A**

How far do you agree that, before the Second World War, leisure opportunities for British people were limited? (20 marks)

**Tip**

*Ensure you give equal space in this essay to both sides of the argument, in order to create a balanced argument, before making a final judgement.*

**ACTIVITY**
**SUMMARY**

**Changing quality of life, 1918-79**

1 Make a graph with 'living standards' on the vertical axis and 'years 1918-79' on the horizontal axis. Plot a line showing your view of the overall changes in British standards of living.

   a) How different would this line be if you focused exclusively on housing, diet or levels of income?

   b) What are the advantages and disadvantages of using such a graph to summarise changes in the standard of living between 1918 and 1979?

2 Choose three sources from this chapter that you think best illustrate the key changes in the British quality of life between 1918 and 1979. Explain your choices, with reference to change and continuity in the quality of life.

3 Which would you argue has experienced the greatest change for British people between 1918 and 1979: their experience of sport, domestic leisure or holidays? How would you justify your choice?

## WIDER READING

**Books**

Akhtar, M. and Humphries, S. *Some Liked it Hot: The British on Holiday at Home and Abroad*, Virgin (2000)

Cawood, I. *Britain in the Twentieth Century*, Routledge (2004)

Clayton, S. *Mass Media Popular Culture and Social Change in Britain since 1945*, Pearson (2010)

Higgins, M., Smith, C. and Storey, J. *The Cambridge Companion to Modern British Culture*, Cambridge University Press (2010)

Hill, J. *Sport, Leisure and Culture in Twentieth-Century Britain*, Palgrave (2002)

Holt, R. *Sport and the British: a Modern History*, OUP (1999)

Middleton, V. *British Tourism: the Remarkable Story of Growth*, Elsevier (2005)

Pearce, *R. Contemporary Britain 1914–1979*, Longman (2004)

Waller, S. *A Sixties Social Revolution?: British Society 1959–1975*, Nelson Thornes (2008)

Walton, J. *The British Seaside: Holidays and Resorts in the Twentieth Century*, Manchester University Press (2000)

**Websites**

*National Archives themed document collections*

The 1930s: www.nationalarchives.gov.uk/education/topics/thirties-britain.htm

The 1950s: www.nationalarchives.gov.uk/education/topics/fifties-britain.htm

The 1960s: www.nationalarchives.gov.uk/education/topics/sixties-britain.htm

Attlee's Britain: www.nationalarchives.gov.uk/education/topics/attlees-britain.htm

# 1.5 What impact did Thatcher's governments (1979–90) have on Britain 1979–97?

**KEY QUESTIONS**

- What were the effects of Thatcher's economic policies?
- To what extent were state intervention and the public sector 'rolled back'?
- How far did political and social division within Britain change 1979–97?
- What were the effects of Thatcherism on politics and party development?

## INTRODUCTION

Margaret Thatcher was the most divisive prime minister of the 20th century. To some, she saved Britain from economic ruin and restored national pride; to others, she promoted greedy individualism and condemned whole communities to hopeless poverty. At the time of her death in April 2013, sympathetic obituaries paid tribute to her as 'the greatest British peacetime Prime Minister'; at the same time, an internet campaign saw the song 'Ding Dong! The Witch is Dead' reach number 2 in the pop charts. These extreme reactions, dictated by political conviction or personal experience of life under Thatcher, continue to be held by many people even after her death. Passionate supporters and critics would both agree that Thatcher, and her legacy, have strongly shaped 21st-century Britain. However, this interpretation should not be taken as given: it is the historian's task to see past emotional responses and to analyse both the impact of her government on contemporaries and the extent of her legacy since 1990. For several reasons, even 'objective', 'neutral' historians disagree about the extent and nature of Thatcher's impact on Britain.

Professional historians do not deliberately present misleading or distorted accounts of the past; they work hard to get as close to the truth as possible (and maintain their academic reputation). To do this they must base their conclusions on clearly referenced, verifiable evidence. However, even in areas where all possible evidence is likely to have been found (for example, the First Crusade), historians using exactly the same information have reached different conclusions. In some cases, this is because they have posed different questions: for example, more recent historians have revisited old evidence with questions about cultural change in mind that were ignored by earlier generations of historians. Even where the questions are the same, differences in expertise or interest can lead to different interpretations: those fascinated by economic history might interpret evidence differently from someone writing a political biography, for instance. Techniques borrowed from other academic disciplines have also affected the way historians approach historical evidence: for example, historians today are far less likely to accept even the most 'neutral' reports at face value thanks to advances in literary criticism.

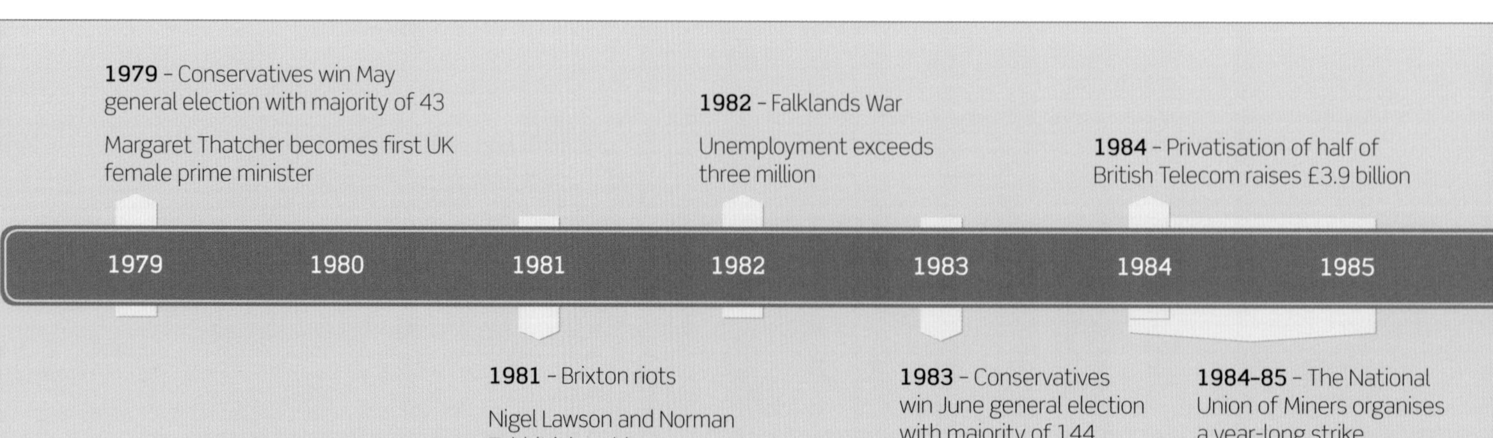

Historians of Thatcherism have additional reasons to reach different conclusions. Proximity to (or direct experience of) the period makes it harder to put aside political sympathies. It also means that historians are living through some impacts of Thatcherism that are yet to play out in full; where this is the case (such as her long-term political or economic legacy), there is more scope for credible interpretation. The complexity of interrelated issues allows for a wide range of conclusions, as does the sheer volume of available evidence (visit the website of the Thatcher Foundation to get some idea of this).

In order to decide which historians' interpretations you find the most convincing, you will need to investigate some of this primary evidence for yourself. When weighing up different interpretations, the key thing is not so much to evaluate the provenance of the extracts (who wrote it, when and for what purpose) but rather to judge the persuasiveness of the argument. Does the historian put the right degree of emphasis on a particular factor? Do they use representative examples? Do they accurately capture the pace or extent of change? Have they conveniently ignored something that might weaken their viewpoint? Does the tone of the language give away their political sympathy? You will only be able to answer such questions when you have gained a solid factual grasp of the impact of Thatcher's governments.

### Evaluating interpretations of history

The job of the historian is to provide judgements about what happened in the past based on research and an assessment of the available evidence. It is inevitable that this process will result in their opinion or beliefs influencing the outcome of their research. This chapter contains a number of interpretations that will help you prepare for section C of your exam.

Although the interpretations historians present are based to some extent on opinion, this does not mean they should be discarded by the student. Evaluating and comparing a number of interpretations of an event can be just as useful as evaluating different primary sources in order to ascertain the truth. Some historians will clearly state their agenda throughout their work, and others will attempt to remain as neutral as possible. Either way, it is important to note that every interpretation created is informed, whether consciously or unconsciously, by factors including the political, religious, moral or cultural viewpoint of its author.

Sound interpretations need to be backed up with evidence, and it is important for the historian to show how they have arrived at their interpretation. When reading the extracts in this chapter, consider the following:

- Is the author actually giving an interpretation or are they simply stating facts?
- Is the interpretation based on generalisations or is it backed up by evidence?
- Does the historian make clear the methods they have used to arrive at their interpretation?
- Do any other interpretations agree with the one given?
- Does the historian appear to have a political agenda?

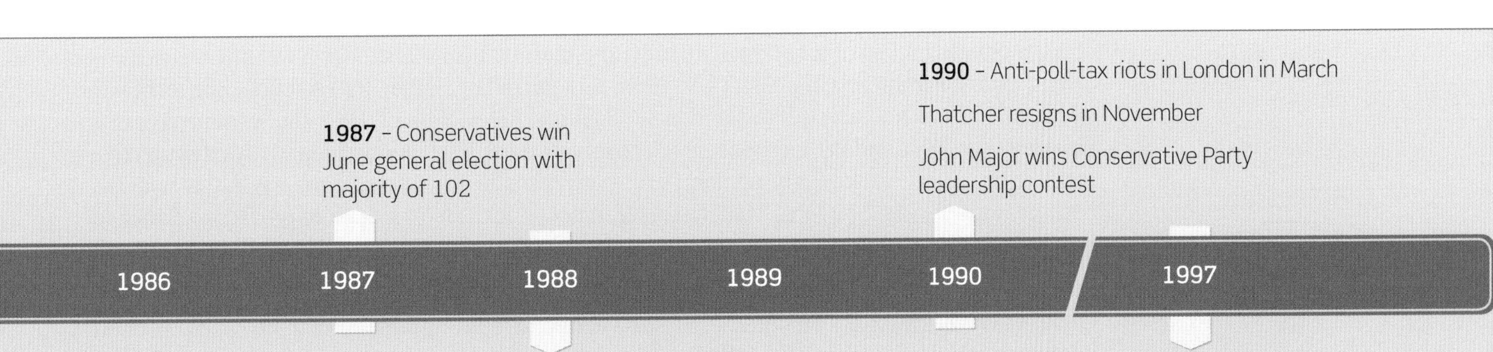

## THINKING HISTORICALLY Interpretations (5a)

**What I believe is how I see**

Below are three descriptions of the perspectives of very famous historians. They have been written for the purposes of this exercise.

| Herodotus | Leopold von Ranke | Karl Marx |
|---|---|---|
| • Research consisted of conversations<br>• Identified that accounts had to be judged on their merits<br>• Some believe that certain passages in his writing are inventions to complete the narrative | • Believed in an evidence-based approach and relied heavily on primary sources<br>• Wanted to find out the 'facts' and discover the connections between them<br>• Stressed the role of the individual in shaping history | • Believed that history would go through stages leading to a state where everybody was equal<br>• Believed that historical changes were ultimately determined by changes to the economy<br>• Was often driven by political considerations and looked for evidence to support his point of view |

Work in groups of three or six.

Each member or pair takes the perspective of one of the above historians and argues from that perspective. Work through questions 1–4 as a group, then answer question 5 individually.

1 Herodotus did not use written evidence to construct his history. Does this mean that his history is less useful than history written by the others?

2 Ranke based his writing almost exclusively on primary sources from the time he was investigating, rather than secondary sources. How might this affect his ability to see larger patterns in history as opposed to the other two?

3 Marx put his philosophy of history, and perhaps politics, first and research second. Would this make his history weaker than the others?

4 'Colourful' individuals populate the writing of Herodotus and Ranke, whilst Marx concentrates on the differences between classes. Write three historical questions that each historian might ask.

5 The three historians mentioned above all had different methods and motivations and yet their writing has been valued ever since it was created. Explain how the prior knowledge that we bring to the history that we write does not invalidate it.

## An overview of Thatcher's career

Margaret Thatcher was born in Grantham, Lincolnshire, where her father Alfred owned two grocery shops. He was very active in local politics and took his daughter along to many of the meetings he attended. Margaret was brought up with a Christian faith that informed a strongly held set of conservative moral values throughout her life.

Having studied chemistry at the University of Oxford, she worked for a few years as a research chemist before training as a barrister. In 1951, she married Denis Thatcher, a wealthy businessman. She never lost her interest in politics and stood as a candidate in the 1950 election. She lost on this occasion and was not selected to stand in 1955, but in the election of 1959 she won the seat of Finchley (in north London) and became a Conservative MP. Thatcher gradually rose through the ranks of the Conservative Party, until in 1970 she was made Education Secretary. In this role she became notorious as 'Margaret Thatcher, milk snatcher' for stopping the free provision of milk for 7–11-year-olds. In 1975, she became leader of the Conservative Party, which was then in opposition, and when her party won the 1979 election became the first female prime minister.

Once in power, Thatcher's first priority was the economy, starting with cutting the supply of money in order to reduce inflation. With inflation reduced, she aimed to reduce government interference in the economy and use the law to smash the power of the trade unions. Thatcher's initial economic policies led to manufacturing output falling by 30 percent, and unemployment doubling between 1978 and 1983, with 3.6 million out of work. Many commentators felt that it was only success against Argentina in the 1982 Falklands War that saw Thatcher re-elected in the 1983 general election.

### EXTEND YOUR KNOWLEDGE

**The Falklands War**

The Falkland Islands lie 300 miles off the east coast of Argentina, 7,500 miles from Britain. The islands possibly have untapped oil reserves beneath them, but it was the lucrative seal trade and whaling that first brought Europeans to the uninhabited land. The French, Spanish, Argentines and British had all laid claim to the island before the British established permanent control from 1833. In 1945, the Argentines began to press their claim to the islands at the UN. The British said that they would only withdraw if and when the inhabitants of the island voted for Argentinian sovereignty; as the population was British, this was never likely to happen.

On 2 April 1982, the Falklands War began when Argentine forces occupied the islands. They had invaded upon the orders of General Galtieri, leader of the military *junta* that ruled Argentina after taking control by force in 1976. Galtieri wanted a swift military victory to distract attention from domestic economic problems and to bolster his own power. While diplomatic negotiations continued with the Argentinians, a British task force was dispatched.

British ships arrived on 19 April and began to land troops on the islands. On 2 May, Margaret Thatcher ordered the submarine HMS *Conqueror* to attack an Argentinian light cruiser called the *General Belgrano*. The *General Belgrano* was torpedoed and sunk with the loss of 368 crew-members.

This divided opinion in Britain: while some approved of her action to protect British troops, reports came back that the *General Belgrano* was not in the Total Exclusion Zone (TEZ) and was sailing away from the islands. The TEZ was an area of around 200 miles around the Falkland Islands within which the British, on 30 April 1982, had declared they would attack any Argentine vessel. Some critics, notably the Labour MP Tam Dalyell, suspected that Mrs Thatcher had ordered the attack to boost her popularity, and to stop any possibility of success for a new diplomatic settlement announced by the Peruvians 14 hours earlier. Thatcher insisted that she did not learn of this plan until after the *General Belgrano* had been sunk.

On 21 May, SAS troops began to land on the islands and, after some tough fighting, proceeded to recapture the airstrip at Goose Green. By mid-June they had recaptured the capital, Port Stanley, and taken almost 10,000 Argentine prisoners.

The war resulted in the deaths of 649 Argentines and 255 British men and had cost the British almost £3 billion. It led to a surge of pride and patriotism among the British, and contributed to the success of Mrs Thatcher in the 1983 election.

Thatcher's second term in office gave her the confidence to expand the privatisation of state-owned assets that had tentatively begun before 1983. She centralised more power in Whitehall at the expense of local authorities and promoted unelected 'political advisers' from the world of business to advance her policies. She took a tough line against a year-long miners' strike in 1984, against the Provisional IRA throughout the 1980s and against the Soviet Union in the last years of the Cold War. These stands were very popular with many British people, who saw her as an almost Churchill-like patriot.

In 1987, she was re-elected for a third term, the only prime minister to achieve this feat in the 20th century. However, a number of policies in her third term, most notably the introduction of the 'Poll Tax' in 1989–90, were very unpopular. She resigned in November 1990. In 1992, she entered the House of Lords as Baroness Thatcher. She was occasionally critical of the Conservative leaders who followed her, especially of their pro-European stance. Although she died in April 2013, many would argue that Thatcherism, or at least her belief in the liberating power of the free market, remains the new **political consensus** in British politics.

### KEY TERM

**Political consensus**
Broad agreement among major parties on issues such as the economy, welfare and foreign policy. Political commentators today talk of a 'post-Thatcher consensus', where the Conservatives, Labour and Liberal Democrats all agree on principles of a market economy, low direct taxation and a smaller role for the state.

# WHAT WERE THE EFFECTS OF THATCHER'S ECONOMIC POLICIES?

## The origin and evolution of Thatcher's views on the economy

Like her views on big government, Thatcher's economic views were based on a mixture of her moral upbringing and the influence of 'new right' thinkers. She herself was more practical than theoretical when it came to economic policy. In her own words: 'Thatcherism stands for sound finance… It stands for honesty, not inflation; it stands for living within your means; it stands for incentives… it stands for the wider and wider spread of ownership of property, of houses, of shares, of savings.' This neatly encapsulates most of what she wanted to achieve with her economic policies: to smash the restrictive and, as she saw it, undemocratic practices of the trade unions in order to promote individualism, overcome the inefficiencies of state-owned industry, promote growth and investment by cutting red tape and lifting the tax burden on successful business people, and fostering a greater sense of public participation in the economy through ownership of shares and property. Before any of this was possible, however, Thatcher had to tackle the 'evil' of inflation to put the economy on a stable path.

### ACTIVITY
### KNOWLEDGE CHECK

**Thatcherism**

1 How would you define Thatcherism in your own words?

2 In what respects does Thatcherism deviate from the post-war political consensus?

## The fight against inflation

While all previous post-war governments had prioritised employment, Thatcher was willing to risk a (temporary) period of higher unemployment in order to tackle inflation. In order to reduce inflation, Thatcher and her advisers believed that access to money should be cut. This meant raising interest rates, and many companies, particularly in the manufacturing industry, struggled to survive. In 1978, inflation stood at 11 percent; by 1980 it had doubled to 22 percent, largely due to spiralling pay demands. Thatcher refused to print money to cover inflation as it punished 'careful savers' and rewarded 'reckless borrowers'. She placed her

KEY TERMS

**Monetarism**
An economic theory that argues governments should prioritise low inflation and should achieve this by controlling the amount of money in circulation in a nation's economy. The idea was popular with conservative economists but had only been tested in the military dictatorship of Chile.

**Supply-side**
An economic theory that argues that governments should encourage production; they should do this by removing regulations and cutting taxes. This theory went against the 'demand-side' post-war consensus, begun under Attlee's Labour government, which argued governments should tax and spend to create demand.

trust in the economic theories of a few experts: Chicago-based economist Milton Friedman argued that inflation could only be effectively tackled by restricting the amount of money in circulation. **Monetarism**, as this theory was called, was given a prominent role in the 1980 'Medium-Term Financial Strategy', but was never fully understood by Thatcher or the British public. A key problem was that no one was quite sure how best to measure how much money was in circulation: should this just mean the total value of notes and coins or should it include money in bank accounts? By 1983, even fans of monetarism such as Chancellor Nigel Lawson began to give up on the idea of setting targets for money supply. A range of **supply-side** policies was introduced to replace monetarism; these included cuts to income tax, cuts to welfare payments where possible and a wide range of deregulation.

The 1980 and 1981 budgets slashed government spending, with especially unpopular cuts made to spending on housing and social security; this had negative consequences for many people in inner-city areas. There were riots in several cities, with the most severe in Handsworth in Birmingham, Chapeltown in Leeds, Toxteth in Liverpool and Brixton in London. While these were partly sparked by racial issues, the poverty in those areas heightened tensions; as one journalist wrote in the *Daily Telegraph* at the time, riots occurred in areas where the general dilapidation was so bad that you would be hard pushed to notice the damage caused by the riots. In 1980 and 1981, manufacturing production fell 14 percent. By 1982, unemployment had risen to over three million, the highest figure since 1930. Ironically, the scale of unemployment benefits payments forced up government spending. Despite this, inflation was reduced to single figures by 1982, and never rose above nine percent for the rest of the 1980s.

## Privatisation

TIMELINE: PRIVATISATION UNDER THATCHER AND MAJOR

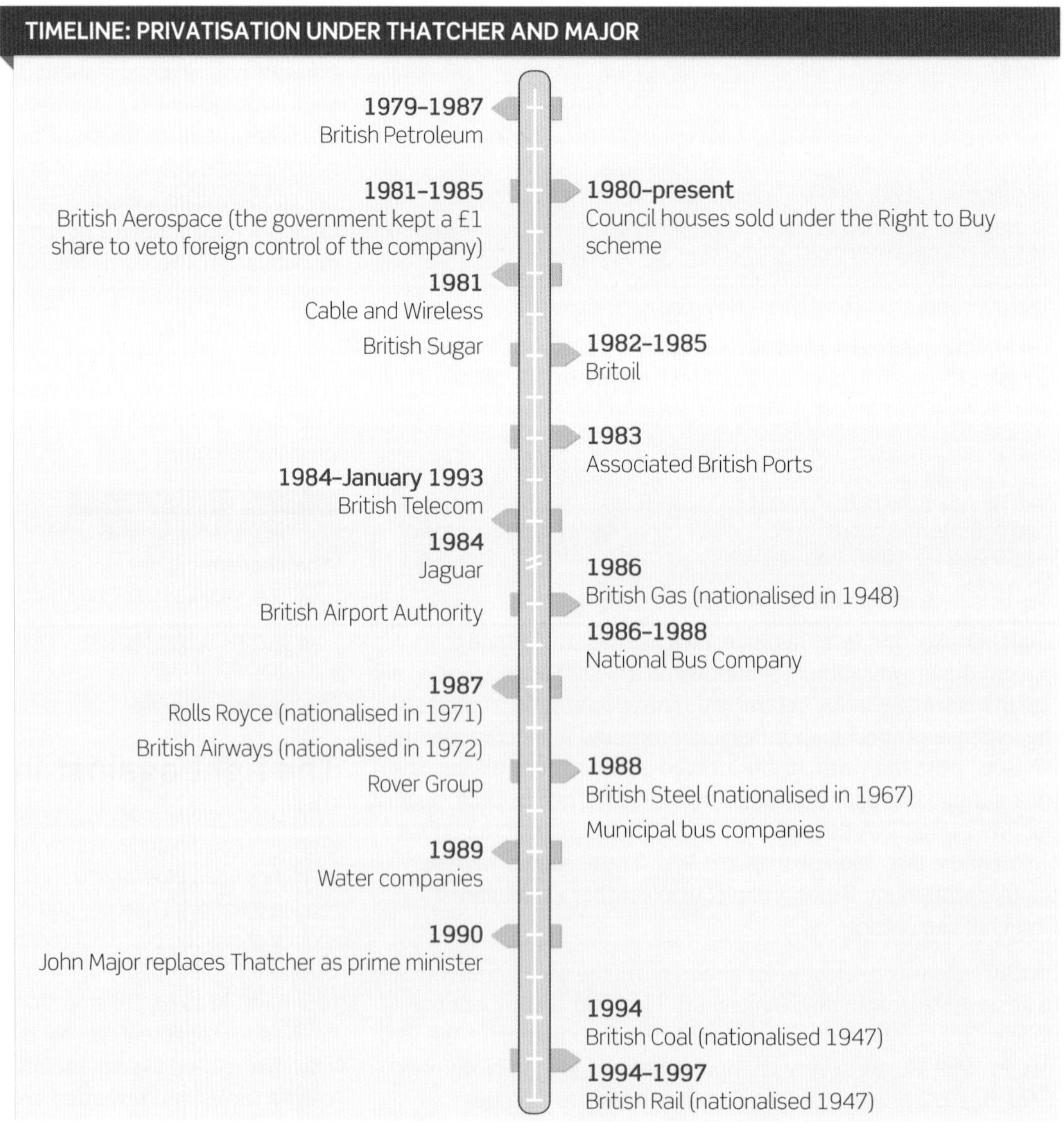

## Privatisation under Thatcher

Thatcher saw the sale of state-owned companies, the removal of government monopolies and the **contracting out** of services as key parts of her crusade to cure Britain's economic stagnation. It would cut government expenditure on loss-making industries and cut the number of civil servants by replacing them with private employees. More than this, privatisation would reinvigorate the British economy by promoting competition and innovation. The revenue generated by the sale of state assets would also fund a reduction in tax, allowing entrepreneurs to invest more wealth in job-creating ventures. Lastly, the sales would help to create a wider ownership of shares; ordinary people would have a greater incentive to work harder, knowing that they owned a slice of the company for which they worked. While there is no doubt that Thatcher was successful in terms of the pace and extent of privatisation, historians are divided over the long-term success of this policy.

Privatisation proceeded slowly at first, but then gathered pace in Thatcher's second term in office. Before 1983, British Aerospace, British Sugar and British Petroleum had all been sold off. However, it was the sale of British Telecom in 1984 and of British Gas in 1986 that really saw the launch of what Thatcher came to call '**popular capitalism**'. Shares were sold cheaply to ensure a quick sale and wide take-up; between 1979 and 1990, the number of shareowners increased from three million to 11 million. However, the distribution of these shares was far more uneven than the Conservatives made out in their 1987 election manifesto: while it spoke of the start of 'a profound and progressive social transformation – popular capitalism', only nine percent of unskilled male workers owned any shares, compared to half of all professional males. More damaging to the long-term success of popular capitalism was the rapid sale of most shares for a quick profit to large pension or investment firms: individuals owned 38 percent of shares in 1975, but only 20 percent in 1990. By far the most successful aspect of 'popular capitalism' was the sale of council houses: over a million were sold between 1979 and 1988.

The longer-term impact of privatisation is disputed and it is clear that the process has had more success in certain sectors than in others. The sum of £19 billion was raised by the sale of state assets, something that former prime minister Harold Macmillan compared to 'selling off the family silver'. This money was used to pay for tax cuts (discussed below). While competition has driven innovation and better customer service in telecoms for example, there was little appreciable difference in the quality of water or gas supply while prices increased faster than inflation to the benefit of shareholders and chief executives with huge salaries.

## Privatisation after Thatcher

The privatisation of British Rail between 1994 and 1997 (which even Thatcher felt was a 'privatisation too far') led to a highly confused situation where the government continued to subsidise private firms that operate the trains; government spending on trains has doubled since 1994, while most commuters would agree that the service has not improved.

A further way in which privatisation was increased after 1990 was the launch of the Private Finance Initiative under Thatcher's successor, John Major, in 1992. **Public–private partnerships** were designed to inject private funding and expertise into traditionally state-run concerns such as hospitals and schools. While the initiative led to the construction of some impressive buildings, it became clear by 1997 that future generations of taxpayers would have to pay a huge amount of money to the private firms who put in the initial investment.

### KEY TERMS

**Contracting out**
To offer contracts for government-funded work or projects to private companies in order to reduce costs.

**Popular capitalism**
The idea that everyone in society should have the opportunity to own property and shares in companies. It aims to create a wider spread of privately owned wealth.

**Public-private partnership**
A collaboration between a public sector body and a private company or companies to provide a government service or launch a private enterprise. The private company usually provides a lot of financial, technical and managerial help in the short term, funded by the state in the long term.

### SOURCE

The privatisation of British Gas raised £5.4 billion for the government. It was accompanied by an advertising campaign encouraging people to buy shares, often with the tagline, 'If you see Sid, tell him'.

THE MINIMUM INVESTMENT FOR BRITISH GAS SHARES WILL BE NO MORE THAN £150.

Everyone can apply for a share of the shares.

British Gas

### ACTIVITY
### KNOWLEDGE CHECK

**Privatisation**

1. How did Thatcher's government attempt to tackle inflation? How successful were they?
2. Why was privatisation beneficial to the government? How could it be argued that the benefits of privatisation were short term?

## Deregulation

Thatcher was keen to remove the rules and regulations that she believed stifled innovation and competitiveness. The first example of this was the removal of exchange controls in October 1979: before 1979, there were limits to how many pounds people could convert into foreign currencies and spend abroad. The end of this restriction fuelled greater overseas investment (which returned profits to Britain), but also led to a huge increase in consumer spending on foreign goods, which drained wealth from Britain. Perhaps the most significant example of deregulation was the 'Big Bang' of October 1986. This relaxed the rules on the ownership and trading operation of banks, resulting in the massive growth in financial services. The City of London rapidly grew to become one of the major financial centres in the world as financial institutions took advantage of the more relaxed rules to offer riskier **financial products** that returned huge profits. In the longer term, deregulation enabled unscrupulous individuals to make a lot of money in an unsustainable (and even illegal) fashion; this culture, not tackled by New Labour after 1997, was a major contributor to the financial crisis of 2008.

British people became more used to borrowing to pay for consumer goods. The 'Big Bang' meant that a great deal of government regulation on the financial industry was scrapped; this modernised the stock market and allowed banks to take more risks with their lending and investments. This had a number of effects on private individuals:

- First, unregulated finance led to the rise in private household debt, which stood at £16 billion in 1980 and increased to £47 billion in 1989.
- Second, easier access to mortgages meant that mortgage debt rose from £43 billion to £235 billion.
- Third, by 2003, personal debt, including mortgages, stood at £1.3 trillion – by far the highest in Europe.

While banks made huge profits, a 2003 Financial Services Authority report estimated that six million families, around 20 percent of the total, faced problems with debt. The rise of credit cards also contributed to this problem: the first credit card was launched in June 1966; by 1980, there were ten million credit cards in Britain, a figure that had risen to 27 million by 1990.

## Taxation and incentives

Thatcher did not believe that taxation should be used to take money from the rich to subsidise the poor. She thought this not only led to a lack of incentive to work hard and generate wealth among high earners but also bred dependence at the bottom of the social scale. Her hope was that tax cuts for the wealthy would promote more investment, more growth and therefore more government income, allowing her to cut taxes further. In the 1980 budget, the top rate of income tax was cut from 83 to 60 percent; in 1988, it was cut again to 40 percent. The cuts in the early 1980s were subsidised by a huge government windfall from the discovery and sale of North Sea oil. The oil had been extracted and sold by a state-owned corporation until Thatcher sold government shares to private investors in 1982. Chancellor Nigel Lawson was happy to point out that, due to a decline in tax avoidance schemes, the wealthiest five percent of individuals paid as much tax in 1988 as they had done in 1978 when they were taxed at 83 percent. The basic rate of income tax was also reduced from 33 to 25 percent and inheritance tax was cut from 75 to 40 percent. However, although income tax fell under Thatcher, the average tax bill rose by six percent between 1979 and 1990. The reason for this was the growth of indirect taxation (Value Added Tax) and National Insurance payments. In 1979, VAT was increased from eight to 15 percent, the figure at which it remained until 1991. Both VAT and National Insurance are **regressive** taxes: they take a higher proportion of income from the poor than the rich. This shift in the tax burden from direct to indirect taxes has contributed to the growing gap between the richest and poorest in British society since the late 1970s.

### KEY TERMS

**Financial products**
Schemes and services that help consumers manage and use money. Everyday examples include bank accounts, credit cards and life insurance, while more exotic examples include complex and risky investment portfolios.

**Regressive**
Whereas under progressive taxes (such as UK income tax) more money is paid as more money is earned, regressive taxes result in those with the lowest incomes having to pay more tax as a percentage of their total income.

### ACTIVITY
KNOWLEDGE CHECK

**Deregulation and tax reform**

What were the positive and negative effects of deregulation and tax reform?

## The fight against the trade unions

### Trade union legislation

Tackling the trade unions was part of Thatcher's overall economic policy to reduce the influence of socialist institutions, and promote individualism and popular capitalism; but the conflict was also an inevitable result of her focus on realigning the British economy away from heavy industry and towards financial services. Thatcher had been part of the Heath government that had lost power partly as a result of the 1974 miners' strike and, although she was keen to smash the power of the trade unions, she was prepared to bide her time and avoid the mistakes made by her predecessor. In her view, trade unions bullied individual workers into joining them, forced them into strike action they often had no wish to take part in and acted irresponsibly with no regard for democratically elected government.

Their power was undermined gradually through a series of Employment Acts:

- The 1980 Act meant workers did not have to join a union when they joined a particular firm (the so-called 'closed shop'); it also meant unions could only organise strikes against their direct employers and were not allowed to strike in sympathy with other workers.
- The 1982 Act meant the unions could be sued for illegal strike action.
- The 1984 Trade Union Act meant that a strike had to be approved by a majority of union members in a secret ballot before it was legal. In the same year, Thatcher also built up coal reserves that would enable the government to resist a miners' strike without resorting to a three-day week as Heath had done.

### The miners' strike and the decline of heavy industry

In the event, Thatcher was fortunate in her enemy: NUM President Arthur Scargill made several tactical errors that undermined the miners' strike. The strike began on 6 March 1984, just as the UK emerged from winter and demanded less energy. Scargill did not ballot NUM members about strike action, choosing instead to launch the strike with 'flying pickets'. This caused miners in Nottinghamshire to leave the NUM and set up their own union, which voted to keep their mines open. Lastly, Scargill lost public sympathy due to what were seen as provocative methods: his public disapproval rating never fell below 79 percent throughout the year-long strike. The strike was finally defeated on 3 March 1985, almost a year to the day after it began, although miners in Kent held out for a further two weeks.

Unions became far more willing to work with government legislation following the defeat of the NUM. The total number of trade union members fell from 13.5 million in 1979 to under 10 million in 1990; the total number of working days lost to strike action fell from 10.5 million in 1980–84 to 0.8 million in 1990–94. The coal industry had become increasingly uncompetitive since the war and pit closures had led to large-scale redundancies since the 1960s. It is likely that the coal industry would have been scaled back at a slower pace had it not been for the strike.

After the bitter struggle with the miners, a series of Employment Acts in 1988, 1989 and 1990 weakened trade unions further. After Thatcher's resignation in 1990, trade union membership fell again to 6.7 million in 1997. The removal of government subsidies for struggling older industries also saw a decline in the percentage of the labour force employed in manual labour from 47 percent in 1974 to 36 percent in 1991. The number of miners fell from 200,000 to 10,000 in the same period.

Many local communities were greatly affected by the end of a major local industry, such as shipbuilding in Sunderland, and steel manufacturing in Sheffield (as depicted in the 1997 film *The Full Monty*). The impact of Thatcher's anti-union legislation and action is a source of emotional disagreement. Critics argue that she caused unnecessary suffering to whole communities who relied on mining and other industries and that not enough was done to encourage other forms of employment in former mining areas.

**EXTRACT**

From *Finding a Role? Britain 1970–1990* (2010), by Brian Harrison, professor of Modern History at the University of Oxford.

Tackling the NUM tested Thatcher's political agility to the full. She shrewdly executed move and counter-move against Scargill's activists... without ever risking undue public loss of face, and always chose her ground carefully... In June 77 per cent of those polled by MORI thought the police had handled the situation well... The 10,372 criminal charges brought during the dispute included three of murder, and by December 1984 thirteen deaths were in some way being attributed to the strike, including two suicides of intimidated working miners. 'Scabs? They are lions,' Thatcher told her party conference in October 1984... For [Norman] Tebbit at Trade and Industry, money spent in resisting the strike was 'money well spent', and the coal industry's productivity now began to rise fast. Ever since 1957, the NUM's membership had been falling – by 1980 to 257,000, by 1990 to 90,000 and by 1998 to a mere 5,000. If Scargill had compromised before or during the strike, the run-down would have been slower and less painful. The miners' loss was the trade union movement's gain, for with the end of the strike the 'new realism' could resume... By mid-decade [1990s] the unions were increasingly cooperating with the government's new legislation.

**EXTRACT**

From Donald Macintyre's article 'How the miners' strike of 1984–85 changed Britain forever'. Macintyre is a journalist who writes for the centre-left daily newspaper *The Independent*. The article was published in the left-leaning *New Statesman* magazine on 16 June 2014.

The secret plan – denied during the strike but admitted by Thatcher in her memoirs – had been to cut 75,000 jobs over three years. This was slightly more than Scargill was later ridiculed for predicting... Thatcher sought not only to avenge the miners' victories of 1972 and 1974, but also to erase the mystique attaching to the NUM, its solidarity reinforced by the small and cohesive communities in which miners lived, by the mutual dependence required by the dangers underground, and by widespread public admiration... About 10,000 NUM pickets were allowed to assemble – suggesting a set-up – and were then forced back by at least 5,000 police officers, using horseback baton charges and snatch squads. The prosecutions against 93 arrested pickets collapsed because the police evidence was unreliable. South Yorkshire Police, sued for malicious prosecution and assault, later paid £425,000 compensation and £100,000 in legal costs to 39 pickets in an out-of-court settlement... Terry Thomas, the left-wing NUM vice-president in South Wales during the strike told me 30 years later at his home in Gowerton, near Swansea: The men returned to work not because they had stopped believing in what they were fighting for... Houses were being repossessed, marriages were breaking up, the kids were going without, and there was no end in sight. Proud, strong miners crying because they were going back to work. Thomas sees it as a 'defeat for the whole working class, a defeat for us all', without which the battery of exploitative employment practices, such as zero-hours contracts, would not have been possible a generation later. It is certainly impossible to separate yawning income inequality from the halving of union membership since its 1979 peak. Because the NUM was the trade unions' Praetorian Guard [an elite Roman military unit], the defeat robbed organised labour of an important source of its self-confidence.

**EXTRACT 3** From Anthony Seldon and Daniel Collings, *Britain Under Thatcher* (1999).

Perhaps most damagingly, the government too often appeared to be acting in the interests of the well-off, white males in England, while showing little concern for the fate of those afflicted by economic policy, most notably the unemployed. This was perhaps the inevitable consequence of [Thatcher's] deliberate attempts to widen inequality in the belief that greater rewards for success and less cushioning of failure would act as an incentive to effort and enterprise.

So, what of Britain under Thatcher?... a Britain with higher unemployment and inflation not yet tamed, but a Britain where more people owned their own shares and their own homes.

**Interpretations (4a)**

**The weight of evidence**

Work in pairs.

Read Extracts 1–3 above, then answer the questions below.

1 Use highlighter pens to colour-code copies of the extracts. Use one colour for 'evidence', another colour for 'conclusions' and a third for language that shows the historian is 'reasoning' (e.g. 'therefore', 'so'). Alternatively, draw up a table with three columns, headed 'Evidence', 'Conclusions' and 'Reasoning language' and copy the relevant parts of the extracts into the columns.

2 How do the extracts differ in terms of the way that the evidence is used?

3 Which of these extracts do you find most convincing? Which has the best-supported arguments?

4 What other information might you want in order to make a judgement about the strength of these claims?

5 Write a paragraph of 200 words explaining the importance of using evidence to support historical claims.

**AS Level Exam-Style Question Section C**

***Study Extracts 1 and 3 before you answer this question.***

Historians have different views about the impact on Britain of Thatcher's governments in the years 1979–97. Analyse and evaluate the extracts and use your knowledge of the issues to explain your answer to the following question.

How far do you agree with the view that Thatcher's economic policies were successful? (20 marks)

**Tip**

*Although Extract 1 focuses closely on the miners' strike, ensure you also make links with privatisation, deregulation and other economic policies.*

**A Level Exam-Style Question Section C**

***Study Extracts 1 and 3 before you answer this question.***

In the light of differing interpretations, how convincing do you find the view that, as a result of Margaret Thatcher's economic policies, there were 'deliberate attempts to widen inequality' (Extract 3, line 5)? (20 marks)

To explain your answer, analyse and evaluate both extracts, using your own knowledge of the issues.

**Tip**

*Consider the issues of trade union reform, privatisation, unemployment and inflation mentioned in the sources, and relate your own knowledge to those issues.*

**ACTIVITY**
**KNOWLEDGE CHECK**

**Trade unions**

1 Why did Thatcher want to limit the influence of trade unions?

2 Was the battle with the miners necessary? Explain your answer.

3 What was the long-term impact of the miners' strike?

# TO WHAT EXTENT WERE STATE INTERVENTION AND THE PUBLIC SECTOR 'ROLLED BACK'?

## The state Thatcher inherited

The post-war political consensus favoured state intervention in the economy and a relatively large state apparatus. Attlee's government (1945–51) built on the welfare state that had been established earlier in the century by Lloyd George. The NHS, family allowances, council housing and unemployment benefits were all part of this 'safety net' designed to act as insurance for British people if they experienced hardship. In the eyes of many Conservatives under Thatcher's leadership, a large public sector led to individuals becoming lazy and dependent on the state, as well as the belief that state monopolies of public services led to complacency from an uncompetitive public workforce.

## The origins of Thatcher's views on government

Margaret Thatcher had a clear, unshakable sense of what was right and wrong for Britain. Her strong moral values were rooted in her Methodist upbringing and respect for her father's hard work, self-reliance, thrift and determination. As an adult, she embraced political views that resonated with her personal experiences: she wanted government to promote the positive moral values from which she had benefited. More than this, she felt that too much state interference in people's lives had been a major reason for British decline: the welfare state had become a 'nanny state' and turned potentially upright, productive citizens into lazy dependants. She thought that state ownership of industry crushed innovation, choice and competition, and led to inferior, uncompetitive products that people did not want to buy. Even worse for her were the high levels of taxation required to pay for large state interference: this drained the wealth of successful individuals who could have used this money for private entrepreneurship. She hated the 'creeping socialism' of the post-war consensus and wanted the Conservative Party to break out of the centre ground.

A number of key influences shaped Thatcher's instinctive moral stance into political policies to 'roll back' the overbearing state apparatus. More than anyone else, it was 'new right' Conservative Keith Joseph who inspired Thatcher with his brand of free-market liberalism. He introduced her to the ideas of Austrian economist Friedrich von Hayek who, in his 1944 book *The Road to Serfdom*, argued that government should provide the conditions of liberty within which individuals can make their own choices, not provide welfare that leads to dependence. Such ideas had been around since the war but had made little impression: too many people associated the free market with the dark days of the Great Depression. Thatcher rose to prominence at exactly the right time for many Conservatives to finally give these **neo-liberal** ideas a chance: by the mid-1970s, government planning and interference seemed responsible for a stagnant economy, high inflation and rising unemployment. The Labour government's application for an IMF bail-out and, above all, the Winter of Discontent, led a large swathe of the British public to agree that something different had to be tried. The acronym TINA, short for 'There Is No Alternative', was frequently used to defend Thatcher's controversial policies in the early 1980s.

Success for Thatcher would have meant leaving Britain with a smaller state bureaucracy, less government interference in people's lives, less government spending and a cheaper tax bill for the British public. She attempted to achieve this by promoting 'efficiency' in administration, privatisation of state-owned assets and 'contracting out' of government services. Her track record in government demonstrates success in some areas but failure in others. Historians have disagreed about the balance of success and failure in this area.

**KEY TERM**

**Neo-liberal**
Neo-liberals believe that the free market is better at allocating goods and resources than the state. They recommend that the state does not interfere in the economy or in people's lives; they argue that government regulations should be relaxed, state services replaced by private provision and state assets sold off.

## The civil service

Thatcher had some success in slimming down the civil service. With 732,000 civil servants in 1980, Britain had three times as many bureaucrats as comparable nations. Thatcher used business-minded colleagues and advisers brought in from outside government to help her achieve the desired reduction. As Environment Minister (1979–83), Michael Heseltine introduced the Management Information System for Ministers (MINIS). This allowed him to more closely monitor the cost and responsibilities of civil servants. Where inefficiencies were uncovered, job losses followed: one in four workers at the Environment Ministry was sacked in just three years. Thatcher abolished the Civil Service Department in 1981. This had existed to supervise and protect its members, but Thatcher saw it as a trade union in all but name.

MINIS was rolled out to other ministries under the Financial Management Initiative. By 1988, 22.5 percent of civil servants had been sacked, saving an estimated £1 billion. The 'Next Steps' report that year promoted a less centralised civil service and the rise of more flexible 'agencies' that would work with the private sector to deliver services. By 1991, there were 57 such agencies, something that historian Brian Harrison considers 'the most substantial revolution within the civil service since the 1850s'. By 1997, 76 percent of civil servants worked in almost 100 different agencies; they remain the key way in which public services are delivered. Examples of these agencies included the Benefits Agency (for the Department of Social Security), the Employment Service Agency (for the Department of Education and Employment) and the Prison Service (for the Home Office).

## Local government

Thatcher not only wanted to slim down local government, but to reduce its independence from central government. The Local Government Act (1985) enabled her to abolish the councils she found to be most troublesome: the Greater London Council and six other metropolitan councils were dissolved. Although this represented increased central government interference, she was more concerned by the 'capture' of some local councils by 'irresponsible' left-wingers who rejected her policies. She cut central government payments (from 60 to 49 percent of funding) and, following council attempts to plug the funding gap by raising local rates, introduced rate 'caps' on 18 councils (Rates Act 1984).

SOURCE 2 Michael Heseltine (second from the left), Margaret Thatcher (centre) and Prime Minister John Major (right) at the Conservative Party conference in 1995. Heseltine was instrumental in the drive for efficiency in the civil service, although he became a rival to Thatcher and stood against her in the leadership contest in 1990.

Local rates were only paid by people who owned or rented property of a certain value; many poorer people did not have to pay them at all. Thatcher hated the fact that some councils could promise ever more generous provision of benefits and services to people who would not have to pay for them. She felt that the capping of local rates was at the heart of what she was trying to accomplish: making people responsible citizens rather than lazy dependants.

Thatcher tried to widen a sense of financial responsibility through the introduction of a 'Community Charge' (1989 in Scotland, 1990 in England and Wales). The 'poll tax' (as it quickly became known) would be based on individuals rather than the value of property. As the charge was the same for everyone, the poor paid a higher percentage of their income than the rich. This was hugely unpopular and mass protests erupted when the tax was rolled out in 1990. The Conservatives were forced to abandon the tax and introduce a revised council tax linked to property values instead.

Thatcher used the example of innovative Conservative councils, such as Wandsworth in London, to promote greater efficiency through the 'contracting out' of council services. This meant that private firms were encouraged to bid for contracts to supply services such as rubbish collection. By 1985, staff numbers had fallen by one-third in Wandsworth; nationally, the total number of local government employees fell from 2.5 to 2.1 million between 1979 and 1995.

Thatcher used a number of methods to detach individuals from reliance on local government. The measure that had the greatest impact was the Housing Act of 1980. This gave some people the 'Right to Buy': it enabled those who had lived in a council house for three or more years to buy their house from the council. The idea was not only to cut council spending on property maintenance, but to promote a sense of pride and responsibility through independent ownership. It was a hugely popular reform: 204,000 council houses were bought in 1982–83 alone and home ownership rose from 55 to 63 percent between 1979 and 1990. While these individuals made substantial personal gains from property price increases, the lack of availability of council houses made it harder and more expensive for councils to house the poorest in society by 1997.

## The National Health Service

Thatcher would have loved to slash the cost and inefficiency of the NHS in the same way she did with the civil service, breaking up the huge state structure and introducing elements of choice and competition. Her preferred solution to the spiralling cost of the NHS would have been to abolish tax funding entirely and enforce private health insurance. However, while the public did not notice the 'revolution' in government bureaucracy, they would certainly have noticed cuts or 'contracting out' in healthcare. The vast majority of the British public approved of the NHS's provision of free, expert care to those in need regardless of wealth or income; for this reason, Thatcher had to tread far more cautiously than she would have instinctively liked. Between 1980 and 1987, spending on the NHS rose by 60 percent; as a percentage of total government spending, the NHS's share rose from 12 to 15 percent between 1979 and 1996.

Her third election victory in 1987 gave Thatcher the confidence to back more radical proposals for NHS reform. The 1989 White Paper 'Working for Patients' called for the creation of an 'internal market' where health authorities would purchase healthcare services from hospital trusts. These trusts would be run by professional managers rather than doctors to ensure performance targets were hit and waste reduced. The idea was that better providers would attract more demand (from GPs) and so success would be rewarded with higher funding. Although the internal market was not introduced until after Thatcher's fall from power in 1990, the introduction of free-market elements into the NHS was very much in line with her overall aims.

The reforms proved to be highly unpopular with doctors and did not deliver cost savings in the way Thatcher had anticipated: while the overall cost of the NHS rose by almost 25 percent between 1985 and 1991, the money spent on NHS managers increased from £25.7 million to £383.8 million. By 1996, 34 NHS trusts were in debt; attempts to cut costs impacted upon the quality of care for non-emergency patients (for example, the loss of two percent of hospital beds between 1990 and 1994). The requirement to 'meet targets' led to demoralisation among doctors and nurses who felt they spent less time caring for patients in order to satisfy managers without medical training.

Although spending on the NHS rose at a slower rate than under previous governments, Thatcher was unable to roll back government provision of healthcare. While numbers of people with private health insurance grew from around 500,000 in 1955 to 6.6 million in 1990, only one percent of manual workers had private cover. The vast majority of the British people continued to depend on the state-provided healthcare that they regarded as the 'jewel in the crown' of welfare provision.

## Education

As with healthcare, the most radical reforms to education came after 1987. Thatcher wanted to raise educational standards and deliver more value for money. She felt that the teaching profession and Local Education Authorities (LEAs) were hostile to the measures required to fulfil these aims; she thought that they were engaged in a conspiracy to protect inadequate teachers and promote 'soft', 'child-centred' learning rather than measurable academic success. Keith Joseph, Education Minister 1981–86, began the process of raising standards and creating a national curriculum by merging the old Certificate of Secondary Education and O-Level into a single GCSE. He was hugely interested in education and insisted on personally approving the new syllabuses before they could be taught in schools. The plans were announced in 1984 and the new courses were first taught in 1986 and examined in 1988.

The 1988 Education Act of his successor, Kenneth Baker, built on Joseph's legacy by imposing a National Curriculum, compulsory for all apart from private schools, and new methods of assessment at several 'Key Stages', including the GCSE examination at the end of Key Stage 4. Exam results formed the basis for league tables, which aimed to empower parents to select better schools for their children and drive up standards. 'Better' schools were quickly oversubscribed and, as demand for housing within such schools' catchment areas increased, poorer families were priced out and their children forced to attend 'worse' schools. The Act also allowed schools to become grant-maintained schools, directly funded by central government; this meant headteachers and governors could control budgets and spending rather than the LEA. Although this aspect of the Act increased the independence of the 1,200 schools (19 percent of all secondary schools) that became grant-maintained, the introduction of a National Curriculum meant that, overall, Thatcher's preferred educational reforms led to an increase in central government interference in this area.

EXTRACT

From Simon Jenkins's book, *Thatcher & Sons – a Revolution in Three Acts* (2006). Jenkins is a journalist who mainly writes for the left-of-centre daily newspaper the *Guardian*.

Attention thus fastened on a group of services whose leadership was at some remove from the heart of government, notably the health service, housing, schools and universities, urban renewal and local government. In most democracies these activities were either constitutionally protected or were regional or municipal in responsibility... To Thatcher these were just the services most afflicted by socialism, since they were in the grip of such incorrigibly socialist institutions as elected local councils and trade unions. They had to be purged by being brought within the penumbra [shadow] of her office... Private sector disciplines were a success in local government... But she brought to public service ceaseless upheaval, blood-letting and top-down reorganisation. This was informed not by public inquiry or consensus but by consultancy out of ideology. The outcome was always contentious. Almost all the public services... never settled down under later prime ministers. They have remained at the top of the league table of public dissatisfaction ever since, demanding ever more money with no diminution of central control.

EXTRACT

From Shirley Letwin's book, *The Anatomy of Thatcherism* (1992). Letwin had been taught by Friedrich von Hayek at the University of Chicago and worked for a Conservative think-tank.

The legislation [on trade unions] was designed to remove obstacles to the thriving of Britain and to the freedom needed by individuals to be independent, efficient and honest workmen... In 1979, socialism, in the sense of dependency of the individual upon the state in a series of vital areas including industry, education, health and housing, was regarded by Britons as 'here to stay'... When Mrs Thatcher proclaimed the need to drive back the tide of socialism, to let freedom of choice and the vigorous virtues flourish, in short to change the course of British history, few if any commentators believed she could do it... Next to the trade unions, Thatcherism's greatest bugbear has been 'local government'. The picture of the Thatcherite relationship to local councils is usually painted in vivid colours: Mrs Thatcher is portrayed as a 'centralist' dictator mounting an all-out attack on ancient bastions of local autonomy and liberty... The reason why the usual picture of the relationship between the Thatcher Government and local government poses such problems is that it is a radically false picture. Local government was not an ancient bastion of local autonomy and liberty; and the Thatcher Government's attack on it was the very opposite of an attempt to centralize.

## Conclusion

Thatcher slimmed down the size of the state where this was politically possible, but failed to cut overall government spending: this made up 43 percent of the value of all wealth produced in Britain in 1977–78, 47 percent in 1983–84 and 39 percent in 1988–89. By 1994, it had risen again to 44 percent. The total tax bill also rose throughout Thatcher's time in office, from 38.5 percent of total wealth produced in 1979 to almost 41 percent in 1990; the tax on an average person rose from 31 to 37 percent of their income.

ACTIVITY
KNOWLEDGE CHECK

**State intervention and the public sector**

1. What were Thatcher's views on the role of the state?
2. In what way did the Thatcher government attempt to make local government and public services more efficient?
3. Create a table with two columns (one for successes and one for failures) and use it to evaluate how far the aims of the Thatcher government were achieved.

Interpretations (3a)

### Differing accounts

Carefully read Extracts 4 and 5, which are both historical interpretations of Thatcher's success in 'rolling back' the state. After you have read them, answer these questions:

1 For each extract, summarise the author's views on:

a) Thatcher's aims and attitudes

b) the success of her attempts to 'roll back' the public sector

c) the popularity of her policies.

2 Use your notes and knowledge to give evidence that supports or challenges each interpretation.

3 In pairs, discuss which interpretation of Thatcher's attempts to 'roll back' the public sector seems the most convincing based on the available evidence.

4 Make a note of any issues that made it difficult to compare the two interpretations directly.

5 Challenge: find another historical interpretation of Thatcher's attempts to 'roll back' the public sector and compare this view to the views you have already explored.

### AS Level Exam-Style Question Section C

***Study Extracts 4 and 5 before you answer this question.***

Historians have different views about the impact on Britain of Thatcher's governments in the years 1979–97. Analyse and evaluate the extracts and use your knowledge of the issues to explain your answer to the following question.

How far do you agree with the view that the role of the state was reduced in the years 1979–97? (20 marks)

**Tip**

*Most content for this question will be covered in the section on public services, but there is some scope for referring to economic policies such as privatisation.*

### A Level Exam-Style Question Section C

***Study Extracts 4 and 5 before you answer this question.***

In the light of differing interpretations, how convincing do you find the view that in the years 1979–89, Conservative governments succeeded in giving 'freedom of choice' (Extract 5, line 5) to the British people? (20 marks)

To explain your answer, analyse and evaluate both extracts, using your own knowledge of the issues.

**Tip**

*The focus of this question is relatively narrow, and should incorporate a contextualised discussion of the impact of Thatcherism on public services.*

# HOW FAR DID POLITICAL AND SOCIAL DIVISION WITHIN BRITAIN CHANGE, 1979-97?

## Political division

### Regional divisions

Apart from her impact on the Conservative and Labour Party (see below), Thatcher had some important effects on the nature of British politics more generally. In most cases these are far from what she would have liked and must be considered as unintended consequences of her time in power. The first division that she helped to accelerate was regional: the Conservatives did far better in the south and east of England and lost support in the north of England, Scotland and Wales. While the Conservatives had won 21 out of 71 available Scottish seats in 1979, this had fallen to ten by 1987;

in 1997, the party was wiped out in Scotland. Scottish and Welsh nationalism gained a boost from the local reaction against the decline of their traditional industries. This movement accelerated with **devolution** under New Labour, something to which Thatcher was utterly opposed.

### Special advisers and career politicians

Thatcher accelerated an earlier trend to use outside advisers rather than career civil servants for policy advice. This continued in the post-Thatcher Conservative governments and especially under New Labour. Some political analysts have linked the fall in voter turn-out to a perception that the votes cast will not change the nature of government. The share of votes for the two main parties also fell. A political divide can be said to have opened up between the career politicians in London and the rest of the country. The number of MPs with a university degree rose from 40 percent in the period 1918–45 to 75 percent in 2010. The fraction of Labour MPs from a manual worker background was around one-third in 1945, declining to one in ten in 2010. The number of MPs from all parties who come from a legal background has also declined since 1979, with more than 70 falling into this category in 1974, diminishing to less than 30 in 1997 (although the number increased significantly at the 2010 election).

Perhaps the most significant statistic is that the number of MPs who have previously worked for political organisations or for politicians increased from three percent in 1979 to 14 percent in 2010. The Conservative Party in the Thatcher years changed the rules of political organisation and other parties had to change their approach in order to succeed.

### Divisions between left and right

The Thatcher years had a profound effect on party development, as discussed in the final section below, but a more general ideological battle was also initiated, which redefined what right- and left-wing meant. Despite Tony Blair adopting many Thatcherite ideas in his attempt to establish a 'third way' in politics between neo-liberal economics and socialism, the battle for the **centre ground** shifted right and has broadly stayed the same ever since.

The post-war consensus (1945–79) was founded on moderate socialist principles. Policies associated with Attlee's Labour government, such as the NHS, state intervention in the economy, progressive taxation and a welfare state, were all accepted by the Conservative governments in power between 1951 and 1964. Both Wilson (Labour) and Heath (Conservative), the titans of British politics in the 1960s and 1970s, were essentially pro-European **centrist** politicians who agreed with many of these principles. With the advent of Thatcherism, many Conservative politicians inevitably lurched to the right, towards free markets and away from state planning, towards traditional family values and away from a liberal attitude towards social reform. The centre ground shifted right as the Labour Party and, to an extent, the Liberal Democrats adopted Thatcherite policies, particularly on the economy.

With a changing centre ground, more radical left-wing ideas that had once been current in the relative mainstream, such as those promoted by Michael Foot as Labour leader in the 1983 general election campaign, were now seen as unusual and did not garner much support in the 1990s.

### Divisions between local and national government

As part of Thatcher's objective to reduce the size of government and roll back the state, the power of local government was reduced. Since Thatcher's resignation in 1996, local government has continued its decline. After its election victory in 1997, Labour continued to cap local spending and allowed local government to raise only 30 percent of its own funding.

Thatcher's distaste for the left meant that Labour-controlled councils were an inevitable target for local government cuts, and many northern councils controlled by Labour saw themselves as warriors against Thatcher's government in the 1980s. Economic powers taken away from local councils in Merseyside and London were replaced by the introduction of development corporations, headed by central government. This style of urban regeneration directed by national government has been influential ever since, and the redevelopment projects in London and Liverpool are now seen as effective.

Thatcher's government also moved to abolish the six metropolitan county councils and the Greater London Council (GLC) in 1986. The GLC leader, Ken Livingstone, who was a major figure on the left of the Labour Party, came to embody everything that Thatcher disliked about local government.

#### KEY TERMS

**Devolution**
A process where some decision-making authority is given over from central government to the Scottish Parliament, the Welsh and Northern Irish Assemblies, and the Greater London Authority.

**Centre ground**
The space in the political spectrum that is accepted as neither left- nor right-wing.

**Centrist**
A person who holds moderate political views.

## Social division

### The gap between rich and poor

Thatcher is often criticised for widening the gap between the richest and poorest sections of British society. A whole host of social problems, from mental illness to obesity, can be directly linked to this gap in wealth and income. A number of Thatcher's policies benefited the wealthy and discriminated against the poor. Regressive taxes took a far higher percentage of the income of the poor for the state. Privatisation benefited the more financially astute middle and upper classes more than the working classes. Policies aimed at cutting inflation not only cut spending on the poor but fuelled unemployment predominantly among manufacturing workers. Other effects of the Thatcher years that increased social divisions include the following:

- Uneven benefits from cuts in income tax. In 1989 the bottom ten percent of earners paid £400 million less in income tax than they did in 1979, whereas the top ten percent of earners paid £9.3 *billion* less in income tax.
- In 1974, those in the top ten percent received 25 percent of all post-tax income. In 1997, this had increased to 35.2 percent.
- By reducing welfare payments, Supplementary Benefit (later called Income Support) was equivalent to 53 percent of average earnings in 1987, down from 61 percent in 1978.
- The proportion of pensioners living below the poverty line increased from 13 percent to 43 percent.
- Cuts to housing benefit, as explained in Extract 6, also led to social divisions.

EXTRACT

From Pete Dorey, 'A farewell to alms: Thatcherism's legacy of inequality', in *British Politics* Vol. 10 (2015).

Housing Benefit was reduced for those whose employment was sufficiently low-paid to render them eligible for assistance with their rent, the precise amount being determined by a formula based on post-tax earnings and weekly rent: the lower the claimant's wage and the higher his/her rent (within reason), the more Housing Benefit s/he could claim. By altering the formula, Ministers could reduce the amount actually paid to each claimant towards their rent, whereupon s/he would either have to pay more out of their net pay, thus leaving them with less money for food, fuel or clothing for their family, or move to cheaper, invariably less salubrious [decent], accommodation.

While the income of the richest ten percent increased by 61 percent between 1979 and 1992, the poorest ten percent saw a reduction of 18 percent in the same period. While the former group held 20.6 percent of UK wealth in 1979, and the latter 4.3 percent, by 1991 these figures had changed to 26.1 and 2.9 percent respectively. A 2010 government report found that the income of top earners increased from three times that of low earners in the late 1970s to four times that of low earners in the early 1990s; this income gap has continued to widen since the 1990s. The middle classes became increasingly divided over Thatcher: although they benefited from rising incomes, many objected to her attack on the public sector. 55 percent of middle-class people voted Conservative in 1987 – fewer than at any time since 1918.

### Regional divisions

Regional divisions in wealth also increased under Thatcher: London and the south-east got richer and became more productive than the north-east and north-west, where productivity actually declined. Political commentators and historians often point out the north–south divide that was created as a result of Thatcher's policies. Thatcher did try to address this problem through 'enterprise zones': these were deprived areas where private firms received government funds to move in and generate growth. This did lead to some impressive urban renewal projects, such as the Albert Docks in Liverpool and the waterfront in Newcastle, but had limited wider success.

The number of economically inactive people (particularly men) in former industrial areas continued to increase between 1990 and 1997, and by 2001 one in five men in the former coalfields were unemployed, up from one in ten in 1981. Some areas fared better at job creation than others in the 1990s, with Yorkshire, South Derbyshire and North Warwickshire bouncing back and South Wales struggling.

## Social divisions in Wales: a case study

Despite some investment in areas that had gone into decline, social divisions were most obvious in former mining towns. South Wales in particular suffered as a result in the decline of the industry. 73,000 people were unemployed in Wales in 1979, rising to 166,000 in 1986. Although there was already a trend in mines closing before Thatcher came to power (the number of those employed in deep mining reduced from 34,000 in 1974 to 28,000 in 1980), just 3,000 people were working in deep mining in Wales by 1990. Across the country as a whole, 90 percent of the workforce was lost. Social problems were created by this decline, and homelessness and drug use became prevalent in former mining towns: 1,308 drug offences were recorded in Wales in 1990, compared with 605 in 1979.

Despite the social divisions created by the decline in industry, Wales, like the rest of the UK, experienced economic growth in other areas to the benefit of ordinary people. Spending on the NHS in Wales increased, from just over £500 million in 1979 to £1.5 billion in 1990. **GDP** per person increased from £7,072 to £20,306 in the same period, and the number of school-leavers seeking further education or training increased from 20 to 47 percent between 1974 and 1991.

**KEY TERM**

**Gross Domestic Product (GDP)**
This is the total value of all goods and services produced within a country's borders over a certain time period, usually one year. It is a common shorthand for gauging the size and health of an economy.

**SOURCE 3** The high street in the former mining town of Blaenavon, South Wales, in a rundown state with boarded-up shops, before a regeneration project was started (1998).

EXTRACT 7

From Norman Lowe, *Mastering Modern British History* (2009). Lowe was head of history at a school in Lancashire for 20 years before becoming a freelance writer and lecturer.

The gap between the rich and poor widened. Successive income tax reductions, particularly in 1988, benefitted the rich more than the poor: the richest 20 per cent gained by almost a third, whereas the poorest 20 per cent gained only 1 per cent in income. Higher direct taxes such as VAT meant that people on low incomes had to pay the same VAT increases as those on the highest incomes, for example on commodities like petrol, and they were relatively worse off... By 1993, the gap between the highest and lowest wages was the widest since records began... Tighter regulations made it more difficult for young people to get social security benefits... With unemployment running permanently at around 3 million, it seemed that Thatcherite policies had created, or at least had been unable to prevent, the emergence of a permanent 'underclass' for whom there was no longer any role in society. And as unemployment and poverty increased, so did the crime rate.

EXTRACT 8

From centre-right newspaper *The Daily Telegraph,* 8 April 2013.

She was a leader who wrenched this nation from the path of demoralisation, diminishment and decline so decisively, so self-evidently successfully, that her victory seems, in hindsight, to be almost an inevitability... Her chief accomplishment was to free British business, not least from the control of the unions. In every part of the economy, she sought to transfer the initiative from the state to the people. Managers were given the right to manage; taxes were cut to shift the balance of spending and encourage wealth creation; the working classes were encouraged to become shareholders and homeowners; the privatisation of nationalised industry opened up competition and created new avenues for investment. In some areas, the process of adjustment from a closed, state-dominated, heavy-industry-based economy to a more open, consumer-centric and entrepreneurial culture was traumatic. But that was not because the changes were unnecessary, but because they had been so long delayed. As a result of Lady Thatcher's efforts, Britain is not only immeasurably richer, but more purely democratic, in that she gave us the freedom to vote with our wallets, where others cared only for raiding them.

THINKING HISTORICALLY

## Interpretations (4b)

**Method is everything**

**Bad history**
- Based on gut feeling
- Argument does not progress logically
- No supporting evidence

**Extract 1**
*An except from a history book with quotes making a point about an event*

**Good history**
- Based on an interpretation of evidence
- Argument progresses logically
- Evidence deployed to support argument

Historical writing can reveal much about the methods by which it was constructed. Read Extracts 7 and 8 and answer the questions below.

Work in pairs.

1 Look carefully at the 'spectrum of methodology'.

a) Where would you place each source on the spectrum of historical practice?

b) What evidence would you use to support your choice?

2 Look at Extract 8. How would you change it to make it the same quality of historical writing as Extract 7?

3 Use a dictionary. Explain the following words in their relation to historical writing: substantiation, deduction, inference, cross-reference.

4 How important is it that historians understand and evaluate the methods used by other historians?

**AS Level Exam-Style Question Section C**

***Study Extracts 7 and 8 before you answer this question.***

Historians have different views about the impact on Britain of Thatcher's governments in the years 1979–97. Analyse and evaluate the extracts and use your knowledge of the issues to explain your answer to the following question.

How far do you agree with the view that deep divisions in society were created by the policies of the Thatcher governments (1979–90)? (20 marks)

**Tip**

*Much of the content for inclusion in this answer can be found in the section on social divisions above, but don't forget to include content from the sections on the economy and the state, as they both had a severe impact on social divisions.*

**Note**

*The question asks you to analyse two opposing views, of one historian and one newspaper journalist. In the actual examination, both extracts would be written by historians.*

**ACTIVITY**
**KNOWLEDGE CHECK**

**Changes in political and social division**

1 What sorts of political divisions were created in the Thatcher years? Which are still with us today?

2 In what ways did the gap between rich and poor widen?

3 Why do political commentators talk about the creation of a north-south divide when discussing the Thatcher years?

# WHAT WERE THE EFFECTS OF THATCHERISM ON POLITICS AND PARTY DEVELOPMENT?

## The Conservative Party

### The impact of Thatcher's approach to politics

The Conservative Party had already begun to change before Thatcher rose to the leadership of the Party in 1975. As a former grammar school boy, Edward Heath had moved the Party away from the domination of elite aristocrats such as Macmillan and Douglas-Home. He tried to modernise the Party and to steer it rightwards but ended up returning to the familiar post-war consensus. Heath had promised to implement free-market policies, including no government interference in setting prices and wage rises, and no bailing out of 'lame duck' industries in financial trouble. When inflation hit 15 percent in 1971, Heath was forced to retreat back to the 'prices and incomes' policy of the previous prime minister, Harold Wilson, whereby the government kept a close eye on inflation and would step in to limit price and wage rises where necessary. When Rolls Royce and the Upper Clyde shipbuilders came close to collapse, Heath decided to bail them out with public money, a complete reversal of his original policy. (For more on the Heath government see Chapter 1.)

Although Thatcher and other right-wing Conservatives hated Heath's U-turn, they were careful not to criticise him before 1974 to avoid splitting the party. Once Thatcher became leader she was aware that her neo-liberal views were a minority taste in 1975, fiercely supported by a few think-tanks but given a cool reception by a party that traditionally preferred pragmatism to radical political or economic theory. She was careful not to alienate the more traditional 'one nation' Conservatives (whom she referred to as 'wets') and enlisted one 'wet', the highly respected William Whitelaw, to help keep them on side (she later said, without a hint of humour, that 'every prime minister needs a Willie').

However, her caution had limits: she set out to save Britain from 'creeping socialism' and needed the Conservatives to take the fight to Labour rather than continue to court consensus. By 1976, she was already claiming to have 'changed everything' about the Conservative Party. She saw herself as a 'conviction politician', a champion of 'middle-class values' and wanted to inject some vigour and self-belief into the Conservatives. A month before the May 1979 general election, she roused the Party faithful by saying, 'the Old Testament Prophets did not say "Brothers, I want a consensus." They said:

"This is my faith, this is what I passionately believe. If you believe it too, then come with me."' Her faith, as outlined above, was founded on free-market liberalism, coupled with a strong sense of patriotism. She rapidly promoted 'dries', men like Norman Tebbit and Nigel Lawson, who loyally shared her faith and, especially after 1983, began to shuffle 'wets' like Ian Gilmour and Francis Pym out of the cabinet.

Thatcher was careful not to ignore Conservative backbenchers (of which Heath had been guilty) or the rank-and-file party members; indeed, on occasions where she faced opposition from her cabinet or the parliamentary party, she was adept at seeking out and securing wider support for her course of action. She used her press secretary, Sir Bernard Ingham, to leak information to newspapers that would damage the reputation of ministers who opposed her. Thatcher loved party conferences and saw them as a valuable annual opportunity to reaffirm her strong connection to the views of ordinary members. Some commentators saw her performances, followed by long standing ovations, as symptomatic of the growing Americanisation of British politics.

### New innovations and changing party make-up

One American innovation that was swiftly adopted by the Conservatives was the use of computers to target and contact potential voters in marginal constituencies. Party Chairman Cecil Parkinson organised a direct mail campaign that reached 500,000 voters before the 1983 general election. The social make-up of the Conservative Party changed more rapidly under Thatcher than in the years before 1979. Although most MPs still went to university, the Party became less 'posh'. The proportion of MPs educated at public schools dropped from 75 to 66 percent between 1974 and 1987. There were more self-made businessmen and fewer men of inherited wealth, more Thatcherites and fewer 'one nation' Conservatives. This trend persisted into the 1990s and beyond.

Men have been the clear focus of the paragraph above and with good reason: Thatcher is fairly accused of doing little to advance women in politics. During her time as prime minister, the number of female MPs only increased from 19 to 41 (and of these only eight and 17 respectively were Conservative MPs). She believed that merit alone should lead to a successful political career and was opposed to any form of positive discrimination in favour of women.

Thatcher's determination to drive forward with policies she believed to be right ultimately led to her downfall in November 1990. By then, she had alienated a long list of Conservatives, '**big beasts**' who were unhappy at being ignored or even rebuked in cabinet. Two of the most senior to be '**handbagged**' were Chancellor Nigel Lawson, who resigned in October 1989 when Thatcher refused to consider linking the value of the pound to the value of the Deutschmark, and Deputy Prime Minister Geoffrey Howe, who resigned in November 1990 over her resistance to further integration with the European Economic Community.

**KEY TERMS**

**Big Beast**
A term used to describe an MP who is so senior and influential that it is very difficult to keep him out of the cabinet. Big beasts under Thatcher included Nigel Lawson, Geoffrey Howe, Norman Tebbit, Michael Heseltine, Douglas Hurd and John Major.

**Handbag**
To crush a person or their ideas with a forceful verbal attack. A term coined by Conservative MP Julian Critchley to describe Thatcher's ministerial style in cabinet meetings. Thatcher famously always carried a handbag in public.

**SOURCE**

An extract from Geoffrey Howe's resignation speech in the House of Commons on 1 November 1990.

Reporting to this House, my Right Honourable Friend [Thatcher] almost casually remarked that she did not think that many people would want to use... a Common Currency. It was remarkable - indeed, it was tragic - to hear... her assert that the whole idea might be open for consideration only by future generations... How on earth are the Chancellor and the Governor of the Bank of England... be taken as serious participants in the debate against this background noise? I believe that the Chancellor and Governor are cricketing enthusiasts ... it is rather like sending your opening batsmen out to the crease only for them to find, the moment the first balls are bowled, that their bats have been broken by the team captain... I have done what I believe to be right for my party and my country. The time has come for others to consider their own response to the tragic conflict of loyalties [to Thatcher and the country] with which I have myself wrestled for perhaps too long.

### The Conservatives after Thatcher

These resignations, together with the unpopularity of the Poll Tax, led to a revolt against Thatcher by a cabinet that feared she would lose them the next election. Thatcher approved of her successor, John Major, because she thought him the most likely of the potential candidates to maintain her legacy. Major's government continued with many of Thatcher's policies, including:

- the privatisation of British Rail in 1994–97

- the extension of trade union legislation with the passing of the Trade Union and Labour Relations (Consolidation) Act of 1992
- a commitment to lower direct taxation: the basic income tax was reduced from 25 percent to 23 percent in 1997
- a preference for indirect taxation, demonstrated when Major's Chancellor, Norman Lamont, increased VAT from 15 percent to 17.5 percent in 1991. The Conservative Party's continued commitment to indirect taxation was demonstrated again when Chancellor George Osborne raised it again to 20 percent in 2010.

While Major did maintain privatisation and low taxation, Thatcher was bitterly disappointed by his moves to promote closer European integration. Rows within the party over Europe, and regular reports of 'sleaze' among leading Conservatives, contributed to a disastrous defeat in the 1997 general election: they gained only 165 seats compared to Labour's 419. Some commentators saw this result as not only a reaction to party problems but also to a more general rejection of Thatcher's legacy. Overall though, the majority of the Party had been converted to Thatcherism, and this commitment to her ideology was made clear when William Hague, who idolised Thatcher as a teenager, became leader in 1997.

## The Labour Party

### Why did the Labour Party need to change?

By challenging 'creeping socialism' so aggressively and so successfully, Thatcher forced the Labour Party to carry out some painful readjustments to make itself electable. It took a disastrous performance in the 1983 general election, when it gained just 28 percent of the vote, before the lessons started to sink in. Labour had suffered from the decline of their traditional northern industrial heartland before Thatcher came to power; her attack on manufacturing in the early 1980s, and closure of coal mines after 1984, accelerated this erosion of 'natural' Labour supporters: working-class union members who would naturally gravitate towards socialism.

At the same time, disillusionment with Labour's record under Wilson and Callaghan in the 1970s led to the growth of extra-parliamentary Labour activism: demonstrations, protests and, through the trade unions, strikes. The popular impression of a leftward lurch of the Party by the early 1980s was typified by Militant Tendency, a group of extreme left-wingers who gained control of the Liverpool branch of the Party. They were attacked in the right-wing press as the 'loony left'. Many moderate Labour supporters grew concerned at this development and switched allegiance to a new centrist party launched in 1981: the Social Democratic Party (SDP).

### Kinnock's reforms, 1983–92

The split between Labour and the Social Democrats made it harder for moderates who remained with Labour to tackle the left-wing of the party. Neil Kinnock, who replaced Michael Foot as Party leader in 1983, had to take action against Militant Tendency and unite the party if Labour were ever to regain power. Although he made some impressive speeches against them in 1985, Kinnock was substantially aided in his fight by Thatcher. By capping local rates, disbanding certain local authorities, the privatisation of state industries and limiting trade union power, she undermined the bases of far-left power within the Labour movement. Kinnock's modernising reforms consisted of the following:

- Unilateral nuclear disarmament was rejected as Labour Party policy.
- He moved Labour to a more pro-Europe stance.
- In 1988, trade unions lost the casting vote on the selection of parliamentary candidates.
- In 1989, the Party dropped its support for union closed-shop practice.

Kinnock stood down after the 1992 Conservative election victory, and was succeeded by John Smith, who was a favourite with MPs and ordinary Labour Party members alike. Smith had little time to build on Kinnock's reforms, however, before he died prematurely in 1994. His successor, Tony Blair, would complete the turnaround in Labour policy started by Kinnock.

SOURCE 5

Tony Blair shakes hands with supporters after winning the 1997 general election. To the right of the photograph is Peter Mandelson, often referred to as one of the architects of New Labour and a proponent of the Thatcherite beliefs that brought Labour back to power.

## Tony Blair and New Labour

When Tony Blair became Labour leader in 1994, he recognised that the Party needed to continue the move away from traditional working-class and trade union support started by Kinnock in order to reach out to the growing number of middle-class voters, the sort who had abandoned the Party in the early 1980s. In 1994, Blair announced that Clause IV of the party constitution, which called for the 'common ownership of the means of production and exchange', would be replaced with a less committal statement; the Party formally embraced free-market policies. In the same year, he rebranded the Party 'New Labour' to make clear to British voters the different direction it had taken since the mid-1980s. The extent to which New Labour, and its key leaders (such as Tony Blair and Gordon Brown), were the real inheritors of Thatcherism has been disputed by political commentators. While some have emphasised their willingness to work with the free market, others have pointed out how New Labour, rather than worrying about creating dependency, spent billions of pounds on trying to help the poorest in society. The commitment of New Labour to Thatcher's ideas is summed up by the following:

- The complete rejection of any commitment to nationalisation.
- The party would aim to continue Thatcher's policy of low direct taxation.
- Big business would be embraced and free markets allowed to flourish.

- There would be no reversal of the anti-trade union laws passed under Thatcher and Major.
- Issues of class politics would no longer be the focus of the Party.

Despite these Thatcherite objectives, New Labour attempted to promote 'inclusiveness' in the following ways:

- There was an emphasis on Labour's commitment to social justice in an attempt to close the gap between rich and poor. The Party aimed to promote an equal distribution of opportunities for everyone, in contrast with the Old Labour commitment to more equal distribution of wealth.
- The Party was committed to a minimum wage, which it introduced in 1998.
- There was massive investment in education in order to create equal opportunities.

**ACTIVITY**
**KNOWLEDGE CHECK**

**Thatcher and the Labour Party**

1 How did the reforms of Blair and Kinnock show a commitment to Thatcherism?

2 Why was Blair not a complete Thatcherite?

## Other parties

### The SDP and the Liberal Party

With the increasing influence of the far left in the Labour Party in the late 1970s and early 1980s, a number of Labour MPs broke away to form the new Social Democratic Party in 1981. The leading figures, known as the 'gang of four', were Roy Jenkins, David Owen, Shirley Williams and William Rodgers. They believed that, in a polarised political climate, with Thatcher representing the right and Foot representing the left, there was a need for a centre-left party. Ironically, many of their beliefs would later be satisfied by the creation of New Labour.

The SDP hoped to claim new members from the Labour Party, but also some disaffected Conservatives unhappy with the direction of the party under Thatcher. In order to mount a serious challenge to the status quo, the SDP allied with the Liberal Party for the 1983 election, where the alliance gained a quarter of the popular votes (but just 23 seats due to the first past the post system). The SDP were unable to capitalise on their early success and formally merged with the Liberals in 1988, to form the Liberal Democrats. Although the Liberal Democrats have always been socially liberal and pro-European, some Thatcherite influence can be seen in the commitment of many of their MPs to free-market principles and low taxation.

### Regional nationalist parties

The realignment of the economy in the Thatcher years hit Wales and Scotland particularly hard. Coal mining was practised in both regions and heavy industries such as shipbuilding were the backbone of the Scottish economy. The Scottish Nationalist Party (SNP) was founded in 1934 and called for greater powers (and later full independence) to be given to Scotland. They performed badly at the 1979, 1983 and 1987 elections but when Thatcher's government decided to use Scotland to trial the Poll Tax before introducing it in other parts of the United Kingdom, existing anti-Thatcher feeling reached a new peak. The Thatcher government was seen as anti-Scottish and although an SNP breakthrough did not materialise until the 2015 general election, they began to make inroads that would result in Scotland voting for devolution and its own parliament in 1997.

The Welsh Nationalist Party, Plaid Cymru, was formed in 1925 and, like the SNP, is generally seen to be on the left of the political spectrum. With increasing dissatisfaction with Thatcher's policies, the Conservative Party went into decline in the late 1980s. This decline helped Labour more than any other party, but Plaid Cymru were able to secure a referendum under New Labour that created the Welsh Assembly.

EXTRACT 9

From Bob Jessop's article, 'Margaret Thatcher and Thatcherism: Dead but not buried', published in the academic journal *British Politics* in 2015.

Margaret Thatcher is widely reputed to have opined, possibly more than once and perhaps mischievously, that her big political legacy was Tony Blair and New Labour. This initially surprising claim can be understood in terms of significant continuities between Thatcherism and the New Labour project. These include... Liberalisation to promote the free-market, deregulation, privatisation, introduction of the state in the residual state sector, reductions in direct taxation, internationalisation to boost the free flow of goods and services... These policies continued under New Labour, whose Blairite wing was also enchanted with and by entrepreneurs, business leaders and the business community more generally. These forces enjoyed privileged access to the Labour Government, playing a key role in policy advice and evaluation, securing critical positions in an increasing range of public-private partnerships, and providing lucrative employment and consultancies when ministers and civil servants retired.

EXTRACT 10

From David Rubinstein's article, 'A New Look at New Labour', published in the academic journal *Politics* in 2000. Rubinstein is a social historian who is an honorary fellow of the University of York.

The evidence is that similarities between present and past Labour governments are as important as the differences... Labour is not a business party and nothing else. No party that brings in minimum wages and lightens, even if only partly, the legal burdens placed on trade unions by the Conservatives, can be so described... In essentials the party's policies have not changed... Under Blair the party's tone has certainly changed. It has changed because Britain is no longer a society with a few wealthy people and a mass of poor ones, in which different social classes inhabit different worlds. Higher incomes, the loss of heavy industry, improved access to higher education, near-universal possession of consumer durables, the influence of the media and other factors have done their work, leading to more sweeping social changes than in any other period of similar length in British history... British Labour governments in the past were composed predominantly of moderate social reformers. So too is the Blair government. It wants to work with, not against the prevailing economic and social structure.

**A Level Exam-Style Question Section C**

***Study Extracts 9 and 10 before you answer this question.***

In the light of differing interpretations, how convincing do you find the view that the centre ground in British politics has changed as a result of the Thatcher governments (1979–90)? (20 marks)

To explain your answer, analyse and evaluate both extracts, using your own knowledge of the issues.

**Tip**

*This question requires you to explore what has happened to party development as a result of Thatcher's reforms. This can include the Labour Party, Conservative Party and others.*

**ACTIVITY**
**KNOWLEDGE CHECK**

**Politics and party development**

1 How did Thatcher's approach to politics shape the Conservative Party?

2 Why had so many senior colleagues become frustrated with Thatcher by 1990?

3 In what ways did John Major show a commitment to Thatcherism?

4 In what ways did Thatcher influence the more minor parties in Britain?

ACTIVITY
SUMMARY

### Thatcherism dinner party

Throughout this chapter you have encountered interpretations of the impact of Thatcher's governments. On separate sticky notes or pieces of paper write down as many named historians as you can find in the chapter, together with a basic description of their beliefs. In the middle of a large piece of paper, draw a dining table and arrange the historians around the table. Your aim is to ensure that historians who would broadly agree with each other sit together and also sit as far away as possible from historians they would disagree with. Provide a key to show why you have made your selections.

Categories you may wish to focus on:

- historians who have commented on Thatcher's economic policies
- historians who have commented on the role of the state
- historians who have focused on the divisions created by Thatcherism
- historians who appear to approve of Thatcher's policies
- historians who appear to disapprove of Thatcher's policies.

Now answer these questions:

1 If conflict was to arise, which two (or more) historians would be involved? Draw lines on the diagram to link historians who might disagree.

2 Where would you seat yourself? Write a paragraph to explain why.

## WIDER READING

**Books**

Harrison, B. *Finding a Role? The United Kingdom 1970-1990*, OUP (2010)

Lynch, M. *Britain 1945-2007*, Hodder (2008)

Rowe, C. and Waller, S. *The Making of Modern Britain, 1951-2007*, Nelson Thornes (2009)

Seldon, A. and Collings, D. *Britain under Thatcher*, Routledge (1999)

Stewart, G. *Bang! A History of Britain in the 1980s*, Atlantic Books (2013)

Thatcher, M. *The Path to Power* and *The Downing Street Years*, HarperPress (2012)

Turner, A. *Rejoice! Rejoice!: Britain in the 1980s* and *A Classless Society: Britain in the 1990s*, Aurum Press Ltd (2013 and 2014)

**Websites**

The Thatcher Foundation: www.margaretthatcher.org

# Preparing for your AS Level Paper 1 exam

## Advance planning

1. Draw up a timetable for your revision and try to keep to it. Spread your timetable over a number of weeks, and aim to cover four or five topics each week.
2. Spend longer on topics that you have found difficult, and revise them several times.
3. Above all, do not try to limit your revision by attempting to 'question spot'. Try to be confident about all aspects of your Paper 1 work, because this will ensure that you have a choice of questions in Sections A and B.

## Paper 1 overview:

| AS Paper 1 | Time: 2 hours 15 minutes | |
|---|---|---|
| Section A | Answer 1 question from a choice of 2 | 20 marks |
| Section B | Answer 1 question from a choice of 2 | 20 marks |
| Section C | Answer 1 compulsory interpretations question | 20 marks |
| | **Total marks =** | **60 marks** |

You should familiarise yourself with the layout of the paper by looking at the examples published by Edexcel. The questions for each section are followed by eight pages of lined paper where you should write your answer.

## Section A questions

Section A questions ask you to analyse and evaluate either cause or consequence. You should consider either the reasons for, or the results of, an event or development. You will be asked for coverage of a period of around ten years, possibly a little longer. For example, a question for Option 1F might be 'Was the involvement of President Truman the main reason for the changing status of black Americans in the years 1945–55?' Your answer should consider the reason(s) given in the question, then look at other relevant points and reach a conclusion.

## Section B questions

Section B questions cover a longer timespan than in Section A, at least one-third of the period you have studied. The questions take the form of 'How far…', 'How significant…', 'To what extent…' or 'How accurate is it to say…'. The questions can deal with historical concepts such as cause, consequence, change, continuity, similarity, difference and significance. Again, you should consider the issue raised in the question, consider other relevant issues, and then conclude with an overall judgement.

## Section C questions

There is no choice in Section C, which is concerned with the historical interpretations you have studied linked to the question 'What was the impact on Britain of Thatcher's governments in the years 1979–97?' You will be given two extracts totalling around 300 words (printed separately) and the question will take the form 'How far do you agree with the view that…?' There is no need to use source analysis skills such as making inferences or considering provenance for Section C answers. You will need to use the extracts and your own knowledge to consider the view given in the question.

## Use of time

This is an issue that you should discuss with your teachers and fellow students, but here are some suggestions for you.

1. Do not write solidly for 45 minutes on each question. For Section A and B answers you should spend a few minutes working out what the question is asking you to do, and drawing up a plan of your answer. This is especially important for Section B answers, which cover an extended period of time.
2. For Section C it is essential that you have a clear understanding of the content of each extract and the points that each extract is making. Read each extract carefully and underline important points. You could approach your answer by analysing the first extract, then the second, and then using your own knowledge before reaching an overall judgement. You might decide to spend up to ten minutes reading the extracts and drawing up your plan, and 35 minutes writing your answer.

# Preparing for your AS Level exams

## Paper 1: AS Level sample answer with comments

### Section A

These questions assess your understanding of the period in breadth. They will ask you about the content you learned about in the four key themes, and may ask about more than one theme. For these questions remember to:

- give an analytical, not a descriptive, response
- support your points with evidence
- cover the whole time period specified in the question
- come to a substantiated judgement.

*Was the rise of the Labour Party the main reason for the decline of the Liberal Party in the years 1918–30? (20 marks)*

#### Average student answer

The First World War ended in 1918 and this marked a period of great change in Britain because of the legacy of the war. It was a time when more people were able to vote – this began to include the working man and increasing numbers of women. By 1930, the Labour Party had taken over from the Liberals as an alternative government to the Conservatives. My essay will try to work out why this happened.

This is a weak opening paragraph because it does not show a clear understanding of the question – the question is not why the Labour Party took over from the Liberals, but whether the increasing strength of the Labour Party was the 'main reason' for the decline of the Liberal Party.

During the 19th century the number of men who could vote increased and by 1918 some women could vote. The Representation of the People Act of 1918 meant that the electorate increased by seven million. By 1928, the Reform Act granted women the vote on the same terms as men. The changes in the nature of the electorate meant that voting patterns changed and this impacted on all the political parties. Women had played an important role on the Home Front in the First World War. Although many were required to stand down when the men came home, their role in the war effort was recognised and their voting rights were extended. By 1923, the Labour Party had won more votes than the Liberals at the General Election: was this to be a permanent change in their relative positions? Was it because of more women voters or had the working-class man decided to vote Labour?

The changing nature of the electorate is a valid factor for this question, but the information is not developed and does not make an explicit link with the question. The final question is highly relevant, but the paragraph does not go on to answer it.

The post-war years saw tough economic conditions. Many British traditional industries such as shipbuilding, iron, steel and textiles found stiff competition from France and Germany. Furthermore, there was the Great Depression of the 1930s. These were challenging times, both for British citizens and governments. It was no surprise therefore to see the growing popularity of socialism, which promised hope to the poor and put the needs of the working man as a priority. Before 1918, the Labour Party had growing support from voters, but it was still very much a minor player. It had begun in 1900 and then was rebranded as the Labour Party in 1906. Socialism helped them to gain power as its policies appealed to the working-class voter. It was clear that the working man was suffering – as shown by the unemployment figures and the General Strike in 1926 – and this discontent helped the Labour Party to grow. There was also a growing distrust of the Liberals amongst the electorate that they did not really understand the needs of the working man and this view was highlighted by the fact that working men did not become candidates for the Liberal Party.

This paragraph touches on the growing appeal of socialism and its link to the popularity of the Labour Party, a valid factor, but fails to draw a connection with the Liberal Party's decline. The growing distrust by the working man of the Liberals is also a valid point, but it has not been effectively linked to the focus of the question.

Party funds were needed to put up candidates in elections and the Labour Party had the help of the trade unions. Clearly the Conservative candidates did not have a funding problem as the Conservative Party was in power for 62 of the 80 years following the First World War. The Liberals had funding problems and this affected the number of candidates they put up in 1922, 1923 and 1924. If a party had insufficient funds for an effective local party machine, then the future looked bleak for them.

Another factor that adversely affected the Liberals and helped with their decline was the growth of divisions within the party. In a sense it was the impact of the war that forced the Liberals to take 'illiberal' policies such as rationing, conscription and tight control of the economy. These policies caused arguments within the party and led to the rivalry between Asquith and David Lloyd George. These divisions weakened the image of the party and led to the need to rely on the Conservatives to remain in government.

Finally, the issue of party leadership must be considered. All three parties saw changes in leadership in these years. Perhaps it was the lure of Baldwin for Liberal voters that did not help their prospects. On the other hand the differences between David Lloyd George and Asquith played their part in weakening the Liberals. As far as Labour was concerned, Ramsay Macdonald's leadership of a minority government gained the confidence of many voters when in coalition with the Liberals after the 1923 election. This was Asquith's misjudgement – he had expected the Labour Party to make mistakes. Instead, it was the Liberals that subsequently paid the electoral price.

There are many factors that contributed to the decline of the Liberal Party between 1918 and 1930. These range from a divided and financially strapped Liberal Party to the increased strength of the Labour Party during a very challenging post-war period in terms of the economic health of the nation.

Party funding was an important factor in this debate. The paragraph gives some facts and figures on funding issues for each of the main parties, but does not go on to link this information to the question. The response needs to draw out the link between Labour's funding strength and the Liberals' shortage of funds, and make a clear statement about how this contributed to the Liberal Party's decline.

Again, this is a relevant factor, but the response needs to develop this point by saying whether the Liberals' internal problems were more or less important than Labour success at this time.

The characters who led the major parties at this time certainly played a part in the fortunes of their respective parties. This is a valid issue, but more focus on the question is required; there is only sufficient development here to imply the link with the question.

The judgement required for this answer, to identify 'the main reason', has not been made; it merely states that a variety of factors were at play.

## Verdict

This is an average answer because:

- there is an attempt to analyse the relevant key features, but there is limited explanation; links to the question are mainly implied. The answer does not really get to grips with linking the growth of the Labour Party as the main factor for the decline of the Liberal Party through reasoned argument and evidence
- the information given is accurate, with some range and depth, which is what takes the answer up to an average level
- the overall judgement is weak and lacks focus on the wording of the question.

Use the feedback on this answer to rewrite it, making as many improvements as you can.

# Paper 1: AS Level sample answer with comments

## Section A

These questions assess your understanding of the period in breadth. They will ask you about the content you learned about in the four key themes, and may ask about more than one theme. For these questions remember to:

- give an analytical, not a descriptive, response
- support your points with evidence
- cover the whole time period specified in the question
- come to a substantiated judgement.

---

*Was the rise of the Labour Party the main reason for the decline of the Liberal Party in the years 1918–30? (20 marks)*

### Strong student answer

Between 1918 and 1930, the fortunes of the Liberal Party dramatically declined from being the alternative government to the Conservatives to being second-best to the increasingly popular Labour Party. The focus of this question is to discover whether the rise of Labour was the main reason for the decline of the Liberals or whether there were other, more significant factors at work.

> This is strong as it explicitly refers to the focus of the question. It also sets out the timeframe covered by the question very clearly.

The Liberals lost voters between 1918 and 1930, which was the outward and visible sign of the party's decline. The evidence for this can be seen in the general election figures of the period. In the election year of 1910, the Liberals gained 43.9%; the Conservatives 46.3% and Labour just 7.1% of the votes. At this stage it was still a two-party race between the Liberals and Conservatives, with Labour very much in a minor position. By the December 1923 election, Labour had polled 30.5 %, the Conservatives 38.1%, and the Liberals crashed with 29.6% of the votes. In this instance, votes had been lost by both the Conservatives and the Liberals, which suggests that it was not just the rise of the Labour Party that weakened the Liberals. Labour's spectacular growth is significant. Many voters were choosing Labour over the other two parties, mainly because of the post-war economic difficulties. Socialism, espoused by Labour, put the needs of the working man first. It would seem that the policies of both the Liberals and the Conservatives were not offering the voters what they wanted at this stage.

> The use of detailed election results sharpens the focus on the question, as does the level of analysis – key for a higher-level answer.

A factor that played into the rise of Labour was the advance of mass democracy. The 19th century had seen the extension of the franchise to most men, but it was not until 1918 (with the Representation of the People Act, which increased the electorate by seven million and gave the vote to the working man) that Labour began to make its mark. The working man made up 80% of the electorate after 1918. Labour's share of the vote increased in the following general election, but the Liberal share declined. Therefore there was a link between the decline of the lacklustre Liberals and the rise of Labour. New voters supported a more vibrant Labour leadership and were attracted to socialism.

> This paragraph shows conceptual awareness. The response shows how the Liberals and Labour reacted to increased democracy, and links their different responses back to the question.

The election of October 1924 offers further evidence of the Liberal decline. Its support dropped to 17.6%, whilst Labour rose to 33% and the Conservatives regained voters with 48.3% of the votes cast. Clearly, the disillusion of Liberal voters had increased, but the other two parties had gained in their share of the vote. Somehow the Liberals failed to reconnect with their disillusioned voters or attract new voters. This suggests that their ideas and middle-class philosophy of reasoned discussion and compromise failed to gain traction with the working man. They supported the constitution, order and the rule of law, which did not connect with the increasingly frustrated unemployed, who were attracted to direct action through trade union and Labour Party membership. This suggests that it was the Liberal Party's inability to reinvent

> More detailed information about the Liberals' appeal to the electorate is given here and used to give a direct answer to the question, suggesting a factor other than the rise of Labour that played a part in the Liberals' downfall.

itself after the election of 1923 that was as much to blame for its ultimate decline as the rise of Labour. Clearly, if the Liberals failed to put up working men as parliamentary candidates then the outward image merely reflected the party's inability to change with the times.

The Liberals not only failed to change their rhetoric to meet the challenges of the 20th century, they also had a funding problem that adversely affected the local party machine. Labour had trade union financial support, whereas the Liberals found themselves unable to put up sufficient party candidates for the elections of 1922–24 because of financial restraints. Internal financial weakness played a part in the decline of the Liberals, as they were unable to 'do battle' effectively in the 1920s. By comparison, the Labour Party had financial backing from the trade unions, showed internal unity and was therefore able effectively to fight elections. The election results of 1922–24 speak for themselves. Here is another strand of the rise of the Labour Party impacting on the decline of the Liberals.

*This paragraph makes an effective and detailed comparison of Liberal and Labour Party funding, and uses the comparison to build the argument.*

The splits in the Liberal Party after 1918 did much damage to their image. The war had required illiberal policies such as rationing, tight control over key industries and conscription. These issues resulted in a split within the party between Asquith and David Lloyd George, which resulted in a coalition government. This split could only weaken the party's image and, unfortunately, it coincided with a period of unity within the Labour leadership and recognition amongst the Conservatives that they needed the support of working-class voters to form a government.

*The splits in the Liberal Party are a valid factor, but the paragraph would be improved if it made a judgement on how important these were in causing the party's decline relative to other factors.*

In 1921, the Irish Free State gained independence from the UK. This resulted in the loss of 80 Irish Nationalist MPs, who had supported the Liberals. In comparison, the Conservatives continued to receive support from about ten Northern Irish MPs after 1921. This was something that was really beyond the control of the Liberals, but the timing could not have been more inconvenient. As the Labour vote was not affected by Irish politics, this dimension of the Liberal decline could not be blamed on their rise.

*This is another valid factor, which could do with a little more development.*

Many would argue that, once Labour started to gain support and its electoral performance began to improve, then the Liberals were doomed. In this sense it was the most important factor in the demise of the party while there was a first-past the post system. There was only room for two parties at the top. However, the outcome, i.e. Liberal decline, was not inevitable in 1923. Unfortunately, unlike the Conservatives, the Liberals failed to take corrective action to keep their core vote and to attract the new working-class voters, in particular when things started to go wrong in the mid-1920s. From this time onwards it could be said that the Liberals only had themselves to blame, and so the rise of the Labour Party was only one of several factors adversely affecting the outcome of elections.

*The conclusion makes a complex argument and makes a good attempt at reaching a judgement using the information that has been discussed.*

## Verdict

This is a strong answer because:

- it deploys appropriate own knowledge accurately and effectively
- it covers a range of factors, which are analysed with explicit references and reference to the question; the treatment of these factors is a little uneven and this is one area for improvement
- of the depth of information and level of analysis given
- the process of coming to a judgement is evident throughout the essay and leads naturally to the reasoning in the conclusion.

# Paper 1: AS Level sample answer with comments

## Section B

These questions assess your understanding of the course in breadth and will cover a period of 30 years or more. They will ask you about the content you learned about in the four key themes, and may ask about more than one theme. The questions will also require you to explore a range of concepts, such as change over time, similarity and difference, as well as significance. For these questions remember to:

- identify the focus of the question
- consider the concepts you will need to explore
- support your points with evidence from across the time period specified in the question
- develop the evidence you deploy to build up your overall judgement
- come to a substantiated judgement that directly addresses the question set.

*To what extent did mass popular culture change attitudes in the years 1945 to 1970? (20 marks)*

### Average student answer

Mass popular culture gained momentum with the arrival of cinema, radio and television during the 20th century. Increasing numbers of people had access to these advances in technology, hence the term 'mass popular culture'. Attitudes changed in the post-war years – some would say from an austere approach to life to that of a consumer society. Was it mass popular culture that drove the change in attitude from needs to an increasing emphasis on wants, and if so, to what extent?

> The introduction gives a reasonable outline of the question, but could be improved by setting out definitions for the key terms.

The Second World War placed economic restrictions on the lives of British citizens through the imposition of rationing as part of the war effort. In many other ways the lives of people were turned upside-down, whether it was because of conscription or the loss of a home or a loved one. It is not surprising that once the war was over attitudes began to change. In the scheme of things people felt safe or certainly safer, so priorities began to change as the straitjacket of austerity was lifted. This did not really come about until the 1950s and continued into the 1970s. This period was to become known as the 'golden era' of western capitalism. I feel that it is the relative feeling of safety that affected people's attitudes the most in the first five post-war years rather than the influence of mass popular culture like television and radio.

> The question asks about the years 1945–70. This paragraph gives a brief description of events before 1945, but this is acceptable as it provides context and helps explain the candidate's point about changing attitudes immediately after the war. However, the point would be made more clearly if this paragraph focused on the 'five post-war years' and left the 'golden era' of the 1950s-70s for a separate paragraph.

There was a rapid rise in real incomes from the 1950s. The increase was 30% in the 1950s and 22% in the 1960s. This increase in real income certainly changed attitudes as people had more income to spend after they had paid for food, fuel and rent. People definitely had options, and there is evidence of the growing influence of mass media on the decisions people made on spending their income. The increase in disposable income coincided with the rise of mass media on the one hand and on the other a flurry of technological developments. This was not only the age of mass media but also mass production. This meant that for the first time all sorts of new gadgets were affordable – fridges, cars and freezers ended up on the list of 'must-haves'. This meant that a consumer society was taking shape, in that attitudes changed so that the ownership of material items was prized above all else.

> There is a hint that perhaps the issue of changing attitudes is complex and does not just include mass media. More explicit development focused on the question and stating how rising incomes changed attitudes is needed.

The BBC was established in 1922, but it was only after 1946 that broadcasts were really up and running. By 1951, 91% of the population had access to radio. By examining the sorts of programmes that people watched or listened to, it is possible

> This paragraph makes a link between individual radio programmes and their potential impact on popular attitudes. The candidate is aware that there were different audiences (older men, older women, young listeners) and the answer could be improved by dealing with each in turn.

to see the kind of influence that this form of mass media had on the public. Some people would argue that in fact the BBC was an instrument of the state in the lives portrayed by the plays and serials the public heard. For example, in the post-war years there was a focus on those at home – mostly women – and the strengthening of national identity through the commemoration of national events often involving the royal family. These were powerful messages, which served either to reinforce existing attitudes or to coax new ones. The relevant programmes were 'Mrs Dale's Diary', 'The Archers', 'Housewives' Choice' and 'Woman's Hour'. Not only were listeners exposed to new ideas but there was a subliminal message, certainly until the 1960s, that the lives of men and women were different. So we can see how the radio was a force to change attitudes and to reinforce others in relation to the home, fashion and child-rearing. As the 1960s developed, the influence of commercial radio changed attitudes towards popular music with the growing popularity of rock'n'roll. Attitudes of the young to fashion linked to this style of music began to change. There was some overlap between music and the cinema with icons such as Elvis Presley and Cliff Richard, who also appeared in films, such as 'Summer Holiday', affecting changes in the attitudes of youths during the 1960s.

However, television was perhaps the biggest influence on post-war attitudes and behaviour. In 1950, only 4% of households had television. By 1955 it was 40% and by 1960 it was 80%. 'Coronation Street', launched in 1960 with 11 million viewers rapidly acquired, is an example of both how television reflected the lives of its viewers and also acted as a change agent of attitudes in British society. Such controversial topics as abortion, homelessness and single mothers were aired and cannot have failed to shape attitudes on moral issues. Some say that the BBC tried to act as a moral guide for the public, but its monopoly was ended in 1955 when commercial stations were allowed. This also opened the way for advertising to operate and it could be seen as a major force in changing attitudes by creating a 'want' or 'must-have item'. Such products as domestic gadgets, fashion and motor cars would feature large in advertising campaigns.

This paragraph looks at the different ways television could influence viewers. It suggests that programmes about abortion, homelessness and single mothers could have shaped attitudes, but doesn't say how attitudes were changed or to what extent.

Cinemas were also popular with many youngsters in this period as the cinema offered a refuge from home and parents. Films were classified in an attempt to 'protect' the young from inappropriate influences and ideas. However, during the 1950s and 1960s, the influence of the cinema was in decline as it fought against television, especially once colour and multi-channel television took off.

Film classification is relevant to the link between media and shaping attitudes, but the idea is not developed or linked to the question. The sentence about the decline of cinema is not really relevant to the question.

Changes in attitudes towards the home, leisure, travel and fashion were fuelled by the increase in disposable income during the 1950s and 1960s. Without this, the inventions in technology and choice of consumer items would have fallen on stony ground; so for mass media to have an impact on attitudes the economic environment had to be right. The extent of the influence of mass media on attitudes varied depending on the cross-match between income and 'the must-have item' and the individual consumer.

The conclusion makes the valid point that mass media helped foster a consumer culture in an economic environment where people had more cash to spare, but does not mention any of the other ways attitudes might have changed, such as changes in attitudes to social issues like abortion.

## Verdict

This is an average answer because:

- it has identified a range of factors to show where attitudes changed, but mostly focuses on the creation of a consumer society
- there is some analysis and some attempt to make links to the question
- the information is mostly accurate, but it could have more depth and range
- there is some understanding of the demands of the question, but a lack of conceptual focus
- there is an attempt to make a judgement in the conclusion.

Use the feedback on this answer to rewrite it, making as many improvements as you can.

# Paper 1: AS Level sample answer with comments

## Section B

These questions assess your understanding of the course in breadth and will cover a period of 30 years or more. They will ask you about the content you learned about in the four key themes, and may ask about more than one theme. The questions will also require you to explore a range of concepts, such as change over time, similarity and difference, as well as significance. For these questions remember to:

- identify the focus of the question
- consider the concepts you will need to explore
- support your points with evidence from across the time period specified in the question
- develop the evidence you deploy to build up your overall judgement
- come to a substantiated judgement that directly addresses the question set.

*To what extent did mass popular culture change attitudes in the years 1945 to 1970? (20 marks)*

### Strong student answer

The period 1945 to 1970 covers the immediate post-war years and what became known as the 'golden era' of western capitalism. In this period, not only did mass popular culture such as television and radio become widely available, but also the process of mass production made all sorts of new products widely available to an increasingly consumer-driven society. This is a society that prized the ownership of items and believed that happiness would be best derived from spending more and more on 'must-have' items. To what extent was mass popular culture the source of this change in attitude from a deeply conservative, austerity-driven society to a more liberal and consumerist society, particularly amongst the working class?

> The introduction shows clear understanding of the question and gives an overview of the social and economic climate and changes in attitudes during the timeframe given in the question.

The general trend in this period was for mass-produced items to become cheaper or more affordable, especially as disposable income was increasing. Attitudes changed about the acquisition of goods that had previously been beyond the financial reach of most people – especially the working class – or had not existed in the 1930s. Now these goods were available, or people were encouraged to think they were, through the medium of mass media advertising. An example of this would be car ownership, which exploded by 25% in the 1950s. The resulting change in attitudes to travel, shopping and hire purchase (to buy the car) cannot just be levelled at mass popular culture. In conjunction with the increase in car ownership, there were changes in the law that facilitated 'shopping'. As well as increased availability of consumer goods, there was an increase in the level of disposable income, which meant that people began to focus on 'wants' after the 'needs' had been paid for. If consumers had not had the money to pay for them, fridges, irons, televisions and other household gadgets would have remained on the shelf in the shop.

> The paragraph makes a direct link between changing attitudes and popular culture, and uses a detailed example – car ownership – to explore the links in depth.

Television ownership rose from 4% of households in 1950 to 40% in 1955, 80% in 1960 and 95% in 1969. Television was particularly influential in changing habits and attitudes, as it affected home dynamics. Watching television became a leisure activity. From 1955 the BBC was no longer allowed a monopoly and the commercial channels were able to compete for the 23% of their free time that men and women spent watching the box. The commercial channels were funded via advertising, which reached into an increasing number of households each year. The contents of programmes and adverts became part of everyday conversation, both in the school playground and at work. Between 1977 and 1979, people on average watched 16 hours of television per week in the summer and 20 hours in winter. Increasingly, television became a powerful element in changing attitudes during this period. These attitudes spanned fashion,

> The paragraph gives some detail on television ownership and refers to a variety of changes in attitude, again showing the interplay between mass popular culture and other forces, in order to address 'to what extent'.

household gadgets and moral codes. In some ways, programmes reflected what was happening in society and for others it was a driver of change. The 1967 Abortion Act did not come about because of television, but attitudes may have been softened with programmes such as 'Up the Junction' in 1965 and 'Cathy Come Home' in 1966. Again, we see that mass popular culture was not alone in changing attitudes to these controversial topics, but television was the most influential form of mass media.

The end of rationing from 1948 marked the start of the change in attitudes and this continued at a brisk pace once rationing was finally abolished in 1964. Expenditure had been controlled by rationing, but with the restraint gradually lifted people got a taste of a wider range of goods, and they were of a better quality too. The rolling back of Retail Price Maintenance on groceries in 1955 and more generally in 1964 meant that supermarkets could slash prices and give shoppers more choice. Attitudes towards 'service' changed as 'self-serve' became the order of the day. In this case, changing attitudes were driven by changes in the economic climate and developments in the commercial world more than mass culture.

This paragraph makes a new point, suggesting that it was not only mass popular culture that changed attitudes.

The role of advertising – whether on television, radio or in magazines – can be seen to be a root cause of creating a change in attitudes towards certain products. Attitudes towards personal hygiene altered for several reasons, not least the increasing availability of hot water on tap in the home. Advertising had a strong influence on the use of deodorant. Prior to 1957, only 32% of women and girls between the age of 16 and 64 used deodorant, and hardly any men used a deodorant as it was regarded as effeminate. By 1969 this figure had gone beyond 50% for both men and women. There can be no doubt that the advertising campaign by Old Spice in 1957 had a dramatic impact on male attitudes on the subject of personal hygiene. This example shows that there were many forces at work to change attitudes in the period between 1945 and 1970 and mass media was just one of these factors.

This paragraph uses a detailed example – deodorant – to explore the question of changing attitudes and their relationship to a specific medium – advertising.

After the 1950s, youth culture emerged with distinct attitudes and clothes. One of main influences on the young for this generational shift in attitudes was the music played by pirate radio stations, in particular, and distinct fashion that identified Mods, Rockers, Teddy Boys and Skinheads, as advertised in magazines and worn by music icons. The emphasis for the youth of the 1950s and 1960s was on having fun and dressing in a particular way to create an identity, both of which set them apart from the older generations. These attitudes were far removed from those of their parents and grandparents, who had lived through the Second World War. The power of popular mass culture cannot be underestimated in driving this generational shift in attitudes in the post-war years.

In this paragraph, the response looks at youth culture, where popular culture had its greatest impact. Some mention of other groups within society as a whole would have made the answer even stronger.

It is clear that popular mass culture did play a part in changing attitudes on a range of issues during the period 1945 to 1970. However, the level of influence varied, particularly with age and gender. It was a complex and usually stealthy process. Without technological advances courtesy of mass production and increased disposable income, the influence of mass popular culture would have been less able to change attitudes than it did.

The conclusion reaches a judgement that reflects the argument in the essay.

## Verdict

This is a strong answer because:

- the key issues relevant to the question are explored in an analytical way
- there is some awareness of concepts and of the relationship between a range of key factors in the period
- it is generally well organised and a judgement is reached on a complex issue.

# Paper 1: AS Level sample answer with comments

## Section C

These questions require you to read and analyse two extracts carefully in order to develop a response that examines and makes an informed judgement about different interpretations. The best answers:

- need to show an understanding of the extracts and identify the key points of interpretation
- deploy own knowledge to develop points emerging from extracts and provide necessary context
- develop a judgement after developing and weighing up different interpretations.

***Study Extracts 4 and 5 (Chapter 5, page 126) before you answer this question.***

*Historians have different views on the impact on Britain of Thatcher's governments in the years 1979–97. Analyse and evaluate the extracts and use your own knowledge of the issues to answer the following question.*

*How far do you agree that the Thatcher government effectively rolled back the frontiers of the state? (20 marks)*

### Average student answer

During the years of Thatcher government between 1979 and 1997, there were many examples of reform that in effect saw state intervention reduced. Thatcher's policy was to free up areas such as industry, education, health and housing from the yoke of socialism and in so doing Britain would be changed for ever.

In Extract 4, Simon Jenkins explains that the health service, housing, schools and universities were to Thatcher 'the services most afflicted by socialism' because they had come under the control of local councils and trade unions. Jenkins goes on to say that as a result of Thatcherite ideology these institutions came under private sector discipline, and as a result public services have been constantly involved in blood-letting and top-down reorganisation.

Extract 5 by Shirley Letwin gives a different view. Letwin and Jenkins agree that Thatcher saw that socialism was impacting adversely on the health service, housing, universities and schools. They also both make reference to Thatcher's negative attitudes towards councils. Jenkins refers to Thatcher's view on councils as being 'incorrigibly socialist institutions' and Letwin says that after trade unions 'Thatcherism's greatest bugbear has been local government'. The strength of Thatcher's feelings, as expressed in these extracts, suggests that it is likely some changes would be made regarding rolling back the frontiers of the state. However, the extracts disagree as Simon Jenkins reflects that despite the changes with the introduction of 'private sector disciplines' to local government, there was actually no reduction in central control. Letwin on the other hand suggests that the changes made were intended to remove obstacles and give people more freedom and independence. One is suggesting that there was a rolling back of the frontiers of the state whilst the other suggests there was not.

Although this paragraph is relevant to the issue, it sounds as though there is conviction in the response that Thatcher did roll back the frontier of the state and is not considering alternative views.

This a weak paragraph as it really only restates the extract. Some own knowledge and reference to the words of the question, i.e. the debate as to whether 'Thatcher rolled back the frontiers of the state effectively', would improve this.

This paragraph is stronger because it makes reference to the strength of feeling Thatcher had about socialism and its impact on various institutions though the authority of local councils. It also makes reference to the central debate of the question.

Thatcher's moral stance, rooted in her Methodist upbringing, meant that she applauded self-reliance, thrift and determination as personal qualities for the success of the individual and nation. In her view, the creeping role of the state in the post-war years had led to decline in Britain as more and more people became dependent on the state and more and more levels of inefficiency were evident in state-run institutions. Thatcher's view was that there was too much state intervention, which resulted in a lack of competition and high taxation. These strongly held opinions led to her personal philosophy becoming Tory party policy once she became prime minister. The backdrop to these ideas gaining acceptance was the Winter of Discontent and the Labour Party having to apply to the IMF for a loan. She pledged to roll back the level of state intervention so that individuals had enough personal choices to not depend on the state. I agree wholeheartedly that the central plank of Thatcherism was to effectively roll back the frontiers of the state.

Local government reform was at the heart of Thatcherism by reducing its independence from central government. The 1985 Local Government Act meant that Thatcher could abolish the Greater London Council and six other metropolitan councils, and her critics pointed out that local power had merely been replaced by Westminster power. This could also be said of the 1988 Education Act, which allowed for grant-maintained schools to be funded by Westminster, but control of budgets came from within the schools themselves rather than from the LEA.

These two paragraphs demonstrate detailed own knowledge, but the information is not used in conjunction with the extracts to assess the validity of the interpretations. The answer would be much improved if it discussed whether or not the information given supports Letwin's interpretation or Jenkins's.

I would agree that Thatcher's government did manage to trim down the size of the state at local level, but in terms of cost of overall spending she did not always achieve her aim – government spending made up 43% of the value of all wealth produced in Britain in 1977–78, rose to 47% in 1983–84, fell to 39% in 1988–89, but rose again to 44% in 1994. Jenkins states 'Private sector disciplines were a success in local government' – in effect socialism was purged from local government so the government effectively rolled back the frontiers of the state. However, this does not seem to be directly linked to the costs incurred. The total tax bill also rose throughout Thatcher's time in office, from 38.5% of total wealth produced in 1979 to almost 41% in 1990; the tax on an average person rose from 31 to 37% of their income. This seems to conflict with Letwin's view that the changes introduced by Thatcher's government were intended to 'remove obstacles to the thriving of Britain and to the freedom needed by individuals to be independent, efficient and honest workmen', as in reality they had paid a high price in taxation. I agree that the frontiers of the state at local level had been rolled back effectively in a variety of areas, but did central control represent freedom or not for the individual?

The concluding paragraph is strong because it combines own knowledge and integrates it with the extracts. It also tries to reach a judgement, taking into account the differing interpretations and their validity. Had this approach been adopted throughout, the answer would have been stronger.

## Verdict

This is an average answer because:

- there is some knowledge of the issues related to the debate and there is some analysis
- the extracts are understood and some of the differences between them are referred to
- it attempts to reach a judgement by making some reference to some key points with limited discussion and limited substantiation.

Use the feedback on this answer to rewrite it, making as many improvements as you can.

# Paper 1: AS Level sample answer with comments

## Section C

These questions require you to read and analyse two extracts carefully in order to develop a response that examines and makes an informed judgement about different interpretations. The best answers:

- need to show an understanding of the extracts and identify the key points of interpretation
- deploy own knowledge to develop points emerging from extracts and provide necessary context
- develop a judgement after developing and weighing up different interpretations.

***Study Extracts 4 and 5 (from Chapter 5, page 126) before you answer this question.***

*Historians have different views on the impact on Britain of Thatcher's governments in the years 1979–97. Analyse and evaluate the extracts and use your own knowledge of the issues to answer the following question.*

*How far do you agree that the Thatcher government effectively rolled back the frontiers of the state? (20 marks)*

### Strong student answer

The question of how effective the Thatcher governments were in rolling back the frontiers of the state has been the subject of much heated debate. As a right-wing Tory, Mrs Thatcher sought to reduce state control over industry, education, housing and health, so reducing the cost to the taxpayer. Jenkins says that 'private sector disciplines were a success in local government', suggesting a positive outcome for her changes, and Letwin points out that, next to trade unions, 'Thatcherism's greatest bugbear was local government', underlining the focus of her changes in the fight against the levels of socialist-driven state intervention. The wording also reveals the strength of her negative feelings on the subject and maybe that of her critics too, by the use of the emotive word 'bugbear'. Measuring the effectiveness of Thatcher's policies is difficult without considering that their impact is still keenly felt by many writers today.

This is a strong introduction because it shows an awareness of dealing with interpretations that need to be assessed for their validity. It is already beginning to suggest differences between the two extracts.

Jenkins raises the question of the nature of a group of services, namely housing, schools, universities, the health service, urban renewal and local government: in 'most democracies these activities were either constitutionally protected or were regional or municipal in responsibility'. This appeared not to be the case under Thatcher. Thatcher viewed them as being afflicted by socialism and often under the control of trades unions, hence the need to 'be purged' of socialist influence. For Thatcher, success meant less state bureaucracy and a cheaper tax bill through efficiency, privatisation and 'contracting out'. The Local Government Act of 1985 meant that some parts of local government were dismantled, for example Greater London Council and six other Metropolitan Councils were axed. She cut central funding for local government from 60% to 49% as a drive for efficiency, and when councils tried to raise the shortfall by increasing local rates, 18 councils were rate-capped. However, what did the reforms bring in terms of rolling back the frontiers of the state? Jenkins is clear on this aspect of her policy: they were 'brought within the penumbra of her office'. In other words, from his view, local control was replaced by control from Westminster so there was never 'a loss of control'. This is a mixed message and serves to demonstrate how interrelated the issues of personal freedom versus state control actually were.

This paragraph is effective, clearly explaining a key interpretation in Extract 4 and using substantial own knowledge to assess the validity of the interpretation.

Thatcher often used the example of innovative Conservative councils such as Wandsworth to demonstrate greater efficiency. Private firms were encouraged to bid for contracts to supply services such as rubbish collection. By 1985, staff numbers had fallen by one-third in Wandsworth. The evidence would suggest that greater efficiency resulted from the application of privatisation (but perhaps only in Tory councils). Certainly, Jenkins partly agrees that 'private sector principles were a success to local government'. However, he also suggests that the picture was not so straightforward, arguing that 'private sector disciplines brought to public services ceaseless upheaval, blood-letting and top-down reorganisation' and 'in reality never a loss of control'. Thatcher's policy of rolling back the frontiers of the state was controversial in institutions like local government; the extent of this policy was felt in a loss of control through central funding and constant upheaval.

Letwin, on the other hand, suggests that it is difficult at this stage to get a fair picture of the relationship between Thatcher and local government as it has yet to be properly understood. Letwin states 'the picture of the Thatcherite relationship to local councils is usually painted in vivid colours'. She suggests that Thatcher's critics painted her as a 'centralist dictator mounting an all-out attack on the ancient bastions of local autonomy and liberty'. Yet she counters this view with the comment that 'the Thatcher government's attack on it [local government] was the very opposite of an attempt to centralise'. Letwin is suggesting that, at this stage, it is not possible to accurately assess the effectiveness of role of the Thatcher government in rolling back the frontiers of the state as the emotions are still raw and the truth has yet to be fully assessed. This probably gives a reasonable verdict on Thatcher and local government.

Here the candidate modifies the analysis presented in the previous paragraph by suggesting that (in 1992) it was too soon to make a final judgement.

Another example of Thatcher's policy to roll back the state was the Housing Act of 1980. This gave people the 'Right to Buy' after three years' council house tenancy. The idea was not only to cut council spending on property maintenance, but to promote a sense of pride and responsibility through independent ownership. It was a hugely popular reform: 204,000 council houses were bought in 1982–83 alone and home ownership rose from 55 to 63% between 1979 and 1990. The individual, according to Thatcher, was 'encouraged' to stand on their own two feet and loosen their dependence on the state. Again, this policy was hugely divisive, with critics saying that the council house stock was so reduced that the poor were robbed of cheap housing and that many council house tenants subsequently sold their houses at a huge profit. Supporters have argued that the Housing Act had served to 'remove obstacles to the thriving of Britain and to the freedom needed by individuals to be independent' (Letwin). It was extremely effective as a policy in rolling back the frontiers of the state and one that has proved to be difficult to reverse.

In this paragraph the question is addressed through reference to the Housing Act, which is not explicitly mentioned in the extracts. However, the answer clearly links to Extract 5.

The extent to which Thatcher effectively rolled back the frontiers of the state is difficult to assess, but the motives of her neo-liberalism are not. She intended through her policies, as Extract 5 says, 'to change the course of British history' and end society's dependence on the state. It was an ambitious project and few thought she could be successful. There is clear evidence of some shift in the frontiers of state intervention, but at what price? In the areas highlighted judgements are emotional as the outcome of her policies were, as Jenkins says, 'always contentious' and, as Letwin implies, history has yet to make a balanced verdict. Whatever the view, all agree that Margaret Thatcher was the most divisive prime minister of the 20th century. To some, she saved Britain from economic ruin and restored national pride with her neo-liberal policies; to others, she promoted greedy individualism and condemned whole communities to hopeless poverty. As the statistics show, the cost of her changes were reflected in the tax paid by individuals, which rose from 31 to 37% of their income; the extent to which she rolled back the frontiers of the state is an opinion upon which there is still much debate.

The concluding paragraph makes a relevant and reasoned judgement, and addresses the validity of the interpretations offered in the two extracts.

## Verdict

This is a strong answer because:

- it has a sharp focus on the question
- it explains the key features of the interpretations in the extracts
- own knowledge is used to explain points in the interpretations
- a reasoned judgement is made that assesses the validity of the interpretation questioned
- the quality of written communication, logical coherence and conceptual understanding are all excellent.

# Preparing for your A Level Paper 1 exam

## Advance planning

1. Draw up a timetable for your revision and try to keep to it. Spread your timetable over a number of weeks, and aim to cover four or five topics each week.
2. Spend longer on topics that you have found difficult, and revise them several times.
3. Above all, do not try to limit your revision by attempting to 'question spot'. Try to be confident about all aspects of your Paper 1 work, because this will ensure that you have a choice of questions in Sections A and B.

## Paper 1 overview:

| AL Paper 1 | Time: 2 hours 15 minutes | |
|---|---|---|
| Section A | Answer 1 question from a choice of 2 | 20 marks |
| Section B | Answer 1 question from a choice of 2 | 20 marks |
| Section C | Answer 1 compulsory interpretations question | 20 marks |
| | Total marks = | 60 marks |

You should familiarise yourself with the layout of the paper by looking at the examples published by Edexcel. The questions for each section are followed by eight pages of lined paper where you should write your answer.

## Section A and Section B questions

The essay questions in Sections A and B are similar in form. They ask you to reach a judgement on an aspect of the course you have studied, and will deal with one or more historical concepts of change, continuity, similarity, difference, cause, consequence and significance. The question stems which will be used will include 'To what extent…', 'How far…', 'How significant was…' and so on. You should consider the issue raised by the question, develop your answer by looking at other relevant points, and reach a judgement in your conclusion.

The main difference between Section A and Section B questions will be the timespan of the questions. Section A questions will cover a period of ten years or more, while Section B questions will be concerned with at least one-third of the period you have studied.

A Section A question for Option 1E might read 'How far was high expenditure on the armed forces responsible for economic decline in the USSR in the years 1964–82?' Your answer should consider the issue of expenditure on the armed forces, look at other issues such as agricultural decline, falling productivity in industry, and Brezhnev's reluctance to undertake economic reforms, before reaching an overall judgement on the question.

A Section B question on the same paper will cover a longer period of time, but have a similar shape. For example, 'How successful were the government's social policies in improving the lives of the Soviet people in the years 1917–64?' Here you should consider various successes, such as full employment, education and healthcare, but also point out policies that were less successful, such as housing and different policies towards women over time. You should conclude by reaching a judgement on the question.

## Section C questions

There is no choice in Section C, which is concerned with the historical interpretations you have studied linked to the question 'What was the impact on Britain of Thatcher's governments in the years 1979–97?' You will be given two extracts totalling around 400 words (printed separately) and the question will take the form 'How convincing do you find the view that…?' There is no need to use source analysis skills such as making inferences or considering provenance for Section C answers. You should approach your answer by analysing both extracts separately, and then use your own knowledge to support, and to counter, the view given in the question, before reaching an overall judgement.

## Use of time

This is an issue that you should discuss with your teachers and fellow students, but here are some suggestions for you.

1. Do not write solidly for 45 minutes on each question. For Section A and B answers you should spend a few minutes working out what the question is asking you to do, and drawing up a plan of your answer. This is especially important for Section B answers, which cover an extended period of time.
2. For Section C it is essential that you have a clear understanding of the content of each extract and the points that each extract is making. Read each extract carefully and underline important points. You might decide to spend up to ten minutes reading the extracts and drawing up your plan, and 35 minutes writing your answer.

# Preparing for your A Level exams

## Paper 1: A Level sample answer with comments

### Section A

These questions assess your understanding of the period in breadth. They will ask you about the content you learned about in the four key themes, and may ask about more than one theme. For these questions remember to:

- give an analytical, not a descriptive, response
- support your points with evidence
- cover the whole time period specified in the question
- come to a substantiated judgement.

---

*To what extent did the changes in educational provision between 1944 and 1965 help to widen opportunities in the workplace? (20 marks)*

#### Average student answer

The 1944 Education Act was a landmark Act that moved the country into a form of selective education; made key changes to the structure of schools in terms of age groups and established 15 as the school leaving age (this came into full effect in 1947). These changes left behind some of the educational reforms of the latter years of the Victorian age – a system known as elementary education that concluded at 14 in theory. There was an emphasis on the three Rs and most pupils left school at 11 or 12 years old. These criteria were no longer seen as fit for purpose, as the post-Second World War years had more complex pressures and demands. From 1944 there were a series of educational reforms that significantly changed educational provision.

The introduction gives a reasonable summary of the backdrop to the 1944 Education Act and looks forward to 'a series of educational reforms', but doesn't say anything about 'opportunities in the workplace'.

During this period, the amount spent on education rose sharply. In 1950, £272 million was spent on education; in 1960 it had risen to £917.3 million; and by 1970 the amount was an eye-watering £2,592 million. This difference was not just about spending more on education; it was also in response to the post-war baby boom. It was a time when the school leaving age went up to 15 and the number of 11–14-year-olds in school increased from 93.1% in 1951 to 100% and the number of 15–18-year-olds in school went up from 12.5% in 1951 to 30% in 1968.

This is useful context, however it has been presented rather like a list, with little development or evaluation. The paragraph does not make any reference to the question.

The Butler Education Act of 1944 introduced what was called the '11-plus' examination. 11-year-olds were 'selected' for the next stage of their education based on their examination performance. The tripartite system created grammar schools, technical schools and secondary moderns. It was hoped that opportunities in the workplace would be widened by this more focused approach to learning. The grammar schools provided an academic focus, which for many students would open the possibility of university, whilst the technical schools gave students the basis for a technical career in industry. In the post-war years there were huge gaps in the world of work and a more highly skilled workforce was needed quickly. The Butler Act increased qualifications for academic pupils, widening their opportunities in the workplace; a debate began as to whether it also widened opportunities for the non-academics. Technical schools gave pupils relevant preparation for a technical career, but there was only a limited number, so there is a mixed picture here.

The analysis here makes some links between relevant factors and the question; the answer shows some good depth of knowledge and some awareness that educational change created debate. However, these ideas have not been fully developed in terms of the question.

In 1951, the General Certificate of Education was introduced for those mainly in grammar schools who planned to go to university. This provided a more specialist approach with standalone qualifications in a range of mainly academic subjects. The old School Certificate was only achievable if a candidate passed all the subjects within it. The new system allowed for candidates to select subjects beyond a core, which allowed them to consider subjects they preferred or were interested in. This could then lead on to a specialism for a job. It also helped those in grammar schools who were contemplating university to consider whether they wanted to be a linguist, scientist, etc. Again, as with the Butler Act, the widening of workplace opportunities seemed to be mainly for academic pupils with the introduction of the GCE: the focus on changing the lives of those who would go to university.

A further relevant factor is raised here, and the paragraph gives a detailed discussion of a specific group. It could be improved by further development, including an assessment of how these changes widened opportunity in the workplace.

The Robbins Committee in the early 1960s recommended that university provision be extended. It was recommended that the number of places offered should be doubled over ten years. This meant that between 1962 and 1970 the number of universities went up from 22 to 46. The traditional subjects offered at the old universities were expanded to include engineering, technical and business schools.

The information here goes beyond the timeframe of the question (1944–65). Instead of mentioning the increase in university numbers to 1970, it would be better to give an example from within the timeframe.

The growing influence of a socialist stance meant that people began to question whether the changes in educational provision allowed equal opportunities for all. The narrowness of a grammar school academic education was questioned, along with the inflexibility of the tripartite system to deliver wider workplace opportunities. The age of 11 was increasingly seen as inappropriate for testing: once a pupil failed the academic test set by the 11–plus, a less successful future seemed likely. A comprehensive school that accepted all abilities began to gain traction as being fairer to all and offering a more flexible approach to pupils as their needs and abilities changed over time. The Labour Party came to power in 1964 pledging to get rid of grammar schools and replace them with comprehensive schools in a document known as 10/65: comprehensives would replace grammar schools and offer more of a community school.

This paragraph offers some insight into the debate surrounding grammar schools and the intended solution – the introduction of comprehensive schools. 'Wider workplace opportunities' are mentioned, but the link between opportunities at school and opportunities in the workplace is not made.

It can be seen that the changes in educational provision between 1944 and 1965 had an impact on the widening of opportunities in the workplace to some extent. It depended on where you lived, as technical schools were not widespread and were limited to towns; some areas adopted comprehensive education faster than others – so again the extent of the impact of the changes was mixed. It was an era of greater opportunity and equality for all and to some extent the changes reflected these ideas.

This is a weak conclusion because, although it tries to answer the question and mentions some valid factors, it does not draw together the points made in this essay.

## Verdict

This is an average answer because:

- the candidate shows an awareness of changes in educational provision within the given timeframe and performs some analysis in terms of the question
- the factors raised are valid but, for the most part, the development does not contribute to forming a sound judgement and this can be seen clearly in the conclusion
- there are signs of organisation, but some passages lose the argument, are descriptive and have limited depth.

Use the feedback on this answer to rewrite it, making as many improvements as you can.

# Paper 1: A Level sample answer with comments

## Section A

These questions assess your understanding of the period in breadth. They will ask you about the content you learned about in the four key themes, and may ask about more than one theme. For these questions remember to:

- give an analytical, not a descriptive, response
- support your points with evidence
- cover the whole time period specified in the question
- come to a substantiated judgement.

---

*To what extent did the changes in educational provision between 1944 and 1965 help to widen opportunities in the workplace? (20 marks)*

### Strong student answer

There was a series of educational changes between 1944 and 1965 that in essence saw a free state system established for ages 5–18. The minimum school leaving age was raised to 15 and, in 1944, entry to secondary education was based on academic ability to three types of selective secondary school – secondary moderns, technical and grammar schools. By the mid-1960s, comprehensive schools were replacing the system set up in 1944. There were also changes in educational provision at university level and in the examination system, which impacted on workplace opportunities. The context for these post-war educational changes was increased acceptance of Keynesian economics, a shift from austerity to the 'golden' age of capitalism and the growing influence of an increasingly liberal outlook, with emphasis on equality and opportunity for all.

> This is a strong introduction that sets out the conceptual framework for the changes in educational provision within the timeline, and also makes reference to the wider social and economic context.

The 1944 Butler Education Act introduced a tripartite selective secondary system, which was free to all. Children in primary schools sat an exam known as the 11-plus to decide which type of school they would attend from the age of 11. This was set up with the intention of widening workplace opportunities, irrespective of background, by giving all children the education that would suit them best. In secondary moderns there was more emphasis on practical subjects, such as needlework and cookery for girls, and metalwork and woodwork for boys. This combination of lessons would help pupils to prepare for life and the world of work. Technical schools allowed pupils to learn a trade. Grammar schools offered more academic subjects. It could be argued that, while grammar schools delivered the academic education they promised, secondary moderns and technical schools were less effective at delivering an education that would lead to increased opportunities in the workplace.

> This paragraph gives a factual description of the tripartite system and sets up the argument for the following paragraphs.

From 1947 the school leaving age was 15. Pupils could take a School Certificate before leaving. Secondary moderns catered for 70% of the school population in the 1950s, but many left with no qualifications, especially after the General Certificate of Education was introduced in 1961. Employers wanted numeracy and literacy skills above all else and, ironically, this was exactly what the secondary moderns focused on. But, without qualifications, it would be harder to compete in the workplace. In terms of secondary modern schools, the extent to which workplace opportunities widened was seen by social and liberal reformers to be very limited indeed.

Before 1965, only 5% of the school population attended technical schools, usually located in towns. The changes meant a small proportion of the school population had wider workplace opportunities than before 1944 by being trained for highly skilled technical jobs, but this was extremely limited to small geographical areas. The technical schools were also for boys only,

> These paragraphs give a brief, but adequate, analysis of the role of secondary moderns and technical schools in extending workplace opportunities, looking at positive and negative contributions.

so offered no advantage to girls. The gender factor was something that became an increasingly sensitive and political issue. By the 1960s, equality of gender was gaining support across all sections of society.

The third arm of the tripartite system was the grammar school. Its curriculum was classically academic. In order to reward highly academic pupils, in 1951 the more specialised General Certificate of Education replaced the School Certificate. Only 20% of the school population were able to take this examination in specific subjects at 'O' level and a smaller percentage at 'A' level, and they were found mainly in grammar schools. A new generation of school pupils were acquiring academic qualifications in specific subject areas, usually linked directly to further study at degree level. Workplace opportunities were widened for a very small percentage of the school population, but in a very big way. By gaining 'O' levels and 'A' levels, students could apply for a university place, putting them on course for a profession such as medicine, law, architecture or teaching. These changes in educational provision meant that workplace opportunities had widened into professional fields on a much greater scale than previously. The limitations of these changes could be found in the social make-up and gender imbalance of university students, showing that the working class and women were under-represented.

The grammar schools are analysed in the context of the question. The answer compares increasing opportunities of different groups as well as increasing opportunities in general.

This process of giving pupils the opportunity to gain more qualifications was aided by the increased provision of university places and the introduction of universal and mandatory means-tested university grants in 1962. Following the Robbins Committee recommendations in the early 1960s, there was an unprecedented growth in university provision between 1962 and 1970 from 26 to 42 establishments. New courses in engineering, business studies and languages challenged the exclusive classical nature of Oxbridge courses. More university places meant more graduates, which widened workplace opportunities, theoretically, for the academic student. The reality was for a gender imbalance to now emerge in favour of males. By the 1960s, those who supported selective education on the basis of ability felt that, by making the system free, they had enhanced workplace opportunities irrespective of wealth or class. Critics argued that this was not true in reality. By the mid 1960s, it was also clear that a disproportionate percentage of pupils in grammar schools and university came from middle-class and wealthy backgrounds. Parity of esteem between the leavers of grammar schools, secondary moderns and technical schools had also clearly failed. So the extent to which the changes in educational provision had widened workplace opportunities by 1965 was limited by class in particular.

This paragraph makes reference to widened university access and also looks at how attitudes changed over the timeframe of the question.

In the post-war years, educational reform was seen by politicians as a weapon to engineer social change. The 1944 Education Act reflected the pre-war norms of a class-driven, patriarchal society. By 1965, elitism and class distinction were being challenged. The changes in educational provision between 1944 and 1965 did widen workplace opportunities to a great extent, in that increased numbers of people began to access managerial jobs and the professions by the 1960s, but it was now gender that was acting as a brake on the extent to which women could take advantage of workplace opportunities.

The conclusion makes a reasoned judgement and addresses the issue with some sophistication, as it refers to hitherto unintended factors not given consideration when the 1944 Education Act became law.

## Verdict

This is a strong answer because:

- the key issues are explored through sustained analysis and they are consistently linked to the key features of the period
- it shows an in-depth and conceptual understanding of the question
- there is some attempt to assess the relative importance of the criteria raised by the question in reaching a judgment.

# Paper 1: A Level sample answer with comments

## Section B

These questions assess your understanding of the course in breadth and will cover a period of 30 years or more. They will ask you about the content you learned about in the four key themes, and may ask about more than one theme. The questions will also require you to explore a range of concepts, such as change over time, similarity and difference, as well as significance. For these questions remember to:

- identify the focus of the question
- consider the concepts you will need to explore
- support your points with evidence from across the time period specified in the question
- develop the evidence you deploy to build up your overall judgement
- come to a substantiated judgement that directly addresses the question set.

*How far do you agree that healthcare improved significantly between 1946 and 1979? (20 marks)*

### Average student answer

In 1946 the ability to seek medical help for ailments rested on the individual's ability to pay, which meant that poor people often found medicine unaffordable. Life in the 1930s and 1940s was tough, as every year thousands died from infectious diseases. At this time, meningitis, pneumonia, diphtheria, polio and tuberculosis were serious killers for all ages. Infant mortality was particularly distressing as 1 in 20 children died before they reached the age of one, which was particularly apparent with the post-war baby boom. There were many soldiers from the war who had gained injuries through fighting for their country, and whose medical needs exceeded their ability to pay. The health system was also a piecemeal system that varied from one part of the country to another. There were growing calls, particularly amongst socialists, to make changes to the existing health system and to replace it with a state-controlled system. Between 1946 and 1979, a National Health Service was introduced, which promoted the principle that healthcare was free at the point of use for everyone irrespective of income and this system came under central control.

The introduction identifies two key issues (affordability and variation in local provision) in 1946, and what was done (the introduction of the NHS) to address these issues by 1979. The introduction would be much stronger if it suggested a definition of 'significantly' in the context of the question.

The National Health Service Act of 1946 applied to England and Wales and made healthcare free at the point of use for all. To achieve this there would be 19 regional health boards to co-ordinate local healthcare and 472 local management committees to run hospitals. The mere fact that healthcare was free – in hospitals, at dentists and with doctors in the community – had the effect of transforming the lives of millions. The system came into being in July 1948 for the populations in Wales and England. It took a little while longer for the system to be introduced into Scotland and Northern Ireland along the same principles. I would agree that in 1948 healthcare was improved significantly at a stroke, and this was the most significant improvement in healthcare between 1944 and 1979.

This paragraph answers the question, with the candidate agreeing that healthcare improved significantly, but for a higher mark it would need to go into more detail.

The impact of an improved healthcare system became apparent very quickly in terms of eradicating infectious diseases. As the system was across England and Wales, it was possible to implement nationwide health programmes such as mass immunisation. For example, there was a 90% drop in whooping cough deaths by 1970 and the number of deaths from tuberculosis fell from 25,000 to 5,000 per year as access to antibiotics was increased. These statistics were just a few of many in this field, but they are clear evidence of just how significant the improvements in healthcare really were and just how effective a nationwide approach could be when dealing with infectious diseases.

In my opinion, another area with significant improvement in healthcare came from the impact of improved midwifery between 1944 and 1979. This impacted on death rates for mothers and babies. Maternal death rates fell from 1 per 1,000 births in 1949 to 0.18 in 1970. This was a truly significant improvement by any standards and this would affect millions of families. Infant mortality rate reduced from 60 per 1,000 in 1944 to 12 per 1,000 in 1979. Specialist knowledge and improved professional standards meant that healthcare in this field improved significantly and led to increased expectations as to what improved healthcare under the NHS could deliver. These improvements, coupled with the contraceptive pill being freely available from the NHS, meant that the lives of women improved beyond recognition.

> Again, these paragraphs are raising valid issues, but they are not building an argument for (or against) a significant improvement in healthcare. The paragraphs would have a tighter focus if they compared the situation in 1946 with the situation in 1979, rather than listing statistics from various years.

Another area of healthcare that seemed to benefit from the NHS was the developments in surgery that impacted upon life expectancy. For example, the first kidney transplant took place in Edinburgh in 1960 and began a whole series of transplant operations as organ rejection was overcome. The NHS began to address the issue of ageing, which was something not really anticipated by Aneurin Bevan when he created the 1946 Act. This meant that treatments for cancer and heart disease began to eat into the NHS budgets and people began to have ever-increasing expectations about what improvements in healthcare could achieve. In 1950, life expectancy for men was 66, and 70 in 1979, and for women it rose from 71 to 75 in the same period. In my opinion, these statistics show how improvements in healthcare had impacted on the lives of men and women in Britain over a 30-year period, but also hint at the positive impact of government 'healthy living' campaigns over the same period – in particular the importance of a healthy balanced diet and the dangers of smoking.

> This paragraph has a better focus on the question. It assesses a range of improvements over the period, against the original position in 1946.

In my opinion, the issue of NHS budgets soon became a key issue in determining the rate of improvement of healthcare. In 1950 the NHS cost 4.1% of GDP and, by 1970, it had risen to 4.8% of GDP. The focus of government began to shift towards advice for a healthier lifestyle, which was blurring the lines of healthcare and health awareness. Along with the introduction of a free healthcare system in 1948, these were the most significant improvements in healthcare if falling death rates are considered. As time progressed and the 'magic bullet' of mass immunisation programmes waned; more complicated diseases and a wider range of patients began to find that significant improvements to healthcare were increasingly costly and, in some cases, the cost was shifted from the NHS to the patient, e.g. spectacles in 1978.

> The final paragraph introduces lots of new ideas, so does not work as a conclusion, which should tie together all the ideas raised in previous paragraphs. If some of the new ideas raised here, about the ever-changing landscape of healthcare requirements, were integrated throughout the answer, it would be much stronger. A stronger answer would also consider other aspects of healthcare beyond the NHS.

## Verdict

This is an average answer because:

- it mostly has adequate depth, but the range of ideas covered is limited
- most of the knowledge deployed is accurate and relevant
- it comes to a weak overall judgement
- it does take an analytical approach and focuses on the question for most of the essay.

Use the feedback on this answer to rewrite it, making as many improvements as you can.

# Paper 1: A Level sample answer with comments

## Section B

These questions assess your understanding of the course in breadth and will cover a period of 30 years or more. They will ask you about the content you learned about in the four key themes, and may ask about more than one theme. The questions will also require you to explore a range of concepts, such as change over time, similarity and difference, as well as significance. For these questions remember to:

- identify the focus of the question
- consider the concepts you will need to explore
- support your points with evidence from across the time period specified in the question
- develop the evidence you deploy to build up your overall judgement
- come to a substantiated judgement that directly addresses the question set.

---

*How far do you agree that healthcare improved significantly between 1945 and 1979? (20 marks)*

### Strong student answer

From 1945, Britain saw efforts to create 'a new Jerusalem' – a transformed Britain that would create a more inclusive, egalitarian society. The state led on these new initiatives for welfare, education and employment. The seeds of change were sown in 1942 with the Beveridge Report, but it was not until 1946, with the National Health Service Act, that the blueprint for sweeping changes in healthcare emerged under Aneurin Bevan. The NHS was the first system in the world to give free healthcare to all citizens at the point of use without further qualifying factors.

> A strong introduction that sets the scene and places changes in healthcare in the wider context of the creation of the welfare state.

Up to 1948, the healthcare a patient received depended on their ability to pay: either by paying fees upfront or through an insurance scheme. Many poorer patients were unable to pay for medicines to deal with contagious infections, such as tuberculosis, meningitis, pneumonia, diphtheria and polio, so thousands of people died or suffered unnecessarily each year. The arrival of free healthcare had a very significant impact on the everyday lives of British people. At a stroke, the lives of millions were changed.

> The paragraph briefly explains how one change – healthcare being free at point of use – had a dramatic impact and links this explicitly to the question.

Healthcare prior to 1945 was piecemeal, unregulated and disorganised. The idea of the NHS was to centralise healthcare as part of post-war reconstruction to create a welfare state. From 1948, healthcare was significantly improved by the introduction of 19 regional health boards co-ordinating healthcare and 472 local management committees running hospitals. The centralised system promised to lead to cheaper running costs because of economies of scale. In 1973, the National Health Service Reorganisation Act came into effect, creating regional healthcare bodies within new local government boundaries. Whilst centralised healthcare had its plusses, the danger of regional health authorities was their unwieldy size, potentially leading to unfair distribution of resources, mirroring the political map.

> The paragraph discusses the advantages and disadvantages of a centralised system – this is key to providing a balanced answer to the question 'How far do you agree?'

Centres of excellence were created in large hospitals, representing a significant change, but not necessarily improved healthcare for all. Part of this national efficiency drive was the closure of over 300 cottage hospitals in the 1960s. The aim was to improve healthcare but, for those without transport or countryside dwellers, these closures adversely affected their healthcare. The centres of excellence forged close links with university medical schools, such as Leeds and Manchester, leading to the development of surgical specialisms like kidney and heart transplants, which improved the range of surgery on offer. These significant developments in healthcare were not envisaged by the founders of the NHS, but they were available to all irrespective of background or ability to pay.

> Again, this paragraph attempts a balanced answer to the question by looking at pros and cons of changes in healthcare during the timeframe of the question.

The centralised healthcare system saw many improvements in the treatment of infectious diseases. National immunisation programmes begun in the 1950s saw the virtual eradication of childhood killers like whooping cough within 20 years; diphtheria and polio cases dropped massively in the mid-1950s. Childhood mortality dropped from 60 per 1,000 children in 1944 to 12 in 1979. Adult deaths from tuberculosis dropped from 25,000 to 5,000 thanks to antibiotics. It was far easier to organise effective immunisation in a national system.

The national immunisation programme is a clear example of significant improvement in healthcare.

Midwifery benefited from centralised standards of training. The number of midwives increased and there was a steep decline in maternal death rates, which fell from 1 per 1,000 births in 1949 to 0.18 in 1970. This significantly improved healthcare for all sections of society, but particularly for those who were poor as, prior to 1948, rich and middle-class women had privately funded options available. The improvement for all came if there was an emergency that required hospital treatment, often in the post-birth phase, when the use of specialist facilities might be required.

Midwifery was a key area, as the statistics suggest. The idea that changes were more significant for some classes than others is introduced here – this could have been developed more fully throughout.

The issue of NHS budgets was key to the rate of improvement of healthcare. In 1950 it cost 4.1% of GDP and, by 1970, it had risen to 4.8%. As the range of treatments increased, the centrally funded budgets became strained and, as basic ailments were treated, this left the issues of an ageing population for the NHS to contend with. Illnesses such as cancer, heart disease and arthritis began to eat into budgets as never before.

NHS budgets were a key factor in the rate of healthcare improvement, but this is a weak paragraph as it does not link effectively with the question.

I would agree that there were many significant improvements in healthcare between 1944 and 1979. Certainly, the changes reflected the sentiments of politicians in post-war Britain – that they should improve the general health of the population. Life expectancy rates for men were 66 in 1950 and 70 in 1979, for women in the same period 71 and 79. The NHS created in 1946 played a significant part in improved healthcare for all British citizens.

The conclusion tries to reach an overall judgement, agreeing with the hypothesis posed in the question. Although this is a strong answer overall, it could have been improved by touching on areas of healthcare outside the NHS, e.g. public health education.

## Verdict

This is a strong answer because:

- it has explored the key issues relevant to the question in an analytical way
- there is contextual cross-referencing of key features in the period; however the depth is uneven, which is the main weakness of the answer
- most of the demands of the question have been met and there is an attempt to reach a judgement that is supported
- it is generally well organised and clearly explained.

# Paper 1: A Level sample answer with comments

## Section C

These questions require you to read two extracts carefully to identify the key points raised and establish the argument being put forward. For these questions remember to:

- read and analyse the extracts thoroughly, remembering that you need to use them in tandem
- take careful note of the information provided about the extracts
- deploy own knowledge to develop the points and arguments that emerge from the extracts and to provide appropriate context
- develop an argument rooted in the points raised in the extracts and come to a substantiated conclusion.

***Study Extracts 7 and 8 (from Chapter 5, page 131) before you answer this question.***

*In the light of differing interpretations, how convincing do you find the view that Thatcher's economic policies widened the gap between rich and poor?*

*To explain your answer, analyse and evaluate the material in both extracts, using your own knowledge of the issues. (20 marks)*

*Note: The question asks you to analyse two opposing views, of one historian and one newspaper journalist. In the actual examination, both extracts would be written by historians.*

### Average student answer

Margaret Thatcher became leader of the Conservative Party in 1975 and then prime minister in 1979. As a neo-liberal, the key elements of her economic policies were privatisation, monetarism and supply-side policies. The priorities for her government were low inflation through the control of money supply, the removal of regulation and lowering of taxes to act as triggers for increased demand. Privatisation meant that state-owned industries were prime targets for sale – British Sugar, BP and British Aerospace were all sold off before 1983; British Telecom was sold in 1984 and British Gas was sold in 1986. In order to tackle inflation, which stood at 11% in 1978, Thatcher was prepared to risk a temporary rise in unemployment that ran counter to the policies of previous post-war governments (who had prioritised cutting levels of unemployment).

> This opening paragraph provides accurate information about Thatcher's economic policies, but is a weak introduction because it does not address the issue of 'interpretations' raised in the question.

Norman Lowe in Extract 7 claims that the gap between rich and poor did widen because 'successive income tax reductions, particularly in 1988, benefited the rich more than the poor'. He goes on to cite various aspects of Thatcher's policies, such as changes in direct taxes (such as VAT), which meant that – as everyone paid the same amount of VAT – the low-paid contributed a larger percentage of their income than the better-off for such commodities as petrol. These comments support his initial comment that the gap between rich and poor widened. However, if one considers that it was the lower paid who were able to buy their council-owned homes at knock-down prices and subsequently sell them at the going market rates the picture painted by Lowe is not so clear cut, especially as the sale of council houses was the most popular aspect of what was dubbed 'popular capitalism': over a million were sold between 1979 and 1988.

Extract 7 also looks at the issue of wages during Thatcher's time in power and asserts that 'By 1993 the gap between the highest and lowest salaries was the widest since records began.' On this basis, the gap between rich and poor had demonstrably widened and this would be a very powerful argument. Extract 7 also says that 'the wages of most people in work rose'. However, is the viewpoint really that simple, for wages are only part of the equation in a person's wealth? Tax is another consideration to bear in mind before reaching a conclusion as to whether Thatcher's policies really did widen the gap between rich and poor. As Extract 8 points out,

> These paragraphs use the extracts with some precision and draw points out from the evidence, but the explanations could be more developed. There are several missed opportunities here to use own knowledge to assess the extracts.

'taxes were cut to shift the balance of spending and encourage wealth creation'. Inflation was reduced to single figures by 1982, and never rose above 9% for the rest of the 1980s, which meant that – if wages were rising and tax was falling – most working people would see an improvement in their standard of living. They had opportunities to make money through house sales and the purchase of shares in previously nationalised industries. I am convinced that there was some widening of the gap between the 'haves' and the 'have-nots', but the overall picture is complicated and very difficult to assess when looked at from a variety of perspectives.

The theory behind the sale of state-owned industries such as British Telecom and British Gas was that lower taxes would result, benefiting all taxpayers, and widespread share ownership was encouraged. In reality, privatisation benefited the more financially astute middle and upper classes rather than the working classes. The sale of council houses only benefited working-class tenants. This cannot be seen as widening the gap between rich and poor, but possibly widened the gap between the employed working class and the unemployed poor, as the lack of availability of council houses made it harder and more expensive for councils to house the poorest in society by 1997.

This paragraph is weak because it makes no reference to the extracts. The focus in a Section C answer should be on assessing interpretations.

It is clear that there are several ways to interpret the impact of Margaret Thatcher's economic policies as to whether she widened the gap between rich and poor. The difficulty of making a convincing argument lies with the complexity of the issues involved and what political standpoint the writer has. In Extract 7, Norman Lowe, writing in 2009, supports his interpretation that 'the gap between the rich and poor widened' by focusing on the impact of wages and tax policies, whereas the 'Telegraph' piece (Extract 8) has a longer perspective as it was written in 2013, some time after the policies were introduced, and places more emphasis on the long-term impact of Thatcher's economic policies for the nation as a whole by saying that 'As a result of Lady Thatcher's efforts Britain is... immeasurably richer.'

The concluding paragraph is better. It makes a judgement that is relevant and shows some awareness of the differences in the extracts. It would have been better if this approach had been taken earlier in the answer.

## Verdict

This is an average answer because:

- it lacks a direct focus on the key words in the question
- it does not always integrate own knowledge with the extracts
- it does not always cross-reference the extracts to highlight areas of agreement and disagreement
- it comes to a relevant judgement, but the supporting reasons are not argued explicitly throughout.

Use the feedback on this answer to rewrite it, making as many improvements as you can.

# Paper 1: A Level sample answer with comments

## Section C

These questions require you to read two extracts carefully to identify the key points raised and establish the argument being put forward. For these questions remember to:

- read and analyse the extracts thoroughly, remembering that you need to use them in tandem
- take careful note of the information provided about the extracts
- deploy own knowledge to develop the points and arguments that emerge from the extracts and to provide appropriate context
- develop an argument rooted in the points raised in the extracts and come to a substantiated conclusion.

***Study Extracts 7 and 8 (from Chapter 5, page 131) before you answer this question.***

*In the light of differing interpretations, how convincing do you find the view that Thatcher's economic policies widened the gap between rich and poor?*

*To explain your answer, analyse and evaluate the material in both extracts, using your own knowledge of the issues. (20 marks)*

*Note: The question asks you to analyse two opposing views, of one historian and one newspaper journalist. In the actual examination, both extracts would be written by historians.*

### Strong student answer

Mrs Thatcher had clear ideas as to how to get Britain's economy working again. The election slogan imprinted on the public mindset was 'Labour isn't working'. The impact of her neo-liberal policies on different social groups, making some winners and some losers, has been the subject of heated debate. In Extract 7, Norman Lowe takes the view that 'The gap between rich and poor widened... Successive income tax reductions particularly in 1988 benefited the rich more than the poor.' These tax reductions were in line with her stated policies, but Lowe is in no doubt about their unfairness. The 'Daily Telegraph' extract sees the issue of lower tax in a different light when it says 'taxes were cut to shift the balance of spending and encourage wealth creation'. It is difficult to assess if the economic policies did widen the gap between rich and poor, because of political convictions and the limited perspective there can be on policies that are less than 50 years old.

> This is a strong introduction because it shows clear awareness of the issue under discussion and the fact that there are differing interpretations of the issue that need to be assessed.

Both extracts acknowledge that Thatcher brought about significant changes in the workplace. Extract 7 makes a strong point about wages by stating, 'By 1993, the gap between the highest and lowest wages was the widest since records began.' The income of the richest 10% increased by 61% between 1979 and 1992, the poorest 10% saw a reduction of 18% in the same period. While the former group held 20.6% of UK wealth in 1979, and the latter 4.3%, by 1991 these figures had changed to 26.1 and 2.9% respectively. These statistics support Lowe's convincing interpretation. Extract 8 emphasises the shifts in workplace practices that aimed to bring about more productivity and 'Managers were given the right to manage'. This change was helped by a number of factors, but not least lessening trade union power, which was challenged gradually through a series of Employment Acts. The 1980 Act meant workers did not have to join a union; it also meant unions could only organise strikes against their direct employers and were not allowed sympathy strikes. The 1982 Act meant the unions could be sued for illegal strike action. The 1984 Trade Union Act meant that a strike had to be approved by a majority of union members in a secret ballot before it was legal. Extract 8 does not make a strong argument against the assertion that wages was an area where criticism of Thatcher's policies is valid.

> This paragraph focuses on the differing interpretations offered by the extracts and uses own knowledge to develop and explain the key features of each interpretation. Own knowledge is also used effectively to test the validity of each interpretation.

Thatcher's economic policies were driven by monetarist principles. She prioritised low inflation and kept the money supply tightly under control. She was prepared to allow unemployment to rise. Deflationary policies not only cut spending on the poor but fuelled unemployment, predominantly among manufacturing workers. This would lay Thatcher open on another front to the charge that it was the poor who suffered most from her policies. As Extract 7 comments, 'With unemployment running permanently at around 3 million... as unemployment and poverty increased, so did the crime rate.' Ironically, the scale of unemployment benefits payments forced up government spending. Despite this, inflation was reduced to single figures by 1982, and never rose above 9% for the rest of the 1980s. This view contrasts sharply with Extract 8, which claims that 'As a result of Lady Thatcher's efforts, Britain is... immeasurably richer.' The relationships between unemployment, the overall wealth of the nation and the battle against inflation are all inextricably linked. If one sees figures referring to inflation up to 1980, a perception is created for part of the picture. By 1982, things had changed in this area, but often it is the original perception that persists and clouds subsequent judgements.

Both VAT and National Insurance are regressive taxes: they take a higher proportion of income from the poor than the rich and both these were increased in the Thatcher years. This shift in the tax burden from direct to indirect taxes has contributed to the growing gap between the richest and poorest in Britain since the late 1970s. Extract 7 supports this by saying that 'Higher direct taxes such as VAT meant that people on low incomes had to pay the same VAT increases as those on the highest incomes, for example on commodities such as petrol.' In 1979, VAT was increased from 8 to 15%, the figure at which it remained until 1991. Yet, as well as VAT being increased, there was also an increase in National Insurance payments. The flip side of the growth of indirect taxation was that the basic rate of income tax was reduced from 33 to 25% and inheritance tax was cut from 75 to 40%. However, although income tax fell under Thatcher, the average tax bill rose by 6% between 1979 and 1990. As this shift was a major plank of Thatcher's economic policy, it becomes increasingly more difficult not to accept Lowe's argument in this context. The 'Telegraph' would counter the charge by saying that people had more purchasing freedom 'in that she gave us the freedom to vote with our wallets, where others cared only for raiding them'. Thatcher believed that low taxation gave people more spending power whilst promoting investment. In the 1980 budget, the top rate of income tax was cut from 83% to 60%; in 1988 it was cut again to 40%.

These sections deploy precise own knowledge to explain the interpretations in the extracts. Here own knowledge is effectively integrated with reference to the extracts.

It has become apparent that it is really the shift in taxation where the heart of this debate rests, as the 'Telegraph' says 'taxes were cut to shift the balance of spending and encourage wealth creation.' Thatcher shifted the balance between direct and indirect taxation that, however, meant that incrementally the poor lost more than the rich, which supports Lowe's conviction. Whether it was wages, VAT, privatisation or taxation, it was the rich who seem to have gained the most, from whatever angle the issue is probed. The monetarist policies required low inflation and a limited money supply even if unemployment rose – which it did. Unemployment, particularly amongst labourers, prompted an emotional response to monetarism that convinced many in Britain that the perceived benefits, such as the Right to Buy and the removal of trade union strangleholds on the workplace, were not worth the pain that seemed to be inflicted on the poor. The increased competition and a more 'entrepreneurial culture' promised a better future, but instead they were seen as a sign of greed and rampant consumerism. Certainly it is right to say that the gap between rich and poor widened thanks to Thatcher's economic policies in many respects, but equally it would be fair to say that the complete picture was not quite so simple.

The concluding paragraph makes a relevant and reasoned judgement, assessing the validity of the interpretations. There is a clear focus on the widening of the gap between rich and poor as a result of Thatcher's economic policies.

## Verdict

This is a strong answer because:

- it has a sharp focus on the question
- it explains the key features of the interpretations in the extracts by integrating own knowledge
- the validity of the interpretations is assessed by reference to own knowledge
- a reasoned judgement is made that assesses the validity of the interpretations on the impact of Thatcher's economic policies on different social groups
- the quality of written communication, logical coherence and conceptual understanding are all excellent.

# The USA, c1920-55: boom, bust and recovery

In 1920, the USA was the world's largest economy. It had been the economic powerhouse behind the Allied victory in the First World War. American industry was the most advanced in the world and American farmers had fed a Europe devastated by war. The 20th century was to be the USA's century.

In 1955, the USA was the world's economic superpower. Outside the communist world, the USA dominated the world economically and militarily. The standard of living in the USA was the highest the world had seen. While rationing of goods was just coming to an end in Britain after the Second World War, most Americans had cars, televisions and refrigerators. American popular culture in cinema and popular music dominated the non-communist world.

Between 1920 and 1955, the USA was transformed and helped transform the world economically and culturally. However, the path to such a dominant position was not smooth or straightforward. The USA went through periods of rapid economic growth but also the worst economic crisis the world had seen: a severe economic depression that began in 1929 and persisted until the outbreak of the Second World War.

The depression led to a major change in US national politics, when the Republican Party, which was associated with boom and bust, was replaced by the Democratic Party under Franklin D. Roosevelt (also known as FDR) as president. He was the only president to be elected four times. In the period from 1933 to his death in 1945, Roosevelt oversaw the USA's recovery from economic depression, and success in the Second World War. Following the Second World War, economic prosperity was maintained, partly through the onset of the Cold War.

In the period 1920–55, huge economic changes were mirrored by great changes in US society. The 1920s was an age of both indulgence and intolerance. Women, who had been given the vote in 1919, began to play an important role in the US economy, outside the home. Their position was greatly improved by opportunities to work on the Home Front created by the Second World War.

**SOURCE 1** Sheet music for a song, 'Viva Roosevelt!', published in 1942 by the RCA recording company.

|  |  |
|---|---|
| 1919 | 18th Amendment of US Constitution introduces national prohibition in 1920<br>19th Amendment to US Constitution introduces votes for women<br>Red Scare |
| 1921 | Emergency Immigration Act |
| 1929 | Wall Street Crash starts the Depression |
| 1933 | First New Deal begins |
| 1940 | Franklin D. Roosevelt becomes first president to be elected for third time |
| 1945 | Franklin D. Roosevelt dies in office having won four presidential elections |
| 1950 | Senator J. McCarthy launches anti-communist attacks on US government |
| 1954 | *Brown v Board of Education* decision by US Supreme Court |

1920 Republicans win presidential election

1927 Sacco and Vanzetti executed

1932 Franklin D. Roosevelt wins presidential election for Democrats

1935 Second New Deal: Wagner Act, Revenue Act and Social Security Act

1941 USA enters Second World War

1948 US armed forces desegregated

1952 Dwight Eisenhower wins presidential election for Republicans

1955 Montgomery Bus Boycott
'Rock around the Clock' by Bill Haley and the Comets is Number 1 in USA and UK

In 1920, black Americans were regarded as second-class citizens and experienced discrimination in employment and housing across the USA. In the Old South (the south-eastern United States), black Americans faced legal discrimination through **segregation**. Blacks and whites were forced to go to different schools and use separate facilities.

**KEY TERM**

**Segregation**
In the former Confederate states in the south-eastern USA, blacks and whites were required by law to use separate schools, live in separate areas, use separate toilets and public transportation. The laws that imposed segregation were known as 'Jim Crow' laws. Many other US states in different parts of the country had unofficial segregation where education and housing were provided separately.

By 1955 black America had gone through a transformation. The US armed forces were desegregated in 1948, and in 1954 and 1955 the US Supreme Court issued rulings demanding the end of segregation in schools. A movement towards full equality was beginning.

The period from 1920 to 1955 saw US popular culture dominate the world. The development of Hollywood meant the USA was the centre of the world's film industry. American film stars were the first global superstars. This dominance also occurred in popular music. Jazz, a uniquely American form of music, became the dominant popular music of the 1920s and 1930s. By 1955 the USA saw the beginning of modern teenage culture, illustrated by the rapid growth and popularity of rock'n'roll.

The USA had been transformed economically by 1955. This transformation, in turn, helped alter profoundly the role of women, black Americans and other minorities in US society. The period laid the foundations of the modern USA.

**EXTEND YOUR KNOWLEDGE**

**How the USA is governed**
The US Constitution, drawn up in 1787, is the document containing the rules of American government. It can be amended only if the Congress and three-quarters of the US states agree.

The USA is a federal state where political power is divided between the central or federal government based in Washington DC, and 50 state governments (48 until 1959). The federal government is responsible for national defence, foreign policy, interstate commerce and trade, and interstate law and order. State governments are responsible for law and order, education and welfare.

The federal government is divided into three parts:

1 *The Executive* headed by the president. He is elected every four years and is responsible for running the government.

2 *The Legislature* is the US Congress and is responsible for law-making and raising taxes. It is made up of two houses. The House of Representatives has 435 members, elected every two years. They are elected on the basis of population, so states such as New York and California have a large number of Congressmen, and low population states, like Wyoming, have just one. The Senate contains 100 senators (96 until 1959), two from each state, irrespective of size or population. They are elected for six years. All major appointments to the government have to receive Senate approval through its power of 'advice and consent'. Both houses have to agree to a proposal before it becomes a law. The president can veto a law but a two-thirds majority in both houses can override his veto.

3 *The Supreme Court* consists of nine judges appointed by the president and approved by the Senate. They hold office for life. They have the very important power of deciding whether laws conform to the US Constitution. If not, these laws are declared illegal.

# Boom and crash, 1920–29

**KEY QUESTIONS**

- Why did the USA experience an economic boom in the 1920s?
- How far did speculation cause the Wall Street Crash?
- To what extent were the 1920s a decade of intolerance?
- Why were the 1920s a period of major cultural change in the USA?

## INTRODUCTION

The period from 1920 to 1929 was known as the Roaring Twenties. The decade saw a period of rapid economic growth that confirmed the USA as the world's greatest economy. Growth in car production and ownership was the most obvious sign to most Americans that the USA was in a period of unprecedented prosperity. The period was also linked to major changes in culture. The growth in popularity of jazz and new forms of dance such as the Charleston gave the impression that the USA had entered a new era of indulgence following the grim years of the First World War. However, not all of the USA experienced these changes. Farmers and those living in rural areas experienced economic hardship, and there was opposition to the rapid social and economic change. The rapid growth of the Ku Klux Klan and its white supremacist views made the 1920s a period of repression for many black Americans. In 1929, the economic boom came to an abrupt end, beginning with a major fall in share prices on the New York Stock Exchange based in Wall Street, New York City.

## WHY DID THE USA EXPERIENCE AN ECONOMIC BOOM IN THE 1920s?

**KEY TERMS**

**Gross National Product (GNP)**
The size of a national economy based on a measurement of the total amount of wealth produced by the economy, including imports and exports and money earned abroad.

**Inflation**
A period of general price rises.

The 1920s was a decade of unrivalled prosperity for the USA. The **Gross National Product** (GNP) rose from $73.3 billion in 1920 to $104.4 billion in 1929. Unemployment remained relatively low at 3.7 percent and **inflation** never rose above one percent. Profits for US businesses increased by 62 percent between 1923 and 1929. Already the world's largest economy, by 1920 the USA rapidly outstripped rivals like Britain, whose economy stagnated in the 1920s, and Germany, which had been devastated by the First World War and its aftermath.

A major underlying advantage possessed by the USA was its size and natural wealth. In 1920, it had a population of 106 million, compared to Britain's 42 million. This provided a large domestic market for goods and services. The USA also possessed considerable natural resources:

- huge coalfields in areas such as West Virginia and Kentucky

**1920** - Warren Harding (Republican) wins presidential election

**1920–1922** - Brief post-war economic recession

**1921** - Revenue Act cuts taxes on rich Federal Highways Act

**1922** - Fordney-McCumber Tariff

1920 | 1921 | 1922 | 1923 | 1924

**1924** - First attempt to aid farmers through McNary-Haugen bill fails

Figure 1.1: The 48 states of the USA and their capitals during the period 1920–55. Alaska and Hawaii joined later, in 1959.

- huge reserves of oil in states such as Texas, Oklahoma and California
- large quantities of metals such as iron, copper and lead, all important for industrial production.

To exploit these natural resources, the USA developed the most advanced transportation system in the world. It had an extensive railway network and a vast river system for the transportation of goods. In the 1920s, the development of the motor car was matched by a nationwide road system.

Exploitation of the USA's natural resources was also made possible by the American 'spirit of enterprise'. The ideal of rugged individualism created a basis for economic advance. The 'American Dream' suggested that anyone, no matter how poor initially, through hard work and talent could become rich. Self-made millionaires like steel magnate Andrew Carnegie and car manufacturer Henry Ford proved by example that it could be done.

Finally, millions of European immigrants provided the cheap labour and hard work to lay foundations for the USA's rapid economic advance.

**1925** – Price of Model T Ford car falls to $290 from $335 in 1920

**1927** – Second attempt to aid farmers through McNary-Haugen bill vetoed by President Coolidge
50 million Americans listen to Dempsey-Tunney heavyweight boxing match on radio

**1929** – Largest 200 corporations own 20 percent of nation's wealth

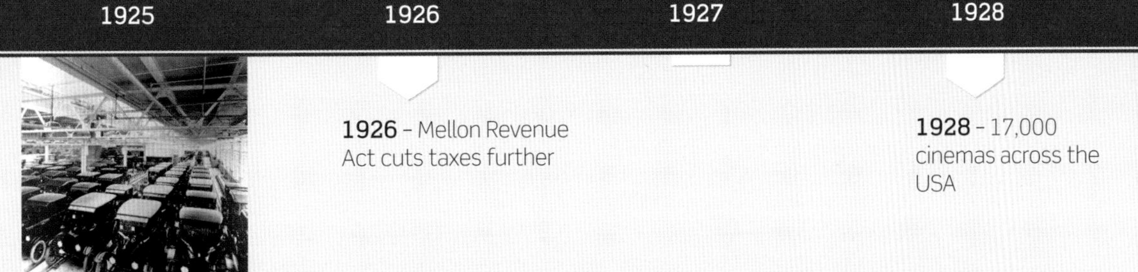


**1926** – Mellon Revenue Act cuts taxes further

**1928** – 17,000 cinemas across the USA

## Mass production

The technological advances of the 1920s made this period a virtual second industrial revolution for the USA.

One of the most important advances was the development of mass production, closely associated with Henry Ford. Ford established a car manufacturing plant in Detroit, Michigan before the First World War. He introduced the production line, which revolutionised car manufacture. On the Ford assembly line individual workers learned how to assemble only one specific part of a car. The assembly line moved at a steady pace, setting the rate of production. This meant low-skilled and semi-skilled workers could be employed.

In 1913, it took 12.5 hours to produce a Ford car. By 1913, through mass production, the time had been reduced to 2 hours 40 minutes.

In 1920, there were eight million cars in the USA. By 1929, that number had risen to 26 million. The most-produced car was the Ford Model T, which famously was only available in black between 1914 and 1926. Mass production led to higher output and lower prices. By 1925, a Model T cost $290, well within the reach of the ordinary American.

Production levels were also increased by combining mass production with scientific management. Frederick Taylor introduced time and motion studies of production. The methods of production were analysed so that new, more time-efficient ways of manufacturing goods could be adopted to improve the manufacturing process, resulting in lower labour costs and higher profits.

Perhaps, the most important advance was the creation of the large industrial corporation. This allowed companies to benefit from economies of scale. Corporations bought up natural resources, and controlled the whole manufacturing process and sales of their products. They could benefit from lower raw material costs and pass on lower costs to their consumers.

The larger corporations could come to control a very large proportion of the market. Samuel Insull controlled 111 separate but linked companies by 1929, with a combined value of $3 billion. By 1929, just 16 companies controlled 90 percent of the USA's electricity supply industry.

Electrification stimulated the development of other advances, such as radios, vacuum cleaners and toasters. In 1912, there were 2.4 million electrical appliances in the USA. By 1929, there were 160 million. However, electrification was centred on towns and cities. By 1929 much of the rural US was still without electricity, though overall 75 percent of Americans had electricity in their homes.

### EXTEND YOUR KNOWLEDGE

**Henry Ford and Fordism**

Henry Ford is the person most closely associated with the economic boom and the growth of the car industry. He built up one of the biggest car companies in US history at Dearborn, Michigan near Detroit. Before the First World War, Ford developed the production line, revolutionising car production. He paid workers $5 a day, a high wage at the time, to encourage hard work. Fordism, Ford's approach to mass production, was the cornerstone of the US manufacturing boom.

**Republican and Democrat economic policy in the 1920s**

The Republican Party in the United States was closely associated with big business, which wanted minimal government interference in economic matters. Up until the mid-1930s, the US Supreme Court tended to support this view.

The Democratic Party became increasingly linked with farmers, trade unions and the urban poor. The Democrats supported anti-trust legislation that attempted to prevent price-fixing by large corporations or groups of corporations, known as trusts.

**SOURCE**

From 'Why this Prosperity?' an article written by Donald Rea Hanson in *The Forum* magazine, July 1929. Hanson was a financial writer for the *Boston Journal*. The article discusses the causes of the economic boom.

Most of us have some idea as to the causes underlying the prosperity of the past six or eight years, but our views are likely to be colored by the prejudices, the political views and the occupation of the individual expressing the opinion. To the banker it might seem that the great expansion of credit has been the basic cause of our prosperity. To the head of a labor union it might seem that high wages and the gradual rise in the standard of living were the basic reasons. The manufacturer would explain our prosperity by pointing to the development of mass production. A Wall Street worker would declare that the confidence inspired by the election of President Coolidge in 1924 was the spark that kindled the flame of prosperity, and the foreign observer would insist that the war, which changed this nation from a debtor to a creditor nation, was the real cause of prosperity.

### AS Level Exam-Style Question Section A

***Study Source 1 before you answer this question.***

Why is Source 1 valuable to the historian for an enquiry into why an economic boom occurred in the USA in the 1920s?

Explain your answer using the source, the information about it and your own knowledge of the historical context. (8 marks)

**Tip**

*You should refer to the fact that Donald Rea Hanson worked as a financial writer and the date of the article. You should also make use of your own knowledge about the causes of the boom.*

## Technological advances and their impact on leisure

Another important stimulant to consumer spending was the development of the advertising and marketing industries, which were aided by the technological advances of radio and cinema. The first major commercial radio station was KDKA in Pittsburgh, Pennsylvania. It began broadcasting in November 1920 and became a model for radio stations across the USA. Popular radio shows were sponsored by corporations advertising their goods. By 1929, there were 619 commercial radio stations in the USA, providing a vast audience for advertisers. By the mid-1930s, 75 percent of all US households possessed a radio. In addition to radio, cinema provided another mass outlet for advertising. By 1929, every town in the USA possessed a picture theatre showing Hollywood films. New roads also provided new opportunities for advertising through billboards.

Not only did the rapid growth in car ownership stimulate the economic boom, it also had a major impact on US society. The car allowed workers to live further away from their place of work, helping the growth of suburbs around towns and cities. Extra mobility allowed Americans to travel, thus stimulating the leisure industry.

Seaside resorts such as Atlantic City, New Jersey grew rapidly as the destination for New Yorkers, while National Parks now became more accessible. Henry Ford said the car would allow a man 'to enjoy with his family the blessings of pleasure in God's open spaces'. These developments were aided by the federal government. In 1921, Congress passed the Federal Highways Act, which gave the government responsibility for building roads. Between 1920 and 1929, the overall length of surfaced roads increased from 350,000 miles to 662,000 miles. This was a major boost to the construction industry.

## The automobile

Perhaps the main driving force behind the economic boom of the 1920s was the motor car. Car registrations increased from eight million in 1920 to nearly 28 million in 1929. In 1920, Ford alone produced 1.25 million cars, one every sixty seconds. Hundreds of thousands were involved in car manufacture, in companies such as Ford, General Motors and Chrysler. Detroit became the world's car manufacturing centre. As the manufacturers flourished, so too did their workers. The car industry directly employed 375,000 workers: Ford's River Rouge plant employed 75,000 workers alone. By 1929, the car industry employed seven percent of the American manufacturing workforce, paying nine percent of all manufacturing wages.

SOURCE

Model T cars from the Ford Factory, Detroit, Michigan, ready for delivery in 1925. The Model T Ford was the most popular model of car in the USA during the 1920s.

Car manufacturing stimulated the growth of other industries as well. Steel, rubber and glass were essential materials for manufacture. As demand for cars increased, so too did demand for these materials. Technological advances in engineering and electrical industries were stimulated by the increased demand for better, more efficient cars. The huge increase in car ownership led to an equivalent, rapid rise in the demand for petrol, thus stimulating the oil industry, and also the emergence of petrol stations, motels and garages to serve motorists.

KEY TERM

**Real wages**
The amount of wages received above the rate of inflation. Inflation is a period of rising prices that leads to a rise in the cost of living. If inflation was one percent and a person received a pay increase of five percent, the rise in real wages would be four percent.

## Hire purchase

The 1920s was a decade of low unemployment and low inflation. **Real wages** rose 13 percent between 1923 and 1929. These factors were the basis of a major consumer boom that provided the demand for mass-produced goods. However, to encourage more consumer spending, firms in the USA offered hire-purchase schemes. These allowed consumers to buy goods by initially paying a small portion of the price and then paying off the rest of the price in monthly instalments. Over 75 percent of cars were bought through hire-purchase schemes. In 1920, consumer borrowing was just over $2 billion. By 1929, it had risen to over $8 billion.

Consumer spending was also stimulated by the belief that the economic boom of the 1920s would be never-ending. The USA, like all western economies, had gone through periods of boom and bust in the past. In 1857, 1873 and 1893, the US suffered major downturns in economic activity, but many believed the USA would avoid this business cycle of growth and depression in the 1920s.

SOURCE 3

From Stuart Chase, *Why Business Prosperity Came: Fact or Myth* (1929). Stuart Chase was a co-founder of Consumers Research Inc., the first product-testing organisation in the USA.

To my mind, the largest single force has been the motor car. The automobile was something which people really wanted with a desire that amounted to a passion. The effect was two-fold. It stimulated business, and it suffused the country with a visible appearance of a prosperity in which everybody seemed to share. Other prosperous periods had been stimulated by foreign trade. But this particular period was stimulated by a large, active, noisy and inescapable article visible on every road. You could see, hear and smell it for miles. It sent the credit structure of the USA spiralling upward, and it certainly made us look prosperous.

Most of us have not tired of this gorgeous toy. Its appeal strikes into our innermost natures. It has captured the psychological interest, as nothing has ever done before, and as perhaps nothing will ever do again.

THINKING HISTORICALLY **Cause and consequence (6a)**

**Seeing things differently**

Different people and groups have different beliefs about how the world works, how human societies should be governed and the best way to achieve economic prosperity. Other people's ideas can be radically different from our own. It is important for the historian to take this into account when considering past attitudes, and be aware of the dangers of judging them against personal beliefs and ideas from our own time.

Source 3 discusses the causes and consequences of the economic boom. Look at the source again and then answer the following questions.

1 How do views on the causes and consequences of the economic boom differ in Source 1 from the reasons put forward in Source 3?

2 If the author of the source had known how events would progress, e.g. that the economic boom would be followed by a major economic depression, do you think the author believing that the motor car was the major cause of the boom would have changed his attitude?

3 Attitudes in the USA in the late 1920s about the causes of the economic boom are different to current attitudes. Are there any other ways in which attitudes in the USA in the 1920s differed dramatically from those that are current now? Why do you think that they are different?

4 How important is it for historians to deal with events in the context of the beliefs and values of people in the past as well as seeing them as part of a greater pattern?

## How did the government's *laissez-faire* policy aid the economic boom?

The 1920s was a decade of dominance for the Republican Party, which won the presidential elections in 1920, 1924 and 1928. Republicans also dominated Congress. Calvin Coolidge, US president from 1923 to 1929, claimed that the 'business of America is business'. Successive Republican governments aided the development of big business through ***laissez-faire*** economic policies. These aimed to lower taxes and reduce government regulation on the development of business.

Some key policies were:

- In 1922, Congress passed the Fordney–McCumber Tariff. This law placed taxes (tariffs) on foreign goods imported into the US such as chemicals, textiles and farm products. By erecting a tariff wall around the US economy, the Fordney–McCumber Tariff increased the profits of the American chemical, dye, steel and aluminium industries. However, it did nothing to deal with the problem of agricultural overproduction and led to a fall in farm product prices.
- Andrew Mellon, Secretary to the Treasury from 1921 to 1932, adopted a low-tax policy. Taxes on the rich were lowered from 50 percent to 20 percent, in a series of revenue acts from 1921 to 1926. For instance, the 1926 Revenue Act lowered the tax rate for high earners, but also lowered taxes on the transfer of property and repealed the gift tax. During his eight years in office, Mellon handed out $3.5 billion in tax reductions. Mellon also supported a reduction in public spending. Mellon actually balanced the federal budget for part of his time in office and, under President Coolidge, the federal government actually operated on a surplus. In 1925, this was $677 million. In addition, Mellon helped reduce the US national debt.
- The Federal Trade Commission and Republican-run state governments reduced regulations on business. Price-fixing by businesses to raise profits was often ignored by the Federal Trade Commission. Little attempt was made to regulate hours of work or the use of child labour, and wage rates were kept low, all of which favoured businesses.
- When Republican President Calvin Coolidge stated that 'the business of America is business', it meant in reality that trade unions faced a difficult time in the 1920s. During the First World War (1914–18) the federal government had protected the rights of workers to join trade unions. By the war's end trade union membership had risen to over four million. Once government controls were lifted, many employers became involved in 'the American Plan', a slogan for reducing union power. No-strike agreements and no-union agreements were forced on many workers. Henry Ford, the car manufacturer, had a strong reputation for anti-union views. By 1929, union membership had declined by nearly a million. The Republican governments played their part. In 1922, Attorney General Dougherty broke the railroad shopman's strike by securing the support of a business-friendly judge against the strike. Between 1921 and 1925, the US Supreme Court made four significant anti-union decisions that restricted union power.

**KEY TERM**

***Laissez-faire***
A French term that roughly translates as 'leave things alone'. In an economic context, it is used to describe a policy of minimum government involvement in the economy. It is associated with low taxes and limited government regulation of business and industry.

## Farmers, black Americans and limits to the boom

The 1920s may have seen the US economy create unrivalled prosperity for many, but several social groups missed out.

### Farmers

US agriculture had boomed during the First World War when Europe was devastated by armed conflict. US agricultural prices rose by 82 percent from 1913 to 1917. However, once the war was over and European agriculture began to recover, demand for US food exports dropped and so did agricultural prices in the USA.

Agriculture was also affected by technological advances, such as the combine harvester. This machine greatly increased productivity in cereal production, but also led to an increase in unemployment among farm workers. Part of the unemployment problem was offset by the growth of towns and cities. By 1929, more Americans lived in urban rather than rural areas for the first time.

KEY TERM

**National prohibition**
The manufacture, sale and consumption of alcoholic drinks was banned across the USA in 1920. Prohibition was brought to an end by the 21st Amendment of the Constitution in 1933. Today, individual states determine their own drinks laws.

In the south-eastern USA in the 1920s, the dominant crop, cotton, was affected by the appearance of a nasty pest, the boll weevil, which caused serious damage to cotton plants. Grain demand fell with the introduction of **national prohibition** in 1920, as wheat and barley are important ingredients in whiskey and beer.

Attempts to aid farmers through legislation such as the McNary–Haugen bill, failed in a Congress dominated by *laissez-faire* ideas on the economy. The McNary–Haugen bill had attempted to stabilise agricultural prices with the government buying up surplus produce.

### Black Americans

Another group who missed out were black Americans. The majority still lived in the south-eastern USA and suffered legal and social discrimination. Many were sharecroppers who were unable to escape poverty. Sharecropping involved poor farmers, both black and white, buying seed and renting land from a large landowner. In return, they would pay back the landowner once the crop was harvested. If the harvest was poor, sharecroppers suffered extreme hardship. Outside the south-east, black Americans were given the most menial and low-paid jobs, and lived in areas of poor-quality housing. Even in the northern states, black Americans often only had jobs such as labourers, railway clerks and domestic servants.

The 1920s saw the biggest mass migration of black Americans in history. Nearly a million left the poverty-stricken south-east for jobs in the prosperous northern industrial cities, such as Detroit, New York and Chicago. By 1929, black Americans were engaged in manufacturing employment in large numbers for the first time.

SOURCE

From 'The Faith of the American Negro', a speech delivered by Mordecai Johnson, a black American educator and clergyman, to the 1922 graduating class of Harvard University. In 1926, he was appointed the first black American president of Howard University, Washington DC.

When the USA set forth its war aims, called upon Negro soldiers to fight, the entire Negro population experienced a profound sense of spiritual release. For the first time since emancipation from slavery they found themselves comparatively free to vote in a real and decisive way and in war found themselves bound with other Americans in a common cause.

At the close of war the Negro's hopes were suddenly dashed to the ground. Southern newspapers began at once to tell Negro soldiers that the war was over and the sooner they forgot the better. 'Pull off your uniform,' they said, 'find the place you had before the war and stay in it.' In connection with this there were attacks on Negro life and property. There came also the increasing boldness of those who engaged in lynching black Americans, who advertised their purposes in advance to their victims. There came vain appeals to the President of the USA and to the houses of Congress. From those terrible days until this day the Negro's faith in the righteous purpose of the Federal Government has sagged. Some have laid the blame on the party in power. Some have laid it elsewhere. But all the colored people believe that there is something wrong, not accidently wrong, at the very heart of the Government.

ACTIVITY
KNOWLEDGE CHECK

**The economic boom of the 1920s**

1 Write down five reasons why the economic boom took place in the 1920s.

2 What do you regard as the most important reason? Give reasons for your answer.

3 Create a spider diagram that identifies different reasons for the economic boom and the links between them.

**A Level Exam-Style Question Section B**

'The economic boom of the 1920s was due more to a consumer boom than to technological advances.' How far do you agree with this statement? (20 marks)

**Tip**

*You need to compare and assess the two factors in the question rather than merely describe the boom with a concluding assessment.*

# WHAT CAUSED THE WALL STREET CRASH?

Throughout the 1920s the economy had been booming and **share** prices had been steadily rising. In October 1929 the boom came to a dramatic end with the **Wall Street** Crash.

## The Wall Street Crash

On Thursday 24 October 1929, also known as Black Thursday, 12.8 million shares changed hands on the New York Stock Exchange, the largest stock exchange in the USA, also known as Wall Street. By the end of that day, the value of shares on the New York Stock Exchange had fallen by almost $4 billion. On the following Tuesday, 29 October, a record 16 million shares changed hands at very low prices. By the end of November 1929, $30 billion had been wiped off share values.

A severe economic slump followed the Wall Street Crash, but was not a direct result of it. Between October and December 1929, the number of unemployed in the USA rose from 500,000 to four million as the share value of companies began to fall and banks that possessed shares in companies began to close down. As a result, companies went bankrupt and workers found themselves unemployed. This triggered a cycle of increased unemployment across the USA.

Many thought the drop in share prices and the downturn in the economy would be temporary. The USA had experienced economic booms and recessions in the past. However, the Wall Street Crash began the biggest economic depression in US and world history. Average real wages fell 16 percent in the period 1929 to 1931. The Gross National Product (GNP) fell 29 percent between 1929 and 1933. By 1932, the US steel industry, the biggest in the world, was operating at 12 percent capacity.

The Wall Street Crash shattered public confidence. By November 1929, share values nationally had fallen from a high of $87 billion to only $56 billion. Share prices continued to fall in the succeeding years. By 1933, these same shares were worth only $18 billion.

### KEY TERMS

**Share**
A certificate which gives the owner a financial stake in a private company. These are traded at stock exchanges.

**Wall Street**
The name for the New York Stock Exchange, based in Wall Street, New York City. Stock exchanges existed across the US. The New York Stock Exchange is the largest and most important.

**SOURCE 5** From the *Philadelphia Evening Ledger* newspaper, 30 October 1929.

Again in yesterday's stock market we are able to see how dangerous a thing the emotion of fright may be when it is artificially created by propaganda and used as a means of control in the field of business. The propagandists of gloom and economic terror certainly should feel proud of their work, whatever the feeling of the country may be when it pauses to think a little later on. The poison of fear was fed liberally to the public mind and so all of a sudden the lords of the nation's credit found themselves trying desperately to stop a fall of price that was even more unreasonable and disturbing than the rise of which they complained in the first place.

### AS Level Exam-Style Question Section A

***Study Source 5 before you answer this question.***

Why is Source 5 valuable to a historian investigating how the Wall Street Crash affected the US economy? (8 marks)

**Tip**

*Refer to the provenance of the source in your answer. When was it written? Who wrote it? What was the intended audience? These questions will help you assess the source's value. To support your answer you should also refer to relevant information from within the source and your own knowledge to place the source in historical context.*

### TIMELINE

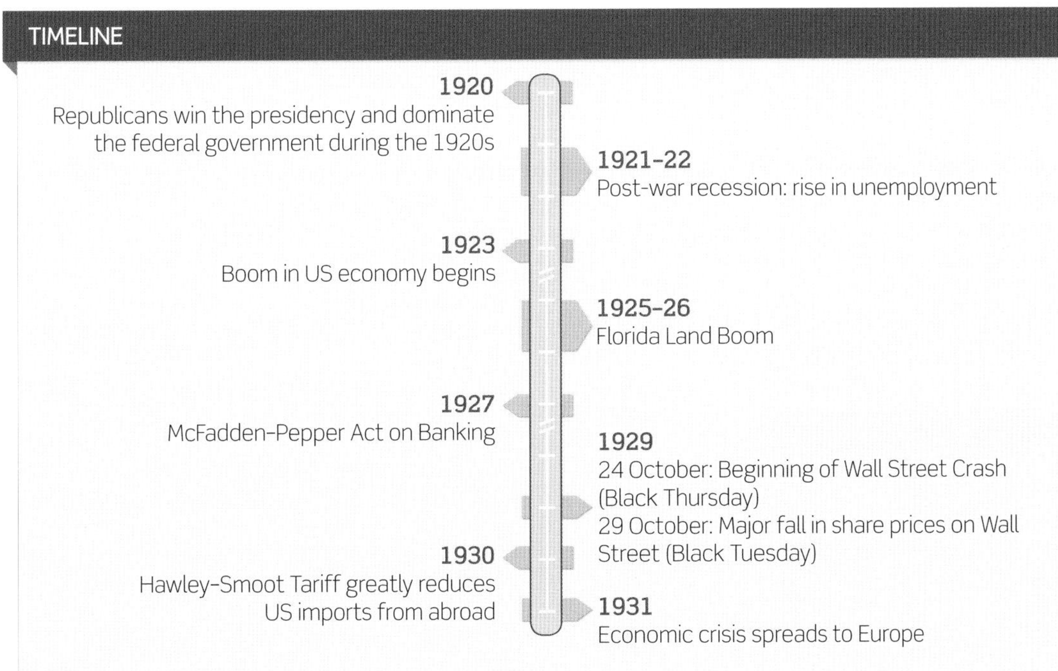

EXTEND YOUR KNOWLEDGE

**Business cycle**

In western economies like the USA and Britain, economic activity traditionally goes through phases of boom and bust. Economic growth normally results in rising employment and inflation. When an economy overproduces, a recession occurs and brings rising unemployment. Prices also drop, a process known as deflation. The lowest point of a business cycle is a depression. This is normally followed by economic recovery, leading to a boom.

In 1929, the depression was so severe that governments across the world were forced to intervene to stimulate recovery. This was usually done through public spending on projects like infrastructure. This occurred in the USA, Britain and Germany in the 1930s.

**Double-barrelled names for Congressional bills and Acts**

US Congressional legislation normally has two names. The first name is that of the Senator who introduces the proposal in the Senate and the second name is that of the Congressman or woman who introduces the proposal in the House of Representatives.

## Overproduction

The 1920s may have been a period of unrivalled prosperity but the people who benefited most were the top five percent of the population. As a result of the low tax policies of the Republican governments in the 1920s, the rich became richer. By 1929, this group owned 33 percent of the nation's wealth. In contrast, the bottom 40 percent of the population owned only 12.5 percent of the nation's wealth. The US economy therefore lacked the spending power to buy all the goods produced. Overproduction became a major problem.

Demand for new goods required spending power across the US population. The belief that the US had entered a new era of continued economic growth encouraged corporations to build more factories to provide goods for an ever-expanding market. By the late 1920s, the US economy had reached capacity in terms of what the domestic market for goods could consume. Part of the economy's problem was the Fordney–McCumber Tariff of 1922, which limited US trade with the rest of the world economy. In retaliation to that tariff, foreign countries put their own tariffs on US goods. Also, much of the European market was affected by the problems associated with the aftermath of the First World War. Germany had to pay huge war damages, known as reparations, to the Allied powers. Potential markets were also lost with the creation of the world's first **communist** state in Russia, after 1917, and the resulting tensions between the new USSR and the capitalist world. Between 1920 and 1929, US manufacturing capacity rose 50 percent but US exports rose by only 38 percent.

KEY TERM

**Communist**

A person who believes in the common ownership of property, land and business. Communists were opposed to the type of capitalist society that existed in the United States.

Consumption within the US was also artificially inflated by the existence of easy credit through hire purchase schemes. Thousands of Americans were buying goods and paying only a small proportion of the price up front. Once confidence in the economy began to wane following the Wall Street Crash, consumer spending dropped rapidly.

The disparity in wealth between the very rich and the bottom third of the US population meant that the economic boom of the 1920s was unsustainable. Too many goods were being produced in an economy that lacked the spending power to purchase them. When the stock market crashed in October 1929, it revealed the underlying weaknesses of the US economy.

## Land speculation

The Wall Street Crash was not the first major economic crisis to face the USA in the 1920s. A prelude to the Crash had occurred in 1926, with land speculation centred on Florida. As many Americans saw the 1920s as a period of unrivalled prosperity and average incomes rose, the idea of owning property in the sunshine state of Florida became very attractive.

Super-rich industrialists such as T. Coleman Du Pont, who owned America's largest chemical company, saw the possibility of buying up land in southern Florida and selling it to the newly prosperous populations who faced cold winters in the north-eastern USA. The growth of the motor car made Florida even more accessible. Hundreds motored down to Florida to buy their dream home. The area around modern-day Miami went through a massive land boom and thousands of new houses were built at Miami Beach, Palm Beach and Coral Gables. Between 1920 and 1925, Miami's population grew from 30,000 to 130,000.

By 1926, the Florida Land Boom had collapsed. Lack of infrastructure, such as railways and roads, impeded development. Swindlers, like the unscrupulous speculators who sold land in the non-existent town of Nettie, gave the land boom a very bad name, causing a loss in confidence. In 1925, the Internal Revenue Service began taxing profits on property speculation, which reduced levels of speculation and confidence. Finally, in September 1926, a major hurricane devastated large parts of southern Florida. The hurricane killed 400 people and left 50,000 homeless. This dissuaded many from investing in property in Florida. The flood of investors buying property in 1925 was reduced to a trickle by 1927.

EXTRACT

This description of the Florida Land Speculation Boom of 1925 is from *The Anxious Decades* by Michael Parrish, published in 1994.

In the Miami Area, where a single edition of the 'Daily News' in 1925 topped 500 pages, mostly crammed with property advertisements, tales of feverish speculation and fabulous wealth abounded. Prime business lots sold for $5,000 a foot. Those on Biscayne Bay commanded $15,000 to $20,000. A woman who purchased a parcel for $25 at the turn of the century sold it for $150,000 in 1925. A man who sold a lot for $2,500 in 1923 claimed he bought it back for $35,000 at the height of the boom. Binders changed hands, sometimes as often as five times a day, each price higher than the last. At a local hotel, a New York reporter overheard an excited conversation: 'Momma! Momma! Is that you, Momma? This is Moe! I bought 10,000 acres today. Yes, 10,000. How should I tell you where this land is? I don't know myself?' A few years later the Marx Brothers captured the madness in their first film, 'Cocoanuts', where property broker Groucho announces, 'Now folks, everybody this way for the grand swindle! Buy a lot. You can have any kind of house you want.'

## The bull market

Another key factor leading to the 1929 crash was over-speculation on future share prices. Even though the USA had experienced **bear markets** in the past, there was a belief among many that the **bull market** of the 1920s would be almost never-ending. The share values on the New York Stock Exchange almost doubled between 1925 and 1929 from $34 billion to $64 billion. The idea that even average Americans could 'get rich quick' through buying shares led to considerable share speculation. By 1929, many Americans were buying shares 'at the margin'. They would borrow money and buy shares at ten percent of the share price. They hoped to pay back the loan through selling the shares at a higher price in the future. As long as share prices kept rising, the practice worked. Once share prices began to fall then speculation in share prices began to unravel. President Hoover, elected in 1928, called it a 'mad orgy of speculation'.

**KEY TERMS**

**Bear market**
A period when share prices fall.

**Bull market**
A period when share prices go up.

In 1929–30, share speculators lost money, many going bankrupt. Once confidence in the value of stock prices began to waver a wave of selling began which triggered a share sale panic.

Some had feared a share price fall by early 1929. Moody's Investment Service and the Harvard Economic Society both warned that share prices had reached unreasonable levels and a downward readjustment in prices was expected. However, these warnings were not heeded by the majority of share purchasers.

## Weaknesses of the US banking system

A strong banking system is the bedrock of any successful economy. In a healthy economy individuals and companies deposit savings at banks, which in turn lend that money at a profit to commercial and private customers. Normally banks keep only a percentage (about eight percent) of the money deposited with them and loan the rest. Banks may pay depositors interest to encourage them to use the bank's deposit facilities, and charge a higher rate of interest for loans.

However, if borrowers fail to repay their loans, banks face the problem of how to pay off depositors. If very large numbers of borrowers fail to repay their loans, banks may be forced to close because they owe more money than they possess. Those who have deposited their money in that bank will lose their money.

In the 1920s various weaknesses in the US banking system contributed to the onset of economic depression.

Under Director Benjamin Strong, in 1927 the **Federal Reserve Board** kept US interest rates low, at 3.5 percent. This helped fuel a considerable amount of borrowing by banks with substantial reserves of money. Unfortunately, much of the money banks invested went into share speculation and property investments instead of loans to commerce and industry, so did not contribute to growing the economy.

**KEY TERM**

**Federal Reserve Board**
The US equivalent of the Bank of England, created in 1914. This acts as the central bank of the USA, and the head of the board is appointed directly by the president. Central banks have the important role of helping set the rate of interest at which money can be borrowed, in order to limit or encourage the amount of lending within the economy. The Federal Reserve Board is also responsible for providing guidance on how to regulate the US economy, including the banking industry. In the 1920s only one third of US banks followed the Federal Reserve Board's regulations.

'Call loans' were a particular problem. These were loans to individuals and companies to buy shares 'on the margin'. This system was profitable as long as share prices rose. Once they began to fall, in the autumn of 1929, it exposed thousands of banks to bad debts, which they could not get borrowers to repay.

These problems would have been minimised if all banks in the USA had followed the regulations laid down by the Federal Reserve Board. However, only one third of US banks worked within this Federal Reserve System. The other two-thirds operated in an unregulated market without clear controls on how they should operate. This led to high-risk lending to businesses that were not in a strong financial position.

The situation in the US was also made worse by the existence of thousands of different banks. US law set limits on bank operations, restricting most to operation within one of the 48 states. These banks had limited stocks of money. When they were faced with bad debt they usually called in loans. This sparked off bank closures when debtors were unable to pay.

**AS Level Exam-Style Question Section A**

How accurate is it to say that the Wall Street Crash caused the Depression in the USA? (20 marks)

**Tip**

*You need to assess the direct relationship between the Wall Street Crash and the onset of depression.*

Between 1921 and 1928, 5,000 banks went out of business. In 1929, 659 suspended operations. As banks were the institutions that provided money for industry through loans, the weakness of the banking system made a major economic depression inevitable.

In 1927, Congress passed the McFadden–Pepper Act. This Act gave big city commercial banks extra powers, which allowed them to compete more strongly against smaller rural banks. Most of the smaller rural banks were outside the Federal Reserve System.

It would take a major banking reform in 1933, the Glass–Steagall Act, to begin the creation of a modern banking system and finally enable the US economy to get out of the severe economic depression it found itself in.

**SOURCE**

From an article entitled 'What caused the panic of 1929?' by Henry Parker Wills in the magazine *North American Review*, February 1930. Wills was First Secretary to the Federal Reserve Board from 1914 to 1918.

This panic was not 'inevitable'. It was the result of gross carelessness or wanton recklessness. The recording of its causes in frank language may help to prevent the recurrence of a similar situation. For generations past it has been expected that our bankers should act to restrain hasty investors, and that they should encourage the advantages of saving as against speculation. Yet within the past two years it has been indisputably true that this whole range of guidelines has been abandoned by our banking community. Through their establishment of financing companies, they have put themselves into a position as issuers of shares. Investment trusts, shares and similar securities of all kinds have poured forth from the banks, while many more have been issued by 'groups' which were practically bankers and banking houses in another form.

The breakdown of 1929 was as nearly the result of wilful mismanagement and violation of the principle of sound finance, which has resulted in untold loss both national and individual.

**ACTIVITY**
**KNOWLEDGE CHECK**

**The Crash**

Give five reasons why you think the economic boom came to an end after October 1929. Place the reasons in order of importance with an explanation for your choice.

**KEY TERMS**

**Supremacists**
Members of the Ku Klux Klan and others, who believed white Anglo-Saxon Protestants (WASPS) were superior to other groups in the USA, including black Americans, Native Americans, white Catholics and Jews.

**Bolshevik (or October) Revolution**
In October 1917, communists, also known as Bolsheviks, took over the government of Russia. The former ruler, the Tsar, had been deposed in an earlier revolution in February 1917. The Bolsheviks aimed to abolish all private property and took all private business under government control. Money invested in Russian companies by foreign investors was confiscated by the Bolshevik government. These actions caused deep concern within the USA.

# TO WHAT EXTENT WERE THE 1920s A DECADE OF INTOLERANCE?

Although the 1920s were a decade of unrivalled prosperity, they also saw major changes in US society.

- The US had been the recipient of millions of European immigrants in the 19th century. The 1920s saw the first restrictions on that immigration.
- The decade saw the reappearance of the white **supremacist** group, the Ku Klux Klan.
- The introduction of national prohibition helped fuel the growth of organised crime.
- Women received the vote in federal elections for the first time and their role in society changed radically.

## Immigration and the 'Red Scare'

From November 1917 the **Bolshevik Revolution** in Russia created the world's first communist state. Communist ideas were seen as a direct threat to the US political and economic system. Immigrants from central and eastern Europe came to be feared in the USA as being susceptible to these 'un-American' ideas. Also, from April 1917 when the USA joined the First World War, Germany and Austria-Hungary were enemy nations and resentment towards immigrants from these countries increased.

The year 1919 was one of considerable industrial unrest. Inflation caused by the war resulted in widespread strikes. Over four million workers were involved nationwide. Extreme left-wing trade unions, like the International Workers of the World (known at the time by the nickname the Wobblies), were seen as causing much of the unrest.

A General Intelligence Division of the federal government was created in August 1919, in order to investigate the scale of socialist and communist activity in the USA. It was the forerunner of the **FBI.**

By January 1920, the federal government began to act. 'Palmer' raids (named after the **Attorney General**) were launched against left-wing newspapers and left-wing activists. 6,000 were arrested. By the middle of 1920, the Red Scare had died down.

### KEY TERMS

**FBI**
Federal Bureau of Investigation. Set up in 1924, it became the US national police force but could only deal with interstate crime.

**Attorney General**
The most senior legal officer of the American government.

### EXTEND YOUR KNOWLEDGE

**Sacco and Vanzetti case**
In May 1920, two Italian immigrants with left-wing views were arrested and put on trial for the murder of a paymaster. The Sacco and Vanzetti case divided the USA. Evidence of their involvement in the crime was based mainly on circumstantial evidence such as the fact they had avoided military service in the war and had supported anarchist ideas (anarchists were opposed to all forms of government). Between 1920 and 1927, Sacco and Vanzetti faced a trial and then an appeal. Finally, in 1927, they were executed for murder. The trial is an indicator of the general climate of fear and intolerance towards people with radical and alternative political views in the US in the 1920s.

### SOURCE

**An extract from 'To the American People: Report on the Illegal Practices of the US Department of Justice', May 1920. The report, written by 12 prominent lawyers and law professors for the National Popular Government League, was an appeal against the Palmer Raids.**

TO THE AMERICAN PEOPLE: For more than six months, we, the undersigned lawyers, whose sworn duty it is to uphold The Constitution and Laws of the United States, have seen with growing apprehension the continued violation of that Constitution and breaking of those Laws by the Department of Justice.

Wholesale arrests both of aliens and citizens have been made without warrant or any process of law; men and women have been jailed and held in secret without access to friends or legal counsel; homes have been entered without search warrant and property seized and removed; other property has been wantonly destroyed; working men and working women suspected of radical views have been shamefully abused and maltreated. Agents of the Department of Justice have been introduced into radical organisations for the purpose of informing upon their members or inciting them to activities. These agents have even been instructed from Washington DC to arrange meetings upon certain dates for the express object of facilitating raids and arrests. In support of illegal acts and to create sentiment in its favour, the Department of Justice has also created itself a propaganda office and has sent newspapers and magazines designed to excite public opinion against radicals, all at the expense of the government.

We make no argument in favour of any radical doctrine, such as communism or anarchism. No one of us belongs to any of these schools of thought. We are concerned solely with bringing to the attention of the American people the utterly illegal acts which have been committed by those whose highest duty is enforcing the law and have brought the name of our country into disrepute.

### ACTIVITY
### WRITING

**Study Source 7 on the Red Scare before answering this question.**

**1** Analyse the language and content used in the source.

**2** Identify any words or phrases you do not understand and research their meanings.

**3** Identify words and phrases that show the writers' feelings towards the Palmer Raids instituted by the federal government.

**4** Write a short paragraph explaining the views of the authors of this source, using quotes from the extract to back up your points.

## Restrictions on immigration

An inscription on the Statue of Liberty in New York Harbour states: 'Bring me your huddled masses yearning to be free'. The USA was a nation of immigrants, overwhelmingly from Europe. However, opposition to unlimited immigration, especially of immigrants who could not speak English, had grown during the First World War. In 1917, Congress overrode the president's veto by a two-thirds majority in both houses, and passed the Immigration Act. This denied entry into the USA to immigrants who could not read or write.

Opposition to immigration continued to grow after the war. In 1921, the Emergency Immigration Act placed the first-ever limit on immigration. It was restricted to three percent of the total number of people from a national group already living in the US, as recorded in the 1910 national census. This greatly favoured immigrants from the British Isles and Western Europe.

The Johnson–Reed Immigration Act of 1924 made these changes permanent. New quotas were two percent from a particular region, based on the US 1890 census. This increased the bias towards immigrants from the British Isles and against those from eastern and southern Europe. Hispanic workers in California were exempt from the Act. By 1929, Congress declared that only 120,000 immigrants could enter the USA per year.

The US had turned its back on unlimited immigration, which had helped transform the economy in the 19th century.

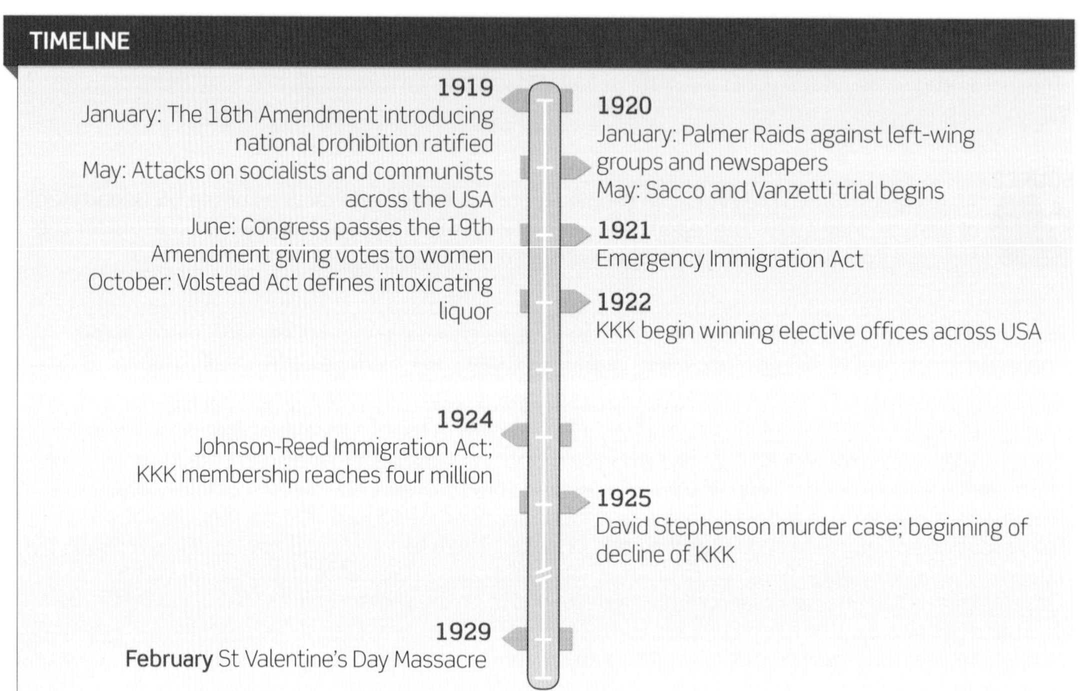


## Rise and decline of the Ku Klux Klan

Many would say the clearest sign of intolerance in the 1920s was the rapid rise, and then decline, of the Ku Klux Klan (KKK). This organisation had been established immediately after the end of the US Civil War (1861–65) in the former **Confederate states** to protect whites and attack and intimidate black Americans, who had been freed from slavery by the war.

In the late 1870s, the Ku Klux Klan went into decline. By that time, most former Confederate states had introduced legal segregation of blacks and whites, so the KKK's tactics of intimidation were no longer in demand.

In 1915, the KKK was revived by William Simmons at Stone Mountain, Georgia. The revival was greatly influenced by two developments. One was the publication of a book, *The Clansman*, a story about the KKK and its activities by Thomas Dixon. Another was the first full-length feature film made by Hollywood, *The Birth of a Nation*, by D. W. Griffith, first shown in 1915. It portrayed the old KKK as heroes of the white race.

The KKK was seen as a way to defend the small-town, rural America of WASPS, who felt threatened by new immigrants as well as established black Americans. From 1915, the KKK also turned against Jews and Catholics.

Although William Simmons refounded the KKK, the people behind its rapid rise were Edgar Young Clark and Elizabeth Tyler. They used public relations techniques to encourage recruitment.

### KEY TERM

**Confederate states**
Between 1861 and 1865, 11 states in the south-east of the USA declared their independence from the USA in order to preserve the practice of enslaving black Americans. These states were Virginia, North and South Carolina, Georgia, Alabama, Mississippi, Arkansas, Tennessee, Texas, Louisiana and Florida. At the end of the Civil War, slavery was abolished throughout the USA.

Following their defeat in the US Civil War, former Confederate states began introducing 'Jim Crow' laws, which deprived black Americans of the right to vote and forced them to live lives separate from whites through legal segregation. This situation lasted until the 1960s.

As the Republican Party had freed the slaves, these states traditionally voted for the Democratic Party.

A small joining fee of $10 got you a white robe and hood, the uniform of the KKK, handed over at an elaborate ceremony. KKK members wore their hooded robes to large gatherings at which they often burned a large wooden cross. This was a way of displaying their power and intimidating their opponents. By 1924, the KKK had a national membership of four million across the whole of the USA. Many state governments, such as those of Indiana and Colorado, were sympathetic to the KKK.

However, the KKK's rapid rise was mirrored by its rapid decline. In 1925, the KKK leader in Indiana, its Grand Dragon, David Curtis Stephenson, was convicted of the rape and murder of a 28-year-old woman. This badly damaged its reputation as attempting to defend 'decent America'. Other KKK members were found guilty of bribery and corruption. By 1929, KKK membership had declined to 200,000.

SOURCE

From 'The Sign of Fear', an article in the *North American Review* by W. E. B. DuBois, published in 1926. DuBois was a leading black American supporter of equal rights.

I was lecturing in Akron, Ohio. Now Ohio is one of those States upon whose essential Americanism and devotion to the finer ideals of democracy I have long banked. There in the Middle West that finer flower of democracy, born in New England, and later choked by the industrialism of the East, had, to my mind, gone for replanting and renewal. I looked for sanity in the United States to come from a democratic appeal to the Middle West. And yet, there in Akron, in the land of Joshua R. Giddings, in the Western Reserve, I found the Klan calmly and openly in the saddle. The leader of the local Klan was president of the Board of Education and had just been tremendously busied in driving a Jew out of the public schools. The Mayor, the secretary of the Y.M.C.A. [Young Men's Christian Association], prominent men in many walks of life, were either open Klansmen or secret sympathizers. I was too astonished to talk. Throughout parts of Ohio, Illinois and Indiana I found a similar state of affairs...

What is the cause of all this? There can be little doubt but that the Klan in its present form is a legacy of the World War. Whatever there was of it before that great catastrophe was negligible. The wages of War is hate; and the End, and indeed the Beginning of Hate is fear. The civilised world today is desperately afraid.

## National prohibition

Between 1920 and 1933, the USA engaged in a major social change. The sale, manufacture and consumption of intoxicating liquor were banned throughout the land.

Prohibition of alcohol sales was introduced by the 18th Amendment of the US Constitution in 1919. However, the amendment did not define 'intoxicating liquor'. Later the same year Congress passed the Volstead Act, which defined intoxicating liquor as any drink with more than 0.5 percent alcohol. This meant that virtually all beer, plus wine and spirits, were illegal.

Although national prohibition began in January 1920, several states had already banned alcoholic drinks before the First World War. Organisations such as the Women's Christian Temperance Union and the Anti-Saloon League campaigned vigorously for prohibition. Wayne Wheeler of the Anti-Saloon League was one of the most effective lobbyists of politicians in the USA.

Supporters of prohibition claimed that alcohol ruined lives. Men drank away their wages, leaving their families to starve. Alcohol caused violence and was linked to gambling and prostitution. It was un-Christian, because it destroyed family life. The biggest support for prohibition came from small towns and rural areas dominated by white Anglo-Saxon Protestants (WASPS). They resented new immigrants from southern and eastern Europe and saw drinking alcohol as a distinctive feature of their cultures. Many of these groups also happened to be Catholic. The WASPS came to see drinking as un-American.

The First World War also helped increase support for national prohibition. Many businessmen opposed the drinking of alcohol by workers who were operating complicated machinery.

During the First World War, anti-German feeling reached its height in the USA. Many breweries, such as Budweiser, Schlitz and Pabst were German-American owned. Supporters of prohibition claimed it was patriotic to support their cause. In addition, they claimed grain used for alcohol manufacture would be better used for food in the wartime emergency.

The issue of prohibition split the Democratic Party. 'Dry' Democrats from the South and West were opposed by 'Wet' Democrats from the big cities.

Of all the laws passed in the USA, national prohibition was the most widely ignored. Even President Harding (1921–23) had alcoholic drinks at White House receptions. Across the USA, thousands of illegal drinking places, known as speakeasies, were set up. People began making alcoholic drinks illegally from scratch, or using industrial or medical alcohol as substitute raw materials. This was called moonshine liquor.

National prohibition also failed for other reasons. For many Americans, such as Irish Americans, Italian Americans and German Americans, drinking alcohol was part of their culture and they were reluctant to stop. The USA had 6,500 miles of land borders with Canada and Mexico. Neither of these countries had introduced prohibition, so large quantities of alcoholic drinks were illegally imported. To enforce national prohibition, the federal government had only 3,000 Prohibition agents, paid on average $2,500 a year. This was a relatively low salary-making them susceptible to bribery. This number was far too few to patrol the borders and enforce national prohibition within the USA.

### Prohibition and organised crime

A major reason for the failure of national prohibition was the involvement of organised crime. Organised crime had been heavily involved in gambling and prostitution. Now it saw that huge profits could be made from importing, manufacturing and selling alcoholic drinks. National prohibition led to these gangs becoming heavily involved in politics. Gangsters bribed the police, judges and local politicians to ensure their huge profits from **bootlegging** would be maintained.

KEY TERM

**Bootlegging**
The illegal transportation and sale of intoxicating liquor.

The large sums of money to be made from selling alcohol led to rivalry between gangs. The centre of bootleg activity was Chicago, and gangs of Italian, Jewish and Irish Americans competed for the trade. On 14 February 1929, an Italian-American gang led by Al Capone wiped out the leaders of his main rivals, a Jewish/Irish-American gang led by Dion O'Banion, in the St Valentine's Day Massacre. This was one of the most publicised examples of the gang violence that flared up across America.

Even after national prohibition was abolished in 1933, organised crime remained a major feature of US life, vying for control of newspapers, politicians, judges and the police. Those who hoped national prohibition would make the USA a more moral country had, inadvertently, helped create the opposite.

President Hoover (1929–33) set up the Wickersham Commission to investigate national prohibition. It reported in 1931, stating that although national prohibition should continue, it was impossible to enforce.

SOURCE

From *The Effect of Prohibition on Crime*, an article by George Gordon Battle, a Democratic Party lawyer from New York, published in 1920.

I believe that the Prohibition laws regarded as in a class by themselves. Very few of our people feel any obligation to observe these laws. But I do not observe that this habitual violation of the Prohibition laws carries with it any general contempt of law. I believe that the great majority of men and women pay no attention to these laws but are as obedient as formerly to other laws. In conclusion, I believe the most dangerous feature of the present situation is in the official corruption which now forms such a scandal in the enforcement of these laws. If steps can be taken to cleanse the Government of this evil, in my opinion, the principal menace of Prohibition will cease to threaten us.

**AS Level Exam-Style Question Section A**

***Study Source 9 before you answer this question.***

How much weight would you give to the evidence in Source 9 for an enquiry into the links between national prohibition and crime? (12 marks)

**Tip**

*Make sure you refer to who wrote the source, when it was written and the intended audience. These are important in your assessment of the source's value as evidence. You will also be expected to use relevant information from the source and your own knowledge to support and sustain your argument.*

## The changing role of women

Not all social change in the USA in the 1920s was associated with intolerance. In 1919, American women received the right to vote in federal elections.

The 1920s were a period of considerable change for American women. One of the most enduring images of the 1920s was the 'flapper'. This term was applied to young, independent-minded women who felt that a woman's place was no longer 'in the home', rearing children and looking after the family.

The economic boom provided women with new opportunities for employment. Becoming secretaries, telephone operators and typists allowed tens of thousands to move to big towns and cities and live independent lives. Their new-found freedom was mirrored in major changes in fashion. Short skirts and short hair became associated with flappers. In addition, women, for the first time in large numbers, began to use cosmetics. Beauty salons opened up across the USA.

Although the 1920s was a period of liberation for many young unmarried women, the women's revolution predicted by many failed to materialise. By 1928, 145 women had won seats in state legislatures and two had become state governors, but politics was still dominated by men, as were business and commerce. The vast majority of universities were male only. Even the prestigious female college, Vassar, still offered courses in 'Wife, Motherhood and the Family'. Flappers were associated with urban living. For the majority of women living in small towns and rural areas, the 1920s brought little change.

An attempt was made in the 1920s to get female equality enshrined in law. The National Woman's Party, led by Alice Paul, campaigned to have an Equal Rights Amendment to the US Constitution. It failed because it did not get sufficient support in the US Congress.

## THINKING HISTORICALLY Evidence (5a)

### Context is everything

Reread Source 7, an appeal by the National Popular Government League against the Palmer Raids, Source 8, in which a black American civil rights campaigner discusses his experiences in a midwestern town, and Source 9, discussing the effects of prohibition on crime.

Work in small groups. Take an A3 piece of paper. In the middle draw a circle about 20 cm in diameter. Label the circle 'evidence' and the space outside it 'context'.

For each source:

1 Think of a question that the source could be helpful in answering.

2 Inside the circle, write a set of statements giving information that can be gleaned only from the source itself without any contextual knowledge.

3 Outside the circle write statements of contextual knowledge that relate to the source.

4 Draw annotated lines to show links between the contextual statements and the information from the source. Does context change the nature or meaning of the information?

Now answer this question:

5 Explain why knowledge of context is important when gathering and using historical evidence. Give specific examples to illustrate your point.

## ACTIVITY KNOWLEDGE CHECK

### Changing society

1 Why was communism seen as such a threat to the USA in 1919?

2 Give three reasons why national prohibition was introduced in the USA in the 1920s.

3 Give three reasons for the revival of the KKK in the early 1920s.

**A Level Exam-Style Question Section B**

To what extent was the rise of the Ku Klux Klan the most important threat facing US society in the 1920s? (20 marks)

**Tip**

*You will need to assess the threat posed by the KKK against other threats to US society.*

# WHY WERE THE 1920s A PERIOD OF MAJOR CULTURAL CHANGE IN THE USA?

With the end of the First World War, and the economic boom of the 1920s, this was also a period of rapid cultural change in music, fashion, sport and literature. The USA dominated new technologies in popular entertainment: the radio and cinema. A suburb of Los Angeles, California, became the movie-making capital of the USA and the world: Hollywood. Although black Americans faced informal and legal discrimination across the USA, the 1920s saw them make a major contribution to US culture and society.

## The Jazz Age

Jazz is perhaps the USA's greatest contribution to world music. Jazz, as a form of music, was first developed by black Americans in New Orleans, Louisiana around 1895. Much of jazz music was improvised playing, which immediately became popular among black Americans in towns and cities. Jazz musicians used a variety of instruments, most notably the saxophone.

During the 1920s, the Great Migration of black Americans began to northern cities such as Chicago, Philadelphia and New York. 850,000 made the journey north to find employment and get away from legal segregation. In doing so, they took their music with them. White musicians soon began to play jazz as well and, by 1929, jazz had become a form of music played across the USA by whites and blacks alike. The development of commercial radio stations greatly aided the process.

Although first associated with instrumental music, jazz became associated with a more general cultural revolution that encompassed singing and dancing. For the first time, black American, and in particular female black American, singers achieved widespread popularity. Bessie Smith and Billie Holiday became household names. Black musicians such as Louis Armstrong began recording records, bought by white and black fans.

Jazz was also the music that accompanied new dance crazes in the 1920s. The Charleston and the turkey trot were new, lively dances. They replaced the sedate waltz, which had been popular in the early part of the century.

The growth of jazz was not universally popular. Jazz was popular in urban areas, but in country areas whites were still attracted to country music, while in black American rural areas the blues remained important. Jazz was denounced by groups such as the KKK and others who saw this and other cultural changes of the 1920s, such as flappers, as bringing the decline of US society. In the 1920s, much of the Midwest and South took part in a Protestant religious revival. Leading preachers, such as Billy Sunday and Aimee Semple McPherson, condemned jazz as the music of the devil.

SOURCE

Frank Farnum, who popularised the Charleston, coaching Hollywood actress Pauline Starke for her role in the film *A Little Bit of Broadway*, in 1925.

## The Harlem Renaissance

Jazz was only one part of the development of black American culture in the 1920s. It was part of a much wider movement, known as the 'New Negro Movement', which encompassed black American achievement in literature, art, plays and music. Singers such as Florence Mills and Ethel Waters, and dancers such as Bill Robinson, performed in a growing number of black American theatres and night clubs, such as the Cotton Club. Noble Sissle helped produce an all-black Broadway play, *Shuffle Along*.

Harlem was a black American ghetto on Manhattan Island, in the middle of New York. It became an important destination in the migration from the South in the 1920s. The black American community in northern cities began to assert its unique identity. Important to this development was a magazine, *The Crisis*, produced by the National Association for the Advancement of Colored People (NAACP). This organisation aimed to celebrate black American achievement and support the struggle for equal rights.

Also important was the Universal Negro Improvement Association (UNIA), founded and led by Marcus Garvey. Garvey believed in **Pan-Africanism**, saying that black people all over the world should be united in a struggle for equality. He founded separate black-only businesses, including a shipping company.

**KEY TERM**

**Pan-Africanism**
This was the idea that all people of black African origin had a common culture and history. Pan-Africanists thought black Americans should support the independence of black African areas that were under colonial rule. They also encouraged self-sufficiency among black people through the creation of black-run businesses.

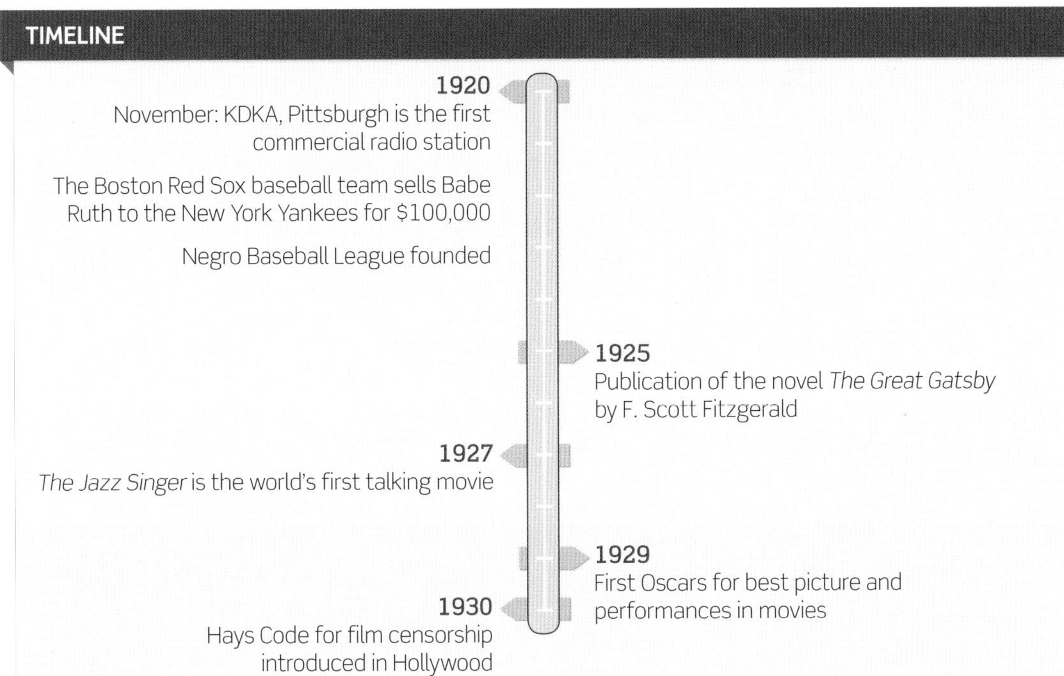


SOURCE 11

This description of Harlem in New York City at the height of the Jazz Age was written by US poet Langston Hughes.

When I came back to New York in 1925 the Negro Renaissance was in full swing... the Savoy Ballroom was open with a specially built floor that rocked as the dancers swayed. Alain Locke was putting together *The New Negro* [an anthology of black American literature]. Art took heart from Harlem creativity. Jazz filled the night air - but not everywhere - and people came from all around after dark to look upon our city within a city, Black Harlem. Had I not had to earn a living, I might have thought it even more wonderful than it was. But I could not eat the poems I wrote. Unlike the whites who came to spend their money in Harlem, only a few Harlemites seemed to live in even a modest degree of luxury. Most rode the subway downtown every morning to work or look for work.

## The growing popularity of baseball

By the 1920s, baseball was fast becoming America's national pastime. The game had first developed during the US Civil War (1861–65), but the 1920s became the sport's first golden age. By 1929, most major cities had a baseball stadium that could hold tens of thousands of spectators. Baseball teams like the New York Yankees and Chicago White Sox became household names and baseball players became national celebrities. In 1920, the Boston Red Sox star player, Babe Ruth, signed for the New York Yankees for $100,000. Known as the 'Sultan of Swat', Ruth became the greatest baseball player of all time. He helped the Yankees to win national championships (known as the World Series) throughout the decade. His record of home runs was only surpassed in the 1970s.

Although it was the national sport, baseball began the decade in controversy. The 1919 World Series final saw the Chicago White Sox team accused and convicted of match fixing against the Cincinnati Reds. Even though the team was acquitted in 1921, several players had admitted taking money to throw games.

Baseball recovered from the controversy quickly for a number of reasons. One was the appointment of Kenesaw Mountain Landis as national baseball commissioner. He helped clean up the image of baseball by stamping out corruption and banning substances he felt enhanced player performance. This involved banning players and coaches who were found guilty.

Baseball also benefited from the growing prosperity of the 1920s. Workers had more money to spend and the consumer boom helped fuel demand for spectator sports. The growth of commercial radio stations also allowed people across the country to listen to baseball matches. Newspapers developed sports sections with extensive coverage of Major League Baseball (MLB).

Finally, the ball used in baseball was standardised with a cork interior. This benefited the hitters rather than the pitchers, making the game more high-scoring. MLB was standardised into two rival leagues, the National League and the American League. The winners of each league met in the highlight of the MLB season, the World Series. This format has lasted until the present day.

Despite its popularity, Major League Baseball remained segregated. The first black American MLB player, Jackie Robinson, only played after the Second World War. In 1920, a Negro Baseball League was created. More poorly financed than its white counterpart, the Negro Baseball League still attracted large crowds of black Americans and gave black American baseball players an opportunity to play the sport professionally.

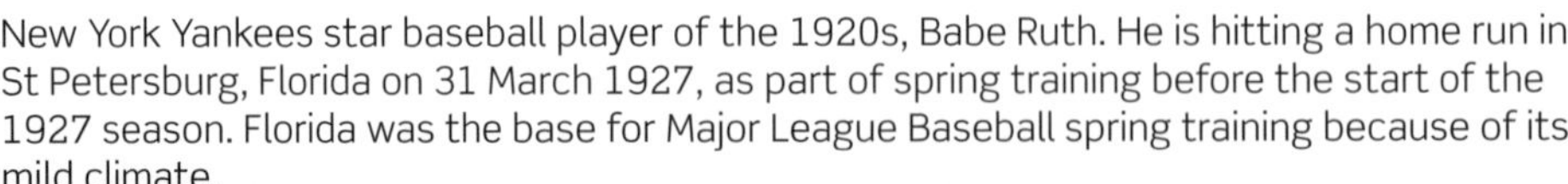

**SOURCE 12** New York Yankees star baseball player of the 1920s, Babe Ruth. He is hitting a home run in St Petersburg, Florida on 31 March 1927, as part of spring training before the start of the 1927 season. Florida was the base for Major League Baseball spring training because of its mild climate.

## Radio and cinema

In no other cultural field did the USA dominate more than in the fields of radio and cinema. The 1920s saw the radio help bring the entire country even closer together through the airwaves.

Until the appearance of radio, Americans visited theatres to watch entertainment shows. These were initially located in big cities and large towns. Broadway, in New York City, became the centre of America's theatre industry. However, radio brought entertainment into the homes of millions of Americans, irrespective of where they lived. No longer did Americans have to leave home to hear professional-quality entertainment or sports. It is hard to believe that jazz, baseball, and popular entertainers, be they comedians or actors, would have ever received national recognition in the USA without radio.

Radio also became an important medium during the religious revival of the 1920s. Aimee Semple McPherson, in particular, used radio to broadcast her religious services and messages across the nation from her church in California. Radio was as important as the motor car in bringing Americans together and making them all believe the USA was the leading country in the modern era.

The growth of radio led to a huge growth in advertising. Following the creation of the first commercial radio station, KDKA, based in Pittsburgh, Pennsylvania in 1920, the USA was soon dotted with stations offering unique opportunities for companies to sell their wares through radio advertising.

If radio helped bring Americans together, cinema allowed them to lead the world in popular entertainment. Hollywood in California became the centre of the world film industry, producing hundreds of films per year. Until 1927, all cinema films were silent, which meant films produced in the USA could be enjoyed all over the world. Initially, before the First World War, Hollywood produced short-length films, many of them comedies. Perhaps the world's first global film star was English-born comedian Charlie Chaplin, who usually played a poor, little man taking on authority. In 1915, the first full-length feature film, *The Birth of Nation*, captured the nation's imagination. It was about the most traumatic episode in US history, the Civil War. Even the president had a private showing of the film at the White House. It was also the film that helped relaunch the Ku Klux Klan.

Comedy was an important ingredient in films of the 1920s. Charlie Chaplin and the Keystone Cops appeared in many silent films. With the advent of talking movies, the comic pair Laurel and Hardy became one of the most popular comic film partnerships. Hollywood also produced comedies, westerns and romances.

By 1929, every small town in the USA had its own picture house showing Hollywood films. By that stage, the industry was dominated by big studios such as Paramount, Warner Brothers and MGM. Owners of Hollywood studios became multimillionaires.

Hollywood helped to create America's own celebrities: film stars. These individuals represented the American Dream, the idea that even poor people through hard work and ability could become rich and famous. Many came from poor backgrounds and small towns, but became world famous and super-rich as a result of the cinema. Douglas Fairbanks played all-action parts and married a famous film sweetheart, Mary Pickford. Living in their Hollywood mansion, Pickfair, they were the Hollywood royalty of the 1920s.

Through newspapers and magazines, the lives of Hollywood stars became almost an obsession for many Americans.

Not everyone was pleased by the rapid spread of cinema. Religious moralists were concerned that Hollywood films could be used to undermine the Christian ethos of the country. In response to this pressure, the film studios appointed Will Hays, former Postmaster General, to produce a code of censorship for the industry. This was adopted in 1930 and lasted until 1968.

In 1927, a revolution took place in Hollywood: the invention of talking pictures, beginning with *The Jazz Singer*, starring Al Jolson. The film made Jolson an international star overnight. Two years later, Hollywood began the Annual Academy Awards, better known as the Oscars. By 1929, films were the premier form of popular entertainment for Americans and made the USA the top country for popular culture in the world.

## Changes in American literature

The 1920s has been given different names, including the Jazz Age and the Roaring Twenties. It was also the period of the 'Lost Generation', those artists who had survived the First World War. Their literature, in particular novels, of the 1920s saw a much greater concentration on realism, reflecting the actual experiences of individual novelists, including moral issues such as breaking the law during prohibition or first-hand experience of the horrors of war.

Perhaps the novelist who encapsulated the spirit of the times more than any other was F. Scott Fitzgerald. He became famous for capturing the spirit of the rebellious youth of flappers, the new rich and those who defied national prohibition. His novel *The Great Gatsby* (1925) deals with a super-rich playboy who made a fortune on the New York Stock Exchange. To Fitzgerald, the 1920s was the 'Age of Excess'.

Another American novelist, Ernest Hemingway, in his first novel *The Sun Also Rises* (1926), traces the lives of Americans living in Paris and Spain, experiencing the excesses of life. In 1929, Hemingway produced *A Farewell to Arms* about his own life as a volunteer ambulance driver on the Italian Front in the First World War, where he was involved in a tragic love affair.

Fitzgerald and Hemingway achieved both national and international acclaim and gave American literature a global reputation for the first time. Their international standing was matched by poets Ezra Pound, T. S. Eliot and Robert Frost. It also saw the USA lead the world in popular culture and reach the world stage in literature.

**ACTIVITY**
**KNOWLEDGE CHECK**

**Cultural developments in the 1920s**

1 What do you regard as the main features of the Jazz Age?

2 In what ways did the Harlem Renaissance change the role of black Americans in US society and culture?

3 Why do you think baseball became such a popular pastime in the USA in the 1920s?

4 What impact did the development of radio and the cinema have on US society in the 1920s?

5 What were the main changes in American literature in the1920s?

**AS Level Exam-Style Question Section B**

How accurate is it to say that American culture went through a revolution during the 1920s? (20 marks)

**Tip**

*You need to assess the degree of change, not just say that it did change.*

**A Level Exam-Style Question Section B**

How far was the development of radio and the cinema responsible for the rapid social change in the USA in the 1920s? (20 marks)

**Tip**

*You need to assess the role of radio and the cinema against other factors such as the changing role of women and the impact of the economic boom.*

ACTIVITY
SUMMARY

**Boom and crash, 1920–29**

Create a spider diagram that shows the main changes in US culture during the 1920s and the links between them. Include changes in:

- The US economy
- Music and dance
- Literature
- Popular entertainment.

## WIDER READING

de Pennington, J. *Modern America, The USA, 1865 to the Present*, Hodder Murray (2005)

Farmer, A. and Sanders, V. *An Introduction to American History, 1860–1990*, Hodder (2002)

Field, R. *Civil Rights in America, 1865 to 1980*, Cambridge University Press (2002)

Murphy, D. *Flagship History – United States 1776–1992*, Collins Educational (2001)

Murphy, D. *Flagship History – United States 1917–2008*, Collins Educational (2008)

Parrish, M. *The Anxious Decades: America in Prosperity and Depression 1920–1941*, WW Norton and Company (1994)

Rowe, C. *USA, 1890–1945*, Nelson Thornes (2008)

Stewart, G. and Barker, L. *The United States 1917–1954: Boom Bust and Recovery*, Pearson (2010)

Willoughby, S. and Willoughby, D. *The USA 1917–1945*, Heinemann (2000)

# Depression and New Deal, 1929–38

**KEY QUESTIONS**

- Why was the Depression so serious for American society and the economy?
- Why did President Hoover fail to end the Depression?
- How successful was President Roosevelt's First New Deal in ending the Depression?
- To what extent had President Roosevelt brought recovery by 1938?

## INTRODUCTION

The Wall Street Crash of October 1929 brought about a major fall in share prices in the USA. There had been stock market crashes in the country's past, which were then followed by a period of economic depression: in 1857, 1873 and 1893 stock market crashes had caused hundreds of business bankruptcies and rising unemployment. However, the economic downturn after the Wall Street Crash was the most severe in both US and world history. By 1932, 25 percent of America's workforce was unemployed. Thousands of companies had gone bust.

The Depression was the main reason why President Hoover lost the 1932 presidential election to Franklin D. Roosevelt (often known as FDR). This brought a major change within the USA, as the Republican Party's dominance of the 1920s came to an abrupt end. The Democrats won the presidency and controlled both houses of Congress: they also controlled most state governments. This situation lasted until after the Second World War.

Roosevelt's presidency (1933–1945) saw a significant change in the role of the federal government. Under programmes called the New Deal, the federal government played a major role in getting the US economy out of economic depression.

## WHY WAS THE DEPRESSION SO SERIOUS FOR AMERICAN SOCIETY AND THE ECONOMY?

### The growth of unemployment and collapse of GDP

Only a small proportion of the US population was affected directly by the Wall Street Crash, since the majority of Americans did not own shares. However, between October and December 1929, the numbers of unemployed in the USA rose from 500,000 to over four million. By the time Franklin D. Roosevelt became president in the spring of 1933, the number of unemployed had risen to 15 million. These figures did not include the hundreds of thousands who were working part-time.

1928 | 1929 | 1930 | 1931 | 1932 | 1933

**1929** – October: Wall Street Crash

**1930** – June: Hawley-Smoot Tariff
November: Midterm elections. Democrats gain control of House of Representatives

**1932** – January: Reconstruction Finance Corporation created
July: Emergency Relief and Construction Act provides £1.5 billion for public works
November: Roosevelt wins presidential election. Democrats gain control of both houses of Congress

**1933** – March: Beginning of 100 Days of First New Deal; creation of alphabet agencies

The Wall Street Crash had shattered public confidence and plunged the USA into deep economic depression.

- Real wages in the USA, between 1929 and 1931, fell by 16 percent.
- The Gross National Product (GNP), the value of all goods and services produced by the US economy, fell dramatically between 1929 and 1933 (see Source 1). GNP is different from GDP because it includes net property income from abroad.
- Construction fell by 78 percent in the period 1929–31.
- Manufacturing went down 54 percent in the period 1929–31.
- Investment went down a massive 98 percent in the period 1929–31.

The federal government was reluctant to intervene for a variety of reasons. Firstly, President Hoover believed the economic downturn would be short-lived, so intervention was not necessary. Secondly, the Republican administration and Republican-controlled Congress were reluctant to change their economic policy of *laissez-faire*. This policy had brought unrivalled prosperity in the 1920s. They believed it would lead to economic recovery.

SOURCE

Statistics on the US economy. From *The Longman Companion to America in the Era of the Two World Wars 1910–1945* (1996).

Gross National Product (GNP) 1920–38

| | 1920 | 1929 | 1933 | 1938 |
|---|---|---|---|---|
| Total ($ billions) | 91 | 103 | 55 | 84 |

Unemployment in the USA 1910–1938

| | 1910 | 1929 | 1933 | 1938 |
|---|---|---|---|---|
| Total (millions) | 2.1 | 1.5 | 12.8 | 10.4 |

## The effects of the Depression on society, 1929-1932

When the Depression struck the USA, the massive rise in unemployment caused huge problems. In 1929, the USA did not have old age pensions or a national system of unemployment welfare. Helping the unemployed was a responsibility of state governments. Only a few of these had unemployed welfare systems. Even these found it almost impossible to cope with the catastrophe. Frank Murphy, Mayor of Detroit, Michigan, home of the world's car industry, stated in 1932 that the city was on the verge of bankruptcy if it did not get federal aid.

SOURCE

This description of the effects of the Wall Street Crash was written by a 16-year-old, Gordon Parks, in November 1929. Parks was living alone and attending high school in St Paul, Minnesota.

By Thursday the entire world knew. 'Market crashes - Panic hits nation!' one headline blared. The newspapers were full of it, and I read everything I could get my hands on, gathering in the full meaning of such terms, Black Thursday, deflation and depression. I couldn't imagine such financial disaster touching my small world; it surely concerned only the rich. But by the first week of November I knew differently; along with millions of others across the nation, I was out of a job. All that next week, I searched for any kind of work. Again it was, 'We're firing not hiring. Sorry nothing doing here.'

### Effects on workers and families

With the collapse of thousands of businesses and hundreds of banks, the main help for the poor and unemployed came from voluntary organisations. President Hoover encouraged **voluntarism**. By 1930, soup kitchens and breadlines were set up in towns to provide direct help to those affected by the Depression. Some unemployed workers began selling apples on street corners to make a few dollars. Nearly a million left home to search for work, riding on railroad freight cars.

KEY TERM

**Voluntarism**
The idea that help for the poor and unemployed should be provided by voluntary organisations like churches.

By 1931, a survey in the state of Colorado noted that all schoolchildren were insufficiently fed, leading to the spread of diseases such as dysentery, typhus and pellagra, which are associated with poor diet and living conditions. Nationally, the

**1935** - US Supreme Court declares NRA unconstitutional.
Beginning of Second New Deal
July: Wagner Act
August: Social Security Act and Revenue Act passed

**1936** - January: US Supreme Court declares AAA unconstitutional
November: F.D. Roosevelt wins landslide victory in presidential election

**1937** - February: Roosevelt introduces his 'Court Packing Plan' which is defeated
April: US Supreme Court upholds Wagner Act and Social Security Act
August: Roosevelt Recession begins

**1938** - February: Second Agricultural Adjustment Act
June: Fair Labor Standards Act

1934 | 1935 | 1936 | 1937 | 1938 | 1939

suicide rate rose 14 percent between 1929 and 1932. Marriages fell by ten percent over the same period and there was a drop in the birth rate. Family breakdowns rose dramatically as unemployed men left home to search for work in other parts of the country. The migration of unemployed workers from state to state caused friction as each state considered helping their own poor and unemployed more important than helping the new arrivals.

### KEY TERMS

**Old South**
The area of the south-eastern USA that comprised the Confederate states during the US Civil War (1861–65). It was made up of Virginia, North and South Carolina, Georgia, Alabama, Mississippi, Arkansas, Louisiana, Tennessee, Florida and Texas. This was the area that had legal segregation of blacks and whites and where much of the violence and intimidation against black Americans was committed.

**Lynching**
The impromptu execution of a person through hanging, usually by a mob. Surprisingly, in the 1930s, lynching was not a federal crime.

### Effects on ethnic minorities

The rapid decline in economic activity led to a rise in racial discrimination. Several employers adopted a preferential hiring system for whites. A particularly serious problem occurred in California when tens of thousands of Spanish-speaking Hispanic workers were adversely affected by a dramatic drop in demand for agricultural products. During the Depression, almost 500,000 Mexican citizens were forced to leave the United States, most before 1933. To encourage Spanish speakers to 'go home', several states barred non-US citizens from public works programmes. Some states were willing to pay the rail fare of these workers to the Mexican border to further encourage them to depart.

The Chinese were another group that experienced discrimination. In 1932, customers in New York City boycotted Chinese laundries in a concerted attempt to drive them out of business.

Black Americans, who had suffered discrimination for generations, faced renewed oppression. Blacks were usually the first to be fired when companies had to downsize. In Milwaukee, Wisconsin, white workers at the Wehr Steel foundry went on strike, demanding that all black American workers be fired. In the **Old South**, discrimination was more extreme. In Louisiana, white mobs attacked black American railway workers, killing ten, in an attempt to drive all black Americans out of their jobs. **Lynching** of blacks increased during the Depression, reaching 24 deaths in 1932.

### Effects on farmers

While workers in towns and cities were laid off with the collapse of businesses, farmers across the USA were even more badly hit. Between 1929 and 1932, farm incomes fell by two-thirds. This was due to a sharp fall in demand and therefore farm prices. Cotton, which was the main crop of the south-east, saw its price fall two-thirds between 1929 and 1932.

Farmers also suffered from the collapse of the banking sector. Most farmers had bank loans and used their farms as security for these loans. When over 600 banks went out of business in 1930, thousands of farmers lost their livelihoods. For instance, Iowa, an agricultural state famous for producing pigs and maize, saw one in eight farms put up for auction between 1930 and 1932.

### A Level Exam-Style Question Section A

***Study Sources 2 and 3 before you answer this question.***

How far could the historian make use of Sources 2 and 3 together to investigate the effects of the Depression on the lives of the American people?

Explain your answer using the sources, the information given about them and your own knowledge of the historical context. (20 marks)

**Tip**

*In your answer it is important to refer to the provenance of both sources: who wrote them, when they were written and their intended audiences. This will allow you to assess their value to the historian. To support your answer ensure that you use relevant information from both sources and your own knowledge of the subject matter to place the sources in historical context.*

### Bonus Army

In 1932, some of those badly affected by the Depression took matters into their own hands. Veterans who had fought in the First World War marched on Washington DC. 21,000 protesters demanded that the bonuses they were due in 1945 should be paid immediately. The army, under General Douglas MacArthur, was ordered to remove the 'Bonus marchers'. On 28 July 1932, at the 'Battle of Anacostia Flats', the army forcibly evicted the Bonus marchers from Washington DC using tanks, with the loss of two lives. President Hoover declared the Bonus marchers a threat to democracy.

**SOURCE**

Meridel Le Sueur was a novelist who also wrote extensively about women's experiences in the USA. In this extract from her short story 'Women on the Breadlines' (1932), she describes the plight of women in the Depression. The extract was written during the Depression.

It's one of the great mysteries of the city where women go when they are out of work and hungry. There are not many women on the bread line. You don't see women lying on the floor at the mission... They obviously don't sleep in the jungle or under newspapers in the park.

Yet there must be as many women out of jobs in cities and suffering extreme poverty as there are men. What happens to them? Where do they go?

I've lived in cities for many months broke, without help, too timid to get into bread lines. I've known many women to live like this until they simply faint on the street from privations, without saying a word to anyone. A woman will shut herself up in a room until it is taken away from her.

## EXTEND YOUR KNOWLEDGE

**Herbert Hoover (1874–1964)**
Republican President of the USA from 1929 to 1933. A mining engineer by profession, after the First World War he gained international acclaim for organising assistance such as food and clothing aid for those displaced by the war. From 1921 to 1928, he was Secretary for Commerce. In 1928, he defeated the Democrat Al Smith to become president. His success as Secretary for Commerce eluded him as president when faced with the economic crisis after the Wall Street Crash.

## Gangsterism

The collapse of the US economy encouraged the development of organised crime or 'gangsterism'. The decline in law and order had begun in the 1920s with the opposition to national prohibition. This opposition was exploited by organised crime gangs. By 1930, gangsters had developed a widespread network of illegal activities connected with the alcohol trade, gambling and other black market trading activity. The centre of such activities was Chicago, Illinois, and the most notorious gangster was Italian-American Al Capone. By 1929, federal officials had begun trying to smash Capone's bootlegging operations. Eventually, his gang was infiltrated by a US Treasury official and Capone was convicted of tax evasion, for which he received 11 years in prison. He died before being released.

Other gangsters ranged across the USA robbing banks. In the period from 1929 to 1933, the most famous and notorious were Bonnie Elizabeth Parker and Clyde Chestnut Barrow, known as Bonnie and Clyde. They led a gang from a hideout in the state of Missouri, robbing banks and committing murder until they were tracked down and killed by the FBI on 23 May 1934. Their activities were the inspiration for the 1967 Hollywood film *Bonnie and Clyde*, starring Warren Beatty and Faye Dunaway.

Another infamous gangster was George Francis Barnes, known as Machine Gun Kelly. Like Bonnie and Clyde, he achieved fame through bank robbery, until he was cornered and caught by the police in Oklahoma in 1933. He spent the last 21 years of his life in prison. These gangsters received national notoriety in the press. In part their notoriety was fuelled by the FBI's decision from 1931 to label certain criminals 'public enemies'. 'Public Enemy Number 1' for part of this period was John Dillinger. A bankrobber, bootlegger and organised crime gangster, Dillinger operated in the Midwest. He was eventually tracked down and shot by the FBI in Chicago in 1934. These gangsters epitomised the lawlessness that affected parts of the USA during the Depression years.

SOURCE

The corpse of gangster John Dillinger, on display at the Chicago County Morgue on 23 July 1934, shortly after being gunned down by the FBI. A large crowd came to view Dillinger's body. He was one of the most notorious gangsters in the years 1929 to 1933 and was on the FBI's 'Most Wanted' list.

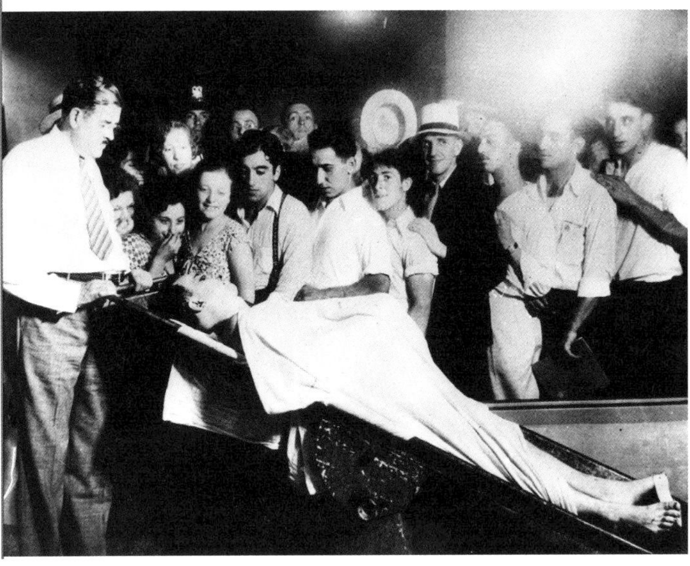

## THE DEPRESSION, 1929–33

**October 1929**
Wall Street Crash; collapse of share prices

**June 1930**
Hawley-Smoot Tariff

**November 1930**
Democrats gain control of House of Representatives

**1931**
Economic crisis spreads to Europe and deepens in USA

**January 1932**
Reconstruction Finance Corporation set up

**July 1932**
Emergency Relief and Construction Act gives $1.5 billion for public works

Federal Home Loan Bank Act

Bonus Army ejected from Washington DC by US Army

**November 1932**
FDR defeats Hoover in presidential election. Democrats gain control of both houses of Congress

ACTIVITY
KNOWLEDGE CHECK

**The effects of the Depression**

The Depression affected many different social groups: workers, families, farmers and ethnic minorities.

**1** Write down ways in which each group was affected by the Depression.

**2** Which social group do you think was affected most? Give reasons for your answer.

# WHY DID PRESIDENT HOOVER FAIL TO END THE DEPRESSION?

As the president who was in power during the Depression, Hoover was vilified, both at the time and since. He was heavily criticised for not taking effective action to end the Depression. His 1928 election campaign slogan had said that he wanted America to have 'a chicken in every pot and a car in every garage'. This was a very distant aim as unemployment spiralled upwards from 1929. He also suffered from the fact that he preceded Franklin D. Roosevelt (FDR) as president. FDR has come to be regarded as one of the USA's greatest presidents. Hoover looked indecisive and lacklustre by comparison.

Hoover faced a number of issues that limited his ability to act decisively. Like most members of the federal government and Congress, Hoover believed the economy would right itself as the business cycle would lead eventually to recovery. Any intervention by the federal government was initially seen as a possible barrier to that recovery. Hoover also believed that the strength of US society was 'rugged individualism', the belief that people should be self-reliant and not be dependent on government financial support.

Hoover also had to contend with the nature of American government. He needed the support of both houses of Congress which, until November 1930, were dominated by his Republican Party, who supported *laissez-faire* economic policies. Also, it was a state and not a federal responsibility to help the poor and unemployed. Hoover had to persuade these groups to support any relief programme.

Early in the Depression, Hoover believed its cause lay outside the USA. After the First World War, Germany was expected to make huge **reparation payments** to the Allied governments. Those Allied governments also owed the USA tens of millions of pounds in war debts. To help prevent the onset of a global economic depression, Hoover negotiated a **moratorium** on inter-Allied war debt in 1931 and the cancellation of German reparation payments in 1932. The aim was to encourage international trade by releasing more money directly into the economy. It could be argued that this was too little, too late.

KEY TERMS

**Reparation payments**
After the First World War, Germany was forced to accept responsibility for starting the war and, as a result, for all the damage caused during the war. In signing the Treaty of Versailles, Germany agreed to make reparation payments to the Allied powers to help repair the damage. The sum to be paid was set at £6.6 billion in 1921. Mainly paid to Britain, France and Belgium, this money would help the Allies repay their own debts to the USA.

**Moratorium**
A temporary suspension. In this case it was a temporary suspension of reparation payments.

## Smoot–Hawley Tariff, 1930

The cancellation of the inter-Allied debts should have helped increase international trade. However, this potential benefit was lost by the implementation of the Smoot–Hawley Tariff on 17 June 1930. This raised import taxes (tariffs) to the highest level in US history, in an attempt to protect the US economy from foreign competition. Average tariffs on imported agricultural and industrial goods rose to 40 percent. This was intended to raise the prices of foreign goods and ensure that domestic producers were protected from foreign competition; however, 1,000 economists signed a petition asking Hoover to veto the tariff.

The Smoot–Hawley Tariff forced other countries to follow suit and raise their own tariff rates in retaliation. By signing this proposal into law, Hoover aided the contraction rather than the expansion of the world economy, making the prospects of economic recovery even more difficult.

## Homelessness and the Hoovervilles

While President Hoover attempted to offer positive words about economic recovery being 'just around the corner', the reality of the Depression was very different. Unemployment spiralled: during Hoover's presidency 13 million Americans lost their jobs, with 62 percent of these being out of work for more than one year. Unemployment rose from 6.9 percent in 1930 to 24.1 percent in 1933. Because the USA lacked a federal welfare system in the period 1929–33, the unemployed had to rely on help from state governments. Many of these failed to offer anything more than short-term help, which led to a rapid rise in homelessness.

A whole new vocabulary of words became fashionable. Pulled-out empty pockets were 'Hoover flags'. A 'Hoover wagon' was a motor car pulled by mules. 'Hoover blankets' were the newspapers people used to keep warm at night while sleeping rough. By 1930, virtually every major town and city had a shanty town to house the unemployed, who had either been evicted for non-payment of rent or were on the road looking for work. The shanty towns became known as 'Hoovervilles'. Homeless people were termed 'hobos' and faced almost constant harassment by the police. Homes in Hoovervilles were makeshift shacks, usually built on wasteland. They had no water supply, sanitation or power and there was no provision for waste collection or sewerage disposal.

**SOURCE 5** A letter from President Hoover to the governor of the state of Illinois, dated 10 July 1931.

Confidential

Hon. Louis L. Emmerson
Governor of Illinois
Springfield, Ill.

My dear Governor Emmerson:

No matter what improvement there may be in our economic situation during the fall, we shall unquestionably have considerable continuance of destitution over the winter. I am wondering if it would not be advisable for us to get the machinery of the country into earlier action than last year in order that there may be provision for funds substantially made before the winter arrives.

Your organization last winter was one of the most admirable in the whole country and I had some thought that if all organizations were to begin their appeals for funds some time in October and run them over Thanksgiving we could make it more or less a national question and thereby support each state committee more effectively.

This, however, is just thinking aloud on the general situation and I would like your views.

I wish again to express my appreciation for the fine courtesies we received at the hands of Mrs. Emmerson and yourself and with kind regards to you both, I am

Yours faithfully,

Herbert Hoover

## The Reconstruction Finance Corporation

Although widely blamed for the Depression, Hoover was faced with the worst economic crisis in US and world history. Although he has been criticised as doing too little too late, he did try to use the federal government to help those suffering from hardship.

At first the federal government attempted to deal with the economic crisis by relying solely on voluntarism. The first major departure from this approach came in January 1932, with the creation of the Reconstruction Finance Corporation (RFC). This was a big U-turn for Hoover and the Republican Party. It was one of the first direct attempts by the federal government to get the USA out of the economic depression. The Corporation was given $2 billion of taxpayers' money to assist directly banks and insurance companies that were in financial trouble. Hoover's newly appointed Secretary to the Treasury, Ogden Mills, stated that 90 percent of the RFC's money went in loans to small- and medium-sized banks. The aim was to help revive the US banking system, but it was only partially successful.

The RFC did help prevent a worsening of the Depression. From February to March 1932, it helped 160 banks, 60 railroads and 18 mortgage companies. The aim was to prevent further banking collapse and to bring stability to the financial and banking sectors of the US economy.

However, the RFC failed to encourage banks to lend more to businesses that were facing severe financial problems and possible bankruptcy. Hoover was downcast by the autumn that there were no signs of economic recovery. Nevertheless, when FDR became president in 1933, he continued to use the RFC as part of his attempt to bring about economic recovery.

## Emergency Relief and Construction Act, July 1932

Once the Hoover administration had decided to use federal money to aid businesses and banks, the logical next step was to directly help the unemployed, previously a responsibility of state governments.

The Emergency Relief and Construction Act, passed on 21 July 1932, was the USA's first massive relief programme. It was passed just as the army were about to evict the Bonus Army marchers (ex-servicemen who had gone to Washington DC to pressure Congress into providing them with federal relief). A corporation similar to the RFC was created, which had the power to give $1.5 billion to state governments to fund public works for the unemployed. This avoided direct payments from the federal government to the unemployed. To qualify for funding, state governments had to prove they were running out of money for unemployment relief. One critic of Hoover, journalist and economist Walter Lippmann, stated that $2 billion would be enough to help just ten percent of America's unemployed.

Like the RFC, the Emergency Relief and Construction Act was a major change in federal government policy. The policy did provide important support for both business and individuals. However, by mid-1932, the economic depression was so deep and business and public confidence so low that a dramatic change was required if the economic crisis was to end.

## Conclusion

Looking back on Hoover's handling of the Depression, it is clear that he failed. It cost him the presidency in November 1932, when FDR and the Democrats swept to power across the USA. In a democracy, that is the ultimate verdict for a politician. However, Hoover faced an unprecedented economic crisis. Also, the global economy went into a serious depression after 1929. The Hawley–Smoot Tariff helped make the global depression worse, but the US economy had already been in a fragile state before the Wall Street Crash. It could be said that Hoover was in the wrong place at the wrong time.

**AS Level Exam-Style Question Section B**

How far was President Hoover personally responsible for the onset of economic depression? (20 marks)

**Tip**

*Your answer should address directly the personal role of Hoover. You will need to provide evidence that Hoover's personal actions brought about the onset of economic depression. To balance your answer you should assess Hoover's role against other factors such as prevailing economic policy, the depth of the depression and the limited power Hoover possessed as president.*

**EXTRACT 1**

From *The Presidency of Herbert C. Hoover* by Martin L. Fausold, published in 1985.

> Few presidents, perhaps none, have been subjected to such a wide range of interpretation as has Herbert Hoover, from hero to villain. Certainly, at least, two questions must be considered, in all fairness. One is whether Hoover attained his goals outlined in his Inaugural Address: justice, order, liberty, equality of opportunity, encouragement of the individual initiative, freedom of opinion, integrity in government, strengthening of the home. The other is whether he attacked the causes of depression. Both questions are readily answered either yes or no. In regard the first was what Walter Lippmann said a president should be, a 'custodian of the nation's ideals'. And with regard to the second, Hoover did attack the causes of the depression with vigor and imagination. Nevertheless, on election day 1932, he was turned out of office by a landslide. He clearly had not met the expectations of most of his fellow Americans.

**EXTEND YOUR KNOWLEDGE**

**Demand management economics**

Demand management economics involved the government playing a major role in the running of the economy by manipulating the level of taxation and public spending. If unemployment rose, a demand management policy would be to increase public spending on projects such as construction, which would create jobs and thus lower unemployment. Demand management economics was closely associated with the New Deal, but could also be applied to the RFC.

ACTIVITY
KNOWLEDGE CHECK

**Hoover and the Depression**

1 Write down reasons why you think it was difficult for President Hoover to take direct action to deal with the Depression during his presidency.

2 What actions did Hoover take to help get the US economy out of Depression?

3 How does Source 5 help you understand Hoover's views on helping the US economy get out of economic depression?

4 a) Write down ways in which you think Hoover helped make the Depression worse in the USA between 1929 and 1932.

b) Write down ways you think Hoover tried to deal with problems created by the Depression.

c) On balance, do you think Hoover was a villain or scapegoat in dealing with the Depression?

# HOW SUCCESSFUL WAS THE FIRST NEW DEAL IN ENDING THE DEPRESSION?

SOURCE

6

Herbert Hoover (left) and Franklin D. Roosevelt (right) on the day Roosevelt was inaugurated president. Both presidents are in formal dress, including top hats. At the end of a US presidency, presidential power is ceremonially handed over from the old president to the new. Hoover accompanied Roosevelt to the Capitol Building, where Roosevelt was sworn in as president on 4 March 1933, four months after winning the presidential election.

Franklin D. Roosevelt (FDR) is the only president in American history to have been elected four times. He dominated US politics from his election in 1932 until his death in April 1945, just before the end of the Second World War. He is also the only disabled person to have served as president. He was struck down with polio in 1921 and for the rest of his life he could only walk with leg irons and assistance. When he came to the presidency, the USA was facing the worst economic crisis in its history. When he died, the USA was on the verge of an Allied victory in the Second World War and was by far the most prosperous nation on Earth.

FDR had been the Governor of New York State in the years prior to 1932 and had first-hand knowledge of the social problems associated with the Depression. On 2 July 1932, he became the Democratic Party candidate for the presidency. In his acceptance speech in Chicago, he promised a 'new deal' for the American people. FDR believed American men required two things: work and security for themselves, and for their wives and children. Up till then, the state governments had held the main responsibility for relieving economic distress. If elected, he would change that.

In the November election, FDR won 22.8 million votes compared to Hoover's 15.8 million. FDR received support from the trade unions, workers in manufacturing, Catholics, Jews and the whites of the Old South. These groups were attracted to the Democrats for a variety of reasons. Whites in the Old South disliked the Republicans because they had won the US Civil War and had imposed political racial equality on the Old South. Jews and Catholics were attracted by the social and economic policies of FDR and disliked the Republican Party because it was dominated by WASPs (White Anglo-Saxon Protestants). Up until the 1932 elections, black Americans had generally supported the Republican Party, which had abolished slavery in 1865. However, from 1932, black Americans began to switch their support to the Democrats, in particular in the northern states. This coalition of voters ensured Roosevelt won again in 1936, 1940 and 1944. However, although FDR was elected at the beginning of November 1932, under the US Constitution he did not take office until early March 1933. The period from November to March is known as the 'lame duck' period, where the outgoing president has very little authority. In that period, Hoover offered to work with FDR to relieve the misery of the Depression. FDR refused. He did not want Hoover to gain any credit for getting the US economy out of depression. This increased the feeling of hopelessness and uncertainty within the USA and made the Depression worse.

On 4 March 1933, in his inaugural speech as president, FDR outlined his bold plan. He claimed that 'the only fear is fear itself – nameless, unreasoning, unjustified terror which paralyses needed efforts to convert retreat into advance... I assume the leadership of this great army of our people dedicated to a disciplined attack on our common problems'. The New Deal aimed at relief, recovery and reform: relief for the poor and unemployed, recovery of the economy and reform of the economic system to prevent a recurrence of the Wall Street Crash. This attack began with a frantic 'Hundred Days' of activity in which Congress, at the insistence of FDR, passed the legislation that formed the basis of the First New Deal. The First New Deal was not a master plan to bring radical change to the USA. FDR claimed that he would experiment with different ways to bring relief, recovery and reform. If one method did not work, he said he would try another.

### AS Level Exam-Style Question Section A

***Study Source 7 before you answer this question.***

Why is Source 7 valuable to the historian for an enquiry into the aims and purposes of the First New Deal?

Explain your answer using the source, the information given about it and your own knowledge of the historical context. (8 marks)

**Tip**

*You should refer to the fact that this is the first public address FDR made as president. You need to mention both the content and style of delivery in your answer.*

**SOURCE**

From Franklin D. Roosevelt's first inaugural address as president, 4 March 1933.

Our greatest primary task is to put people to work. This is no unsolvable problem if we face it wisely and courageously. It can be accomplished in part by direct recruiting by the Government itself, treating the task as we would treat the emergency of a war, but at the same time, through this employment, accomplishing greatly needed projects to stimulate and reorganise the use of our natural resources.

Hand in hand with this we must frankly recognize the overbalance of population in our industrial centers and, by engaging on a national scale in a redistribution, endeavor to provide a better use of the land for those best fitted for the land.

I am prepared under my constitutional duty to recommend the measures that a stricken Nation in the midst of a stricken world may require. I shall seek, within my constitutional authority, to bring a speedy adoption.

But in the event that the Congress shall fail to take one of these courses, and in the event that the national emergency is still critical, I shall not evade the clear course of duty that will then confront me. I shall ask the Congress for the one remaining instrument to meet the crisis - broad Executive power to wage a war against the emergency, as great as the power that would be given to me if we were in fact invaded by a foreign foe.

**FRANKLIN D. ROOSEVELT AND THE FIRST NEW DEAL**

**4 March 1933**
FDR inaugurated as president

**9 March 1933**
Emergency Banking Act

**20 March 1933**
Economy Act imposes cuts on public sector pay in federal government

**22 March 1933**
Beer Act overturns Volstead Act

**31 March 1933**
Civilian Conservation Corps (CCC) created

**19 April 1933**
FDR takes US currency off the Gold Standard

**12 May 1933**
Creation of Federal Emergency Relief Administration (FERA)

**18 May 1933**
Creation of Tennessee Valley Authority (TVA)

**16 June 1933**
Glass-Steagall Banking Act; creation of National Recovery Administration (NRA)

**November 1933**
Civil Works Administration (CWA), Agricultural Adjustment Administration (AAA) created to aid farmers

**19 June 1934**
Silver Purchase Act

**6 November 1934**
Democrats make big gains in midterm elections

## Emergency relief

When Franklin D. Roosevelt became president in March 1933 one in four Americans was out of work. Soup kitchens and bread lines run by voluntary organisations were in every major city. Also, on the outskirts of virtually every town and city, makeshift Hoovervilles housed the homeless. If Roosevelt was going to tackle the problems created by the economic depression, emergency relief would be one of his top priorities.

## Public works

Roosevelt thought one way of bringing immediate employment to those out of work was through publicly funded work schemes. It might take time before private businesses had enough confidence in the future and enough funds to bring about economic recovery on their own. Public works were a way of kick-starting the economy. They would help bring down the rate of unemployment and they would put money in the pockets of those employed on public works projects. This money would then be spent, thus stimulating the private sector of the economy.

## The Alphabet Agencies

The First and Second New Deals created a wide variety of federal agencies. Some had overlapping responsibilities. All were known by their initials – hence the name Alphabet Agencies.

| Agency | Date of Creation |
|---|---|
| Civilian Conservation Corps (CCC) | March 1933 |
| Federal Emergency Relief Administration (FERA) | May 1933 |
| Agricultural Adjustment Administration (AAA) | May 1933 |
| Tennessee Valley Authority (TVA) | May 1933 |
| Public Works Administration (PWA) | June 1933 |
| National Recovery Administration (NRA) | June 1933 |
| Works Progress Administration (WPA) | April 1935 |
| Rural Electrification Administration (REA) | May 1935 |
| National Youth Administration (NYA) | June 1935 |

**Figure 2.1**: The Alphabet Agencies.

### Helping regions: the Tennessee Valley Authority (TVA), May 1933

The Tennessee River Valley was an area notorious for flooding, poor infrastructure and a low standard of living. The area comprised seven states: Tennessee, North Carolina, Georgia, Alabama, Mississippi, Virginia and Kentucky. It contained approximately two million people and covered 40,000 square miles. It was an area of strong loyalty to the Democratic Party. The TVA established a network of dams to control the flow of the river and create hydro-electric power. In 1933, only two percent of Tennessee valley farms had electricity. By 1945, this had risen to 75 percent. Flooding and soil erosion were prevented, increasing the agricultural yield of the area.

The TVA was a model of federal-state government co-operation.

**SOURCE**

From the Tennessee Valley Authority Act, 1933.

An Act to Improve the Navigability and to Provide for the Flood Control of the Tennessee River: To Provide for Reforestation and the Proper Use of Marginal Lands in the Tennessee Valley; to Provide for the Agricultural and Industrial Development of Said Valley; to Provide for the National Defense by the Creation of a Corporation for the Operation of Government Properties at and near Muscle Shoals in the State of Alabama, and for Other Purposes May 18, 1933.

Be it enacted by the Senate and House of Representatives of the United States of America in Congress assembled, That for the purpose of maintaining and operating the properties now owned by the United States in the vicinity of Muscle Shoals, Alabama, in the interest of the national defense and for agriculture and industrial development, and to improve navigation in the Tennessee River and to control the destructive flood waters in the Tennessee River and Mississippi River Basins, there is hereby created a body corporate by the name of the "Tennessee Valley Authority" (hereinafter referred to as the "Corporation"). The board of directors first appointed shall be deemed the incorporators and the incorporation shall be held to have been effected from the date of the first meeting of the board. This Act may be cited as the "Tennessee Valley Authority Act of 1933."

### Helping Businesses: National Recovery Administration (NRA), June 1933

Perhaps the most visible and controversial alphabet agency of the First New Deal was the NRA, led by General Hugh Johnson. As part of the recovery plan, the NRA was to issue codes of practice for each industry. These codes aimed to ensure fair competition, fair wages and hours of work. Under the NRA codes, child labour was banned below the age of 16 years. The most significant part of the NRA, as far as trades unions were concerned, was Section 7(a). This allowed unions to collectively bargain for wage rates for their members. In addition, the NRA had $3.3 billion to spend. If a company or industry adopted the NRA codes, it received the NRA Blue Eagle sign, the most recognisable symbol of the First New Deal.

In all, the NRA issued 557 codes of practice. Unfortunately, many of the codes proved unworkable and some large companies, such as the Ford Motor Company, refused to participate. Ultimately, the NRA's activities were declared unconstitutional by the US Supreme Court in 1935. Also, Hugh Johnson's enthusiasm alienated as many people as it pleased.

Although Johnson claimed that the NRA put two million back to work, the wages offered under NRA codes were low and most workers did not experience any improvement in their working conditions, even if their company displayed the Blue Eagle logo. Even before the US Supreme Court intervened, it was clear that the regimentation of business by the NRA was not leading to rapid economic recovery.

### Civilian Conservation Corps (CCC), March 1933

FDR had made it plain in his statements on the New Deal that his priority was to put the USA back to work.

His first programme, the Civilian Conservation Corps (CCC) was his own idea. It was an inter-departmental agency involving the Labor Department, Interior Department and Forest Service of the Department of Agriculture. The CCC programmes were supervised by the army and offered work, mostly manual labour, to young men aged 18 to 25 years, for a minimum of six months, up to two years. The launch involved taking 250,000 off the unemployment lists in cities and rural areas. They lived on-site in camps, which were segregated between blacks and whites. Pay was set at $1 a day plus lodging and food. Of the $30 they received a month, $25 was sent home to their families.

The CCC lasted until 1942 and, in all, three million young men took part in the programme. The CCC built 125,000 miles of road, 46,854 bridges and planted three billion trees. Facilities in many of the National Parks, such as Shenandoah in Virginia, and State Parks such as Edisto Beach, South Carolina, were built by the CCC.

### Federal Emergency Relief Administration (FERA), May 1933

The New Deal's first attempt to aid the unemployed directly was FERA. It was put under the control of a former social worker from Iowa, Harry Hopkins. He believed that work would give the unemployed self-respect, instead of them just being given welfare payments. With a budget of $500 million, it provided work that resulted in the building of over 5,000 public buildings. FERA oversaw state-organised relief for the unemployed. Hopkins used the threat of withdrawal of federal funding to force reluctant states like Georgia and Oregon to take part in the scheme.

### Civil Works Administration (CWA), November 1933

In the winter of 1933–34, Hopkins was given an even bigger job by FDR. The onset of winter meant millions of unemployed faced severe hardship. The CWA was a temporary administration created to meet the problems caused by the winter of 1933–34. With an additional budget of $400 million, Hopkins hired over 4.2 million workers in four months. Under the CWA, workers built over 400 airports and 255,000 miles of road. Much of this work was done over the winter to keep people in employment. Although emergency relief was the main reason for the creation of the CWA, it did provide valuable infrastructure for the US economy, which encouraged future economic growth.

### Public Works Administration (PWA), June 1933

The PWA was created as part of the National Industrial Recovery Act and was placed under Harold Ickes, head of the Department of the Interior. Unlike FERA and the CWA, which offered emergency relief, the PWA aimed at a more long-term programme of stimulating economic growth. It had a budget of $3.3 billion. Harry Hopkins had been accused of providing jobs that aimed merely to give the unemployed emergency work. These were described as 'boondoggle' jobs that had no real purpose. Ickes aimed to provide real, long-term jobs.

Eventually the PWA was responsible for building 13,000 schools and 50,000 miles of road. However, Ickes was accused of spending federal money too slowly. Hopkins's aim was to reduce unemployment as quickly as possible and to this end he spent $5 million in a few hours. The PWA spent only $110 million of its $3.3 billion budget in six months.

Although there was tension between Hopkins and Ickes about how to spend federal funding, FDR was able to use them to help bring about recovery. By 1934, the FERA, PWA and CWA had offered work to 20 percent of the US workforce, an astonishing achievement.

SOURCE

From Franklin D. Roosevelt's 'Fireside Chat to the American People', broadcast on the radio, 7 May 1933. He outlines aspects of the First New Deal. FDR was the first US president to communicate directly with the American people in this way.

The legislation which has been passed or in the process of enactment can properly be considered as part of a well-grounded plan.

We are giving opportunity of employment to one-quarter of a million of the unemployed, especially the young men who have dependents, to go into the forestry and flood prevention work. This is a big task because it means feeding, clothing and caring for nearly twice as many men as we have in the regular army itself. In creating this civilian conservation corps we are killing two birds with one stone. We are clearly enhancing the value of our natural resources and second, we are relieving an appreciable amount of actual distress. This great group of men have entered upon their work on a purely voluntary basis, no military training is involved and we are conserving not only our natural resources but our human resources. One of the great values to this work is the fact that it is direct and requires the intervention of very little machinery.

Our next step in seeking immediate relief is a grant of half a billion dollars to help the states, counties and municipalities in their duty to care for those who need direct and immediate relief.

SOURCE

Political cartoon, dated 1935, by Clifford Berryman, showing FDR encircled by Alphabet Agencies, including the WPA, PWA and AAA.

## Help for farmers

### The Agricultural Adjustment Administration (AAA), June 1933

A nationwide plan to assist farmers and improve agriculture came with the passage of the Agricultural Adjustment Act in May 1933. The McNary–Haugen bills of the 1920s had been an attempt to stabilise farm prices through the government purchase of agricultural surpluses. Overproduction had brought prices down. At the same time, sales of farm products had fallen due to the Depression and foreign tariffs on American food exports.

Under the leadership of Agriculture Secretary Henry Wallace, the AAA set about stabilising prices by a variety of methods. They introduced an allotment plan whereby, to prevent agricultural surpluses, farmers would reduce the acreage under cultivation or reduce their production. At a time of malnutrition in many towns and cities, the sight of farmers killing piglets, burning crops or pouring away surplus milk was hard to comprehend. However, many farmers slaughtered piglets because it was more economical than to raise them to maturity, and crops were burned to provide cheaper fuel. By 1935, 35 million **acres** had been removed from cultivation but farm incomes rose in the same period from $4.5 billion to $6.9 billion.

Not all farmers benefited. Many black American **sharecroppers** in the Old South still lived in abject poverty. In 1935, most rural parts of the USA were still without electricity. Climatic changes and poor agricultural methods resulted in the **Dustbowl**, centred on Oklahoma and Arkansas. By the mid-1930s, thousands of poor farmers fled that area, travelling along Route 66, for a better life working in southern California.

ACTIVITY
KNOWLEDGE CHECK

**Emergency relief, public works and the Alphabet Agencies**

1 Identify four ways in which the First New Deal provided emergency relief for Americans suffering during the Depression.

2 Write down the ways the following Alphabet Agencies provided emergency relief and work:

a) The Civilian Conservation Corps (CCC)

b) Federal Emergency Relief Administration (FERA) and Civil Works Administration (CWA)

c) Public Works Administration (PWA)

Which one do you think was most successful? Explain your answer.

3 How did the First New Deal attempt to aid farmers?

## Reforming the financial system

To most Americans, the Crash and subsequent economic depression were due to problems associated with banks and other financial institutions. To regain public confidence, and prevent a repeat of the economic depression in the future, financial reform was essential. These issues were the major cause of the fear mentioned by FDR in his inaugural speech.

### The Emergency Banking Act, March 1933

The key priority for FDR was to restore faith in the banking system. He acted decisively. Two days after his inauguration as president, he ordered a national bank holiday from 6 to 9 March. In that period he persuaded Congress to pass the Emergency Bank Act, which it did in a record seven hours. During the bank holiday the US Treasury investigated all the banks threatened with collapse and only those approved by the Treasury were allowed to reopen for business on 10 March. Monies from the Reconstruction Finance Corporation were used to prevent banking collapse. Within a week of becoming president FDR had effectively restored confidence in the US banking industry.

### Glass-Steagall Banking Act, June 1933

With public confidence restored, FDR had to reform the system. The Glass–Steagall Act separated **commercial** from **investment banking**. The latter was seen as a major contributory factor in causing the Wall Street Crash. The act also created the Federal Deposit Insurance Corporation (FDIC), which guaranteed all bank deposits to the value of $5,000.

#### KEY TERMS

**Acre**
The standard use of area measurement in USA. An acre is equivalent to about two-fifths of a hectare.

**Sharecropper**
Sharecropping was a form of farming associated with the Old South. A farmer, known as a sharecropper, would rent farmland from a landowner and receive seed to plant as part of the deal. The farmer would pay off use of the land and seed by giving a share of the crop to the landowner.

**Dustbowl**
Area encompassing parts of Kansas, Oklahoma, north Texas and Arkansas. It was affected by drought and poor farming methods, which led to soil erosion. Droughts and serious soil erosion occurred in 1934, 1936 and 1939. Thousands of farmers were ruined and forced to sell or give up their farms. Many travelled down Route 66 (now Interstate 40) to southern California to find work. The exodus of 'Okies' and 'Arkies' along Route 66 was immortalised in John Steinbeck's novel *The Grapes of Wrath* in 1939.

**Commercial banking**
Banking services for the general public and businesses, including holding money on deposit or processing financial transactions.

**Investment banking**
Investment banks loan large sums of money for creating businesses and factories and for construction projects.

Between them, these two Acts restored confidence in the banking system. In 1936, for the first time in 60 years, no US bank closed for business. With a stable banking system the economic recovery, which FDR pledged to bring about, was placed on a sound footing.

**KEY TERM**

**Share speculation**
People bought shares hoping they would increase in value, so they could then sell them on at a profit. The system worked well as long as share prices consistently rose. When prices fell, as in October 1929, it led to share-selling panic.

### The Federal Securities Act, May 1933

Another perceived cause of the Wall Street Crash had been **share speculation**. The purpose of the Federal Securities Act was to regulate the whole system of buying and selling shares. All new share purchases had to be registered with the Federal Trade Commission. In June 1934, FDR created the Securities and Exchange Commission, which regulated all share transactions and stock exchanges across the US. Joseph Kennedy (future president John F. Kennedy's father) was put in charge and the frenzied speculation in shares came to an end.

### The Gold Reserve Act, January 1934, and Silver Purchase Act, June 1934

FDR attempted to bring currency stability to the US through two Acts. The Gold Reserve Act devalued the US dollar against the rate of gold. He hoped this would make US exports cheaper. The Silver Purchase Act hoped to raise prices by increasing the amount of silver in US coinage. The aim was to increase the money supply in order to encourage more economic activity.

Unfortunately, neither Act achieved the hope of reviving US trade. This was mainly due to FDR's belief that the causes of economic crisis were domestic and not international. This was opposite to the view of his predecessor, Herbert Hoover, who had thought the causes of the economic crisis lay abroad. FDR's main efforts in the First New Deal were aimed at getting the USA working.

A key development was the London Economic Conference of July 1933. Other nations wanted to stabilise the value of currencies in order to stimulate international trade: FDR simply wanted to work on his own. By hindering international co-operation, FDR may have harmed the US economy as he prevented foreign economies from growing sufficiently to start importing US-made goods.

## THINKING HISTORICALLY — Cause and consequence (6b)

**Attitudes and actions**

Individuals can only make choices based on their context. Prevalent attitudes combine with individual experience and natural temperament to frame the individual's perception of what is going on around them. Nobody can know the future or see into the minds of others.

Read the following information then look at the questions below. Answer them individually first, then discuss in small groups.

| Context | Action |
|---|---|
| The Republican government under Hoover failed to offer policies that reduced unemployment.<br>FDR felt that a completely new approach to the role of the federal government was required to get the USA out of deep economic depression.<br>FDR believed that the federal government could play a major role in ending the economic depression.<br>The Democratic Party won a landslide victory in both the presidential and congressional elections of 1932, which gave FDR the platform to embark on a major reform programme. | On 4 March1933, FDR announced in his first address as president that he would embark on a bold new programme to get the USA out of deep economic depression. This was the announcement of the New Deal and, in particular, the 100 Days programme of March–June 1933. |

1 Why might FDR have believed that his New Deal programme would get the USA out of economic depression?
2 Why might he have thought that a radical change in the role of the federal government would work when other policies had failed?
3 What other information would have been useful to him to help him decide on his course of action?
4 How reasonable was FDR's course of action given what he understood about the situation at the time?
5 How far should the historian try to understand the context of the beliefs and values of people in the past when explaining why individuals make choices in history?

ACTIVITY
KNOWLEDGE CHECK

**Reforming the banking system**

1 Identify three ways FDR attempted to reform the financial and banking system in the USA in the First New Deal.

2 Which reform or reforms do you think were the most successful? Give reasons for your answer.

## Opposition to the First New Deal

In the midterm elections of November 1934, the Democratic Party achieved great success. The Democrats gained nine seats in the Senate, giving them a majority of 45, and in the House their majority rose to 219. This was a ringing endorsement of the First New Deal. However, not everyone in the USA was satisfied with what FDR had achieved in his first two years as president. Opposition to the First New Deal came from both those who opposed the more activist role of the federal government in economic and social affairs, and those who felt the First New Deal had not gone far enough in tackling the USA's problems.

### The American Liberty League

This group was formed in the summer of 1934 and pledged to defend and uphold the Constitution, to foster the right to work, earn, save and acquire property, and to preserve the ownership and lawful use of property. The League was a mix of FDR's enemies and those who opposed the new, active role of the federal government. Old enemies within the Democratic Party, such as 1928 presidential candidate Al Smith, joined. Those who financially backed the American Liberty League were a 'who's who' of big business, and included the Du Pont family, who owned the USA's largest chemical company, Alfred Sloan of General Motors and Nathan Miller of US Steel.

Even though the First New Deal had brought stability to the financial sector and saved the economy from complete collapse, the American Liberty League believed FDR was planning to change the country in a fundamental way that was alien to the business culture that had made the USA great. Liberty Leaguers tended to support the Republican candidate, Alfred Landon, in the 1936 election. He received 16 million votes, 11 million less than FDR.

### Father Charles Coughlin and Francis Townsend

One of the most important media in the debate over the First New Deal was radio. As early as 12 March 1933, FDR had directly addressed the American people through radio, in what became known as his 'Fireside Chats'. These were used to explain FDR's policies.

By 1930, a Roman Catholic priest, Father Coughlin, had 35 million listeners nationwide for his weekly radio show, *The Golden Hour of the Little Flower*. Initially it seemed that Coughlin backed the underlying aims of the New Deal. He blamed bankers for the economic catastrophe. However, by 1934 he had formed the National Union of Social Justice as an alternative to the First New Deal. Coughlin wanted monetary reform, such as more silver coinage and a policy that encouraged inflation. Inflation would help wipe out financial debt. Coughlin also attacked Jewish members of FDR's administration.

Another radical voice that opposed FDR's policies was that of a retired doctor from California, Francis Townsend. He supported the idea of federal-funded old-age pensions as a way of stimulating demand in the economy. Under his plan, everyone over 60 years old would receive a federal pension of $200 per month. By 1935, over 500,000 people had joined Townsend Clubs across the USA in support of his plan.

In the 1936 presidential election, both Coughlin and Townsend backed William Lemke, presidential candidate of the Union Party, a party created specifically to fight the elections of 1936. He polled only 892,000 votes compared to FDR's 27.8 million.

### Huey P. Long

A serious threat to FDR from within his own party was the governor of Louisiana, Huey Long, known as the Kingfish. In February 1934, Long launched his Share Our Wealth campaign against the First

New Deal. He believed economic recovery would be stimulated if every American family received a minimum annual income of $2,000 and a 'homestead' allowance of $5,000. The cost of this scheme would be met by raising taxes on the rich, such as income and inheritance tax. By early 1935, Long had created 27,000 Share our Wealth clubs across the USA. These clubs acted as pressure groups supporting Long's Share Our Wealth campaign. He was seen as a serious contender for the Democratic nomination for president in 1936 but was assassinated in September 1935.

### The US Supreme Court

By far the most serious opposition to the First New Deal came from the US Supreme Court. The nine justices were political appointments and the majority had been nominated by Republican presidents. The Chief Justice, Charles Evans Hughes, had been the Republican candidate in the 1916 presidential election. The Court had the power to declare Acts of Congress, actions by the president or state laws unconstitutional. FDR's defence of New Deal measures was that he believed they could be justified because they promoted the general welfare clause of the US Constitution.

In 1935, the Court declared various key parts of the First New Deal unconstitutional. The National Industrial Recovery Act, which had created the NRA and PWA, was declared unconstitutional in May 1935. In what became known as the Schechter 'Sick Chicken' case, the Court declared that the federal government had exceeded its powers by trying to regulate commerce within a state, New York. In January 1936, the Court declared the Agricultural Adjustment Administration illegal in the case *US v Butler* on similar grounds. The Court ruled that the federal government levied a tax on farm products, a power that was reserved to the states under the 10th Amendment of the US Constitution. In all, the US Supreme Court declared 11 First New Deal laws illegal because they were deemed contrary to the US Constitution. The impact of these US Supreme Court decisions was to make large parts of FDR's First New Deal unworkable. Almost singlehandedly, the US Supreme Court had nearly wrecked the First New Deal by early 1936.

**SOURCE**

From 'Share our Wealth' by Huey P. Long, 23 May 1935. This was a statement issued by the Share Our Wealth campaign that Huey P. Long believed would bring the fundamental reform required to get the USA out of economic depression and create a more equal society. Long was seen as a major contender against Franklin D. Roosevelt for the Democratic Party nomination as presidential candidate in the 1936 elections. It was also feared that he might run as a third party candidate if unsuccessful in gaining the Democratic Party nomination and so split the vote.

It is impossible for the United States to preserve itself as a republic or as a democracy when 600 families own more of this Nation's wealth – in fact twice as much – as all the balance of the people put together. 96% of our people live below the poverty line, while 4% own 87% of the wealth. America can have enough for all living in comfort and still permit millionaires to own more than they can ever spend and to have more than they can ever use; but America cannot allow the multi-millionaires and the billionaires, a mere handful of them, to own everything unless we are willing to inflict starvation on 125 million people,

Here is the substance of the share-our-wealth movement:

1. Every family to be furnished by the Government a homestead allowance, free of debt, of not less than one-third the average family wealth of the country.
2. The yearly income of every family shall not be less than one-third of the average family income, no family's annual income would be less than $2000-$2500.
3. To limit the hours of work to prevent overproduction.
4. An old age pension to persons over 60.
5. To balance agricultural production.
6. To pay veterans of our wars what we owe them.
7. Education and training to all children.
8. To raise revenue and taxes to support this program.

**A Level Exam-Style Question Section B**

To what extent did the First New Deal bring relief and recovery to the US economy? (20 marks)

**Tip**

*This question requires a balanced answer in which you should point out and explain the areas where the First New Deal brought relief and recovery to the US economy. You should deal with relief and recovery separately rather than both together. You will also be expected to explain the limitations of the First New Deal in both areas before writing a concluding judgement.*

**ACTIVITY**
**KNOWLEDGE CHECK**

**The First New Deal**

What do Sources 7, 8 and 9 tell us about how the USA could get out of the problems created by the economic depression?

# TO WHAT EXTENT HAD PRESIDENT ROOSEVELT BROUGHT RECOVERY BY 1938?

Normally, halfway through a president's first term of four years in office, his political party loses seats in Congress in the midterm elections. However, in November 1934, the Democrats greatly increased their support in both houses and also in state government elections across the country. Congress was now filled with New Deal Democrats who wanted FDR to be more radical in dealing with the problems of the Depression.

## THE SECOND NEW DEAL

**1935**

April: Emergency Relief Appropriation Act creates Works Progress Administration

1 May: Resettlement Administration created

11 May: Rural Electrification Administration created

26 June: National Youth Administration created

5 July: Wagner Act passed

14 August: Social Security Act passed

30 August: Revenue Act passed

8 September: Huey Long assassinated

**1936**

6 January: US Supreme Court declares AAA unconstitutional

3 November: FDR wins landslide victory in presidential election; Democrats increase their majority in Congress

**1937**

5 February: FDR submits Court Packing bill to Congress

12 April: Supreme Court upholds Wagner Act and Social Security Act

22 July: Senate rejects FDR's Court Packing proposal

August: Beginning of Roosevelt Recession

**1938**

16 February: Second Agricultural Adjustment Act passed

25 June: Fair Labor Standards Act passed

## The Wagner Act, June 1935

In July 1935, Congress passed the national Labor Relations Act, known after the senator who proposed it, Robert Wagner. The Wagner Act is regarded as a milestone in giving trade unions basic rights. The 1930s saw the greatest increase in trade union membership in US history. The major national labour organisation up to 1935 was the American Federation of Labor (AFL), which mainly had members in craft occupations. In the autumn of 1935, a new, more militant organisation was created, called the Congress of Industrial Organizations (CIO). It organised members in the steel, car, textile, coal and rubber industries, which had semi-skilled and unskilled workers.

Trade unions were also major supporters of the Democratic Party. Initially, Section 7(a) of the National Industrial Recovery Act (1933) had given trade unions the right to collectively bargain for better pay and conditions on behalf of their members. In May 1935, the US Supreme Court declared that Act unconstitutional. The Wagner Act gave the right to collective bargaining back to the unions. Individual workplaces were given the right to join trade unions, following a secret ballot of their members. Finally, the federal government established the National Labor Relations Board, consisting of three independent members to ensure both employers and trade unions acted correctly.

Other legislation in the Second New Deal meant that FDR provided the basis for modern US labour relations. The Guffey–Snyder Act of 1935 and the Guffey–Vinson Act of 1937 enabled a national coal commission to set minimum wages in the coal industry. In 1938, a Fair Labor Standards Act prohibited child labour.

However, the Wagner Act excluded agricultural and service workers, public employees and those employed outside interstate commerce. These were excluded because of opposition within Congress. Therefore, many black Americans, Hispanic Americans and women, whose employment was concentrated in these areas, received very little benefit from the Act.

## The Social Security Act, June 1935

Until 1935, the USA did not possess a national government system for the elderly. Germany had introduced one in 1889 and Britain introduced old age pensions in 1908. The Social Security Act was a response to Francis Townsend's criticism of the First New Deal. It was the responsibility of the USA's first woman cabinet member, Frances Perkins of the Department of Labor. The social security system was to be funded by equal contributions from employers and workers and would provide minimal payments to unemployed workers, the elderly and dependents of deceased breadwinners. Pensions were to be paid out at a rate of between $10 and $85 per month. Unemployment benefit was to be paid at a maximum of $18 per week for 16 weeks only. This was a major break with the past. Until 1935, unemployment was regarded as a state government responsibility. The Act was not completely comprehensive as it excluded those workers who needed it most: farm workers, domestic servants and the self-employed.

On 17 January 1940, the first person to receive a pension under the act was Ida Fuller, a 76-year-old from Vermont.

**SOURCE 12** On 2 September 1935 Frances Perkins, Secretary of Labor, gave a radio address, outlining what she regarded as the major features of the Social Security Act to the general public.

Old people who are in need, unemployables, children, mothers and the sightless, will find systematic regular provisions for needs. The Act limits Federal aid to no more than $15 per month for the individual, provided the State in which he resides appropriates the same amount. There is nothing to prevent a State from contributing more than $15 per month in special cases.

The social security measure looks primarily to the future and is only a part of the administration's plan to promote sound and stable economic life. We cannot think of it disassociated from the Government's program to save the homes, the farms, the businesses and the banks of the Nation.

The passage of this act is deeply significant of the progress which the American people have made in thought in the social field and awareness of the methods of using cooperation through government to overcome social hazards against which the individual alone is inadequate.

THINKING HISTORICALLY **Evidence (6a)**

**Arguments and facts**

Read Sources 8, 9, 11 and 12.

Work in groups and discuss the following questions:

1 In what ways do Sources 9 and 11 disagree? Which one do you think is correct? Explain your answer.

2 How do Sources 8 and 12 differ in the ways they attempt to give US workers opportunities during the Depression?

3 Do you think that the authors of Sources 8 and 12, which offer different solutions to the problems facing American workers during the Depression, differ in terms of facts and focus? Explain your answer.

4 All of these sources give detailed information about the significance of the New Deal and a suggested alternative. Which do you think is more important?

5 If we accept that Source 9 is dated before an assessment could have been made of the effectiveness of New Deal programmes, should we discount Source 11 as being useful? Explain your answer.

6 Why are facts important in history?

**AS Level Exam-Style Question Section A**

***Study Source 12 before you answer this question.***

How much weight would you give the evidence of Source 12 in an enquiry into the reasons why the Social Security Act was passed in 1935?

Explain your answer using the source, the information given about it and your own knowledge of the historical context. (12 marks)

**Tip**

*You need to look at the provenance of the source and explain why this may be important in judging the value and weight it can be given. Also, identify relevant sections of Source 12 that help you explain the importance and possible impact of the Social Security Act.*

## The Revenue Act, August 1935

The First and Second New Deals involved spending billions of dollars on schemes to offer relief to the unemployed, put Americans back to work and pay for social security. To help pay for these programmes, Congress passed the Revenue Act (also known as the Wealth Tax Act) in August 1935. It increased the rate of income tax from 63 to 79 percent on incomes over $5 million. This change raised an additional $250 million a year, a tiny sum compared to the huge amounts the federal government spent on New Deal projects. Fewer than one American household in 20 paid federal income tax and only ten percent of US families earned more than $3,200 a year. Most Americans paid state taxes only.

In addition, the Act also increased taxes on property and introduced an undistributed profits tax to force large companies (corporations) back into the stock market to raise money for more investment in the economy.

The Revenue Act of 1935 was more of a political showpiece than a fundamental change in the tax system. It was a move to thwart the Share Our Wealth campaign by Huey P. Long, the Louisiana Kingfish. When the proposal was read in the Senate, Long claimed credit for the idea.

Even though the Act made limited changes to the federal tax system, it aroused huge criticism from the rich, including William Randolph Hearst, a major newspaper owner. What annoyed many of the rich was the fact that FDR also came from a very wealthy background. They called him a class traitor.

## More aid to farmers

Two major Second New Deal initiatives specifically aided rural communities. The Resettlement Administration of 1935 helped relocate 45,000 farming families from the areas in Oklahoma, Texas and Kansas most badly affected by the Dustbowl.

The Rural Electrification Administration (REA), also created in 1935, gave low interest loans to rural co-operatives to allow them to provide electricity. In 1930, only ten percent of rural communities had electricity. By 1945, 40 percent of farms had electricity, mainly as a result of the REA.

## Assessment

The Second New Deal brought fundamental reform to the USA. FDR aimed to reform and strengthen the American social and economic system, not to destroy it. The proof of the Second New Deal's popularity came in the presidential and Congressional elections of November 1936. FDR improved on his electoral performance of 1932. He polled 27.8 million votes against Republican Alfred Landon's 16.7 million.

William Lemke of the Union Party and Norman Thomas, the Socialist candidate, both offering more radical alternatives to the New Deal, polled just under one million votes between them.

Under the US electoral system, popular votes were counted within each state. States were apportioned Electoral College votes based on their combined seats in the Senate and House of Representatives. FDR won every state except Maine and Vermont, winning 523 Electoral College votes to Landon's eight, a massive landslide victory.

**EXTEND YOUR KNOWLEDGE**

**The Electoral College**

Under the United Sates Constitution, a president and vice president are elected by the states, not directly by popular vote. On the first Tuesday in November every four years, voters cast their ballots, then in December the Electoral College casts its votes. Each state has as many Electoral College votes as it has seats in the Senate and House of Representatives combined. Wyoming, for example, has three Electoral College votes. New York State has over 40.

Members of the Electoral College are meant to follow the wishes of voters in their state and vote for the candidate who won a majority. Rarely, some Electoral College members vote for the candidate they prefer! It is possible for a candidate who has won the popular vote nationwide to lose the election because of the Electoral College vote. This happened in 1976 and, possibly, in 2000.

In 1940, FDR won 27.3 million votes and won 449 Electoral College votes. His Republican opponent, Wendell Wilkie won 22.3 million votes and only 82 Electoral College votes. In Congress the Democrats had a majority of 229 in the House and 56 in the Senate. They also won control of many state governments.

### Jobs, jobs, jobs

Many of the Alphabet Agencies of the First New Deal aimed to create public sector jobs to aid economic recovery. Under Harry Hopkins, FERA and the CWA provided emergency jobs for the unemployed. Under the Second New Deal, Hopkins was given a more ambitious project. The Emergency Relief Appropriation Act of April 1935 created the Works Progress Administration (WPA). It received the substantial budget of $4 billion to get Americans back to work.

From 1935 until its demise in 1943, the WPA spent over $11 billion, ultimately employing eight million workers, one-fifth of America's entire workforce. Thousands of hospitals, schools, parks and rural roads were constructed by WPA workers. It also helped groups such as women, black Americans, artists and musicians. In 1936, the WPA set up CCC-style camps for young women. The Federal Writers' Project aided writers, especially black Americans; the Theatre Project employed 12,000 performers and production companies. Two Oscar winners, Orson Welles and John Huston, were funded by the project.

The National Youth Administration encouraged education and part-time work for students, while its Negro Division, headed by black American Mary McLeod Bethune, ensured that black Americans benefitted from WPA and NYA programmes.

## Opposition to the Second New Deal

The 1936 presidential and Congressional elections were a major triumph for FDR and the New Deal. However, within two years, FDR's personal popularity had fallen significantly. In the midterm Congressional elections of November 1938, the Democrats lost seven seats in the Senate and 70 in the House of Representatives. What brought about this change?

### Socialists, communists, strikes and sit-ins

FDR wanted to reform the American economic system. Socialists and communists wanted to destroy it and replace it with an economic system that they regarded as more fair. The capitalist economic system of the USA allowed private ownership of property, business, agriculture and industry. Although this economic system had enabled the USA to become the world's biggest economic power, it also allowed wealth and economic power to be concentrated with a small number of people. Individuals like Henry Ford, and families like the Rockefellers and Du Ponts, had millions of dollars. The gap between rich and poor in the USA was immense. In his second inaugural address as president in January 1937, FDR claimed that one-third of the USA was still poor.

Socialists and communists wanted to replace private ownership of industry, agriculture and business with government ownership they hoped that the government would share out the USA's wealth more equally. Communists, in particular, looked to the USSR as the model economy to follow. Although these groups received a lot of publicity, their impact on elections was marginal. In 1936, the Communist presidential candidate, Earl Browder, received a mere 79,000 votes. Norman Thomas, the Socialist candidate, got slightly more with 187,000, compared to the millions of votes polled for the Democratic and Republican candidates. Although trade unions generally supported the Democrats, industrial unrest grew in the USA in the mid-1930s. Led by the CIO, unions such as the United Automobile Workers' Union, organised strikes. Many of the union leaders were socialists or communists. In December 1936, a new phenomenon affected US labour relations. In Flint, Michigan, auto workers occupied the factory owned by the Cleveland Fisher company. A month-long sit-in by workers prevented the factory from operating.

In 1936 there had been over 2,000 strikes, involving 788,000 workers. In 1937 this rose to 4,470, involving 1.9 million workers.

### The Roosevelt Recession, 1937–38

A major contributory factor in the rise of trade union militancy was the Roosevelt **Recession**. In 1937, at the beginning of his second term as president, FDR ordered substantial cuts in federal government spending. The Federal Reserve Board also feared a rise in inflation and limited the supply of money in the US economy. On 19 October 1937, another stock market crash occurred when 17 million shares were offloaded by investors. Employment in manufacturing fell by 23 percent, and the GNP dropped by 13 percent. Work relief offered by the WPA grew by 500 percent. By the summer of 1938, it seemed that the American economy was reverting back to the days before FDR was elected in 1932.

**KEY TERM**

**Recession**
A period of slowdown in an economy, less severe than an economic depression. A depression was avoided at least in part, thanks to the passage of important federal legislation under the First and Second New Deals.

### The Court Packing Plan, 1937

The biggest setback FDR faced was his attempt to change the composition of the US Supreme Court. In February 1937, he submitted a bill known as the Judicial Procedures Reform bill to Congress. The aim was to force all Supreme Court justices to retire at 70 years of age. In 1937, six of the nine Supreme Court justices were over 70. If passed, this would have allowed FDR to appoint six new justices, transforming the political balance of the Supreme Court. He also wanted the number of justices increased from nine to 15. If passed, this change would have given FDR immense power. The plan provoked massive criticism in the media and Congress and FDR's popularity suffered a major decline. Even though the Democrats had a majority in the Senate, that body rejected his plan by 70 to 20.

Fortunately for FDR, the US Supreme Court began to allow progressive legislation to become law. The first instance of this was their decision to uphold a minimum wage act from Washington State in March 1937. Then, on 12 April 1937, they upheld the Wagner Act, one of the cornerstones of the Second New Deal. Later in the same year, one of the most conservative justices, Willis van Devanter, retired, allowing FDR to nominate his replacement. After 1937, the US Supreme Court no longer acted as the major opponent of the New Deal. However, in the process FDR had lost considerable support within Congress. There was a Third New Deal from 1937 to 1939, but this lacked the radical changes of the previous two.

**A Level Exam-Style Question Section B**

To what extent did the Second New Deal bring fundamental reform to the USA? (20 marks)

**Tip**

*The answer requires a balanced judgement. You will need to assess the Second New Deal's level of success. It is important you offer a definition of the word 'fundamental' in your answer.*

**ACTIVITY**
**KNOWLEDGE CHECK**

**Second New Deal**

1 Sources 11 and 12 offer different views on how to deal with the problems created by the economic depression in the USA. Why do you think they are so different? You will need to consider the dates of the sources, who produced them and the intended audience for each.

2 Source 10 is a political cartoon. What statement do you think it is trying to make about the Alphabet Agencies? Do you think this political cartoon supports or opposes Franklin D. Roosevelt's policies? Explain your answer.

**ACTIVITY**
**SUMMARY**

**The First and Second New Deals**

1 Write down ways the First New Deal brought:

a) relief for those affected by the Depression

b) reform of the US economic system as a way of preventing future depressions

c) recovery of the US economy.

2 a What were the key changes the Second New Deal made to the lives of American citizens?

b Which do you regard as the more successful in achieving its aims, the First or Second New Deal? Give reasons for your answer.

## WIDER READING


Clements, P. *Prosperity, Depression and the New Deal, Access to History*, Hodder (2005)

de Pennington, J. *Modern America, The USA, 1865 to the present*, Hodder Murray (2005)

Farmer, A. and Sanders, V. *An Introduction to American History, 1860–1990*, Hodder (2002)

Field, R. *Civil Rights in America, 1865 to 1980*, Cambridge University Press (2002)

Murphy, D. *Flagship History - The United States 1776–1992*, Collins Educational (2001)

Murphy, D. *Flagship History - The United States 1917–2008*, Collins Educational (2008)

Parrish, M. *The Anxious Decades: America in Prosperity and Depression 1920–1941*, WW Norton and Company (1994)

Rowe, C. *USA, 1890–1945*, Nelson Thornes (2008)

Stewart, G. and Barker, L. *The United States 1917–1954: Boom Bust and Recovery*, Pearson (2010)

Willoughby, S. and Willoughby, D. *The USA 1917–1945*, Heinemann (2000)

# 2a.3 Impact of the New Deal and the Second World War on the USA to 1945

**KEY QUESTIONS**

- How successful was the New Deal in bringing economic recovery to the USA by 1940?
- How far did the New Deal affect the lives of ethnic minorities within the USA?
- How far did the period to 1945 bring social and cultural change to the USA?
- To what extent did the Second World War affect the performance of the economy between 1941 and 1945?

## INTRODUCTION

The New Deal was a major turning point in US history. Politically, it saw the decline in popularity of the Republican Party and the rise to dominance of the Democrats. A 'New Deal coalition' was created, comprising southern whites, Jewish Americans, Irish Americans, black Americans, trade unionists and manufacturing workers. This combination of voting groups lasted until the 1960s. The New Deal also had profound effects on the US economy. The New Deal programmes, implemented by the Alphabet Agencies saved the US from economic catastrophe. They brought work and relief to millions of Americans and helped transform the USA's infrastructure of roads, bridges and energy supply.

However, when the US became directly involved in the Second World War on 7 December 1941, the USA still had high levels of unemployment and many industries were plagued with strikes. America's war years (1941–45) completed what the New Deal had begun. Unemployment plummeted, the economy boomed and, as President F. D. Roosevelt (FDR) said, the USA became the main provider of the war material that clinched Allied victory.

The New Deal and the Second World War also had profound social effects. The lives of black Americans, Native Americans, Hispanic Americans and women were in several areas changed beyond recognition. A new era in US domestic history had begun.

The New Deal and Second World War also changed the USA culturally. Help to writers and musicians, new job opportunities for minorities and a growth in the cultural influence of radio and cinema were dominant themes of this period. The Second World War completed a period of transformation and change that had begun with FDR's election in November 1932.

**1933** – F. D. Roosevelt (FDR) becomes president and the New Deal begins

**1934** – Indian Reorganisation Act

**1935** – Wagner Act establishes trade union rights
Works Progress Administration (WPA) created
Federal Writers' Project
Federal Music Project
National Youth Administration created
Split at AFL leads to creation of the CIO

**1939** – Cash and carry programme

1933 | 1934 | 1935 | 1936 | 1937 | 1938 | 1939

# HOW SUCCESSFUL WAS THE NEW DEAL IN BRINGING ECONOMIC RECOVERY TO THE USA BY 1940?

When Roosevelt became president in March 1933, the USA was on the brink of economic collapse. Banks had closed by the hundred. Unemployment had risen to 32.6 percent at the end of 1933.

## The impact of the New Deal

### The New Deal and unemployment

The New Deal aimed at relief for the unemployed, economic recovery and economic reform. In these aims, by 1939 FDR was only partially successful. Through the Alphabet Agencies, such as the CCC, PWA and WPA, the federal government for the first time engaged in bringing help and assistance to the unemployed through directly funded works programmes. However, in no year after 1933 did unemployment fall below 14 percent of the workforce: 9.5 million Americans, 17.2 percent of the workforce, were still out of work in 1939. Some New Deal measures, such as the National Recovery Administration and the gold-buying experiment, did more harm than good. FDR's decision to concentrate on domestic solutions to the USA's economic problems had the adverse effect of prolonging the global depression and was seen by many as depressing US exports. There were claims that the PWA offered 'boondoggle' jobs, which provided work of dubious economic value, like scaring pigeons away from public parks.

The combined personal income of the USA was $72.9 billion in 1939, compared to $85.8 billion in 1929, although the population had grown by nine million. In 1939, one in five Americans received some form of government relief. Three-quarters of those who were receiving government relief had been out of work in 1933. Of all the major industrial economies, such as Britain and Germany, the USA continued to be most seriously affected by depression.

The economic problems had been made worse by the Roosevelt Recession of 1937–38, when the rate of economic decline was sharper than in late 1929. Over a ten-month period, industrial production fell 33 percent. Nearly four million people lost their jobs, with unemployment rising to 11.5 percent. GNP fell by 12 percent. FDR was at least partially responsible through cutting federal expenditure sharply: the government's contribution to purchasing power fell from $4.1 billion in 1936 to less than $1 billion in 1937.

Within the context of the 1930s, in the search for economic growth, the New Deal was a failure, but it did prevent economic collapse and laid the foundations for rapid economic growth in the Second World War.

### The New Deal and national infrastructure

Even though the New Deal did not bring full economic recovery, it did have a profound impact on the **national infrastructure** of the USA. The Alphabet Agencies played a central role in this. The Works Progress Administration (WPA), created in 1935 by the Emergency Relief Appropriation Act, helped transform the USA. In seven years, from 1935 to 1943, workers of the WPA built 2,500 hospitals, 5,900 schools, 350 airports, 570,000 miles of road and 8,000 parks.

**KEY TERM**

**National infrastructure**
The road, rail, river and canal network.

The Civilian Conservation Corps (CCC) was heavily involved in helping the development of US National Parks and State Parks. Roads, tree planting and the building of tourist facilities were some of the more substantial legacies of the CCC that can still be seen today. Roads made National Parks accessible. Mesa Verde National Park in southern Colorado, the road system of Yellowstone National Park, and the tourist facilities at Shenandoah National Park, Virginia were all CCC projects and are still in use today.

The development of regional infrastructure was also an important New Deal legacy. The Tennessee Valley Authority (TVA) of 1933 helped transform an area blighted by soil erosion and economic under-development. The Tennessee River was made navigable from its junction with the Ohio River to Knoxville, in the Appalachian Mountains. This was achieved through building locks and dams. The dams also provided hydro-electric power for both domestic and industrial use: the dam at Muscle Shoals helped power the Alcan aluminium factory. In 1937, the Booneville Power Administration was created, which provided similar facilities on the Columbia River in Oregon, in the Pacific Northwest.

**1941** - March: Lend-Lease programme
7 December: US enters the Second World War

**1943** - June: Race riots in Detroit and Los Angeles

**1945** - April: FDR dies in office and is succeeded by Vice President Harry Truman

1940 | 1941 | 1942 | 1943 | 1944 | 1945

**1942** - January: War Labor Board created; War Production Board created
April: War Manpower Commission created

**1944** - July: Bretton Woods Agreement
November: FDR re-elected for a record fourth time

In May 1935, FDR created the Rural Electrification Administration (REA), headed by Morris Llewellyn Cooke. He persuaded private power companies to extend power lines into farm areas, offering low-interest loans to the power companies to do the work. He also created non-profit co-operatives to do the work where private firms failed to do so. The provision of electricity transformed rural life across the USA. It powered labour-saving equipment and enabled new industries to locate in rural areas. By 1941, 40 percent of the nation's farmers had received electricity, increasing to 90 percent by 1950. However, even with rural electrification, acreage under cultivation did not really increase in the New Deal years. In 1929 it was one billion acres, rising slightly to 1.05 billion in 1939.

FDR may not have brought full economic recovery, but by 1940 the New Deal had provided millions of jobs and transformed the road network, the schools system and hospital provision. Rural areas went through a revolution in energy provision and regions such as the Upper South in the Tennessee Valley Authority (TVA) area and Oregon had major boosts to their economies.

## Women and the New Deal

Until 1933, US national politics was dominated by men from a white Anglo-Saxon Protestant (WASP) background. FDR's New Deal had a profound effect on a variety of people. For Catholics (Irish, Italian and German), Jews and trade unionists there was more opportunity to influence federal government policy. For women of all religions and backgrounds, the New Deal opened up more job opportunities.

In 1930, 10.7 million of the USA's 60.6 million women worked. By 1940 this figure had risen to 12.5 million out of 65 million women. The New Deal played an important part in opening up opportunities for the female population. For instance, women benefited from the Civilian Conservation Corps and employment in the Alphabet Agencies created in both the First and Second New Deal. Women's Civilian Corps camps, nicknamed 'She She She camps', mirrored the CCC camps of men. Federal employment offered opportunities that did not exist before 1933 for women from a wide variety of backgrounds. The numbers involved in the She She She camps were extremely small when compared to those in the CCC camps. In some cases, women also played a central role in how the New Deal operated.

### Eleanor Roosevelt, First Lady

The president's wife, known as the First Lady, has always played an important role in the USA. Up to 1933, this role was overwhelmingly ceremonial. First Ladies supported their husbands during social functions and trips around the USA. In 1933, things changed: for the first time, the First Lady played an important role in deciding policy. Eleanor Roosevelt, more than any other First Lady, before or since, helped forge the direction of national policy. Her intelligence, powerful personality and social and political links gave her influence. Eleanor Roosevelt regularly advised her husband on aspects of federal policy and championed the position of women and ethnic minorities. She became an unofficial member of FDR's advisory team.

**SOURCE 1** Eleanor Roosevelt (right) with a volunteer collecting books to be sent to US servicemen overseas. The scene is typical of her hands-on active approach to the role of First Lady.

Eleanor Roosevelt's impact was almost immediate. Two days after FDR was inaugurated president, she held her first press conference. During the New Deal years, she held 348 such conferences, explaining to the press what she felt ought to be done. In particular, she highlighted the plight of young people faced with extreme poverty and lack of opportunity. Her link to the American public was also enhanced through letter-writing. She encouraged Americans to write to her at the White House. Over 300,000 letters, mainly from young Americans, were received. Eleanor Roosevelt used the information she received through the letters to influence the president's actions and policies. Many 'Dear Mrs Roosevelt' letters asked for simple necessities like clothing.

Eleanor Roosevelt also had her own syndicated regular newspaper article 'My Day', an early version of a blog, explaining to the American people what she did day-by-day. In 1936, 'My Day' appeared six days a week. During her husband's presidency, Eleanor Roosevelt travelled nearly 300,000 miles across the USA, asking questions and supporting New Deal policies. She visited coal mines, sharecroppers and slum dwellers. She was as much the face of the New Deal as her husband. Her high national profile increased her ability to influence the president on policy issues.

Eleanor Roosevelt thought there should be more women in government and encouraged her husband to appoint women wherever possible. When FDR established the Civilian Conservation Corps (CCC) for young men in 1933, she campaigned for a female equivalent. She eventually got her wish in 1936, when the work camps for young women known as 'She She She' camps, were established. There were 90 residential work camps for women that together employed on average 5,000 women per year.

Eleanor Roosevelt's support for US youth was an important factor in the creation of the National Youth Administration to provide work and educational opportunities for young people. However, it was affordable housing that was a special concern and she worked with the PWA and the Washington DC Housing Authority to support 'greenbelt' towns. Eleanor Roosevelt also played a key role in the Federal Arts Projects of the Works Progress Administration (WPA) from 1935, and defended them against attacks in Congress and accusations that federal money was being wasted.

Of all the supporters of the New Deal, Eleanor Roosevelt was the strongest advocate for civil rights for black Americans. She met with Walter White, head of the National Association for the Advancement of Colored People (NAACP), and supported the appointment of Mary Bethune. In the same year, an opinion poll by the research firm Gallup saw her gain a national approval rating of 67 percent against her husband's rating of 58 percent.

### Frances Perkins, first woman cabinet member

In March 1933, Frances Perkins became the first woman cabinet member in US history, taking on the role of Secretary of Labor, which she held until June 1945. She played a pivotal role in establishing the Civilian Conservation Corps (CCC), which was an interdepartmental New Deal agency involving the Labor Department, Interior Department and Agriculture Department and supervised by the army. Her greatest contribution to the New Deal was crafting the Social Security Act of 1935 which, for the first time, gave direct federal aid to the aged and unemployed through a form of insurance. The Social Security Act was seen by many as the New Deal's most important act. For the first time the federal government provided direct welfare support to American citizens.

Perkins also helped pass a federal minimum wage for workers, for the first time, in the Fair Labor Standards Act of 1938.

### Mary McLeod Bethune, black American adviser and activist

The most prominent black American in the New Deal became FDR's special adviser on minority affairs in 1935, the year she founded her own civil rights organisation, the National Council of Negro Women. The following year, she became the chairperson of an informal 'Black Cabinet', a group of federally appointed black American officials to help plan priorities for the black American community. In 1936, she achieved national prominence through her appointment as the Director of the Negro Affairs Division of the National Youth Administration (NYA). She held that post from 1936 to 1944. She constantly demanded that black American youth should receive federal aid in numbers that reflected their proportion of the national population, but with very limited success. She also campaigned for the rights of black Americans to get the same pay as whites in the federal government, although this was only partially successful.

## EXTEND YOUR KNOWLEDGE

### Eleanor Roosevelt (1884–1962)

The future First Lady was born into one of America's most privileged families, the Roosevelts. In 1905, she married another Roosevelt, Franklin, a distant cousin. In the 1920s she began her own political career, speaking on issues such as women's rights, labour unions and black equality.

When FDR became president, Eleanor championed these issues throughout the New Deal and war years. She constantly pressured FDR to appoint women and minority members to federal positions of influence, and supported the appointment of Mary McLeod Bethune to the National Youth Administration.

In the Second World War, she was a major defender of the black American Tuskegee airmen against white criticism in Congress. A fighter training school had been established at Tuskegee for black airmen but many white politicians from the southern states thought black Americans should not have combat roles.

Eleanor survived her husband, who died in April 1945, by 17 years. Under his successor, President Truman, she represented the USA in the United Nations.

### SOURCE

An extract from 'Women in Politics', an article by Eleanor Roosevelt that appeared in the magazine *Good Housekeeping* in April 1940. She had developed a national reputation through her involvement in political matters by 1940. In that year, her husband was planning to stand for re-election. *Good Housekeeping* was a magazine bought and read by women, mainly from middle-class backgrounds.

I find the influence of women emerging into a more important sphere. There was a time when no one asked 'What will the women think about this?' Now that question comes up often. It is true that we have more women in elective positions than ten years ago; but I think the change is so slight that it is just a temporary fluctuation, and due to the fact that women haven't yet gained confidence in themselves in that type of competition. Women are quite willing to compete in an examination that tests their knowledge even though there is still a prejudice against appointing them in certain positions because of their sex. To come out and fight a political campaign, however, is still difficult for most women. That is one reason why a woman who does hold office, either elective or appointive, so often obtains it at her husband's death or as a result of his interests. She is continuing work she might never have taken up on her own initiative.

### AS Level Exam-Style Question Section A

***Study Source 2 before you answer this question.***

Why is Source 2 valuable to the historian for an enquiry into the impact of the role of Eleanor Roosevelt in US politics?

Explain your answer using the source, the information given about it and your own knowledge of the historical context. (8 marks)

**Tip**

*Make sure you comment on the provenance of the source and the audience it is aimed at.*

## Evidence (5b)

### The importance of context

Documents like Source 2 are like small pieces torn from a larger tapestry. Historians have to reconstruct the larger pattern into which documents might fit in order to construct accounts of the past. The problem is that texts can have multiple contexts. Historians often debate how best to contextualise the documents that they interpret.

Source 2 is an interview with the USA's First Lady, Eleanor Roosevelt, the wife of President F. D. Roosevelt. Unlike many of her predecessors, as First Lady Eleanor Roosevelt was an active force in trying to get extra rights for women in the USA.

**1** Summarise some key points from Source 2. Does the document indicate that the New Deal opened up greater opportunities for women in the USA?

**2** In which areas do you think the New Deal had the biggest impact on assisting women in getting greater opportunities?

**3** In which areas did Eleanor Roosevelt think women still had a way to go to achieve greater equality with men?

**4** Did she have a timetable for when this would or could take place?

As well as noting the contents of Source 2, it is important to consider the audience of the source. *Good Housekeeping* was a magazine designed for and read by women in the USA.

The timeline below provides a possible context for the document in the wider story of the New Deal. Look at the timeline and then answer the question that follows.

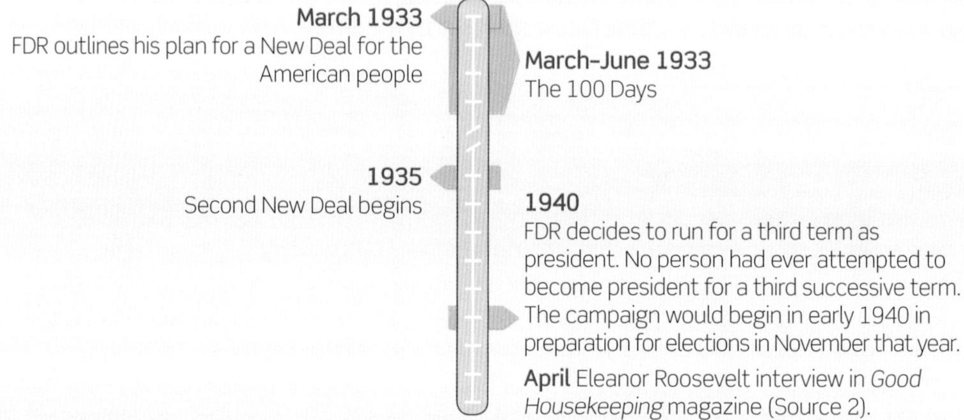


**5** How does Source 2 fit into the pattern of events? Why might Eleanor Roosevelt have shared these thoughts about the role of women and the policies associated with her husband, the president, in April 1940?

The document takes on one meaning when interpreted in the context of the New Deal and presidential elections in the USA, but a contrasting interpretation can be made if we locate it in another context.

There is good reason to think that the role of women in the USA, and the future role of women in US politics in particular, may not have been of such importance as Eleanor Roosevelt has suggested. Consider this timeline and answer the question that follows.

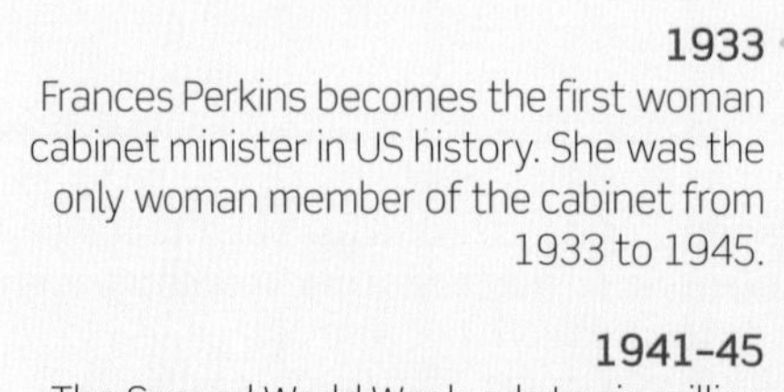


*Continued*

6 Why might Eleanor Roosevelt have shared her thoughts about the role of women and future role of women with a national women's magazine in April 1940?

Consider both timelines together and answer the following questions.

7 Use information from both timelines to construct a possible context for what Eleanor Roosevelt said in April 1940 - why might she have said these things to a select audience of women who subscribed to the *Good Housekeeping* magazine at that time?

8 Why is it important for historians to spend time thinking about possible contexts for a document before they start to use it to draw conclusions about the past?

## The state of the US economy in 1940

By 1940, Europe was at war and the US had staved off economic collapse and gone through a partial economic recovery. With unemployment still at 8.1 million (14.6 percent of the workforce), trade union membership had increased considerably. In 1930, trade union membership was 3.4 million, comprising 11.6 percent of the workforce. This had risen to 8.7 million in 1940, 26.9 percent of the workforce. The beginnings of national welfare provision had begun with the Social Security Act of 1935. The workforce had more protection on pay and conditions than ever before.

However, economic power was still in the hands of big corporations. In 1939, the top five corporations in the USA controlled 84.5 percent of all income generated by business. This compared to 84.3 percent in 1929, on the eve of the Depression. Industrial unrest was still a feature of many American manufacturing towns.

Nevertheless, infrastructure changes made by the New Deal laid the foundation for future recovery, none more so than in education. By 1940, the number of 17-year-olds graduating from high school had risen to 50.8 percent, compared to 29 percent in 1930. These positive changes also occurred in higher education. Thanks to increased federal funding, the number of universities and colleges grew from 1,400 to 1,700 during the New Deal years. A better-educated population meant that the human capital (skills level) of the US economy improved, thus aiding future economic growth.

The New Deal halted the economic depression in the USA. However, full recovery of the economy only came with the onset of the Second World War when the US became a major source of war production. In September 1939, FDR persuaded Congress to amend the Neutrality Acts that prevented the USA from offering aid to countries at war. This led to the **'cash and carry' programme**. In 1939 and 1940, the British and French government placed large orders for war goods and materials with US firms.

### KEY TERM

**'Cash and carry' programme**
Under the terms of this programme the US would supply war materials to Britain and France, provided these two nations transported the goods in their own ships. In March 1941, after the fall of France, it was replaced by Lend-Lease programme, in which the US supplied war materials to Britain and other countries.

### ACTIVITY
KNOWLEDGE CHECK

**The role of women**

1 How far did the role of women change during the New Deal years?

2 How important was Eleanor Roosevelt in aiding women and minorities during the period from 1933 to 1945?

**The New Deal and the economy**

1 Write a description of how the US economy changed between 1933 and 1940.

2 What were the major changes that took place in the economy?

3 What problems still remained in the US economy in 1940?

### AS Level Exam-Style Question Section B

To what extent did the New Deal improve job opportunities for women? (20 marks)

**Tip**

*This question requires a balanced response in which you need to assess the ways women's job opportunities increased and were aided by the New Deal, and where you think the position of women in society and the economy remained limited.*

**A Level Exam-Style Question Section B**

'The New Deal offered only limited opportunities for women in the years 1933–39.'

How far do you agree with this statement? (20 marks)

**Tip**

*You will need to address the statement made in the question directly. Provide evidence that women, in some areas, may have had limited opportunities during the New Deal years. To balance this, you can refer to the success of specific women such as Eleanor Roosevelt, Mary Bethune and Frances Perkins.*

# HOW FAR DID THE NEW DEAL AFFECT THE LIVES OF ETHNIC MINORITIES WITHIN THE USA?

## The impact of the New Deal on black Americans

Black Americans comprised approximately ten percent of the US population. Until the 20th century, they had generally lived in the south-east of the USA where, until 1865, they had been slaves. Even though slavery was abolished in 1866 and black Americans received the right to vote in 1870, they still faced considerable racial discrimination. By the beginning of the New Deal, many states in the south-east of the USA had introduced legal segregation and, through intimidation and **Jim Crow laws**, black Americans were treated as second-class citizens. Even though almost one million black Americans moved north in the 1920s and 1930s, known as the Great Migration, they found that they did not escape racial discrimination and lived in separate housing areas, often referred to as **ghettos**.

When the Depression hit the USA after 1929, it was black Americans who bore the brunt of job losses. The New Deal relief agencies offered hope. For instance, in the large industrial city of Cleveland, Ohio the federal government became the largest employer of black Americans, and their jobless numbers fell from 50 percent to 30 percent.

The New Deal also opened up opportunities for black Americans in the federal government. In 1934, a black American, Robert Weaver, was appointed as FDR's special adviser on the 'Economic Status of the Negro'. His rise was in large part due to Harold Ickes, the Secretary of the Interior from 1933 to 1946. Ickes had been a former president of the Chicago branch of the National Association for the Advancement of Colored People (NAACP) and, in his role in the Public Works Administration (PWA), in particular its housing division, Ickes directly aided black Americans. The housing division, which became the US Housing Authority, introduced **racial quotas** for its construction projects and, by 1940, black Americans occupied one-third of its housing units.

The biggest relief agency set up by the New Deal was the Works Progress Administration, under Harry Hopkins. Between 1936 and 1940, the WPA provided work for 350,000 black Americans every year. Its educational programmes employed over 5,000 black American teachers and taught 250,000 black Americans how to read and write. In the National Youth Administration, Mary McLeod Bethune provided skills training for 500,000 young black Americans.

However, the New Deal did not always provide help. Poor black American farmers received very little aid from the AAA. Its cotton section was headed by Cully Cobb, a southern white conservative who gave priority to whites. Similarly, the CCC was headed by another southern white conservative, Robert Fechner, who was equally discriminatory. Although 200,000 black Americans received placements under the CCC between 1933 and 1942, most were low-skill and most CCC camps were racially segregated.

In 1935, the trade union body, the Congress of Industrial Organizations, was created, comprising predominantly blue-collar and unskilled workers. The CIO actively recruited black American members, who felt more empowered with union support. They also benefitted from the Second New Deal legislation. The Wagner Act of 1935 offered trade union recognition and the Social Security Act provided pensions. The National Labor Relations Board, in 1938, required the Pullman railroad company to sit down with the all-black Brotherhood of Sleeping Car Porters, led by A. Philip Randolph, to discuss pay and conditions. It achieved partial success.

### KEY TERMS

**Jim Crow law**
Legislation passed in southern states aimed at preventing black Americans gaining civil and political equality. The laws segregated facilities and provided major obstacles to voter registration for blacks.

**Ghetto**
A term used to describe an area of housing occupied by one ethnic group. They are usually poor, densely populated areas in inner cities.

**Racial quota**
As black Americans comprised ten percent of the US population, ten percent of jobs created by federal programmes were to be allocated to them.

However, by the end of the New Deal, FDR had done nothing to end legal racial segregation in the Old South or informal racial segregation in other parts of the country. The decision not to change legal segregation was heavily influenced by the fact that southern whites were an important group within the Democratic Party in Congress, and FDR could not afford to upset them. The southern whites also had the influence to block anti-lynching proposals. Attempts by black American activists, such as the NAACP and Mary McLeod Bethune, to make lynching a federal offence in 1937, and again in 1940, came to nothing. Small advances had been made, but black Americans remained second-class citizens.

SOURCE

From an article by W. E. B. DuBois that appeared in the black American magazine, *The Crisis* in January 1934. Dubois was a black American founder of the National Association for the Advancement of Colored People (NAACP), a major black American organisation that aimed to gain full civil and political equality for black Americans.

In the recent endeavour of the United States government to redistribute capital so that some of the disadvantaged groups may get a chance for development, the American Negro should voluntarily and insistently demand his share. Groups of communities and farms inhabited by colored folk should be voluntarily formed. In no case should there be any discrimination against whites and blacks. But, at the same time, colored people should come forward, should organise and conduct enterprises, and their only insistence should be that the same provisions be made for the success of their enterprise that is being made for the success of any other enterprise. It must be remembered that in the last quarter of a century, the advance of colored people has been mainly in the lines where they themselves working by and for themselves, have accomplished the greatest advance.

### AS Level Exam-Style Question Section A

***Study Source 3 before you answer this question.***

Why is Source 3 valuable to the historian for an enquiry into the views of black Americans during the New Deal years? (8 marks)

**Tip**

*Study the provenance of the source to determine its value. Think about who wrote it, when it was written and the intended audience. You should also use information from the content of the source to determine how much insight it offers into the position of black Americans in the New Deal years.*

### A Level Exam-Style Question Section A

***Study Sources 2 and 3 before you answer this question.***

How far could the historian make use of Sources 2 and 3 together to investigate the effects of the New Deal on the USA before 1940?

Explain your answer, using both sources, the information given about them and your own knowledge of the historical context. (20 marks)

**Tip**

*You will need to refer to the provenance of both sources and the audiences at which they were directed. It is important that you address the 'how far' instruction by providing a balanced answer.*

## The impact of the New Deal on Native Americans

Black Americans comprised approximately 12 million of the USA's 122 million people in 1930. Native Americans comprised only 330,000 of the population, with the majority of the Native American population living in the West. Previous US governments had moved many eastern tribes to areas such as Indian Territory, which became part of Oklahoma when it became a state in 1907.

Up to the New Deal, many Native Americans were affected by the Dawes Severalty Act of 1887, which gave the Plains Indians of the West such as the Sioux land and full US citizenship. Citizenship was extended to the so-called Five Civilised Tribes of Oklahoma in 1901: the Choctaw, Chickasaw, Creek, Cherokee and Seminole. These groups constituted only part of the Native American population. It was not until 1924 that all Native Americans became US citizens.

Much of the land given to Native Americans under the Dawes Severalty Act had been sold off to speculators by the time of the New Deal. By 1934, only one-third of the land given to Native Americans in 1887 was still in their hands. Oil and gas were discovered on many Native American reservations, which encouraged white speculators to purchase land and exploit these natural resources.

The remaining land was of poor quality. The Sioux and Northern Cheyenne, who had been nomadic until the 1880s, were moved to reservations in South Dakota, such as Pine Ridge, which was noted for its poor agricultural land. The Navajos of Arizona and New Mexico lived on a reservation that was mostly desert. Adversely affected by poverty, drunkenness and disease, the quality of life on many reservations was extremely poor.

**Figure 3.1**: Main locations of Native American settlement in the 20th century.

### The Indian Reorganisation Act of 1934

Native American issues at federal level were handled by the Bureau of Indian Affairs, which was starved of funding and regarded as a very low priority by successive federal administrations. However, in 1934, the Indian Reorganisation Act replaced the Dawes Severalty Act and offered radical change. FDR appointed John Collier as the new Commissioner of Indian Affairs. For the first time an attempt was made to preserve Native American culture. Native tribes were organised into self-governing bodies with an elected tribal council. They were able to write their own constitutions and have their own legal system, enforced by their own police force. For instance, the Pine Ridge Reservation forbade the sale of alcohol even after national prohibition was abandoned.

Although proclaimed as the 'Indian New Deal', 75 of the 245 native tribes including the largest tribe, the Navajos, rejected the provisions of the Act. These tribes were opposed to further government interference in their affairs. Nevertheless, Collier ensured that key New Deal Alphabet Agencies, such as the Civilian Conservation Corps (CCC) and the Public Works Administration (PWA), offered relief from unemployment to Native Americans.

Overall, the Indian Reorganisation Act made little difference to the position of Native Americans within the US economy. It brought some administrative changes but did virtually nothing to improve their economic plight. Although the Indian Reorganisation Act was regarded as the Native American New Deal, it in fact did very little to lift many Native Americans out of poverty. Not until 1944 was the National Congress of American Indians created as a forum to voice Native American concerns.

## How did the New Deal affect Hispanic Americans?

During the 1930s, the majority of Hispanic Americans in the USA were engaged in agriculture and were predominantly **migrant workers**. Most of them came originally from Mexico. The biggest concentration of such workers was in southern California (in areas such as the San Joaquin and Imperial valleys), Arizona, New Mexico, Texas and Colorado. They worked on citrus farms picking oranges and harvesting grapes and other agricultural produce.

**KEY TERM**

**Migrant worker**

A migrant worker is a person who moves to a different area or country to work. In the USA migrant workers were primarily employed in agriculture, carrying out seasonal work such as harvesting crops. Thousands of Mexicans, who were not US citizens, worked on American farms. They lived in temporary, poorly maintained housing and had very few civil rights.

When the Depression struck the USA, many migrant workers were deported back to Mexico. The number of Mexican-American migrant workers dropped from 600,000 in 1930 to 400,000 in 1940. Many of those allowed to stay had had children while in the USA. These children were legally American citizens.

Those who remained saw their wage rates slashed. In southern California, migrant workers saw their wages cut from 35 cents an hour in 1928 to 14 cents an hour by 1933. Hispanic Americans, like other migrant workers, lived in poor, temporary accommodation, usually shanties built by farmers at the lowest cost.

Hispanic Americans suffered a similar fate to black Americans when trying to visit restaurants and cinemas. Racial discrimination was widespread and even included the public school system.

Unfortunately for migrant workers, much of the New Deal legislation excluded them. Section 7(a) of the National Industrial Recovery Act of 1933 gave workers the right to organise into trade unions, but this excluded migrant workers. This was also the case with the Wagner (National Labor Relations) Act of 1935. Even the Fair Labor Standards Act of 1938, which established a national minimum wage, excluded them. Without trade union support, their pay and conditions worsened during the New Deal years.

In other ways the New Deal even made their lives worse. The Agricultural Adjustment Act of 1933 attempted to stabilise farm prices by reducing production. This meant that fewer workers were required. Of all the ethnic minority groups, perhaps Hispanic, and in particular Mexican, migrant workers fared the worst.

**SOURCE**

An extract from 'A New Deal for American Indians, the Annual Report on the Position of Native Americans'. The report was issued by John Collier, head of the Federal Bureau for Indian Affairs, 1938.

We define our Indian policy as follows: So productively to use the moneys appropriated by Congress for Indians as to enable them, on good, adequate lands of their own, to earn decent livelihoods and lead self-respecting, organised lives in harmony with their own aims and ideals, as an integral part of American life. Under such a policy, the ideal end result will be the ultimate disappearance of any need of Government aid or supervision. This will not happen tomorrow: perhaps not in our lifetime; but with the revitalisation of Indian hope due to the actions and attitudes of this Government during the last few years, that aim is a possibility and a real one.

A major aim, then, of the Indian Service is to help the Indians to keep and consolidate what lands they have now and to provide more and better lands upon which they may effectively carry out their lives. Just as important is the task of helping Indians make such use of land as will conserve the land, insure Indian self-support, and safeguard or build up the Indian's social life.

THE IMPACT OF THE NEW DEAL ON ETHNIC MINORITIES

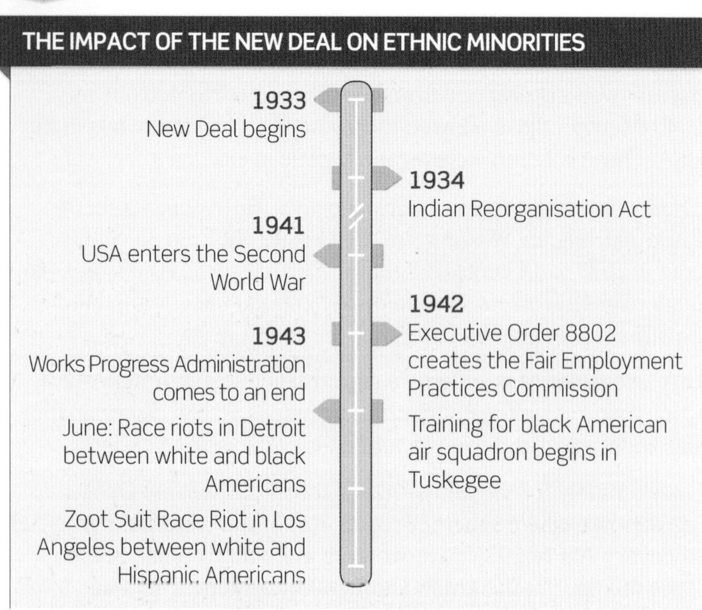


ACTIVITY
KNOWLEDGE CHECK

**The impact of the New Deal on ethnic minorities**

1 Identify the ways the New Deal affected the lives of:
   a) Black Americans
   b) Native Americans
   c) Hispanic Americans.

2 On balance, do you think the New Deal improved the lives of different ethnic minorities within the USA? Explain your answer.

## The contribution of ethnic minorities to the war effort, 1941–45

The Second World War saw the USA play a pivotal role in the Allied victory, both in Europe and in the Pacific. More than any other Allied nation, the USA provided the ships, planes, tanks and guns that won the war. US armed forces were also central to victory.

Until 1948, the US armed forces were segregated on racial lines. When the USA entered the Second World War in December 1941, there were fewer than 4,000 black Americans serving in the US military and only 12 black Americans were officers. This was a very small proportion compared to whites. By the end of the war, 21.2 million black Americans were in the forces, either on the Home Front or in Europe and the Pacific, including female black Americans in the auxiliary armed forces. As before the war, only a tiny proportion of black Americans became officers and only a few of these fought in combat roles.

Black Americans faced racial discrimination in the armed forces. All-white draft boards decided which branch of the armed forces a person would be allocated to or whether they would be accepted for military service. Even when they were accepted for military service, the majority of black Americans served in non-combat roles such as supply or transportation. This was an act of racial discrimination, as many politicians believed black Americans would perform poorly in combat or combat areas.

Even in non-combat roles, black Americans served with distinction in the warzone, for example those who served in the 'Red Ball Express', which carried supplies to US forces serving in France after D-Day, in 1944.

### Tuskegee Airmen

The most celebrated black American combat unit was the 332nd Fighter Group of the 15th US Army Air Force. They trained at Tuskegee in Alabama and were known as the Tuskegee Airmen. Men and officers were all black. The Tuskegee Airmen, known as the 'Red Tails' because of the distinctive tail markings on their P521 Mustang fighters, engaged in bomber escort duty, flying over 15,000 sorties. From May 1943 to June 1945, the Red Tails never lost a single bomber they were escorting to enemy fighters. Even so, they faced considerable criticism from white southern Congressmen. These Congressmen disliked black Americans gaining combat experience. They also disliked the fact that many of the Tuskegee pilots were given officer status. Eleanor Roosevelt helped champion the airmen's cause and keep the group operational.

SOURCE

5 Tuskegee Airmen in 1942. The Tuskegee Airmen were one of the most celebrated fighter squadrons in the US Army Air Force. They helped destroy the myth that black Americans would not be effective members of the US military.

### Navajo code talkers

One of the great contributions of this numerically small ethnic minority was the inspiration of Philip Johnston, a Protestant missionary who worked with the Navajos in the south-west of the USA. He persuaded Lieutenant Colonel Jones of the Signal Corps to employ Navajos as communications soldiers, serving in the Pacific theatre of operations. The Navajo language is so complex that the Japanese could not crack the communications made between them. By the end of the war, 420 Navajo men were code talkers, out of a population of only 50,000 people. They served in the Pacific war zone from 1942 to 1945.

**SOURCE 6** Adapted from an interview with Peter MacDonald, a Navajo code talker, remembering his time in the Second World War, posted online on 7 April 2014. This was one of a number of interviews made by college students for the Navajo Nation to celebrate the contribution of Navajo code talkers during the Second World War.

We were trained at Fort Pendleton to learn how the codes were meant to work. We learnt code names and code words. Only 400 of us code talkers knew the words and we had to remember the 600 code words. These were kept under lock and key. To show you how the code words worked a group of marines were pinned down by Japanese fire on a Pacific island and requested military help. A Navajo code talker was asked to transmit a message for help which was sent to another Navajo code talker at headquarters, Navajo words such as deer, rabbit, sick horse were used in the transmission. These were code words and even an ordinary Navajo listening in to the conversation could not understand what was being said. Navajo Code Talkers saved thousands of lives and helped win the war.

### Japanese Americans

Of all the ethnic minorities within the USA, Japanese Americans suffered the most. Following the Japanese attack on Pearl Harbor in December 1941, all of the US Japanese-American population, who lived mainly on the West Coast, were forced to leave their homes and were relocated to internment camps in the desert areas of the west. 400,000 were relocated in this fashion.

Japanese Americans in the USA were divided into two groups: *Issei* were Japanese who immigrated to the USA; *Nisei* were Japanese Americans born and educated in the USA. Even though the USA was also at war with Germany and Italy, German and Italian Americans were not treated as a whole ethnic group for internment and loss of their civil rights. Several lawsuits challenged the right of the US government to intern *Nisei*. In *Hirabayashi v the United States* on 21 June 1943, the US Supreme Court upheld the right of the US government to intern the entire Japanese-American population. However, Supreme Court Justice Frank Murphy stated the internment programme was very close to 'the very brink of constitutional power.' He said the US government policy resembled that accorded to members of the Jewish race in Germany.

Ethnic minorities made up a relatively small proportion of the US population, just over ten percent, but they played an important part in winning the war. However, even though they served bravely, they faced racial discrimination in the military and many were forced into separate racially segregated units. When ethnic-minority servicemen returned home, they still found that they were barred from whites-only facilities such as restaurants, dance halls and hotels.

## The 1943 race riots

The US entry into the Second World and the work of the Federal Employment Practices Commission helped bring an end to racial discrimination in defence industries as black Americans could benefit from the employment created by the war. However, they faced racial discrimination, which erupted into race riots across the USA in 1943. The first was in Beaumont, Texas, but the most serious were in Detroit, Michigan and Los Angeles, California.

Racial tensions had been high in Detroit since 20,000 defence industry white workers walked out when a small handful of black American workers were given promotion in the spring of 1943. The Detroit Race Riots began on 20 June at an integrated amusement park called Belle Isle. Beginning with fights between black and white teenagers, the trouble escalated when white sailors from the Naval Armoury joined in. This spread quickly to involve over 5,000 whites, stirred up by a false rumour that a black man had raped a white woman. The rioting lasted three days and was only brought to an end when the president sent 6,000 troops to occupy the city. The occupation took six months to restore and maintain order. 25 blacks and nine whites were killed. 17 of the blacks were killed by white police. The material damage was calculated at $2 million.

In July, another riot involving hundreds occurred in the black American neighbourhood of Harlem, New York City, and also had to be quelled by troops.

On 3 June 1943, the Zoot Suit Riots occurred in Los Angeles. On that day, white sailors claimed to be attacked by a Mexican American wearing a new fashion suit associated with ethnic minorities, the 'zoot suit'. Fifty sailors then went around LA, stripping anyone wearing a zoot suit. The riots reached a peak on 7 June when sailors beat up a Mexican-American youth for wearing a zoot suit, and only came to an end on 8 June when white sailors were confined to their barracks. Eleanor Roosevelt caused uproar by writing directly to the female head of the California State Chamber of Commerce, claiming the riots were racially motivated attacks against Mexican Americans.

## The Double 'V' campaign

On the Home Front, the desire to serve the US in the armed forces during the war and the need to fight racial discrimination at home led to the Double V (for victory) campaign. It was inspired by one of the biggest-selling black American newspapers, the *Pittsburgh Courier*, with sales of 200,000 nationwide. It began with a letter to the editor of that paper from James G. Thompson of Kansas at the end of 1941. In his letter, he suggested that black Americans should fight injustice overseas by serving in the armed forces and fight racial injustice at home by campaigning against racial segregation and racial discrimination in the workplace. The Double V campaign was part of the wider campaign for black American racial equality. Other newspapers with large black American readerships joined in the campaign.

As a result of the Thompson letter, the *Courier* began its Double V campaign on 7 February 1942 and continued it weekly until 1943. To promote patriotism, the *Courier* included an American flag with every subscription to the campaign and a request that those involved bought US government war bonds to help finance the war. Double V clubs were founded across the country to promote the ideal of racial equality by publicising racial discrimination and campaigning against it. The campaign received support from white Hollywood stars, such as Lana Turner, and 1940 Republican presidential candidate Wendell Wilkie. After the war, in 1946, the campaign insignia changed from a Double V to a single V, demanding racial equality at home now that victory had been won abroad.

Part of the Double V Campaign was to end racial discrimination in sports. All Major League Baseball teams were all-white. However, it took until 1947, when the Brooklyn Dodgers signed black American Jackie Robinson, for racial segregation in baseball to begin to come to an end. Other Major League Baseball clubs followed the lead of the Brooklyn Dodgers and began signing black American players during the 1950s.

Inspired by the Double V campaign, the leader of the Brotherhood of Sleeping Car Porters, A. Philip Randolph, planned a march of black Americans on Washington DC in 1941, to demand the end of racial segregation. The plan was to encourage five million black Americans to participate. The Roosevelt government was so concerned about the planned march that FDR agreed to issue Executive Order 8802, which outlawed racial discrimination in defence industries, in return for the cancellation of the march.

SOURCE

From the *Pittsburgh Courier*, 14 February 1942. 'The Courier's Double 'V' For a Double Victory Campaign Gets Country-Wide Support.'

Last week, without any public announcement or fanfare, the editors of *The Courier* introduced its war Slogan - a double "V" for a double victory to colored America. We did this advisedly because we wanted to test the response and popularity of such a slogan with our readers. The response has been overwhelming. Our office has been inundated with hundreds of telegrams and letters of congratulations proving that without any explanation, this slogan represents the true battle cry of colored America. This week we gratefully acknowledge this voluntary response and offer the following explanation: Americans all, are involved in a gigantic war effort to assure the victory for the cause of freedom - the four freedoms that have been so nobly expressed by President Roosevelt and Prime Minister Churchill. We, as colored Americans, are determined to protect our country, our form of government and the freedoms which we cherish for ourselves and the rest of the world, therefore we have adopted the Double "V" war cry - victory over our enemies on the battlefields abroad. Thus in our fight for freedom we wage a two-pronged attack against our enslaved at home and those abroad who would enslave us. WE HAVE A STAKE IN THIS FIGHT... WE ARE AMERICANS TOO!

## EXTEND YOUR KNOWLEDGE

### What's in a name?

The name given to America's ethnic minorities has changed over the years.

- Black Americans in the 19th and first half of the 20th century were called either 'negro' or 'colored', terms used by black Americans themselves. Today, the term African American is widely used.
- Hispanic Americans are now also referred to as Latinos.
- Native Americans were once called Red Indians or American Indians.

These name changes are reflected in primary source documents.

### W. E. B. DuBois (1868–1963)

Black historian, writer and civil rights activist, DuBois was Professor of Latin and Greek at Wilberforce University, Ohio from 1894–96. He then became Professor of Sociology at the University of Atlanta, Georgia from 1897 to 1910. In 1903, he produced a major study of black Americans called *The Souls of the Black Folk*. He was one of the founders of the National Association for the Advancement of Colored People (NAACP) in 1909.

He was also a writer for and editor of *The Crisis*, the NAACP magazine from 1910 to 1934, when he decided to leave the NAACP after a dispute about the future of black Americans in the USA in the 1930s. In 1945, he joined the American Communist Party.

## ACTIVITY
KNOWLEDGE CHECK

**The impact of the Second World War on ethnic minorities**

1 How did the war affect the lives of the following:

   **a)** Black Americans
   **b)** Native Americans
   **c)** Hispanic Americans
   **d)** Japanese Americans.

2 Which ethnic group do you think was affected most by the war? Explain your answer.

### AS Level Exam-Style Question Section B

How accurate is it to say that all ethnic groups in the USA benefited from the New Deal? (20 marks)

**Tip**

*You will need to provide a balanced answer in which you mention in what ways and how far ethnic groups benefited from the New Deal. You should consider the impact of the New Deal period on black Americans, Hispanic Americans and Native Americans.*

### A Level Exam-Style Question Section A

***Study Sources 6 and 7 before answering this question.***

How far could the historian make use of Sources 6 and 7 together to investigate the issues facing ethnic minorities in the years 1933 to 1945? (20 marks)

**Tip**

*In your answer you should consider the provenance of both sources to assess their value and use to the historian. In addition, you should refer to relevant information from within the content of both sources and outside knowledge as part of your overall assessment.*

### A Level Exam-Style Question Section B

To what extent did the position of ethnic minorities improve in the years 1933 to 1945? (20 marks)

**Tip**

*You will be expected to assess the degree to which the position of ethnic minorities changed. This should include reference to their social, economic and political position within the USA. You should mention black Americans, Hispanic Americans and Native Americans. Also, you should be able to compare and contrast the position of each of these ethnic minority groups in terms of the change in their position.*

# HOW FAR DID THE PERIOD TO 1945 BRING SOCIAL AND CULTURAL CHANGE TO THE USA?

The tail-end of the Depression and the years of the Second World War saw considerable social and cultural change across the USA. For the first time the federal government played a significant role in bringing about social and cultural change. Previously, government involvement had usually meant state government. Now, the federal government played an important role. Several important changes in social and cultural life were due to federal government policy.

By 1945, the USA had changed almost beyond recognition compared to the dark days of the Depression.

## Works Progress Administration (WPA): support for writers and musicians

A unique aspect of the New Deal was support for the arts. In December 1933, the federal government began a long involvement in the production of public art. By 1937, thousands of artists had created more than 15,000 individual pieces of art, such as murals, paintings and posters. Much of this work was produced through the Federal Art Project under the Works Progress Administration from 1935. It employed 6,600 people, made up of everyday professionals, but also notable writers such as Saul Bellow, who went on to win the Nobel Prize for Literature.

Also, in 1935 the WPA began the Federal Writers' Project (FWP). Like other WPA programmes, the FWP aimed to offer employment to out-of-work teachers, librarians and writers who could be better employed than digging ditches and other manual work associated with programmes like the Civilian Conservation Corps. Two of the most well-known projects were American State Guides and *America Eats*. One State Guide had already been produced for the state of Connecticut under the federal Emergency Relief Administration (FERA) in 1933. The aim was to produce a written portrait of the cultural diversity and richness of American life. The American Guide, under the guidance of Katherine Kellok, covered all 48 states and was, perhaps, the most lasting achievement of the FWP. Each state was responsible for its own guide and it was an important aid to developing tourism.

In 1935, Saul Bellow and other writers were given the task of documenting America's food and eating habits in *America Eats*. This included information on the origins of American cuisine and regional specialties, including recipes. In addition, FWP workers collected oral histories, including interviews with former slaves, Native Americans and immigrants from across Europe about their experiences on arriving in the USA. Under the FWP, over 275 books and 700 pamphlets were published.

In 1935, support was offered to musicians. Under the Federal Music Project (FMP), from May 1935 to 1939, and the WPA Music Program of 1939 to 1943, help was given to unemployed musicians. These included instrumentalists, singers and music teachers. Under the leadership of Dr Nickolai Sokoloff, former conductor of the Cleveland Orchestra, the FMP attempted to produce high-quality music and singing in a variety of forms.

The WPA Federal Music Project sponsored many New York City musical groups that appeared on the local city radio station, WNYC. These included the WNYC Concert Orchestra, the Waverly Brass Band, Juanita Hall's Negro Melody Singers and the Brooklyn Symphony Orchestra. In 1936 alone, almost half of WNYC's broadcast hours were supported by the FMP.

In the four years of the FMP, it funded 7,332 compositions by 2,258 American composers. FMP-funded concerts were given in front of over 148 million people. The programme gave under-represented groups such as black Americans, women and Hispanics a chance to play music and be paid for it. It also encouraged a revival of traditional music and folk songs with the creation of a national archive. The FMP offered low-cost or free concerts to the poor and underprivileged, and courses in musicianship, providing the USA with a pool of musical talent that would have otherwise gone untapped.

**SOCIAL AND CULTURAL CHANGE IN THE USA TO 1945**

**1935**
WPA creates the Federal Writers' Project and Federal Music Project

**1939**
Federal Music Project ends and is replaced by Federal Music Program

**1942**
Office of War Information created

Civil Defence Organisation attracts tens of thousands of young volunteers

*Mrs Miniver* wins Best Film Oscar

**1943**
Glenn Miller and Artie Shaw go on tours to entertain troops

Executive Order 9346 extends power of Fair Employment Practices Commission

**1945**
350,000 women have served in US armed forces

6 million women have worked in US economy during the Second World War

**EXTRACT 1**

From 'Constructing the "People's Music": The Federal Music Project, Nationalism and the New Deal, 1935–1939' by J. A. Gronbeck-Tedesco, published in the *NeoAmericanist* magazine, autumn 2005.

By the time of the FMP's termination, Earl Vincent Moore had succeeded Sokoloff as the FMP's final director in May 1939. The Federal Music Project changed to the WPA Music Program in September of 1939 and finally dissolved in 1943. In his "Final Report of the Federal Music Project," Moore described the FMP as an agency that had helped America on the road to recovery. By citing dozens of reviews in periodicals such as *Fortune, New York Times, Harpers,* and *Ladies Home Journal*, Moore deems the Federal Music Project a success. America had grown culturally richer as a result of the FMP, for there was a "notable advance in the interest in and consciousness of music in many parts of the country."

He credits the FMP with generating music appreciation across America: "As a matter of attestable fact there has been revealed in America a vast eagerness and hunger for music that was suspected only dimly four years ago."

## Changes in the role of women and black Americans

The Second World War brought unparalleled prosperity to the USA. The Home Front was transformed with war industries, helping to eradicate unemployment. It was a time of enormous opportunity for groups that had previously been minorities in America's industrial workforce.

### The Second World War and the role of women

The Second World War helped transform the role and status of women in the USA. Traditionally, the role of women had been to marry and raise children. The social changes of the 1920s opened up new opportunities in employment, but these paled into insignificance compared to the millions of jobs created by the Second World War. Even before the USA formally entered the Second World War, it was producing a considerable amount of war material for Britain under the Lend–Lease Act of 1941. Between 1941 and 1945, the USA mobilised 11.9 million men. With a massive increase in war production, their jobs had to be filled. Women stepped into the vacuum.

### Black Americans and the Fair Employment Practices Commission (FEPC)

On 25 June 1941, six months after the US entered the Second World War following the attack on Pearl Harbour, FDR signed Executive Order 8802, creating the Fair Employment Practices Commission (FEPC). The Executive Order outlawed racial discrimination based on colour or national origin.

The FEPC gave black Americans opportunities for employment and helped encourage further migration from the Old South to the northern cities associated with war production, such as Detroit, Cleveland and Philadelphia. However, living conditions were overcrowded and many black Americans were forced to live in segregated housing areas. Reluctant employers were forced to take on black American workers, but usually gave them low wages and menial jobs. Even where black Americans got skilled jobs, as at the shipyard in Galveston, Texas, they received low-skilled wage rates. While white workers saw their average wages rise 60 percent during the war, black workers saw only a 40 percent rise.

In 1943, Roosevelt decided to strengthen the power of the FEPC with Executive Order 9346, after being informed of violations by employers of his Executive Order 8802. He increased the FEPC's budget by $500,000 and replaced its part-time staff with full-time professionals. By 1945, at the war's end, eight percent of defence jobs were held by black Americans, compared to only three percent at the start of the war. In 1946, Congress decided to end the FEPC. There were two attempts to recreate the FEPC on a permanent basis in 1946 and, again in 1948, but both of these failed to pass a Republican-controlled Congress.

**KEY TERMS**

**Propaganda**
Information and opinions, which may be biased or even untrue, shared with the general population through the media to persuade them to support a policy or point of view.

**War bonds**
These were sold to the American public as a way of financing the war. People who bought war bonds were guaranteed their money back with the addition of some interest once the war was over.

## Wartime domestic propaganda

The USA, like other countries fighting the Second World War, helped gain popular support for the war through **propaganda**. The war involved maximum effort, not just by those fighting at the front, but by Americans at home. To ensure that the hearts and minds of the US people were completely behind the efforts of their government, propaganda was as important as bullets, ships and aeroplanes.

In 1942, shortly after the USA joined the war, the federal government created the Office of War Information (OWI). Its aim was to communicate the government's views on the war. Posters appeared across the USA in public places such as railroad stations, billboards on highways and in public buildings and schools. To encourage women to participate in war industries, OWI created the character Rosie the Riveter, and posters with the slogan 'Woman power'. Posters warning against spies, spreading gossip or telling people about their own war work included slogans such as 'Loose lips cost ships'.

National War Bond campaigns also swept the country. **War bonds**, bought by ordinary Americans, were a major source of funding for the war. In 1945, the marine soldiers who raised the US flag on Mount Surabachi in the Battle of Iwo Jima against Japan, featured in a nationwide government advertising campaign.

Propaganda could also be negative and was used to demonise the enemy. Germans and Japanese were depicted as bestial, almost sub-humans, who were determined to destroy the US way of life.

SOURCE

When the Second World War began, women became involved in occupations that were normally the preserve of men. The government developed a character, Rosie the Riveter, to acknowledge and highlight the vital contribution of women to the American war effort.

EXTRACT 2

From *The Unfinished Journey* by William H. Chafe, published in 1994. It discusses the importance of government propaganda.

One of the greatest problems American leaders faced was how to make the war real at home. The first link was through propaganda - the public portrayal of soldiers and war issues through advertising, the mass media, music and songs. The Office of War Information, formed shortly after the war began, produced films, posters and radio broadcasts of its own, while offering guidelines to magazines and networks on how they might speed up the process of mobilizing the Home Front. In one of its most popular manifestations, this campaign took the form of vivid reminders that what took place in war factories and kitchens directly affected the fate of GI Joe. One hard-line ad asked, 'Are you comfortable, brother? That's good brother. Just sleep right through the war. What's it to you that a kid got bumped off in the Solomons because you couldn't be bothered with scrap collection.' In another version of the same theme, a short film from Bataan featured a wounded GI exhorting his family not to waste food. 'We haven't had anything but a little horsemeat and rice for days'. Lest the message be lost the film ended with an announcement that the soldier died in hospital after making the film.

## The power of Hollywood

The USA possessed a very powerful propaganda weapon in **Hollywood** and this was used to full effect. A Senate subcommittee in September 1941, before the American entry into the war, launched an investigation into whether Hollywood was playing its part in the campaign to support Britain in the war. The committee hoped that pro-British messages in films would help the cause of supplying Britain with Lend–Lease war materials.

**KEY TERM**

**Hollywood**
The suburb of Los Angeles which was, and is, the centre of the US film industry.

In 1941, actor Gary Cooper won the Best Actor Oscar for his portrayal of Sergeant York, a fictional US soldier who captured 20 German prisoners of war in the First World War. In 1942, the Best Film Oscar went to *Mrs Miniver*, a film about how a fictional British family was standing up to the Germans on the Home Front. Famous Hollywood director John Ford was employed by the US Navy to make films about the naval war in the Pacific. Ford also made a Hollywood film about that war, starring John Wayne, called *They Were Expendable*.

Several Hollywood stars, such as Clark Gable and James Stewart, volunteered and joined the air force. In all, 12 percent of Hollywood actors joined up and 25 percent of Hollywood employees fought in the war. Many others joined government efforts in supporting the war. Bing Crosby and Bob Hope, among others, sold war bonds.

One studio that made a major contribution to the war effort was the Walt Disney Company, maker of animated films. In 1942, many of Disney's most popular cartoon characters, such as Mickey Mouse and Donald Duck, appeared in magazines such as the *Coronet,* dressed as marines and Red Cross volunteers. Disney's biggest Home Front role was working with the Treasury Department. Disney produced two income tax films and produced numerous cartoon posters selling war bonds, such as the Fifth War Bond drive of 1944, discouraging wartime waste and backing the government. One of the most successful Disney campaigns aimed to encourage Americans to grow their own food in 'victory gardens'. Disney characters became enormously popular and were often to be seen painted on warplanes.

Overall, Hollywood proved to be a most effective weapon in raising morale, explaining US war aims and supporting government programmes. In 1942, the Office of War Information (OWI) set up two subagencies to supervise Hollywood.

**SOURCE 9** 1942 Oscar winners, including Greer Garson for her role in *Mrs Miniver*. On the left is actor Van Heflin, who joined the armed forces.

The Bureau of Motion Pictures produced educational films and the Bureau of Censorship oversaw the export of Hollywood films, in particular to neutral countries in areas such as South America. They ensured that negative images of the USA, such as gangsterism and racial discrimination, were not exported.

## The growing power of radio

FDR had shown the power of radio in his 'Fireside Chats' during the New Deal era. As most Americans had access to a radio, it was an effective way to get over the government's message. In 1941, radio stations broadcast a series of talks called 'Speaking of Liberty' and, in 1942, 'You can't do business with Hitler'. The US Treasury sponsored many radio shows where war bonds were sold in commercial breaks. Sitcoms were popular and some were used to deal directly with issues such as petrol rationing, buying war bonds and playing a full part in the USA's war effort at home.

## Popular music goes to war

Leading popular music stars played their full part in the war effort. Swing, a type of band music, was the most popular style of the war years. Band leader Glenn Miller joined the army and his band toured European battlefields. Glenn Miller died in the war, in 1944, while travelling by plane from Britain to France to entertain US troops. Band leader Artie Shaw served in the US Navy and led a jazz band that toured the Pacific combat zone playing to troops. Popular singing trio the Andrews Sisters went on tours of troop camps within the USA and overseas to entertain troops and lift morale. Musical entertainment was part of the government's plans to ensure that troops received effective moral support, support that also included regular mail and decent food.

### EXTEND YOUR KNOWLEDGE

**Glenn Miller (1904–44)**

Alvin Glenn Miller was a famous wartime bandleader who is well known for entertaining US troops in the European theatre of war to 1944. He was born in the Midwestern state of Iowa. During the 1930s, his swing band was one of the most popular in the USA, with such songs as 'In the Mood', 'Pennsylvania 65,000' and 'Tuxedo Junction'. In 1942, Miller enlisted in the US Army and was assigned to lead the Army Air Force Band. He boosted the morale of the troops with his many popular songs before his mysterious disappearance.

On 15 December 1944, Miller boarded a transport plane to take him from England to Paris. He intended to organise a series of concerts for Allied troops there but his plane never arrived. It is thought to have crashed into the English Channel but Miller's body was not found. His memorial is at the US Military Cemetery at Madingley, Cambridge.

In 1954, a Hollywood film entitled *The Glenn Miller Story* was released. It was based loosely on Miller's life. The actor who played Miller was James Stewart, who served in the 8th US Army Air Force in Norfolk during the war. Miller's original recordings continue to sell millions of copies.

ACTIVITY
KNOWLEDGE CHECK

**The impact of the Second World War on the USA**

1 How did the USA's involvement in the Second World War affect the lives of women?

2 In what ways, and with what effect, did the government attempt to use propaganda to assist in the American war effort?

3 How useful were Hollywood films, the radio and popular music in supporting the American war effort?

4 What do you regard as the most important impact of the war on the American Home Front? Explain your answer. As a group discuss which changes were most important.

**AS Level Exam-Style Question Section B**

To what extent did the federal government help bring cultural change in the years 1933 to 1945? (20 marks)

**Tip**

*It is important that you provide a balanced answer in which you identify the various ways the federal government helped bring cultural change, such as through WPA support for writers and musicians and through wartime propaganda. You will also need to point out in what ways the federal government's involvement in cultural change was limited and that cultural change also took place without the involvement of the federal government.*

# TO WHAT EXTENT DID THE SECOND WORLD WAR AFFECT THE PERFORMANCE OF THE ECONOMY BETWEEN 1941 AND 1945?

The Second World War transformed the US economy. In the four wartime years of 1941–45, national income, wealth and industrial production more than doubled. In 1940, Gross National Product was $99.7 billion. In 1945, it had risen to $211 billion. By 1947, the US was producing 57 percent of the world's steel, 43 percent of its electricity and 62 percent of the world's oil. It was the global economic power.

In July 1944, the federal government led the way in creating the post-war international economic system. The Bretton Woods Agreement created the International Monetary Fund, to stabilise national currencies, and the International Bank for Reconstruction and Development, to lend money to other countries for post-war reconstruction.

To finance the war, the federal government had to raise taxes. Tax revenue raised $137 billion of the total cost of the war of $304 billion. To cover the cost of the shortfall of $167 billion, the US Treasury used war bonds. Beginning on 1 May 1941, the government launched a number of war bond drives to sell as many as they could to the American public. Bonds would repay the purchaser with an interest rate of 2.9 percent after ten years. By 1946, when war bond selling came to an end, 85 million Americans had purchased $185 billion of bonds.

The war also greatly increased the federal government's role in economic affairs. Agencies such as the Office of Price Administration were set up in April 1942 to set price ceilings for almost all consumer goods. In January of the same year, the War Production Board, under Donald Nelson, took overall control of the domestic war economy. In April, the War Manpower Commission under General P. V. McNutt controlled the flow of workers in war industries. In July 1942, the War Labor Board set wage increases for workers in the steel industry.

## The collapse of unemployment

When FDR came to power in 1933, there were 12.8 million out of work, 25 percent of the workforce. By 1940, after six years of the New Deal, unemployment had fallen to 8.1 million, 14.6 percent of the workforce. By 1945, unemployment had fallen to one million, 1.9 percent of the workforce. By conscripting nearly 12 million men into the armed forces, and placing the economy on a war footing, FDR had brought unrivalled prosperity. The war created 17 million new jobs, with average wages rising 30 percent.

The war also saw a drop in wealth inequality. The share of national wealth owned by the top five percent of the population dropped from 23.7 percent to 16.8 percent during the war.

## Women and the war effort

Many women joined the armed forces, with 100,000 serving in the Women's Army Corps alone. Others joined the navy and air force equivalents. In all, 350,000 served in the armed forces. Thousands became nurses. However, the greatest contribution women made was on the Home Front in wartime industries. Six million women entered the workforce for the first time. By the war's end, 18 million women had worked to help the USA win the war, most working six days a week. While many filled the roles of telephonists and secretaries, others became involved in traditionally male-dominated industries. Women ended up doing welding, machining, building aircraft and repairing tanks. The most dangerous work was manufacturing explosives, such as shells and bombs. During the war, over 200,000 women were disabled permanently and 37,000 died, many working in explosives factories.

During the war, women, many with husbands serving overseas in the armed forces, were still expected to look after their families. They also received less pay than men for doing the same job. For example, in 1944 the average wage for a woman was just $31.21 per week, compared to $54.64 per week for a man doing the same or a similar job. With the aid of the FEPC, black American women were able to get wartime work too, but they received even less money than white women workers.

The independence many women achieved through earning their own money was short-lived, however. They were all expected to give up their wartime work once the war had ended, leaving jobs open for returning armed servicemen.

SOURCE

An extract from 'We were Determined to Stay', by Celia Sapersteen Yanish, who worked as a machinist in New York City during the Second World War. She highlights the opposition many women faced from male workers who resented the employment of women. Celia's memories were recorded after the Second World War and appeared in a collection on the experiences of American women working on the Home Front called *The Life and Times of Rosie the Riveter*, published in 1982.

The men were afraid women were taking away jobs and they resented us. They complained they wouldn't be able to undress in the shop and work half nude like they did before. They said women would interfere with their work, would distract them.

I was about 24 at the time and I knew how to handle myself. I didn't laugh at the men's dirty jokes. But another girl who was only 17 did laugh and so the men got more and more brazen. They would be looking up her skirt until she would start to cry.

We worked on a competitive system. You had to keep up with the man standing next to you. Because he made more money if he could increase his production. If you slowed down, they would say, 'we knew these women would be no damn good.' We were exhausted all the time. The men would go home and sit down to a prepared meal but when the women came home they had to get the meal ready for their family.

It was rough for a while but we were determined to stay, and eventually, the majority of men learned to accept us and respect us as co-workers and union sisters.

**AS Level Exam-Style Question Section A**

***Study Source 10 before you answer this question.***

Why is Source 10 valuable to the historian for an enquiry into the experiences of women workers in the Second World War?

Explain your answer using the source, the information given about it and your own knowledge of the historical context. (8 marks)

**Tip**

*It is important that you comment on who wrote the source and how far it illustrates the type of work and experience of American women more generally in the Second World War. The source contains recollections recorded after the end of the Second World War. Will that affect its value to the historian?*

## The contribution of young people to the war effort

With 11.8 million men serving in the military and over 17 million women working in the war economy, 16- to 18-year-olds, who were old enough to work but not yet old enough to be conscripted into the armed forces, began to play an important role.

Almost 20 million became junior members of the American Red Cross, engaging in activities such as producing toys, clothing and furniture, and putting on entertainment programmes at military camps and hospitals. Many other young people entered the workforce to help fill the void left by adults in agriculture and industry.

With so many adults involved in Home Front and military activities, young people played an important role in Civil Defence. Young Civil Defence volunteers engaged in coast watching and watching for enemy aircraft. On the West Coast, fears of a Japanese invasion began with the attack on Pearl Harbour on 7 December 1941 and persisted until June 1942, when the Japanese aircraft carrier force was destroyed at the Battle of the Midway, one of the most decisive naval battles of the war. On the East Coast, volunteers watched for German **U-boat** activity. By mid-1942, the US Civil Defence Organization had ten million volunteers, the vast majority being young people.

**KEY TERM**

**U-boat**
German submarines were known as U-boats. During the Battle of the Atlantic (1939–45), Germany used submarine warfare to sink Allied ships transporting food and other essential supplies to Britain. The aim was to starve Britain into submission. Following the German declaration of war on the USA in December 1941, U-boats attacked American shipping close to the East Coast of the USA. It was not until mid-1943 that British and American naval and air forces began to sink U-boats in large numbers.

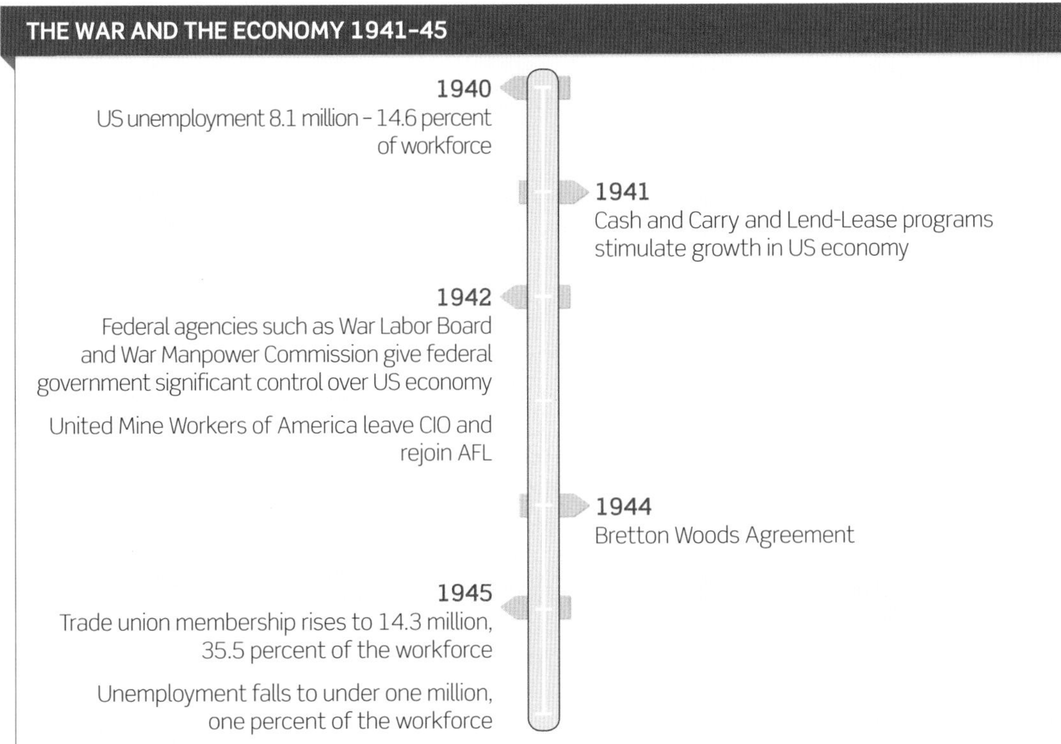


## The growing power of trade unions

An important feature of the years 1933 to 1945 was the considerable growth in trade union membership. This was aided by the legislation passed by the Roosevelt administration, which greatly helped trade union development. In 1933, Section 7(a) of the National Industrial Recovery Act (NIRA) gave unions the right of **collective bargaining**. Even though the US Supreme Court declared the NIRA unconstitutional in 1935, the Wagner Act of that year ensured trade unions kept this power.

**KEY TERM**

**Collective bargaining**
When a trade union negotiates with an employer for better pay and conditions on behalf of all its members.

The pattern of trade union membership reflected its growing power. In 1930, unions had 3.4 million members, 11.6 percent of the workforce. Most of these were skilled workers associated with a union organisation called the American Federation of Labor (AFL). In 1935, membership had risen slightly to 3.5 million. In 1940, the numbers almost doubled to 8.7 million (26.9 percent) of the workforce. By the war's end, union membership had reached 14.3 million (35.5 percent of the workforce, its highest-ever percentage). A significant part of this increased membership was due to the unionisation of semi-skilled and unskilled workers. In 1936, these unions formed the Congress of Industrial Organizations (CIO).

When the war began, the government and businesses needed every worker they could get. 11.8 million of the potential workforce were away in the armed forces. This greatly increased union power, and both government and businesses wanted to negotiate directly with one body rather than individual workers. When war broke out, most unions agreed with FDR's call for a 'no strike' agreement. Also, the War Labor Board, set up by FDR, introduced a 'maintenance of membership' policy where every employee at a unionised workplace had to join a union.

This does not mean there were no labour problems during the war. Unofficial strikes became a problem from 1942. The biggest problem, however, was with the United Mine Workers of America (UMWA), the most important union with the Congress of Industrial Organizations (CIO). In 1942, union leader, Jon L. Lewis, attempted to raise coal-miners' wages, but faced opposition from the War Labor Board. So incensed was Lewis that he left the CIO, which he had helped to form, and rejoined the AFL. He also became estranged from the FDR administration. In 1943 alone, Lewis called the 500,000-strong UMWA out on strike four times.

In November 1943, Lewis and the Secretary of the Interior, Harold Ickes, signed an agreement that broke the War Labor Board's attempt to limit pay rises as an attempt to stop inflation. Soon other major unions demanded the same treatment. By the war's end, union member wages across the USA had shown a marked increase. It also led to major national strikes after the war.

**SOURCE 11**

In 1942, the CIO made a no-strike agreement as part of the American war effort. This is a statement made by a CIO member in support of revoking the agreement at the Annual Meeting of the organisation's Michigan State Council in 1943.

Some time ago labor made a very noble gesture. That was a matter of giving a no-strike pledge. Arguments to the contrary notwithstanding, there were certain commitments that were made to labor at that particular time. Does anyone question that these commitments have not been lived up to by this Government? When it comes to the question of giving labor its just due, it seems that the Government seems not to be able to find any money to do anything with but when it comes to the question of building factories for corporations who have already more than they need, they find billions of dollars to do that with. Is that giving labor a square deal? I don't think so. My personal sentiments are on the question that the no-strike pledge should be revoked here and now.

## Migration to urban and industrial centres

When millions of Americans joined the military, they moved to bases away from home. So did millions of military civilian employees. However, more important permanent shifts in population occurred because of the war. 15 million Americans moved permanently. Black Americans continued the Great Migration of the 1920s and 1930s, moving north from the Old South. 700,000 left the Old South, many taking the traditional route to Chicago, Philadelphia and New York. However, a new trend in population movement was occurring, with many people moving to the Pacific Coast, with its war industries such as aircraft production and shipbuilding. 120,000 black Americans, for instance, moved west into the Los Angeles area. In all, California gained two million in population due to the war.

Many used the war to escape rural poverty. In 1940, just under half of all white families and 90 percent of black families living in rural areas lived in poverty. The new opportunities offered by war industries in the towns accelerated a trend away from rural living. The number of people living in towns with populations of 25,000 or more increased from 53 million in 1940 to 63 million by 1950, 42 percent of the entire US population.

Whole new cities grew up around specific war industries, such as Wichita, Kansas, which was associated with aircraft production, in particular the B24 bomber, the Liberator.

SOURCE 12

From President Roosevelt's State of the Union address delivered to both houses of Congress on 11 January 1944. Roosevelt challenged Congress to pass legislation that would guarantee the rights outlined in the speech in law. The speech is nicknamed 'the Second Bill of Rights'.

We have come to the realization of the fact that true individual freedom cannot exist without economic security and independence. People who are hungry and out of a job are the stuff of which dictatorships are made.

In our day these economic truths have become accepted as self-evident.

Among these are:-

The right to a useful and remunerative job in the industries or shops or farms or mines of the Nation;

The right to earn enough to provide adequate food and clothing and recreation;

The right of every farmer to raise and sell his products at a return which will give him and his family a decent living;

The right of every businessman, large and small, to trade in an atmosphere of freedom from unfair competition and domination by monopolies at home or abroad;

The right of every family to a decent home;

The right to adequate health care;

The right to a good education.

After this war is won we must be prepared to move forward, in the implementation of these rights, to new goals of human happiness and well-being.

## The growth of new industries

The drive to win the Second World War acted as a stimulus for new industries to develop. The most innovative and significant was the programme to produce the world's first atomic weapon. Known as the Manhattan Project, the programme involved the construction of large industrial plants and employed the world's top scientists outside Nazi Germany and the USSR. The Manhattan Project cost $2 billion and employed more than 100,000 in facilities such as Oak Ridge, Tennessee, where the atomic bombs were constructed, and the research laboratories at Los Alamos, New Mexico. With the onset of the **Cold War** with the USSR after 1945, the new nuclear industry formed an increasingly important part of the US defence industry and also provided nuclear-powered electricity.

The aircraft industry helped stimulate the growth of the war economy as a whole. Aircraft production was the largest single section of the war economy, costing $45 billion, almost a quarter of all money spent on military production. An example of the development of aviation as a result of this new industry was the production of the B29 Boeing Superfortress bomber. It was the aeroplane that delivered the two atomic bombs dropped on Hiroshima and Nagasaki in Japan in August 1945. Its production involved hundreds of thousands of workers in four major factories and $3 billion in government spending. Overall, 125,000 aircraft were produced during the war, employing two million workers.

Technological development was mirrored in ship production. The US devised a new prefabricated way of making merchant ships, known as Liberty Ships, which could be built in days rather than months. Overseen by the US Maritime Commission, 5,777 merchant ships were built in the Second World War, at a cost of $13 billion. The most sophisticated and important naval ship built in the war was the aircraft carrier. It formed the mainstay of the naval war in the Pacific and helped defeat German U-boats in the Battle of the Atlantic.

These war industries stimulated the development of electronics, radio communications, new methods of construction and weaponry. It also led to a growing interdependence between US industry, the US government and military production, which became a dominant feature of the Cold War after 1945.

### KEY TERM

**Cold War**
A period of international confrontation between the USA and its allies and the USSR and its allies, which lasted from 1945 to 1991. It involved a propaganda war, an arms race and wars in the developing world in which the USA and USSR provided support for the opposing sides, such as the Korean War (1950–53), the Vietnam War (1965–73) and the war in Angola (1975–99).

### ACTIVITY
KNOWLEDGE CHECK

**The war and the economy, 1941–45**

1 The Second World War had a profound impact on the US economy and those who worked in it.

Identify ways in which the following were affected by the Second World War:

**a)** The level of unemployment **b)** New industries **c)** Trade unions.

2 How far did the Second World War affect the role of women in the US economy and society?

## Change (6a)

### Separately and together

In thematic histories a historian focuses on a particular aspect of change. For example, an economic history of the British Empire would focus on trade and the economic reasons for the expansion of the empire, whereas a political history of the empire would focus on governance of the colonies and strategic reasons for its expansion. Below are some different types of thematic history.

| Political history | Economic history | Social history |
|---|---|---|
| Ethnic minority history | Cultural history | International history |

**1** Working in groups, write a definition for each type of history.

Here are some events in our period.

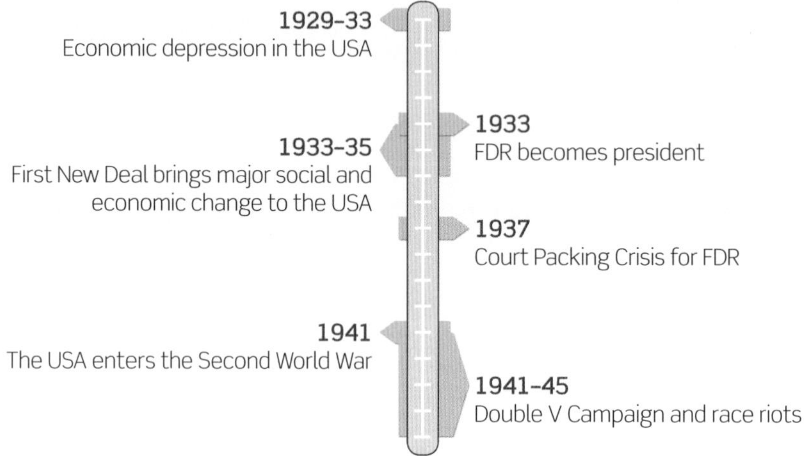


Working on your own, answer the following questions, then discuss your answers in groups.

**2** The first two events can be classified as 'political'.

**a)** Why was the economic depression of 1929–33 such an important event in US history?

**b)** What other area of history does this take it into?

**3** What political change came about due to the economic depression of 1929–33?

**4** Was the New Deal of 1933–45 political or economic or both? Explain your answer.

**5** What was the social impact of the USA's entry into the Second World War on America?

**6** Did the US entry into the Second World War have political aspects as well as social and economic?

Working in pairs:

**7** Write a statement attacking 'thematic history'.

**8** Write three statements defending 'thematic history'.

**9** Discuss why historians take a thematic approach.

ACTIVITY
SUMMARY

**The USA, the New Deal and the Second World War**

Work with another member of your class.

1 a) How far did the New Deal change American society and the economy? To support your answer, provide specific examples of how it affected national infrastructure, unemployment and the role of women.

b) What do you regard as the most important change brought about by the US involvement in the Second World War? Explain your answer.

2 a) Identify ways the New Deal years impacted on the USA.

b) Identify ways the Second World War affected the USA on the Home Front.

c) On balance, which had a bigger impact on American society and the economy: the New Deal years or the Second World War? Explain the reasons for your answer.

3 What major changes took place in the US economy in the New Deal and war years? Create a spider diagram of changes that you have identified.

## WIDER READING

Brogan, H. *The Penguin History of the USA*, Penguin (1999)

Clements, P. *Prosperity, Depression and the New Deal, Access to History Series*, Hodder Murray (2005)

de Pennington, J. *Modern America, The USA, 1865 to the present*, Hodder Murray (2005)

Farmer, A. and Sanders, V. *An Introduction to American History, 1860–1990*, Hodder (2002)

Kennedy, D. *Freedom from Fear: The American People on Depression and War, 1929–1945*, Oxford University Press (2001)

Leuchtenberg, W. *Franklin D Roosevelt and the New Deal: 1932–1940*, Harper Perennial (2009)

Murphy, D. *Flagship History – United States 1917–2008*, Collins Educational (2008)

Parrish, M. *The Anxious Decades: America in Prosperity and Depression 1920–1941*, WW Norton and Company (1994)

Rowe, C. *USA, 1890–1945*, Nelson Thornes (2008)

Stewart, G. and Barker, L. *The United States 1917–1954: Boom Bust and Recovery*, Pearson (2010)

Willoughby, S. and Willoughby, D. *The USA 1917–1945*, Heinemann (2000)

# 2a.4 The transformation of the USA, 1945–55

**KEY QUESTIONS**

- How far was the US economy transformed in the period 1945–55?
- To what extent did the Cold War affect life within the USA?
- To what extent did American culture change in the years 1945–55?
- How far did the civil rights of minorities improve in the period 1945–55?

**KEY TERMS**

**Cold War (1945–91)**
The Cold War was a period of international history that involved political and military confrontation between the capitalist USA (and its allies) and the communist Soviet Union (and its allies). The USA and USSR had completely different political and economic social systems and ideologies. The USA feared that the USSR planned to turn the world communist and outlaw the private ownership of business and property. The USA saw itself as the leader of the free world, which allowed private ownership of businesses and property. The USA claimed it was defending the non-communist world against dictatorship but, in reality, supported anti-communist dictatorship in areas such as Latin America.

**Communist**
Communism is an anti-democratic system of government. In a communist state the government controls the entire economy, and private control of businesses and private ownership of property are outlawed. Many communists were atheists, who did not believe in God. The success of communism in Russia in 1917 was due to the activities of a small group of dedicated revolutionaries, rather than a mass movement of support.

## INTRODUCTION

In 1958, the US economist and future US ambassador to India, J. K. Galbraith, published a study of modern America called *The Affluent Society*. The USA had reached a level of economic wealth and development that made it the leading global nation, with the highest standard of living. The USA had become the world's first consumer society.

Even though the USA was experiencing continued economic growth, it faced major problems in international relations, in particular with the Soviet Union. From 1945, the USA was engaged in the **Cold War**, a political, economic, military and ideological confrontation with the Soviet Union, its former ally from the Second World War.

Fear of **communist** infiltration of US society was a pronounced and recurrent theme in the period 1945–55. It not only affected US government but pervaded every aspect of US society, including Hollywood and the media.

However, while the US was gripped by anti-communist fears, the period also saw the beginnings of the black American civil rights movement. Major advances were made in making black Americans equal citizens with other Americans. By 1955, the first major moves towards full equality had begun.

**1944** – GI Bill of Rights

**1945** – September: Second World War ends

Beginning of the Cold War

1946

**1947** – House Un-American Activities Committee begin investigation into communist subversion

Loyalty Oath introduced for government employees

**1948** – *The Goldbergs* sitcom appears on US television

*The Ed Sullivan Show* begins on US television, originally called *Toast of the Town*

**1949** – Levitt Town opens in New York State

# HOW FAR WAS THE US ECONOMY TRANSFORMED IN THE PERIOD 1945–55?

By the end of the Second World War, the USA dominated the world economy. Economic rivals Germany and Japan had lost the war and were devastated. In Germany, heavy bombing and fighting had destroyed factories, housing and roads on a major scale. Japan suffered heavy bombing and a major economic blockade that gravely damaged production. Allies such as Britain were virtually bankrupt and the USSR had lost over 20 million people, with much of the western part of the republic a virtual wasteland because of war.

The US economy, having grown rapidly during the war, continued its exceptional growth rate after 1945.

## Changing employment opportunities

The continued expansion of the US economy after 1945 increased employment opportunities for many Americans. The development of the aircraft and shipbuilding industries during the war continued into peacetime due to the emerging tensions of the Cold War. Unlike after the First World War, the USA remained in a period of military preparedness in anticipation of global conflict with the USSR and communism. Events such as the **Berlin Airlift Crisis** of 1948–49 and the **Korean War** of 1950–53 meant government expenditure remained high and demand for military material kept the domestic economy buoyant.

The growth of disposable income sustained domestic demand (as shown in Source 1). Demand for cars became a major indicator of consumer demand. In 1946, car production was two million. By 1955, it had risen to eight million. This meant that new job opportunities were created for skilled employment involving higher wages. The growth of the clerical sector in these industries also opened up greater job opportunities for women, who were under-represented in manufacturing jobs. Companies like General Motors, Ford and Chrysler expanded to become some of the biggest corporations in the USA. This in turn led to increased demand for oil.

Another major area for new employment opportunities came with the expansion of the US retail sector. In 1945, there were only eight shopping centres across the USA. By 1960, there were almost 4,000. The new stores offered thousands of new job opportunities for unskilled and semi-skilled workers. The new shopping centres sold televisions, washing machines, dishwashers, refrigerators, toasters and other labour-saving domestic appliances, and so the expanded retail sector helped create jobs for those workers making these goods.

### KEY TERMS

**Berlin Airlift Crisis (1948–49)**
An international crisis started by the Soviet Union's decision to close all land routes between western Germany and western sectors in Berlin. The USA and Britain launched an airlift that successfully supplied West Berlin with food and fuel. The USSR ended the blockade in June 1949. These events led directly to the creation of NATO and the states of West Germany and communist East Germany.

**Korean War (1950–53)**
The first major armed confrontation in the Cold War. In June 1950, communist North Korea invaded South Korea. The USA and its United Nations' allies, such as the UK, provided military support for South Korea. The North Korean invasion was repelled by UN forces, but the attempt to defeat North Korea came to an end when communist China entered the war on the side of North Korea at the end of 1950. By 1953, a ceasefire was agreed and the border of North and South Korea has remained approximately the same as the division at the beginning of the war in 1950 to the present day.

**1950** – McCarthy's Wheeling Speech

Korean War begins

**1951** – Rosenbergs found guilty of espionage

*I Love Lucy* sitcom begins on US television

1952

**1953** – HCR 108 on Native American Reservations

**1954** – *Brown* case outlaws school segregation

**1955** – 'Rock Around the Clock' becomes a pop music hit

Montgomery Bus Boycott

Federal Highways Act

All these changes were fuelled by advertising. During the 1950s, advertising expenditure increased by a thousand percent.

New employment opportunities were also provided with the development of the aircraft industry. With the development of the jet engine, the aircraft industry was transformed. Initially, jet aircraft were purchased by the US Air Force. In 1952, the UK produced the de Havilland Comet jet airliner. By 1958, the US firm Boeing had produced the 707 four-engine jet airliner. The development of domestic civilian aviation led to a decline in the importance of railways and greatly increased air travel within the USA. It also created more new job opportunities in the aeronautical engineering industry, involving high-skilled jobs offering higher wages compared to traditional manufacturing industries.

Technological development also created opportunities in computing. In 1944, Harvard University, in association with International Business Machines (IBM), produced the first general-purpose computer, which had 500 miles of wiring. By 1947, the US Army had produced its own computer. By the early 1950s, computers began to appear in US business and industry, leading to a communications and data revolution.

The growth of the US economy led to a major increase in **white-collar** jobs, in offices and in management. In 1956, for the first time in US history, the number of white collar workers outnumbered **blue-collar workers**. For instance, the chemical industry saw a three percent increase in blue-collar workers between 1947 and 1952, but the white-collar workforce increased by 50 percent. A major centre of the chemical industry was the state of Delaware, on the east coast, where the DuPont chemical corporation was based. However, major chemical industries also developed in the states of Ohio and California.

Although tens of thousands of jobs were created thanks to growth in the economy, new employment opportunities disproportionately favoured white men.

## Government policies to encourage growth

A pivotal factor in the creation of new job opportunities and US economic growth was the policies followed by the federal government. The federal government actively attempted to stimulate economic growth through an increase in defence spending, supporting the industries that had grown up to support the USA's involvement in the Second World War.

Technological breakthroughs made in the period 1941–45 had led to new industries and greater productivity. The new industries were in areas such as nuclear physics, aerospace, electronics and chemicals. After 1945, the federal government sold many of its industrial facilities, such as aluminium plants and aircraft factories, to private buyers, who created some of the country's fastest-growing businesses. Productivity rose dramatically. For instance, it took 310 labour hours to make a car in 1945. By 1960, this figure had dropped to 150 hours.

The Cold War brought increased federal government spending. The government began to play an increasing role in the US economy, so much so that the outgoing president in 1961, Dwight Eisenhower, talked of a **military-industrial complex** in the USA, where business and the military worked together. Direct and indirect federal funding provided money for scientific research in fields such as plastics, where government funding increased 600 percent during the 1950s.

The funding fuelled the development of the 'knowledge revolution' in the USA, where the number of jobs in professional and technological work grew enormously. The number of salaried middle-class workers rose 61 percent between 1947 and 1957.

The rapid increase in government military expenditure also helped lead to a concentration of industrial power in the hands of a few giant corporations, such as General Motors, McDonnell Douglas Aircraft and the Dow Chemical Corporation. These were some of the major beneficiaries of the 'military-industrial complex'.

### KEY TERMS

**White-collar workers**
Workers who work in offices doing clerical, secretarial or managerial work.

**Blue-collar workers**
Workers who do physical and manual work in manufacturing and construction. The term is applied to both unskilled and skilled workers, such as carpenters, labourers, electricians and machinists.

**Military-industrial complex**
A term first used by President Eisenhower in his farewell speech as president in January 1961. It referred to the close relationship between the government and large corporations that manufactured military equipment. It also encompassed politicians in Congress who used military contracts to create employment opportunities in their own congressional districts. Although never an official policy or policies, this relationship developed as part of the US response to the Cold War confrontation with the Soviet Union after the Second World War.

Another effect of the increased growth and drive for efficiency was limitations on the power of the trade unions. In 1945, 35.5 percent of the US workforce were in unions, the highest ever percentage of union members. As the war ended and inflation rose, the USA was affected by a wave of strikes by workers demanding higher wages. After the 1946 midterm elections, the Republicans regained control of Congress and in 1947 passed the Taft–Hartley Act, which considerably reduced trade union rights, in particular the right to call a strike. This helped reduce the number of industrial disputes.

### EXTEND YOUR KNOWLEDGE

**Taft-Hartley Act, 1947**

Passed by a Republican-controlled Congress, the Act outlawed the 'closed shop', whereby all workers in a factory had to belong to a trade union. It also outlawed union practices such as 'featherbedding', where workers received payment for work not done, and making contributions to political parties, usually the Democrats. All union leaders had to take oaths that they were not members of the Communist Party.

Employers gained the right to sue unions for breach of contract. The Act forbade strikes by federal government employees and introduced a cooling-off period of 80 days for any strike that the president found to be dangerous to public health and safety.

President Truman vetoed the proposal, but it became law because two-thirds of each house of Congress supported it.

## Provision for veterans

An important stimulant to economic growth was the **GI** bill, passed by Congress in 1944. Also known as the Servicemen's Readjustment Act, it meant veterans returning from the war received a range of benefits. Those wishing to start businesses could get a guaranteed loan of $2,000 from the Veterans' Administration, a branch of the federal government.

The most important federal assistance to veterans came with home-buying. The Federal Housing Authority (FHA) was willing to support veteran mortgage applications for up to 90 percent of a house's value. The Veterans' Administration also gave returning servicemen low-interest mortgages. The veterans did not have to have a deposit in order to secure a mortgage. These benefits helped stimulate a major construction boom in the late 1940s and early 1950s, which greatly aided economic development. By 1956, 4.3 million home loans had been made, with a combined value of $33 billion.

The GI bill also gave veterans educational opportunities. Just over half of the 7.8 million returning servicemen attended colleges and technical schools through grants given under the provisions of the bill. Between 1944 and when it ended in 1956, the GI bill cost the federal government $14.5 billion.

### KEY TERM

**GI**
A slang term for a member of the US armed forces, from the term 'government issue'.

SOURCE

This table originally appeared in *America in the Twentieth Century*, by James Patterson (1994).

US Economic Growth, 1946–55

| Year | GNP (in billion $) | % Change in GNP of preceding year | Disposable income (in billion $) |
|---|---|---|---|
| 1946 | 208.5 | −1.6 | 160.0 |
| 1950 | 284.8 | +11 | 206.9 |
| 1951 | 328.4 | +15.3 | 226.9 |
| 1952 | 345.5 | +5.2 | 238.3 |
| 1953 | 364.6 | +5.5 | 252.6 |
| 1954 | 364.8 | +0.1 | 257.4 |
| 1955 | 398.0 | +9.1 | 275.3 |

### AS Level Exam-Style Question Section A

***Study Source 1 before you answer this question.***

Why is Source 1 valuable to the historian for an enquiry into the development of the US economy after the Second World War?

Explain your answer using the source, the information given about it and your knowledge of the historical context. (8 marks)

**Tip**

*You need to identify relevant data from the source that helps explain how the US economy developed after the Second World War and would allow the historian to make an assessment of the nature and degree of change. It would be useful, in your answer, to identify the rate of economic growth between years.*

## Growing mobility

The post-war economic boom and subsequent transformation in the USA was greatly aided by the growth of the car industry. Between 1946 and 1955, car production quadrupled. In 1950, the USA produced two-thirds of all the world's cars and trucks. By 1955, the US produced 9.2 million cars and trucks. The UK, which was the second largest producer, turned out only 1.3 million. Japan produced a mere 69,000. In that year, the industry was dominated by three giant corporations, all based in Detroit, Michigan: General Motors, Ford and Chrysler. The widespread availability of cars led to greater mobility for Americans and was directly linked to the growth of suburbs around towns and cities. It also aided the growth of the domestic tourist industry, as Americans could now drive to visit other parts of the USA.

Car sales were fuelled by a major increase in credit purchasing by consumers, helped by the introduction of the world's first credit card, Diner's Club, in 1950, followed by American Express in 1951. Short-term credit, mainly spent on consumer purchasing, rose from $8.4 billion in 1946 to $45.6 billion in 1958. Demand for cars was also increased by clever advertising and what became known as 'built-in obsolescence': each year, manufacturers brought out new models, with innovations such as tail fins, two-tone colour, extra chrome and white-walled tyres. In 1955, Pontiac produced the Sensational Strato-Streak V-8, which could go twice as fast as the official speed limit. Car production was also aided by federal construction of highways. Federal spending went from $79 million in 1946 to $2.6 billion by 1960.

## Growth of suburbs and the rise of Levittown projects

Greater mobility supplied by the rapid growth in car ownership helped the growth of suburbs, new housing developments built on the edges of towns and cities. Prior to the rapid growth in car ownership, the ability of Americans to live outside a town or city centre was limited. More remote areas now became accessible to commuters. The number of people living in suburbs rose ten percent during the 1950s and the number of suburban houses nearly doubled, as 18 million people moved out of the inner cities. Cheap land and mass construction reduced house building costs, and the greater availability of financial credit to purchase suburban houses increased demand. Suburban living was seen as a very attractive proposition.

Also fuelling demand for suburban housing was the assistance in acquiring mortgages and social developments provided by the GI bill. Many former GIs bought houses in the newly developed suburbs. After the Second World War, the number of marriages doubled. In 1948, two million couples were still living with their relatives. These factors led to a rise in demand for new housing that suburban development provided.

An important individual in the development of suburbia was William Levitt from New York State. In 1947, he bought 1,200 acres of farmland on Long Island, New York and built 10,600 houses, which were quickly bought up and occupied by more than 40,000 people. Levitt had realised that the government guarantee of veterans' mortgages under the GI bill had created a great opportunity. He reduced the costs of building by using prefabricated walls and door and window frames that could be assembled quickly on site. 'Levitt Town' (as Levitt's development was known) also encouraged sales by including swimming pools, schools, athletic fields and tennis courts in the development, making living in suburbia even more attractive.

Levittown houses in the Pennsylvania developments originally sold at $6,990. Each one had a white picket fence, a fully equipped kitchen and a green lawn. However, William Levitt made sure that his homes were sold only to whites. In 1953, Levittown, New York contained 70,000 people, the largest housing development in the USA without black Americans. This policy of racial segregation was declared illegal by US courts in the 1960s.

In California, suburbs were constructed around Los Angeles by Henry J. Kaiser and Henry Doelger. The developments offered ranch-style housing with front lawns and backyards, a huge change from inner-city living.

SOURCE 2 New houses at Levittown, New York in 1949.

## The new consumer society

By 1955, the USA had become the world's first consumer society. Suburban housing developments, cars, televisions and easy consumer credit were all features of this affluent society that placed considerable weight on recreation. During the 1950s, the average family in suburbia earned $6,500, which was 70 percent higher than the rest of the country. Suburban dwellers purchased boats, built swimming pools and many went on foreign holidays. Cars led to greater mobility, encouraging the development of drive-in restaurants, drive-in movie theatres and out-of-town shopping centres.

In 1954, in San Bernardino, California, near Los Angeles, Ray Kroc devised a new way to serve hamburgers and French fries to meet the new demand for eating out – McDonalds was born! McDonalds and similar fast food outlets provided food in a completely differently way from traditional sit-down restaurants.

Despite this prosperity, in 1960 nearly 40 million Americans (22 percent of the population) lived below the poverty line of $3,000 a year for a family of four. The inner cities, which the middle class had left to live in the suburbs, fell into economic decline and became associated with crime and poverty.

**ACTIVITY**
**KNOWLEDGE CHECK**

**Economic transformation**

1 Identify how the post-war US economy offered new job opportunities for many Americans.

2 In what ways, and how, did government policies encourage economic growth in the years 1945 -55?

3 Explain why suburbs grew rapidly in the years 1945–55.

4 What do you regard as the most important development that led to the economic transformation of the USA in the years 1945–55? Explain your answer.

**AS Level Exam-Style Question Section B**

How accurate is it to say that the US became the world's first consumer society in the years 1945 to 1955? (20 marks)

**Tip**

*It is important that you offer a definition of the term 'consumer society'. This will involve reference to the ability of Americans to purchase goods and services and the range of goods and services available to most Americans. The ownership of cars and purchasing of housing are two important aspects that require explanation. It is important to provide a balanced account, so you should also include any information that shows not all Americans benefited from the rapid economic growth in the years 1945–55.*

**A Level Exam-Style Question Section B**

To what extent did federal government policy stimulate the economic growth of the years 1945 to 1955? (20 marks)

**Tip**

*This question requires a balanced answer. You will need to identify and assess ways in which the federal government assisted economic growth such as the GI bill, aid to veterans, the military-industrial complex and road construction. To balance the role of the federal government, you will be expected to identify and assess other factors, such as new styles of housing development and the increased mobility offered by a rapid growth in car ownership.*

# TO WHAT EXTENT DID THE COLD WAR AFFECT LIFE WITHIN THE USA?

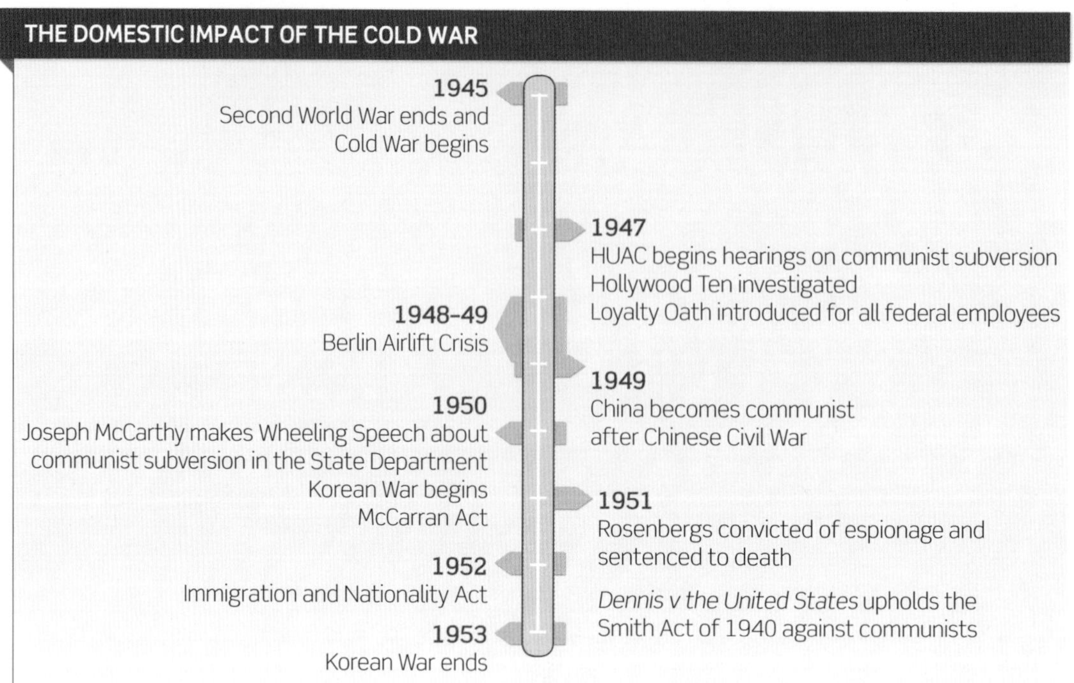


**KEY TERM**

**Red Scare**
A growing fear that communist ideas would spread and perhaps lead to a communist revolution and creation of a communist dictatorship in the USA. Communists and other radical left-wing groups were known as 'Reds'. The first major Red Scare took place in 1919 when the federal government launched the Palmer Raids.

## Anti-communism and the Cold War context

In one way, the endings of the First and Second World Wars were similar. After each war the USA was gripped by a **Red Scare**. In 1919, this was in direct response to the success of the Bolshevik Revolution in Russia, which created the world's first communist state. Supporters of Bolshevik Russia within the USA wanted to see similar revolutionary change in the United States.

After 1945, the second Red Scare occurred. Although Allies against Nazi Germany, the USA and the Soviet Union soon fell out, in particular over the post-war division of Europe. All of Eastern Europe became communist between 1945 and 1948. Winston Churchill, Britain's wartime prime minister, claimed an 'Iron Curtain' had descended on Europe, dividing the continent in two.

Fear of communist spying and subversion were exacerbated by the following events. In 1945, hundreds of secret State Department documents were discovered in the offices of the communist-sponsored magazine *Amerasia*. In the following year, Canadian government employees were caught handing over atomic secrets to Soviet spies. The discovery of communist activity on the USA's doorstep and the handing over of atomic secrets to the USSR was seen as a serious threat to US security. Until 1949, the USA was the world's only power with nuclear weapons. In 1949, the USSR successfully tested its own atomic weapon, confirming fears that spies and subversion had provided the USSR with the information to produce nuclear weapons. From 1949, the Cold War was a confrontation between the USA and USSR of both conventional and nuclear weapons.

In 1947, President Truman, in the wake of these developments, introduced new loyalty and security checks on all federal employees to see if they had communist sympathies. Under Executive Order 9835, the Federal Employee Loyalty Program was created. It investigated every aspect of employees' lives, including who they associated with and their own private beliefs. Between 1947 and 1951, nearly 3,000 federal employees resigned over the program and 300 were dismissed.

## The House Un-American Activities Committee (HUAC) and Joseph McCarthy

Originally created in 1938, the Un-American Activities Committee (HUAC) was set up by the House of Representatives to protect the USA against Nazi German spying and subversion. After the Second

World War, it was used against communist subversion. The HUAC was aided by the passage of the Smith Act of 1940: this Act allowed the prosecution of anyone who supported and promoted communism. When the Republican Party gained control of the House of Representatives after the midterm elections of 1946, the HUAC became a powerful tool in the campaign against communism within the USA.

President Truman helped foster the growing anti-communist feeling. In March 1947, he made a speech advocating massive US aid to Europe to help reconstruction after the war. In his attempt to gain Congressional support, he stated that the Soviet Union was a major threat to democracy in Europe and the free world. This led to the Republican-dominated Congress agreeing to the European Recovery Plan (also known as the Marshall Plan) and providing aid to Greece and Turkey, which both faced communist subversion.

The HUAC investigated communist infiltration across American society. It attempted to expose communist supporters in the federal government, the trade union movement and even in Hollywood. Its investigations were filmed and broadcast on television so, across the USA, average Americans could watch the **witch hunt** against anyone suspected of being a 'Red'.

**KEY TERM**

**Witch hunt**
A process whereby accusers deliberately set out to find a person or persons guilty of a crime, irrespective of the strength of evidence.

Democrat president Harry S. Truman was re-elected in 1948. After the election, who the HUAC investigated one of its most celebrated cases, involving a State Department official, Alger Hiss, who was accused of being a communist sympathiser. Hiss was president of the Carnegie Endowment for International Peace and had served in several government departments. He was accused of giving secret US government documents to Whitaker Chambers, a self-confessed former communist, in 1938. Although Hiss denied the charges, he was convicted for lying to the HUAC in January 1950. The case was publicised nationwide.

The Republicans claimed the Truman administration had been soft on communism, which among other things had led to the victory of the communists in the Chinese Civil War (1946–49). The communist victory in China was blamed on Truman and his administration, in particular, the State Department, which was responsible for conducting foreign policy. The Republicans believed Truman should have offered more effective assistance, which, in their opinion, would have prevented a communist victory. The case also brought to national prominence a junior Congressman from California who attacked Hiss. He was Richard Nixon, who later became vice president (1953–61) and then president (1969–74).

The HUAC greatly increased national hysteria against communists. The fear of 'Reds under the bed', undermining the American way of life, became a recurrent theme. However, the height of anti-communist feeling came with the rise of a junior senator from Wisconsin, Joseph McCarthy.

**SOURCE**

From 'How Not to Get Investigated, Ten Commandments for Government Employees' by Thurman Arnold, which appeared in *Harper's Magazine*, November 1948. Although it sounds comically extreme, this was meant to be a serious article, which illustrates the degree of concern felt within the federal government about possible communist subversion.

1. Do not attend any social gathering, no matter how large, at which 'a subversive' may also be present. This includes dances.
2. Never talk, even to your neighbours or at social gatherings, about controversial issues. If your views offend someone, they may show up in a report in a distorted fashion and you will never even know who gave the information.
3. Do not subscribe to... any liberal publication. Maybe it's communist and you don't know it. Don't read any books about Russia even out of curiosity.
4. If anyone sends you as a gift a publication of the sort described in the foregoing Commandment, cancel it at once.
5. Do not ever attend the large annual reception at the Russian Embassy.
6. Do not contribute any money for the legal defense of some old acquaintance or college classmate charged with disloyalty.
7. Do not marry anyone who... had radical associations.
8. Be particularly careful never to ride in an automobile in which a "subversive" may be another rider.
9. Do not yourself be unduly critical of Fascists or Nazis.
10. If any relative, no matter how distant, has ever been a "radical" do not take a government position at all.

## Senator McCarthy and McCarthyism

Senator McCarthy is the person most closely associated with the anti-communist movement within the USA in the early stages of the Cold War. In February 1950, at Wheeling, West Virginia, he announced that the State Department had been infiltrated by communists who were undermining the USA's conflict with world communism. He claimed that the State Department was full of communists and communist sympathisers. This statement propelled McCarthy into the national limelight.

McCarthy has been called an opportunist who saw the popularity of anti-communism and wished to exploit it for his own political ends. When pressed to produce the names, he said he had 205, then 57, and then said he had a lot of names. A Senate Committee appointed to look into McCarthy's claims found no evidence to support them. However, this did not stop McCarthy. He went on to attack other government departments, such as the American Bar Association, the American Medical Association and the teaching profession. In a poll in 1950, 61 percent of Americans said that, if a person was proved to be a communist sympathiser, they should be dismissed from the teaching profession. In the 1950 midterm elections, McCarthy's tactics seemed to have worked, with two anti-McCarthy senators losing their seats and big gains for the Republicans.

Even though his claims were never substantiated, McCarthy was popular. He offered simple answers to questions many Americans were asking: why was the USA, the most powerful country on earth, with (from 1945 to 1949) a monopoly in nuclear weapons, the world's greatest economy, and a military force that, according to many Americans, had won the Second World War, being outdone by the Soviet Union? The Soviet Union had spread communism across Eastern Europe and helped China become communist in 1949. When the Soviet Union successfully exploded its own atomic bomb in 1949 and communist North Korea invaded South Korea in June 1950, and almost defeated the South Korean and US army units based there, concern grew further.

McCarthy's answer was that people within the USA were undermining the country, that they were giving secrets to the USSR. Catholics supported McCarthy because they saw how their co-religionists in Eastern Europe and Asia suffered persecution under communism. Fear of communism was also widespread among businessmen. Also, McCarthy's anti-establishment and anti-privilege stance won support in the Midwest and West. In spite of its great power, the USA was believed to be being undermined from within.

The activities of the HUAC and Senator McCarthy gave the Republican Party a vote-winning formula. The Democrats had dominated the presidency since 1933 and, until 1946, they had dominated Congress. The anti-communist crusade gave Republicans a popular appeal. The Democrats had been outwitted by Stalin in Europe and had 'lost China' to communism. From June 1950 to June 1953, US forces, with their UN allies, were fighting a bloody war against communism in Korea.

In 1948, congressmen Richard Nixon supported a bill in the House of Representatives that required all of the USA's 60,000 communists to register with the government. In 1950, Pat McCarran, the Republican Senator for Nevada, was able to pass the Internal Security Act, also known as the McCarran Act. This required all communist and communist-front organisations to register with the Subversive Activities Control Board, which would also investigate any group reported to be 'ideologically suspect'. It empowered the federal government to order the arrest of any persons suspected of **subversive** activity in times of national emergency. As the McCarran Act was passed shortly after the outbreak of the Korean War, the country was already in such a state.

**KEY TERM**

**Subversive**
An act regarded as undermining the government and/or society of a country.

In 1952, Senator McCarran helped pass another law, the Immigration and Nationality Act. It established new, stricter quotas on immigration and set up procedures to screen out any potential subversives from entering the USA.

The activities of the HUAC and McCarthy were heavily criticised by President Truman, the Democrats and the American Civil Liberties Union. They believed this legislation undermined individual freedom in the USA and undermined the US Constitution. However, in 1951, in the case *Dennis v United States,* the US Supreme Court upheld the Smith Act of 1940. The Smith Act had allowed law enforcement officers to arrest and detain known communists. This decision led to the conviction and imprisonment of 11 top communists.

McCarthy's attacks on the State Department in particular, and government departments in general, weakened morale in the federal government and created a climate of fear and accusation that helped undermine American life. Fear of 'Reds under the bed' in every US town and institution became a feature of US life in the early 1950s.

**SOURCE**

Senator McCarthy at a Senate Investigating Committee hearing in April 1953. The Senate Investigating Committee gave McCarthy a national stage to put forward his views, as senate hearings were held in public and filmed for television broadcast. This photograph is typical of the media coverage that brought McCarthy's hearings into the living rooms of American homes.

SOURCE

From a speech given at Wheeling, West Virginia, 9 February 1950 by Senator Joseph McCarthy. It was delivered in front of the Ohio County Women's Republican Club at the height of the Alger Hiss trial. 1950 was a key election year for the US Congress and State governments. In his speech Senator McCarthy accuses the US State Department of communist sympathies.

Ladies and gentlemen, can there be anyone here tonight who is so blind as to say that the war is not on? Can there be anyone who fails to realize that the Communist world has said, "The time is now" that this is the time for the show-down between the democratic Christian world and the Communist atheistic world? Unless we face this fact, we shall pay the price that must be paid by those who wait too long. At war's end we were physically the strongest nation on earth and, at least potentially, the most powerful intellectually and morally. Ours could have been the honor of being a beacon in the desert of destruction, a shining living proof that civilization was not yet ready to destroy itself. Unfortunately, we have failed miserably and tragically to arise to the opportunity. The reason why we find ourselves in a position of impotency is not because our only powerful potential enemy has sent men to invade our shores, but rather because of the traitorous actions of those who have been treated so well by this Nation. It has not been the less fortunate of members of minority groups who have been selling this Nation out, but rather those who have had all the benefits that the wealthiest nation on earth has had to offer - the finest homes, the finest college educations and the finest jobs in Government we can give. This is glaringly true in the State Department. There the bright young men who are born with silver spoons in their mouths are the ones who have been worst offenders.

### The downfall of McCarthy

The strength of McCarthy's anti-communist crusade paid dividends for the Republican Party. For the first time in 20 years, in November 1952 they won the presidential election. Once the Republicans were in power in 1953, much of McCarthy's political usefulness had gone. However, he did not stop making accusations about communist infiltration into America's most prestigious institutions. What was most embarrassing to the Eisenhower administration was his claim that the armed forces were under suspicion.

The US Senate became increasingly irritated by McCarthy's accusations and behaviour. He was known to be a heavy drinker and was seen as an embarrassment to the Senate. From 22 April 1954, McCarthy faced questioning in the Senate Caucus Room for 35 days, with as many as 20 million Americans watching the proceedings on television.

For nearly five years, McCarthy had dominated the national scene. His accusations helped undermine government, the teaching profession and other professional bodies. In the nuclear age, where the USA's dominant position in the world was being threatened by communism, his claims of domestic treachery hit a raw nerve.

## The reality of the nuclear age

At the end of the Second World War, the USA saw itself as the world's greatest power. It alone possessed nuclear weapons. Its main rival, the Soviet Union, had lost 20 million people in the war and much of the western Soviet Union was devastated by war. However, by 1949, the Soviet Union had exploded its own nuclear weapon.

From 1949 to the end of the Cold War in 1991, the two superpowers faced each other with nuclear weapons. For the very first time, US home territory was under serious threat of attack by the most destructive weapon in history. This threat led directly to a growing fear that the US's position in the world could be undermined by communist subversion at home. People were particularly concerned about how the USSR had acquired the knowledge to make a nuclear weapon so quickly. Suspicion fell on Soviet spies and communist sympathisers in the USA giving away state secrets.

The reality of the nuclear age seemed to affect all of American life. At school children were taught what to do in the case of a nuclear attack on the USA. In regular drills they practised hiding under their desks when they heard the nuclear attack warning. Families that could afford it built anti-nuclear war shelters either under their houses or in their yards. Large cities had public shelters in case of nuclear attack. Civil defence plans were drawn up. The Federal Highways and Defense Act of 1956 was passed, partly to enable the rapid evacuation of cities in case of nuclear attack.

### The Rosenberg case

In early February 1950, the British arrested Klaus Fuchs, a scientist who worked on the US atomic weapon at the Los Alamos laboratory, New Mexico during the Second World War. He admitted to passing on the USA's nuclear weapons secrets to the Soviets. He also implicated two Americans, Ethel and Julius Rosenberg.

On 17 July 1950, Julius Rosenberg, an electrical engineer with the US Army Signal Corps, was arrested. On 11 August 1950, his wife Ethel was also arrested. Both Rosenbergs had been former members of the American Communist Party. Their arrest was based partly on evidence provided by Ethel's brother-in-law, David Greengrass, and a Philadelphia chemist, Harry Gold, who admitted his own espionage activities. Much of the evidence against the Rosenbergs was circumstantial. They claimed they had been singled out because they were Jewish. They appealed to the US Supreme Court seven times, claiming they did not have a fair trial. However, in the virulent anti-communist atmosphere of the early 1950s, they were found guilty under the Espionage Act of 1917 and sentenced to death. The executions took place on 19 June 1953. The death sentence received popular support. All major media sources were in agreement except *The Daily Worker*, the newspaper of the American Communist Party, and the *Jewish Way Forward* magazine.

Both Rosenbergs claimed their innocence but, since the declassification of the Soviet archives in the 1990s, after the collapse of the USSR, it has become clear that Julius was a communist who passed on secret information to Soviet agents. The trial confirmed the belief of many Americans that the main threat to the US's position in the world came from within.

**SOURCE**

**6** From the summary statement of Irving Saypol, the prosecuting lawyer in the Rosenberg trial, 1951.

Ladies and gentlemen, you have heard statements of defense counsel here concerning the injection of communism in this case. I repeat again, these defendants are not on trial for being Communists. I don't want you to convict them merely because of their Communist activity. Communism, as the testimony has demonstrated, has a very definite place in this case because it is the Communist ideology which teaches worship and devotion to the Soviet Union over our own government. It has provided the motive and inspiration for these people to do the terrible things which have been proven against them. It is this adherence and devotion which makes clear their intent and motivation in carrying out this conspiracy to commit espionage. We ask you to sustain the charge of the grand jury in a verdict of guilty against each of these three defendants, on one basis and one basis alone; the evidence produced in this courtroom as to their guilt of the crime of conspiracy to commit espionage; that proof as to each defendant has been overwhelming. The guilt of each one has been established beyond any peradventure of doubt.

**AS Level Exam-Style Question Section A**

***Study Source 6 before you answer this question.***

How much weight do you give the evidence in Source 6 for an enquiry into McCarthyism in the early 1950s?

Explain your answer using the source, the information given about it and your own knowledge of the historical context. (12 marks)

**Tip**

*The provenance of the source is important in determining its value. You will be expected to refer to the significance of its authorship and the intended audience for the speech. To support your answer you should also mention relevant sections of the source that provide information about McCarthy's claims and the need for action.*

**ACTIVITY**
**KNOWLEDGE CHECK**

**The end of post-war euphoria and the beginning of the Cold War**

1. How important was the House Un-American Activities Committee in dealing with communist subversion?
2. Senator McCarthy was a controversial figure in US politics in the early 1950s. Do you think his influence was useful in dealing with possible communist subversion in the USA? Explain your answer.
3. How did the Cold War impact on the lives of ordinary Americans?

**AS Level Exam-Style Question Section B**

How accurate is it to say that the failures of the Truman administration were responsible for the rise of Senator Joseph McCarthy to national prominence? (20 marks)

**Tip**

*This question requires a balanced answer. You will need to give information that supports the view that failures of the Truman administration were responsible for McCarthy's rise, for example the victory of the communists in China and the Soviet takeover of Eastern Europe. You will need to balance this with reference to the general concerns many Americans had about possible communist subversion and the impact of the Cold War on the USA. At the end of your answer make a concluding assessment.*

**A Level Exam-Style Question Section A**

***Study Sources 5 and 6 before you answer this question.***

How far could the historian make use of Sources 5 and 6 together in an investigation into the anti-communist witch hunt in the USA between 1947 and 1953?

Explain your answer using the sources, the information given about them and your own knowledge of the historical context. (20 marks)

**Tip**

*The two sources reflect concern felt by many Americans about the threat of communist subversion after the Second World War. In your answer you will be expected to refer to the provenance of both sources. This should include who wrote it and who the intended audience was. Your answer should also deal directly with the idea of a 'witch hunt' against possible communists. In dealing with this aspect of the answer you should consider the style and tone of both sources.*

# TO WHAT EXTENT DID AMERICAN CULTURE CHANGE IN THE YEARS 1945–55?

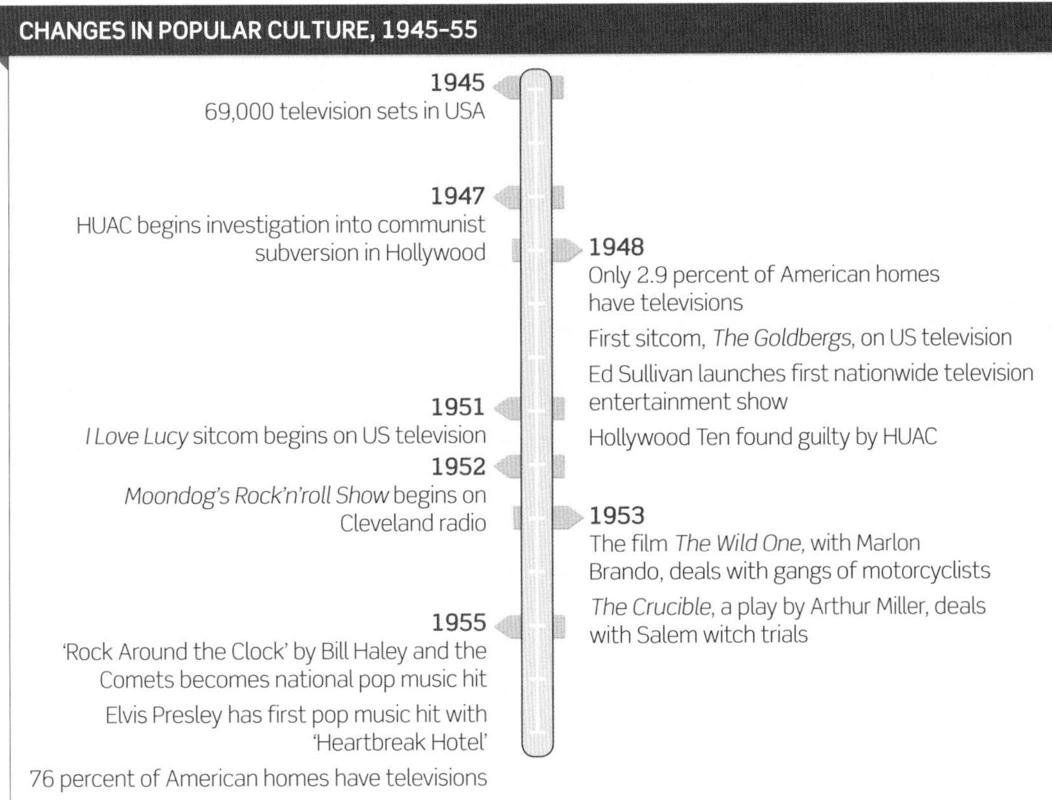


## Hollywood and the Cold War

During the Second World War, Hollywood had played its part in 'winning the war'. Films with a patriotic theme were produced to support the war effort. Hollywood directors like John Ford and William Wyler made films about the US Navy and Air Force.

During the Cold War, Hollywood was at the forefront of the confrontation with the USSR, off the screen as well as on. After 1945, Hollywood was affected by labour problems, leading to strikes, while the Hollywood branch of the Communist Party openly supported Soviet policy in Eastern Europe. In 1947, the House Un-American Activities Committee decided to investigate America's film industry. It was aided by the head of the Screen Actors' Guild, the B-movie actor Ronald Reagan, who would later be president from 1981 to 1989. The most dramatic part of the investigation involved a group of screenwriters known as the Hollywood Ten, who refused to co-operate with the HUAC.

## EXTEND YOUR KNOWLEDGE

### The Hollywood Ten

The ten individuals who defied the House Un-American Activities Committee ( HUAC) were Alvah Bessie, Herbert Biberman, Lester Cole, Edward Dmytryk, Ring Lardner Jr, John Howard Lawson, Albert Maltz, Samuel Ornitz, Robert Adrian Scott and Dalton Trumbo.

In November 1947, the Ten were charged with contempt of Congress. They had refused to co-operate with the committee and its investigation into communist activity in Hollywood and the US film industry. In April 1948, they were found guilty, forced to pay a $1,000 fine and given one year in prison. Eventually, in 1951, one of their number, Edward Dmytryk, decided to co-operate with HUAC and gave it the names of 20 Hollywood workers who he claimed were communists.

The investigation and conviction of the Hollywood Ten split Hollywood. Supporters of the Ten included many of the major film stars of the day, including Humphrey Bogart, Henry Fonda, Gene Kelly, Katharine Hepburn and Frank Sinatra. They formed the Committee for the First Amendment, the amendment that guaranteed freedom of speech. The Committee campaigned to defend the right of Americans to free speech. In particular, they disliked the HUAC tactic of expecting witnesses to name supposed communists and communist sympathisers. Others supported the purge of communists from the film industry. These included Walt Disney, Ronald Reagan, John Wayne and Gary Cooper.

Initially, the public tended to support Hollywood workers in the investigation. However, when many refused to answer questions about whether or not they had been or were members of the Communist Party, opinion began to change.

Of longer-lasting significance was a blacklist that was produced of Hollywood actors and writers who would not be employed in the film industry. The Motion Picture Association of America declared that it would blacklist anyone who it regarded as a communist. This meant they would dismiss them without compensation. This blacklist lasted until the 1960s and included several of Hollywood's most famous names, such as comic actor Charlie Chaplin, the black American Paul Robeson and the actor/director Orson Welles. These actors and entertainers were forced to work overseas. Many blacklisted writers continued to work under false names. Dalton Trumbo won an Oscar in 1953 for the screenplay for *Roman Holiday*, which he scripted under an assumed name.

Following the hearings and convictions, Hollywood tended to avoid controversial topics for its major films. In the early 1950s, films such as Gene Kelly's song-and-dance *An American in Paris* and circus film *The Greatest Show on Earth* won best picture Oscars. However, writer Arthur Miller produced a play in 1953 called *The Crucible*, about the Salem witch trials in 1692. This was a veiled attack on the activities of the HUAC. Miller co-operated with the HUAC investigation in respect of his own past but refused to name other supposed communists. As a result, he was not blacklisted.

The HUAC investigations had greatly affected Hollywood. It led to the end of many careers and ensured that, for over a decade, Hollywood would stay away from producing films that had a strong political message.

**SOURCE**

From the testimony of Ronald Reagan as President of the Screen Actors' Guild in front of the HUAC on communist influence in Hollywood, 1947. He is being questioned by Mr Stripling, a member of the HUAC investigation team.

*Mr. Stripling*: Mr. Reagan, what is your feeling about what steps should be taken to rid the motion-picture industry of any Communist influences?

*Mr. Reagan*: Well, sir, ninety-nine percent of us are pretty well aware of what is going on, and we have done a pretty good job in our business of keeping those people's activities curtailed. On that basis we have exposed their lies when we came across them, we have opposed their propaganda, and I can certainly testify that in the case of the Screen Actors' Guild we have been eminently successful in preventing them from their usual tactics in opposing those people.

Whether the Party should be outlawed, that is a matter for the Government to decide. However, if it is proven that an organization is an agent of a foreign power, or in any way not a legitimate political party - and I think the Government is capable of proving that - then that is another matter. I happen to be very proud of the industry in which I work; I happen to be very proud of the way in which we conducted the fight.

Interpretations (5c)

**Good questions/bad questions**

Below are summaries of the interests of three individuals at the height of anti-communist feeling in the USA in the late 1950s and early 1960s. They are generalisations for the purpose of this exercise.

| *Harper's Magazine* journalist | Joseph McCarthy | Ronald Reagan |
|---|---|---|
| Interested in ways federal employees could avoid being investigated as a possible security risk | Interested in highlighting the amount of possible communist subversion in the US State Department | Has views on communist influence in Hollywood and the role of the Screen Actors' Guild in dealing with it |
| (see Source 3) | (see Source 5) | (see Source 7) |

Working in groups:

1 Discuss what makes a good historical question and agree on three criteria.

2 Consider what you know about the issue of communist subversion in the USA after the Second World War, then each write a historical question based on that subject matter.

3 Put the questions in rank order, with the best question first, based on your criteria.

4 Using a piece of A3 paper write '*Harper's Magazine* journalist', 'Joseph McCarthy' and 'Ronald Reagan' at the points of a large triangle.

5 Write your questions in the triangle so that their positions reflect how likely it is that each person would be interested by that question. For example, a question about federal employees with communist sympathies might interest the *Harper's* journalist and Joseph McCarthy more than Ronald Reagan, so you would put this on the side of the triangle connecting the journalist and McCarthy.

6 Add some further questions. Try to think of questions that only one of the three would be interested in.

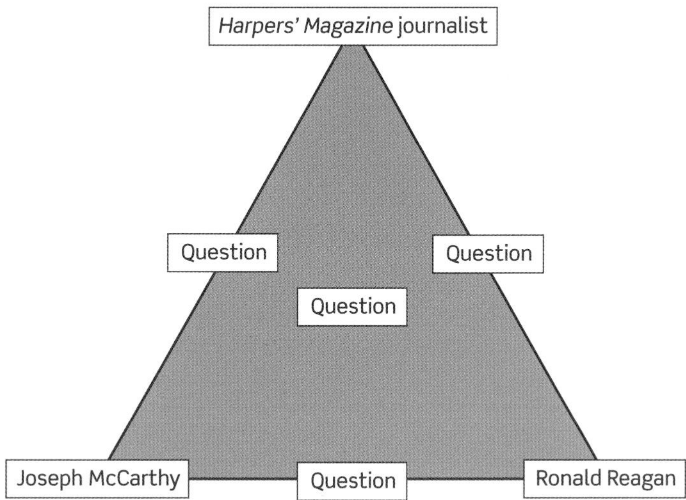


7 Take it in turns to try to answer the questions you have created from the point of view and in the style of one of the three people. See if the other members of the group can guess which it was.

8 Explain why each of the three people's particular interests and focus help create useful sources for the study of the past.

**AS Level Exam-Style Question Section A**

***Study Source 7 before you answer this question.***

How much weight do you give the evidence of Source 7 for an historical enquiry into the level of communist activity in Hollywood after the Second World War?

Explain your answer using the source, the information given about it and your own knowledge of the historical context. (12 marks)

**Tip**

*In your answer you should refer to the provenance of the source, in particular, the comments of Ronald Reagan, who was head of the Screen Actors' Guild and held an important position within Hollywood. Also consider the occasion of his statement – he was speaking in front of the House Un-American Activities Committee. This might provide you with a motive for what he said. You should also make reference to the content of his statement and the degree to which he offered his own opinion.*

## The growing power of television

A huge rise in television ownership transformed popular entertainment in the USA. In 1948, only 2.9 percent of households possessed a television. By 1955, this had risen to just over 76 percent. The Federal Communications Commission (FCC) gave commercial licences to six television stations in 1946. This rose to 442 by 1956.

Television brought high-quality entertainment and news programmes into the most humble of homes in both rural and urban areas. For the first time, people on low incomes could experience shows, sports and popular entertainment that had been the preserve of the middle class and the rich. A survey in 1950 showed that junior high school students (9- to 13-year-olds) with a television in their home watched an average of 27 hours per week. As a result, any publication associated with television sold well: by 1960, the *TV Guide* outsold all other magazines. Television also led to a change in eating habits. In 1954, the first 'TV dinner' was marketed. People did not have to leave their sofas as they could watch and eat at the same time. It also transformed the advertising industry, which was not slow to see the potential of television advertising. By 1955, it had become one of the main media for the industry. It also had a major impact on other forms of entertainment: average weekly attendance at movies fell from 90 million in 1946 to 47 million in 1956.

## Popular entertainment and sitcoms

Television allowed millions to see top-level sporting events for the first time. In 1947, this included Major League Baseball's premier event, the World Series. This was a series of baseball games between the two best baseball teams in the USA. In 1955, the World Series was shown for the first time in colour on NBC. By then, US television was dominated by three national networks: the American Broadcasting Corporation (ABC), the National Broadcasting Corporation (NBC) and Columbia Broadcasting Systems (CBS). These networks were responsible for programming that included sitcoms and news bulletins as well as sporting occasions.

Some of the most popular television shows in the late 1940s transferred from radio. Programmes such as the *Jack Benny Show* first appeared on radio and then became a popular television show. In 1948, a situation comedy (sitcom) series, *The Goldbergs,* told the story of a Jewish working-class family living in a Bronx **tenement** in New York City.

### KEY TERM

**Tenement**
A block of flats (apartments) usually of poor standard in low-income areas of inner cities. One of the worst areas for tenements in New York City was the Bronx, a borough north of Manhattan Island. All major US cities had tenement areas.

However, with the growth of suburbia and rise in living standards, other shows came along to replace it. *Father Knows Best* first appeared in 1953. It focused on life in a new suburb, 'Springfield', and the Anderson family, who lived in a large house. Its main star, Robert Young, had appeared in Hollywood films. As Jim Anderson, he was portrayed as the typical middle-class father. The show made no reference to politics and Jim did not have any strongly held views and never had a bad day at the office. His wife was played by Jane Wyatt, who kept perfect order in her home, kept her opinions to herself and was a supportive wife to Jim.

The most popular sitcom of the 1950s had a female star. *I Love Lucy* focused on the home life of Lucille Ball, loyal wife of her musician husband in the show and real life, Desi Arnaz. It ran from 1951 to 1957. When Lucy had a baby in the series, almost 70 percent of the nation's television sets were tuned in to watch.

Game shows also proved popular. *You Bet Your Life*, with comedian Groucho Marx, mixed winning money with Groucho's ability as a comedian. It began on radio and transferred to television in 1950. The most popular game show was *The $64,000 Question*, which began in June 1955. Sponsored by cosmetic firm Revlon, it placed contestants in isolation booths to answer demanding questions. An early star contestant was Charles van Doren, who seemed to be a genius until it was discovered that he was given the questions before the show!

## Stereotyping of women and ethnic minorities

Women like Mrs Anderson in *Father Knows Best* and Lucille Ball in *I Love Lucy* were housewives who were always loyal, subordinate partners to their middle-class husbands. Only the feisty Molly Goldberg, in the late 1940s sitcom *The Goldbergs*, was outspoken. Ethnic minorities were almost always portrayed in servile roles such as domestic servants. A popular comedy series, *The Jack Benny Show*, which ran from 1950 to 1965, starred Jack Benny, who always appeared with his black American servant and chauffeur, Rochester. It would take until 1965 before a black American received a starring role in a popular television series. That was *I Spy* with Bill Cosby.

Some television shows did provide high-quality debate, however. Edward Murrow's *See It Now* (1951–58) looked at serious issues, such as the McCarthy anti-communist crusade in 1953. McCarthy's record was analysed and it was the beginning of the end of McCarthyism. Nevertheless, television was criticised for offering 'low-brow' programmes and contributing to low scores for students who, many believed, spent too much time watching it rather than doing schoolwork.

SOURCE

A scene from *I Love Lucy*, one of the most popular sitcoms, and the only one with a female star. The episode first aired on 26 October 1952. Lucille Ball is on the left and her real-life and on-screen husband, Desi Arnaz, is on the right.

EXTRACT

From *Blacks and White Television* by J. Fred MacDonald, a study of African Americans in television since 1948, published in 2009. MacDonald assesses the importance of *The Ed Sullivan Show*, a major national entertainment show, in bringing black Americans onto US national television in the late 1940s and early 1950s.

From the inception in 1948 of his *Toast of the Town* (later called *The Ed Sullivan Show*), Sullivan liberally seasoned his Sunday evening variety program with African-American celebrities. Despite periodic letters of criticism from prejudiced viewers and anxious advertisers, Sullivan persisted in welcoming entertainers as diverse as singers Sarah Vaughan, Ella Fitzgerald, Harry Belafonte, and The Fisk Jubilee Singers; comedian Dewey "Pigmeat" Markham; rhythm and blues performers Billy Ward and the Dominoes; operatic soprano Marian Anderson; dancers Peg Leg Bates, Bunny Briggs, and the Will Mastin Trio with Sammy Davis, Jr.; and Dr. Ralph Bunche, United Nations Commissioner and recipient in 1950 of the Nobel Peace Prize for his role in settling the Arab-Israeli war. Even former heavyweight boxing champion Joe Louis appeared on *Toast of the Town* in an unsuccessful venture as a song-and-dance entertainer.

Sullivan felt that by bringing black personalities directly into the homes of Americans, TV would undermine racism. He believed that white adults and children, seeing and appreciating black talent, would be forced to reassess racist stereotyping and their own prejudices. Sullivan was particularly sensitive to the impact such images would have upon children, for it was they, he suggested, "who will finally lay Jim Crow to rest."

## Origins of teenage culture

The idea of rebellious youth had been associated with the 1920s when the 'flapper', new dances and music were frowned on by many adults. However, the 1950s saw the true rise of the teenager. Not only were young people in their teens rebellious, they now had the financial power to buy, thanks to the post-war economic boom. They were also given more independence by their parents, who wanted to offer them something different from the harsh economic conditions of the Depression years and the strict regimentation of life during the Second World War, which they had grown up with. Teenagers benefited from the availability of cars and the development of fast food. Business saw opportunities and developed teenage fashion. Most of all, teenage culture was associated with a new form of popular music known as rock'n'roll.

Television programming and films helped develop the idea of the new social group in society. Teenagers were often portrayed as 'juvenile delinquents', disrespectful of adults and society in general. The media claimed gangs of youths roamed inner cities, engaging in violence. The 1953 film *The Wild One*, starring Marlon Brando, captured the mood. Brando led a motorcycle gang that intimidated small communities. *Rebel without a Cause*, first shown in 1955, starred one of the 1950s most popular film stars, James Dean, and dealt with teenage alienation. Youths cruising in their cars or riding in motorcycle gangs, wearing leather jackets, using their own slang and greasing their hair, shocked many adults. At the time, there were attempts to explain these new developments. Margaret Mead, in *The School in American Culture*, published in 1951, claimed that growing disrespect for teachers was due to the rapid change in US society, where many young people began to regard formal education as irrelevant.

The USA was also shocked by the findings of Alfred Kinsey and his team at the Institute of Sexual Research at Indiana University. He published *Sexual Behaviour in the Human Male* in 1948 and *Sexual Behaviour in the Human Female* in 1953. Kinsey's findings claimed that 95 percent of males had been sexually active by the age of 15 years. Similar findings were made about the sexual behaviour of American females. Kinsey's work fuelled the idea that the current generation of teenagers was very different from previous generations who, allegedly, respected their parents and conformed with adult society.

In 1954, Fredric Wertham published *Seduction of the Innocent*, claiming that comic books helped corrupt the young. By 1955, 13 states had passed laws regulating the content and places of sale of comic books to prevent overt references to sex and immoral behaviour. Also in 1955, the national magazine *Time* produced a special edition called 'Teenagers on the Rampage'. This reinforced the belief among many parents that teenage culture in the early 1950s was rebellious and unlike their own teenage years.

**SOURCE**

From a letter written by a parent in the early 1950s to Dr Frederic Wertham, a psychiatrist, who was a critic of comic books. It revealed the concerns of many middle-class parents about teenage culture at that time.

> Dear Dr Wertham,
>
> We have two boys, 7 and 13, with unusually high intelligence and excellent ability in school and sports. They have a library of fine books of their own, and read library books almost daily, yet in the presence of comic books they have appeared as if drugged, and will not lift their eyes or speak when spoken to. What we would like to know is, what can be done about it before it is too late? My boys fight with each other in a manner that is unbelievable in a home where both parents are university graduates and perfectly matched. We attribute the so-called 'hatred' that they profess for each other as harmful influence of these books plus movies and radio.
>
> We consider the situation to be as serious as the invasion of the enemy in war time, with as far-reaching consequences as the atom bomb. If we cannot stop the wicked men who are poisoning our children's minds what chance is there for mankind to survive longer than one generation, or half of one?

### The birth of rock'n'roll

The art form most closely associated with this distinct teenage culture was popular music. Rock and roll epitomised the new teenage culture. It stood in marked contrast to the music popular with adults during the Second World War, which usually involved ballads sung by male artists, such as Frank Sinatra. With financial independence, teenagers could buy records or listen to new records on jukeboxes, which started appearing in cafes and fast food outlets.

The origins of rock'n'roll were in black American music from the Old South associated with the Great Migration to northern cities. Transferred to the north, southern Blues produced a new, distinct sound. The first time it received media attention was in 1952, on a new programme on radio station WXEL in Cleveland, Ohio, called *Moondog's Rock'n'roll Party*. Alan Freed, who coined the phrase 'rock'n'roll', played music by black American artists. It was so popular that the show moved to New York City, to radio station WINS, in 1954, and helped make rock and roll a national craze. The first successful record in this style, recorded by black American Big Joe Turner in Kansas City, Missouri in 1954, was called 'Shake Rattle and Roll'. In the same year, another black American, Chuck Berry, produced 'Johnny B. Goode'.

Even though its origins were in black American culture, rock'n'roll music only took off when performed by white artists. This reflected the degree of racial discrimination against black American entertainers at the time. In 1955, Bill Haley and the Comets performed 'Rock Around the Clock', which appeared in *The Blackboard Jungle*, a film about teenage rebellion at a high school, released in 1955. 'Rock Around the Clock' became a nationwide success. The artist who really gave rock'n'roll national appeal was a southern white from Tupelo, Mississippi – Elvis Presley. His sexy dance moves, good looks and powerful voice propelled Elvis to national fame. In 1955, he had his first number one hit song, 'Heartbreak Hotel', with RCA. Rock'n'roll had found its first national teenage idol.

**ACTIVITY**
**KNOWLEDGE CHECK**

**Cultural change**

1. Identify ways in which Hollywood and the US film industry were affected by the Cold War.
2. Why do you think television became such a popular form of entertainment in the period 1945-55?
3. Write down the ways women and ethnic minorities were portrayed in US television in the years 1945-55.
4. What does Source 9 tell us about the feelings of many middle-class parents towards changes in culture in the USA after 1945?

**AS Level Exam-Style Question Section B**

How accurate is it to say that television was a major influence on US society in the years 1945 to 1955? (20 marks)

**Tip**

*You will be expected to provide a balanced answer in which you should produce evidence to support the view that television was a major influence in US society. You should also produce evidence to support the view that the influence of television changed over time. You could, for example, mention that the number of televisions available in the USA increased over this period, so its influence varied.*

**A Level Exam-Style Question Section B**

How far did the USA experience a revolution in popular culture in the years 1945 to 1955? (20 marks)

**Tip**

*You will be expected to provide a balanced answer in which you define and explain how far a revolution had taken place in popular culture. You will also be expected to explain what is meant by 'popular culture', which needs to include film, television and popular music. You may decide that a revolution may have occurred in one area of popular culture and not in others. Whatever you decide, you need to provide evidence to support your case.*

## HOW FAR DID THE CIVIL RIGHTS OF MINORITIES IMPROVE IN THE PERIOD 1945-55?

In 1945, the position of black Americans had seen an improvement since the outbreak of the Second World War. Their share in defence-related employment rose from three to eight percent. The Tuskegee airmen had achieved national recognition for their role in the 15th Air Force. Almost half a million black Americans had joined the National Association for the Advancement of Colored People (NAACP). In 1944, black American Adam Clayton Powell was elected to the House of Representatives.

However, when the war came to an end, black Americans suffered disproportionately. Like women in traditionally male workplaces, workers from ethnic minorities were usually the first to lose their jobs as wartime production moved over to a peacetime economy and demobilised servicemen returned to their old jobs.

Returning black servicemen were attacked because racist whites feared their combat experience might make them less accepting of their inferior status. There were 56 attacks between June 1945 and September 1946 across the USA. The National Emergency Committee against Mob Violence, which included NAACP leader Walter White, urged President Truman to take action to end racial abuse in September 1946. The National Emergency Committee against Mob Violence issued its final report, *To Secure these Rights*, in October 1947. It suggested greater racial equality, including equality in federal employment.

## Desegregation of the armed forces, 1948

At the start of his presidency, Harry S. Truman looked as if he would not be interested in the issue of civil rights. He had been chosen as Franklin D. Roosevelt's (FDR's) running mate as vice president because he was from a former slave state and it was believed this would make FDR more attractive to southern white voters. When he became president in April 1945, after Roosevelt died in office, Truman at first did little to aid black Americans openly. He refused to allow the Fair Employment Practices Commission (FEPC) to order Washington DC's transit system to hire black workers and black American lawyer Charles Houston resigned from the FEPC in disgust.

However, in July 1948 President Truman issued Executive Order 9981, which brought to an end the segregation of the US armed forces. Ever since black Americans had been allowed to join the armed forces, they had faced worse pay and conditions than whites and usually had white officers. The timing of the decision seemed to have a lot to do with the presidential election of that year. The Democratic Party was facing a serious challenge from the Republican Thomas Dewey. It was also splitting up. Henry Wallace, a left-wing Democrat, was standing for the presidency as a Progressive. He wanted more social reform and greater federal support for welfare programmes. Strom Thormond of South Carolina was standing as a Dixiecrat, a southern white Democrat in favour of legal segregation of the races. He was totally opposed to any improvement in black American civil rights. Executive Order 9981 was seen by some as a cynical attempt to get black American votes. In the 1948 election, Truman received two-thirds of the black American vote.

### EXTEND YOUR KNOWLEDGE

**President Harry S. Truman (1884–1972)**

Harry S. Truman was from the state of Missouri and was a US Senator from 1934 to 1944. He rose to national prominence in the Second World War because of his role as Chairman of the Senate Committee on Military Affairs, which investigated abuses in government military contracts.

He became president on the death of FDR in April 1945. As president, he authorised the dropping of the atomic bomb on Japan in August 1945, and was the first Cold War president. In 1947, he proclaimed the Truman Doctrine, which openly opposed the growth of communism in the world.

He won re-election as president in 1948 and sent US troops to the Korean War.

### KEY TERM

**Poll tax**

A tax introduced by some states in which those who wished to vote had to pay. Poor people, usually black Americans, could not always afford the tax and so were unable to vote. The tax was declared unconstitutional in 1964.

In fact, the desegregation of the armed forces was the culmination of a number of attempts by Truman to improve civil rights. The report *To Secure these Rights*, commissioned by the Truman administration in October 1947, advocated a bold approach. It allowed civil rights groups, including the NAACP, to put forward their views. It called for a permanent civil rights division of the Justice Department, the creation of a Commission on Civil Rights, anti-lynching laws, the abolition of the **poll tax,** enactment of a permanent FEPC, self-government for the District of Columbia (which was previously ruled directly by the federal government), and desegregation of the armed forces. In Executive Order 9980, Truman created the Fair Employment Board to ensure equal treatment in hiring for federal jobs. This had a significant impact on job opportunities for black Americans.

On 2 February 1948, six months before desegregating the armed forces, Truman, without conferring with congressional leaders, sent a civil rights message to Congress, in which he called for both a federal law against lynching and desegregation of the armed forces.

By the end of his presidency, Truman had made clear attempts to advance the cause of black American civil rights. The Korean War (1950–53) was the first conflict where black and whites fought together and, by 1952, the army, air force and navy were all integrated. Yet it was only a partial success, as Executive Order 9981 did not apply to the National Guard or to reserve forces. These important military groups remained segregated because of opposition from state governments.

SOURCE

EXECUTIVE ORDER 9981 by President Harry S. Truman, July 1948. The order desegregated the US armed forces.

Establishing the President's Committee on Equality of Treatment and Opportunity In the Armed Forces.

WHEREAS it is essential that there be maintained in the armed services of the United States the highest standards of democracy, with equality of treatment and opportunity for all those who serve in our country's defense:

NOW THEREFORE, by virtue of the authority vested in me as President of the United States, by the Constitution and the statutes of the United States, and as Commander in Chief of the armed services, it is hereby ordered as follows:

1. It is hereby declared to be the policy of the President that there shall be equality of treatment and opportunity for all persons in the armed services without regard to race, color, religion or national origin. This policy shall be put into effect as rapidly as possible, having due regard to the time required to effectuate any necessary changes without impairing efficiency or morale.

2. There shall be created in the National Military Establishment an advisory committee to be known as the President's Committee on Equality of Treatment and Opportunity in the Armed Services, which shall be composed of seven members to be designated by the President.

3. The Committee is authorized on behalf of the President to examine into the rules, procedures and practices of the Armed Services in order to determine in what respect such rules, procedures and practices may be altered or improved with a view to carrying out the policy of this order. The Committee shall confer and advise the Secretary of Defense, the Secretary of the Army, the Secretary of the Navy, and the Secretary of the Air Force, and shall make such recommendations to the President and to said Secretaries as in the judgment of the Committee will effectuate the policy hereof.

Harry Truman

The White House

July 26, 1948

## Integration in professional sports and popular entertainment

Black Americans had been prominent in professional sport before 1945, but this was due to their superior talent rather than an aspect of racial equality. In the 1930s and 1940s, the World Heavyweight champion, Joe Louis, known as the Brown Bomber, won more titles than any other World Heavyweight in defence of his title. Sugar Ray Robinson dominated middleweight boxing in the 1950s. In the 1936 Olympics, Jesse Owens won the 100 metres and long jump. Hitler famously left the stadium in disgust. And, when Owens returned in triumph to the USA, President Roosevelt refused to welcome him at the White House.

In 1947, a racial breakthrough did take place in Major League Baseball (MLB). The Brooklyn Dodgers signed Jackie Robinson as the first-ever black professional at the top level. He faced considerable prejudice, but fought through it to become one of the all-time baseball greats. When he retired, his number, 42, was withdrawn by all MLB teams in his honour. However, the majority of black Americans still faced racial segregation in most sports, where they faced difficulty in acquiring jobs, particularly in coaching and getting the same pay and conditions as whites. Many black American sportsmen also faced verbal abuse from white spectators.

In popular entertainment, black Americans tended to get supporting roles in menial positions in Hollywood films. The first black American to win an Oscar was Hattie McDaniel, who played a domestic servant in the film *Gone with the Wind* in 1939. In music, Nat King Cole became a popular ballad singer but found it difficult to tour in the Old South. Rock'n'roll gave black American singers a real chance to get national recognition. Chuck Berry and Little Richard eventually became national stars.

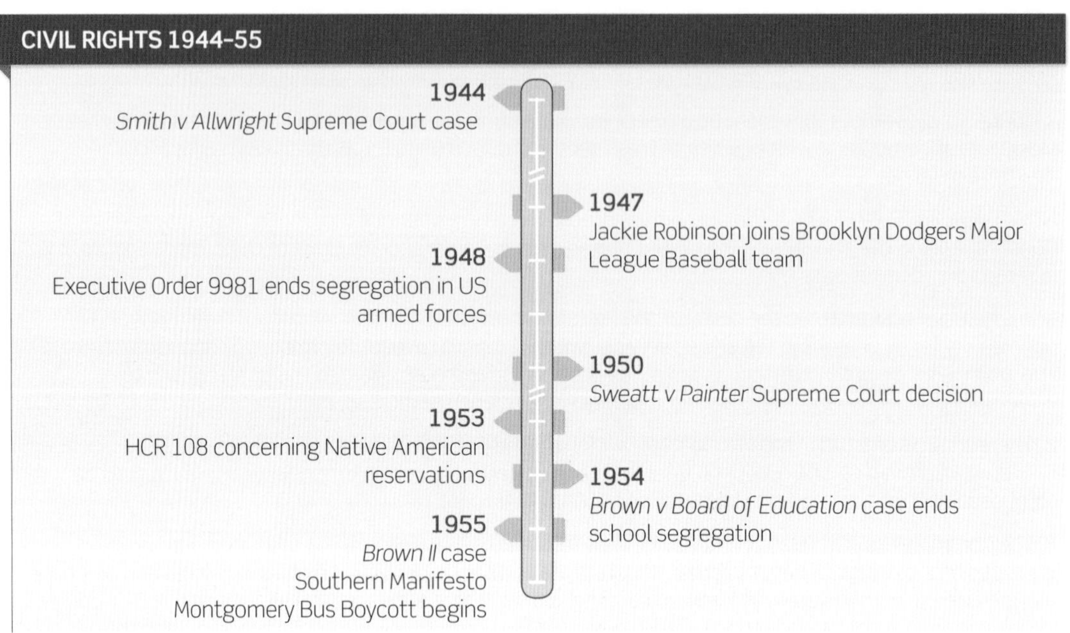


## The growth of the NAACP

The National Association for the Advancement of Colored People had been founded in 1909 by black Americans and white liberals. Its aim was to gain full civil rights for black Americans through legal means, mainly through using the US court system. The leading black American in its leadership was W. E. B. Dubois. He edited the NAACP magazine, *The Crisis*, from 1909 to 1934. An early victory for the NAACP came in 1930, when NAACP lobbying prevented President Hoover appointing arch-segregationist John Parker of North Carolina to the US Supreme Court. The NAACP's membership grew rapidly during the Second World War, from 50,000 to 450,000. Although originally a rather elite organisation of northern liberals, many of the new members were black Americans from the segregated South.

While the NAACP received national notoriety through the publication of *The Crisis* and its actions in court cases, it also worked at a grass-roots level. Charles H. Houston, one of the NAACP's leading figures during the Depression years of the 1930s, supported the idea of organising southern blacks who faced the greatest discrimination. Southern branches of the NAACP were established or reformed, and many blacks in trade unions joined the organisation. In its southern strategy, the NAACP supported activities such as voter registration and campaigned for the abolition of the poll tax. In 1941, the NAACP joined with other organisations, such as the trade union bodies the American Federation of Labor, Congress of Industrial Organizations and the National Negro Congress, to co-sponsor the National Committee to abolish the poll tax.

After 1945, the NAACP worked closely with other civil rights groups, such as the CIO's Political Action Committee, to fight for black American rights. The NAACP made representations to the President's Committee on Civil Rights and the committee's report, in October 1947, *To Secure These Rights*, owed a lot to NAACP evidence.

## The Brown case of 1954 and the end of school segregation

The greatest achievement of the NAACP in legal cases came on 17 May 1954. The US Supreme Court, in a unanimous decision (9–0), declared school segregation unconstitutional. The court ruled that it contravened the 14th Amendment of the US Constitution, passed in 1868 after the Civil War, which guaranteed US citizens equal protection of the law. Legal segregation had been introduced after the Civil War in many southern states. In 1896, black Americans challenged segregation in the US Supreme Court case, *Plessy v Ferguson*. The US Supreme Court, however, upheld legal segregation, proclaiming 'separate but equal' facilities were legal. In the years after 1896, black Americans got separate facilities, but they were far from equal. In particular, black American schools had less funding and offered a poorer level of education.

**SOURCE 11** The NAACP legal team outside the US Supreme Court on 17 May 1954 after the *Brown* decision. Thurgood Marshall is in the middle, flanked by E. C. Hayes on the left and James Nabrit Jr on the right. The case to end legal racial segregation in public schools was led by black Americans. The main lawyer defending the separate but equal position was white. His name was John Davis and he had been the Democratic candidate for the presidency in 1924.

The NAACP brought a number of cases against segregated education to the Court. *Brown v the Board of Education of Topeka, Kansas* was alphabetically the first. However, it also had greater significance. Kansas was outside the Old South – it was not a former Confederate state and had been against slavery in the Civil War. Racial segregation in Kansas public schools was therefore particularly significant. The NAACP legal team, led by Thurgood Marshall, argued that there was psychological as well as educational discrimination involved in having separate schools for blacks and whites.

Already, in 1950, in the case *Sweatt v Painter,* the US Supreme Court had demanded an upgrade of the black American Prairie View University, Texas, because it argued its educational facilities were inferior, so a recent precedent had been set. In its ruling on *Brown v the Board of Education*, the Supreme Court declared all racially segregated school systems were unequal. The US Supreme Court believed segregation bred a feeling of inferiority in black American children.

The key factor in the change in the US Supreme Court's view on legal segregation was the appointment, by President Eisenhower, of a new Chief Justice, Earl Warren, in 1953. Warren would lead the Court in a period of judicial activism, where it played a key role in improving minority rights. Although the US Supreme Court made the decision in the *Brown* case, it was up to the president, government, Congress and the states to implement that decision. It proved to be very controversial. White-dominated state governments in the Old South showed extreme reluctance in implementing the decision. Southern white Congressmen were opposed to racial desegregation and used their power to thwart implementation, and the president feared losing white electoral support if he forced desegregation on the Old South.

The *Brown* decision was regarded as a great triumph for the NAACP and black American civil rights. If separate but equal facilities were unconstitutional in education, then other forms of legal segregation could be challenged. Thurgood Marshall later became the US Supreme Court's first black American justice in the 1960s.

SOURCE

From 'The Atlanta Declaration', 19 May 1954, by the NAACP, made two days after the *Brown* judgement of the US Supreme Court.

All Americans are now relieved to have the laws of the land declare in the clearest language 'in the field of public education the doctrine of "separate but equal" has no place. Separate educational facilities are inherently unequal.' Segregation in public education is now not only unlawful it is un-American. True Americans are grateful for this decision. Now that the law is made clear, we look to the future. Having canvassed the situation in each of our states we approach the future with utmost confidence.

We stand ready to work with other law-abiding citizens who are anxious to translate this decision into a program of action to eradicate racial segregation in public education as speedily as possible.

We look upon this memorable decision not as a victory for Negroes alone, but for the whole American people and as a vindication of America's leadership of the free world.

### AS Level Exam-Style Question Section A

***Study Source 12 before you answer this question.***

How much weight do you give the evidence of Source 12 for an enquiry into the improvement in minority rights in the USA in the years 1945 to 1955?

Explain your answer using the source, the information given about it and your own knowledge of the historical context. (12 marks)

**Tip**

*It is important to study the provenance of the source to assess its value and weight as evidence. You need to consider who wrote the source, when it was written and the intended audience of the source. To support your answer you should use information from the content of the source to support your answer. You may wish to refer to the factual content and tone of the source.*

## Civil rights: the extent of change by 1955

By 1955, the modern civil rights movement had begun. In 1948, the desegregation of the armed forces by President Truman was an important step towards racial equality. The *Brown v Board of Education* decision by the US Supreme Court in 1954 was the breakthrough case that would ultimately lead to the dismantling of legal segregation within the USA. In 1955, the *Brown II* Supreme Court case declared that school desegregation should take place with all deliberate speed.

However, the degree of change was very limited. By 1955, virtually all the segregated public schools were still segregated. So were a variety of other public facilities such as public toilets, park benches, drinking fountains, and public transportation. Although some important changes to the law at federal level had been made, in the Old South black Americans still lived second-class lives in a legally segregated society. Outside the Old South, black Americans still faced considerable racial discrimination in housing and employment. The beginnings of change had taken place but black Americans were far from civil, political and social equality.

Opposition to the end of legal segregation proved to be a major obstacle to change. In 1955, 100 congressmen signed 'The Southern Manifesto', which declared that the *Brown* case was a clear abuse of judicial power. Across the South, White Citizens Councils were created to defend legal segregation. Even by the end of 1956, not one school in the Deep South was integrated.

### Rosa Parks and the Montgomery Bus Boycott

In March 1955, in Montgomery, the state capital of Alabama, black American Mrs Rosa Parks boarded a public bus. Montgomery operated a system where the front rows of seats were always reserved for whites. Rosa Parks refused to give up her seat near the front of the bus and was arrested. This sparked the Montgomery Bus Boycott of 1955 to 1956, in which black Americans refused to use public transport until it was desegregated. Eventually, in December 1956, the US Supreme Court declared segregated public transport unconstitutional. The boycott was also important in other ways. Most notably it saw the rise to prominence of a local black American religious minister, Dr Martin Luther King. He was to be a central figure in the civil rights movement until his assassination in 1968.

SOURCE

From the resolution of a mass meeting of black American citizens held at Holt Baptist Church, Montgomery, Alabama on 5 December 1955 on the Montgomery Bus Boycott. The resolution set out what the Montgomery Improvement Association (MIA) wanted to achieve. The MIA was the organisation that ran the boycott with local Baptist minister Martin Luther King as the leader of the boycott.

Be resolved as follows:-

That the citizens of Montgomery are requesting that every citizen in Montgomery, regardless of race, color or creed, to refrain from riding buses owned and operated in the city of Montgomery by the Montgomery City Lines, Incorporated until some arrangement has been worked out between said citizens and Montgomery Bus Lines, Incorporated.

That every person owning or who has access to automobiles use their automobiles in assisting other persons to get to work without charge.

That the employers of persons whose employees live a distance from them, as much as possible afford transportation to your own employees.

That the Negro citizens of Montgomery are ready and willing to send a delegation of citizens to the Montgomery Bus Lines, Incorporated to discuss their grievances and to work out a solution at the same time.

### The Congress of Racial Equality

The NAACP was not the only organisation campaigning for civil rights. In 1942, in Chicago, black American James Farmer created the Congress of Racial Equality. It was a multiracial organisation that advocated non-violent campaigning to achieve full racial equality. It took its inspiration from Indian nationalist leader, Mahatma Gandhi. It was ultimately to play an important role in the 1960s civil rights campaigns.

## Residual discrimination

Even though black Americans did see an improvement in their civil rights, they still suffered discrimination in housing and employment. In the north, black Americans lived in black ghettos such as Harlem, New York City and the south side of Chicago. Many lived below the **poverty line**. In the Old South, many blacks were disenfranchised. The poll tax meant that poor blacks (and whites) were prevented from voting. Also, intimidation by white supremacist groups such as the Ku Klux Klan helped maintain black Americans' second-class status.

**KEY TERM**

**Poverty line**
A measurement of the income needed to maintain a certain standard of living.

Hispanic Americans made very limited headway in gaining extra rights. Many Mexican Americans had been deported during the Second World War. After 1945, agricultural improvements led to the addition of an extra 7.5 million acres of land in the south-west. Many Mexican American migrants were attracted to seasonal agricultural work there. However, the Eisenhower administration, from 1953, shipped more than three million illegal migrants back across the border. Of those who stayed, almost one-third lived below the poverty line.

After the war, Hispanics from Puerto Rico, an American-owned Caribbean island, began to come to the USA in large numbers. Many ended up in ghettos like east Harlem, New York City and were regarded as second-class citizens by white American citizens.

The position of Native Americans was mixed. In 1944, the National Congress of American Indians (NCAI) was created, which, for the first time, included all Native American tribes. It attempted to emulate the NAACP in getting legal redress for their problems. In 1953, Congress, pressured by timber and mining interests, passed House Concurrent Resolution (HCR) 108, which ended Native American status as wards of the USA and called for the end of the reservation system. It transferred more than 500,000 acres of Native American land to non-Indians. The Federal Voluntary Relocation Program attempted to remove Native Americans from their reservations with aid for moving costs and assistance in finding jobs and housing.

In 1955, the USA was on the cusp of a great awakening by minorities into an organised campaign for equality. They were aided by an activist US Supreme Court, but faced resistance from whites in the Old South, politicians in Congress and state governments in the South that did not want change.

### AS Level Exam-Style Question Section B

To what extent did black Americans achieve greater equality in the USA between 1945 and 1955? (20 marks)

**Tip**

*Your answer should provide a balanced view of the issue of greater equality for black Americans. On one side of the argument you may wish to discuss the desegregation of the armed forces and the Brown case of 1954 as examples of greater equality. On the other hand, by 1955, the vast majority of black Americans still faced discrimination through legal and informal segregation of facilities.*

### A Level Exam-Style Question Section A

***Study Sources 12 and 13 before you answer this question.***

How far could the historian make use of Sources 12 and 13 together to investigate how black Americans helped to achieve improvement in their civil rights in the 1950s?

Explain your answer using the sources, the information about them and your knowledge of the historical context. (20 marks)

**Tip**

*The sources deal with two important issues in the early civil rights movement: the Brown case and the Montgomery Bus Boycott. You will need to mention why together these were important developments. In assessing the value of the sources you will be expected to comment on who wrote them, when they were written and the intended audience. Your answer should also be supported with reference to relevant information extracted from both sources.*

ACTIVITY
KNOWLEDGE CHECK

**The changing status of minorities**

1 In what ways did the federal government aid the improvement of civil rights for ethnic minorities in the USA in the years 1945–55? Focus in particular on the role of the president and the US Supreme Court.

2 How far did the position of ethnic minorities improve in professional sports between 1945 and 1955?

3 In what ways did the NAACP aid the development of black American civil rights in the years 1945–55?

4 How far did the position of ethnic minorities such as black Americans improve in the years 1945–55?

Cause and consequence (5b)

**Causation relativity**

Historical events usually have many causes. Some are crucial, while some are less important. For some historical questions, it is important to understand exactly what role certain factors played in causing historical change.

These are some of the significant factors in the timing and nature of the Civil Rights Movement:

| | | |
|---|---|---|
| In the southern states of the USA black Americans faced legal segregation. | The Declaration of Independence and US Constitution declared that US citizens were equal and deserved equal protection of the law. | The Double 'V' Campaign in the Second World War demanded freedom at home and overseas and received widespread support from black Americans. |
| In 1948, President Truman desegregated the US armed forces. | The US Supreme Court declared segregated public schools unconstitutional in the *Brown v Board of Education* case of 1954. | The Montgomery Bus Boycott of 1955–56 was a major event in the Civil Rights movement. Its success led to the rise of Martin Luther King. |

Answer the following questions on your own:

1 How important was the Supreme Court Brown decision in explaining the timing of the rise of the Civil Rights Movement?

2 In what ways was the decision to desegregate the armed forces due to the role of black Americans in the armed forces during the Second World War? To what extent did this precipitate the growth of a civil rights movement?

3 How could President Eisenhower have delayed the growth and development of the civil rights movement?

4 How far did the Declaration of Independence and the civil rights guaranteed under the US Constitution to all US citizens change the attitudes of the people who became involved in the civil rights movement?

5 What role did the above factors play in the way that the civil rights movement aimed to gain equality and justice for black Americans?

6 Would the nature of the civil rights movement have been the same if the US Supreme Court had not made the *Brown v Board of Education* decision of 1954?

7 What roles did each of the above causal factors play in determining the nature and timing of the development of the civil rights movement? Write them out in order of importance.

ACTIVITY
SUMMARY

**The USA transformed?**

1. Using the information in this chapter, write down ways in which you think the US economy experienced radical change in the years 1945 to 1955.
2. Identify ways in which the USA faced the problem of communist subversion in the years 1945-55. What do you regard as the most serious example of communist activity in the USA in this period?
3. What do you regard as the most important change in US society in the years 1945 to 1955 - cultural change or the changing status of minorities? Explain your answer.
4. In what ways did popular culture and sport change in the period 1945-55?
5. Do you think the position and status of ethnic minorities improved in the years 1945-55? Give examples to support your view.

ACTIVITY
WRITING

1. Analyse Source 10, an extract from Executive Order 9981 issued by President Truman in July 1948. The order desegregated the US armed forces.
   a) Identify any words or phrases you do not understand and research their meanings.
   b) Identify words and phrases that show that this is an official government document.
   c) Write a short paragraph explaining how the Executive Order planned to bring about the desegregation of the US armed forces, using quotes from the source to back up your points.
2. Use the words below to complete the sentences so that they best describe the changing status of minorities in the USA in the years 1945-55.

| desegregated | US Supreme Court | boycott | equality |
|---|---|---|---|
| latent | discrimination | dependent | thwarted |

In 1948, through Executive Order 9981 President Truman .............. the US armed forces, which was regarded as an important step towards greater .............. for black Americans. However, even with this reform, black Americans faced racial .............. in a wide variety of areas, such as professional sports, public schools and public transportation.

In bringing about change in the public schools system, the NAACP brought a case before the .............. In the *Brown* case of 1954 separate public schools for blacks and whites were declared unconstitutional. However, the implementation of the *Brown* case decision was .............. by action by state governments. The *Brown* case also brought about the prospect of .............. opposition by southern state governments, which were dominated by whites. Black Americans in Montgomery also tried the tactic of a .............. to achieve their aims.

**WIDER READING**

Diggins, J. P. *The Proud Decades, America in War and Peace, 1941 to 1960*, W. W. Norton Inc. (1989)

Murphy, D. *United States 1776 to 1992, Flagship History*, Collins Educational (2001)

Murphy, D. *United States 1917 to 2008, Flagship History*, Collins Educational (2008)

# Preparing for your AS Level Paper 2 exam

## Advance planning

1. Draw up a timetable for your revision and try to keep to it. Spread your timetable over a number of weeks, and aim to cover four or five topics each week.
2. Spend longer on topics that you have found difficult, and revise them several times.
3. Above all, do not try to limit your revision by attempting to 'question spot'. Try to be confident about all aspects of your Paper 2 work, because this will ensure that you have a choice of questions in Section B.

## Paper 2 overview:

| AS Paper 2 | Time: 1 hour 30 minutes | |
|---|---|---|
| Section A | Answer 1 compulsory two-part source question | 8+12 marks = 20 marks |
| Section B | Answer 1 question from a choice of 3 | 20 marks |
| | Total marks = | 40 marks |

You should familiarise yourself with the layout of the paper by looking at the examples published by Edexcel. The questions for each section are followed by eight pages of lined paper where you should write your answer.

## Section A question

Each of the two parts of the question will focus on one of the two contemporary sources provided. The sources together will total around 300 words. The (a) question, worth 8 marks, will be in the form of 'Why is Source 1 useful for an enquiry into …?' The (b) question, worth 12 marks, will be in the form of 'How much weight do you give the evidence of Source 2 for an enquiry into …?' In both your answers you should address the value of the content of the source, and then its nature, origin and purpose. Finally, you should use your own knowledge of the context of the source to assess its value.

## Section B questions

These questions ask you to reach a judgement on an aspect of the topic studied. The questions will have the form, for example, of 'How far…', 'How significant…', 'To what extent…' or 'How accurate is it to say…'. The questions can deal with historical concepts such as cause, consequence, change, continuity, similarity, difference and significance. You should consider the issue raised in the question, consider other relevant issues, and then conclude with an overall judgement.

The timescale of the questions could be as short as a single year or even a single event (an example from Option 2C.2 could be, 'To what extent was Russia's involvement in the First World War responsible for the fall of the Provisional Government in 1917?'). The timescale could be longer depending on the historical event or process being examined, but questions are likely to be shorter than those set for Sections A and B in Paper 1.

## Use of time

This is an issue that you should discuss with your teachers and fellow students, but here are some suggestions for you.

1. Do not write solidly for 45 minutes on each question. For Section A it is essential that you have a clear understanding of the content of each source, the points being made, and the nature, origin and purpose of each source. You might decide to spend up to ten minutes reading the sources and drawing up your plan, and 35 minutes writing your answer.
2. For Section B answers you should spend a few minutes working out what the question is asking you to do, and drawing up a plan of your answer before you begin to write your response.

# Preparing for your AS Level exams

## Paper 2: AS Level sample answer with comments

### Section A

Part A requires you to:

- identify key points in the source and explain them
- deploy your own knowledge of the context in which events took place
- make appropriate comments about the author/origin/purpose of the source.

***Study Source 1 (Chapter 1, page 170) before you answer this question.***

*Why is Source 1 valuable to the historian for an enquiry about the causes of prosperity in the United States in the 1920s?*

*Explain your answer using the source, the information given about it and your own knowledge of the historical context. (8 marks)*

#### Average student answer

The source has value to historians writing about the causes of prosperity in the United States in the 1920s. The source says that prosperity in the United States was due to a number of reasons. It says that the great expansion of credit was an important reason and so was the gradual rise in the standard of living. These reasons would help explain why prosperity took place, so would give historians important information about the subject. Also, from my own knowledge I know that the policies of President Coolidge helped with the growth of prosperity because he lowered taxes and encouraged businesses to grow. Mass production, in particular by Henry Ford in car production, helped stimulate the US economy. All these points help explain why the source would be of value to historians writing about prosperity in the 1920s.

Clearly the reasons for prosperity in the United States during the 1920s were many and varied. The source is valuable because it is written by someone towards the end of the 1920s, so will be able to comment on the whole decade. The source is also by someone who has some financial knowledge, because the attribution of the source states that the author is a financial writer for 'The Boston Journal'. This means he would be looking at financial reasons for the causes of prosperity rather than more general reasons.

The source material provides lots of information about different reasons why prosperity occurred in the USA in the 1920s. From my own knowledge I know that mass production, the widespread availability of credit, higher wages and government policies all helped bring prosperity. Therefore, the source has considerable value to historians writing about the subject.

The paragraph is linked to the 'value' aspect of the question because it refers directly to the value of the date of writing and to the authorship of the source, suggesting that a person who has a financial background is useful to historians writing about the causes of prosperity.

The opening paragraph is linked directly to the issue in the question. It refers to the issue of value to historians and also refers directly to the source material, and selects and summarises information from it. There is also an attempt to deploy some outside knowledge about Coolidge's policies, which expands and confirms details mentioned in the source material. However, information taken from the source is limited and the response does not make clear links between the information extracted and reasons why this source material may be valuable.

The concluding paragraph provides an overview of the source's value and is linked, in general terms, to the reasons associated with the economic prosperity of the 1920s.

### Verdict

This is an average answer because:

- it demonstrates some understanding of the source material and offers some analysis
- it provides some contextual evidence to expand and explain information from the source
- it discusses how useful the source is, though this is limited to noting the provenance of the source and making brief reference to the author.

Use the feedback on this answer to rewrite it, making as many improvements as you can.

# Paper 2: AS Level sample answer with comments

## Section A

Part B requires you to:

- interrogate the source
- draw reasoned inferences
- deploy your own knowledge to interpret the material in its context
- make a judgement about the value (weight) of the source in terms of making judgements.

***Study Source 4 (Chapter 1, page 173) before you answer this question.***

*How much weight do you give the evidence of Source 4 for an enquiry into the position of black Americans in US society in the 1920s?*

*Explain your answer using the source, the information given about it and your own knowledge of the historical context. (12 marks)*

### Average student answer

The source would carry weight and value for any enquiry into the position of black Americans in US society in the 1920s. The source states that black Americans faced considerable discrimination, in particular in the Old South where southern newspapers suggested that they should adopt an inferior position in society again when they 'pulled off their uniforms', having returned from military service in the First World War. The source also highlights the fact that black Americans faced attacks on their property and, on occasion, lynching. It also refers to the fact that black Americans could not look to help from the US national government. The source claims black Americans were not listened to. For much of the 1920s, black Americans faced discrimination in jobs and housing and were intimidated by the Ku Klux Klan, a white supremacist organisation that supported the idea that black Americans were second-class citizens.

The introduction makes reference to the weight and value of the source, but goes on to paraphrase information from the source without evaluating it.

Weight can be placed on the evidence presented in the source because it is written by a black American in the 1920s. The author is a highly educated black American because he went on to be the first black American president of Howard University in Washington DC.

The student deals with the weight of the source material through reference to the authorship of the source and the author's background and position. This assessment is supported, in very limited form, by the student's use of their own knowledge about the status of Harvard University.

The source only touches on some aspects of the position of black Americans in US society in the 1920s. This is shown by the fact that it was written in 1922 and, therefore, does not cover the whole period. Even though the author gives the impression that he is a highly educated individual, it is still only one person's point of view, and to ascertain the true importance of the source as evidence other information will need to be studied by the historian.

The concluding paragraph makes explicit reference to the date of the source, and says that as it dates from the early 1920s it is limited as evidence for the whole decade.

### Verdict

This is an average answer because:

- it identifies some key information from the source but does not directly link this information to the weight a historian would place on the evidence
- it makes some use of background contextual information about the position of black Americans in US society in the 1920s
- it makes a limited judgement about the weight and value of the source, mainly in the conclusion.

Use the feedback on this answer to rewrite it, making as many improvements as you can.

# Paper 2: AS Level sample answer with comments

## Section A

Part A requires you to:

- identify key points in the source and explain them
- deploy your own knowledge of the context in which events took place
- make appropriate comments about the author/origin/purpose of the source.

***Study Source 1 (Chapter 1, page 170) before you answer this question.***

*Why is Source 1 valuable to the historian for an enquiry about the causes of prosperity in the United States in the 1920s?*

*Explain your answer using the source, the information given about it and your own knowledge of the historical context. (8 marks)*

### Strong student answer

The source is of immense value for an enquiry about the causes of prosperity in the United States in the 1920s because it reveals a wide variety of reasons why prosperity arose from the perspective of a variety of groups within the USA. It makes direct reference to the importance of the availability of credit, which the banking sector saw as vital to the creation of businesses and the purchasing of goods and services. Linked to that cause was the provision of higher wages, which increased demand and was popular with trade unionists. The success of many enterprises that provided mass production both increased the number of goods available, such as cars, and helped lower the cost of goods available.

A very strong opening that is sharply focused on the specific question and indicates a top-level response. There is some thorough deployment of the student's own knowledge, which places the information in the source in broader historical context and makes links between different causes of prosperity clear.

Clearly, the causes of economic prosperity were varied and many and the source deals with several key causes. However, it looks at the causes of prosperity from the viewpoint of one person, writing in July 1929. The source was written by a person with considerable financial knowledge as he was the financial writer for 'The Boston Journal'. The date of the source increases the value of the information as it was written in July 1929, allowing the writer to look back over the preceding decade to assess the causes of prosperity.

This section places the value of the source in broader historical context through assessment of its provenance.

The nature of the source, its content, authorship and the date it was written makes it of considerable value to the historian through the provision of reference to a variety of causes. However, all the causes mentioned have a strong financial and economic basis, and broader causes, such as the nature of US society and the geographical and raw material advantages of the USA, are not mentioned specifically.

### Verdict

This is a strong answer because:

- it has sharp focus on the specific question
- it make use of evidence in the source and in the introduction to the source
- it deploys appropriate own knowledge accurately and effectively.

# Paper 2: AS Level sample answer with comments

## Section A

Part B requires you to:

- interrogate the source
- draw reasoned inferences
- deploy your own knowledge to interpret the material in its context
- make a judgement about the value (weight) of the source in terms of making judgements.

***Study Source 4 (Chapter 1, page 173) before you answer this question.***

*How much weight do you give the evidence of Source 4 for an enquiry into the position of black Americans in US society in the 1920s?*

*Explain your answer using the source, the information given about it and your own knowledge of the historical context. (12 marks)*

### Strong student answer

The source would carry considerable weight and value for an enquiry into the position of black Americans in US society in the 1920s. The author, Mordecai Johnson, was an important black American educator and preacher, and had been educated at one of the USA's top universities before going on to become the first black American president of Howard University in Washington, DC. He relates his experiences and feelings about the position of black Americans in the years following the end of the First World War and the early 1920s. The fact that he is writing in 1922 means that the source has considerable value as evidence of the position of black Americans at the beginning of the decade, but fails to offer evidence of the plight of black Americans for the rest of the 1920s. In fact, his views are substantiated by subsequent events in the 1920s, when black Americans faced discrimination and intimidation by white supremacist groups such as the Ku Klux Klan.

A focused and well-balanced introduction that comments on the value of Mordecai Johnson as a witness and makes effective use of specific references.

Johnson's attitude on the position of black Americans is particularly valuable in shedding light on what happened to them following demobilisation from the US armed forces after the First World War. He explains specifically what happened to many black Americans in the southern states and how they faced discrimination. He is also able to place the position of black Americans in broader perspective by referring to the inactivity of the federal government, in this case the president and Congress not acting on requests from the black community for justice. Johnson confirms the problems faced by black Americans, not just in the southern states. Discrimination in jobs, housing and education were commonplace throughout the USA.

The answer identifies, illustrates and explains some of the key points emerging from the source. The student deploys their own knowledge effectively to support and develop points.

Clearly, the source only touches on some aspects of life for black Americans in US society in the 1920s, but it confirms and provides graphic illustration of some key features. There are inevitably limits to the value of the testimony of an individual. Certainly it would be good to know more about what personal experiences Johnson had faced. However, the source comes across as an honest account with some specific testimony, which makes it valuable in studying the position of black Americans in US society in the 1920s.

### Verdict

This is a strong answer because:

- it interrogates the source and selects and comments on key specific points
- it makes effective use of the background information provided
- it brings in some own knowledge and links this source to other witness accounts and evidence from the time
- it makes an overall judgement about the value of the source.

# Paper 2: AS Level sample answer with comments

## Section B

These questions assess your understanding of the period in some depth. They will ask you about the content you learned about in the four key themes, but may not ask about more than one theme. For these questions remember to:

- give an analytical, not a descriptive, response
- support your points with evidence
- cover the whole time period specified in the question
- come to a substantiated judgement.

---

*How accurate is it to say that the Second New Deal (1935 to 1938) brought fundamental change to the US economy and society?(20 marks)*

### Average student answer

It is accurate to say that the Second New Deal brought fundamental change to the USA but it was not all successful.

This is an example of how not to start an answer. This brief introduction does not make any substantial point, nor is there any judgement here. A stronger opening paragraph would be longer than this single sentence. See the sample strong answer on page 272.

Firstly, one way in which the Second New Deal brought change to the USA was President Roosevelt's decision to introduce laws that helped the unemployed. On 8 April 1935, the government created the Works Progress Administration, which was run by Harry Hopkins. The Works Progress Administration, also known as the WPA, pumped billions of dollars into the US economy to provide work for the unemployed. It helped create a variety of projects to help specific types of worker. Federal Project One helped musicians and actors and the Theatre Project gave employment to directors and theatre workers. The WPA also helped artists and writers. Most important of all the WPA paid workers to build schools, roads, airports and parks. As a result, the WPA provided tens of thousands of jobs over the years to 1943, and built on the work of the First New Deal where the Public Works Administration and Civil Works Administration provided work for the unemployed. The policies of the government did bring work to thousands, but in 1937 there was a rise in unemployment as Roosevelt cut the amount of money given to the WPA and other New Deal programmes. So although Roosevelt did help the economy with the creation of the WPA, during part of the Second New Deal unemployment did not disappear but actually rose in 1937.

This paragraph considers the importance of the Works Progress Administration in dealing with one of the most important problems facing the US economy in the 1930s: unemployment. It displays a lot of accurate knowledge but much of it is deployed in a narrative-descriptive way with only limited analysis. Although it makes a limited judgement, clear reference to 'fundamental change' is limited.

Secondly, another way in which the Second New Deal brought change to the USA was through the Wagner Act, which improved trade union and workers' rights. Until the Second New Deal, trade unions in the USA had only limited rights. Many big companies like the Ford Motor Company were anti-trade union. An attempt was made under the National Recovery Act of 1934 to give trade unions extra rights but that act was declared illegal by the US Supreme Court. To replace it the Roosevelt administration passed the Wagner Act in 1935, which gave trade unions the right to bargain for better pay and conditions for its members. It was called 'a new deal for labour'. This act was a major landmark in bringing benefits to trade unionists and workers and was one of the most long-lasting laws passed during the Second New Deal.

During the Second New Deal trade unions grew in numbers and a brand new trade union organisation was formed called the Congress of Industrial Organisations and included important unions such as the miners and car workers.

There is a lot going on in this paragraph, not all of it relevant or focused. The paragraph does mention an important part of the Second New Deal and the paragraph contains accurate factual information. However, much of this information is used descriptively. Judgement and assessment is limited and undeveloped. There is some analysis of the importance of the Wagner Act, but there is also some irrelevant information about the creation of the Congress of Industrial Organisations, which is not used to help develop an argument linked directly to the question.

Thirdly, the Second New Deal brought in the Social Security Act of 1935, which provided welfare support for Americans by the federal government directly. The Social Security Act was mainly the work of Frances Perkins, the USA's first woman cabinet minister. It introduced old-age pensions for the first time. In many ways it was an attempt to win support of voters who were attracted to Francis Townsend's Old Age Revolving Plan. The Act provided government financial help for pensions but both employers and businesses also had to contribute. This was one of the most long-lasting changes made by the Second New Deal. However, many classes of worker were not allowed to participate in the scheme and it didn't start until 1940.

Some relevant points are hinted at here, such as the fact that this was the first time that the federal government introduced a national system of welfare support for the elderly. However, again, factual material on the Social Security Act is used descriptively rather than as supporting evidence to an analysis of fundamental change. No attempt is made to link the Act to social change as opposed to the economic changes proposed under the WPA.

However, the Second New Deal period of 1935 to 1938 did not always bring positive change. The Works Progress Administration did attempt to give tens of thousands of jobs to the unemployed, but the reduction in federal government expenditure in 1936 to 1937 led to the Roosevelt Recession of 1937, which actually saw unemployment rise. So, in that sense the Second New Deal did not bring positive change. Also, although the Wagner Act gave trade unionists extra rights the Second New Deal did not end industrial disputes. In 1937, serious industrial disputes broke out in the car manufacturing industry in the state of Michigan, the centre of the US car-making industry. Workers occupied factories in sit-down strikes. Even with all the reforms passed in the Second New Deal, the US economy did not experience full recovery by 1938. In that year unemployment still stood at nearly 20%, when it had been just over 23% when Roosevelt took office at the height of the depression in March 1933.

This is a reasonable paragraph which offers a balanced coverage of the topic. A clear attempt is made to provided information which shows the limits of change made during the Second New Deal.

An important part of the Second New Deal was the Revenue Act of 1935, which helped provide the money to pay for New Deal programmes. The Revenue Act increased the rate of income tax for the rich. It meant that Roosevelt was using the tax system to ensure that those who could pay, the rich, helped finance programmes designed to help the poor. It was regarded by many rich people as the 'soak the rich act'. Through a tax system that expected the rich to pay more tax than the poor it brought about a major change in the way the US government raised revenue and income.

These are accurate points. It displays a sound understanding of the underlying principles of Roosevelt's tax changes and provides a link to the question in the final sentence.

Thus I have shown that the Second New Deal brought many benefits to the USA in the years 1935 to 1938 – it helped create jobs to help the unemployed and introduced a system of old-age pensions. It also gave trade unionists and workers extra rights, which was regarded as a 'new deal for labour'. However, there were some problems such as the Roosevelt Recession of 1937, which saw unemployment rise and strikes continue to affect several major industries such as car-making. But, overall, the Second New Deal brought about important changes to both the US economy and US society. It made more important changes than those made by the First New Deal with many long-lasting like the Social Security Act and the Wagner Act.

Overall, the successes of the Second New Deal outweighed the problems still experienced by the US economy and society.

The response should not use a phrase such as 'Thus I have shown' in the conclusion: a simple 'To conclude' will suffice. The response is attempting to reach a conclusion, but note that this is achieved by repeating points made in the body of the answer rather than drawing them together to make a final point.

## Verdict

This is an average answer because:

- there is some attempt at explanation, but there are descriptive passages, including some that do not appear directly relevant
- the material included is accurate, but is lacking in depth in several places
- there is an attempt to reach an overall judgement, but it is not entirely secure
- it is organised around the question and the general trend of the argument is reasonably clear, but a couple of paragraphs are fairly free-standing and could be improved with sharper links to the question overall.

Use the feedback on this answer to rewrite it, making as many improvements as you can.

# Paper 2: AS Level sample answer with comments

## Section B

These questions assess your understanding of the period in some depth. They will ask you about the content you learned about in the four key themes, but may not ask about more than one theme. For these questions remember to:

- give an analytical, not a descriptive response
- support your points with evidence
- cover the whole time period specified in the question
- come to a substantiated judgement.

*How accurate is it to say that the Second New Deal (1935 to 1938) brought fundamental change to the US economy and society? (20 marks)*

### Strong student answer

When F. D. Roosevelt became president of the USA in March 1933 he faced the most serious economic depression in the country's history. During the course of 1933 to 1934, he introduced a variety of measures aimed to combat the worst excesses of the Depression, a programme known as the First New Deal. From 1935 to 1938, Roosevelt embarked on a second, more radical set of measures, known collectively as the Second New Deal. The president aimed to go far beyond the emergency measures associated with the First New Deal. In the years 1935 to 1938, Roosevelt aimed to transform the US economy and US society. Supported by strong majorities in both houses of Congress, Roosevelt planned to permanently change the way the federal government was financed and how American workers and the elderly lived their lives. The First New Deal prevented economic collapse; the Second New Deal aimed to bring economic recovery and reform American society. I believe that many of the Second New Deal programmes did bring about positive change to the US economy and US society. However, whether these changes were fundamental in bringing permanent change is open to historical debate. By 1938, US society and the US economy were very different from the position at the beginning of 1933, but were these changes fundamentally different and were the changes equally significant to both the economy and society as a whole?

> This is a strong opening paragraph that places the Second New Deal in context of the wider programmes of the Roosevelt administration since 1933. It also offers a comparison between the aims of both the First and Second New Deals. The response also challenges the question by offering a brief definition of what constitutes 'fundamental change' and whether or not the degree of change was different in relation to the economy and society.

One area in which Roosevelt in the Second New Deal brought fundamental change to US society was the introduction of old-age pensions under the Social Security Act of 1935. The Act changed completely the role of the federal government in welfare matters, which had traditionally been a state government responsibility. The Act introduced a pension for most employed workers based on a joint contribution of government, employee and company. The scheme, which became operable in 1940, meant that the federal government had laid the foundation of a sort of welfare state within the USA. However, not all classes of worker were eligible for pension. For instance, those working in the laundry industry were not included, mainly because southern white Congressmen opposed giving pensions to an industry dominated by black American women.

What could also be classified as bringing fundamental change in the US economy was the creation of the Works Progress Administration (WPA) in 1935. This organisation provided tens of thousands of jobs and could be regarded as a continuation of unemployment relief programmes adopted under the First New Deal, such as the Public Works Administration and Civil Works Administration. Assistance led to jobs in construction involving the building of schools, airports, bridges and parks. Where the WPA was different, and with what could be regarded as a fundamental change in government relief programmes, was the financial support given to theatres, actors, musicians, artists and writers. For instance, the Federal Writers' Project provided invaluable financial assistance to the USA's writing community.

> These are well-developed paragraphs. The response addresses directly the issue of fundamental change, offers a brief definition and provides analysis of potential fundamental change affecting, firstly, society and then the economy. Accurate factual evidence is used to support and sustain argument and is not used descriptively.

An important group supporting Roosevelt and the Democratic Party was the trade unions. In 1935, this group were rewarded for their support when Congress passed the Wagner Act, regarded by many as a 'new deal for labour'. The Act was partially required because the US Supreme Court had declared the National Recovery Act of 1934, in the First New Deal, unconstitutional and therefore illegal. Under that Act trade unions had the right to represent their members in negotiating pay and conditions for their members. The Wagner Act reintroduced this important trade union right. However, its impact went further than the mere terms of the Act. The Wagner Act was responsible for the growth of trade union membership, which had been rapid in the 1930s. However, the Wagner Act did not solve the USA's labour problems. In 1937, it was affected by a wave of labour disputes as unemployment rose during the Roosevelt Recession. Many of these disputes involved sit-down strikes in the car manufacturing industry. Therefore, although the Wagner Act was an important milestone in the achievement of trade union and workers' rights, it did not bring industrial peace. Another Act, in 1938, the National Labor Relations Act, introduced a National Labor Relations Board, which aimed at solving labour disputes impartially. Overall, the Second New Deal did bring fundamental change to trade union and workers' rights.

This paragraph continues and sustains the argument about fundamental change in the USA. It offer analysis supported by relevant factual evidence and also provides balanced coverage by referring to limitations in labour matters.

The radical policies associated with the Second New Deal, such as the Social Security Act and the WPA, involved a considerable amount of federal government expenditure. A way the Second New Deal brought fundamental change to US society was the way the federal government financed its programmes. It adopted a policy of increasing taxation on the rich to finance programmes to assist the poor and unemployed. This involved a major change in the distribution of wealth within the US that lasted far beyond the end of the Second New Deal. The main proposal bringing in these changes was the Revenue Act of 1935. It increased significantly the rate of taxation for the rich.

The response sustains a strong analytical approach that supplements and builds on the arguments made in previous paragraphs and provides a strong argument on the issue of fundamental change.

Although it is clear that aspects of the Second New Deal brought fundamental change, in particular, to US society, it was not a complete success. The problem of unemployment still affected the US economy. In fact, a reduction in government expenditure following the 1936 presidential election led to the Roosevelt Recession. Unemployment rose to 20% of the workforce, a mere 3% lower than the unemployment level when Roosevelt took office in March 1933. Unemployment was a major problem in the USA until the outbreak of the Second World War. Only a partial economic recovery had taken place within the USA. Similarly, labour disputes continued to plague the economy up to 1941.

In conclusion, the Second New Deal aimed to bring radical reform to the US economy and US society, and to a degree it achieved several of its aims. Social Security meant the federal government became directly involved in welfare provision for the first time. The Wagner Act laid the foundations of modern industrial relations in the USA and the WPSA provided financial assistance to much innovative work, which helped transform economic infrastructure and cultural offerings. However, the Second New Deal seemed to be more successful in bringing fundamental change to US society rather than the economy. It took the Second World War to bring full economic recovery.

This is a strong evaluative conclusion. The response makes a clear assessment of the role of the Second New Deal in bringing fundamental change in both the economy and society. The comments and evaluation in the conclusion flow logically from the analysis.

### Verdict

This is a strong answer because:

- the key issues relevant to the question are all explored, and the impact of the Second New Deal in bringing fundamental change in both economic and social matters is addressed directly
- there is a wide range of accurate material deployed to support the points made
- the argument throughout it is well-organised, coherent, logical and persuasive.

# Preparing for your A Level Paper 2 exam

### Advance planning

1. Draw up a timetable for your revision and try to keep to it. Spread your timetable over a number of weeks, and aim to cover four or five topics each week.
2. Spend longer on topics which you have found difficult, and revise them several times.
3. Above all, do not try to limit your revision by attempting to 'question spot'. Try to be confident about all aspects of your Paper 2 work, because this will ensure that you have a choice of questions in Section B.

### Paper 2 overview

| AL Paper 2 | Time: 1 hour 30 minutes | |
|---|---|---|
| Section A | Answer 1 compulsory source question | 20 marks |
| Section B | Answer 1 question from a choice of 2 | 20 marks |
| | Total marks = | 40 marks |

You should familiarise yourself with the layout of the paper by looking at the examples published by Edexcel. The questions for each section are followed by eight pages of lined paper where you should write your answer.

### Section A questions

This question asks you to assess two different types of contemporary sources totalling around 400 words, and will be in the form of 'How far could the historian make use of Sources 1 and 2 together to investigate …?' Your answer should evaluate both sources, considering their nature, origin and purpose, and you should use your own knowledge of the context of the sources to consider their value to the specific investigation. Remember, too, that in assessing their value, you must consider the two sources, taken together, as a set.

### Section B questions

These questions ask you to reach a judgement on an aspect of the topic studied. The questions will have the form, for example, of 'How far…', 'To what extent…' or 'How accurate is it to say…'. The questions can deal with historical concepts such as cause, consequence, change, continuity, similarity, difference and significance. You should consider the issue raised in the question, then other relevant issues, and conclude with an overall judgement.

The timescale of the questions could be as short as a single year or even a single event (an example from Option 2C.2 could be, 'To what extent was Russia's involvement in the First World War responsible for the fall of the Romanovs in 1917?'). The timescale could be longer depending on the historical event or process being examined, but questions are likely to be shorter than those set for Sections A and B in Paper 1.

### Use of time

This is an issue that you should discuss with your teachers and fellow students, but here are some suggestions for you.

1. Do not write solidly for 45 minutes on each question. For Section A it is essential that you have a clear understanding of the content of each source, the points being made, and the nature, origin and purpose of each source. You might decide to spend up to ten minutes reading the sources and drawing up your plan, and 35 minutes writing your answer.
2. For Section B answers you should spend a few minutes working out what the question is asking you to do, and drawing up a plan of your answer before you begin to write your response.

# Preparing for your A Level exams

## Paper 2: A Level sample answer with comments

Section A

You will need to read and analyse two sources and use them in tandem to assess how useful they are in investigating an issue. For these questions remember to:

- spend time, up to ten minutes, reading and identifying the arguments and evidence present in the sources, then make a plan to ensure that your response will be rooted in these sources
- use specific references from the sources
- deploy your own knowledge to develop points made in the sources and establish appropriate context
- come to a substantiated judgement.

***Study Sources 5 and 7 (Chapter 4, pages 247 and 250) before you answer this question.***

*How far could a historian make use of Sources 5 and 7 together to investigate the anti-communist witch hunt in the USA between 1947 and 1953?*

*Explain your answer using both sources, the information given about them and your own knowledge of the historical context. (20 marks)*

### Average student answer

Source 5 outlines the fears expressed by Senator Joseph McCarthy about communist subversion within the State Department of the federal government. He makes the claim that, although the USA was one of the world's greatest military powers and was the world's largest economy, it was incapable of facing up to the communist world. His claim was based on the belief that within the US government communists were working to undermine the US position in the Cold War. He said, 'The reason why we find ourselves in a position of impotency is not because our only powerful potential enemy has sent men to invade our shores, but rather because of the traitorous actions of those who have been treated so well by this Nation.' McCarthy was a Republican senator and the year he delivered the speech was 1950, a key election year for the Republican Party. They had not controlled the federal government since 1933 and McCarthy was making accusations against his political opponents, the Democrats.

The opening paragraph deals only with one source, Source 5. It concentrates on offering a description of the content of the source but also provides some contextual evidence about the Cold War. To support the argument the response offers a direct quotation from the source. In addition, the response makes a direct reference to the provenance of the source. This is not developed but is linked to some contextual information concerning the 1950 elections.

Source 7 also offers valuable information that could be used by the historian for an investigation into the anti-communist witch hunt in the USA. The source makes direct reference to a House of Representatives investigation into possible communist activity in the Hollywood film industry in 1947. This was a time of extreme tension in the early Cold War when President Truman outlined the Truman Doctrine, and the Marshall Plan was introduced to help prevent communist takeovers in western and central Europe. Ronald Reagan, the head of the Screen Actors' Guild takes a less dramatic approach to the possibility of communist subversion. The tone of his comments to the committee are measured and seem thoughtful. However, he is under oath facing questions from Congressmen on the issue of communist infiltration into the film industry.

The second paragraph also deals with one source, Source 7. Although early references to the source are descriptive, the response does provide historical context to the timing of the source and its relationship with events in the early Cold War. It goes farther than coverage of Source 5 by making a direct reference to the language and tone of Ronald Reagan's comments and places them within the context of appearing as a witness before an important Congressional committee.

I therefore think that both sources offer valuable evidence to the historian writing about the communist witch hunt in the USA. Source 7 provides evidence from 1947. It is an important Congressional committee hearing and Ronald Reagan was an important witness. The fact that a Congressional committee was investigating possible communist influence in the US film industry shows how seriously Congress regarded the threat. Similarly, Source 5, from 1950, shows how important an issue communist infiltration had become because Senator McCarthy was using the topic as a major election issue. Taken together the two sources offer coverage of much of the period 1947 to 1950. However, they do not offer evidence of the post-1950 period when McCarthy became a national political figure leading a witch hunt against communists.

The final, concluding paragraph attempts to bring the information about the sources together as part of an assessment of the value of both sources to an investigation. There is clear evidence that the response has attempted to assess the value and potential limitations of the two sources as evidence. There is also an attempt to link the source material to the time parameters within the question and the candidate does provide some contextual evidence on the post-1950 period.

## Verdict

This is an average answer because:

- it makes direct reference to both sources and selects relevant material from both to illustrate their key features
- it provides some historical context to explain and support inferences in the sources, which expands and confirms material in both sources
- there is reference to the provenance of both sources
- there is limited integration of own knowledge with the source material until the final paragraph.

Use the feedback on this answer to rewrite it, making as many improvements as you can.

# Paper 2: A Level sample answer with comments

## Section A

You will need to read and analyse two sources and use them in tandem to assess how useful they are in investigating an issue. For these questions remember to:

- spend time, up to ten minutes, reading and identifying the arguments and evidence present in the sources; then make a plan to ensure that your response will be rooted in these sources
- use specific references from the sources
- deploy own knowledge to develop points made in the sources and establish appropriate context
- come to a substantiated judgement.

***Study Sources 5 and 7 (Chapter 4, pages 247 and 250) before you answer this question.***

*How far could a historian make use of Sources 5 and 7 together to investigate the anti-communist witch hunt in the USA between 1947 and 1953?*

*Explain your answer using both sources, the information given about them and your own knowledge of the historical context. (20 marks)*

### Strong student answer

The two sources provide very different perspectives on the anti-communist witch hunt in the USA in the years 1947 to 1953. Senator Joseph McCarthy is a Republican politician speaking during an important election year for the US Congress against the incumbent Democratic administration of President Harry S. Truman. He makes a persuasive case that communist subversion within the USA is a problem. He points out that the USA, which was the world's greatest power, faced international competition from the communist world. McCarthy saw the conflict as one between Christian civilisation and democracy on one hand and the communist, atheist world on the other. He suggests the USA was not in a position to confront effectively the communist world because of communist subversion at home. Ronald Reagan's testimony to the House Un-American Activities Committee, made in 1947, three years before McCarthy's speech, takes a more measured view of possible communist subversion, this time within the US film industry in Hollywood. Although not dismissing the possibility of communist subversion, he took the view that Hollywood, and in particular the Screen Actors' Guild, had a very good view of what was happening in the US film industry and any possibility of communist subversion would be identified and dealt with effectively.

A strong opening, which explains the background of both sources and contrasts McCarthy's dramatic speech with Reagan's more measured testimony.

The speech by Senator McCarthy in 1950 raises clear concerns about why the USA was perceived as not winning the global Cold War against communism. By 1950, Eastern Europe was under communist control. The 'Iron Curtain' had been put in place and in 1948–49, the Cold War in Europe reached crisis point with the Berlin Airlift Crisis. More importantly, by 1949, communists had won the Chinese Civil War. By the time McCarthy spoke, the largest country on earth, the USSR, and the most populous, China, were both communist. The USA and its allies seemed to be on the defensive. McCarthy clearly feels that the US position cannot be explained by events overseas alone. He argues that the US position in the world was being undermined by federal officials within the USA, and in particular those in the State Department responsible for foreign policy.

Ronald Reagan, in Source 7, as President of the Screen Actors' Guild, is answering questions about possible communist subversion in the film industry. He is testifying in front of a Congressional committee and his answers to questions are measured. He sees part of his job as defending the Screen Actors' Guild and refers to its activities in a positive way. However, like McCarthy he is concerned about the activities of the communist party and its supporters. He points out that the Screen Actors' Guild in particular, and the US film industry in general, were fully aware of possible subversion and were on the lookout for any possible activity. Reagan's testimony was made at the beginning of the Cold War, in 1947. This was the year that saw communist takeovers in Eastern Europe and communist activity in the Greek Civil War. The source also shows how wide-ranging the House Un-American Activities Committee investigations were, given that they decided to interview someone from the US film industry.

Both sources are in a style appropriate to their purpose. McCarthy is trying to score political points against the Democrat-controlled federal government. He sets the scene for his audience by stating: 'Ladies and gentlemen, can there be anyone here tonight who is so blind as to say that the war is not on? Can there be anyone who fails to realize that the Communist world has said, "The time is now."' This is a call to action, which McCarthy uses to highlight the need to confront communism within the USA as well as around the world. Ronald Reagan is explaining to the House Committee that he is aware of possible communist subversion but also realises he is defending the integrity of his organisation the Screen Actors' Guild when he states: 'I happen to be very proud of the industry in which I work; I happen to be very proud of the way in which we conducted the fight.' They both react to the issue of possible communist subversion. Neither source however provides any specific evidence that communist subversion actually took place.

*The last two paragraphs identify key points made in the sources and illustrate them with specific references and some effective contextual knowledge.*

## Verdict

This is a strong answer because:

- it is rooted in the sources and identifies and illustrates their key features
- it deploys a sound range of own knowledge to support the points and provide context
- it sustains focus and develops a clear and balanced argument
- there is a clear judgement that follows on from the arguments put forward.

# Paper 2: A Level sample answer with comments

## Section B

These questions assess your understanding of the period in some depth. They will ask you about the content you learned about in the four key themes, but may not ask about more than one theme. For these questions remember to:

- give an analytical, not a descriptive, response
- support your points with evidence
- cover the whole time period specified in the question
- come to a substantiated judgement.

*To what extent was the changing status of black Americans due to their own actions in the years 1945 to 1955? (20 marks)*

### Average student answer

In many ways, the status of black Americans changed in the years 1945 to 1955. Black Americans had long been regarded as second-class citizens in the USA even though slavery had been abolished at the end of the US Civil War in 1865. In some parts of the USA, like the Old South, black Americans faced legal discrimination. They had to attend different schools to whites and use different seating on public buses and trains. Many black Americans attempted to bring about change so that they could make sure they were treated equally with whites. In the years 1945 to 1955, many changes took place and black Americans helped bring this about.

The respondent has clearly decided to deal directly with the issue in the question. Some contextual information is provided but it is of a general nature. Nevertheless, direct reference is made to the role of black Americans in bringing about change.

During the Second World War, black Americans who served in the armed forces had to do so in racially segregated units. Only a few black Americans became officers. However, some black units achieved fame like the Tuskegee airmen. Also, black Americans ran the Double V campaign for victory abroad and victory for equality at home. In 1948, a move towards equality occurred when President Truman sign an executive order that desegregated the US armed forces. From 1948, all US armed forces units were racially integrated. In the Korean War of 1950 to 1953, black and white Americans served in the same armed forces units. So the status of black Americans was changed in 1948 and the person who made this change was the US president.

This paragraph offers some detailed factual information. It also attempts to place the period from 1945 in historical context through references to the black American experience during the Second World War. An important change is identified and the response offers some detailed information. However, not all US armed forces were desegregated. National Guard and reserve units in several states remained segregated after 1948. A brief, undeveloped assessment is made at the end of what is a narrative-descriptive paragraph.

Another way black Americans had their status changed was in sports, in particular Major League Baseball. The Brooklyn Dodgers baseball team was the first major team to sign a black American in the person of Jackie Robinson. Although Jackie Robinson faced racial abuse, he established himself as a major player through his own ability as a very fine baseball player. So it might be said that in the person of Jackie Robinson black Americans improved their status through their own actions.

Again a descriptive paragraph that contains accurate information, but not all of it is directly relevant to the issue of changing status because the response concentrates on the experience of a single individual.

The change in status of black Americans was changed dramatically by the US Supreme Court decision 'Brown v the Board of Education' in 1954. By a unanimous majority the Court declared racial segregation in public schools to be against the US Constitution because it went against the 14th Amendment right of equal protection of the law. It reversed a previous Supreme Court decision of 1896, 'Plessy v Ferguson', which declared that it was possible to have separate but equal provision of public schooling. This allowed the formation of white-only and black-only schools. However, the Supreme Court declared that white and black schools were separate but not equal and that from 1954 all public schools had to be racially integrated. In the following year, 1955, the Supreme Court made another decision, known as the 'Brown II' case. It declared that all public schools should be integrated with all deliberate speed. However, by 1955 only a tiny fraction of desegregated schools had been integrated. So it was an important decision, but had limited impact by 1955 and was the work of the US Supreme Court, not black Americans.

Once again this is a relevant paragraph in terms of the content. However, the information, though accurate, is used descriptively with a link to the wording of the question only appearing in the final sentence.

In 1955, black Americans became involved in a major bus boycott. In that year a black American, Mrs Rosa Parks, was arrested for not giving up her seat to a white person on a public bus in Montgomery, Alabama. This led to a boycott of all public buses by black Americans in that city. The boycott was led by Martin Luther King and lasted into 1956. It was successful as the bus companies decided to integrate their buses racially and allow blacks and whites to occupy any seat on a bus. So in this case black Americans did achieve a change in their status through their own actions.

The response begins to deal with an issue where black Americans played a major role in changing their status through their own actions. It provides accurate information that is deployed in a narrative-descriptive way. Links to the question are limited and appear in the last sentence of the paragraph.

Overall, therefore, the status of black Americans changed a lot in the years 1945 to 1955. The armed forces were desegregated in 1945 and black Americans like Jackie Robinson were allowed to play in major league sports like baseball. The most important changes took place between 1954 and 1955. In 1954, the landmark Supreme Court decision of Brown v Board of Education allowed the racial integration of schools and the following year the Montgomery Bus Boycott led to the racial integration on public buses in Montgomery. Most of the changes were made by people other than black Americans except for the Montgomery Bus Boycott.

The conclusion is brief and consists largely of repetition of points made in the body of the answer.

### Verdict

This is an average answer because:

- it has a tendency to provide narrative-description rather than analysis
- the knowledge deployed deals directly with the issue of the status of black Americans but only in a limited way
- there is an attempt to reach a judgement, but it is limited in its range and needs greater supporting material to make the judgement stand up
- it is well organised and quite logical in places but does not develop clear links between the different factors that resulted in a change of status of black Americans.

Use the feedback on this answer to rewrite it, making as many improvements as you can.

# Paper 2: A Level sample answer with comments

## Section B

These questions assess your understanding of the period in some depth. They will ask you about the content you learned about in the four key themes, but may not ask about more than one theme. For these questions remember to:

- give an analytical, not a descriptive, response
- support your points with evidence
- cover the whole time period specified in the question
- come to a substantiated judgement.

---

*To what extent was the changing status of black Americans due to their own actions in the years 1945 to 1955? (20 marks)*

### Strong student answer

The years 1945 to 1955 witnessed major changes for the black American community. In 1948, for the first time, the US armed forces were desegregated. In 1954, a landmark US Supreme Court decision desegregated all public schools, ending one of the most contentious aspects of legal segregation. In the following year, in Montgomery, Alabama, a bus boycott attracted national attention and brought about another major challenge to legal segregation of black Americans. The decade following the Second World War saw major advances in black American rights and the move towards racial equality with whites. But how far were these changes due directly to the actions of black Americans themselves?

In 1945, the position of black Americans was one of general second-class citizenship. In the Old South legal segregation treated black Americans separately. So did the US government within the armed forces. However, changes in the position of black Americans during the Second World War suggested the possibility for advancement. The Federal Employment Practices Commission (FEPC) had provided job opportunities for blacks on federal projects and programmes. The war also afforded several black American military units such as the Red Tails squadron of Tuskegee airmen opportunities to gain recognition and respect. Yet these advances for black Americans were very limited.

The decision to segregate the US armed forces was taken primarily by President Harry S. Truman in Executive Order 8891 in 1948. He had been consistently pressured by black American groups to do so but it was ultimately his decision. The 1948 decision brought a major change in black American status. The Korean War of 1950–53 was the first major conflict where the racially integrated armed forces participated. Undoubtedly, black American performance in the Second World War and black American demands for equal treatment were contributory factors but it was primarily an act by the presidency to bring this important change.

Another area of considerable change in the position of black Americans from 1945 was their advancement in professional sport, most notably in Major League Baseball. The signing of black American Jackie Robinson by the Brooklyn Dodgers baseball team was the first time a black American played at the highest level of US baseball. Robinson's outstanding ability and the manner in which he conducted himself against racist slurs and provocation helped paved the way for other black American sportsmen to participate in Major League Baseball and other sports such as basketball. In that sense, although Robinson was signed by white baseball executives it was his own actions that paved the way for the growth of black American involvement in US sports.

This is a strong start to the answer. The response places the answer within the context of major changes in the position of black Americans in US society. It is focused, covers the period mentioned in the question and poses a rhetorical question in the last sentence that will offer the opportunity for balanced analysis within the rest of the answer.

These paragraphs address directly the issues raised in the question. The first paragraph provides some initial historical context and goes on to explain who was primarily responsible for black American advancement, notably the US president.

This analytical approach is sustained in the third paragraph, which offers contrast by choosing an area where black Americans aided their own advancement in the area of professional sports.

The most important areas where black Americans played a key role in improving their status within US society took place towards the end of the period mentioned in the question. In 1954, one of the most important US Supreme Court decisions in the 20th century was made. In the case of 'Brown v the Board of Education, Topeka, Kansas' the Court declared that 'separate but equal' educational facilities for blacks and whites, confirmed by the Supreme Court decision of 'Plessy v Ferguson' of 1896 that allowed legal segregation in education, did not exist in practice. In a 9–0 unanimous decision the Court declared that the status of black Americans in public schools was inferior to those of whites and that a completely integrated system should be introduced across the USA where it did not already exist. In 1955, another Supreme Court decision, known as the 'Brown II' decision, declared that integration should take place with all deliberate speed. The case would not have reached the US Supreme Court without the efforts of the National Association for the Advancement of Colored People (NAACP), a predominantly black organisation that aimed to change the status of black Americans through legal means. It was the black American NAACP legal team that won the Brown case and brought about the end of legal segregation in public schools. However, the appointment of Earl Warren as US Supreme Court Chief Justice in 1953 was also important in winning the Brown case. He ensured, through persuasion, that his fellow justices would support this important change in the status of black Americans.

This paragraph sustains the analytical approach of the answer. The paragraph begins with an analytical statement, which is then supported and sustained by accurate, detailed supporting evidence. The paragraph also qualifies the role of black Americans by referring to the role of Chief Justice Earl Warren.

In the same year as the Brown II case, 1955, black Americans were prominent in their attempt to end segregation in public transport in Montgomery, Alabama. The bus boycott began when a black American, Mrs Rosa Parks, refused to move from her seat on a public bus for a white passenger and was arrested. A very effective boycott of the Montgomery bus system developed, organised by the black American pressure group the Montgomery Improvement Association (MIA). It was headed by Dr Martin Luther King, who was able to offer clear leadership to the boycott and ensured that the vast majority of black Americans in Montgomery joined the boycott. The boycott received national attention and galvanised black Americans' demands for a changed status and equality with white Americans. However, the eventual success of the boycott was ensured by another US Supreme Court decision, 'Browder v Gayle', which declared legal segregation on the Montgomery public buses unconstitutional.

A strong answer to this question must consider benefits and costs, and weigh these up before reaching a judgement. This is what the respondent has done in this conclusion.

In conclusion, the status of black Americans within the USA changed considerably in the years 1945 to 1955. The desegregation of the armed forces and the opening up of professional support to black Americans were important developments at the beginning of the period of the question. However, the most significant changes affecting black Americans took place in 1954 and 1955 in the Brown case and the Montgomery Bus Boycott. In changing their status black Americans played a prominent role. The NAACP and the MIA were instrumental in bringing change in the period 1954 to 1955. However, change in status was also due to the actions of the Federal government, in particular, the role of the president in 1948 on the issue of integrating the armed forces and the US Supreme Court in both the Brown case and the desegregation of public buses in Montgomery.

### Verdict

This is a strong answer because:

- it puts both sides of the case, looking at both the actions of black Americans and the actions of other agencies and individuals, and sustains a focus on the question set
- it uses a wide range of evidence to support the points made
- it reaches a secure concluding judgement
- it is well organised and communication of material is clear and precise.

# The USA, 1955–92: conformity and challenge

The years 1955–92 were a period of both conformity and challenge for the USA. In many ways the period saw a continuation of traditional values, with an emphasis on family life. Traditional values were associated with the Republican Party, which controlled the presidency and federal government for 25 out of the 37 years covered in this period. However, the period also saw major challenges to the status quo. One of the most significant was the development of the civil rights movement, which called for greater equality for black Americans, Native Americans, gay people and women.

The period 1955 to 1992 also saw major changes in popular culture and the economy. By 1992, the USA had changed considerably from the society and economy it had been in 1955.

Following the Second World War, the USA had become the world's first consumer society. By 1955, the USA was the world's largest economy and dominated the non-communist world. The American standard of living far outstripped Europe and the rest of the world. The majority of Americans owned cars, televisions, refrigerators and their own homes. However, by 1992, American economic dominance was being challenged as the European Union (founded as the European Economic Community in 1957), began to enjoy similar standards of living to those once associated with the USA.

One area where the USA remained dominant was popular culture. In the 1950s the USA was the birthplace of rock'n'roll and teenage culture. The USA continued to generate new movements within popular music. Hollywood dominated world cinema. If there was a challenge to Hollywood it came from within the USA, with the development of television.

The growth of teenage and youth culture eventually led to youth protest movements. The 1960s and 1970s saw protest movements across the USA against government policies. By the 1970s the USA was becoming a divided society. Many, mainly in urban areas, supported rapid social change. At the same time, a growth in conservative values led to growing support for the Republican Party and Christian religious groups. By the mid-1970s the Republican Party was gaining increasing political support. From the election of Ronald Reagan as president in 1980 to 1992, the Republican Party was the dominant force in US politics.

SOURCE 1 A civil rights protestor in Monroe, North Carolina, August 1961.

1955
1955 – Montgomery Bus Boycott in Alabama
Rise of Martin Luther King as civil rights leader

1957
1957 – Southern Christian Leadership Conference (SCLC) founded

1963
1963 – Civil rights march on Washington DC
Civil rights protests in Birmingham, Alabama
President J. F. Kennedy assassinated

1965
1965 – Malcolm X assassinated by a member of Nation of Islam
President Johnson launches Great Society programme
Voting Rights Act

1970
1970 – Four students protesting against US invasion of Cambodia shot dead by Ohio National Guard at Kent State University

1973
1973 – *Roe v Wade* US Supreme Court decision on abortion
First major oil crisis affects non-Communist world as world price of oil quadruples following Arab-Israeli War

1977
1977 – Jimmy Carter becomes US president
US faces inflation and energy crisis

1981
1981 – Ronald Reagan becomes US president
AIDS identified as major illness within the USA
Sandra Day O'Connor appointed first female US Supreme Court justice

1992
1992 – Rodney King race riots in Los Angeles
Bill Clinton elected US president

Perhaps the greatest achievement and most significant social and political change that took place between 1955 and 1992 was the success of the civil rights movement. Beginning in the **Old South**, black Americans led a campaign to gain political, civil and social equality and gain the rights they had been promised in the wake of the US Civil War, 100 years before. By 1992, black Americans had gained political and civil equality with other Americans, although considerable social inequality still existed.

By 1992, the USA had gone through major civil, social and political change. Yet the USA weathered these changes. With the collapse of the Soviet Union and communist rule in Eastern Europe, the USA returned to its dominant position in world affairs. At home, protest had given way to the conservative rule of the Republican Party. The political and social stability, which was a feature of 1955, had largely returned.

However, in 1992, a serious race riot occurred in Los Angeles, and in the presidential election of that year, Republican control of the presidency came to an end when Democrat Bill Clinton defeated Republican George H. W. Bush to become president.

### KEY TERM

**Old South**
The area of the south-eastern USA that comprised the Confederate states in the US Civil War of 1861 to 1865: Virginia, North and South Carolina, Georgia, Florida, Alabama, Mississippi, Louisiana, Tennessee, Arkansas and Texas. In these states segregation of facilities between blacks and whites was permitted by law. They were politically dominated by a white-controlled Democratic Party.

1956 — 1956 – Elvis Presley has first US hits: 'Heartbreak Hotel' and 'Hound Dog'

1961 — 1961 – J. F. Kennedy becomes youngest US president

1964 — 1964 – Civil Rights Act

1968 — 1968 – Martin Luther King assassinated
American Indian Movement (AIM) founded
Nixon wins US presidential election

1972 — 1972 – Watergate break-in
Nixon wins landslide victory in 1972 presidential election

1974 — 1974 – Richard Nixon resigns as president

1979 — 1979 – World oil price doubles following Iranian Revolution

1984 — 1984 – Black American, Jesse Jackson, runs for Democratic Party nomination for president

**Figure 1:** The 48 contiguous states of the USA and their capitals. Alaska to the north-west of Canada and Hawaii in the Pacific Ocean are also states of the USA, both joining the Union in 1959.

| | |
|---|---|
| 1953–61: Dwight Eisenhower (Republican) | 1961–63: John F. Kennedy (Democrat) |
| 1963–69: Lyndon Johnson (Democrat) | 1969–74: Richard Nixon (Republican) |
| 1974–77: Gerald Ford (Republican) | 1977–81: Jimmy Carter (Democrat) |
| 1981–89: Ronald Reagan (Republican) | 1989–93: George H. W. Bush (Republican) |

**Figure 2:** US presidents 1955–92.

# 2b.1 Affluence and conformity, 1955–63

## Key questions

- To what extent did the USA experience considerable urbanisation and affluence in the years 1955 to 1963?
- How important were changes in culture in the years 1955 to 1963?
- How successful was the civil rights movement in achieving more rights for black Americans in the years 1955 to 1963?
- Did J. F. Kennedy's New Frontier programme achieve its aims?

## INTRODUCTION

By 1945, the USA was the world's largest military power. It had played a major role in the defeat of Germany and Japan in the Second World War, which had also transformed the US economy. In the four wartime years of 1941–45, national income, wealth and industrial production more than doubled. In 1940, the total value of goods and services supplied by the USA and its income from foreign investment, known as Gross National Product (GNP), was $99.7 billion. In 1945, it had risen to $211 billion. By 1947, the USA was producing 57 percent of the world's steel, 43 percent of its electricity and 62 percent of the world's oil. It was the global economic power. By 1945, the USA had full employment. The decade after the Second World War saw the USA maintain its dominance in the global economy. During this period the US economy developed the world's first consumer society.

## TO WHAT EXTENT DID THE USA EXPERIENCE CONSIDERABLE URBANISATION AND AFFLUENCE IN THE YEARS 1955 TO 1963?

The 1950s was a period of affluence. US gross national product rose from $99.7 billion in 1940 to $284.8 billion in 1950. By 1960, it had leapt again to $503.7 billion. Wages rose and consumer credit, an indicator of personal buying power, rose from $8.4 billion in 1950 to $45 billion in 1960. However, there were important differences between white and non-white Americans. In 1953, the median income of a white family was $4,392 per year compared to only $2,461 for non-white families. By 1960, the gap had grown to $5,835 for white families and $3,233 for non-white families.

**1947** – First Levittown built in New York State

**1955** – Disneyland opens near Los Angeles, at Anaheim, California

**1956** – National Interstate and Defense Highways Act
First time white-collar jobs outnumber blue-collar jobs in US economy

## The changing nature of cities

By 1955, the USA was changing rapidly both in size of population and where people lived. The population rose from 130 million in 1940 to 165 million by the mid-1950s, the biggest increase in the history of the country. A considerable number of people were moving from rural areas and small towns into cities. Numbers living in urban areas rose from 96.5 million in 1950 to 124.7 million in 1960. At the same time the number of people living on rural farms fell from 23 million in 1950 to 13.4 million in 1960. Many took the opportunity to have a new life where consumer goods were plentiful and the standard of living higher. Black Americans continued to escape rural poverty and racial discrimination in the Old South by moving to northern cities, just as they had in the Great Migration of the 1920s and 1930s. In the 1950s, the USA's 12 largest cities gained 1.8 million non-white residents. This led to increased racial tension.

By the 1960s, many cities were becoming racially segregated and city centres were becoming the preserve of non-whites. Areas such as the Watts district of Los Angeles, west and north Philadelphia, the South Bronx and Harlem in New York City were becoming black American areas. On the edges of cities new suburbs were dominated by white Americans. Where interracial tension in the past had been centred in the Old South, now interracial tensions were developing in northern and western cities as the settlement patterns of these cities changed.

Matters were made worse by federal housing policy. The Federal Housing Administration (FHA) supported anti-Jewish and anti-black **restrictive covenants** on new suburban housing developments. The FHA's aim was to ensure neighbourhoods had racial cohesion. It meant that non-white residents of cities were barred from much suburban development. Instead they were forced to live in privately owned rental accommodation in inner city areas, which became rundown racial ghettos. In addition, many cities failed to provide the public housing required for these areas. In the period 1949 to 1959, only 320,000 houses were funded under President Truman's Public Housing Act. Even where public housing areas were provided, known in many cities as 'the projects', much of the accommodation was cramped. To save on cost the projects were built in massive high-rise blocks. As a result, densely populated areas with poor public amenities became a feature of many inner cities. Northern, eastern and western cities were developing into two societies: a predominantly non-white inner city and a predominantly white suburbia. In the Old South, racial segregation in housing was maintained in the new suburbs.

## The expansion of the suburbs

While American cities grew in size, the centre of many cities declined. In the 1950s, many white residents left city centres for life in the suburbs, leaving old city centre residential areas to non-whites. The rapid growth of cities in the 1950s was essentially the growth of suburbia. However, it was also aided by developments such as **Levittowns**, purpose-built new communities of affordable private housing, initially for whites only. Levittowns of over 17,000 houses each were built in New York State and Pennsylvania. Growth was also helped by cheap home loans from organisations such as the Veterans Administration and Federal Housing Administration. The latter financed 30 percent of all new homes in the USA in the 1950s.

### KEY TERMS

**Restrictive covenant**
A list of conditions attached to the sale of a house. In many suburban developments covenants stated that houses could not be sold to Jewish or black American buyers.

**Levittown**
A type of new suburb built near New York City and in eastern Pennsylvania in the late 1940s and early 1950s, which was regarded as typical of suburban development across the USA. Levittowns discriminated against black Americans and other minorities through the use of restrictive covenants on house sales. Levittowns were white and middle-class.

**1957** - Soviet Union launches first satellite, Sputnik, into outer space

**1960** - 75 percent of American households own at least one car

1957 1958 1959 1960

**1959** - McDonalds opens 100th restaurant

By 1960, home ownership had become the norm for the first time in American history, with three in five families owning a home. Between 1950 and 1960, 18 million people moved to the suburbs. By 1960, a new term had come into use to describe the suburban growth from Boston, Massachusetts to Washington DC, which encompassed New York City, Philadelphia and Baltimore: megalopolis.

Not only did people migrate from inner cities to suburbs, they also migrated across the USA. Many deserted the north-east for life in the 'Sun Belt'. Cities in Florida, Texas and California all grew rapidly in the 1950s. These included Dallas, San Diego, Los Angeles, Houston and Miami. By 1970, 80 million Americans lived in suburbs, 15 million more than lived in central areas of cities.

**SOURCE 1**

Based on US government data on economic growth, 1950–60, in billions of dollars. From J. Patterson, *America in the Twentieth Century: a history* (2011)

| Year | GNP | Disposable personal income |
|---|---|---|
| 1950 | 284.8 | 206.9 |
| 1952 | 345.5 | 238.3 |
| 1954 | 364.8 | 257.4 |
| 1956 | 419.2 | 318.8 |
| 1958 | 447.3 | 318.8 |
| 1960 | 503.7 | 350.0 |

**AS Level Exam-Style Question Section A**

***Study Source 1 before you answer this question.***

Why is Source 1 valuable to the historian for an enquiry into how the USA experienced economic growth in the period 1955 to 1963?

Explain your answer using the source, the information about it and your own knowledge of the historical context. (8 marks)

**Tip**

*It is important that you make use of evidence contained within the provenance of the source as well as the data itself. You will be expected to refer to the importance of GNP (Gross National Product) and disposable personal income as important measurements of the degree of wealth produced within an economy. Make sure you also look at changes and the degree of change between years.*

## Highway development

The rapid growth of suburbia went hand in hand with a growth in demand for cars and increased highway construction. Between 1945 and 1960, the number of cars in the USA increased by 133 percent. The most important development in road construction was the National Interstate and Defense Highways Act of 1956. President Eisenhower regarded it as his greatest achievement as president in the years 1953 to 1961. This was the culmination of a number of federal initiatives to improve the USA's highway structure.

In 1938, during Franklin D. Roosevelt's presidency, Congress passed the Federal-Aid Highways Act, which required the Bureau of Public Roads to assess the feasibility of building six major toll roads. However, with the USA entering the Second World War in December 1941, major highway construction was delayed. A further Highways Act of 1944 aimed to construct 40,000 miles of highway as the basis of a national system of interstate highways. In 1952, President Truman proposed $25 million to pay for highway construction on a 50:50 basis with state governments. By the time Eisenhower became president in 1953, state governments had completed only 6,500 miles.

In 1956, Eisenhower gained Congressional support for a new highways act. The National Interstate and Defense Highways Act set up a ten-year programme, at the cost of $25 billion, to construct a nationwide network of 42,500 miles of interstate highways, between four and eight lanes wide. This would be 90 percent of the cost of construction. State governments would provide ten percent. This federal aid went hand in glove with federal support for new housing developments in suburbia. The Act gave a great stimulus to the construction industry, the car industry and the rapid growth of suburbia.

The title of the Act also underlined another motive for highway construction. At the height of the **Cold War** with the Soviet Union, Eisenhower (who had served as a general in the Second World War) claimed the interstate network would facilitate the rapid movement of troops and military equipment across the country. The Eisenhower interstate network still provides the basis of the US highway network. It is hard to imagine the significance of the car in US society without this important highway network.

**KEY TERM**

**Cold War (1945–91)**
The Cold War was a period of international history that involved political and military confrontation between the capitalist USA (and its allies) and the communist Soviet Union of Russia (and its allies). The USA and USSR had completely different political and economic social systems and ideologies. The USA feared that the USSR planned to turn the world communist and would outlaw the private ownership of business and property. The USSR feared encirclement by countries that disliked communist rule. The creation of NATO, CENTO and SEATO, all military organisations that were anti-communist, seemed to confirm Soviet fears.

## Growing ownership and use of cars

By 1955, the USA had become the first society where the car was the central consumer product. Car production soared. In 1946, the USA produced two million cars a year. By 1955, this had risen to eight million. Detroit became the car-producing centre of the world. It was dominated by three car-producing companies: General Motors, Ford and Chrysler. One in seven Americans worked in an industry linked to car manufacture. One million workers were members of the UAW (United Automobile Workers), the nation's most prominent trade union. By 1960, 75 percent of Americans owned at least one car and 15 percent owned more than one car per family.

The growth in car ownership meant that people could move to the suburbs but still work in the inner city. Of the 12 largest cities in the USA, only Los Angeles saw a rise in population in the 1950s and suburbia developed outside the city boundaries. By 1956, 75 million cars and trucks were on the USA's roads. A car-based culture developed across the country. In that year, 3,000 new drive-in movie theatres opened. There were also multilevel car parks and motels to cater for the new car owners. By the mid-1950s, 1,800 out-of-town shopping malls had been built, contributing to the decline of inner cities as retail centres. In 1954, Ray Kroc bought the rights to open a fast-food hamburger outlet in San Bernardino, a suburb of Los Angeles, to cater for drivers. McDonald's as we know it today was born. By 1959, he had opened his 100th restaurant, selling 50 million hamburgers annually at 50c a burger.

Car ownership, particularly in the suburbs, fuelled the growing teenage culture. American teenagers were more mobile than ever before. Rock'n'roll music went alongside a new 'hot rod' car culture in which young men bought and customised fast cars.

Car ownership helped develop the tourist industry within the USA. For the first time the country's national parks became accessible to millions of car owners. Car ownership also reflected the need for the most up-to-date consumer goods. During the 1950s, approximately seven million cars were discarded every year as the affluent wanted the latest car model. Car manufacturers deliberately changed the style and facilities available year on year. Built-in obsolescence became a feature of car sales. New colours, chrome-plated metal parts, white-walled tyres, air conditioning, better radios: all these developments were used to encourage car purchasing.

Of all the consumer goods that separated the USA from the rest of the world in the 1950s and early 1960s, it was the car more than anything else that demonstrated the superiority of the American standard of living. Car ownership reflected the age of affluence.

SOURCE 2

From the Federal Highways Act, 1956.

NATIONAL SYSTEM OF INTERSTATE AND DEFENSE HIGHWAYS. INTERSTATE SYSTEM.

It is hereby declared to be essential to the national interest to provide for the early completion of the "National System of Interstate Highways", as authorized and designated in accordance with section 7 of the Federal-Aid Highway Act of 1944.

It is the intent of the Congress that the Interstate System be completed as nearly as practicable over a thirteen-year period and that the entire System in all the States be brought to simultaneous completion. Because of its primary importance to the national defense, the name of such system is hereby changed to the "National System of Interstate and Defense Highways". Such National System of Interstate and Defense Highways is hereinafter in this Act referred to as the 'Interstate System'.

**A Level Exam-Style Question Section A**

***Study Sources 1 and 2 before you answer this question.***

How far can the historian make use of Sources 1 and 2 together to investigate why the period 1955 to 1963 experienced rapid economic growth?

Explain your answer using both sources, the information given about them and your knowledge of the historical context. (20 marks)

**Tip**

*You will be expected to point out the value to the historian of each source in relation to its provenance: both are from official federal government sources. You will also be expected to provide information from within each source that could be used to explain why the period 1955 to 1963 was an age of affluence.*

SOURCE

Car and appliance ownership statistics, 1949–55. This table originally appeared in *Postwar Economic Trends*, by Ralph E. Freeman, in 1960.

| Year | % families owning | | | |
|---|---|---|---|---|
| | Cars | TVs | Fridges | Washing machines |
| 1949 | 56 | 10.1 | 79.2 | 68.6 |
| 1950 | 60 | 26.4 | 86.4 | 71.9 |
| 1951 | 65 | 38.5 | 86.7 | 73.5 |
| 1952 | 65 | 50.2 | 89.2 | 76.2 |
| 1953 | 65 | 63.5 | 90.4 | 78.5 |
| 1954 | 70 | 74.1 | 92.5 | 81.3 |
| 1955 | 71 | 76.1 | 94.1 | 84.1 |

## White-collar jobs and service industries

In 1956, for the first time in American history, the number of **white-collar** workers outnumbered **blue-collar** workers as the USA became the world's first consumer society. The Second World War had offered a major stimulus to this development. It opened up job opportunities in large numbers to women. In 1960, twice as many women were at work as in 1940 and 40 percent of all women over 16 held a job. Female employment was increasing at a rate four times faster than that of men.

**KEY TERMS**

**White-collar jobs**
White-collar jobs are those associated with office work and service industries such as banking, insurance, tourism, advertising and retailing. White-collar workers include managers, secretaries, office workers and shop staff.

**Blue-collar jobs**
Blue-collar jobs are associated with manufacturing industries. Workers wear overalls and work clothes instead of shirts and ties. Traditionally these jobs were done by men, though many women did blue-collar work during the Second World War.

The Truman government cut defence spending savagely between 1945 and 1948 so that it was significantly lower than that of the USSR in that time, but it increased spending dramatically in 1950. From 1950 to 1953, the Cold War actually became a 'hot war', with fighting in Korea between the USA and its United Nations allies and communist China and North Korea. Defence spending created hundreds of thousands of jobs in the 1950s. Defence contractors such as Lockheed, Boeing and McDonnell Douglas provided military aircraft and missiles for the world's greatest military, as well as economic, power. Throughout the 1950s, defence spending stood at approximately $40 billion a year, accounting for 60 percent of the federal budget and ten percent of GNP. By 1957, the federal government employed eight million workers, double the number in 1940, the majority of whom did white-collar work.

In 1961, in his farewell address to the American people, outgoing President Eisenhower, himself a former general, spoke of the '**military-industrial complex**', the link between the federal government and defence corporations that involved high federal defence expenditure.

**KEY TERM**

**Military-industrial complex**
This was the vested interest of the federal government, Congress and military defence firms to maintain high levels of military spending. Both the federal government and Congress would benefit from the creation of large numbers of jobs in the defence industry.

The growth of white-collar jobs was also fuelled by the growth of service industries. During the 1950s, the average family in suburbia earned $6,500 a year, 70 percent higher than the average income of the rest of the nation. Service industries grew to tap this new wealth. Motels, shopping malls and drive-in movie theatres catered for this new consumer. The internal tourist industry also grew. In 1955, Disneyland opened its doors, in Anaheim, southern California.

## Consumerism and domestic technology

The consumer boom of the 1950s and 1960s was made easier by the ready availability of credit to buy goods and services. In 1950, Diner's Club introduced the first credit card. In 1958, American Express introduced its own credit card. By 1960, the mail order company Sears Roebuck had ten million customers who bought on credit. By the early 1960s, middle-class credit card use was becoming commonplace.

During the period 1955 to 1963, US consumers were presented with a wide variety of products to buy. New models of car, television set, refrigerator, dishwasher and radio appeared on the American market in larger numbers and in a wide variety of models, along with cultural consumables like vinyl records.

The nature of the American retail industry changed to meet this new consumer demand. Old city-centre retail areas declined and were replaced by new, out-of-town shopping centres. In 1945, there were only eight shopping centres in the whole country. By 1960, this had risen to over 4,000. New wealth and demand for new domestic technology turned shopping into a major recreational activity.

In 1957, the Soviet Union shook American society when it launched the world's first satellite into space, the Sputnik. This event intensified the Cold War by adding the new dimension of a space race between the USA and the USSR. In 1961, President J. F. Kennedy (JFK) announced that a priority for the USA was to land a man on the moon by the end of the 1960s. Technology developed for the US space programme soon appeared on the domestic consumer market. Products included non-stick cooking pots and pans, transistors, home computers and advanced electronics.

The increased affluence of many Americans, particularly those in suburbia, was another factor in shaping the teenager as a new class of consumer. Teenagers and their spending power fuelled the growth of the popular music industry. By the early 1960s, popular music idols like Elvis Presley were nationally known personalities earning huge sums of money. Radio stations played rock'n'roll to attract advertisers keen to communicate with teenagers, generating more spending by teenagers who heard the adverts.

With so many labour-saving devices on sale, quality of life for many families improved, freeing up more leisure time. Watching television, attending sports fixtures or travelling in cars became the norm rather than the exception for many Americans.

**AS Level Exam-Style Question Section B**

How accurate is it to say that the growth of suburbia was more as a result of the economic boom than a cause of it in the period 1955 to 1963? (20 marks)

**Tip**

*In your answer you will be expected to provide evidence of how suburbia, and its growth, was an important stimulant to the economic boom of the years 1955 to 1963. You need to compare the growth of suburbia with other factors such as the growth of white collar jobs, car ownership and the growth of new industries in bringing about an economic boom. At the end of your answer you need to make a judgement that directly answers the question.*

**ACTIVITY**
**KNOWLEDGE CHECK**

**Urbanisation and affluence**

1 Identify reasons why cities developed rapidly in the period 1955 to 1963.

2 How important was car ownership and highway construction to the growth of suburbs?

3 Why did the number of white-collar jobs increase in the USA in the years 1955 to 1963?

4 Identify ways in which the USA could be regarded as a consumer society by 1963.

# HOW IMPORTANT WERE CHANGES IN CULTURE IN THE YEARS 1955 TO 1963?

## Suburban conformity and social change in film and television

The years 1955 to 1963 proved to be a period of public protest, political assassination, a youth **counterculture** and a divided society.

Looking back on the 1950s and early 1960s in decades to come, this period seemed like a period of stability, affluence and tranquillity to many Americans. The dominant social change of the period was the rapid growth of suburbia, the heartland of conformity.

Suburbia was characterised by similar housing developments offering young families the chance of a happy family life with all the modern amenities, such as a garage, washing machine, dishwasher, television and a backyard for barbeques and family recreation. Suburbs such as the Levittowns encouraged uniformity and conformity. Suburbs were predominantly white. In 1960, only five percent of suburban dwellers were black Americans, and of the 65,000 residents of Levittowns only 57 were black.

The 1950s and 1960s was the era of the baby boomers. Following years of economic depression and war, causing low birth rates, the young couples who got married in the 1950s had children and brought them up in the suburbs, rapidly increasing the US population. Middle-class family life in the suburbs was portrayed as the 'American Way of Life'. In 1956, *Life* magazine produced a special issue featuring an 'ideal' middle-class woman, 32 years old, 'pretty and popular', the mother of four children and married at 16. She was shown as an excellent wife, volunteer and home manager.

However, suburban life was not a popular theme with US film audiences. In 1957, a film on suburban life, *No Down Payment*, was a flop. The films that dominated American film theatres in the period 1955 to 1963 were mainly escapist, blockbuster films about war and adventure. *Around the World in 80 Days* was voted best Hollywood film in 1957 by the Oscar committee of the Academy of Film Sciences. A war film about British troops in a Japanese prison camp, *The Bridge on the River Kwai*, was best picture in 1958, and *Lawrence of Arabia*, a film about British involvement in the Arab Revolt in the First World War, in 1963. In 1961, a musical called *West Side Story*, based on Shakespeare's *Romeo and Juliet* and set in the Hispanic American neighbourhood of New York City, packed the movie theatres.

Those films about everyday life in the USA that did draw a popular following tended to portray young people who found growing up in 1950s suburbia stifling. *Rebel without a Cause* (1955) was regarded as a sensation at the time and made an instant star of James Dean, the main actor. Dean played a moody youth who represented the 'quiet generation' of young people in the 1950s. Dean's own career was cut short by a car accident later in the same year, aged 24.

However, the image of happy suburban life was mirrored on the ever-growing television networks. Ownership of televisions grew rapidly in the 1950s and early 1960s. A key feature of US television programming was the situation comedy or 'sitcom'. The two most popular television shows of the 1950s were set in middle-class suburbia: *I Love Lucy* and *Father Knows Best*. These were followed by the domestic bliss of the *Dick Van Dyke Show* (1961–66).

*Father Knows Best* first appeared in 1953. It centered on life in a new suburb, 'Springfield', and the Anderson family who lived there in a large house. Its main star, Robert Young, had appeared in Hollywood films. As Jim Anderson he portrayed a typical middle-class father who made no reference to politics, had no strongly held views and never had a bad day at the office. His wife was played by Jane Wyatt, who kept perfect order in her home, kept her opinions to herself and was a supportive wife to Jim.

The most popular sitcom of the 1950s offered one of the only starring roles for a woman. *I Love Lucy* centered on the home life of Lucille Ball, loyal wife of her musician husband in the show and real life, Desi Arnaz. It ran from 1951 to 1957. When Lucy had a baby in the series (shortly after the real-life birth of her son), almost 70 percent of the nation's television sets were tuned in to watch.

*The Dick Van Dyke Show* was on a similar theme. Dick was a happily married man living in the suburb of New Rochelle, near New York City. Dick had a loving wife, young child, good job, lovely private house and friendly neighbours: the suburban ideal.

**KEY TERM**

**Counterculture**
An alternative culture. The US counterculture of the 1960s criticised the American political, economic and social systems and favoured ideas such as new forms of religion, different types of music and dance and opposition to traditional social values such as life-long marriage.

Game shows also proved popular. The most popular was the *$64,000 Question*, which began in June 1955. Sponsored by cosmetic firm Revlon, it placed contestants in isolation booths to answer demanding questions. An early star contestant was Charles van Doren, who seemed to be a virtual genius until it was revealed that he was given the questions before the show!

There were very few opportunities in either film or television for black American actors. When they did appear it was usually in minor subservient roles like the butler Rochester in the popular television programme *The Jack Benny Show*. However, in 1963, for the first time, a black American actor, Sidney Poitier, won the Best Actor Academy Award (Oscar) for his role in *Lilies of the Field*.

**SOURCE 4** Middle-class bliss: *The Dick Van Dyke Show* ran from 1961 to 1966 and was one of the USA's most popular television shows.

**EXTRACT 1** An extract from *Daytime to Primetime: The History of American Television Programs*, by James Roman (2005).

Although Lucille Ball of 'I Love Lucy' was the biggest television star in the 1950s, close behind her was Robert Young. In the show 'Father Knows Best', Young played the role of Jim Anderson, a manager at the General Insurance Company and the consummate father. In that role he exuded a warmth and confidence that endeared him to the fans of the program. The show was a testimony to the intimacy of the American family and its cherished traditions. There can be no doubt that Jim was a faithful husband to his wife, played by Jane Wyatt; a good provider; and an understanding father to his three children, Betty (nicknamed Princess), James Jr (nicknamed Bud) and Kathy (nicknamed Kitten). It appeared on the CBS, NBC and ABC networks from 1954 to 1963 for a total of 203 episodes.

'Father Knows Best' became a fixture of American pop culture, touching the fabric of our institutions. Its ability to enunciate family values and promote civic responsibility was viewed as a valuable asset on the part of the government.

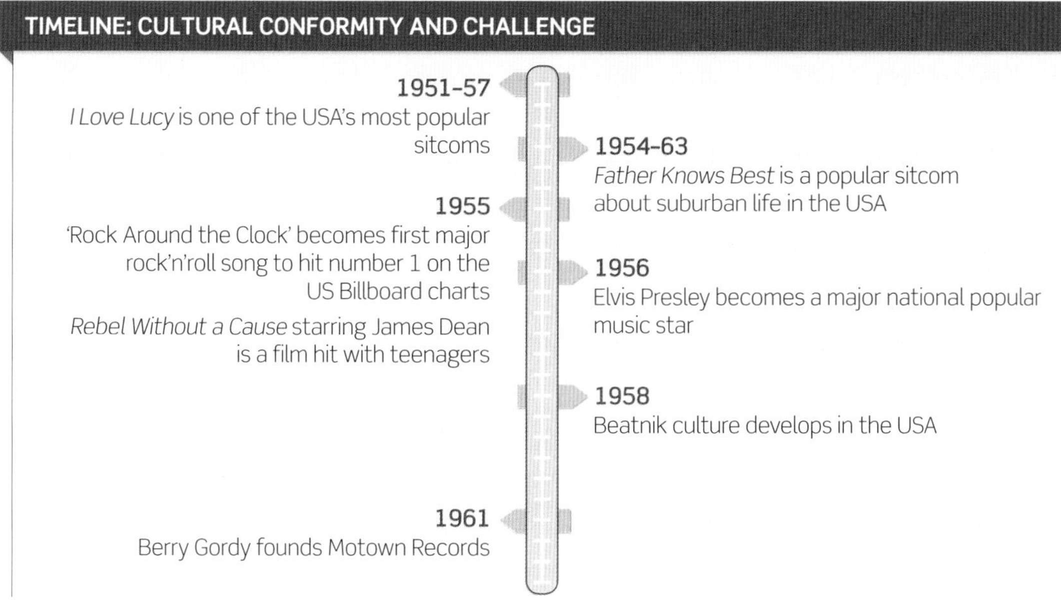


## Advertising

An important stimulus to consumer spending in the age of affluence of the 1950s and early 1960s was the advertising industry, which persuaded the new consumers to buy more. An important aspect of advertising in this period was the development of television. By the early 1960s, almost every US home possessed a television. Television was replacing Hollywood films and variety theatres as the main source of popular entertainment, watched by millions. Unlike other countries, such as the UK, which had government-funded broadcasting, US television was wholly financed through advertising during and between programmes. Television companies' advertising revenue grew by 1000 percent in the 1950s. Overall, advertisers spent $10 billion a year during the 1950s and early 1960s persuading consumers to spend.

## The challenge of teenage culture and music

### Origins of teenage culture

The 1950s is closely associated with the rise of the teenager. Not only were young people in their teens rebellious, they now had the financial power to buy, thanks to the post-war economic boom. They received money from their parents and many had part-time jobs. They were also given more independence by their parents, who had grown up in the Depression years and the Second World War. Teenagers benefited from the availability of cars and the development of fast food. They were regular users of drive-in movie theatres. Business saw opportunities and developed teenage fashion.

Television programming and films helped develop the idea of a new social group in society. Teenagers were often portrayed as 'juvenile delinquents', disrespectful of adults and society in general. The media claimed gangs of youths roamed inner cities engaging in violence. The 1953 film *The Wild One*, starring Marlon Brando, captured the mood. Brando led a motorbike gang that intimidated small communities. *Rebel without a Cause*, first shown in 1955, starred one of the 1950s most popular film stars, James Dean, and dealt with teenage alienation. Youths cruising in their cars or riding in motorbike gangs, wearing leather jackets, using their own slang, and males greasing their hair, shocked many adults.

At the time there were attempts to explain these new developments. Margaret Mead in *The School in American Culture*, published in 1951, claimed that growing disrespect for teachers was due to the rapid change in US society, where many young people began to regard formal education as irrelevant. Americans were also shocked by the findings of Alfred Kinsey and his team at the Institute of Sexual Research at Indiana University. He published *Sexual Behaviour in the Human Male* in 1948 and *Sexual Behaviour in the Human Female* in 1953. Kinsey's study claimed that 95 percent of males had been sexually active by the age of 15 years. Similar findings were revealed in his book on female behaviour.

Kinsey's work fueled the idea that the current generation of teenagers was very different from previous generations who (allegedly) respected their parents and conformed with adult society. In 1954, Fredric Wertham published *Seduction of the Innocent*, claiming that comic books helped corrupt the young through inappropriate depictions of sexual content or by presenting views which ran counter to traditional family life. By 1955, 13 states had passed laws regulating the sale of comic books and censoring depictions of inappropriate behaviour. Also in 1955 the national magazine *Time* produced a special edition called 'Teenagers on the Rampage'.

**EXTRACT 2**

From P. H. Ennis *The Seventh Stream: The Emergence of Rock'n'roll in American Popular Music* (1992). The extract places rock'n'roll within the context of the development of US popular music after the Second World War.

A new music arrived in the US around 1950 and by 1965 it had fully matured as the 7th stream of American popular music, surviving the six other streams that gave it life. These other streams are called pop, black pop, country pop, jazz, folk and gospel. Each of these musics, from their central cores and from their boundary zones with the others, successively touched and mixed, producing rock and roll. It was a boisterous and infectious music, directed to, and embraced almost exclusively by, young people. Rock and roll began with teenagers and was adopted later by college students and those of college age. Together they forged a musical ambience in which they could sing and dance and that would accompany them on a journey of confrontation with the adults who ruled their homes, their schools and their nation.

## Music and teenage rebellion

Most of all, teenage culture was associated with the new form of popular music known as rock'n'roll. Rock'n'roll stood in marked contrast to the music popular with adults during the Second World War, which usually involved 'swing' music and ballad singing by male artists such as Frank Sinatra, also known as 'the Voice'. With financial independence, teenagers could buy records or listen to new records on jukeboxes, which appeared in cafes and fast-food outlets. The person who first coined the term 'rock'n'roll' was Alan Freed on the radio station WINS, in New York City, in 1954 and he helped make rock'n'roll a national craze. The first successful record in this style was by black American Big Joe Turner, made in Kansas City, Missouri in 1954, called 'Shake Rattle and Roll'. In the same year another black American, Chuck Berry, produced 'Johnny B. Goode'.

Racial discrimination, particularly in the Old South, meant that rock'n'roll music only really took off when performed by white artists. In 1955, Bill Haley and the Comets performed 'Rock Around the Clock', which appeared in the film *The Blackboard Jungle* about teenage rebellion at a high school, released in 1955. 'Rock Around the Clock' became a nationwide success.

The artist who gave rock'n'roll truly national appeal was a southern white from Tupelo, Mississippi, Elvis Presley. His sexy dance moves, good looks and powerful voice propelled him to fame. In 1955, he had his first number one hit single, 'Heartbreak Hotel', with RCA. Rock'n'roll had found its first national teenage idol.

While rock'n'roll, and Elvis Presley in particular, dominated popular music in the late 1950s, by 1961 changes were taking place. In 1959, black American Berry Gordy founded the Motown record label in Detroit, the centre of the US car industry. It developed a distinctive northern black American sound and launched the careers of The Four Tops, and Diana Ross and the Supremes. It laid the platform for nationwide popularity of black American popular music not seen since the appearance of jazz in the 1920s.

Rock'n'roll tapped into the growing rebellious nature of American youth in the late 1950s and early 1960s. While popular music (and film) offered youth culture an expression of their feelings, national television tended to ignore developments in youth culture, instead reinforcing the image that suburbia and the 'American Way of Life' was based on happy marriage, domestic tranquility and stability. When Elvis Presley first appeared on the nationally popular *Ed Sullivan Show*, on 9 September 1956, he sang his hit single, 'Hound Dog'. Television producers ensured that only his upper body was shown: his dance moves (which earned him the nickname 'Elvis the Pelvis') were felt too provocative for an American television audience.

**SOURCE 5**

Extract from a *New York Times* article on Elvis Presley and teenagers by Jack Gould, which appeared in September 1956.

Some parents are puzzled or confused by Presley's almost hypnotic powers; others are concerned; perhaps more are a shade disgusted and content to permit the Presley fad to play itself out. Neither criticism of Presley or the teenagers who admire him is particularly to the point. Presley has fallen into a fortune with a routine that in one form or another has always existed on the fringe of show business; in his gyrating figure and aggressive gestures the teenagers have found something that for the moment seems exciting and important.

Quite possibly Presley just happened to move in where society has failed the teenager. Greater in their numbers than ever before they may have found in Presley a rallying point. Family counsellors have wisely noted that ours is still a culture in a stage of frantic transition. With even 16-year-olds capable of commanding $20 to $30 a week in their spare time, with access to automobiles at an early age, with communications media of all kinds exposing them to new thoughts very early in life, theirs indeed is a high degree of independence. Inevitably it has been accompanied by a lessening of parental control.

## Evidence (5b)

### The importance of context

Documents (texts) are like small pieces torn from a larger tapestry (the context). Historians have to reconstruct the larger pattern into which documents might fit in order to use them to construct accounts of the past. The problem is that texts can have multiple contexts. Historians often debate how best to contextualise the documents that they interpret.

Source 5 contains an explanation of why the rock'n'roll star Elvis Presley was popular with teenagers and gives a strong indication of the impact of rock'n'roll among young people in the USA in the 1950s. It was written and published in 1956.

Working alone, summarise the key points made in Source 5.

Now, in groups, discuss the following:

1 Does the source indicate why rock'n'roll was so popular with teenagers?

2 What aspects of rock'n'roll gave cause for concern?

As well as noting the contents of the source, remember to consider the audience.

The timeline below provides a possible context for the source in the wider story of American youth culture and popular music. Look at the timeline and answer these questions.

3 How does Source 5 fit into the pattern of events?

4 Why might 1956 be regarded as an important year in the development of rock'n'roll as part of American teenage culture and popular music?

| | |
|---|---|
| 1948-53: Alfred Kinsey produces studies on sexual behaviour of males and females and claims Americans becoming sexually active in their teenage years<br>1953: Hollywood film *The Wild One* starring Marlon Brando | |
| 1955: 'Rock Around the Clock' becomes first major rock'n'roll hit single in the USA<br>1955: *Rebel Without a Cause* starring James Dean is a film hit with teenagers<br>1956: Elvis Presley become a major national popular music star<br>1958: Beatnik culture develops in USA | September 1956: Publication of *New York Times* article |

There is good reason to think that rock'n'roll was a transitory phenomenon, and that traditional values such as support for family life were more significant and widespread within American culture than enthusiasm for rock'n'roll.

Look at the timeline below, then answer this question:

Why might the New York Times have decided to publish an article on the impact of rock'n'roll on teenage culture in 1956?

| | |
|---|---|
| 1951-57: *I Love Lucy* is one of America's most popular sitcoms | |
| 1954-63: *Father Knows Best* is a popular sitcom about suburban life in USA<br>1961: Berry Gordy founds Tamla Motown Records | September 1956: Publication of *New York Times* article |
| 1961-66: *The Dick Van Dyke Show*, about blissful family life in suburban New York City, is one of the top shows on US television | |

Consider both timelines together and answer the following questions:

5 Why might an adult, middle-class audience be interested in current trends in teenage culture and rock'n'roll music in 1956?

6 Why is it important for historians to spend time thinking about possible contexts for a document before they start to use it to draw conclusions about the past?

**EXTEND YOUR KNOWLEDGE**

**Elvis Presley (1935–77)**
Elvis Aaron Presley was born in Tupelo, northern Mississippi, to a poor white family. He began singing in his church choir. In 1953, he recorded some songs for Sun Records, Memphis, but his career only took off when Colonel Tom Parker (an illegal immigrant from the Netherlands who had never really been a colonel) became his manager. In 1956, he released his first breakthrough single 'Heartbreak Hotel', which sold millions of copies. In his career he released 45 singles, including 'Hound Dog', 'Love Me Tender' and 'Jailhouse Rock'. He also made many low-budget Hollywood films such as *Loving You* (1957), *King Creole* (1958) and *GI Blues* (1960).

Elvis combined good looks with a great voice and latent sexuality, which made him the idol of the teenage population. In the late 1950s, he served two years in the US Army in Germany. Although his career flagged in the early 1960s, he made a comeback in Las Vegas in 1969, which rekindled his early popularity. Known as 'the King', Elvis died suddenly of a heart attack in 1977. He is still one of the most popular music performers of all time.

**SOURCE**

Elvis Presley performing in Hollywood, California on 22 June 1956. It was Presley's stage act as much as his singing voice that gained him widespread popularity. His performances caused controversy but also set the style for many popular music performers who followed him.

## Beatnik culture

An important element in the 'alternative' culture of the USA in the late 1950s and early 1960s was the development of a 'beatnik' culture. The beatnik movement offered its followers an alternative to the conformity and craving for consumer goods that they saw as the main features of American society.

Beatniks were known for experimenting with drugs such as marijuana, for rejecting the affluent society associated with suburbia, for their interest in Asian religions such as Hinduism, and for their opposition to developments such as the arms race with the Soviet Union. Support for sexual liberation and new forms of literature and music were also important parts of the beatnik counterculture. Beatniks wore berets, loose pullovers and were to be seen hanging around in coffee bars discussing society, particularly in the Greenwich Village area of Manhattan, New York City.

The terms 'beat' and 'beat generation' were first used by novelist Jack Kerouac, a French Canadian, in 1948, but the term 'beatnik' was used more generally from the late 1950s onwards. The name linked 'beat' with part of the Russian word 'sputnik', the space satellite, launched in 1957. Because of their anti-conformist views some saw beatniks as possibly pro-communist.

The individuals who were the main creators of the beatnik culture all attended Columbia University in New York City: Allen Ginsberg, Jack Kerouac and Lucien Carr. Jack Kerouac's book *On the Road,* published in 1957, became one of the best examples of Beat literature. It was an account of Kerouac's travels across the USA. Beatnik culture also helped develop the popularity of rhythm and blues and folk music, drawing young singer/composers like Bob Dylan into their culture.

Eventually, beatnik culture developed into the hippie counter-culture and the protest movements of the 1960s.

**AS Level Exam-Style Question Section B**

To what extent did teenage culture change in the USA in the period 1953 to 1963? (20 marks)

**Tip**

*Your answer should give a balanced view of the issue in the question. You will need to explain what you mean by 'teenage culture' and give examples of ways in which it changed. To balance the answer you will also be expected to mention ways in which teenage culture remained the same. At the end of your answer you will be expected to assess the degree of change.*

ACTIVITY
KNOWLEDGE CHECK

**Cultural conformity and challenge**

1 In what ways was suburban conformity portrayed on television?

2 How did the subject matter of popular films in the years 1955-63 differ from what was popular on US television?

3 What do you regard as the main features of teenage culture in the years 1955-63, including beatnik culture?

4 What do you regard as the most important change in US culture in the period 1955-63? Explain your answer.

5 Do you agree that the main characteristic of American life in the period 1955-63 was the stability of suburban life? Set up a debate on this subject.

# HOW SUCCESSFUL WAS THE CIVIL RIGHTS MOVEMENT IN ACHIEVING MORE RIGHTS FOR BLACK AMERICANS IN THE YEARS 1955 TO 1963?

The 'age of affluence' and the move to suburbia were essentially white phenomena. The ten percent of the American population who were black saw their incomes rise at a much lower rate than whites; however, their average income was still about that achieved in Britain and Western Europe at the time. In 1953, the median income of a white family was $4,392 per year compared to only $2,461 for non-white families. By 1960, the gap had grown to $5,835 for white families and $3,233 for non-white families. And, although slavery had been abolished at the end of the American Civil War (1861–65) and all Americans were guaranteed equal protection under the law in 1868, black Americans faced considerable racial discrimination. In the Old South, legal segregation had been introduced in the years 1877 to 1900.

Legal segregation continued into the 1950s with separate schools, benches, public toilets, drinking fountains and seats on public transport set aside for whites and blacks. In other parts of the country, black Americans faced discrimination in housing and jobs. Suburbs were areas of white residence. Black Americans lived in inner cities and rural areas, usually in poor accommodation. The 'American Dream' that hard work and effort would bring prosperity was open to all Americans, except, it seemed, blacks and other non-whites. All was to change in the years after 1955.

**EXTEND YOUR KNOWLEDGE**

Jim Crow Laws

The name given to the laws discriminating against black Americans that were introduced in states of the Old South after 1877. The laws required segregation of blacks and whites at public schools, lunch counters, toilets, drinking fountains and park benches and on public transport. The US Supreme Court reinforced legal segregation in the 1896 case *Plessy v Ferguson*, which declared 'separate but equal' facilities were legal. Unfortunately, white and black facilities were far from equal.

The Jim Crow laws also prevented many black Americans from voting. Poll taxes were introduced in several states, which were charged when voters went to the polls. These discriminated against the poor, both white and black, but as black Americans tended to be poorer than whites it affected them most. Literacy tests to register for voting also discriminated against blacks, who had lower literacy levels.

## The civil rights movement - activism and protest

### Montgomery Bus Boycott, 1955-56

In 1955, Montgomery, the state capital of Alabama, received national attention when an attempt was made to desegregate public transport. In December 1955, a black American woman, Mrs Rosa Parks, boarded a public bus in Montgomery. Mrs Parks had been an activist in the civil rights movement in the city of Montgomery and took this step as a provocative act to highlight segregation on public transport. Montgomery operated a system where the front seats were always occupied by whites. Rosa Parks refused to give up her seat near the front of the bus and was arrested.

**AS Level Exam-Style Question Section A**

***Study Source 7 before you answer this question.***

Why is Source 7 valuable to the historian for an enquiry into why the Montgomery Bus Boycott began?

Explain your answer using the source, the information about it and your own knowledge of the historical context. (8 marks)

**Tip**

*In assessing the source's value you will be expected to comment on its provenance. Think about whose views are mentioned and why would these be valuable to the historian. You will also be expected to comment on the content. The races were not always separated and you could include the specific exceptions mentioned in the source.*

This sparked the Montgomery Bus Boycott of 1955 to 1956, where black Americans refused to use public transport until it was desegregated. Eventually, in December 1956, the US Supreme Court declared segregated public transport unconstitutional. The boycott was important in other ways. Most notably it saw the rise to national prominence of a local black American religious minister, Dr Martin Luther King. He was to be a central figure in the civil rights movement until his assassination in 1968. The success of the Montgomery Bus Boycott led to the creation of the Southern Christian Leadership Conference (SCLC), a black civil rights organisation that mobilised support against legal segregation across the Old South.

**SOURCE**

From the Montgomery City Code on the Operation of Public Buses, 1955. The code laid down rules for how public buses should be operated within Montgomery, Alabama. This code was in operation when Rosa Parks refused to give up her seat to a white passenger on the request of the white bus driver. Her refusal led to her arrest and sparked the Montgomery Bus Boycott.

*Section 10. Separation of the Races - Required*

Every person operating a bus line in the city shall provide equal but separate accommodations for white people and negroes on his buses, by requiring the employees in charge thereof to assign passengers seats on the vehicles in such manner as to separate the white people from the negroes, where they are both white and negroes in the same car; provided, however, that negro nurses having charge of white children or sick or infirm white persons, may be assigned seats among white people. Nothing in this section shall be construed as prohibiting the operators of such bus lines from separating the races by means of separate vehicles if they see fit.

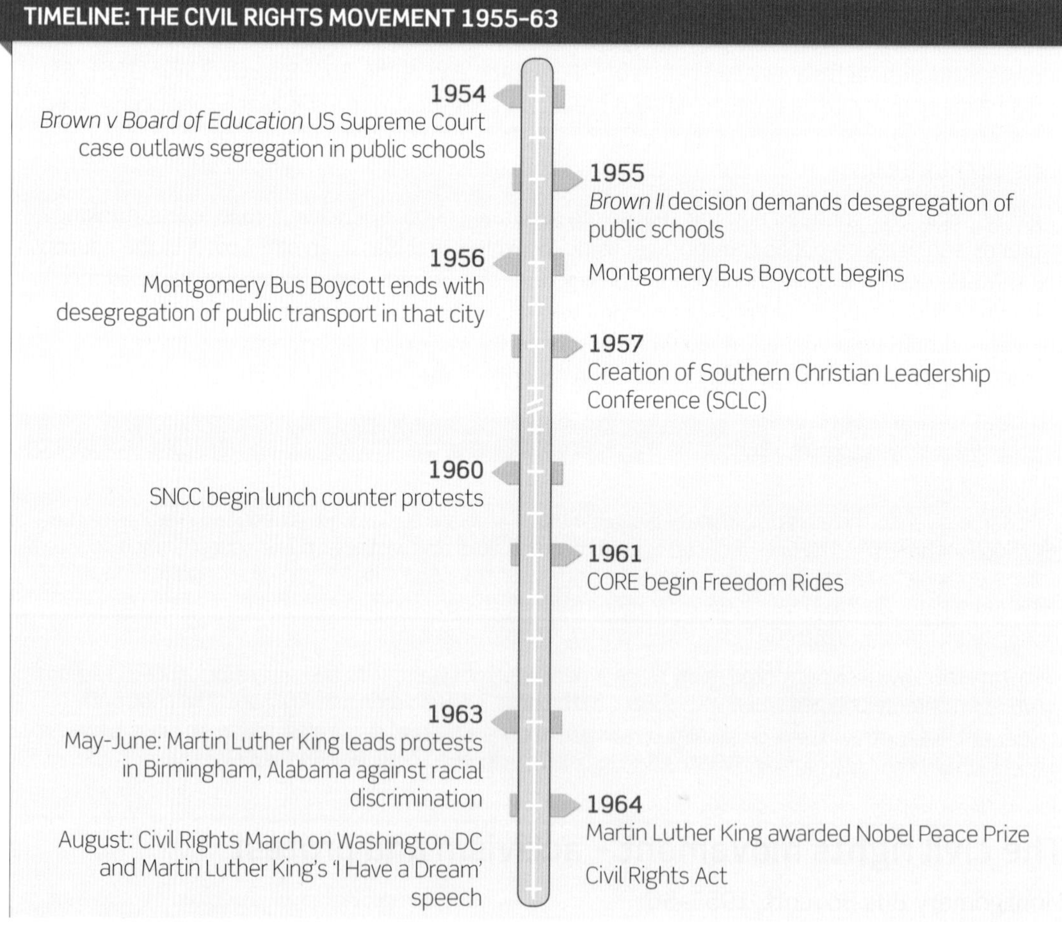


## SNCC and CORE

Although Martin Luther King was seen as the unofficial leader of the demand for full black American rights, he and the SCLC (Southern Christian Leadership Conference) were not the only ones trying to achieve equality. In February 1960, a group of students in Greensboro, North Carolina, began a campaign to allow black Americans to be served at lunch counters in Woolworth stores. Up until then these had been reserved for whites only. In April their actions helped create the Students Non-Violent Co-ordinating Committee (SNCC). These non-violent protests forced stores across the Old South to end racial discrimination at lunch counters.

Also, in 1961, black and white students of the Congress of Racial Equality engaged in Freedom Rides. They took Greyhound buses and ignored segregated waiting areas. They were testing the US Supreme Court decision of 1960, *Boynton v Virginia*, which outlawed segregation on interstate buses. Attacked by mobs in Alabama, the Freedom Riders gained national publicity and forced the federal government to protect them.

**EXTEND YOUR KNOWLEDGE**

School desegregation

By 1955, the modern civil rights movement had begun. In 1948, President Truman had desegregated the armed forces. In 1954, the landmark US Supreme Court decision, *Brown v Board of Education of Topeka, Kansas*, outlawed racial segregation in all public schools across the USA. In 1955, *Brown II* declared that desegregation needed to occur with 'all deliberate speed'. These decisions were met with considerable white opposition, particularly in the Old South.

One of the most controversial incidents in school desegregation occurred at Central High School, Little Rock, Arkansas in 1957. An attempt to enrol nine black students led to a riot. President Eisenhower had to send in troops of the 101st Airborne Division to restore order and to accompany the black students to and from school for a whole year.

In 1962, an attempt to allow a black American student, James Meredith, to attend the University of Mississippi resulted in a major confrontation between the federal government and the state of Mississippi and whites who were opposed to desegregation of education. President J. F. Kennedy had to dispatch hundreds of US Marshals and troops to enforce law and order at the university when violence erupted. Although Meredith was admitted to the university, he was later shot and wounded.

### Birmingham, Alabama, 1963

Martin Luther King continued to be the voice of the civil rights movement. His national prominence was confirmed by a major confrontation with police in Birmingham, Alabama. King had been invited to lead a campaign by the Reverend Fred Shuttlesworth, pastor of the Baptist Bethel Church, who had formed the Alabama Christian Movement for Human Rights, which was linked to the SCLC. King decided to concentrate on three demands: desegregating lunch counters, fitting rooms and toilets in department stores; increasing the hiring of black Americans in business; and creating a multiracial committee to help desegregate facilities across the city of Birmingham.

King organised non-violent demonstrations in Birmingham. The demonstrations led to his arrest and imprisonment for two days, which made national television news. King was released on bail only after the intervention of President Kennedy and his brother, Robert, the Attorney General. A key feature of the non-violent demonstrations in Birmingham was the use of black schoolchildren. The City Police Chief, Eugene 'Bull' Connor, was determined to end demonstrations and used police dogs, water cannon and police clubs to break up demonstrations and arrested 2,500 demonstrators. The sight of police dogs and heavy-handed police tactics on prime-time television horrified most Americans. The federal government forced both sides to reach an agreement and, although King did not get all that he wanted, the Kennedy government did introduce new civil rights legislation. Kennedy went on national television to announce his intention of introducing a civil rights act to give black Americans equality. After Birmingham, the magazine *Newsweek* conducted an opinion poll of black Americans that found that 95 percent regarded Martin Luther King as their most successful spokesman.

**SOURCE**

An extract from a national televised speech given by President Kennedy on 11 June 1963 following protests in Birmingham, Alabama.

We are confronted primarily with a moral issue. It is as old as the Scriptures and is clear as the American Constitution. The heart of the question is whether all Americans are to be afforded equal rights and equal opportunities; whether we are going to treat our fellow Americans as we want to be treated.

If an American, because his skin is dark, cannot eat lunch in a restaurant open to the public; if he cannot send his children to the best public schools available; if he cannot vote for the public officials who represent him; if in short, he cannot enjoy the full and free life which all of us want, then who among us would be content to have the color of his skin changed and stand in his place?

Now the time has come for this nation to fulfill its promise. The events in Birmingham and elsewhere have so increased the cries for equality that no city or state or legislative body can prudently choose to ignore them.

## The impact of the march on Washington DC, August 1963

By August 1963, black American civil rights was a major national issue. Americans had seen for themselves in television news broadcasts the brutality black Americans had been facing in the Old South. In August, 250,000 people converged on Washington DC for a national rally. About a quarter of the marchers were white, including Hollywood stars such as Charlton Heston. Martin Luther King gained international prominence through his keynote 'I have a dream' speech on the steps of the Lincoln Memorial on the National Mall, in which he set out his vision of a completely integrated America. Such was the power of King's oratory and vision that he elevated black American civil rights into an international issue. In 1964, he appeared on the front of *Time* magazine, one of the most influential magazines in the USA. He was credited with 'an indescribable capacity for empathy that is the touchstone of leadership'. In the same year, he was awarded the Nobel Peace Prize. Martin Luther King was now one of the most respected Americans in the world. The march on Washington DC and King's part in that event also had a major national impact within the USA.

The issue of black American civil rights was now one of the most important in US politics. President J. F. Kennedy promised to introduce a Civil Rights bill to Congress to end racial discrimination. He was assassinated before the bill was passed. However, his successor, President Lyndon Johnson, ensured that proposal became law as the Civil Rights Act of 1964.

## The Ku Klux Klan and White Citizens' Committees

The civil rights movement was noted for its non-violent nature. Martin Luther King supported non-violent protest as did SNCC and CORE. However, opposition to the demands for desegregation and racial equality was not always non-violent. Whites in the Old South used a variety of methods to prevent the end of legal segregation.

In the wake of the historic US Supreme Court decision of *Brown v Board of Education, Topeka, Kansas* southern politicians went on the offensive. In March 1956, 100 congressmen and senators from the Old South signed 'The Southern Manifesto', drafted by Senator Sam Ervin of North Carolina. It pledged to support segregation by all legal means. Southern politicians had considerable power. The vast majority were in the Democratic Party, which controlled Congress in the late 1950s. Under the **seniority rule** many of these southern Democrats controlled the powerful committees of both houses of Congress.

In 1957, they worked together to ensure that a civil rights act would have very little impact on segregation. They did it by amending the proposal so that it would be difficult to enforce. After 1961, when Democrat J. F. Kennedy became president, they made it very difficult for his administration to pass legislation to aid black Americans.

A more direct menace to black Americans seeking an end to segregation was the revival of the Ku Klux Klan (KKK). This was a white supremacist organisation set up after the American Civil War in 1866. It had declined in the 1870s, but revived again after 1915 and into the 1920s. Now with the threat to legal segregation its popularity grew again.

Throughout the period 1955–63, the KKK offered a public image of white intimidation of black Americans. KKK groups paraded through towns and set fire to large crosses. Attempts to register black Americans to vote, a key civil rights aim, were met by constant intimidation. It is difficult to quantify how many black Americans were dissuaded from registering to vote or engaging in peaceful protest.

Terror attacks on black Americans were the KKK's trademark. In 1955, in Money, Mississippi, a black American teenager, Emmett Till, on holiday from Chicago, was murdered for talking to a white girl. The alleged perpetrators were put on trial but acquitted. Throughout the period 1955–63, black Americans suffered attacks and intimidation by KKK members. Members of the Montgomery Improvement Association (MIA), which organised the bus boycott in 1955–56, suffered death threats and mob attacks by KKK supporters.

In 1961, Freedom Riders faced violence when they tried to use a whites-only waiting room in Alabama and a Greyhound bus carrying Freedom Riders was firebombed in Anniston, Alabama by a white mob. This was one of a number of violent attacks made by whites against Freedom Riders.

On 12 June 1963, just hours after President Kennedy made a nationwide television address supporting further black American civil rights, Medgar Evers, the **NAACP** (National Association for the Advancement of Colored People) secretary for Mississippi, was assassinated by a member of the KKK, Byron Beckwith. He was never brought to trial.

In the media the KKK was portrayed as the ugly face of white opposition to desegregation. The White Citizens' Councils and committees created across the Old South to oppose desegregation had a broader base of support. They were called 'country club' Klans because of their middle-class membership. They held mass meetings and lobbied politicians. White Citizens' committee members made up much of the crowd that prevented the nine black students attending Central High School, Little Rock on the first day of term in September 1957 and helped pressure Governor Faubus to oppose school desegregation. In 1961–62, these white groups in Mississippi forced Governor Ross Barnett to oppose James Meredith's attempt to enter the University of Mississippi.

### KEY TERMS

**Seniority rule**
Both houses of Congress allocated the chairmanship of important committees on the seniority principle. Chair positions were allocated to those members who had the longest continuous service in both houses of Congress. Southern Democrats tended to served longer as congressmen and senators as the Democrat Party invariably always won seats to the US Congress over a long period of time (from 1877 to 1970s). The longer the continuous service, the greater the likelihood of being made a committee chairman in Congress.

**NAACP**
The National Association for the Advancement of Colored People was established in 1909 by a mixture of black Americans and white supporters. Its aim was to improve the position of black Americans in US society. One of its most effective methods was to use the law to get black Americans the rights promised to them under the US Constitution. The *Brown v Board of Education* case of 1954 was brought to the US Supreme Court by the NAACP.

White Citizens' councils and committees were very effective at forcing southern politicians to oppose desegregation. However, they could not prevent federal government intervention such as the deployment of the 101st Airborne Division in Little Rock in 1957 or the use of federal marshals and troops by President Kennedy at the University of Mississippi in 1962. Ultimately, the federal government had the power to intervene, but it did so primarily to implement US Supreme Court decisions that declared legal segregation as unconstitutional in a series of decisions from 1954. By 1963, only nine percent of school districts in the Old South were desegregated. In Mississippi and Alabama the figure was even lower. This was due to local white opposition in state government. Education, under the US Constitution, was a responsibility for the states rather than the federal government.

**SOURCE 9** A member of the Ku Klux Klan in Atlanta, Georgia in the early 1960s wearing the KKK uniform of white, hooded clothing, with their symbol, a fiery cross.

**A Level Exam-Style Question Section B**

***Study Sources 8 and 10 before you answer this question.***

How far could the historian make use of Sources 8 and 10 together to investigate why the struggle for black American civil rights in the years 1956 to 1963 was so difficult?

Explain your answer using both sources, the information given about them and your knowledge of the historical context.
(20 marks)

**Tip**

*In your answer you will be expected to refer to the provenance of the two sources. Who wrote them, when they were written and the intended audience of both sources will require comment from you. To support your assessment of the sources' usefulness you should also use information from within both sources.*

**SOURCE 10**

The Southern Manifesto, March 1956. Signed by 100 senators and congressmen of the southern states following the *Brown v Board of Education* decision by the US Supreme Court that declared legal segregation in public schools unconstitutional.

The unwarranted decision of the Supreme Court in the public school cases is now bearing the fruit always produced when men substitute naked power for established law.

We regard the decisions of the Supreme Court in the school cases as a clear abuse of judicial power. It climaxes a trend in the Federal Judiciary undertaking to legislate, in derogation of the authority of Congress, and to encroach upon the reserved rights of the States and the people.

This unwarranted exercise of power by the Court, contrary to the Constitution, is creating chaos and confusion in the States principally affected. It is destroying the amicable relations between the white and Negro races that have been created through 90 years of patient effort by the good people of both races. It has planted hatred and suspicion where there has been heretofore friendship and understanding.

**ACTIVITY**
**KNOWLEDGE CHECK**

**The civil rights movement**

1. In what ways did white Americans attempt to resist the improvement of black American civil rights in the years 1955-63?
2. What role did Martin Luther King play in the attempt to increase the civil rights of black Americans in the years 1955-63?
3. Write down the different methods black Americans used to campaign for equality in civil rights in the period 1955-63. Which do you regard as the most effective? Give reasons for your answer.

**THINKING HISTORICALLY** **Evidence (5a)**

**Context is everything**

Reread Sources 7, 8 and 10.

Work in a small group. Take an A3 piece of paper. In the middle draw a circle about 20cm in diameter. Label the circle 'evidence' and the space outside the circle 'context'.

For each source:

1. Think of a question that the source could be helpful in answering.
2. Inside the circle, write a set of statements giving information that can be gleaned only from the source itself without any contextual knowledge. Outside the circle, write down statements of contextual knowledge related to the source. Draw annotated lines to show links between the contextual statements and the information from the source. Does context change the nature or meaning of the information?
3. Explain why knowledge of context is important when gathering and using historical evidence. Give specific examples from this exercise to illustrate your point.
4. Why do you think historical context is so important in assessing historical sources?

# DID J. F. KENNEDY'S NEW FRONTIER PROGRAMME ACHIEVE ITS AIM?

J. F. Kennedy became US president on 20 January 1961 after winning the presidential election of November 1960 by the narrowest of margins, 113,000 votes out of 68 million. He also faced considerable conservative opposition in Congress. Republicans and conservative Democrats from the Old South had a great deal of influence and were opposed to major social change. However, Kennedy planned to embark on an ambitious programme of change known as the New Frontier. In his inaugural speech he said: 'We stand today on a new frontier, a frontier that will demand of us all the qualities of courage and conviction. For we are moving into the most challenging, the most dynamic, revolutionary period of our existence – the 1960s. The next ten years will be years of incredible change and growth – years of unprecedented tasks for the next president of the United States.'

## EXTEND YOUR KNOWLEDGE

### John F. Kennedy (1917-63)

John F. Kennedy (JFK) was the 35th and youngest person to become US president at the time of his election. He was also the first Roman Catholic to be president in a country that prided itself on its Protestant heritage. He came from a very wealthy Boston family. His father, Joseph Kennedy, had been US ambassador to Britain just before the Second World War. JFK received a privileged education at Choate School and Harvard University. In the Second World War, while serving as an officer in the US Navy in the Pacific, he was decorated for his bravery in saving members of the crew of his torpedo boat, PT 109, after it had been sunk by a Japanese destroyer.

He became a congressman in 1947 and a US senator in 1953. In 1956, he was chosen as the Democratic Party vice-presidential candidate but lost in the election that re-elected Dwight Eisenhower as president. In the 1960 presidential election he won by a very narrow margin over Republican Richard Nixon.

His presidency was noted for major foreign policy crises: a failed attempt to invade Castro's Cuba in April 1961, the Berlin Wall Crisis of August 1961, and most serious of all the Cuban Missile Crisis of October 1962, which saw JFK establish a reputation as an international statesman. He was also responsible for increasing US military involvement in Vietnam.

At home, JFK was less successful. He faced a hostile Congress and had to deal with crises associated with the civil rights movement.

On 22 November 1963 he was assassinated on a visit to Dallas, Texas, by Lee Harvey Oswald. Since his death, innumerable conspiracy theories about who was behind his assassination have developed. He was succeeded by his vice president, Lyndon Johnson (1963-69), who persuaded Congress to pass many of JFK's proposals.

## TIMELINE: THE JFK PRESIDENCY

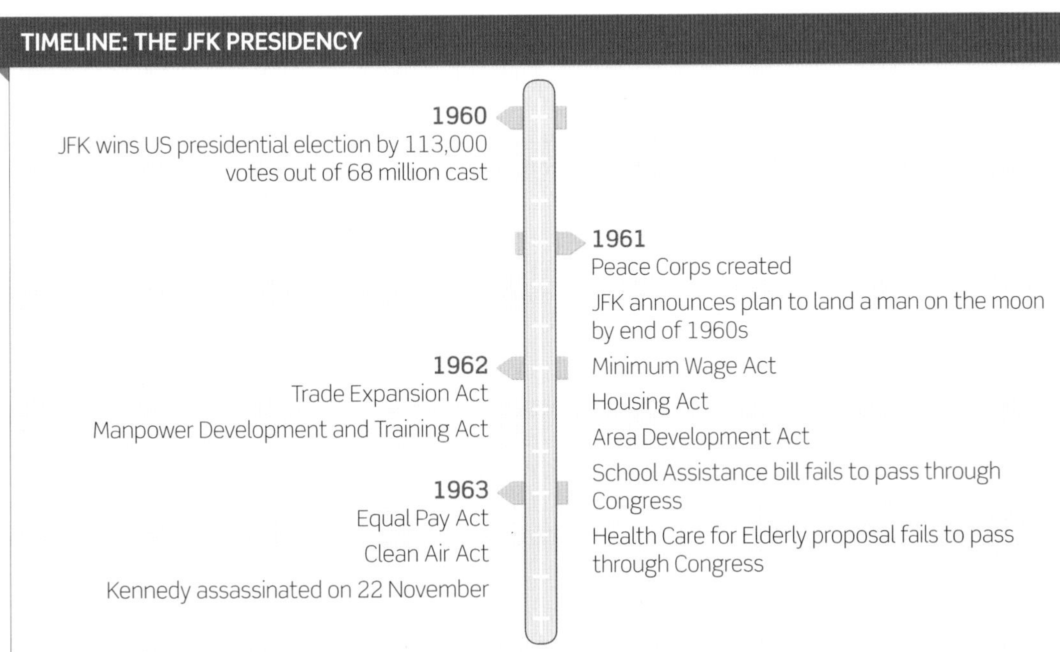

KEY TERM

**Recession**
A downturn in economic activity usually associated with rising unemployment.

## Social welfare and unemployment programmes

An important part of the New Frontier was Kennedy's welfare programme to help the poor and unemployed. He took office during an economic **recession**. Unemployment had risen to 6.5 percent of the workforce and inflation stood at 3.5 percent. And while much of the USA had benefited from the affluence of the 1960s, not all areas or sectors of society had fared equally well. For example, Appalachia, an area of the eastern United States in the Appalachian mountain range that includes West Virginia and parts of eastern Kentucky and Tennessee, was particularly noted for high levels of poverty and economic under-development. Elderly Americans on low incomes lacked health care provision.

In May 1961, Kennedy was able to increase the minimum wage for some low-paid workers. He proposed to increase the minimum wage from $1 per hour to $1.25. Congress passed the proposal, but Southern Democrats, led by Carl Vinson of Georgia, ensured that certain groups of workers were excluded. 350,000 poorly paid workers, including 150,000 laundry workers, working in industrial laundries servicing hospitals, schools and other large institutions, did not benefit from the rise. These low-skilled, low-paid workers included a high proportion of black Americans.

Kennedy was the first president since Herbert Hoover (1929–33) who did not have a woman in his cabinet. However, in 1963, he did propose and pass the Equal Pay Act. It aimed to get women equal pay to men for the same job. Unfortunately, it did not cover all women in work and had no enforcement powers.

Healthcare for the elderly fared no better. JFK planned to increase social security taxes by 0.25 percent to help pay for Medicare for the poor and to help the elderly. However, the House Ways and Means Committee, whose chairman, Wilbur Mills, was a southern Democrat from Arkansas and long opponent of social security healthcare, 'killed off' the measure by refusing to give it enough time to be discussed.

One Kennedy proposal that was passed was the Area Development Act of 1961. This Act provided $394 million over four years to aid areas such as Appalachia. Around 26,000 new jobs were created. However, an attempt to provide an extra $455 million in 1963 was blocked in Congress by the conservative coalition of Republicans and southern white Democrats.

Kennedy had greater success with the manpower Development and Training Act of 1962, which provided job training for the poorly educated. 40 states applied for funding under the Act. He also found less opposition in Congress for the Housing Act of 1961, one of his greatest successes in domestic legislation. Congress voted $4.8 billion to fund housing projects for the poor. This was an attempt to get the USA out of the economic recession that faced the country at the start of the 1960s.

In educational reform JFK faced many problems. In February 1961, he submitted the School Assistance bill to Congress. He asked for $2.3 billion over three years to help construct new schools and raise teachers' salaries. As the USA's first Roman Catholic president JFK was very sensitive about providing federal money to support parochial (church-run) schools, including Catholic schools. As a result, church-run schools were excluded from his proposals. Roman Catholic bishops across the country opposed the bill and, although it passed the Senate, it was defeated in the House of Representatives. However, through the use of **executive orders**, JFK did increase school lunch and milk programmes for the poor. This enabled 700,000 children to enjoy a daily free school lunch and free fresh milk. JFK was also able to get the Higher Educational Facilities Act passed in 1963, which gave $145 million in grants for graduate schools in science, languages and engineering. To co-ordinate efforts to help inner cities, JFK created the Department of Urban Affairs.

KEY TERM

**Executive orders**
A decision made by the US president that did not require a law passed by the US Congress.

In 1962, one of JFK's most significant accomplishments for the longer-term prosperity of the US economy was the Trade Expansion Act. This was the result of the Kennedy round of negotiations in an international organisation, the General Agreement on Tariffs and Trade, set up after the Second World War to encourage more international trade. The Act led to cuts in tariffs (taxes on imports and exports) on average of around 35 percent between the USA and the European Economic Community (later to become the European Union). It also gave the president power to cut tariffs up to 50 percent with other countries that would welcome US goods.

An important measure to help minorities gain employment came in March 1961. Kennedy created, by Executive Order, the Committee on Equal Employment Opportunity (CEEO), to allocate a proportion of federal jobs to black Americans. He placed Vice President Lyndon Johnson in charge.

It was the first attempt by the federal government to introduce affirmative action policies that ensured that minorities like black Americans were to receive the opportunity of federal employment. Johnson got a majority of the largest federal contractors to sign up to his 'Plans for Progress Program' under the CEEO, but by the end of 1961 the *New York Times* stated little change had taken place in the level of black American unemployment, which was twice as high as white unemployment.

SOURCE

President Kennedy's public message on the signing of the Minimum Wage bill, 5 May 1961.

I WANT TO EXPRESS my great satisfaction in signing the bill to increase the minimum wage to a dollar twenty-five cents an hour, and to extend the coverage to three million, six hundred thousand people today who are not covered by this most important piece of national legislation.

This is the first time since the act came into existence under the administration of President Franklin Roosevelt in 1938 that we have been able to expand the coverage. I don't believe that there's any American who believes that any man or woman should have to work in interstate commerce, in companies of substantial size, for less than a dollar twenty-five cents an hour, or fifty dollars a week. That itself is a very minimum wage, and I therefore want to commend the Members of the Congress in the House and the Senate, the Chairmen of the Subcommittees who were particularly involved, under the leadership of the House and Senate, for their untiring efforts.

I also want to commend the leaders of organized labor, the AFL-CIO, who are here today with Mr. Meany, for their long interest. Every member, pretty much, of their unions is paid more than a dollar and a quarter, but they have been concerned about unorganized workers who have been at the bottom of the economic ladder who have not benefited from our growing prosperity in this country as a nation over the long number of years and who need our help.

This doesn't finish this job, but it is a most important step forward, and as a former Member of the Senate who is particularly interested in it, I must say that I am delighted to sign it. I congratulate those who worked for it. They are one group of our citizens who deserve our assistance more, and I think that we can move from this improvement into greater gains in the months and years to come.

## Environmentalism and the expansion of the National Park Service

By the time JFK became president, the environmental effects of a modern industrial society were becoming a national issue. Pollution, environmental degradation and destruction of wildlife habitats were attracting national attention. An important development in environmentalism was the publication in 1962 of *Silent Spring* by Rachel Carson, a former member of the US Fish and Wildlife Service. She highlighted the impact on the food chain of chemical insecticides such as DDT. Kennedy set up an advisory committee on pesticides, partly influenced by *Silent Spring*. In 1963, Congress passed his proposal for a Clean Air Act, which limited pollution emissions from cars and factories. Concern for the environment and the USA's natural heritage in its wilderness areas helped forge an important part of JFK's policies.

An important feature of JFK's domestic achievements was the expansion of the National Park Service. The first national park had been created in 1872, in Yellowstone, Wyoming. Since that date, the Park Service had developed to include national parks, national historic sites, national recreation areas and national monuments. In January 1961, Kennedy appointed Stewart Udall as Secretary of the Interior. He was to serve in that post under both presidents Kennedy and Johnson (1961–69). During that time Udall, a keen environmentalist, made major improvements to the service. In 1963, Udall produced the bestselling book *The Quiet Crisis*, which warned of the dangers of pollution and the threats to the USA's natural resources and called for a nationwide plan to protect the country's wild places. In the same year, Udall appointed George Hertzog as head of the service to help implement Udall's aims. Under Kennedy, Point Reyes National Seashore, California was added to the service. During his time as Secretary of the Interior, Udall helped acquire 3.85 million acres of land for the National Park Service. Udall was also responsible for the addition of six national monuments, nine national recreation areas, 20 historic sites, 50 wildlife refuges and eight national seashores, and for laying the groundwork that allowed Canyonlands in Utah, Redwood in California, North Cascades in Washington State and Guadalupe Mountains in Texas to become national parks in the years following Kennedy's assassination in November 1963.

## The Peace Corps

Of all the changes brought about by the Kennedy administration, the most enduring was the creation of the Peace Corps. Kennedy himself saw it as one of his greatest achievements. It was born out of the Cold War conflict with the Soviet Union. In his inaugural address as president on 20 January 1961, JFK had made a clarion call to the USA: 'Ask not what your country can do for you, ask what you can do for your country.' On 1 March 1961, by executive order, JFK created the Peace Corps, which would send American men and women to developing countries. In its first two years, 5,000 volunteers, mostly young, helped carry American economic and technical aid to 46 countries. Critics saw it as an extension of 'Yankee Imperialism' but its supporters saw it as the USA reaching out to the developing world and giving a helping hand. It has been a permanent fixture of both Democrat and Republican administrations ever since.

**AS Level Exam-Style Question Section A**

***Study Source 12 before you answer this question.***

Why is Source 12 valuable to the historian for an enquiry into the activities of the Peace Corps in the period 1961 to 1963?

Explain your answer using the source, the information about it and your own knowledge of the historical context. (8 marks)

**Tip**

*In your answer refer to the provenance of the source. The fact that it is from an official Peace Corps publication is important. The content is also of value as it describes activities of the Peace Corps, including work by its director, Sargent Shriver. However, it is only one piece of evidence and is only the second newsletter produced by the Peace Corps. It doesn't refer to events after 1961.*

**SOURCE 12** The Peace Corps Volunteer Newsletter, December 1961, Volume 1, Number 2. Sargent Shriver was the first director of the Peace Corps.

*Shriver Visits Corps Projects On Africa Tour*

'You ask how is the Peace Corps doing in Ethiopia? Well, let me put it this way. Those in our government who a month ago were saying, "YOU invited the Peace Corps to Ethiopia..." are now saying, "When WE invited the Peace Corps to Ethiopia."'

The young official from the Ministry of Education was talking to Peace Corps Director Sargent Shriver, who had just arrived in the capital city of Addis Ababa after three days of visiting Volunteers in their classrooms throughout the country. Ethiopia was the first stop on Shriver's recent three-week tour of Peace Corps projects in East Africa. In Tanganyika, Shriver had an opportunity to view Peace Corps.

*Co-op and Loan Programs Broaden Peace Corps Work in Latin America*

The establishment of credit co-operatives and savings-and-loan programs as Peace Corps projects in facilities and marketing opportunities. The institution of credit and market co-operatives is expected to raise substantially both the living standards and the quality of agricultural production.

## The space programme

Another enduring legacy of the Kennedy administration was the space programme, which aimed to land a man on the moon. This was an important part of the 'space race' between the USA and the Soviet Union. The race really began when the USSR successfully launched the first satellite into outer space, the Sputnik, in 1957. The American response to this global Soviet achievement was swift. In 1958, President Eisenhower created the National Aeronautics and Space Administration (NASA) to co-ordinate American efforts in space. The USSR achieved another spectacular success at the beginning of JFK's presidency, when it successfully launched the first man in space, Yuri Gagarin, in April 1961. This was a huge propaganda success for the Soviet Union and the alleged superiority of the Soviet communist system.

On 25 May 1961, JFK delivered a special message to Congress requesting an additional $7–9 billion for the US space programme over the next five years. He proclaimed that 'this nation should commit itself to achieving the goal before the decade is out, of landing a man on the moon and returning him safely to earth'.

Within the year, two American astronauts had travelled in space, Alan Shepard and Virgil Grissom. However, it took until 20 February 1962 before an American, John Glenn, matched Gagarin's achievements of orbiting the earth.

The space programme had significant propaganda value as it meant that the USA would challenge the USSR in space exploration. The space programme also acted as an important stimulant to research and development in computing, electronics and aeronautical engineering.

When the USA was the first nation to land men on the moon in June 1969, they had allegedly won the space race. To date, no other country has successfully landed a man on the moon. This was an important Kennedy legacy, because it was his vision and drive that created the NASA space programme.

SOURCE 13

A NASA photograph of J. F. Kennedy and John Glenn examining Glenn's space module Friendship 7 on 23 February 1962. John Glenn had just returned from being the first US astronaut to orbit the earth, equalling the achievement of Soviet cosmonaut, Yuri Gagarin. Vice President Lyndon Johnson is also in the photograph, behind Kennedy.

SOURCE 14

President Kennedy's message to a Joint Session of Congress on the space programme, delivered 25 May 1961.

If we are to win the battle that is now going on around the world between freedom and tyranny, the dramatic achievements in space which occurred in recent weeks should have made clear to us all, as did the Sputnik in 1957, the impact of this adventure on the minds of men everywhere, who are attempting to make a determination of which road they should take. Since early in my term, our efforts in space have been under review.

I believe we possess all the resources and talents necessary. But the facts of the matter are that we have never made the national decisions or marshaled the national resources required for such leadership. We have never specified long-range goals on an urgent time schedule, or managed our resources and our time so as to insure their fulfillment.

Recognizing the head start obtained by the Soviets with their large rocket engines, which gives them many months of lead-time, and recognizing the likelihood that they will exploit this lead for some time to come in still more impressive successes, we nevertheless are required to make new efforts on our own. For while we cannot guarantee that we shall one day be first, we can guarantee that any failure to make this effort will make us last. We take an additional risk by making it in full view of the world, but as shown by the feat of astronaut Shepard, this very risk enhances our stature when we are successful. But this is not merely a race. Space is open to us now; and our eagerness to share its meaning is not governed by the efforts of others. We go into space because whatever mankind must undertake, free men must fully share.

### A Level Exam-Style Question Section A

***Study Sources 11 and 14 before you answer this question.***

How far could the historian make use of Sources 11 and 14 together to investigate the policies of the Kennedy administration of 1961 to 1963?

Explain your answer using both sources, the information given about them and your knowledge of the historical context.
(20 marks)

**Tip**

*You will be expected to point out the value to the historian of each source in relation to its provenance. This should include the date of the source, who wrote the source and the intended audience of the source.*

**A Level Exam-Style Question Section B**

To what extent was Kennedy's New Frontier programme thwarted by Congressional opposition? (20 marks)

**Tip**

*This type of question requires a balanced answer that addresses directly the assertion concerning Congressional opposition. You will need to provide evidence that Congressional opposition thwarted JFK's New Frontier proposals. You will need to balance that evidence against information which provides evidence that, at least in part, JFK was able to get enacted important parts of his programme.*

## The extent of Kennedy's domestic achievements

Kennedy is remembered by the public as one of the USA's better presidents. However, much of his legacy lay in the field of foreign policy. In domestic affairs his success was very limited. One reason for this was that he lacked a strong mandate from the electorate: his margin of victory over Richard Nixon had been one of the smallest ever in a presidential election. In addition, he had major problems in winning support in the US Congress for his reforms. According to Robert Dallek in his biography of Kennedy, 'Aside from area redevelopment, the White House had no major legislative achievements. Kennedy's high priority items, tax reform, federal aid to elementary and secondary education, and health insurance for the aged, never got out of Congressional committees.' The conservative coalition of southern Democrats and Republicans helped block many JFK proposals. Kennedy stated, 'When I was a Congressman I never realised how important Congress was. I do now.' Kennedy had a minor success early in his presidency, on 30 January 1961, when he was able to increase the membership of the House Rules Committee, which decided which proposals could be debated in the House of Representatives. However, for the rest of his administration his proposals were either rejected or watered down. Some of his most important successes, such as the CEEO and the Peace Corps, were made by Presidential Executive Order, not passed by Congress.

Kennedy had limited success in dealing with the demands of the civil rights movement. He moved cautiously and only took action when he thought it absolutely necessary.

When Kennedy died in November 1963, the recession that had affected the US economy was over and the country was experiencing a period of economic prosperity. Kennedy's trade reform and aid to depressed areas had helped bring this about. After Kennedy's death, his successor, Lyndon Johnson, implemented many of the stalled proposals thanks to his political skill and large Democrat majorities in both houses of Congress.

**ACTIVITY**
**WRITING**

Study Sources 2 and 10.

1 Identify words and phrases you don't understand and research their meanings.

2 Identify words and phrases that show the writers' attitude towards changes in legislation.

3 Write a short paragraph explaining the type of language used in both sources which shows that these are public announcements.

**ACTIVITY**
**KNOWLEDGE CHECK**

**Kennedy's New Frontier**

1 Write down five areas where Kennedy attempted to bring reform to the USA as part of his New Frontier programme.

2 What problems did JFK face in implementing his programme?

3 Which of the following do you regard as JFK's greatest domestic achievement during his administration:

a) Expansion of the National Park Service

b) The Peace Corps

c) The space programme?

Give reasons for your choice.

ACTIVITY
SUMMARY

**Conformity and challenge**

1 Write a description of the major changes that took place in the USA in the period 1955-63.

a) What changes had the most impact on working families?

b) What were the key turning points in the development of US culture and society in the period 1955-63?

2 Create notes on the following as an aid to revising this subject:

a) The impact of suburbia on American society

b) Changes in US culture in the period 1955–63

c) The main events in the civil rights movement from 1955–63

d) The changes made by Kennedy's New Frontier programme.

## WIDER READING

**Books**


Bunce, R. *Pursuing Life and Liberty: Equality in the USA, 1945–1968*, Pearson (2009)

Carson, C. (ed.) *The Eyes on the Prize - Civil Rights Reader: Documents, Speeches and Firsthand Accounts from the Black Freedom Fighters, 1954–1990*, Prentice-Hall (1992)

Cook, R. *Sweet Land of Liberty?: The African-American Struggle for Civil Rights in the Twentieth Century*, Routledge (1997)

Dallek, R. *John F. Kennedy, An Unfinished Life*, Penguin (2003)

Damms, R. V. *The Eisenhower Presidency 1953–61*, Pearson (2002)

de Pennington, J. *Modern America: 1865 to the present*, Hodder (2005)

Farmer, A. *An Introduction to American History, 1860–1990*, Hodder (2002)

Field, R. *Civil Rights in America, 1865–1980*, Cambridge University Press (2002)

Ling, P. J. *Martin Luther King Jr*, Routledge (2006)

Murphy, D. *Flagship History - United States 1776–1992*, Collins Educational (2001)

Paterson *et al. Civil Rights in the USA, 1863–1980*, Heinemann (2001)

Patterson, J. T. *Grand Expectations: The United States, 1945–1974*, Oxford University Press (1998)

Sanders, V. *Access to History: Civil Rights in the USA 1945–68*, Hodder (2008)


**Web**

Fordham University:

Modern social movements www.fordham.edu/Halsall/mod/modsbook56.asp

Pop culture www.fordham.edu/Halsall/mod/modsbook60.asp

The USA as a world leader www.fordham.edu/Halsall/mod/modsbook48.asp

National Archives:

Civil rights movement in the 1950s and 1960s www.nationalarchives.gov.uk/education/topics/civil-rights.htm

Martin Luther King www.nationalarchives.gov.uk/education/heroesvillains

**Video**

ABC *The Century America's Time* - documentary

*Parkland* (2013) - dramatisation of JFK's assassination

# Protest and reaction, 1963–72

## Key questions

- How did the quest for civil rights change between 1963 and 1972?
- To what extent did protest and personal freedom change in the years 1963 to 1972?
- How successful was President Johnson's Great Society programme of 1964 to 1968?
- How important were reactions to the counterculture in the years 1968 to 1972?

## INTRODUCTION

If the years 1955 to 1963 are regarded as a period of affluence and conformity, the period 1963 to 1972 is often regarded as a time of protest. Protest took many forms. The demand for equal civil rights for the USA's ethnic minorities continued. It was no longer limited to the Old South and spread across the USA. The nature and focus of black American civil rights campaigning also changed. More radical views and methods than those adopted by Martin Luther King were put forward by individuals and groups such as Malcolm X and the Black Panther movement. Black Power was copied by Red Power, demands for greater rights for Native Americans. Demands for equality also spread to include other groups. Women's and gay liberation became national campaigns.

In the middle of this period, President Johnson introduced major social reforms, which had been promised but not delivered by the Kennedy administration of 1961–63. Johnson's Great Society programme was intended to eradicate poverty through considerable spending on projects run by the federal government.

The period 1963–73 also saw major changes to US society through the development of a counterculture that offered radical alternatives to contemporary US society. It was characterised by opposition to the **Vietnam War** and a desire for more sexual freedom. However, these changes led to a conservative backlash at the end of the 1960s. The backlash helped bring Republican president Richard Nixon to power.

## HOW DID THE QUEST FOR CIVIL RIGHTS CHANGE BETWEEN 1963 AND 1972?

### The significance of Malcolm X, Black Power and the Black Panthers

By the mid-1960s, approximately 70 percent of black Americans lived in urban areas, many in black-only ghettos in northern cities. There many young blacks faced unemployment, racial discrimination and poor housing. In 1965, race riots broke out in the Watts district of Los Angeles, followed by race riots in other northern cities. These were a reaction to the riots in Watts but also against the poor living and working conditions faced by many black Americans.

**KEY TERM**

**Vietnam War**
The war in Vietnam lasted from 1960 to 1975. Powerful allies supported both sides in the war. Communist North Vietnam received support from communist countries the Soviet Union and China. The USA, along with allies Australia and New Zealand, was opposed to the spread of communism and supported government forces in the non-communist South Vietnam with ground troops from 1965. They fought not only the conventional army of North Vietnam but also the South Vietnamese communist guerrilla army, the Viet-Cong.

**1963** – May: Civil Rights Demonstrations in Birmingham, Alabama
August: Civil Rights March on Washington DC
November: President Kennedy assassinated, Lyndon Johnson becomes president

**1964** – Johnson launches Great Society Program
Economic Opportunity Act
Civil Rights Act passed

**1965** – Voting Rights Act passed
Watts Riots
Malcolm X assassinated
Rise of Black Power

1963 | 1964 | 1965 | 1966

EXTEND YOUR KNOWLEDGE

**The Watts Race Riots, 1965**

Watts is an area of central Los Angeles, known today as South Central LA. When a young black American called Marquette Faye was arrested by a white police officer on 11 August, riots were triggered that raged for six days and resulted in $40 million worth of damage. During the riots, 14,000 California National Guardsmen were mobilised and sent to Watts. Once order was restored the death toll was 34, with over 1,000 injured and 4,000 arrested. The governor of California claimed the riot was started by agitators from outside the area but an inquiry claimed that it was caused by longstanding grievances such as high unemployment, poor housing and inadequate schools. In 1992, another major riot occurred in the same area when Rodney King, also a black American, was beaten by Los Angeles police officers (see Chapter 4).

In this climate a number of new alternatives to the old civil rights movement appeared. Up to 1963, the black American civil rights movement had been centred in the Old South and concentrated on ending legal segregation. It was dominated by black Christian ministers: Martin Luther King, Ralph Abernathy and Fred Shuttleworth. With the rise of Malcolm X this position began to change rapidly.

## Malcolm X

Malcolm X offered a radically different programme for equality from Martin Luther King and the mainstream civil rights movement that appealed to black Americans living in ghettos in northern cities. He was born Malcolm Little in 1925, in the midwestern state of Nebraska. His mother was originally from the West Indies and his father was a Baptist preacher. Malcolm's family were supporters of the Universal Negro Improvement Association (UNIA) founded by Marcus Garvey, which campaigned for black nationalism and an end to European colonies in Africa and the West Indies.

When Little was six, his father was murdered by a white supremacist group called the Black Legion. His family home was also burned down. Little later became a petty criminal and was imprisoned for seven years. In prison he learned about the Nation of Islam (NOI) and its leader, Elijah Muhammad. Like the UNIA, the NOI supported separate black communities. In 1952, on his release from prison, Little joined the NOI and changed his name to Malcom X. He explained that 'Little' was a name given to his ancestors by white slave owners and as he didn't know his real African name he was taking the surname X.

Malcolm X was an excellent orator and gained national attention with his radical views. Based at an NOI temple (mosque) in Harlem, New York, Malcom X offered poor black Americans a more radical message than Martin Luther King. He supported complete black separation and attacked King for not speaking about the ways in which whites had repressed black Americans.

In March 1964, Malcolm X split from the Nation of Islam. After a pilgrimage to Mecca he returned to the USA to found the Organisation of Afro-American Unity (OAAU) in June 1964. He wanted to unify all people of African descent and demanded social and economic independence for all blacks across the world. His career was cut short on 21 February 1965: while speaking in Harlem he was murdered by gunmen from the Nation of Islam.

Malcolm X is less important for what he actually achieved than his influence on other black American radicals. After his death northern black radicalism was carried on by the Black Panthers and the Black Power movement.

## Black Power and the Black Panthers

The Student Non-violent Coordinating Committee (SNCC) had been very important in helping desegregate lunch counters, including those in department stores. In December 1966, the SNCC's ten-man Central Committee voted to expel all whites from the SNCC and, in May 1967, Stokely Carmichael was replaced as chairperson by Henry 'Rap' Brown, a radical who supported black armed defence against the police. On 25 July 1967, Rap Brown, in a speech in Cambridge, Maryland, called on black Americans to take over white-owned stores in black ghettos, if necessary by violence. This led to a race riot where Brown was wounded.

**1968** – Martin Luther King assassinated
Nixon wins presidential election

**1970** – Four students shot dead in anti-Vietnam protest at Kent State University, Ohio

1967 | 1968 | 1969 | 1970

**1969** – Nixon's 'Silent Majority' speech
Stonewall Riots in New York City
*All in the Family* sitcom begins on US television

### EXTEND YOUR KNOWLEDGE

**Stokely Carmichael (1941–1998)**
A West-Indian born, radical black American activist, who moved to the USA from Trinidad in 1951. He joined the SNCC while at university. In 1961, Carmichael became a Freedom Rider, travelling on Greyhound buses across the Old South to bring attention to the segregation of bus station facilities. Many Freedom Riders were attacked by whites. Carmichael became chair of the SNCC in 1966 and was a strong supporter of Black Power. He opposed the Vietnam War and later helped found the All-African People's Revolutionary Party and changed his name to Kwame Toure.

### KEY TERMS

**Apartheid**
A form of legal segregation of blacks, whites and 'coloureds' introduced in South Africa in 1948.

**Reparations**
Financial payments as compensation for wrongs done in the past.

In 1966, the Congress for Racial Equality (CORE) chose Floyd McKissick as chairperson. Like Malcolm X and the new radical leaders of SNCC, he was attracted to the demand for black freedom across the world. Wars of liberation were taking place in Africa, in the Portuguese colonies of Angola and Mozambique. There was also opposition to the white supremacist government in South Africa because of its **apartheid** policy. In July 1966, at the CORE annual convention in Baltimore, Maryland, the organisation endorsed the idea of Black Power. This term had been first used the year before by Stokely Carmichael. McKissick and Carmichael also became opponents of US involvement in the Vietnam War. However, by 1967, the word 'multiracial' was removed from the CORE constitution and in the summer of 1968 whites were excluded from CORE. At the end of that year McKissick was replaced as chairperson by Roy Innis, who advocated more radical direct action to achieve full equality for black Americans.

In October 1966, in Oakland, California, the idea of Black Power was taken a stage further with the creation of the Black Panther Party by Bobby Seale, Eldridge Cleaver, and Huey P. Newton. The Black Panthers advocated the black nationalism of Marcus Garvey and Malcolm X and wore a distinctive black uniform with black berets and Afro-style haircuts. They also carried rifles and advocated self-defence of black communities. They admired communist revolutionaries like Che Guevara of the Cuban Revolution and demanded **reparations** for centuries of persecution by whites. They also wanted blacks to be exempt from compulsory military service, partly because there was a widespread belief that disproportionate numbers of blacks were being called up to serve in the US armed forces in the Vietnam War.

### EXTEND YOUR KNOWLEDGE

**Huey P. Newton (1942–89)**
A co-founder, in 1966, of the Black Panther Party. The aim of the Black Panther Party was to protect black Americans against police brutality and racial discrimination. Newton was convicted of second-degree murder (manslaughter) of a policeman in 1967. The conviction was later overturned. In 1974, Newton fled to Cuba to avoid another murder charge. He later returned to the USA but was murdered in 1989 by Tyrone Robinson, a known drug dealer and member of the Black Guerrilla Family, a rival radical group to the Black Panthers.

Black Power came to international attention at the Olympics medal award ceremony in Mexico City in 1968 for the men's 400 metres. Two black American athletes, Tommy Smith and John Carlos, made the Black Power salute wearing black leather gloves. Their protest meant that neither athlete would ever represent the USA again, as the US Olympic Committee was opposed to athletes making political statements.

### KEY TERM

**FBI**
The Federal Bureau of Investigation was created in 1924. It was the USA's national police force and dealt with federal and interstate crimes.

A number of armed confrontations took place between members of the Black Panther party and the police, including the **Federal Bureau of Investigation (FBI)**. In 1969, 28 members of the Black Panthers were killed by the police in shootouts, including the Chicago Black Panther leader, Fred Hampton. Hundreds more were imprisoned. By 1972, the Black Panther Party was in decline following a major clampdown by the FBI and other law enforcement agencies. Its association with violence also alienated many black Americans, and even at its height it had only 5,000 members.

However, Malcolm X and the Black Panthers had helped transform the nature of black American protest within the USA. They offered an alternative to the non-violent methods of Martin Luther King and spread black protest from the Old South and the home of legal segregation to the whole country, most notably large urban areas like Oakland, California, Chicago and New York City.

SOURCE 1 Black Power activists giving the Black Power salute at a Black Panther Rally in 1970.

SOURCE

From 'What We Want', an essay by Stokely Carmichael, who had been elected chairperson of the SNCC in May 1966. The essay discussed Black Power and was published in the *New York Review of Books* on 22 September 1966.

White America will not face the problem of color, the reality of it. The well-intended say, 'We are all human, everybody is really decent, we must forget color.' But color cannot be 'forgotten'. White America will not acknowledge that the ways in which this country sees itself are contradicted by being black. Whereas most of the people who settled in this country came here for freedom, blacks were brought here to be slaves. Our vision is not merely a society in which all black men have enough to buy the good things in life. When we urge that black money go into black pockets, we mean the communal pocket. We want to see money go back into the community and used to benefit it. We want to see black ghetto residents demand that an exploiting storekeeper sell to them at minimal cost. The society we seek to build among black people is not a capitalist one. It is a society in which the spirit of the community and human love prevail.

Cause and consequence (6a)

**Seeing things differently**

Different times and places have different beliefs about how the world works, how human societies should be governed and the best way to achieve economic prosperity. Other people's ideas can be radically different from our own. It is important for the historian to take this into account when considering past attitudes and be aware of the dangers of judging them against our personal beliefs and ideas from our own time.

Reread Source 2 and answer the following questions.

1 What do you think gave rise to the notion of Black Power as put forward by Stokely Carmichael?

2 If Carmichael had known how events would progress to the present day, do you think he would have changed his attitude?

3 Carmichael's attitudes to civil rights and the place of black people in the world are different from those held by other black leaders in United States, like Malcolm X. Why do you think that they are different?

4 How important is it for historians to deal with events in the context of the beliefs and values people held at the time, as well as seeing them as part of a greater pattern? Explain your answer.

**AS Level Exam-Style Question Section A**

***Study Source 2 before you answer this question.***

How far could the historian make use of Source 2 to investigate the views of black American civil rights campaigners in the years 1963 to 1972?

Explain your answer using the source, the information given about it and your knowledge of the historical context. (12 marks)

**Tip**

*In your answer, comment on the provenance of the source. Who wrote it? When was it written? What was the intended audience? To support you answer you should also refer to the content of the source and the language and tone.*

## Martin Luther King's changing priorities, 1963–68

Martin Luther King continued to be the dominant force in the black civil rights movement. Until his assassination in Memphis, Tennessee, in April 1968, he was the focal point of attempts to gain social and political equality for black Americans.

In 1964, King had been present in the White House when President Johnson signed into law the Civil Rights Act. This saw the end of most of the legal segregation against black Americans. However, it did not end violence against blacks. Nor did it stop attempts to prevent blacks from registering to vote. During the 'Freedom Summer' of 1964, civil rights activists made a major attempt to register black voters in Mississippi. They were met with violence and even murder from extremist white groups such as the Ku Klux Klan.

In March 1965, King aimed to pressure the federal government into action by leading a protest march from Selma, Alabama to the state capital, Montgomery. The march achieved national media coverage, and when the marchers were attacked by Alabama state police at Pettus Bridge on 7 March, the events took place in full view of television cameras from the national press. President Johnson was forced to intervene to protect the marchers and put Alabama police under federal control. The march contributed directly to the passage of the 1965 Voting Rights Act, which guaranteed black Americans the right to vote, first promised in the 15th Amendment of the Constitution in 1870. This was one of King's greatest triumphs, but after 1965 his influence began to decline as more radical leaders took over organisations such as the SNCC and CORE, and Black Power won wider support. The Watts Riots in Los Angeles, in August 1965, showed the limit of King's influence and achievements.

In 1966, King attempted to lead a campaign to desegregate housing in the northern city of Chicago. The Southern Christian Leadership Conference (SCLC), which arranged the protest, was poorly organised. It also faced opposition from Chicago's powerful mayor, Richard Daley. A major confrontation took place at Gage Park, an all-white suburb of Chicago: when King attempted to lead a march through Gage Park the protestors were met by massive white resistance. King and his supporters were attacked with bricks and stones and the campaign had to be called off. Although King had been successful bringing an end to legal segregation in the Old South, he failed to end housing discrimination in the North. He seemed to have underestimated white resistance to the idea of racially integrated neighbourhoods.

King's influence declined further in 1967 when he openly opposed US involvement in the Vietnam War and lost the support of President Johnson. By 1968, his priorities were changing towards tackling the poor social and economic position of many black Americans. In early 1968, he supported the Poor People's Campaign for greater social equality. He began to question the entire social and economic system of the USA.

In April 1968, he arrived in Memphis, Tennessee to support a sanitation workers' strike for better conditions. There he was assassinated at the Lorraine Motel by a white sniper. King's assassination sparked off race riots across many cities in the USA. His funeral in Atlanta, Georgia was attended by major US political figures such as the Republican Richard Nixon and the Democrat, Robert F. Kennedy. His tomb is at the Martin Luther King Centre for Non-violent Social Change in Atlanta, Georgia.

## King's achievements

Martin Luther King was seen by most of the media, black Americans and the USA's political establishment as the unofficial leader of the black civil rights movement. His monument in central Washington DC reflects his influence, as does Martin Luther King, Jr Day, a national holiday in the USA.

King's support of non-violent protest won him the support of both blacks and whites and enabled him to gain influence with the federal government. He was an exceptional speaker and a master at achieving national publicity. By provoking white police and white politicians in the Old South into violent reactions against his non-violent protests, King gained national television coverage and publicity for his message, and notoriety for the white authorities. However, King also benefited from a sympathetic US Supreme Court, which supported the end of legal segregation and had a sympathetic federal administration and Congress during the early Johnson years of 1963 to 1967.

However, from 1966 the black civil rights movement began to split, as radicals took over CORE and the SNCC. Many young black Americans believed King had not gone far enough in campaigning for full social and economic equality for black Americans and that he had concentrated too single-mindedly on gaining civil equality before the law. King also lost influence with the federal government because of his stance on the Vietnam War.

**EXTRACT**

From John White, *Martin Luther King Jr and the Civil Rights Movement in America* (1991).

From his emergence during the Montgomery bus boycott in 1955 to his death in Tennessee 13 years later, Martin Luther King Jr was widely regarded as the leader of the civil rights movement, the individual best able to dramatize the situation by his words and actions, and to communicate black aspirations to sympathetic whites. In effect, King was the catalyst, able to focus attention and support on campaigns usually begun by others. As Ella Baker, a former staff member of the Southern Christian Leadership Conference, has argued persuasively, 'The movement made Martin rather than Martin making the movement'. But King's most fitting tribute was the citation which accompanied his posthumous award of the Presidential Medal of Freedom on 4 July 1977:-

*Martin Luther King Jr was the conscience of his generation. A Southerner, a black man, he gazed upon the great wall of segregation and saw that the power of love could bring it down. From the pain and exhaustion of his fight to free all people from the bondage of separation and injustice, he wrung his eloquent statement of his dream of what America could be.*

## Cesar Chavez and the Chicano movement

The black American civil rights movement inspired other ethnic groups. Hispanic Americans also faced social and political discrimination. The area that saw most militant activity was California, where Hispanic American agricultural workers faced poor pay and conditions. Under Cesar Chavez, the United Farmworkers' Union began to champion workers' rights. Chavez' first major campaign, in 1965, was a strike by grape workers and a national boycott of California grapes. The strike lasted five years and grew into a wider movement for Hispanic civil rights. The United Farmworkers' Union registered 100,000 new Hispanic voters. The strikers and their supporters adopted the name 'Chicano' (a formerly derogatory term for poor Hispanics) to make their image more radical and militant, along similar lines to the Black Power movement.

The Chicano movement split over plans to include Hispanic university students. Groups such as the Brown Berets in Los Angeles, the Crusade for Justice in Denver, Colorado and the

Mexican American Youth Organisation in Texas developed to support fair treatment for Hispanic Americans. Unfortunately, these groups were not successful in gaining improved rights for Hispanic Americans. By the early 1970s, the Chicano movement began to splinter into moderate and radical factions like the black civil rights movement.

**EXTEND YOUR KNOWLEDGE**

Cesar Chavez 1927–93

Cesar Chavez, leader of the Chicano Movement, was born in southern Arizona to a fairly prosperous Mexican American farming family. In 1948, at the age of 21, Chavez took part in his first strike, to protest against the poor living and working conditions of California's migrant farm workers. He then joined the Community Services Organization and became its general director in 1958. He adopted a strategy of non-violence, following the example of Martin Luther King. In 1962, he formed his own organisation, the National Farm Workers' Association, and in 1965 led a strike of California's grape pickers, which attracted extensive national media coverage. In 1968, Chavez began fasting to draw public attention to the plight of farm workers. In the 1970s, he organised a successful series of strikes and boycotts to improve the pay and working conditions of grape and lettuce workers.

**AS Level Exam-Style Question Section B**

How far did the struggle for civil rights change in the USA in the years 1963 to 1972? (20 marks)

**Tip**

*Your answer requires a balanced assessment of the degree of change in the struggle for civil rights in 1963–72. You should refer to the role and importance of Martin Luther King and his tactics and the development of alternative elements in the civil rights movement such as Malcolm X, Black Power and the Black Panthers. You should also mention that the struggle for civil rights did not just involve black Americans, and include other elements such as the Chicano movement.*

**ACTIVITY**
**KNOWLEDGE CHECK**

Civil rights

1 What were the aims and achievements of Black Power and the Black Panther Party?

2 How successful was Martin Luther King in advancing black American rights in the years 1963 to 1972?

3 In what ways and why did Malcolm X's aims and methods differ from those of Martin Luther King's on the issue of black American civil rights?

4 In what ways and with what success did Cesar Chavez attempt to improve the rights of Hispanic Americans?

# TO WHAT EXTENT DID PROTEST AND PERSONAL FREEDOM CHANGE IN THE YEARS 1963 TO 1972?

## Student protest

During the period of affluence in the 1950s, the numbers of Americans engaged in further education (college) after the age of 18 rose sharply. By the late 1960s, 50 percent of over-18s went to college, with 20 percent achieving degrees. College campuses became centres for political and social debate, activism and protest.

In 1964, one of the first student demonstrations took place at the University of California at Oakland. The demonstration was organised by the Free Speech Movement, and protestors called for the university to overturn its ban on political activity on campus. In 1968, 221 major demonstrations took place, covering a wide variety of issues such as opposition to the Vietnam War, greater student participation in university governance and greater student freedom. By 1972, university campuses seemed to be places of revolution and left-wing activity.

One of the most important student protest groups was Students for a Democratic Society (SDS). It was founded at the University of Michigan in 1960 by Tom Hayden and Al Haber. In 1962, Hayden produced the 'Port Huron Statement', which set out SDS's aims. Hayden stated: 'We are the people of this generation, bred in at least moderate comfort, housed in universities, looking uncomfortably to the world we inherit.' He claimed the USA was dominated by large corporations, the government and universities that aimed to oppress the individual. Hayden called for 'participatory democracy' to win back control of university education for the students.

The other major issue fuelling student protest was opposition to US involvement in the Vietnam War. Many SDS supporters were inspired by civil rights militants such as Ray 'Rap' Brown and the Black Power movement. In 1965, Hayden organised a march on Washington DC. He tried to emulate the civil rights march of 1963 but achieved little impact on the media or government.

In the spring of 1967, 500,000 marchers went to New York City's Central Park to protest against the Vietnam War. Some protestors burnt their draft cards (which called them up for compulsory military service). Others criticised American military policy in Vietnam. Two incidents in particular encouraged student protest: the Tet Offensive and the My Lai massacre. In January 1968, the Johnson administration was claiming the USA was winning the Vietnam War. However, at the end of that month the communist forces launched the Tet Offensive, which attacked all the major cities of South Vietnam. They even entered the grounds of the US Embassy in Saigon, the capital. Anger and disillusionment with the war grew as a result, even within President Johnson's particular political party, the Democrats. In February 1968, many students backed Eugene McCarthy as Democrat candidate for president against Johnson.

As a result of the Tet Offensive, many Americans now believed the US would not win the war. In 1969, the announcement that US troops had massacred unarmed men, women and children at the village of My Lai caused outrage.

Student protests were an important part of the anti-Vietnam movement within the USA. By February 1968, many Americans believed the US would not win the war and blamed the president. Facing rising criticism across the USA, even from within his own political party, President Johnson decided not to seek re-election at the end of March 1968.

The most dramatic year of student protest was 1968. Campuses across the USA were affected by student protestors who wanted to take over university education and end the Vietnam War. At the Democratic Party Convention to choose the Democrat presidential candidate, in Chicago in August 1968, widespread rioting occurred in the streets outside the convention centre. In addition to the SDS, an extreme political group, the Youth International Party (also known as Yippies) caused mayhem. Richard Daley, mayor of Chicago, sent in 12,000 police to confront the rioters and quelled the riot.

In the aftermath of the Chicago riots the student movement fragmented into various groups. In 1969, an extremist terrorist group known as the Weather Underground Organization was created. The Weather Underground was a small radical group that received considerable national publicity. In 1969 and 1970, it engaged in a series of bombings of government buildings and universities, which resulted in the deaths of innocent people. The appearance of the 'Weathermen' led to a federal response and several arrests. The group was used by the federal government to illustrate how radical some aspects of student protest had become.

In 1970, the federal government published *The US President's Commission on Campus Unrest*. It declared that the unrest that plagued the nation was rooted in the new youth culture, which rejected the work ethic, materialism and the traditional view of American society. Although the Vietnam War was partly responsible, it was part of a wider movement of teenage rebellion affecting the western world, not just the USA. It helped fuel the rise of what President Nixon called the 'silent majority'.

**SOURCE**

An extract from 'Two, Three, Many Columbias', an article in the 15 June 1968 issue of *Ramparts* magazine. The article was written by Tom Hayden, a leading member of Students for a Democratic Society (SDS), a group heavily involved in student protests. Columbia University in New York City is one of the USA's leading universities.

[The student strike at Columbia] opened a new tactical stage in the resistance movement from the overnight occupation of buildings to permanent occupation; from mill-ins to the creation of revolutionary committees; from symbolic civil disobedience to barricaded resistance...

In the future it is conceivable that students will threaten destruction of buildings as a last deterrent to police attacks... Raids on the offices of professors doing weapons research could win substantial support among students...

The Columbia students... did not even want to be included in the decision-making circles of the military-industrial complex that runs Columbia; they want to be included only if their inclusion is a step toward transforming the university.

### AS Level Exam-Style Question Section A

***Study Source 3 before you answer this question.***

Why is Source 3 valuable to the historian for an enquiry into why students protested in the period 1968–72?

Explain your answer using the source, the information about it and your own knowledge of the historical context (8 marks)

**Tip**

*In your answer you should refer to the provenance of the source: who wrote it, when it was written and what was the purpose behind writing the source.*

## Counterculture and its key features

The 1960s were also a period of a youth counterculture, with origins in groups such as the beatniks of the late 1950s. An outward sign of the counterculture was a major change in youth fashion, such as long hair, beads, and faded jeans. Young women sometimes discarded bras. young people flouted the conventional views on sex. Another important aspect of this counterculture, which can be traced back to the beatnik era, was experimentation with drugs such as marijuana and heroin.

The city most associated with the counterculture was San Francisco, California, in particular the district of Haight-Ashbury. The year 1967 saw San Francisco become the centre of the 'flower power' movement. 'Make Love not War' was a key slogan. In the same year, The Beatles released their hit single 'All You Need is Love'. The rejection of traditional fashion, social and sexual behaviour and support for society caused a major split between the youth generation and their parents.

The counterculture also led to a revolution in popular music. In the late 1950s and early 1960s rock'n'roll and protest folk music, associated with singer/songwriters like Bob Dylan, were popular. However, after 1963 popular music fashion changed. Bands like the Rolling Stones and the Doors were linked with rebellion and drug-taking. In 1969, at Altamount, California, the Rolling Stones employed Hell's Angels motorcycle gangs to keep order at their concert.

The most significant event of this period in popular music came in the summer of 1969 at Yasgur's Farm in upper New York State. The Woodstock Music Festival attracted over 40,000 young people. Performers included Joan Baez, a leading protest folk singer who was active in the civil rights movement, Jimi Hendrix, the Grateful Dead and Janis Joplin. Woodstock was the first of many massive outdoor music concerts. It became the subject of a film and epitomised the counterculture of the 1960s.

SOURCE 4 Woodstock Festival, August 1969.

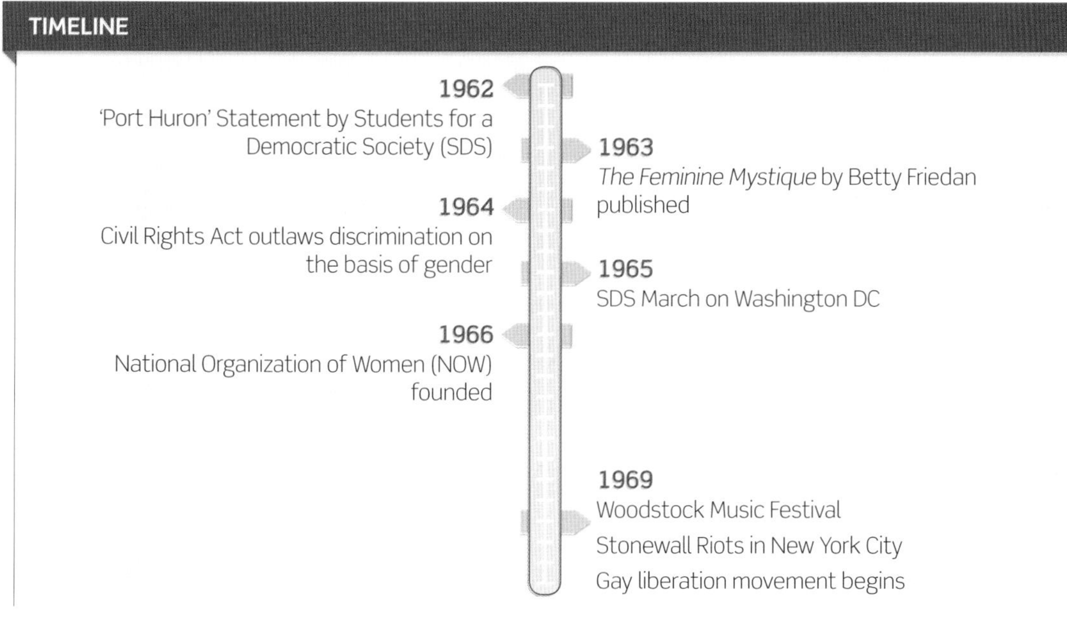

TIMELINE

**1962**
'Port Huron' Statement by Students for a Democratic Society (SDS)

**1963**
*The Feminine Mystique* by Betty Friedan published

**1964**
Civil Rights Act outlaws discrimination on the basis of gender

**1965**
SDS March on Washington DC

**1966**
National Organization of Women (NOW) founded

**1969**
Woodstock Music Festival
Stonewall Riots in New York City
Gay liberation movement begins

## Growth of the women's movement

One of the most important developments of the period 1963 to 1972 was the growth of the women's movement.

Television programmes such as *Father Knows Best* and the *Dick Van Dyke Show* had suggested that a woman's place was in the home, bringing up children. However, the role of women in US society was changing. By 1965, more than 25 million women were in regular employment. Almost 40 percent of married women with young children held full- or part-time jobs by 1968. Between 1964 and 1973, the proportion of women in the age group 20 to 24 years in employment rose from 50 percent to 61 percent.

In addition, the appearance of the contraceptive pill in the early 1960s allowed women to plan whether or not to have children. The social and economic position of women was changing rapidly.

In 1963, the book *The Feminine Mystique* by Betty Friedan was published. Friedan was a university graduate who had married and raised three children during the 1950s. Friedan said middle-class domestic bliss in the suburbs was 'a comfortable concentration camp' and thought women should have the opportunity to experience alternative lifestyles.

The 1964 Civil Rights Act also encouraged women to seek equality with men. Section VII of the Act outlawed discrimination in employment, not just on account of race and religion but also on account of sex.

In 1966, the basis of a women's movement was created in the USA. In that year, Friedan and 300 feminist activists founded the National Organization of Women (NOW). They felt federal government attempts to give women equal work opportunities (including the 1964 Civil Rights Act) had failed. NOW led a campaign to get equality for women in jobs, obtain federal and state support for childcare centres and to legalise abortion. NOW made complaints to the Equal Employment Opportunities Committee (EEOC) regarding job discrimination against women. One of the first cases was lodged by air stewardesses, who claimed their industry was female-only and that job guidelines demanded a particular age, appearance and weight. The EEOC ruled that airlines must not fire women when they got married or reached a certain age.

In 1967 and 1968, a network of young female activists began organising what became known as the Women's Liberation Movement, a more radical organisation than NOW. This new movement reached national attention in 1968 when members of the Women's Liberation Movement protested against the Miss America beauty pageant in Atlantic City, New Jersey. They regarded such pageants as degrading to women.

The women's movement achieved a major success in 1972. Under Section XI of the Education Act, if schools and colleges were to continue to receive federal funding they had to eliminate sex discrimination in their institutions, including athletic programmes. In 1971, only seven percent of students on athletic programmes were female.

In the same year, the US Congress overwhelmingly approved an Equal Rights Amendment to the US Constitution, intended to enshrine the idea of sexual equality. Within a year, 28 states had ratified (supported) the amendment. However, it failed to gain support from 75 percent of states and so was not permanently added to the Constitution.

By 1972, women's organisations such as NOW and the Women's Liberation Movement had placed women's issues at the centre of national debate and helped persuade lawmakers to make major changes. The idea that a woman's place in adult life was in the home as a dutiful wife was becoming a thing of the past. Section VII of the 1964 Civil Rights Act was ultimately used to force employers to offer better pay and conditions to women. Pressure from women's groups helped persuade Congress to pass the Equal Pay Act. Finally, in 1973, pressure from women's groups and changes in attitude led the US Supreme Court to declare abortion legal in the court case *Roe v Wade*.

**SOURCE 5**

**To many feminist activists the National Organisation of Women (NOW) was not radical enough. The more radical Redstockings was formed in 1969. The Redstockings Manifesto was issued in New York City on 7 July. It first appeared as a flyer, designed for distribution at women's liberation events.**

Women are an oppressed class. Our oppression is total, affecting every facet of our lives. We are exploited as sex objects, breeders, domestic servants and cheap labor. We are considered inferior beings, whose only purpose is to enhance men's lives. Our humanity is denied. Our prescribed behaviour is enforced by the threat of physical violence. [...]

We identify the agents of our oppression as men. Male supremacy is the oldest, most basic form of domination. [...] All power structures throughout history have been male-dominated and male orientated. [...]

We also reject the idea that women consent or are to blame for their own oppression. Women's submission is not the result of brainwashing, stupidity or mental illness but of continued, daily pressure from men. We do not need to change ourselves, but to change men. [...]

We identify with all women. We identify our best interest as that of the poorest, most brutally exploited woman.

We repudiate all economic, racial, educational or status privileges that divide us from other women. [...]

We call on all our sisters to unite with us in struggle.

We call on all men to give up their male privileges and support women's liberation in the interests of our humanity and their own.

*For the full text of the Manifesto see the Redstockings Women's Liberation Archives for Action at www.redstockings.org.*

## The impact of sexual liberalisation

The student protest movement, youth counterculture and the women's movement were all associated with increasing sexual liberalisation in the USA. In the period 1963 to 1972, relations between the sexes and attitudes to sex changed rapidly.

The introduction of the contraceptive pill had a major impact. It was approved for use in 1960 by the Federal Drug Administration, and by 1962 1.2 million women were using the Pill, rising to 6.5 million by 1965. This led to a much greater degree of sexual activity, in particular premarital sexual relations, resulting in what contemporaries called a sexual revolution. During the 1960s, casual sex became much more common and by the mid-1970s a survey of eight colleges showed that 76 percent of women and 75 percent of men had engaged in sexual intercourse by their junior (third) year. The youth counterculture of the 1960s became associated with the idea of 'free love'.

The traditional idea that the vast majority of Americans married for life was disappearing rapidly. The divorce rate rose almost 100 percent during the 1960s and increased another 82 percent by

1982. The number of people living alone rose from 10.9 percent in 1964 to 23 percent by 1980. These developments had a profound impact on US society. Traditional ideals of married life and family began to decline. By the 1970s, society and attitudes to family and relationships were radically different from the 1950s.

## The origins of gay rights

Another important change in the period 1963 to 1972 was growing awareness and acceptance of homosexuality. In 1963, being gay was still illegal in the USA. In the Second World War thousands of men and women had been dishonourably discharged from the military if they were found to be gay. In 1953, President Eisenhower had issued an executive order claiming that homosexuality was a sufficient reason to fire a federal employee. Gay communities existed before the 1960s as underground groups in large cities such as San Francisco, New York and Los Angeles, but gay men and women were subject to intimidation by the police and random attacks or 'gay bashing' from members of the public.

The first male group supporting gay rights, the Mattachine Society, was created in 1950. Five years later, in 1955, a lesbian rights group, the Daughters of Bilitis, was set up in San Francisco. In 1965, a small group marched in front of the White House to protest at repression of gay people in Cuba and the USA. However, the first major development occurred on 17 June 1969. On that day, the New York City police raided the Stonewall Inn, a working-class gay bar in Greenwich Village, Manhattan. The customers fought back and three days of rioting followed.

The Stonewall riots led directly to the creation of a gay liberation movement inspired by both the civil rights and women's liberation movements. One of its early campaigns was to get the American Psychiatric Society to remove homosexuality from its list of mental illnesses. The society finally removed homosexuality from the list in 1973. The gay liberation movement also encouraged gay men and women to 'come out' and declare their homosexuality. By 1973, almost 800 gay and lesbian organisations had been formed across the USA. Gay churches, synagogues, bars, restaurants, community centres and health clinics were established. The Haight-Ashbury district of San Francisco became an openly gay district. In 1977, San Francisco elected its first openly gay elected official when Harvey Milk was chosen as supervisor for District 5 in San Francisco. He was later assassinated because of his sexuality.

**SOURCE**

An extract from 'A Walk on the Wild Side of Stonewall', an article by Robert Amsel, who witnessed the Stonewall Riots of July 1969. He was present in the Stonewall Bar when it was raided by the New York City police. The article was published in *The Advocate* magazine on 15 September 1987.

Stonewall management found it difficult to keep their customers inside Saturday night, since all the action was outside. Shouts of 'Gay Power!' echoed along 6th and 7th Avenues.

There was a strong feeling of gay community and a strong fighting spirit, an intoxicating sense of release. It was 'us against them, and by God, we're winning.' Crowds are growing, as if from the pavement. The owner of a gay bookstore reported that some gay men were barricading the streets and not allowing heterosexual drivers to pass. The New York Tactical Police arrived and were unprepared for the guerrilla war that awaited them.

These streets were gay territory. Gay people knew every doorway and side street. Gay men on roofs hurled bottles at the cops. A gay group leader shouted 'Get the bastards!'. The cops were running away at full gallop, a lynch mob on their heels.

A year later diverse gay groups and independent gays marched in brotherhood and sisterhood. Annual gay pride days would follow.

### A Level Exam-Style Question Section A

***Study Sources 5 and 6 before you answer this question.***

How far could the historian make use of Sources 5 and 6 together to investigate why there was a growing demand for greater personal freedom in the period 1963 to 1972?

Explain your answer using both sources, the information given about them and your knowledge of the historical context. (20 marks)

**Tip**

*In assessing the importance of the source you should refer to the provenance of the sources: who wrote them, when were they written and what were the intended audiences for each source. You should also use information from the content of the sources and your own knowledge from this chapter to support your answer.*

**ACTIVITY**
**KNOWLEDGE CHECK**

**Protest and personal freedom**

1 In what ways and why did many students protest in the years 1963 to 1972?

2 What were the main features of the American counterculture?

3 Why did a women's movement develop in the years 1963 to 1972 and what impact did it have on US society?

4 In what ways did gay people's position in society change in the USA in the years 1963 to 1972?

# HOW SUCCESSFUL WAS PRESIDENT JOHNSON'S GREAT SOCIETY PROGRAMME OF 1964 TO 1968?

In the period 1933–45, Franklin D. Roosevelt's (FDR's) domestic policy for social and economic reform was called 'the New Deal'. J. F. Kennedy's programme was 'the New Frontier'. From 1964, Lyndon B. Johnson's (LBJ's) programme for change was 'the Great Society'. In many ways it was a continuation of Kennedy's programme, with an emphasis on civil rights, aiding the poor and improving the economy.

**SOURCE**

From a speech by President Johnson setting out the aims of the Great Society. It was delivered on 22 May 1964 to a packed football stadium at the University of Michigan, Ann Arbor. However, it was intended, and seen as, a speech to the American people.

Our society will never be great until our cities are great. It will be the task of your generation to make the American city a place where future generations will come, not only to live but to live the good life.

A second place where we begin to build a great Society is in our countryside. We have always prided ourselves on being not only America the strong and America the free, but America the beautiful. Today beauty is in danger. The water we drink, the food we eat, the very air we breathe, are threatened with pollution.

A third place to build the Great Society is in the classrooms of America. There your children's lives will be shaped. Our society will not be great until every young mind is set free to scan the farthest reaches of thought and imagination. We are still far from that goal.

These are three of the central themes of the Great Society. While our government has many programs directed at those issues, I do not pretend that we have the full answer to those problems.

So, will you join in this battle to give every citizen the full equality which God enjoins and the law requires, whatever his belief, or race, or the color of his skin?

## THINKING HISTORICALLY Cause and consequence (6b)

### Attitudes and actions

Individuals can only make choices based on their context. Prevalent attitudes combine with individual experience and natural temperament to frame the individual's perception of what is going on around them. Nobody can know the future or see into the minds of others.

| Context | Action |
|---|---|
| • Vice-President Lyndon Johnson became president on the assassination of J. F. Kennedy.<br>• Johnson was a congressman in the 1930s and a keen supporter of President F. D. Roosevelt's New Deal programme for getting the US economy out of the Depression and helping the poor and unemployed.<br>• Johnson believed he had a duty to fulfil the aims and policies of J. F. Kennedy, who wanted to bring major social and economic change to the USA.<br>• 1964 was a presidential election year and Johnson was planning to be the Democratic Party candidate. | On 22 May 1964, President Lyndon B. Johnson made a speech that laid out the aims of his Great Society programme. This was Johnson's plan to transform American society. He wanted to use the powers of the federal government to bring about fundamental social and economic change. Later he referred to his plans as a 'war on poverty'. |

Answer the following questions individually, then discuss your answers in a group.

1 Why might Johnson have believed that the federal government had a major role to play in changing US society and the economy?

2 Why might Johnson have thought the federal government could achieve his aims of a Great Society?

3 What other information would have been useful to him to help him decide on his course of action?

4 How reasonable was Johnson's course of action given what he understood about the situation at the time?

5 How far should the historian try to understand the beliefs and values of people in the past when explaining why individuals make choices in history?

## Tackling poverty and unemployment

A key feature of LBJ's Great Society was the 'war on poverty'. Even though the USA was the wealthiest country in the world, poverty was still an issue. In the early 1960s, the top 20 percent of Americans owned 77 percent of the wealth, while the bottom 20 percent owned 0.5 percent of the wealth. In 1962, 20–25 percent of Americans had barely enough money to buy food and pay for accommodation.

The central feature of the attack on poverty was the Economic Opportunity Act of 1964. It created a new federal agency, the Office of Economic Opportunity (OEO), which had the task of co-ordinating a variety of initiatives to eradicate poverty within the USA. One such programme was a domestic version of JFK's Peace Corps, Volunteers in Service to America or VISTA. It gave middle-class people the opportunity to directly help the needy in the US. By 1968, 3,000 people had volunteered.

The most controversial part of the Economic Opportunity Act was the creation of Community Action Programmes (CAPs). The aim was to allow the poor to play a part in federal programmes, and in part to empower southern black Americans in determining policies that affected them for the first time, after long years of legal segregation. Unfortunately, in some northern cities CAPs were taken over by militants who criticised LBJ for not doing enough.

The Great Society also introduced the Jobs Corps to improve the skills of unemployed inner-city youths. The Jobs Corps programme faced some difficulties, as much of the training was done in camps where there were discipline problems. However, large companies like IBM got involved in the programme and the Jobs Corps eventually had success in placing youths in 10,000 jobs.

LBJ also continued work begun under JFK. The Appalachian Regional Development Act of 1965 allocated $1.1 billion to programmes to raise the standard of living in the Appalachian mountain region.

Eventually, the 'war on poverty' cost $10 billion.

According to the US Census, the number of families in poverty dropped from 40 million in 1959 to 28 million in 1968 and to just over 25 million in 1970. Part of this was due to a thriving economy, but part was due to LBJ's programmes. He had the support of a big Democratic majority in Congress, particularly after the 1964 elections, and very good relations with Congressional leaders. He had built up an in-depth knowledge of how to deal with Congress as leader of the Senate in the 1950s. In many ways, LBJ succeeded where JFK had failed. He was able to pass into law many of the proposals that JFK had hoped to introduce but which had been stalled by opposition politicians in Congress.

### EXTEND YOUR KNOWLEDGE

**Lyndon Baines Johnson (1908-73)**

Lyndon B. Johnson (LBJ) was a southerner, born in Texas. He trained and worked as a teacher before entering Congress as a strong supporter of FDR's New Deal social and economic programmes. He remained a Congressman until 1948, when he was elected to the Senate. He was Senate majority leader 1954-60, dominating the Senate and becoming one of the USA's most powerful politicians. In 1960, JFK defeated him to become the Democrat presidential candidate, but he accepted JFK's offer to become vice-presidential candidate and did much to ensure southern Protestant Democrats would lend their support to JFK, who was a Roman Catholic from the north-east. As Vice President, Johnson was also put in charge of the space programme.

When JFK was assassinated in 1963, Johnson became president in accordance with the terms of the US Constitution. One of his lasting legacies was his decision to send ground troops to Vietnam in March 1965. The resulting US involvement in the Vietnam War eventually cost the USA the lives of over 58,000 people. Johnson decided not to run for the presidency in 1968, primarily because of growing opposition to US involvement in the war.

## Improving housing and cities

LBJ continued JFK's work in housing. The 1965 Housing and Urban Development Act provided for the construction of 240,000 houses and $2.9m for urban renewal. He also set up a new federal department, the Department of Housing and Urban Development (HUD), under the first black American Cabinet member, Robert Weaver. HUD was able to implement LBJ's policies on housing such as the Housing and Urban Development Act.

The most innovative act passed as part of the Great Society programme was the Demonstration Cities and Metropolitan Act of 1966. The federal government offered local government 80-percent grants to deal with issues such as crime prevention, healthcare and job creation. In 1966, Congress authorised spending of $412m, which rose to $512m in 1967. Unfortunately, Congress cut funding in 1968 which limited the impact of LBJ's reforms, but the initial programme did have some success in improving life in metropolitan areas.

In 1968, Johnson saw one of the most ambitious acts to help inner-city development passed. The Housing Act proposed to build 26 million homes in ten years. For the first three years, Congress provided $1.7m in funds. There were few planning restrictions on developers as LBJ wanted the houses built quickly, and the Act led to the building of cheap, poorly built homes. This attracted criticism of the programme and in 1969, under President Nixon, federal funding was reduced.

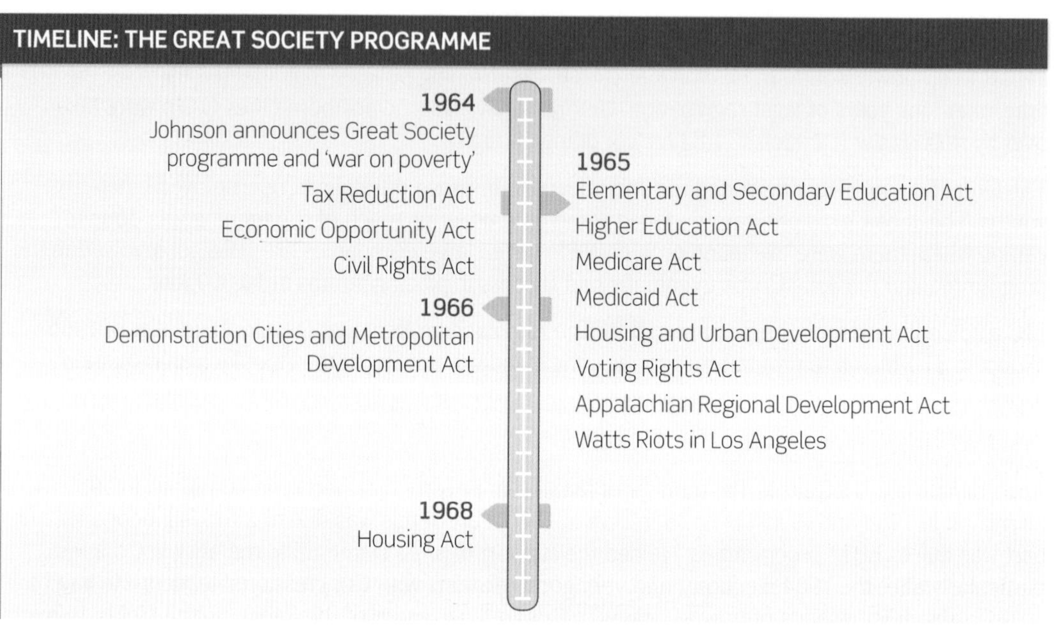


**SOURCE 8** From a message delivered to Congress on 3 March 1964 by President Johnson, introducing the Economic Opportunity bill.

Our fight against poverty will be an investment in the most valuable of our resources - the skills and strength of our people. And, in the future, as in the past, this investment will return its cost manyfold to the entire economy. If we can raise the annual earnings of 10 million among the poor by only $1000 we have added $14 billion a year to our national output. In addition we can make important reductions in public assistance payments, which now cost us $4 billion a year, and in the large costs of fighting crime and delinquency, disease and hunger,

This is only part of the story.

Our history has proved that each time we broaden the base of abundance, giving more people the chance to produce and consume, we create new industry, higher production, increased earnings and better income for all. Giving new opportunity to those who have little will enrich the lives of all the rest. Because it is right, because it is wise, for the first time in our history, it is possible to conquer poverty.

### AS Level Exam-Style Question Section A

***Study Source 8 before you answer this question.***

Why is Source 8 valuable to the historian for an enquiry into why Johnson introduced the Great Society program?

Explain your answer using the source, the information about it and your own knowledge of the historical context. (8 marks)

**Tip**

*It is important to assess the provenance of the source to assess its value. Who wrote it, when was it delivered and what was its intended audience. To support your answer you should refer to information within the content of the source and your own knowledge to place the source in historical context.*

## Improving education

Education was an issue close to LBJ's heart: earlier in his career he had trained to be a teacher. In the USA, until the 1960s, education was a state government responsibility. However, LBJ saw improvements in education as a key part of his 'war on poverty'. In the Elementary and Secondary Education Act of 1965, he aimed to use federal funding to aid deprived children. He believed children from poor backgrounds needed more help in education than those from wealthier backgrounds. As a result, the Act allocated $1 billion a year to schools with a high concentration of low-income children. LBJ said the Act would help 'five million educationally deprived children overcome their greatest barrier to progress: poverty'. Instead of granting aid to all schools, this Act gave aid to specific schools – a significant change in the way federal funds for education were allocated. The Act also gave aid to church-run schools. In 1968, the Act was amended, resulting in the Bilingual Education Act, offering more aid to non-English speakers.

The Headstart programme, which encouraged children from low-income families to attend pre-school classes, benefited eight million children.

The Higher Education Act, passed in 1968, aimed to strengthen the educational resources of colleges and universities and provide financial assistance for students in higher education. The Act provided loans for students to pay college fees, allowing many children from low-income families to have a university education they could not have afforded otherwise. The importance of the Act is demonstrated by the fact it was reauthorised by Congress in 1968, 1972, 1976, 1980, 1986, 1992, 1998 and 2008.

Johnson's educational reforms gave many Americans from poor backgrounds access to higher education for the first time. The provision of university-level education grew as a result of his reform and many state universities, such as Florida State University and Michigan State University, expanded rapidly. Johnson's educational reforms were one of the more effective ways of dealing with problems of inner cities and one of the most significant achievements of his Great Society programme.

## Medicare and Medicaid

On the issue of federal aid for healthcare, Johnson succeeded where presidents Truman and Kennedy had failed. Medicare was introduced in 1965 and proved to be a popular and well-administered programme. It provided medical care for those 65 years old and above who did not have health insurance. In 1965, only about half of those 65 and over had private hospital insurance and only a few could afford insurance covering their surgical or out-of-hospital doctor's costs. Medicare was financed equally by the federal government and the individual. In its first year, over 19 million Social Security recipients registered for the programme.

While Medicare was a plan designed for the elderly, Medicaid was a programme designed to aid the poor who had no medical cover from insurance. This was financed by both the federal and state governments and was administered by the states. As a result, the quality of healthcare offered to poorer citizens through the Medicaid programme varied in impact and quality from state to state.

## Civil rights legislation

Perhaps the most significant and long-lasting changes made by LBJ in domestic policy were in the field of civil rights. Johnson became president at the height of the civil rights movement protests against legal segregation in the Old South. In the months before his assassination, JFK promised a new civil rights act to meet many of the demands of the civil rights movement. However, JFK had problems dealing with Congress, where he faced a conservative coalition of southern Democrats and Republicans, and was assassinated before he could see these proposals become law.

When LBJ became president, he promised to fulfil JFK's hopes of civil rights reform. With the help of LBJ's influence in Congress, pressure from the civil rights movement and a general desire to fulfil the wishes of the assassinated president, the Civil Rights Act was passed in 1964.

The Act was a milestone in American history. It outlawed discrimination on the basis of race, religion or sex in public places, including restaurants, theatres, motels, sports stadiums, cinemas and concert halls. This was the most important piece of civil rights legislation since the Civil War (1861–65). It offered black Americans civil equality and brought an end to legal segregation, a major aim of the civil rights movement.

**SOURCE 9**

From President Johnson's special message to Congress on civil rights, delivered March 1965. Johnson had submitted a Voting Rights bill to Congress in January 1965 but was having difficulties getting it voted through. Also in March 1965, Martin Luther King began his civil rights march from Selma to Montgomery. The Voting Rights Act was eventually passed on 5 August that year.

There is no Negro problem. There is no Southern problem. There is no Northern problem. There is only an American problem. And we are here tonight as Americans - not as Democrats or Republicans; we are met here as Americans to solve a problem. Many of the issues of civil rights are very complex and most difficult. But about this there can and should be no argument: every American citizen must have an equal right to vote. There is no reason which can excuse the denial of that right. There is no duty which weighs more heavily on us than the duty we have to insure that right. Yet the harsh fact is that in many places in this country, men and women are kept from voting simply because they are Negroes. Every device of which human ingenuity is capable has been used to deny this right. The Negro citizen must go to register only to be told that the day is wrong, or the hour is late, or the official in charge is absent. And if he persists and, if he manages to present himself to the registrar, he may be disqualified because he did not spell out his middle name, or because he abbreviated a word in the application. The registrar is the sole judge of whether he passes the test. He may be asked to recite the entire Constitution or explain the most complex provisions of state law.

This time, on this issue, there must be no delay, or no hesitation, or no compromise with our purpose. We cannot, we must not, refuse to protect the right of every American to vote in every election that he may desire to participate in.

### A Level Exam-Style Question Section A

***Study Sources 8 and 9 before you answer this question.***

How far could the historian make use of Sources 8 and 9 together to investigate how President Johnson was able to persuade Congress to support his domestic reforms?

Explain your answer using both sources, the information given about them and your knowledge of the historical context. (20 marks)

**Tip**

*In your answer you will be required to assess the provenance of both sources as a way to explain how the historian could use them. Who wrote them, when were they written and what was the intended audience? To support your answer you should use information from the content of each source and your own knowledge to place the sources in historical context as a way of assessing their importance.*

The Attorney General of the USA (the federal government's senior law officer) was given the power to take legal action in federal courts against any violation of the Act. A key feature of the Act gave power to the federal government to withhold federal funding from any state not complying with it. As state government relied heavily on federal funding, this aspect of the Act was very significant. In one fell swoop Johnson had ended legal segregation in the USA, a key demand of Martin Luther King and the civil rights movement.

In the same year, 1964, an important amendment was made to the US Constitution. The 24th Amendment outlawed the use of poll taxes at elections, which had had been used to prevent many black Americans (and poor whites) from voting in some southern states.

In 1965, Congress passed the Voting Rights Act with Johnson's encouragement and ultimate assent. This Act outlawed literacy tests for voter registration and appointed federal examiners to ensure voter registration was handled correctly. The Act had a profound effect on voter registration in the southern states. Before the Voting Rights Act, only six percent of blacks were registered in Mississippi. After the Act, the figure rose to 60 percent. In Alabama the figures were 18 percent before the Act and 54 percent after. In other southern states the changes were less impressive. In Virginia, 44 percent of blacks were registered before the Act and only 43 percent after it was passed. In Florida, it was 51 percent before the Act and 54 percent after.

The civil rights legislation of Johnson's administration has rightly been regarded as a landmark in aiding black Americans to get civil rights. However, Johnson was depressed both personally and professionally by the Watts Riots of 1965 in Los Angeles, where black Americans engaged in days of rioting, and the rise of Black Power.

## Johnson's achievement in domestic policy

The years of the Great Society programme were a period of immense domestic reform. In the period 1963 to 1969, 435 bills were submitted to Congress. It was one of the great reforming periods in US history. Johnson was aided by a buoyant economy: the Gross National Product increased by seven percent in 1964, eight percent in 1965 and nine percent in 1966. Johnson's Tax Reduction Act of 1964 cut taxes by $10 billion, which encouraged this economic growth. The Great Society increased the number of students, particularly from low-income families, able to attend college and university. It reduced poverty levels. It brought to an end legal discrimination against black Americans.

However, the Great Society programme did not solve the key problems of inner cities, which were in decline due to the rise of suburbia. Wealthier Americans, mainly white, were leaving the inner cities to live in the suburbs, most of which were outside city boundaries. This left cities underfunded, exacerbating the issue of inner-city decline. Crime, drug-trafficking and poverty plagued these areas. Legal discrimination against black Americans may have ended, but they still faced social and economic discrimination in housing and jobs.

In 1966, the **mid-term elections** saw a major drop in support for Great Society policies. In Congress the Democrats lost seats in both the House and Senate to the Republicans.

In March 1968, LBJ went on prime-time national television to announce that he would not stand for re-election as president later that year. The main reason was the failure to win the war in Vietnam. However, the fact that the Great Society programme had not achieved all its very ambitious aims, such as eradicating poverty, also played a part. The Great Society programme demonstrated that federal funding on a vast scale might not be the best way of dealing with social and economic problems: local efforts by city and state governments might be more effective. Since 1968, no federal administration has tried to repeat the kind of massive federal funding of social projects that was associated with the Great Society programme.

**KEY TERM**

**Mid-term elections**
These take place every four years, halfway between presidential elections. All Congressmen and women in the House of Representatives and one third of the Senate are elected, as are many state governments and state governors. Midterm elections are a very good indicator of the popularity of a president and the federal government.

**ACTIVITY**
**KNOWLEDGE CHECK**

**Johnson's Great Society, 1964–68**

1 In what ways did Johnson attempt to deal with poverty and unemployment?
2 How did Johnson's administration attempt to improve housing and education?
3 Why do you think it was thought necessary to introduce Medicare and Medicaid?
4 How far did Johnson advance the cause of civil equality for black Americans in his administration?
5 What do Sources 7, 8 and 9 tell us about the aims of Johnson as president in domestic affairs?

# HOW IMPORTANT WERE REACTIONS TO THE COUNTERCULTURE IN THE YEARS 1968 TO 1972?

## The rise of the silent majority

On 3 November 1969, President Nixon addressed the American people on US involvement in the Vietnam War. The speech was broadcast on both radio and television. Nixon called for 'peace with honour' and proposed handing over most of the fighting to the South Vietnamese armed forces. In the speech he made an appeal to the 'silent majority' of the American people to support him. Nixon's proposal was a very different take on ending US involvement to the withdrawal advocated by student protestors. In Nixon's view, the anti-war demonstrators who had taken to the streets in large numbers in 1968 and 1969 were a militant minority.

A Gallup poll carried out after the speech showed that 77 percent of those polled supported Nixon's Vietnam policy. Also, more than 300 Congressmen and 40 senators supported Nixon's policies.

Although Nixon's speech was the first time the term 'silent majority' was used, the backlash against student demonstrations and the counterculture of the 1960s had been growing for some time. Working-class and middle-class Americans who grew up in the late 1940s and 1950s were known as 'baby boomers'. These were the people who benefited from the age of affluence of the 1950s and were able to buy homes in suburbia. They were also brought up in a period where traditional American values of family and patriotism were commonplace. The upheavals of the 1960s threatened their view of society.

Many ordinary Americans had been appalled by the sight of Yippies and other demonstrators trying to disrupt the Democratic Party National Convention in August 1968, and the university campus anti-war demonstrations in the same year. This was an important factor in the rise of the silent majority.

The perceived attack on family values, premarital sex and drug-taking, all associated with the counterculture particularly offended Christian church communities. They were also offended by women's groups' calls for legalising abortion. The Christian right became an increasingly important source of support for the Republican Party and this support lasted into the 21st century.

Some of the changes in US society had directly affected the white population of the Old South. Many had resisted the end of legal segregation. They found a champion for their views in former Alabama governor George Wallace. He stood for the presidency in 1968 as the American Independence Party candidate, polled 9.9 million votes and won 46 Electoral College votes. Wallace's intervention in the election campaign helped split the traditional Democrat vote, allowing the Republican candidate, Nixon, to win the election with 31 million votes.

### EXTEND YOUR KNOWLEDGE

**The Electoral College**

Under the United Sates constitution, a president and vice president are elected by the states, not directly by popular vote. On the first Tuesday in November every four years, voters cast their ballots. In December, the Electoral College casts its votes. Each state has as many Electoral College votes as it has seats in the Senate and House of Representatives combined. Wyoming, for example, has three Electoral College votes. New York State has over 40.

Members of the Electoral College are meant to follow the wishes of voters in their state and vote for the candidate who won a majority. Rarely, some Electoral College members vote for the candidate they prefer. It is possible for a candidate who has won the popular vote nationwide to lose the election because of the Electoral College vote. This happened in 1976 and, possibly, in 2000.

Nixon narrowly won the presidential election of 1968, partly as a result of Democratic disunity, but also through the support of those voters who wanted a return to traditional values, an end to demonstrations and riots and an honourable end to US involvement in Vietnam. The silent majority formed the bedrock of those who supported the Republican Party in the 1970s and 1980s. It was this group that helped Nixon win a landslide victory in the 1972 presidential election.

**SOURCE 10**

**From President Richard M. Nixon's address on television to the American people on the war in Vietnam, made on 3 November 1969.**

In San Francisco a few weeks ago, I saw demonstrators carrying signs reading: "Lose in Vietnam, bring the boys home."

Well, one of the strengths of our free society is that any American has a right to reach that conclusion and to advocate that point of view. But as President of the United States, I would be untrue to my oath of office if I allowed the policy of this Nation to be dictated by the minority who hold the point of view and who try to impose it on the Nation by mounting demonstration in the street.

For almost 200 years, the policy of this Nation has been made under our Constitution by those leaders in the Congress and the White House elected by all of the people. If a vocal minority, however fervent its cause, prevails over reason and the will of the majority, this Nation has no future as a free society.

And so tonight - to you, the great silent majority of my fellow Americans - I ask for your support.

I pledged in my campaign for the Presidency to end the war in a way that we could win the peace. I have initiated a plan of action which will enable me to keep that pledge.

The more support I can have from the American people, the sooner that pledge can be redeemed; for the more divided we are at home, the less likely the enemy is to negotiate in Paris.

Let us be united for peace. Let us also be united against defeat. Because let us understand: North Vietnam cannot defeat or humiliate the United States. Only Americans can do that.

## The role of the media in influencing attitudes

The formation of public opinion in the USA was heavily dependent on the media and, in particular, television. By 1968, the vast majority of American homes owned at least one television: it had become the main source of both entertainment and news and so had a powerful influence on the formation of opinion in the USA.

The moulding of US opinion on the Vietnam War was heavily influenced by television. Every night news programmes broadcast vivid images of the war in Vietnam. The media had been given unprecedented access to the fighting. One of the most influential television newsmen was CBS's Walter Cronkite. He visited Vietnam at the beginning of 1968 and witnessed the Tet Offensive. On his return he said on national television that he thought the only rational option for the USA was to accept that they had not won the war and negotiate an honourable withdrawal.

A public opinion poll after the broadcast revealed that 70 percent of Americans trusted Walter Cronkite more than any other public figure. LBJ said that if he had lost the support of Walter Cronkite he had lost the support of the American people. A month later he ordered an end to bombing of North Vietnam, and at the end of March announced he would not stand for re-election as president.

In television sitcoms the most popular show was *All in the Family*. It began in 1969 and was based on the BBC show *Till Death Us Do Part*. The leading character was Archie Bunker, an opinionated, white, working-class father. He hated the counterculture and the social changes of the 1960s. His liberal son-in-law was always the butt of his anger as he railed against students, demonstrators, permissive social and sexual behaviour and ethnic minorities. Bunker's views reflected the attitude of many white Americans, contributing to the show's popularity.

The older generation's reaction to the counterculture, youth culture and student protests of the 1960s was a rise in support for the Republican Party in state governments. Ronald Reagan was elected Republican governor of California, the wealthiest US state, from 1967 to 1975. Nixon was re-elected president in November 1972 by a landslide. The majority of those who voted showed their distaste for what they saw as the counterculture.

**TIMELINE: COUNTER-CULTURE AND SILENT MAJORITY**

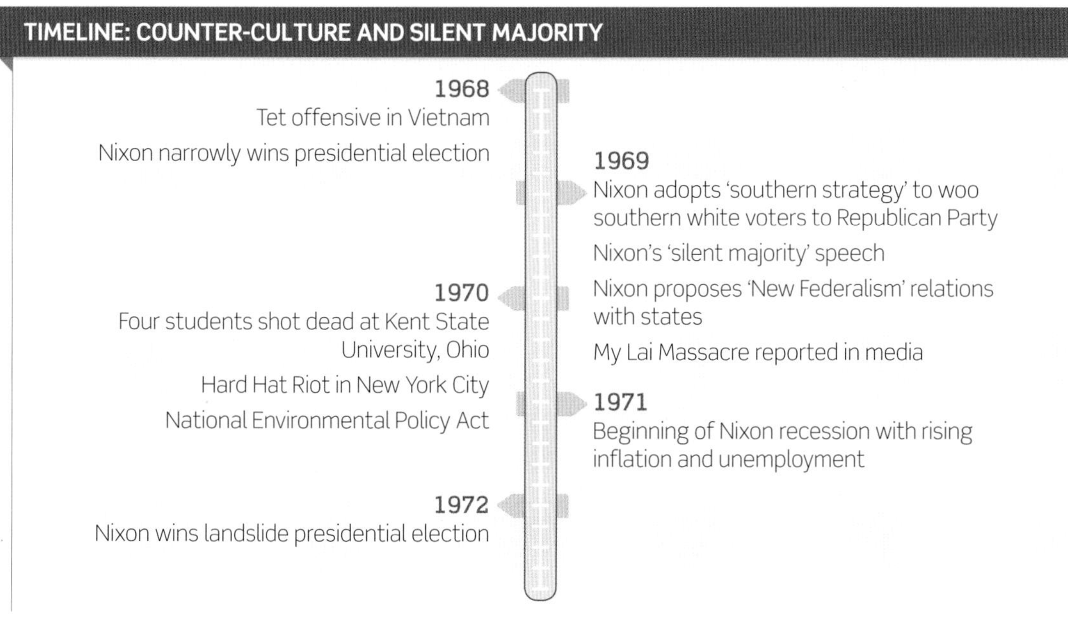


## The impact of events in Vietnam and at Kent State University, Ohio

The most divisive domestic issue in American history since the US Civil War (1861–65) was US involvement in the Vietnam War. LBJ had committed US ground troops to the conflict between the South Vietnamese government and its communist opponents in March 1965. By the end of 1968, US troop levels had reached over 500,000 and thousands of Americans had died. As the US depended on compulsory military service (known as 'the Draft'), many ordinary American males feared being sent to Vietnam.

In January and February 1968, Vietnamese communist forces launched the Tet Offensive, attacking all major cities in South Vietnam. The offensive was a military failure. All the attacks were defeated and communist forces in South Vietnam suffered heavy casualties. After 1968, much of the fighting against the US military forces was conducted by the North Vietnamese Army. However, the Tet Offensive convinced many Americans that the war could not be won. Daily television footage of US planes bombing Vietnam and troops setting fire to Vietnamese villages also alienated many. For the first time, through the medium of television, ordinary Americans were able to watch what was happening in a foreign war and this intensified domestic opposition. The main opponents were young people who feared the Draft. They were faced with graphic images of the fighting in Vietnam on their televisions every night and knew casualty rates were rising. College protestors feared the Draft and also disliked US military tactics.

In 1969, newspapers reported that in March 1968 US troops had engaged in a massacre of old people, women and children at a village called My Lai, in central Vietnam. Over 200 unarmed civilians were killed. During the next two years, Americans learned more about what had happened as the leading troops faced court martial. 25 officers were charged with complicity in the massacre and its cover-up by the military. In the end, at the end of March 1971, only Lieutenant William Calley was convicted of murder. In a public opinion poll, over 70 percent disagreed with the verdict – most thought Calley had been made a scapegoat. Shortly afterwards, Nixon reduced Calley's sentence to house arrest. This caused uproar and led to increased student protests against the war.

The most serious anti-war protest occurred on 4 May 1970. In an attempt to end the war, Nixon had ordered the invasion of Cambodia, a neutral country neighbouring South Vietnam and allegedly the base for communist forces. On 30 April 1970, Nixon appeared on national television to announce the invasion and the need for 150,000 extra US troops for the war. When students learned what Nixon had done, demonstrations broke out across the USA. On 4 May, a major student demonstration at Kent State University, Ohio, led to the state governor sending in 900 members of the Ohio **National Guard** to quell rioting. In the ensuing confrontation, 28 National Guardsmen fired on the students, killing four. Almost 500 colleges shut down or were disrupted by student protests because of the killings. A grand jury indicted eight of the Ohio National Guardsmen, but charges against them were dismissed through lack of evidence. A photograph of the dead students won a Pulitzer Prize. The shootings, along with Nixon's decision to escalate the war, caused national outrage among students and many members of the general public, fuelling the anti-war movement.

### KEY TERM

**National Guard**
The National Guard is the US equivalent of the territorial army in the UK. It is a part-time, volunteer force organised on a state-by-state basis under the control of the state governor. As Commander-in-Chief of the US armed forces, the US president could bring the National Guard under federal control when it was considered necessary.

US involvement in the war was given another blow in June 1971, when the *New York Times* published 'the Pentagon Papers', which had been leaked by Dr Daniel Ellsberg, a Defense Department employee. They showed how the US government under Johnson had not told the full story of the Gulf of Tonkin Incident in 1964, an incident that had been used to justify greater military involvement in South Vietnam. Nixon attempted to block publication but was overruled by the US Supreme Court, which allowed the Pentagon Papers to be read by the American public. They proved to be a damning indictment of US involvement in the Vietnam War.

### EXTEND YOUR KNOWLEDGE

**Gulf of Tonkin Incident, 2–4 August 1964**
This incident allowed President Johnson to gain the support of the US Congress to use whatever military power the president thought fit to intervene directly in the Vietnam War. Under the US Constitution only Congress had the power to declare war. The incident occurred between 2 and 4 August 1964 in the Gulf of Tonkin, the area of the South China Sea adjacent to North Vietnam. Two US destroyers, the USS *Maddox* and the USS *C. Turner Joy*, patrolling in international waters, were allegedly attacked by North Vietnamese torpedo boats. President Johnson used the incident to pass the Gulf of Tonkin Resolution through Congress. The Resolution allowed Johnson to send US ground troops into South Vietnam and to increase US military assistance. In March 1965, the first US ground troops landed at Da Nang, South Vietnam and in the same month Johnson launched an aerial bombing campaign of North Vietnam called Operation Rolling Thunder.

Although Nixon had promised 'peace with honour' in the 1968 presidential campaign, US military involvement continued until January 1973. Nixon's policies in Vietnam continued to divide the nation. While students protested against the war, others supported it. In the so-called 'Hard Hat Riot' in New York City on 8 May 1970, 200 construction workers demonstrated in favour of Nixon's policies and called for the US to bomb Hanoi, the capital of North Vietnam. They chanted 'All the Way, USA' and 'Love it or leave it'. The workers were joined by hundreds of others and they attacked anti-war student demonstrators in Manhattan. The Hard Hat Riot showed that some of the silent majority would not remain silent.

SOURCE 11 Student shot dead at Kent State University, May 1970.

## Nixon's appeal and his attack on the Great Society

Richard Nixon won the 1968 presidential election over Democrat Hubert Humphrey by a narrow margin – 31.7 million votes to 31.2 million. However, during his first term as president (1969–73) he was able to appeal to the American people by offering a new direction in domestic as well as foreign policy.

In domestic policy he attacked what he saw as the excesses of LBJ's Great Society programme. Expenditure of $1.4 billion had not brought peace and stability to the USA. Riots occurred in many American cities in 1968 and student unrest continued into the early 1970s. The Black Panther Party and the Weathermen advocated violence.

On 8 August 1969, in an address to the American people, Nixon set out his vision for domestic reform. A key feature of politics throughout US history was the relationship between the federal and state governments. Under the Great Society programme, the federal government had grown in size and importance at the expense of state government. Nixon advocated 'New Federalism', where more power would be handed back to the states. He supported revenue-sharing, where federal funding would be given to the states, which would decide on their own priorities.

Another major attempt by Nixon to attack the Great Society was to introduce his own alternative, entitled the Family Assistance Plan. This proposed to end hand-outs to the poor. Low-income households were guaranteed an annual income of between $1,500 and 2,000 per year for a family of four. If a parent refused work offered, the parent's income support would be stopped. The plan upset both conservatives and liberals. Conservatives believed the plan did not go far enough and liberals disliked the idea of restricting aid for the poor. The measure was defeated in the Senate, still dominated by Democrats, and dropped.

However, Nixon's domestic programme was regarded by many as too progressive for a conservative politician. In 1972, the Educational Standards Act laid down that colleges must set up affirmative-action programmes to ensure equality of opportunity for women. He also introduced the Philadelphia Plan, which required trade unions working on federal projects to accept quotas for black American workers. In 1970, the Democrat-controlled Congress passed the Occupational Health and Safety Act, which increased social security benefits by linking them to the rate of inflation.

SOURCE 12 An article from the *New York Times*, 4 May 1970, describing the shooting of four students at Kent State University, Ohio.

**4 Kent State Students Killed by Troops**

**8 Hurt as Shooting Follows Reported Sniping at Rally**

*By John Kifner*

Special to The New York Times Kent, Ohio, May 4 — Four students at Kent State University, two of them women, were shot to death this afternoon by a volley of National Guard gunfire. At least 8 other students were wounded.

The burst of gunfire came about 20 minutes after the guardsmen broke up a noon rally on the Commons, a grassy campus gathering spot, by lobbing tear gas at a crowd of about 1,000 young people.

In Washington, President Nixon deplored the deaths of the four students in the following statement:

"This should remind us all once again that when dissent turns to violence it invites tragedy. It is my hope that this tragic and unfortunate incident will strengthen the determination of all the nation's campuses, administrators, faculty and students alike to stand firmly for the right which exists in this country of peaceful dissent and just as strong against the resort to violence as a means of such expression."

In Columbus, Sylvester Del Corso, Adjutant General of the Ohio National Guard, said in a statement that the guardsmen had been forced to shoot after a sniper opened fire against the troops from a nearby rooftop and the crowd began to move to encircle the guardsmen.

Frederick P. Wenger, the Assistant Adjutant General, said the troops had opened fire after they were shot at by a sniper.

"They were understanding orders to take cover and return any fire," he said.

This reporter, who was with the group of students, did not see any indication of sniper fire, nor was the sound of any gunfire audible before the Guard volley. Students, conceding that rocks had been thrown, heatedly denied that there was any sniper.

Gov. James A. Rhodes called on J. Edgar Hoover, director of the Federal Bureau of Investigation, to aid in looking into the campus violence. A Justice Department spokesman said no decision had been made to investigate. At 2:10 this afternoon, after the shootings, the university president, Robert I. White, ordered the university closed for an indefinite time, and officials were making plans to evacuate the dormitories and bus out-of-state students to nearby cities.

Robinson Memorial Hospital identified the dead students as Allison Krause, 19 years old, of Pittsburgh; Sandra Lee Scheuer, 20, of Youngstown, Ohio, both coeds; Jeffrey Glenn Miller, 20, of 22 Diamond Drive, Plainsview, L.I., and William K. Schroeder, 19, of Lorain, Ohio.

At 10:30 P.M. the hospital said that six students had been treated for gunshot wounds. Three were reported in critical condition and three in fair condition. Two others with superficial wounds were treated and released.

Students here, angered by the expansion of the war into Cambodia, have held demonstrations for the last three nights. On Saturday night, the Army Reserve Officers Training Corps building was burned to the ground and the Guard was called in and martial law was declared.

Today's rally, called after a night in which the police and guardsmen drove students into their dormitories and made 69 arrests, began as students rang the iron Victory bell on the commons, normally used to herald football victories.

A National Guard jeep drove onto the Commons and an officer ordered the crowd to disperse. Then several canisters of tear gas were fired, and the students straggled up a hill that borders the area and retreated into buildings.

A platoon of guardsmen, armed - as they have been since they arrived here with loaded M-1 rifles and gas equipment - moved across the green and over the crest of the hill, chasing the main body of protesters.

The youths split into two groups, one heading farther downhill toward a dormitory complex, the other eddying around a parking lot and girls' dormitory just below Taylor Hall, the architecture building.

The guardsmen moved into a grassy area just below the parking lot and fired several canisters of tear gas from their short, stubby launchers.

Three or four youths ran to the smoking canisters and hurled them back. Most fell far short, but one landed near the troops and a cheer went up from the crowd, which was chanting "Pigs off campus" and cursing the war.

A few youths in the front of the crowd ran into the parking lot and hurled stones or small chunks of pavement in the direction of the guardsmen. Then the troops began moving.

SOURCE

An address to the American people on television by President Richard Nixon, given on 8 August 1969. In the address Nixon puts forward his views about the relationship between federal and state governments with regard to federal funds.

We can no longer have effective government at any level unless we have it at all levels. There is too much to be done for the cities to do it alone, for Washington to do it alone, or for the States to do it alone. For a third of a century, power and responsibility have flowed toward Washington, and Washington has taken for its own the best sources of revenue. We intend to reverse this tide, and to turn back to the States a greater measure of responsibility - not as a way of avoiding problems, but as a better way of solving problems.

In the area of environmental legislation, Nixon seemed to outdo the Great Society when the National Environmental Policy Act of 1970 created the Environment Protection Agency. However, the Act was mainly the work of Democrat-controlled Congress, not Nixon himself. To limit the influence of the Environment Protection Agency, Nixon appointed William Rogers, a conservative in environmental affairs, as its first director.

Nixon wanted to portray himself as a consensus politician appealing to the silent majority of voters. However, from 1969 to 1971, he had to deal with a Congress dominated by Democrats. They controlled 58 out of 100 seats in the Senate and 243 out of 435 seats in the House of Representatives. As a result, many of the acts passed in this period owed as much to the Congress as the president.

Politically, Nixon also gained support through his 'southern strategy'. He deliberately attempted to appeal to white Democrat voters in the Old South. He opposed the extension of the Voting Rights Act of 1965 and wanted to modify the Housing Act of 1968, an Act that favoured black Americans. He tried to appoint southern white judges to the US Supreme Court but was thwarted by the Democrats in the Senate.

On a wider level, Nixon claimed credit for reducing violence and bringing stability back to the USA. In 1967, the CIA had launched Operation Chaos against radical groups. This was supported by the FBI's COINTELPRO (Counter-Intelligence Program), which aimed to destroy the Black Panther Party. These measures help explain why, by 1972, radical groups were in decline.

However, Nixon's first term suffered from economic problems. In 1971–74, the economy experienced the 'Nixon Recession'. Massive federal spending on the Great Society and Vietnam War had resulted in a large government deficit. Both inflation and unemployment rose. In 1971, the USA took the monumental decision of abandoning the **Bretton Woods Agreement** and began floating the US dollar on foreign exchanges. This led to the end of the fixed exchange rate system by the rest of the western world in 1972.

### KEY TERM

**Bretton Woods Agreement, 1944**
An international agreement that aimed to stabilise the global economy after the Second World War. It included a measure designed to bring trading stability by fixing currency exchange rates.

Even though Nixon faced economic problems he was popular in the US. His attack on the Great Society and his opposition to student protests and radical groups won him support from the silent majority. His foreign policy, which included improved relations with the USSR and communist China, gave him a strong reputation as an international statesman. In November 1972, Nixon won a landslide victory in the presidential election over the Democrat candidate, George McGovern. Although Nixon was far more popular than McGovern, many of the tactics used by the Nixon campaign team were regarded with suspicion. Nixon's election victory was short-lived. His campaign tactics led to the Watergate Scandal, which forced him resign his office in August 1974. No other US president before or after Nixon has had to resign.

SOURCE

From President Nixon's first State of the Union address to both houses of Congress, 22 January 1970. In the State of the Union address the president assesses government performance over the past year and outlines plans for the future.

Today, let me describe the directions of our new policies. Our concern in our relations with both these nations [South Vietnam and Cambodia] is to avoid a catastrophic collision and to build. At heart, the issue is the effectiveness of government. Ours has become - as it continues to be, and should remain - a society of large expectations. Government helped to generate these expectations. It undertook to meet them. Yet, increasingly, it proved unable to do so. As a people, we had too many visions - and too little vision. Now, as we enter the seventies, we should enter also a great age of reform of the institutions of American government.

Our purpose in this period should not be simply better management of the programs of the past. First, we cannot delay longer in accomplishing a total reform of our welfare system. When a system penalizes work, breaks up homes, robs recipients of dignity, there is no alternative to abolishing that system and adopting in its place the program of income support, job training, and work incentives which I recommended to the Congress last year.

Second, the time has come to assess and reform all of our institutions of government at the Federal, State, and local level. It is time for a New Federalism, in which, after 190 years of power flowing from the people and local and State governments to Washington, D.C., it will begin to flow from Washington back to the States and to the people of the United States.

Third, we must adopt reforms which will expand the range of opportunities for all Americans. We can fulfil the American dream only when each person has a fair chance to fulfil his own dreams. This means equal voting rights, equal employment opportunity, and new opportunities for expanded ownership. Because in order to be secure in their human rights, people need access to property rights.

The people of the United States should wait no longer for these reforms that would so deeply enhance the quality of their lives.

I am confident that the Congress will act now to adopt the legislation I placed before you last year. We in the Executive have done everything we can under existing law, but new and stronger weapons are needed in that fight.

### AS Level Exam-Style Question Section B

How accurate is it to say that there was a backlash against the campaigns for more personal freedom in the years 1968 to 1972? (12 marks)

**Tip**

*In your answer you should produce evidence to support the view suggested in the question that there was a backlash against campaigns for more personal freedom (e.g. campaigns for women's and gay rights). You should also balance that information with evidence suggesting the rise of a silent majority was due to other factors before drawing a final conclusion.*

### A Level Exam-Style Question Section A

***Study Sources 10 and 14 before you answer this question.***

How far could the historian make use of Sources 10 and 14 together to investigate why Nixon appealed to many American voters in the years 1968 to 1972?

Explain your answer using both sources, the information given about them and your knowledge of the historical context. (20 marks)

**Tip**

*It is important that you refer to the provenance of both sources in gauging their importance to the historian: who wrote the sources, when were they written and what were their intended audiences should all be considered. As well as using information from the sources to explain Nixon's appeal to US voters you should also use your own knowledge.*

### ACTIVITY
### KNOWLEDGE CHECK

**Reactions to the counterculture, 1968–72**

1. What reasons can you give for the rise of the 'silent majority' in the years 1968 to 1972?
2. How important was the media in influencing attitudes in the USA in the period 1968 to 1972?
3. In what ways and with what impact did events in Vietnam and at Kent State University affect US society in the years 1968 to 1972?
4. How successful do you think Nixon was as president, in the years 1969 to 1972?

### ACTIVITY
### WRITING

Study Source 14, then:

1. Identify any words or phrases you don't understand and research their meanings.
2. Identify words and phrases that show the ways President Nixon attempted to appeal to American voters in his speech.
3. Write a short paragraph explaining Nixon's views, using quotes from the extract to back up your points.

ACTIVITY
SUMMARY

**Protest and reaction 1963–72**

1. What do you regard as the most important improvement to black American civil rights in the period 1963 to 1972? Give reasons for your choice.
2. How important were protest and demonstration in bringing change in the USA in the period 1963 to 1972?
3. To what extent was personal freedom improved in the USA in the years 1963 to 1972?
4. What do you regard as the most significant development in US domestic history in the period 1963 to 1972? Give reasons to support your answer.

## WIDER READING

**Books**

Carson, C. (ed.) *The Eyes on the Prize – Civil Rights Reader: Documents, Speeches and Firsthand Accounts from the Black Freedom Fighters, 1954–1990*, Prentice-Hall (1992)

Cook, R. *Sweet Land of Liberty?: The African-American Struggle for Civil Rights in the Twentieth Century*, Routledge (1997)

de Pennington, J. *Modern America: 1865 to the present*, Hodder (2005)

Farmer, A. *An Introduction to American History, 1860–1990*, Hodder (2002)

Field, R. *Civil Rights in America, 1865–1980*, Cambridge University Press (2002)

Ling, P. J. *Martin Luther King Jr*, Routledge (2006)

Murphy, D. *Flagship History – United States 1776-1992*, Collins Educational (2001)

Paterson, D. *et al. Civil Rights in the USA, 1863–1980*, Heinemann (2001)

Patterson, J. T. *Grand Expectations: The United States, 1945–1974*, Oxford University Press (1998)

Sanders, V. *Politics, Presidency and Society in the USA 1968–2001*, Hodder (2008)

X, M. *Autobiography of Malcolm X*, Penguin (2007)

**Web**

Fordham University:

Modern social movements www.fordham.edu/Halsall/mod/modsbook56.asp

Pop culture www.fordham.edu/Halsall/mod/modsbook60.asp

The USA as a world leader www.fordham.edu/Halsall/mod/modsbook48.asp

National Archives:

Civil rights movement in the 1950s and 1960s www.nationalarchives.gov.uk/education/topics/civil-rights.htm

Martin Luther King www.nationalarchives.gov.uk/education/heroesvillains

**Video**

*The Century, America's Time* – documentary

*All the President's Men* (1976)

*Malcolm X* (1992)

*Mississippi Burning* (1988)

*Nixon* (1996)

# 2b.3 Social and political change, 1973–80

**KEY QUESTIONS**

- How far was there a crisis in political leadership in the years 1973 to 1980?
- What was the impact of economic change on US society in the years 1973 to 1980?
- How far did popular culture change in the years 1973 to 1980?
- To what extent did individual and civil rights improve in the years 1973 to 1980?

## INTRODUCTION

The period 1973 to 1980 saw the USA go through a period of significant political, economic and social change. The beginning of the period saw US politics engulfed in a major political crisis, which resulted in President Nixon resigning, the only time in American history this had happened. The decade continued in an atmosphere of political change and uncertainty under two presidents, Ford and Carter.

The domestic crisis was mirrored by a crisis in the country's position overseas. US involvement in the Vietnam War ended in 1973, but by the end of 1975 communist forces had taken control of South Vietnam, Cambodia and Laos. In the Middle East in 1979, the US ally the Shah of Iran was overthrown and replaced by a radical Islamist government.

A crisis also occurred in the US economy. The world economy was adversely affected by two oil crises, which saw the global price of oil first quadruple in 1973, then double again in 1979. The period 1973 to 1980 in the USA was one of **stagflation** – a period of rising inflation and rising unemployment.

**KEY TERM**

**Stagflation**
A period in which prices are rising (inflation) and the number of jobs is falling (unemployment). The word is a combination of 'stagnation' and 'inflation'. Stagflation can occur in either a stagnant economy or one facing an economic recession.

Yet, the period was also associated with the development of civil rights and personal freedom. Women's rights were extended with the US Supreme Court decision in *Roe v Wade*, which legalised abortion. Native Americans followed the example of black American radicals and created the American Indian movement. Finally, the status of many black Americans changed as a result of the achievement of civil equality in the years before 1973. These changes were reflected in popular culture, in cinema, television, popular music and sports.

If the 1950s could be seen as an age of affluence and the 1960s as an age of protest, the 1970s was an age of crisis.

**1973** – *Roe v Wade* US Supreme Court decision legalises abortion
Global oil crisis – global price of oil quadruples

**1974** – President Nixon resigns over Watergate scandal
Gerald Ford becomes president
Indian Self-Determination Act passed by Congress
Ford introduces WIN campaign to control inflation

1975

**1976** – Carter defeats Ford to become president

# HOW FAR WAS THERE A CRISIS OF POLITICAL LEADERSHIP IN THE YEARS 1973 TO 1980?

## The impact of Watergate on politics and the presidency

President Nixon was re-elected in November 1972 by one of the biggest margins in US history. He won 47.1 million votes against 29 million for his main challenger, Democratic candidate George McGovern. In the Electoral College the margin was even greater – 520 votes to a mere 17 for McGovern. However, within two years Nixon was forced to resign as president, the only president to do so in the history of the USA. How did such a dramatic change in Nixon's popularity come about?

The reason was the Watergate scandal. This began with the discovery of a burglary at the Democratic Party's presidential campaign headquarters, in the Watergate building, Washington DC in 1972. Subsequent investigation by journalists of the *Washington Post* newspaper and Congressional committees linked the burglary to widespread illegal political activities by the Nixon White House, including bugging the offices of opponents and ordering government agencies including the FBI to harass political activists. Not only were the burglars convicted, but so too were Nixon's two senior advisers, John Erlichman and Robert Haldeman. In the middle of the crisis, Vice President Spiro Agnew was forced to resign on charges of tax evasion not linked directly to the Watergate scandal. Agnew stood down in October 1973 and was replaced by Gerald R. Ford. Eventually, in August 1974, Nixon resigned because he faced impeachment by Congress.

The crisis engulfed the USA for two years and destroyed Nixon's position as president. Nixon's actions also severely damaged the reputation of the office of the presidency.

On the eve of the Watergate scandal, the US president had amassed considerable political power. As commander-in-chief, he controlled the world's greatest nuclear weapons arsenal and the world's greatest military forces. Through executive orders he could pass laws without the need for Congressional support. Nixon used these powers in a way that greatly increased presidential power at the expense of Congress.

As a result of Nixon's use of military forces in South East Asia, Congress had passed the War Powers Act in 1973. This limited the power of the US president to use military force abroad. In response to the Watergate Scandal there were further limitations on presidential powers. Investigations by Congress into the Central Intelligence Agency, the National Security Agency and the Defense Intelligence Agency found these organisations were virtually laws unto themselves and recommended new controls on their activities. In 1975, the Hughes–Ryan Amendment to the Privacy Act of 1974 required the president to report to Congress on all undercover operations by intelligence agencies. In 1977, both the Senate and the House set up committees to investigate the intelligence communities on a regular basis. In 1978, Congress passed the Ethics in Government Act, which required all senior government officials to disclose their finances. It also created the Office of Government Ethics.

**1977** - Carter attempts to control inflation and deals with energy crisis

**1978** - Harvey Milk and Mayor George Moscone assassinated in San Francisco

US Supreme Court 'Bakke case' confirms affirmative action

**1979** - Iranian Revolution sparks second global oil crisis

Iranian Hostage Crisis

**1980** - Reagan defeats Carter in presidential election

Following the resignation of Nixon, his successors, Ford and Carter, adopted a more open approach to presidential government. The real winners in the Watergate scandal were the press, who had uncovered the scandal; Congress, which investigated the scandal; and the US Supreme Court, which supported Congress. The balance of power within the federal government had changed and the so-called 'imperial presidency' came to an end, at least for a while.

### EXTEND YOUR KNOWLEDGE

**Richard M. Nixon (1913–94)**
Richard M. Nixon was the 37th president of the USA. A Republican, he came to office in 1969 and resigned in 1974.

Nixon was born in Yorba Linda, in southern California, and brought up as a member of the Society of Friends, also known as the Quakers, a religious group well-known for their support for pacifism. He attended the local university at Whittier before serving in the US Navy in the Pacific in the Second World War.

In 1946, Nixon was elected to the House of Representatives on a strong anti-communist ticket and, in 1950, entered the US Senate. He initially rose to national prominence when he took a leading role in the campaign against communist influence in government, in particular with the Alger Hiss case, in which he successfully branded Alger Hiss, a former State Department official, as a supporter of communism.

When Dwight Eisenhower won the US presidential election in 1952, Nixon was his vice-presidential running mate. From 1953 to 1961, he served as vice president. In 1960, he lost by the narrowest of margins to J. F. Kennedy in the presidential election. In 1962, he lost the election to be governor of California. In 1968, Nixon was finally elected president.

During his presidency he was responsible for US withdrawal from the Vietnam War and restoring diplomatic relations with communist China. He also improved relations with the Soviet Union.

Nixon's fall from power was caused by the Watergate scandal, which began during the 1972 presidential campaign. He was accused of a number of underhand tactics targeting political opponents. When these issues were investigated, Nixon made matters worse by obstructing investigations and failing to supply evidence, including recordings he had made of his own conversations.

When Nixon was threatened with impeachment (formally accusing a public official of wrong-doing), he resigned, in August 1974.

### AS Level Exam-Style Question Section A

***Study Source 1 before you answer this question.***

Why is Source 1 valuable to the historian for an enquiry into the Watergate scandal and the subsequent resignation of President Nixon?

Explain your answer using the source, the information about it and your own knowledge of the historical context. (8 marks)

**Tip**
*You will need to consider the provenance of the source to assess its value. This is Nixon's own resignation speech on 8 August 1974 and as such does give a strong insight into the reasons for his resignation that he chose to share. However, using your own knowledge you will be expected to place Nixon's comments in their historical context, which may lead you to suggest other reasons why he chose to stand down.*

**SOURCE 1** From President Nixon's resignation statement, delivered on 8 August 1974.

I shall leave office with regret at not completing my term. But with gratitude for the privilege of serving you as your President for the past five and a half years. These years have been a momentous time in the history of our nation and the world. They have been a time of achievement in which we can all be proud. For more than a quarter of a century in public life I have shared in the turbulent history of this era. I have fought for what I believe in. I have tried to the best of my ability to discharge those duties and meet those responsibilities that were entrusted to me. Sometimes I have succeeded and sometimes I have failed.

When I took the oath of office as President, I made [a] sacred commitment, to consecrate my office, my energies, and all the wisdom I can summon to the cause of peace. I have done my very best in all the days since to be true to that pledge.

To have served in this office is to have felt a personal sense of kinship with each and every American. In leaving it, I do so with this prayer: May God's grace be with you in all the days ahead.

## Ford, Carter and a new style of leadership

On the resignation of Richard Nixon, Vice President Gerald Ford became president. Ford had been appointed to the post in October 1973 after Spiro Agnew resigned, so had never been elected. This makes him the only person in American history to become president without winning an election. Ford faced a number of very difficult problems, including the humiliation of the fall of South Vietnam, Cambodia and Laos to communist forces. The USA also faced serious economic problems with rising inflation and unemployment.

Above all, Ford had to restore the reputation of the presidency. While Nixon was regarded as devious, highly intelligent and capable of engaging in dirty tricks to get his way in politics, Ford was seen as the opposite. During his long political career in Congress, Ford had developed a reputation for honesty. To some extent, this characteristic helped Ford re-establish confidence in the office as he attempted to heal the divisions caused by Nixon. In doing so he also courted controversy. On 8 September 1974, only a month after Nixon's resignation, he gave Nixon a full pardon for 'any and all crimes' committed during his presidency. This prevented Nixon from going to prison, and was a further setback to the reputation of the presidency.

The quest for a more open, less imperial-type president dominated the 1976 presidential campaign. Although Ford fought hard, he lost out to the Democrat, James Carter, a peanut farmer from Georgia, who had been governor of that state. Carter was not tainted by any links to Washington politics. In addition to winning the presidency, the Democrats increased their control of both the Senate and House in the US Congress.

Carter offered the USA a new style of leadership. He broke tradition at his inauguration by walking back from the Congress building to the White House after being sworn in in as president, instead of travelling by limousine. He also preferred barbecues on the White House lawn to formal dinners, and was often seen in casual clothes with his wife and young daughter, Amy.

In the early years of his presidency, Carter went around the country attending town council meetings and engaging with ordinary citizens in a style that was open, unpretentious and homely. He liked to be called Jimmy, which implied he was an 'ordinary guy'.

## Growing political disillusionment

Following the Watergate scandal, there was increasing political disillusionment in the USA. This was reflected in the turnout for federal elections. In the 1950s and 1960s, in every presidential election, there was a voter turnout of at least 60 percent. In 1976, the turnout had fallen to 54 percent and in 1980 to 53 percent. In midterm Congressional elections turnout was even lower: in 1978, it hit a new low of less than 38 percent of eligible voters going to the polls.

The biggest fall in political participation was amongst the young. In 1969, the Constitution had been amended to lower the voting age from 21 years to 18 years. Younger voters were the least likely to turn out for elections. Voter turnout also dropped in low-income areas, which traditionally had a lower voter turnout. Voter participation rates for Congressional elections fell on average 20 percent between 1968 and 1976. In low-income areas of New York City, such as South Bronx and Bedford-Stuyvesant, the turnout rate for congressional elections was 21.8 percent and 18.8 percent respectively.

Disillusionment with Ford was demonstrated by the fact that he barely won his own party's nomination for the presidency in 1976 and only narrowly beat the governor of California, Ronald Reagan. Similarly, the Democrats shunned their Washington-based leaders and chose an obscure former governor, Jimmy Carter.

Although Carter began his presidency with an air of optimism, it soon changed to one of growing disillusionment with his administration. One of Carter's biggest assets as a presidential candidate was his lack of links to federal politics. He was seen as an outsider not corrupted by the type of politics that produced Nixon and his White House advisers.

Once in power, Carter's lack of experience became a liability. He surrounded himself with advisers from his own state, known as the 'Georgia Mafia', adopted an aloof style and tried to micromanage the government. The Speaker of the House, Tip O'Neill, a fellow Democrat, said that in his view Carter found it difficult to work with Congress.

Carter faced a number of very difficult economic problems. In 1973, as a result of the Yom Kippur War in the Middle East, global oil prices rose fourfold. As the world's greatest consumer of oil, the USA was badly hit by high fuel prices: many American cars were known as 'gas guzzlers' because of their very heavy fuel consumption. By the time Carter became president, the US economy was suffering stagflation (high inflation and rising unemployment). These developments created an atmosphere of disillusionment within the USA, and in particular with national politicians, who were accused by many of allowing stagflation to take place in what had been the world's greatest economy since the Second World War.

Carter hoped to stimulate domestic demand to encourage economic recovery. In 1977, Carter's first year as president, unemployment fell from eight percent to seven percent. However, it then began to rise, hitting ten percent by the end of 1978. At the same time inflation rose, reaching 13 percent by 1980. Interest rates, the cost of borrowing money from banks, rose to a staggering 20 percent.

The economy was regarded as the most important domestic issue. Support for the Carter administration fell as living standards in the USA fell. Carter had entered the White House with the expectation that he was a new kind of leader who would return the USA to economic prosperity. His failure to do so led to general disillusionment about the economy and a growing feeling that national politicians, including the president, lacked the ability to revive the economy.

SOURCE

From President Carter's State of the Union address to a joint session of both houses of Congress, 19 January 1978. President Carter is attempting to show that he is a new style of president and wants to work closely with Congress on key economic issues.

I want to speak to you tonight about where we are and where we must go, about what we have done and what we must do. And I want to pledge to you my best efforts and ask you to pledge yours. [...]

Every day we spend more than $120 million for foreign oil. This slows our economic growth, it lowers the value of the dollar overseas, and it aggravates unemployment and inflation here at home.

Now we know what we must do — increase production. We must cut down on waste. And we must use more of those fuels which are plentiful and more permanent. We must be fair to people, and we must not disrupt our Nation's economy and our budget. [...]

Our main task at home this year, with energy a central element, is the Nation's economy. We must continue the recovery and further cut unemployment and inflation. [...]

Now, I didn't have any simple answers for all these problems. But we have developed an economic policy that is working, because it's simple, balanced, and fair. It's based on four principles:

First, the economy must keep on expanding to produce new jobs and better income, which our people need. The fruits of growth must be widely shared. More jobs must be made available to those who have been bypassed until now. And the tax system must be made fairer and simpler.

Secondly, private business and not the Government must lead the expansion in the future.

Third, we must lower the rate of inflation and keep it down. Inflation slows down economic growth, and it's the most cruel to the poor and also to the elderly and others who live on fixed incomes.

And fourth, we must contribute to the strength of the world economy.

The failure of national politicians to deal with the USA's economic problems created a feeling of disillusionment with national politics in general. However, disillusionment with Carter personally was mainly affected by foreign affairs. In January 1979, one of the USA's main allies in the Middle East, the Shah of Iran, was overthrown in a revolution. He was replaced by an Islamist regime led by a Muslim cleric, the Ayatollah Khomeini, who was anti-American. On 4 November 1979, a mob surrounded the US Embassy in the Iranian capital, Tehran, and took 66 Americans hostage. This began 444 days of crisis. In April 1980, Carter authorised a military mission to free the hostages but this ended in disaster: US military planes and helicopters crashed in the Iranian desert. Images were shown on television worldwide and the US Secretary of State, Cyrus Vance, resigned because he held himself responsible for the failure of the mission. Following extensive negotiations by Carter the crisis only came to an end after he had left office: Iran was only willing to formally end the crisis once Reagan had replaced Carter as president in January 1981.

Carter's popularity was also badly affected at the end of 1979 when the USSR invaded and occupied Afghanistan from 27 December. This was another humiliation and marked a serious deterioration in the Cold War. Carter's response was controversial: he announced that the US would boycott the 1980 Moscow Olympic Games. A total of 64 nations eventually joined the boycott.

In the 1980 presidential election, Carter faced the Republican candidate, Ronald Reagan. The sluggish nature of the economy, Carter's inability to work with Congress and his failings in foreign affairs cost him the election. Reagan won comfortably, with nearly 44 million votes against Carter's 35.5 million. The gap was worse in the Electoral College. Out of the 50 states Carter won only four: Georgia, Minnesota, West Virginia and Hawaii.

EXTEND YOUR KNOWLEDGE

Jimmy Carter (1924–)

James Earl Carter (known as Jimmy), was 39th president of the USA and served one term as president, from 1977 to 1981.

Carter was a member of the Democratic Party from the state of Georgia. Like Nixon, he had served in the US Navy, and later became a peanut farmer. He entered the Georgia State legislature in 1962 and went on to become governor of the state.

In the aftermath of the Watergate scandal voters were looking for a candidate from outside the Washington elite and Carter's down-to-earth background helped him succeed in the 1976 elections.

During his presidency Carter successfully mediated in the Arab-Israeli conflict in the Middle East and helped produce the Camp David peace agreement between Israel and Egypt. He also oversaw the return of the Panama Canal Zone from US to Panamanian control.

Carter's biggest foreign policy failures were the Iranian hostage crisis and the Soviet invasion of Afghanistan. At home he failed to deal effectively with stagflation.

After losing the presidency to Ronald Reagan, Carter became an unofficial ambassador of peace around the world. He was awarded the Nobel Peace Prize in 2002.

## The political impact of environmentalism

Although growing disillusionment with the traditional political parties and political system were a feature of the period, one issue that did attract younger voters was concern for the environment. Ever since *Silent Spring*, Rachel Carson's book about the adverse effect of pollution and insecticides had been published in 1963, the environment had been a national issue. The Johnson and Nixon administrations saw the passage of many environmental Acts. Congress set up the Environmental Protection Agency (EPA) and the Occupational Safety and Health Administration (OSHA) in 1970. Congress also passed the Clean Air Act in 1970, the Endangered Species Act in 1973 and a Toxic Substances Control Act in 1976. These Acts went a long way to dealing with the USA's environmental problems. Pollution in cities was reduced considerably.

Congressional action was heavily influenced by environmental pressure groups and individuals, including Ralph Nader, founder of Public Citizen, an **NGO** that campaigned on issues such as product safety, corporate accountability and the environment. Other activists took a more direct approach. Edward Abbey's book *The Monkey Wrench Gang*, published in 1975, highlighted tactics such as activists chaining themselves to trees to preserve forests from destruction.

KEY TERM

NGO

NGO stands for non-governmental organisation. Examples include the Red Cross or other private aid agencies.

In the Carter years (1977–81) three major environmental issues grabbed national headlines.

- In 1978, Love Canal, near Niagara Falls, in upper New York State became an issue because it was full of foul-smelling industrial waste. Residents living nearby suffered from chromosomal damage linked to the pollution. The outcry led to a Senate enquiry and New York State spending $30 million to clean up the canal.
- In March 1979, the most serious nuclear accident in American history took place at Three Mile Island, Pennsylvania. A nuclear reactor at a power station nearly exploded. 10,000 people nearby fled their homes. Even though nuclear power stations continued to operate, no new ones were built as a result.
- A plan to build Tellico Dam on the Little Tennessee River in east Tennessee was opposed by environmentalists, as they argued its construction would threaten wildlife, including the snail darter fish, which could become extinct if the dam was built. Using the Endangered Species Act of 1973, environmentalists got the US Supreme Court to declare against the proposed dam in 1978. Nevertheless, the dam was built, after Congress voted for a rider to the Energy and Water Development Appropriation Act ordering the Tennessee Valley Authority to complete the dam.

In 1980, environmentalists had some victories; for example, they helped force through the Alaska Lands Law, which doubled the acreage of land set aside for national parks and wildlife refuges. Wildlife refuges and national park extensions were developed across the USA, including the Elk Wildlife Refuge at Jackson Hole, Wyoming. There was also a superfund created by Congress that would spend $1 billion a year clearing up toxic sites such as in Love Canal.

Carter was sympathetic to the environmental cause and during his presidency he strengthened the powers of the EPA to act on pollution.

SOURCE

From testimony given by James L. Clark , a nearby resident of Love Canal, before the Senate Subcommittee on Environmental Pollution and Hazardous Waste in Love Canal, in Upper New York State on 28–29 March 1979.

I am James L. Clark. I am a disabled American Veteran having served 14 years in various paratroop, Green Beret and guard units. I have lived over 8 years in the Love Canal area. Since living there my family has suffered many serious health problems. The adverse health effects in that area are real. These people need to be immediately evacuated from that contaminated area.

With hundreds of chemicals, of dioxin, of radiation, how much longer will these people be forced to stay? Niagara Falls itself is a scenic wonder. Why are we allowing it to be turned into a chemical dump? There is no such thing as a secure landfill. While being the greatest industrial nation in the world, we are using antiquated methods of waste disposal and of regulating it. What we are doing is regulating the slow, systematic poisoning of our citizens. The people want this dumping to stop. We have letters from trade unions and religious leaders to this effect. The technology of a total, safe method of waste treatment exists.

The Niagara frontier will be a perfect place to initiate a pilot program with over 50 chemical dumps identified and more being built.

Gentlemen, to show what Love Canal really means, a little girl in the neighbourhood asked me to show you this photo. Her condition came about when the digging started and it has grown steadily worse. Several doctors have said it is definitely not teenage acne. Last Friday she was taken to hospital. They did not know what caused the severe rash. That girl, Gentlemen, is my daughter.

**A Level Exam-Style Question Section A**

***Study Sources 2 and 3 before you answer this question.***

How far could the historian make use of Sources 2 and 3 together to investigate the problems facing the Carter presidency in the years 1977 to 1980?

Explain your answer using both sources, the information given about them and your knowledge of the historical context. (20 marks)

**Tip**

*You will be expected to comment on the provenance of each source in assessing how the historian could use them in an investigation. You will also be expected to use your own knowledge to place both sources in the historical context of the Carter presidency.*

**ACTIVITY**
**KNOWLEDGE CHECK**

**The crisis of political leadership**

1. Make a list of reasons why Richard Nixon resigned as president.
2. In what ways did the leadership styles of presidents Ford and Carter differ from President Nixon's?
3. Why were environmental issues regarded as important during the years 1973 to 1980?
4. Write down five reasons why American voters became increasingly disillusioned with national politics in the years 1973 to 1980.

## WHAT WAS THE IMPACT OF ECONOMIC CHANGE ON US SOCIETY IN THE YEARS 1973 TO 1980?

The USA went through a period of considerable economic change in the years 1973 to 1980. In 1973, the USA was the world's largest economy with a high standard of living. However, in the years to 1980 the USA faced a number of economic shocks, such as rapidly rising energy prices and rising unemployment. These developments, collectively known as stagflation, had a profound impact on US society.

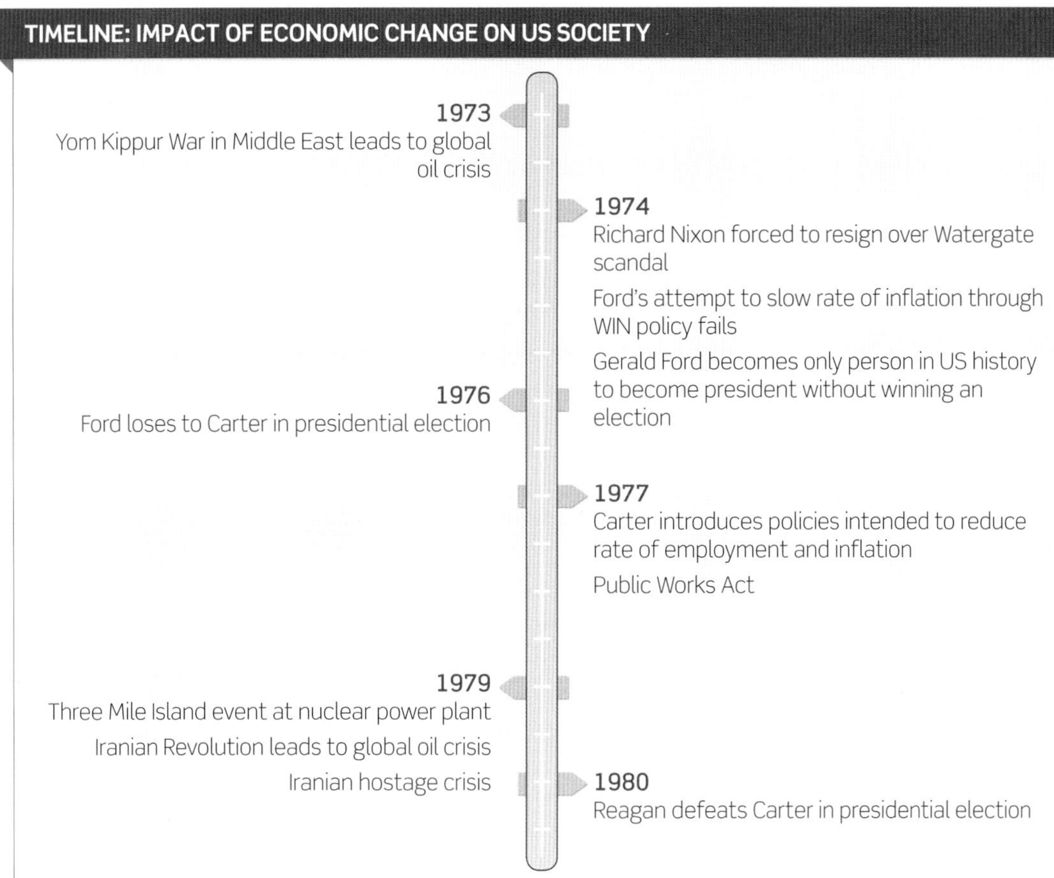


## The effects of inflation on family incomes

One of the biggest problems facing the people of the USA during the 1970s was inflation, a period of rising prices. When Carter took office in 1977, inflation was five percent per year. Within a year it had doubled to ten percent.

The cost of living doubled between 1968 and 1978 and continued to rise until 1982. The cost of a postage stamp was eight cents in 1974, rising to 20 cents in 1981. A McDonald's burger cost 15 cents in 1967, rising to 50 cents by 1981. In addition, interest rates, the cost of borrowing money from banks, reached record highs of around 20 percent. This led to a drop in investment in the economy and a drop in house-buying. Even though the federal minimum wage rose from $2.10 in 1975 to $3.35 in 1981, it failed to keep pace with rising prices caused by inflation.

At the same time as rising prices the US economy experienced sluggish growth. During the period 1972 to 1978, industrial productivity rose only one percent compared to an average of 3.2 percent for the years 1948 to 1955. The USA's major economic rivals, West Germany and Japan, had productivity levels of four to five percent. Real incomes in the USA fell by two percent each year from 1973 to 1981. To make matters worse, from 1975 the US economy suffered from stagflation. Inflation stood at 11 percent, while unemployment rose to nine percent. All of this meant that family incomes and living standards fell. By the mid-1970s, the US standard of living fell to fifth in the world, behind countries like Switzerland, Sweden and Denmark.

The once-mighty US manufacturing sector of the economy went through a process of adjustment. Traditional industries such as steel- and car-manufacturing faced stiff foreign competition. Industrial plants closed or relocated to other parts of the US where labour costs were cheaper. In 1967, two-thirds of all manufacturing jobs were in the Northeast and Midwest. By 1992, this had dropped to 50 percent. States like New York and Michigan lost thousands of jobs. These areas became known as the 'Rust Belt' as businesses relocated to the 'Sun Belt' of the south and west. As a result, the distribution of wealth changed within the USA. Traditionally, the wealthiest part of the country was the north-east: now it began to move to include areas formerly associated with agriculture.

**KEY TERM**

**Foreclosure**
When a house-buyer takes out a mortgage (loan) in order to pay for a house but then fails to keep up the regular repayments on the mortgage, the lender, usually a bank, can 'foreclose'. This means they take possession of the house in place of the repayment of the loan, and usually results in the people living there having to move out.

## The growth of homelessness

With inflation and rising unemployment, household debt rose rapidly, leading to **foreclosures** by banks and greater homelessness. Unlike Britain, the USA does not have a national welfare system: each state is responsible for providing social welfare to its citizens when they are unemployed. On occasion, as in the New Deal in the 1930s and again in the 1970s, the federal government would supplement state provision.

The stagflation of the 1970s brought increasing poverty levels. According to government statistics, the proportion of the population living in poverty remained stable at 12 percent, but immigration in the 1970s drove a rise in population of more than 25 million, so in numerical terms more people were living in poverty.

In addition, in some areas mechanisation of certain industries in a bid to increase productivity also increased unemployment. Areas such as the Mississippi Delta in the South and Appalachia in the East, dependent on textile manufacture and coal-mining, suffered particularly badly.

Philadelphia, Pennsylvania was a good example of what happened to a north-eastern city in this period. In 1951, manufacturing provided 46 percent of its jobs. This had fallen to 24 percent in 1977. The number of Philadelphians on welfare jumped from around 200,000 in 1970 to nearly 340,000 in 1980, more than 20 percent of the population. With fewer jobs, rising prices and limited welfare provision, many Philadelphians were driven to homelessness. Homelessness increased everywhere, but the highest numbers became homeless in those states with the most limited welfare provision, such as Mississippi.

Matters were made worse through the passage of Proposition 13 in the state of California, in June 1978. By a margin of 2:1 a state-wide referendum agreed to reduce state taxes by 57 percent. This was followed by other states where the population faced serious financial problems due to the poor state of the economy. Proposition 13 saved taxpayers money, but had a serious impact on state support services like welfare.

## The oil crisis and the end of cheap energy

The stagflation of the 1970s was caused by a number of factors, such as rising federal debt and foreign manufacturing competition. However, another significant factor was the oil crises that affected the global economy in 1973 and 1979. In 1973, the Arab–Israeli Yom Kippur War in the Middle East created uncertainty about the future availability of oil as the war was taking place in a major oil-producing region. As a result, a global oil-producing cartel, the Organization of Petroleum Exporting Countries (OPEC), decided to quadruple the international price of oil. In 1979, the Islamic revolution in Iran and the fall of the Shah led to a doubling of the global price of oil. In the USA, oil prices rose from $3 dollars a barrel in 1973 to $34 dollars a barrel by the summer of 1979. On 13 June 1979, 58 percent of the USA's petrol stations closed through lack of petrol. These developments made many Americans feel that they were no longer in control of their own economy.

Of all the countries in the world, the USA was most vulnerable to rising oil prices as it was the greatest consumer of oil. In 1970, the USA imported $4 billion worth of oil. By 1980, this figure had risen to $80 billion.

The oil crisis clearly damaged the overall US economy. The US Gross National Product (GNP) dropped by 2.5 percent in the first three quarters of 1973. After the oil price rise of 1973, it fell another 3.2 percent in the winter of 1974 to 1975. By 1979, 55 percent of all Americans believed that 'next year will be worse than this year'. Nearly 90 percent believed inflation was a permanent feature of the US economy.

SOURCE 4

A US petrol station during the energy crisis of 1973. The large cars in the petrol station are typical for the US at this time. This type of car could only travel 8–10 miles per gallon (approximately 4.5 litres) of fuel used.

## The impact of foreign competition

The US economy was heavily dependent on petrol-driven transportation. Up to the 1970s, with the relatively cheap price of oil, the US had produced cars that had poor petrol consumption. These cars, known as 'gas guzzlers', were very susceptible to rising oil costs. By comparison, imported cars from West Germany and Japan had far better fuel consumption. In 1974, the USA's three biggest car manufacturers, General Motors, Ford and Chrysler, laid off 224,000 workers. By 1980, the USA's third largest car producer, Chrysler, faced bankruptcy and only survived through a federal bailout of $1.3 billion. At the same time, car imports rose by 33 percent.

Foreign competition was not just limited to West Germany and Japan. The European Economic Community had been created in 1957, and after 1973 contained nine European countries, including the United Kingdom. This area formed a very important trading bloc that rivalled the US in foreign trade. It was not only in car production that the US faced foreign competition. In electronics the USA faced strong competition from Japanese companies such as Hitachi, Sony and Toshiba. From Europe companies such as Philips and Siemens, and Sud Aviation in aerospace technology, began to both penetrate the US market and challenge the US in global trade.

Foreign competition increased pressure on US manufacturing, resulting in both factory closures and restructuring, which usually involved 'downsizing' and worker redundancies.

## The government's response

Following the oil crisis of 1973 and the rise in inflation, President Ford, who took office in August 1974, attempted a policy of voluntary restraint by businesses and individuals. It was called Whip Inflation Now (WIN). Ford even took to wearing a WIN lapel badge. Ford also cut federal spending to curb rising prices. Unfortunately, Ford's policies failed to deal with the severe economic problems facing the USA. His policies to limit inflation were voluntary, not compulsory, and the problems facing the global economy caused by the oil crisis and the impact of foreign competition required a far more radical response from the federal government. An economic recession occurred in the 1974–75 period with unemployment rising to 11 percent. In 1976, Ford lost the presidential election to Jimmy Carter by a narrow margin – 49.9 percent of the popular vote for Carter compared to 47.9 percent for Ford.

Carter offered the American people a new start from a person who prided himself as not being part of the Washington elite of politicians. In his first year he cut taxes and used public works programmes to get the USA out of economic recession. In the Public Works Act of 1977, Carter introduced what he thought would be a stimulus package to get the economy back on track. It included a $4 billion public works programme and an enlargement of other social policies. This included the Earned Income Tax Credit (EITC), a programme of tax credits for low-income working families with children that had begun in 1975. In the late 1970s, Congress expanded the means-tested food stamps programme. By 1980, this programme alone supported 21 million people on welfare.

However, Carter would not support the Humphrey–Hawkins bill, which was supported by the US Trade Union organisation (the **AFL–CIO**). This bill aimed to allow the federal government to protect workers' jobs at times of economic recession by becoming the employer in the last resort. It passed Congress in October 1978 but had limited effect on the problems facing the US economy.

In dealing with the energy crisis, Carter produced a comprehensive energy programme. A National Energy Plan (NEP) was announced in April 1977. It outlined the deregulation of natural gas prices, but it was not until October 1978 that Congress passed an act implementing this proposal. In 1977, the president also created a Department of Energy, which promoted the conservation of domestic oil reserves and speed limits on car use to reduce fuel consumption. The Department also began to promote alternative sources of energy such as solar power and a form of tax credit to manufacturers who made more fuel-efficient products such as cars and home appliances. Eventually, US energy consumption fell ten percent between 1979 and 1983.

**KEY TERM**

**AFL–CIO**
The US national trade union organisation created in 1955 from an amalgamation of the American Federation of Labor (AFL) and the Congress of Industrial Organizations (CIO). Traditionally, the AFL represented skilled workers and the CIO semi-skilled and unskilled workers.

**AS Level Exam-Style Question Section A**

***Study Source 5 before you answer this question.***

Why is Source 5 valuable to the historian for an enquiry into why the USA was facing an energy crisis in the years 1977 to 1980?

Explain your answer using the source, the information about it and your own knowledge of the historical context. (8 marks)

**Tip**

*Refer to the provenance of the source in your answer. When did Carter make the address and who was he speaking to? To support your answer you should also refer to relevant information from within the source and your own knowledge to place the source in historical context.*

SOURCE

From a television address by President Carter on the energy crisis, 18 April 1977. Jimmy Carter had become president on 20 January that year.

Two days from now, I will present to the Congress my energy proposals. Its members will be my partners and they have already given me a great deal of valuable advice. Many of these proposals will be unpopular. Some will cause you to put up with inconveniences and to make sacrifices.

The most important thing about these proposals is that the alternative may be a national catastrophe. [...]

I know that some of you may doubt that we face real energy shortages. The 1973 gasoline lines are gone, [...] and our homes are warm again. But our energy problem is worse tonight than it was in 1973 or a few weeks ago in the dead of winter. It is worse because more waste has occurred, and more time has passed by without our planning for the future. And it will get worse every day until we act.

The oil and natural gas we rely on for 75 percent of our energy are running out. In spite of increased effort, domestic production has been dropping steadily at about six percent a year. Imports have doubled in the last five years. Our nation's economic and political independence is becoming increasingly vulnerable. Unless profound changes are made to lower oil consumption, we now believe that early in the 1980s the world will be demanding more oil than it can produce.

The world now uses about 60 million barrels of oil a day and demand increases each year about five percent. This means that just to stay even we need the production of a new Texas every year, an Alaskan North Slope every nine months, or a new Saudi Arabia every three years. Obviously, this cannot continue. [...]

The second change took place in this century, with the growing use of oil and natural gas. They were more convenient and cheaper than coal, and the supply seemed to be almost without limit. They made possible the age of automobile and airplane travel. Nearly everyone who is alive today grew up during this age and we have never known anything different.

Because we are now running out of gas and oil, we must prepare quickly for a third change, to strict conservation and to the renewed use of coal and permanent renewable energy sources, like solar power. [...]

World consumption of oil is still going up. If it were possible to keep it rising during the 1970s and 1980s by 5 percent a year as it has in the past, we could use up all the proven reserves of oil in the entire world by the end of the next decade. [...]

We will feel mounting pressure to plunder the environment. We will have a crash program to build more nuclear plants, strip-mine and burn more coal, and drill more offshore wells than we will need if we begin to conserve now. Inflation will soar, production will go down, people will lose their jobs. Intense competition for oil will build up among nations and among the different regions within our own country. [...]

If we fail to act soon, we will face an economic, social and political crisis that will threaten our free institutions.

But we still have another choice. We can begin to prepare right now. We can decide to act while there is time.

In a bid to stimulate the economy, Carter introduced the Airline Deregulation Act of 1978. This abolished the Civil Aeronautics Board in a bid to create greater competition in the airline industry. He introduced similar legislation for the lorry and communications industries. Greater market competition, he hoped, would lead to lower prices for consumers and encourage economic growth. These laws did help stimulate and grow the economy in the 1980s but had little effect on the economic problems facing Carter in the late 1970s.

By late 1978, unemployment had dropped to five percent, yet Carter did little to control inflation. This rose from six percent in 1977 to ten percent in 1978. Following the midterm elections of 1978, when the Democrats lost seats to the Republicans, Carter changed his economic policy. In the summer of 1979, Carter was achieving a mere 26 percent approval rating in opinion polls, lower than Richard Nixon received at the height of the Watergate scandal. He held a ten-day high level conference of advisers at the presidential retreat, Camp David, and then announced a new energy policy. The main outcome was a programme of research into the production of synthetic fuel to limit US dependence on oil and gas. However, this research programme did not offer an answer to the US economy's immediate energy problems. Carter additionally cut public works programmes and delayed tax reductions. By 1980, the economy reverted to stagflation, with unemployment at 7.5 percent, mortgage rates at 15 percent, interest rates at an all-time high of 20 percent and inflation averaging 12–13 percent.

The 1979 *Economic Report of the President* pointed out that inflation was a big problem for the US economy. It recommended a plan for the voluntary control of prices and wages. Unfortunately, voluntary restraint failed to control inflation. By 1979, the American public saw inflation rather than unemployment as the major economic problem, and was losing faith in the Democratic Party. Carter also had faced a number of embarrassing setbacks in foreign policy such as the Iran Hostage Crisis and the Soviet invasion of Afghanistan. In the 1980 presidential elections, Carter's failures helped ensure Democrat defeat. Republican presidential candidate Ronald Reagan won by a landslide, with 489 Electoral College votes to a mere 49 for Carter. Democrats also fared badly in the Congressional election. They lost 33 seats in the House of Representatives to the Republicans and nine in the Senate. These results show how little the electorate rated Carter and the Democrat-controlled Congress's response to the economic problems facing the USA.

**SOURCE 6** From a televised speech by President Carter on the issue of inflation, 24 October 1978.

This has been a long-time threat. For the last 10 years, the annual inflation rate in the United States has averaged six and a half percent. And during the three years before my inauguration, it had increased to an average of eight percent.

Inflation has, therefore, been a serious problem for me ever since I became president. We've tried to control it, but we have not been successful. It's time for all of us to make a greater and more co-ordinated effort.

If inflation gets worse, several things will happen. Your purchasing power will continue to decline, and most of the burden will fall on those who can least afford it. Our national productivity will suffer. The value of our dollar will continue to fall in world trade.

We've made good progress in putting our people back to work over the past 21 months. We've created more than six million new jobs for American workers. We've reduced the unemployment rate by about 25 percent, and we will continue our efforts to reduce unemployment further, especially among our young people and minorities.

But I must tell you tonight that inflation threatens this progress. If we do not get inflation under control, we will not be able to reduce unemployment further, and we may even slide backward.

Inflation is obviously a serious problem. What is the solution?

I do not have all the answers. Nobody does. Perhaps there is no complete and adequate answer. But I want to let you know that fighting inflation will be a central preoccupation of mine during the months ahead, and I want to arouse the nation to join me in this effort.

There are two simplistic and familiar answers which are sometimes proposed - simple, familiar, and too extreme. One of these answers is to impose a complicated scheme of Federal government wage and price controls on our entire free economic system. The other is a deliberate recession which would throw millions of people out of work. Both of these extreme proposals would not work, and they must be rejected.

I've spent many hours in the last few months reviewing with my own advisers and with a number of outside experts every proposal, every suggestion, every possibility in eliminating inflation. If there's one thing I have learned beyond any doubt, it is that there is no single solution for inflation.

### THINKING HISTORICALLY Evidence (6a)

**Arguments and facts**

Reread Sources 3, 5 and 6.

Working in groups:

1 Discuss why facts are important in history.

2 In what ways do Sources 3 and 5 disagree?

3 In what ways do Sources 5 and 6 disagree? Which one do you think is correct? Explain your answer.

4 Do you think that the different dates of Sources 5 and 6 explain the different emphasis on energy? Explain your answer.

5 If we accept that Source 3 deals only with a specific issue in one part of the USA, do we discount Source 3 as being useful? Explain your answer.

**A Level Exam-Style Question Section B**

How accurate is it to say that President Carter was a weak president? (20 marks)

**Tip**

*Work out first what qualities a president should display and then weigh Carter's achievements and failures against these qualities before reaching a supported judgement.*

ACTIVITY
KNOWLEDGE CHECK

**The impact of economic change on society**

1 Write down what you think was the most serious economic problem facing the US economy in the years 1973–80. List the reasons for your choice.

2 Make two lists – one of ways in which Ford attempted to deal with the USA's economic problems and one for the ways Carter tackled economic problems. Compare the lists and evaluate their success.

# HOW FAR DID POPULAR CULTURE CHANGE IN THE YEARS 1973 TO 1980?

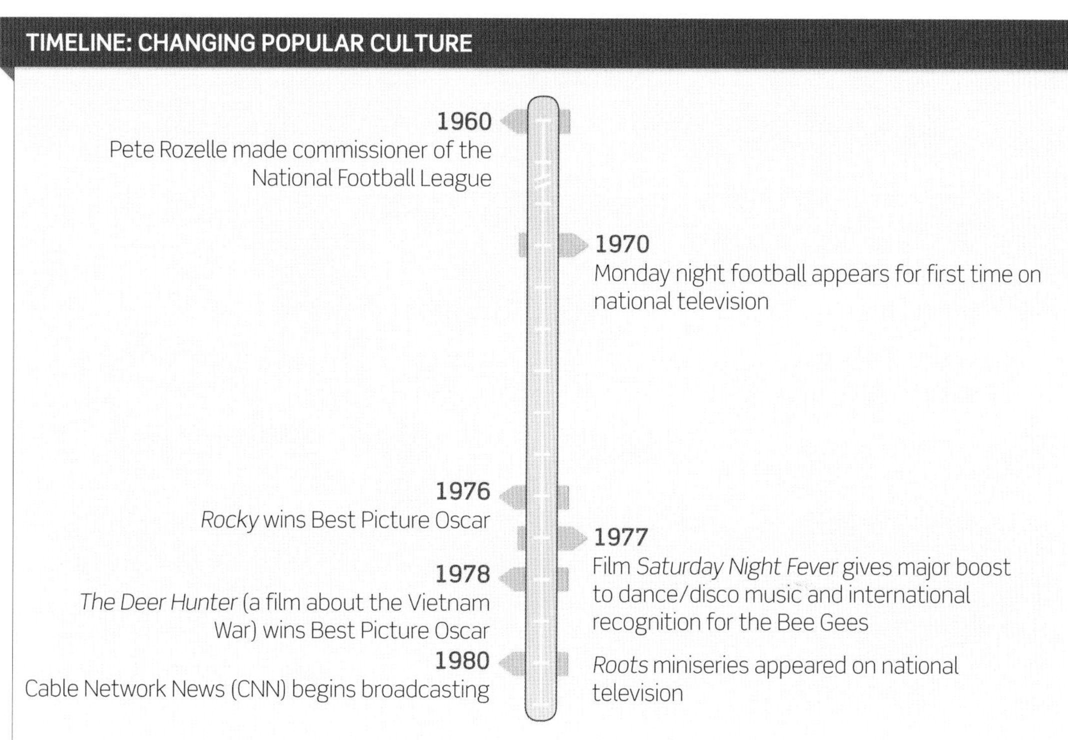


## Business interests in sports

In US popular culture, sports have always played a major role. The national game until the 1960s was baseball. Every year the World Series competition determined the best baseball team in the USA. Most major cities had a major league baseball team. Baseball players were household names and their national reputation was made by newspapers and radio. However, by the 1970s, television became the major medium for sports, and a much wider range of sports was broadcast, attracting business sponsorship and generating revenues for the broadcasters through the advertising shown during games.

Sports such as basketball, boxing, motor racing and golf all attracted new audiences through being broadcast on television, but the sport that benefited most was American football. Up to the 1960s, the most popular American football competitions were those between universities. Universities like Notre Dame in South Bend, Indiana, attracted massive home attendances and a nationwide following. The University of Nebraska in Lincoln had sell-out home games from 1962 onwards, with a stadium that could hold 86,000 spectators. But in the 1970s professional (rather than university) American football became the national game, mainly because of television.

SOURCE 7 The Pittsburgh Steelers score a touchdown at Super Bowl X, played on 18 January 1976 at the Miami Orange Bowl, Florida. The Steelers went on to beat the Dallas Cowboys 21–17. A 30-second advert during the game cost $110,000.

One of the most important individuals in transforming the situation was Pete Rozelle. In 1960, Rozelle was appointed as commissioner of the National Football League (NFL), and in 1962 he negotiated a $9.3 million television deal with the Columbia Broadcasting System (CBS) television network to broadcast NFL games. To cement NFL television popularity, Rozelle negotiated with CBS for a weekly Monday night NFL game, which became a national institution. Advertising during NFL games became an extremely important marketing platform for businesses. The impact of television on NFL football was immense. In the 1960s, the main source of NFL club revenue was ticket sales: by 1980, it was television revenues.

American football replaced baseball as the USA's most popular sport because it was more suitable for television. Regular stoppages allowed more opportunities for advertising during matches. This in turn encouraged business sponsorship of teams and key sporting events. The NFL Super Bowl, played by the two best NFL teams became an unofficial national holiday. On 14 January 1973, Super Bowl VII saw the Washington Redskins defeat the Miami Dolphins. The television audience was 53 million and the advertising cost during the match was $88,000 per 30-second advertisement. By Super Bowl XIV, in 1980, when the LA Rams defeated the Pittsburgh Steelers, the television audience had risen to 76 million and advertising revenue was $222,000 per 30-second advertisement. NFL players' salaries also rose over this period. In 1970, the average annual wage was $23,000: by 1975, this had risen to $56,000 and by 1980 had reached $75,000 per year.

The impact of television was not limited to professional American football. Professional basketball also benefited. In 1979, the National Basketball Association (NBA), signed a lucrative contract with television company ESPN. This channel showed highlights of all major sports and aided the popularity of the NBA with television audiences. The NBA also signed a contract with cable company USA Network. This cable channel showed NBA matches on Thursday nights. This contract pumped millions of dollars into the sport. By 1980, two of the NBA's star players had become household names: Larry Bird of the Boston Celtics and Magic Johnson of the LA Lakers. In only his second season in the NBA Magic Johnson was offered a contract of $25 million a year.

Soft drinks giants Coca-Cola and Pepsi became major sponsors of sport. Coca-Cola sponsored the 1978 FIFA World Cup in Argentina. In the USA, Coca-Cola sponsored NASCAR (car racing), basketball and American football. Pepsi also sponsored these popular sports. A close relationship also grew up between beer companies and sport. Coors, based in Colorado, sponsored the National Hockey League stadium. Anheuser-Busch, the company that brews Budweiser beer, was a key sponsor of the NFL. The link between products like beer and sporting equipment, traditionally marketed to men, became an enduring feature of US professional sports.

By 1980, the impact of television contracts had transformed professional American football and basketball. These changes were also experienced by other sports such as professional baseball, ice hockey and golf. The massive rise in audiences, thanks to television, led to increased business sponsorship of sport. With massive exposure to millions of television viewers, sport had become big business. Coca-Cola, Pepsi, Coors, Anheuser-Busch and electronics companies such as Hitachi now saw sports sponsorship as an effective way to market their products.

## The fragmentation of popular music

The 1960s were a great period of change and innovation in popular music. Ballad singing by individual artists such as Frank Sinatra and Elvis Presley had given way to the rise of the group or band. British bands such as the Beatles and Rolling Stones achieved phenomenal success in the USA. Their success was matched by American bands such as the Beach Boys, the Grateful Dead and the Doors, and solo music stars like Joan Baez, Janis Joplin and John B. Sebastian. The changes in popular music were encapsulated in the Woodstock Festival of 1969. Woodstock was a massive popular music festival in upper New York State that attracted tens of thousands to watch some of the world's top music stars. Following Woodstock, music festivals became popular across the USA.

The years 1973 to 1980 saw major changes again. Popular music in the USA fragmented into many different styles to give the decade of the 1970s a unique place in the developing history of popular music. Dance music became popular with the development of disco and club music. Progressive rock (or prog rock) developed from the rock bands of the 1960s. Tamla Motown northern black music developed into soul and funk. Further, more rebellious, genres were punk and new wave. Finally, in 1979, hip hop emerged.

Disco and dance music tracks were played at the increasingly popular discotheques that replaced dance halls featuring live music. The highpoint of the disco dance music craze came with the release of the film *Saturday Night Fever* in 1977. It made an overnight star of John Travolta, made male disco dancing cool and helped the Bee Gees to become international stars. Bee Gee hits such as 'Jive Talking' epitomised disco music.

A major evolution of the rock band genre of the 1960s was the growth of progressive rock. This took rock music and experimented with elements of classical music and opera. This genre was heavily influenced by British bands like Pink Floyd, Queen and the Electric Light Orchestra (ELO). American bands such as Grand Funk Railroad and Kansas offered a similar blend of rock, jazz, classical and blues in their music.

Perhaps the most sensational development of the 1970s was the appearance of punk rock. Again, the main thrust came from Britain. The Sex Pistols offered a new, rebellious and irreverent style of rock music. One of their best known tracks was a punk version of 'God Save the Queen'. Overtly taking drugs and consuming excessive amounts of alcohol, the Sex Pistols aimed to shock. Their style stood in marked contrast to other popular music artists at the time.

The 1970s also saw a rise in popularity of northern-based black American music. Taking its inspiration from 1960s artists like James Brown, a new 'funky' form of soul music developed. It was played by groups such as Sly and the Family Stone, Kool and the Gang and Earth, Wind and Fire. Funk used electronic psychedelic sounds associated with drug culture. More family-friendly groups appeared later in the 1970s such as the Jackson 5, featuring a young Michael Jackson. A more rebellious version of black American music developed in the rundown area of South Bronx in New York City from 1979, known as hip hop. It combined traditional black music forms with rap music.

Another genre of music popular in the 1970s was folk-pop music, associated with singer-songwriters like Bob Dylan, Joni Mitchell, Joan Baez and Carly Simon. Many of their songs had strong folk roots and links to the protest movements of the 1960s and 1970s. The most popular group was Crosby, Stills and Nash, later to include singer-songwriter Neil Young. Young wrote songs about environmentalism and the Kent State University shootings of 1970.

By 1980, the band was still a dominant format of popular music, but it had developed into a variety of different directions since the 1970s.

## Contradictions in film and television

American film went through a time of change in the period 1973 to 1980. Important political and social issues received significant attention and films about the Mafia and the Vietnam War provided powerful themes.

However, several of the most popular films offered escapism from the problems facing the USA in the 1970s such as the political scandal of Watergate, the energy crisis and stagflation. In 1975, the film that dominated the Academy Awards (Oscar) ceremony was *One Flew over the Cuckoo's Nest*, a black comedy set in a mental hospital. In the following year, *Rocky* saw the major acting debut of Sylvester Stallone playing the lead role of a down-and-out part-time boxer who is given a shot at the World Heavyweight title, which he almost wins. It encapsulated the American Dream of a rags-to-fame story and spawned a whole series of sequels up to *Rocky V* and *Rocky Balboa*.

Towards the end of the decade Hollywood began to deal with the most controversial and divisive issue in US politics since the Second World War: the war in Vietnam. *The Deer Hunter*, starring Robert de Niro, won the Best Picture Award in 1978 and dealt with the experiences of three Pennsylvania steelworkers during and after the war. 1978 also saw a Best Actor Oscar for Jon Voight in the film *Coming Home*, about the return of a paralysed ex-serviceman from Vietnam. In 1979, the director Francis Ford Coppola made *Apocalypse Now*, a very brutal, realistic depiction of the Vietnam War. Coppola had made his reputation earlier in the decade with his films *The Godfather* and *The Godfather Part II* about the rise of a Mafia family in the USA after the Second World War. These powerful themes in film contrasted with the traditional family values of the silent majority.

American television also offered important new developments. Nostalgia was an important theme. The series *The Waltons*, which ran from 1971 to 1981, was about life in the mountains of Appalachia in the Depression and war years, following the lives of a close-knit white family, the Waltons. *Little House on the Prairie*, set in the latter part of the 19th century in the West, followed the life of the Ingalls family and ran from 1974 to 1983. Its folksy stories evoked a rose-tinted past of idyllic family life on the western plains. A popular soap opera was *General Hospital*, which began in 1963 (and is still going) and dealt with the daily traumas and crises in a typical urban hospital. A contrasting show was the soap opera *Dallas*, which portrayed the opulent lifestyle and power politics of an oil-rich family called the Ewings. The main character, J.R. Ewing, played by Larry Hagman, became a national hate figure.

However, television did address some very serious issues. *M.A.S.H.* was the most-watched comedy of the 1970s and ran from 1972 to 1983. It dealt with the lives of personnel in a military field hospital in the Korean War, but clearly had a strong message about American involvement in Vietnam. The most significant drama series of the decade was shown in 1977. *Roots* dealt with the highly controversial issue of American slavery, tracing the lives of a black American family from enslavement in the late 18th century to the end of the Civil War. *Roots* subsequently appeared on the history curriculum in many US states.

## Developments in news media

Though the USA had no national newspaper coverage in the years 1973 to 1980, it did possess a wide-ranging newspaper industry where most news was local and regional, followed by national. Newspaper circulation remained remarkably buoyant in the 1973 to 1980 period. Daily circulation of all newspapers was 26 million in 1973, rising to 32 million in 1980, in a national population of over 200 million.

The newspaper most associated with national events was the *Washington Post*. It received national recognition in the period 1972 to 1974 when two of its journalists, Bob Woodward and Carl Bernstein, helped uncover the Watergate scandal involving the Nixon presidency. Their exploits later appeared in a book and film entitled *All the President's Men*.

Most Americans received their national news from national television networks such as CBS with *Evening News*, NBC with *Nightly News* and ABC with *World News Tonight*. The networks also produced morning and evening news programmes offering coverage of significant events, such as the fall of Saigon, in Vietnam in 1975, and the Iran Hostage Crisis of 1979. In-depth news coverage came with programmes like CBS's *60 Minutes* which went on the air for the first time in 1968.

The dominance of these national networks was broken in June 1980 when Ted Turner set up Cable Network News (CNN). CNN offered constant up-to-the-minute news coverage on the ever-increasing cable network.

**EXTRACT**

In *From Daytime to Primetime, the History of American Television Programs* by James Roman, published in 2005, Roman discusses the impact of the series *Roots*, broadcast on US television in 1977.

On the ABC television network from January 23-30, the mini-series 'Roots' was broadcast on eight consecutive nights, instead of weekly instalments, creating a new scheduling pattern for the genre. Prior to 'Roots', the mini-series was scheduled as a weekly event. The program was adapted from [black American] Alex Haley's 'symbolic' novel of the same name and became a viewing phenomenon with American television audiences. At the time it generated the highest rating of any prime time network television program, with 85% of all television homes having watched all or part of the series. Although executives at ABC had concerns about the viability for success of a mini-series featuring blacks in leading roles and about the audience reaction to the brutality of white slave-owners towards their chattel, they decided to produce the program. In an effort to mediate the harshness of the white characters, scriptwriters created the role of the ship's captain plagued by his conscience about transporting the first 'cargo' of slaves. This character and some others did not appear in the novel.

No one at the network or in the entertainment business could have predicted the enormous success of 'Roots'. During the eight-night run, business at bars, restaurants, and movie theatres suffered as people stayed at home to watch the show.

**ACTIVITY**
**KNOWLEDGE CHECK**

**Changing popular culture**

1. Make a list of ways in which business and professional sport become more closely connected in the years 1973 to 1980. What effects did this have on sport?
2. How did television help transform the popularity of sport within the USA in the years 1973 to 1980?
3. What changes were there in the popular music scene in the years 1973 to 1980?
4. Did television and film depict the political and social tensions within the USA? Suggest some reasons as to why this might be.
5. In what ways did the news media change in the USA in the years 1973 to 1980?

# TO WHAT EXTENT DID INDIVIDUAL AND CIVIL RIGHTS IMPROVE IN THE YEARS 1973 TO 1980?

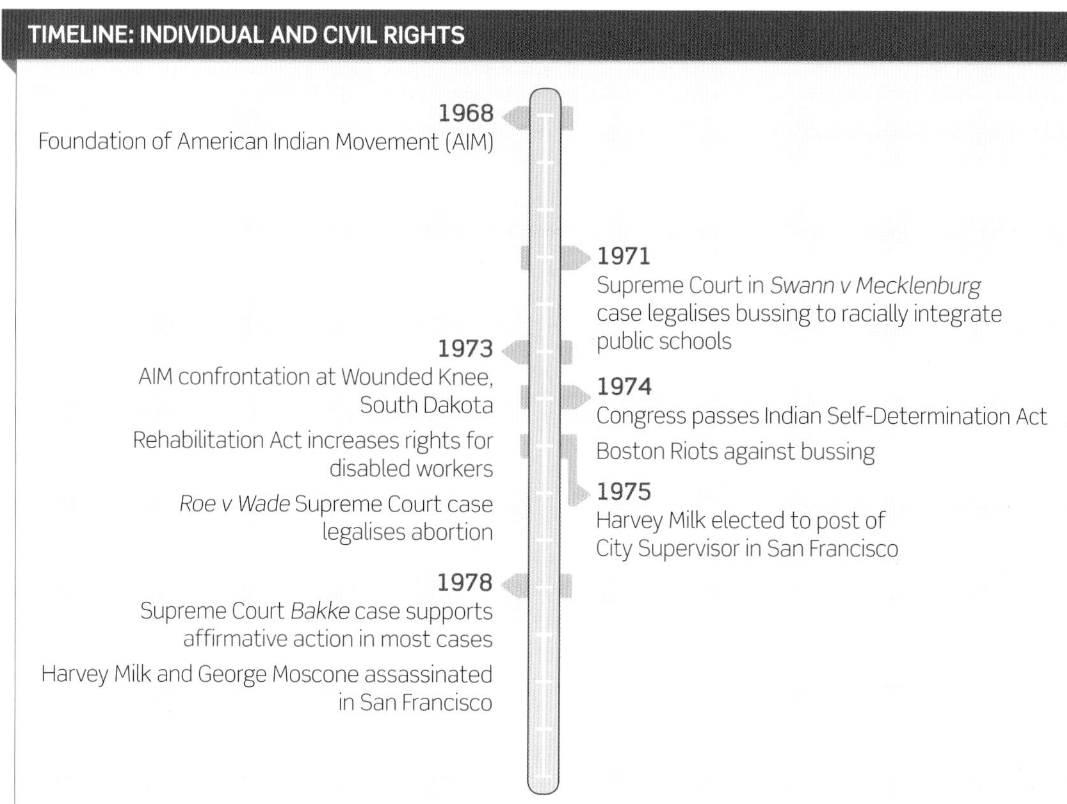


## The political and social Impact of *Roe v Wade*

The period 1973 to 1980 saw the rise to national prominence of the National Organization of Women (NOW). NOW had pushed for the Equal Rights Amendment to the US Constitution in 1972. The organisation achieved another breakthrough with a decision by the US Supreme Court on 22 January 1973 in the case *Roe v Wade*. The Supreme Court decision declared that state laws that forbade abortion were unconstitutional. The Court claimed women had constitutional rights to privacy and to control their own bodies. The ruling allowed abortions to take place in the first three months of pregnancy. Following the Court decision, the number of abortions increased dramatically, rising to 1.7 million legal abortions in 1977.

Although the *Roe v Wade* decision was regarded as a triumph for the feminist and women's movement, it also led to a political backlash by conservative groups within US society. It was an important milestone in the growth of the 'new right' in US politics. The new right became an important factor in the eventual success of the Republican Party from 1981. What began with the concept of the silent majority during Nixon's presidency culminated in Ronald Reagan's triumph in the 1980 presidential election.

Important groups opposed to *Roe v Wade* were the Right to Life organisation, the Catholic Church and fundamentalist Protestant Christian churches. These groups put pressure on government. Shortly after *Roe v Wade*, they successfully lobbied Congress to pass a Human Life Amendment, which attempted to negate the Supreme Court decision. In addition, Senator Jesse Helms was able to amend the Foreign Assistance Act in order to ban federal funds being used for abortion services. In 1974, the Hyde Amendment to the Health, Education and Welfare department budget outlawed the use of federal funds for abortion unless the mother's life was threatened. This position was upheld by the US Supreme Court in a case in 1977. After that date the number of abortions began to fall.

The pro-life groups also became actively involved in the 1976 elections, opposing pro-abortion candidates. Senator Frank Church of Utah was defeated partly because of this opposition.

In 1979, Francis Schaeffer and Dr Everett Koop made a four-hour film, at a cost of $1 million, entitled *Whatever Happened to the Human Race?* It urged voters to oppose abortion and was screened in 20 US cities. In the same year, the Reverend Jerry Falwell founded the Moral Majority, a new right pressure group, to support Reagan's candidacy for the presidency.

EXTEND YOUR KNOWLEDGE

United States Supreme Court

The US Supreme Court is the highest court in the USA and was created under the Judiciary Act of 1789.

It is presided over by nine justices. Each is nominated by the US president, but can only take up the post following a two-thirds vote of approval from the US Senate. Once appointed, a justice remains in the job for life.

The Supreme Court is the highest court of appeal for all federal and state law cases. Its major role is interpreting the US Constitution, a right established in the early 19th century under Chief Justice Marshall.

Under Chief Justice Earl Warren (1953–72) and Chief Justice Warren Burger (1973–80), the Supreme Court took an active role in interpreting the Constitution in controversial areas including abortion and civil rights.

## Women's rights

The move to increase women's rights was a constant theme in the period 1973 to 1980. The Equal Rights Amendment passed Congress in 1972, but ultimately failed to gain support from three-quarters of the states. The women's movement also began to fragment. The moderate NOW faced more radical feminist groups such as the Women's Liberation Front, the Redstockings and the October 17th Movement. These groups challenged the idea of the traditional family and wanted full political, civil, social and economic equality with men. They supported women's centres, communes and collectives and demanded women's studies programs at universities.

In politics, women made important advances. In 1974, Ella Grasso was elected governor of the state of Connecticut, while in the following year the military academies for the army at West Point, the navy at Annapolis and the air force at Colorado Springs began admitting female cadets. These advances in women's rights were mirrored by increasing numbers of women in the workforce. In 1960, 38 percent of women over 16 years were in the workforce. By 1970, the percentage had risen to 43 percent and by 1980 to 52 percent. Opportunities also opened up in higher education, where most male-only colleges and universities opened their doors to women in the 1970s and 1980s.

AS Level Exam-Style Question Section A

***Study Source 8 before you answer this question.***

Why is Source 8 valuable to the historian for an enquiry into why women's rights changed in the USA between 1973 and 1980?

Explain your answer using the source, the information about it and your own knowledge of the historical context. (8 marks)

**Tip**

*It is important you refer to the provenance of the source in your assessment of its value. Who wrote the statement, when was it written and what was its intended audience? You also need to support your answer with direct reference to the content of the source and use your own knowledge of the subject to place the source in its historical context.*

SOURCE 8

The following is an extract from US Supreme Court's majority judgement in *Roe v Wade* in 1973. It was written by Supreme Court Justice Blackmun.

The Constitution does not explicitly mention any right to privacy. In a line of decisions however the Court has recognised that a right of personal privacy does exist under the Constitution. This right of privacy is broad enough to encompass a woman's decision whether or not to terminate her pregnancy. The determinant that the state would impose upon the pregnant woman by denying this choice altogether is apparent. Specific and direct harm medically diagnosable even in early pregnancy may be involved. Maternity, or additional offspring, may force upon the woman a distressful life and future. Psychological harm may be imminent. Mental and physical health may be taxed by child care. There is also the distress associated with bringing an unwanted child into a family already unable, psychologically, to care for it. In other cases the additional difficulties and continuing stigma of unwed motherhood may be involved. All these are factors the woman and her responsible physician necessarily will consider in consultation.

## Workers' rights

The period 1973 to 1980 was not a good one for US workers. Rising prices (inflation) and rising unemployment saw a fall in living standards. In addition, foreign competition and the relocation of businesses from the Rust Belt to the Sun Belt destroyed whole communities in the Northeast and Midwest. Meanwhile, Sun Belt areas such as Florida and Texas saw economic growth. In 1975, New York City faced bankruptcy with President Ford refusing federal aid. Municipal hospitals and city parks closed. Thousands of teachers, police and sanitation workers lost their jobs.

All of these developments increased unemployment, increased workers' insecurity concerning employment and weakened workers' ability to protect their rights. In 1979, the third-biggest car manufacturer, Chrysler, faced bankruptcy. On this occasion the Carter administration did provide federal money to bail out the company, but only after thousands had lost their jobs and under pressure from the AFL–CIO.

However, some workers' rights were enhanced. The Equal Pay Act and the Safety at Work Act, both passed in 1970, improved workers' pay and conditions. Employers were required to treat female and male workers equally and ensure greater safety for employees in the workplace.

In the early 1970s, disability rights activists lobbied Congress and marched on Washington, asking for civil rights for people with disabilities to be included in the 1972 Rehabilitation Act. In 1973, the Rehabilitation Act was passed, and for the first time in history, the civil rights of people with disabilities were protected by law. The Rehabilitation Act of 1973 (Section 504) provided equal opportunity for employment within the federal government and in federally funded programs, prohibiting discrimination on the basis of either physical or mental disability.

When Democrat Jimmy Carter became president in 1977, hopes were high for pro-union legislation. Lane Kirkland, the head of the AFL–CIO, wanted to abolish the National Labor Relations Board, set up in 1938. Kirkland felt the Board was siding with employers in labour disputes. An attempt to extend workers' rights was put forward in a Labor Law Reform bill in 1978. Although it passed Congress, it was amended so drastically that it gave very few extra rights to workers at a time of economic recession.

## Gay rights

Following the Stonewall Riots in New York City's Greenwich Village area in 1969, the gay movement in the USA became more visible and radical. Gay and lesbian bars, newspapers and magazines began to be published, and gay and lesbian marches to raise awareness and draw attention to the discrimination gays experienced became a regular event in many US cities in the 1970s. By 1973, almost 800 gay and lesbian organisations had been formed across the USA. Gay people also became more actively involved in local politics. In Miami, Florida, St Paul, Minnesota and in Wichita, Kansas, gay activists helped repeal laws discriminating against gay and lesbian people.

The election of George Moscone as mayor of San Francisco, California in 1975 and of Edward Koch in New York City in 1977 were partly due to endorsements from the gay community. A big breakthrough was the election of Harvey Milk as a city supervisor (a member of the city council) in San Francisco in 1975. Milk was openly gay and was subsequently assassinated for his sexual orientation, along with Mayor Moscone, on 27 November 1978. The assassin was a disgruntled policeman, Dan White. The event was followed by riots and peaceful candlelight vigils in the city. White was convicted of involuntary manslaughter and received a sentence of five years. He was released in 1986.

Milk's election, and subsequent murder, brought the gay community into the national consciousness. By 1980, the gay community was becoming an accepted and permanent feature of life in most US cities. However, the growth of the gay rights movement, like the women's movement, provoked a conservative backlash. The Reverend Jerry Falwell, founder of the Moral Majority movement, which supported Ronald Reagan's bid for the presidency in 1980, claimed, 'homosexuality is so abominable in the sight of God that he destroyed the cities of Sodom and Gomorrah because of this terrible sin.'

SOURCE

From a speech Harvey Milk, a city supervisor on San Francisco City Council, gave to his supporters. Milk was the first openly gay man to be elected to a public office in California, in 1978. Later the same year Harvey Milk was assassinated, along with Mayor George Moscone.

My name is Harvey Milk and I'm here to recruit you.

I've been saying this one for years. It's a political joke. I can't help it - I've got to tell it. I've never been able to talk to this many people before, so if I tell you nothing else you may be able to go home laughing a bit.

About six months ago, Anita Bryant in her speaking to God said that the drought in California was because of the gay people. On November 9, the day after I got elected, it started to rain. On the day I got sworn in, we walked to City Hall and it was kinda nice, and as soon as I said the word "I do," it started to rain again. It's been raining since then and the people of San Francisco figure the only way to stop it is to do a recall petition. That's the local joke.

So much for that. Why are we here? Why are gay people here? And what's happening? What's happening to me is the antithesis of what you read about in the papers and what you hear about on the radio. You hear about and read about this movement to the right. That we must band together and fight back this movement to the right. And I'm here to go ahead and say that what you hear and read is what they want you to think because it's not happening.

## Native American rights and the impact of Red Power

In the 1970 National Census, the Native American population stood at 800,000, a mere 0.4 percent of the US population, rising to 1.4 million by the time of the 1980 census. The majority of Native Americans lived in the West on reservations, where unemployment, poverty and alcoholism were features of everyday life.

Taking its lead from the black American civil rights movement, in 1968 the American Indian Movement (AIM) was formed, in Minneapolis, Minnesota. The movement for Native American rights was nicknamed 'Red Power', a reference to Black Power. One of AIM's founders, Dennis Banks, explained that it was needed because Native Americans faced slum housing conditions, the highest unemployment rate in the country and police brutality.

In 1969, AIM captured national headlines when a group of armed AIM activists occupied the former federal prison of Alcatraz in San Francisco Bay, as a way to highlight the plight of Native Americans. In 1972, AIM activists occupied the Bureau of Indian Affairs for six days. The following year there was a major confrontation with law enforcement agencies at Wounded Knee, on the Pine Ridge Reservation, South Dakota. Two people were killed and 12 wounded. Wounded Knee had been the scene of a massacre of Sioux elders, women and children in 1890. To add to the publicity, Hollywood actor Marlon Brando refused to accept his Best Actor Oscar in person, instead sending along a Native American woman to accept it and explain the problems Native Americans faced.

Red Power paid off with the Indian Self-Determination Act, passed by Congress in 1974. The Act allowed tribes to assume administrative responsibility for federally funded programmes run by the Bureau of Indian Affairs and by the Indian Health Service.

## The status of black Americans

The 1960s saw black Americans achieve civil equality with other Americans. The 1970s saw major changes in black American communities. Many black Americans benefited from civil equality and the affirmative action programmes of the federal government, which established quotas for federal jobs. By 1972, affirmative action embraced 300,000 firms that worked on federal contracts. This meant a certain number of federal jobs were reserved for black Americans. As a result, 35 percent to 45 percent of black American families achieved a middle-class lifestyle during the 1970s, with well-paid jobs and houses in the suburbs.

However, affirmative action was challenged in the 1970s. In 1978, the *Bakke* case was decided by the US Supreme Court. Allan P. Bakke had applied to join the University of California Law School and although his test scores were higher than others, his place was awarded to a black American student under affirmative action. In a split 5–4 decision the Court declared Bakke had been treated unfairly

SOURCE 10 A Native American protestor at Wounded Knee, on the Pine Ridge Reservation in South Dakota, 1973.

but upheld the principle of affirmative action. In 1980, in *Fullilove v Klutznik*, the Court declared that ten percent of federal jobs should be allocated to ethnic minorities.

Although many black Americans benefited from improvements in civil rights and affirmative action, black Americans living in inner-city slums faced continued poverty, unemployment and poor housing. Black family income declined from 60 percent of a white family income in 1971 to 58 percent by 1980. This bifurcation of black American society became a feature of post-1970 America.

In an attempt to bring greater opportunities to black Americans in poor communities, the US Supreme Court demanded school integration between predominantly black and white schools. In 1971, in *Swann v Charlotte Mecklenburg Board of Education*, the Court instituted the controversial idea of bussing black and white children across school districts to create full racial integration in public schools. In Boston, Massachusetts, in the north-east of the USA, major riots occurred in September 1974 when an attempt was made to bus school children between predominantly white, Irish American south Boston and black areas in north Boston. Similar riots occurred in other cities, including Kansas City, Missouri, but by the end of the decade, bussing to achieve racial integration in public schools across the USA became the norm.

SOURCE 11

From Supreme Court Justice Thurgood Marshall's dissenting decision in the *Bakke* case on affirmative action in July 1978. Justice Marshall was the first black American to serve on the US Supreme Court and was formerly a leading lawyer for the National Association for the Advancement of Colored People. He speaks about the status of black Americans in 1978.

The position of the Negro today in America is the tragic but inevitable consequence of centuries of unequal treatment. Measured by any benchmark meaningful equality is a distant dream for the Negro.

A Negro child today has a life expectancy which is shorter by more than five years than that of a white child. The Negro child's mother is three times more likely to die of complications in childbirth, and the infant mortality rate for Negroes is nearly twice that of whites. The median income of the Negro family is only 60% that of the median income of a white family, and the percentage of Negroes who live in families with incomes below the poverty line is nearly four times greater than that of whites.

When the Negro child reaches working age, he finds that America offers him significantly less than it offers his white counterpart. For Negro adults, the unemployment rate is twice that of whites, and the unemployment rate for Negro teenagers is nearly three times that of white teenagers.

The relationship between those figures and the history of unequal treatment afforded to the Negro cannot be denied.

## Interpretations (5c)

### Good questions/bad questions

Below are summaries of the positions of three famous individuals connected with civil rights in the USA in the 1970s. They are generalisations for the purpose of this exercise.

| **Justice Harry Blackmun** | **Harvey Milk** | **Justice Thurgood Marshall** |
|---|---|---|
| A justice of the US Supreme Court during *Roe v Wade* in 1973. In this case the Court judged that abortion should be permitted by law. (see Source 8) | A local politician in San Francisco who campaigned for gay rights in the USA. (see Source 9) | The first black American to be made a justice of the US Supreme Court, he believed black children growing up in the USA in the 1970s were disadvantaged compared to white children. (see Source 11) |

Work in groups.

Discuss what makes a good historical question and agree on three criteria.

1 Consider what you know about civil rights in the USA in the 1970s then each write a historical question based on that subject matter.

2 Put the questions in rank order, with the best question first, based on your criteria.

3 On a piece of A3 paper, write 'Justice Harry Blackmun', 'Harvey Milk' and 'Justice Thurgood Marshall' at the points of a large triangle.

4 Write your questions in the triangle so that their positions reflect how likely it is that the individuals would be interested by that question. For example, a question about constitutional civil rights would interest Justice Blackmun and Justice Marshall more than Harvey Milk, so write it near the line that joins Marshall and Blackmun.

5 Add some further questions. Try to think of questions that only one of the three would be interested in.

6 Take it in turns to try to answer the questions you have created from the point of view and in the style of one of the individuals. See if the other members of the group can guess which it was.

7 Explain why each of the three people's particular interests and focus help create useful sources for the study of the past.

ACTIVITY
KNOWLEDGE CHECK

**The extent of change in individual and civil rights**

1 In what ways did the individual and civil rights of women, gay people and workers change in the period 1973 to 1980?

2 How did the rights of Native Americans and black Americans change in the years 1973 to 1980?

3 Which group do you think benefited most from improvements in their individual and civil rights in this period: gay people, black Americans, workers or Native Americans? Which group benefited the least? Give reasons for your answer.

ACTIVITY
SUMMARY

**Social and political change, 1973–80**

1 Write a description of the major changes that took place in the USA in the period 1973 to 1980.

a) How did the style of presidential leadership change in the period?

b) What were the key changes in politics and the economy in the period?

2 Create notes on the following as an aid to revising this subject:

a) The impact of Watergate on US politics

b) The main developments in individual and civil rights

c) Changes in popular culture in the period 1973 to 1980.

**WIDER READING**

**Books**

Carson, C. (ed) *The Eyes on the Prize – Civil Rights Reader: Documents, Speeches and Firsthand Accounts from the Black Freedom Fighters, 1954–1990*, Prentice-Hall (1992)

Cook, R. *Sweet Land of Liberty?: The African-American Struggle for Civil Rights in the Twentieth Century*, Routledge (1997)

de Pennington, J. *Modern America: 1865 to the present*, Hodder (2005)

Farmer, A. *An Introduction to American History, 1860–1990*, Hodder (2002)

Field, R. *Civil Rights in America, 1865–1980*, Cambridge University Press (2002)

Murphy, D. *Flagship History – United States 1776–1992*, Collins Educational (2001)

Paterson, D. *et al. Civil Rights in the USA, 1863–1980*, Heinemann (2001)

Sanders, V. *Politics, Presidency and Society in the USA 1968–2001*, Hodder (2008)

**Web**

Fordham University:

Modern social movements www.fordham.edu/Halsall/mod/modsbook56.asp

Pop culture www.fordham.edu/Halsall/mod/modsbook60.asp

The USA as a world leader www.fordham.edu/Halsall/mod/modsbook48.asp

**Video**

*The Century, America's Time* – documentary

*Milk* (2008)

**A Level Exam-Style Question Section A**

***Study Sources 9 and 11 before you answer this question.***

How far could the historian make use of Sources 9 and 11 together to investigate how far the years 1973 to 1980 saw an improvement in individual and civil rights in the USA?

Explain your answer using both sources, the information given about them and your knowledge of the historical context.
(20 marks)

**Tip**

*In your answer you should assess the provenance of the sources as part of your answer in determining their value to an investigation. When the sources were written, who wrote them and their intended audiences are important parts of your answer. You should also use relevant content to support your answer and your own knowledge of the subject as a way of placing the sources in historical context.*

# Republican dominance and its opponents, 1981–92

**KEY QUESTIONS**

- How successful were Presidents Reagan and Bush (Senior) in dealing with the USA's economic problems?
- To what extent was the Religious Right influential in the period 1981 to 1992?
- How far were the years 1981 to 1992 a period of cultural challenge for American youth?
- To what extent did the position of ethnic minorities and women improve in the years 1981 to 1992?

## INTRODUCTION

The 1980s was a period of great change in the USA. The election of Ronald Reagan inaugurated a decade of Republican dominance of the federal government. Between 1980 to 1992 the Republicans won three successive presidential elections. The decade was characterised by the dominance of conservatism, not just in politics but also in social affairs. The Religious Right, which had helped Reagan win the presidency, led a backlash against the liberalisation of society that had taken place in the 1960s and 1970s. However, the idea that the 1980s was just a decade of conservatism would be incorrect. Popular culture saw the continuance of liberal views, which clashed with the views of the Religious Right.

The 1980s also saw a change in status of ethnic minorities and a change in the status of women. However, by 1992, the Republican dominance of politics came to an end with the election of Democrat Bill Clinton to the presidency and a return of racial tension with the Rodney King case.

## HOW SUCCESSFUL WERE PRESIDENTS REAGAN AND BUSH SENIOR IN DEALING WITH THE USA'S ECONOMIC PROBLEMS?

### The impact of Reagan's policies on workers and the family

Ronald Reagan inherited a US economy with many problems. During the 1970s, unemployment averaged 6.2 percent per year compared to 4.1 percent in the 1960s. Inflation reached double figures. Reagan's response was the 'Program for Economic Recovery'. This economic plan abandoned the

**1981** – Ronald Reagan becomes president

Reagan survives assassination attempt

Omnibus Reconciliation Act and Economy Recovery Tax Act reduce taxes and federal spending

**1981** – IBM sells first personal computer

Sony launch Walkman cassette player

MTV broadcasts for first time

Sandra Day O'Connor is first woman justice at US Supreme Court

**1982** – Equal Rights Amendment fails to become part of US Constitution

Nancy Reagan begins Just Say No campaign

1983

**1984** – Carl Lewis wins four gold medals at Los Angeles Olympics

Reagan heavily defeats Democrat challenger Walter Mondale in presidential election

1985

**1986** – Federal budget deficit rises to $221 billion

demand management approach of his immediate predecessor, Democrat Jimmy Carter. Carter had attempted to end stagflation by increasing government spending and manipulating the rate of direct taxes, such as income tax. Reagan supported 'supply-side' economics. This aimed to create economic growth through improvements in productivity (output per worker). The main architect of the changes in federal spending was the Director of the Office of Management and Budget (OMB), the 31-year-old David Stockman.

## EXTEND YOUR KNOWLEDGE

### Demand-side and supply-side economics

For most of the period 1933 to 1981, successive federal governments followed demand-side economic policies. These were based on the belief that low inflation and high employment could be maintained through federal government intervention in the economy. This would be achieved through manipulating the rates of direct taxes such as income tax and changing the amount of federal government spending. In the New Deal (1933–45), President F.D. Roosevelt used heavy federal spending to reduce unemployment and end the Depression.

The 1970s witnessed both rising prices (inflation) and rising unemployment. When Ronald Reagan became president he abandoned demand-side economics in favour of supply-side economics. His approach to encouraging economic growth was to cut federal spending and lower taxes. Reagan also aimed to remove obstacles to growth, such as trade unions and extensive government regulations. These changes gave people more money to spend, thus stimulating demand for goods. This also increased productivity as people were encouraged to work longer hours because they were paying less tax and therefore receiving more money in their pay packets. Initially, from 1981 to 1983, there was an economic recession but for the rest of the 1980s the US economy experienced economic growth.

The principal features of the new economic policy were major tax cuts and a reduction of $35 billion in public spending. In 1981, Reagan's first year in power, Congress passed the Omnibus Reconciliation Act and the Economic Recovery Tax Act. To reduce the budget deficit the Omnibus Reconciliation Act cut government spending on over 300 programmes. This would result in a reduction in spending of $963 billion over the period 1981 to 1987. The second Economic Recovery Tax Act reduced personal income tax by 25 percent. Both these acts were passed by a Democrat-controlled Congress.

This was a fundamental change in federal economic policy with a significant impact. Real GNP (the rate of growth above inflation) grew by 11 percent between 1981 and 1984, one of the fastest growth rates in the US economy since the Second World War. However, these changes came at a cost to many Americans. Many of the programme cuts affected the poorer sections of US society. These included Medicare, which provided healthcare support for the elderly, and Medicaid, which provided healthcare aid to the poor. Another important source of federal support for the poor was the AFDC program (Aid to Families with Dependent Children), and food stamps given to unemployed workers with which they could buy food from shops. In 1981, when Reagan took office, approximately

1987 | 1988 | 1989 | 1990 | 1991 | 1992

**1988** – George Bush (Senior) defeats Michael Dukakis to become president

**1990** – Bush agrees budget deficit reduction plan with Congress

Bush agrees to raise federal taxes

Economic recession begins

**1991** – Rodney King affair

Clarence Thomas becomes the second black American Supreme Court justice

**1992** – Rodney King Riots

*Planned Parenthood v Casey*, Supreme Court case upholds *Roe v Wade* on the right to an abortion

Bill Clinton defeats Bush in presidential election

3.7 million families were receiving help under AFDC, about 20 million people received food stamps and a further 21.6 million received help under Medicaid. The Omnibus Reconciliation Act cut AFDC and food stamp support by approximately 13 percent between 1982 and 1985. Child nutrition programs were cut by 28 percent. The number of people defined as 'poor' increased from 11.7 percent of the population in 1979 to 15 percent by 1982.

Spending on a number of federal government departments was also slashed. For instance, the Department of Housing and Urban Development (HUD) budget was cut by 57 percent between 1981 and 1987. Overall, social spending – which had risen under the previous five presidents from Kennedy to Carter – fell by an average annual rate of 1.5 percent under Reagan.

Another important feature of the Omnibus Reconciliation Act was the introduction of 'workfare'. If a family was to receive AFDC they had to do community service. By January 1987, 42 out of the 50 states had followed the federal government's lead and introduced welfare programmes that linked welfare payments to some sort of work. In 1988, the Family Support Act ensured this approach to welfare support became a permanent feature of American society.

### The effect on workers

Reagan's economic policies also had a significant impact on workers.

His economic revolution involved large-scale economic deregulation. The aim of this was to promote economic growth by cutting funding to federal bodies that regulated industry. Reagan's predecessor, Carter, had already begun the process in 1978. Under Reagan, the Office of Surface Mining (part of the Department of the Interior) lost around 40 percent of its workforce between 1981 and 1982.

Reagan appointed pro-business members to the National Labor Relations Board, which subsequently made several pro-business and anti-trade union judgements. Reagan's biggest confrontation with the trade unions involved the deregulation of air traffic control. Seven months after Reagan took office, 11,300 members of the Professional Air Traffic Controllers (PATCO) went on strike against the deregulation plans. Reagan demanded that all air traffic controllers return to work within 48 hours or face the sack. When they did not return Reagan sacked them all. Union members were replaced by non-union labour and Reagan broke the strike.

Reagan's victory emboldened large corporations to resist union demands. In 1983, the Greyhound Bus Company, Eastern Airlines, Continental Airlines and the *Chicago Tribune* newspaper all refused to give in to union demands for better pay and conditions. Failed strikes in these companies led to a sharp decline in union militancy.

Although Reagan's cuts were unpopular in some quarters, the growth in the US economy between 1981 and 1984 increased the spending power of middle-class families, and helps explain why Reagan won a landslide victory in the 1984 presidential election.

## The trade and budget deficits

When campaigning against Jimmy Carter for the presidency in 1980, Reagan criticised his predecessor for amassing a $73.8 billion federal debt. However, Reagan's policies led to a massive increase in that debt. In addition, Reagan stated in 1980 that he was committed to reducing federal government spending, but it rose by $321 billion during his presidency to more than a trillion dollars. The main budget cuts came in social spending, which comprised only 17 percent of the federal budget. Reagan instead greatly expanded military spending, which was a prime cause of the budget deficit.

At the same time as making major cuts in federal social spending and spending on regulation, Reagan dramatically increased spending on defence, leading to the biggest military build-up in peacetime in US history. Annual defence spending rose from $171 billion at the end of the Carter administration to $242 billion by 1986. By 1983, federal spending on defence was 23.5 percent of GDP. As a result of the increased spending, the number of federal employees (which had been cut in other areas) actually went up from 2.9 million in 1981 to 3.1 million by 1983. This had a major impact on the federal budget deficit. In every one of his budgets Reagan had a deficit of in excess of $100 billion, raising the national debt from $914 billion in 1980 to $2.7 trillion by 1989.

In addition to a federal budget deficit, Reagan's economic policies led to a major trade deficit with the rest of the world. By 1986, the trade deficit amounted to $170 billion. This deficit transformed the USA's relations with the rest of the global economy. For most of the post-Second World War period, the US had been a creditor nation, with other countries owing the US money. Reagan changed this to the point where the USA became the world's greatest debtor nation, owing billions of dollars to foreign countries.

In a bid to deal with these deficits Congress passed the Balanced Budget and Emergency Deficit Control Act of 1985, also known as the Gramm–Rudman Act after its sponsors in Congress. The aim was to gradually reduce the federal budget deficit until it disappeared by 1991. By the time Reagan left office, in early 1989, this act was far from reaching its goal.

Reagan's policies disproportionately hit the poor and massively increased the budget and trade deficits. However, they did benefit the military and those corporations involved in military technology, and helped bring growth to the economy.

In the 1984 presidential election campaign, Reagan campaigned on the idea that he was returning the USA to prosperity and its place in the world as the world's greatest military power. Under the campaign slogan 'Morning Again in America', Reagan won a landslide victory over his Democrat opponent, Walter Mondale. Reagan won 54.4 million votes against 37.7 million for Mondale. In the Electoral College, the margin of victory was even greater. Reagan won 525 Electoral College votes compared to only 13 for Mondale. This meant Reagan won a majority of votes in virtually every state.

SOURCE

From Ronald Reagan's inaugural speech as president in January 1981, entitled 'Government is not the Solution'. Reagan outlines his views on the role of the federal government.

It is my intention to curb the size and influence of the federal establishment and to demand recognition of the distinction between the powers granted to the federal government and those reserved to the states or to the people. All of us need to be reminded that the federal government did not create the states; the states created the federal government. Now, so there will be no misunderstanding, it is my intention not to do away with government. It is rather, to make it work - work with us, not over us; to stand by our side; not to ride on our back. Government can and must provide opportunity, not smother it; foster productivity, not stifle it. It is no coincidence that our present troubles parallel and are proportionate to the intervention and intrusion in our lives that result from unnecessary and excessive growth of government.

Can we solve the problems confronting us? Well, the answer is an unequivocal and emphatic yes. To paraphrase Winston Churchill, I did not take the oath with the intention of presiding over the dissolution of the world's strongest economy.

**AS Level Exam-Style Question Section A**

***Study Source 1 before you answer this question.***

Why is Source 1 valuable to the historian for an enquiry into the aims of Ronald Reagan as president?

Explain your answer using the source, the information about it and your own knowledge of the historical context. (8 marks)

**Tip**

*In your answer it is important to refer to the provenance of the source as a way of assessing its value. Who wrote it? When was it written? What was its intended audience? To support your answer, use relevant information from the content of the source and your own knowledge to help place the source in its historical context.*

## The significance of George Bush Senior's decision to raise taxes

Since the 1950s, the US Constitution has stated that a president can only serve two terms. As a result, in his mid-70s Reagan stood down as president in 1988. He was replaced as Republican presidential candidate by his Vice President, George Herbert Walker Bush. In the 1988 presidential election, Bush defeated Democrat Michael Dukakis. George Herbert Walker Bush is also known as Bush Senior or Bush 41 (because he was the 41st president) to differentiate him from his son George W. Bush, or Bush 43, who was president from 2001 to 2009.

### EXTEND YOUR KNOWLEDGE

**George Herbert Walker Bush (Bush Senior) (1924–)**

George Herbert Walker Bush came from a rich New England family who sent him to Yale University in Connecticut, one of the most prestigious universities in the USA. He became a navy fighter pilot in the Pacific during the Second World War. His plane was shot down but he was rescued by a US submarine. After the war he became an oilman in Texas. In 1976–81, Bush was Director of the Central Intelligence Agency. From 1981 to 1989, he served as Vice President under Ronald Reagan.

As president, Bush Senior carried on the work of Reagan in reducing nuclear weapons by signing an Intermediate Nuclear Forces treaty with the Soviet Union in 1989. His most famous foreign policy success was the formation of an international coalition of countries that defeated Iraqi leader Saddam Hussein's invasion of Kuwait in 1991. In spite of his foreign policy success, he lost the presidential election of 1992 to Democrat Bill Clinton.

His son, George W. Bush, was US president from 2001 to 2009. Another son, Jeb, became governor of Florida.

During the campaign and in the early months of his presidency, Bush Senior continually repeated his election slogan, 'Read my lips, no new taxes'. However, he faced a number of very serious economic problems that would make it impossible for him to deliver on this promise. Many of these problems were inherited from the Reagan administration.

- The US national debt was \$2.7 trillion when Bush Senior became president, three times higher than in 1980.
- Bush also inherited very large budget and trade deficits. By 1992, the federal budget deficit had risen to \$400 billion. This was, in part, caused by economic recession in the early 1990s, which led to reduced tax revenues. The Gramm–Rudman Act of 1985 required the federal government to balance the budget. Bush Senior tried to do this but had not achieved his goal by the time he left office.

- There was a major crisis in the savings and loan industry. Savings and loan associations financed the US housing market, and were similar to building societies in the UK. When he came to office in 1989, Bush Senior produced a federal rescue plan to save these companies from bankruptcy. The plan predicted expenditure of $50 billion. By April 1990, the federal bailout bill had gone up to $325 billion.

To deal with these serious economic difficulties, Bush Senior tried a combination of spending cuts and tax rises – which meant he had to go back on his election promise.

- In 1990 the rate of federal income tax was raised from 28 percent to 31 percent.
- Military and domestic expenditure was cut by $492 billion.
- The Federal Reserve Board, the USA's central bank, lowered interest rates to 3.5 percent in an attempt to stimulate economic growth. The rate change was not enough to counter the effects of the recession and had little impact.

These economic changes failed to save Bush Senior's presidency. In the 1992 presidential election he faced two serious rivals: Democrat Bill Clinton and the independent candidate Ross Perot, a Texan billionaire. In the November election Bush Senior received 38 million votes. However, Bill Clinton received 44.9 million votes and Ross Perot 19 million. In the Electoral College Clinton won 370 votes as against Bush Senior's 168. After only one term in office Bush Senior had lost the presidency, bringing to an end 12 years of Republican dominance of federal government.

**SOURCE**

From 'Reaganomics: The Revolution in American Political Economy', an article by Charles Jacobs, professor of political science at Rutgers University, originally published in *Law and Contemporary Problems Journal* in 1985. It offers an assessment of changes Reagan made in social and economic policy in his first term as president. The Oval Office, mentioned in the source, is the president's private office within the White House in Washington DC.

The first year of the Reagan Administration produced a set of changes in political-economic relationships so novel as to merit the denomination "revolutionary". Reaganomics is used in this article's title on purpose to emphasize the importance of President Reagan's personal role in engineering great change. Although the reorientation of the tax structure constitutes the centerpiece of Reaganomics, it must be noted that the economic package also includes reductions in domestic programs, bureaucracies, and support.

Moreover, another aspect of the Reagan Administration's revolutionary reallocation of state values has taken the form of non-incremental increases in defense spending. Evidence of revolution may be found in authoritative policy enactments which document historic change. On February 5, 1981, President Reagan spoke to the nation from the Oval Office and called for a reduction in personal taxes of 30% over a three-year period. In addition, speaking further to the supply-side ethos, the President proposed accelerated depreciation rewards to business to encourage investment and growth.

On February 18, the President submitted the details of his tax cut plan along with proposed budgetary reductions of $49 billion in domestic program spending in a special "white paper", which constituted the Administration's revision of the Carter Economic Report of 1981.

**ACTIVITY**
**KNOWLEDGE CHECK**

**New directions in economic policy**

1 What changes in economic policy did Reagan introduce in 1981?

2 Why did Reagan's policies result in both an increased budget and trade deficit?

3 What evidence is there to suggest that Reagan and Bush Senior failed in their economic policy?

4 Write down five ways in which Reagan's social and economic policies impacted on workers and the family.

5 Compare and contrast Reagan's own views on economic policy put forward in Source 1 and with Charles Jacobs' analysis in Source 2.

**AS Level Exam-Style Question Section B**

How accurate is it to say that President Reagan brought fundamental change to economic policy in the USA? (20 marks)

**Tip**

*In your answer you will need to define the term 'fundamental change' and say whether or not Reagan's policies brought such a level of change to the USA. You will need to support any assessment you make with relevant evidence.*

**A Level Exam-Style Question Section A**

***Study Sources 1 and 2 before you answer this question.***

How far could the historian make use of Sources 1 and 2 together to investigate the approach of Republican presidents towards economic policy?

Explain your answer using both sources, the information given about them and your knowledge of the historical context.
(20 marks)

**Tip**

*In your answer it is important to refer to the provenance of both sources as part of your assessment of their importance. When were the sources written, who wrote them, and what was the intended audience for each source? Make sure you support your assessment with relevant information from both sources and use your own knowledge to place the source material in historical context.*

# TO WHAT EXTENT WAS THE RELIGIOUS RIGHT INFLUENTIAL IN THE PERIOD 1981 TO 1992?

## The promotion of traditional values

The dominance of the Republican Party in the 1980s was due to a number of factors. One was the poor performance of the American economy in the late 1970s under Democrat president Jimmy Carter. Another was Carter's poor performance in foreign affairs, when dealing with events such as the Iran Hostage Crisis and the Soviet invasion of Afghanistan. However, a third significant factor was the rise of the Religious Right. This group supported 'traditional values' and believed the family and Christianity should play a central role in American society. The traditional values message had a large potential audience. In 1980, the USA was the most religious nation in the western world. An opinion poll conducted in the late 1970s found that approximately 50 percent of Americans said they prayed every day and 80 percent said they believed in an afterlife.

The best-known individual associated with the Religious Right was the Reverend Jerry Falwell, a Baptist preacher from Lynchburg, Virginia. He believed in the literal truth of the Bible, which he maintained subordinated wives to their husbands in marriage. He began his national career with a popular radio show, *The Old Time Gospel Hour*, broadcast on more than 300 radio stations nationwide, with a potential audience of 1.5 million people. In 1979, he founded the Moral Majority, to promote traditional values and realise the potential powerful political influence of those who identified with those values.

**SOURCE 3** Students from across the United States on the steps of the Capitol in Washington DC, home of the US Congress, in the early 1980s. They are campaigning for daily prayers to be part of public school activities.

Television evangelists, or 'televangelists', also played a major role in the rise of the Religious Right. The Reverend Pat Robertson ran the Christian Broadcasting Network (CBN) and even ran for the Republican nomination for president. The Reverend Jim Bakker founded the Praise the Lord ministry in 1974 and had his own television network and religious theme park. The top eight televangelists in 1980 made $310 million from their programmes and reached an audience of 20 million.

## EXTEND YOUR KNOWLEDGE

### Jerry Falwell (1933–2007)

Jerry Falwell was born on 11 August 1933 in Lynchburg, Virginia. He attended the Baptist Bible College and shortly after graduation established the Thomas Road Baptist Church. In 1956, he began his media career, hosting the *Old Time Gospel Hour*. He founded the Lynchburg Christian Academy in 1967 and Liberty Baptist College in 1971.

Falwell supported a fundamentalist view of Christian moral teaching and was opposed to many of the liberal social movements of the 1970s. He was an outspoken critic of feminism and gay rights.

In 1979, Falwell founded the Moral Majority and used his media following and influence to raise money for Ronald Reagan's bid for the presidency. He continued to be president of the Moral Majority until 1987. Meanwhile, his media empire included the *National Liberty Journal*, a monthly publication, and a cable network, the Liberty Channel.

In 1983, *Hustler*, a soft pornographic magazine, published a phony article claiming Jerry Falwell had had an incestuous relationship with his mother. Falwell sued the magazine owner, Larry Flint. In *Hustler Magazine, Inc. v Falwell* the US Supreme Court ruled in 1988 that public figures who suffered emotional distress due to stories published in the media could not receive libel damages in recompense as this would affect the publisher's right to free speech.

In 1989, Falwell dissolved the Moral Majority claiming it had achieved its aims and returned to running Liberty College.

This powerful group influenced the Reagan campaign for the presidency in 1980. During that campaign Reagan expressed his support for traditional family values, traditional gender roles and the rights of unborn children. Falwell helped raise $100 million for Moral Majority causes, far more than was raised by the Democratic Party.

During his time as president Reagan appointed conservative-minded justices to the US Supreme Court, including Sandra Day O'Connor in 1981 – the first woman to become a justice of the Supreme Court. In 1986, Reagan nominated the conservative William Rehnquist and Antonin Scalia as Supreme Court justices. In 1987, Anthony Kennedy was elevated to the Court. All these appointments made the Supreme Court less activist and more conservative. However, despite his campaign promises, and the Supreme Court appointments, on a more general level Reagan failed to deliver on much of the Moral Majority's agenda.

**SOURCE**

**From a speech made by President Reagan at a prayer breakfast in Dallas, Texas on 23 August 1984. In the speech he outlines his views on the relationship between politics and religion in the USA in the 1980s during his presidency.**

These past few weeks it seems that we've all been hearing a lot of talk about religion and its role in politics, religion and its place in the political life of the Nation. And I think it's appropriate today, at a prayer breakfast for 17,000 citizens in the State of Texas during a great political convention, that this issue be addressed.

I believe that faith and religion play a critical role in the political life of our nation - and always has.

I submit to you that the tolerant society is open to and encouraging of all religions. And this does not weaken us; it strengthens us, it makes us strong. You know, if we look back through history to all those great civilizations, those great nations that rose up to even world dominance and then deteriorated, declined, and fell, we find they all had one thing in common. One of the significant forerunners of their fall was their turning away from their God or gods.

Without God, there is no virtue, because there's no prompting of the conscience. Without God, we're mired in the material, that flat world that tells us only what the senses perceive. Without God, there is a coarsening of the society. And without God, democracy will not and cannot long endure. If we ever forget that we're one nation under God, then we will be a nation gone under.

AS Level Exam-Style Question Section A

***Study Source 4 before you answer this question.***

Why is Source 4 valuable to the historian for an enquiry into the influence of the Religious Right in American politics in the years 1981 to 1992?

Explain your answer using the source, the information about it and your own knowledge of the historical context. (8 marks)

**Tip**

*It is important to assess the provenance of the source as a way of gauging its value to the historian in an enquiry. You should also refer to relevant information within the content of the source to support your assessment and use your own knowledge to place the source within the historical context, making reference to the influence of the Religious Right.*

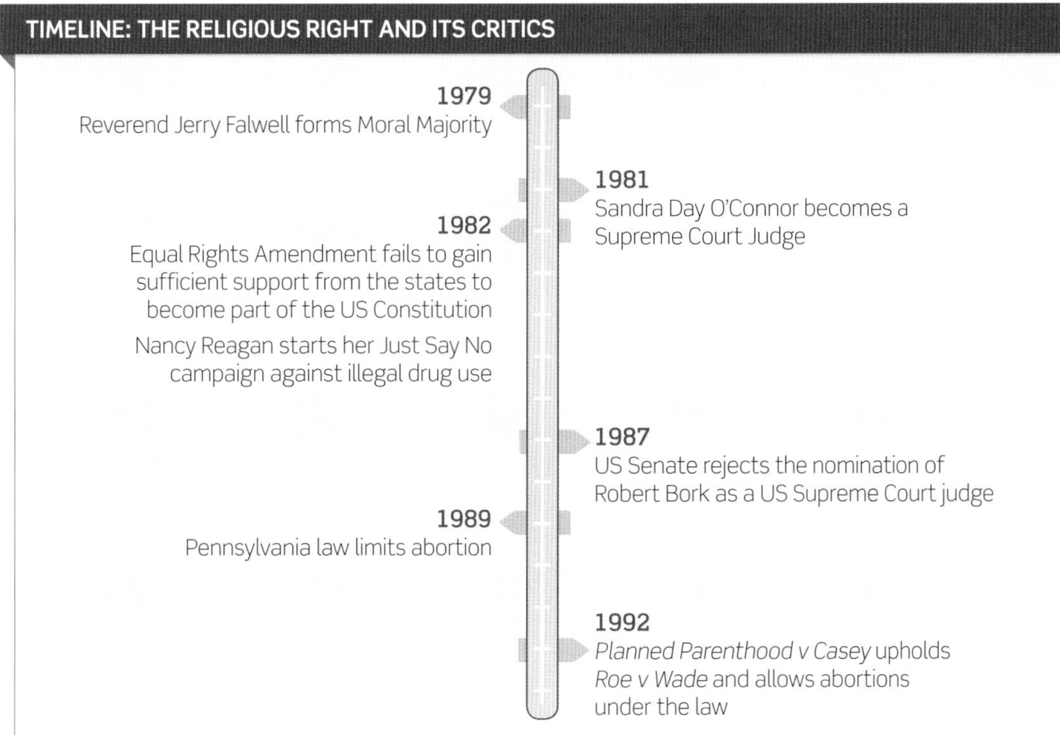


## Campaigns against abortion and homosexuality

The US Supreme Court decision to legalise abortion in the *Roe v Wade* case, the women's movement and the legalisation of pornography in some states led to a conservative backlash targeted at each of these issues (see Chapter 3).

One of the key individuals in the campaign against abortion was Phyllis Schlafly, a Catholic Republican supporter from the state of Illinois. Known as the 'Sweetheart of the Silent Majority', Schlafly led a campaign against the *Roe v Wade* decision, with the support of the Roman Catholic Church. Partly as a result of Schlafly's activities, the National Conference of Catholic Bishops created the National Right to Life Committee which, by 1980, had 11 million supporters from a wide variety of religious denominations.

Traditional values were also supported by conservative Protestants. In 1979, Beverley La Haye, the wife of a Baptist minister from San Diego, southern California, formed Concerned Women for America (CWA). The CWA opposed abortion and no-fault divorce laws. Like Phyllis Schlafly, the CWA was also against the Equal Rights Amendment (ERA), which both Schlafly and La Haye regarded as anti-family. By the mid-1980s, the CWA had 500,000 members, which made it larger than the National Organization of Women, the foremost force in the women's movement.

The activities of these campaigners and traditional values groups helped prevent the Equal Rights Amendment to the constitution being adopted, even though it had initially received support from both houses of Congress in 1972. To become a constitutional change, a proposal had to pass both houses of Congress and then gain support from three-quarters of US states within ten years. Pressure from groups on the Religious Right and defenders of traditional values ensured that by 1982, the necessary support from the states failed to materialise, and the ERA did not become part of the US Constitution.

Another issue that attracted significant criticism from the Religious Right was homosexuality: they believed that being gay went against Bible teaching. The Religious Right's opposition to homosexuality was fuelled by the rise of AIDS in the early 1980s as a higher proportion of gay men contracted the condition. To members of the Religious Right, AIDS was sent by God as a punishment for homosexuality.

## Nancy Reagan's Just Say No campaign

As wife of the president, Nancy Reagan was the USA's First Lady, giving her a prominent public position and platform. During Reagan's presidency she led the Just Say No campaign, to discourage children and young people from becoming involved with drugs. This was one area where the Reagan presidency did engage with a major social issue facing the USA.

Nancy Reagan claimed during the presidential campaign of 1980 that that she was impressed by work at the Daytop Village, a substance-abuse treatment centre in New York. When she became First Lady, Nancy Reagan visited several treatment centres across the USA and met with the Board of Directors for the National Federation of Parents for a Drug Free Youth. In mid-1982, she addressed the National Legislative session of the Parent Teacher Association on drug abuse, and on 11 October of the same year she attended the first National Conference for Drug Free Youth.

In 1982, Nancy Reagan began the Just Say No campaign, a nationwide campaign against illegal drug use by young Americans. She said, 'Drugs take away the dream from every child's heart and replace it with a nightmare, and it's time we in America stand up and replace those dreams.' In her campaign the First Lady travelled 250,000 miles and visited 65 cities in 33 states. In April 1985, she invited the wives of world leaders to attend the First Ladies Conference on Drug Abuse at the White House in Washington DC and was joined by 18 wives of world leaders. In the following year, President Reagan signed the National Crusade for a Drug Free America anti-drug abuse bill into law. The year also saw the first official Just Say No to Drugs week. Finally, on 25 October 1988, Nancy Reagan addressed the United Nations General Assembly on the issue. By 1988, 12,000 Just Say No Clubs had been founded across the USA.

The impact of Nancy Reagan's campaign was a reduction in illegal drug use by the USA's youth. Cocaine use by high school students (14–18-year-olds) dropped by one third from 6.2 percent in 1986 to 4.3 percent in 1987. In addition, while more than ten percent of high school leavers in 1978 said they used marijuana daily, this had dropped to around three percent by 1987. Perhaps more than any First Lady since Eleanor Roosevelt in the 1930s and early 1940s, Nancy Reagan played a full and active role in creating a national campaign. Her efforts were clearly in line with the aims and aspirations of the Religious Right.

SOURCE

From a national address by Nancy Reagan, delivered from the West Wing of the White House on 14 September 1986. She explains why she became involved in what became known as the Just Say No campaign.

As a mother, I've always thought of September as a special month, a time when we bundled our children off to school, to the warmth of an environment in which they could fulfil the promise and hope in those restless minds. But so much has happened over these last years, so much to shake the foundations of all that we know and all that we believe in. Today there's a drug and alcohol abuse epidemic in this country, and no one is safe from it - not you, not me, and certainly not our children, because this epidemic has their names written on it. Many of you may be thinking: "Well, drugs don't concern me." But it does concern you. It concerns us all because of the way it tears at our lives and because it's aimed at destroying the brightness and life of the sons and daughters of the United States. [...]

Now you can see why drug abuse concerns every one of us - all the American family. Drugs steal away so much. They take and take, until finally every time a drug goes into a child, something else is forced out - like love and hope and trust and confidence. Drugs take away the dream from every child's heart and replace it with a nightmare, and it's time we in America stand up and replace those dreams. Each of us has to put our principles and consciences on the line, whether in social settings or in the workplace, to set forth solid standards and stick to them. There's no moral middle ground. Indifference is not an option. We want you to help us create an outspoken intolerance for drug use. For the sake of our children, I implore each of you to be unyielding and inflexible in your opposition to drugs. [...]

And finally, to young people watching or listening, I have a very personal message for you: There's a big, wonderful world out there for you. It belongs to you. It's exciting and stimulating and rewarding. Don't cheat yourselves out of this promise. Our country needs you, but it needs you to be clear-eyed and clear-minded. I recently read one teenager's story. She's now determined to stay clean but was once strung out on several drugs. What she remembered most clearly about her recovery was that during the time she was on drugs everything appeared to her in shades of black and gray and after her treatment she was able to see colors again.

**A Level Exam-Style Question Section B**

How far were traditional values important in framing federal government policy in the 1980s? (20 marks)

**Tip**

*Define what people in the USA meant by 'traditional values', and then work whether, in your judgement, they really did underpin policies rather than policies being determined by other factors.*

## The growth of bitter political divisions

When Reagan sought re-election in 1984 he used the slogan 'Morning Again in America' to suggest that he had brought back stability and prosperity. However, during the Reagan years the gap between rich and poor increased. Between 1980 and 1988, the top 20 percent of wage earners saw their share of national income go up from 41.6 percent to 44 percent, while the bottom 60 percent saw their share drop. The very wealthiest top one percent of earners saw their share of national income go up from nine percent to 11 percent. The Reagan years were a very good time for the super-rich.

The economic changes brought about by Reagan's policies also deepened political divisions. For the whole of Reagan's presidency the House of Representatives had a Democrat majority. Although the Republicans controlled the Senate from 1980 to 1984, they lost control after the 1986 midterm elections.

Many Democrats were against Reagan's conservative policies and on occasion they were able to thwart his proposals. In 1987, Reagan attempted to get Robert Bork nominated as a US Supreme Court judge. Bork was a federal judge and an outspoken conservative who had served under Richard Nixon. He opposed the Civil Rights Act of 1964 and affirmative action to help ethnic minorities to get jobs. His nomination caused a great division between the president and Democrat members of the Senate. A two-thirds majority vote in the Senate was required before a Supreme Court judge could be confirmed in post. In acrimonious nomination hearings, Bork was subjected to intense questioning by Senate Democrats. In the end Bork's nomination was rejected by 58 votes to 42.

Further ideological confrontation between Democrat and Republican came with Reagan's attempts to limit the power of federal regulatory bodies. Reagan attempted to reduce funding to federal agencies that he regarded as guided by liberal policies, such as the Housing and Urban Development Department (HUD) and the Health and Human Services Department (HHS).

Perhaps the biggest division came over Reagan's attempt to redefine the relationship between the federal government and the states. Shortly after he became president, in April 1981 Reagan set up the Presidential Advisory Committee on Federalism and the Coordinating Task Force on Federalism. In his 1982 State of the Union message, Reagan announced his plan to reduce federal spending. He claimed he wanted to bring government closer to the people by giving money directly to the states, to use as they saw fit. However, Reagan's plans failed to pass Congress where the Democrats controlled the House of Representatives.

Where Reagan had caused division, Bush Senior attempted to bring greater consensus. He saw himself as a moderate Republican and even denounced Reaganomics as 'voodoo economics'. To emphasise the contrast in the approaches of the two Republican presidents, in 1990, Bush Senior got Congress to pass a Clean Air Act and in 1992 he signed the Energy Policy Act, which aimed at greater energy conservation and support for renewable energy.

However, in 1992 Bush Senior raised income tax and cut federal spending in order to eradicate a large budget deficit. Cutting spending alienated Democrats and raising taxes alienated Republicans. As a result, in 1992 Bush Senior was not re-elected and lost the presidency to Democrat Bill Clinton.

**SOURCE**

From Walter 'Fritz' Mondale's acceptance speech after he was selected as the Democratic Party's candidate for the 1984 presidential election, facing Ronald Reagan. Mondale highlights the main divisions between Democrats and Republicans in 1984.

First, there was Mr. Reagan's tax program. What happened was, he gave each of his rich friends enough tax relief to buy a Rolls Royce - and then he asked your family to pay for the hub caps.

Then they looked the other way at the rip-offs, soaring utility bills, phone bills, medical bills.

Then they socked it to workers. They encouraged executives to vote themselves huge bonuses.

Mr. Reagan believes that the genius of America is in the boardrooms and exclusive country clubs. I believe that the greatness can be found in the men and women who built our nation; do its work; and defend our freedom.

If this administration has a plan for a better future, they're keeping it a secret.

Here is the truth about the future: We are living on borrowed money and borrowed time. These deficits hike interest rates, clobber exports, stunt investment, kill jobs, undermine growth, cheat our kids, and shrink our future.

Whoever is inaugurated in January, the American people will have to pay Mr. Reagan's bills. The budget will be squeezed. Taxes will go up. And anyone who says they won't is not telling the truth to the American people.

To the corporations and freeloaders who play the loopholes or pay no taxes, my message is: Your free ride is over.

To the Congress, my message is: We must cut spending and pay as we go. If you don't hold the line, I will: That's what the veto is for.

I challenge tonight, I challenge Mr. Reagan to put his plan on the table next to mine - and then let's debate it on national television before the American people. Americans want the truth about the future - not after the election.

## Cause and consequence (5b)

### Causation relativity

Historical events usually have many causes. Some are crucial, while some are less important. For some historical questions, it is important to understand exactly what role certain factors played in causing historical change.

These are some of the significant factors in the timing and nature of Republican dominance in the 1980s.

| Poor economic performance of the US economy under President Carter (1977-81) | Poor foreign policy performance of the Carter administration in handling the Iran Hostage Crisis | Economic reforms made by presidents Reagan and George Bush Senior |
|---|---|---|

Working alone, answer these questions exploring why the Republicans became dominant at this time.

1 How important was Reagan's economic policy in explaining the timing of the Republic dominance in the 1980s?

2 In what ways was the success of Reagan in the presidential election of 1980 due to the poor performance of the Carter presidency (1977–81)?

3 To what extent could Ronald and Nancy Reagan be held personally responsible for the Republican dominance of the 1980s?

Working alone, answer the following questions looking at the nature of the Republican dominance.

4 How far had social and economic changes in the 1970s changed the attitudes of the people towards the Republican Party under Ronald Reagan?

5 What role did the above factors play in the way that the Reagan and Bush administrations approached social and economic policy?

6 Would the nature of the Republican dominance have been the same if the Religious Right had not developed in the late 1970s and 1980?

Discuss in a group:

7 What roles did each of the above causal factors play in determining the nature and timing of the Republican dominance of the 1980s?

## ACTIVITY
KNOWLEDGE CHECK

### The Religious Right and its critics

1 What were the 'traditional values' promoted by the Religious Right?

2 How did the Religious Right organise campaigns against abortion and homosexuality?

3 What evidence is there in Source 5 to explain why the Just Say No campaign was so important to Nancy Reagan?

4 Why do you think the campaign for traditional values caused political divisions within the USA in the years 1981 to 1992?

## AS Level Exam-Style Question Section B

How accurate is it to say that the Religious Right was successful in its aims in the period 1981 to 1992? (20 marks)

**Tip**

*In your answer you will be expected to mention the aims of the Religious Right and to explain the degree of success the Religious Right achieved in fulfilling these aims. Make sure you use relevant information and examples to support and sustain the arguments you make.*

**A Level Exam-Style Question Section B**

'The Reagan administration was marked more by the divisions it created than by its achievements.'

How far do you agree with this statement? (20 marks)

**Tip**

*Analyse the positive achievements of the Reagan administration and weigh these against the divisions in society and in politics that were the outcome of the implementation of his administrations's policies.*

# HOW FAR WERE THE YEARS 1981 TO 1992 A PERIOD OF CULTURAL CHALLENGE FOR AMERICAN YOUTH?

## The impact of technology on popular youth culture

Young people are most likely to engage with new technology, so changing technology also affects the way they consume and contribute to popular culture. Since the 1950s, US popular culture had been based on a limited number of technologies. For example, to watch newly released films Americans had to visit the cinema. This form of entertainment was supplemented by listening to radio or vinyl records or perhaps watching television at home. Otherwise live entertainment was the alternative.

The 1980s saw a revolution in technology that greatly increased availability and ease of access to popular culture, and laid the foundations of today's technology-based popular culture.

The most revolutionary technological development was the personal computer. Computers had been around since the Second World War, when they were used by Allied governments to break enemy codes. These early computers were huge and extremely expensive devices.

Computers were being used by some bigger businesses by the 1950s, but a breakthrough came in August 1981 when the IBM corporation released the IBM 5150 personal computer. Compared to today's personal computers, the IBM 5150 was slow and very basic, with a 16KB memory on removable floppy disks, but it was small enough and simple enough to be used by ordinary people in their own homes. The basic IBM 5150 system, including a VDU (monitor), cost around $1600. It was also possible to link the IBM 5150 to the family television. Later, IBM produced an updated model with a double diskette drive (to take two floppy disks) and printer, which sold for $4000. While IBM was the first company in this area, by 1992 many other companies, including Apple, had entered the personal computer market. Soon floppy disks were supplemented by hard drives, dramatically increasing the computer's memory. Personal computers allowed people to write and store text and data. They could also play early computer games such as *Ship of Doom* released by Artic and *Arcadia* by Imagine.

Games could also be played on the new games consoles such as the Atari 2600, which went on sale in 1977. A breakthrough came with the arrival of *Space Invaders* in 1980, which became hugely popular. It was shortly followed by *Pac-Man*. Initially, the market for game consoles was dominated by Atari and Mattel, but in 1985 Nintendo appeared. Nintendo came to be a major player in the market and provided a wide variety of computer games. By 1992, home entertainment had acquired a new dimension beyond radio and television.

The biggest technological change in the music industry came with the appearance of the compact disc (CD). The first CD player was the Philips CD100, launched in August 1982, followed by Sony's CDP-101 in October. Retailing initially at $1000, they entered a market that had been dominated by audio cassette tapes (and a declining market for vinyl). The sound quality of CDs far exceeded vinyl or cassette. When the cost of CDs dropped to rival audio cassette tapes, the CD revolution had arrived. In 1984, the US music industry saw CD sales of $103.4 million. The first album to appear on CD was Billy Joel's *52nd Street* and the first single released on CD was 'The Visitors' by ABBA. In 1985, the first CD album to sell one million copies was *Brothers in Arms* by Dire Straits.

Although CDs improved the quality of music recording, the development of the Walkman portable audio cassette player revolutionised where and when people could listen to music. It was initially launched by the Sony Corporation in Japan in 1979 and became an instant hit. Although very chunky by modern iPod standards, the Walkman gave young people a completely new mobile way to listen to music. By 1989, 50 million Walkmans had been sold. Although a trade name, the term Walkman appeared in the *Oxford English Dictionary* in 1986.

**SOURCE 7** A Sony Walkman audio cassette player, launched in the USA in 1980. A user displays the size and convenience of use of this new technology.

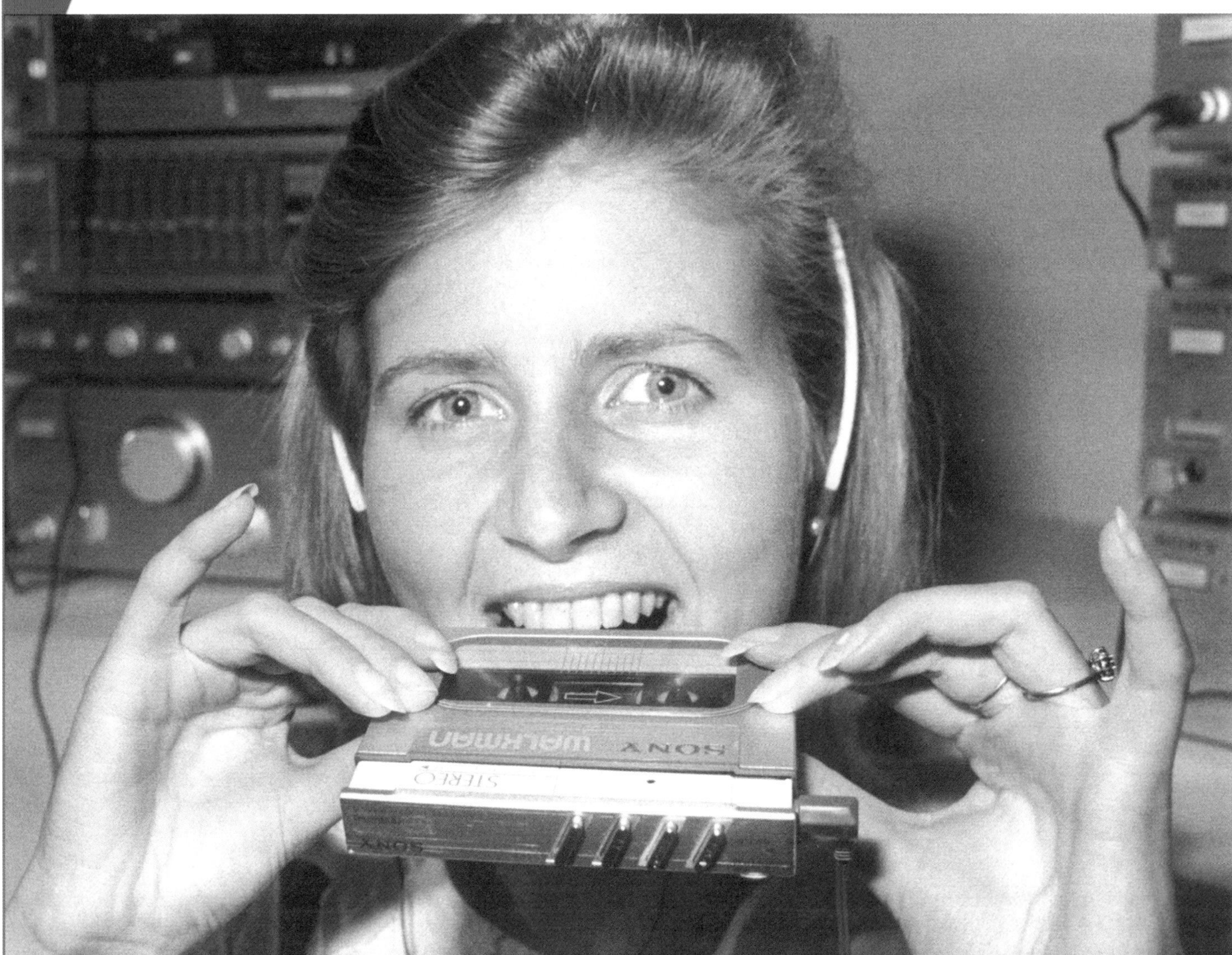


In terms of home entertainment, the development of the video cassette and with it the video cassette player enabled people to watch recently released films, sporting events and music concerts in their own home. Initially expensive and split between two delivery systems, Betamax and VHS, the video cassette took off in terms of sales in the 1980s when the VHS system began to dominate the market. A Betamax video cassette recorder (VCR) cost $2,000 in 1975. By 1987, a VHS VCR cost $250, with a blank VHS videotape selling for just $5. Unfortunately, the development also led to the growth of a lucrative pirate industry in videos.

Linked with the appearance of the video cassette and VCR was the camcorder, which appeared in 1983 and quickly replaced 8mm film home movie cameras. This enabled individuals to make their own cassettes to be watched at home. It spawned a massive boom in amateur home movie-making, which television series like *You've Been Framed* have exploited ever since.

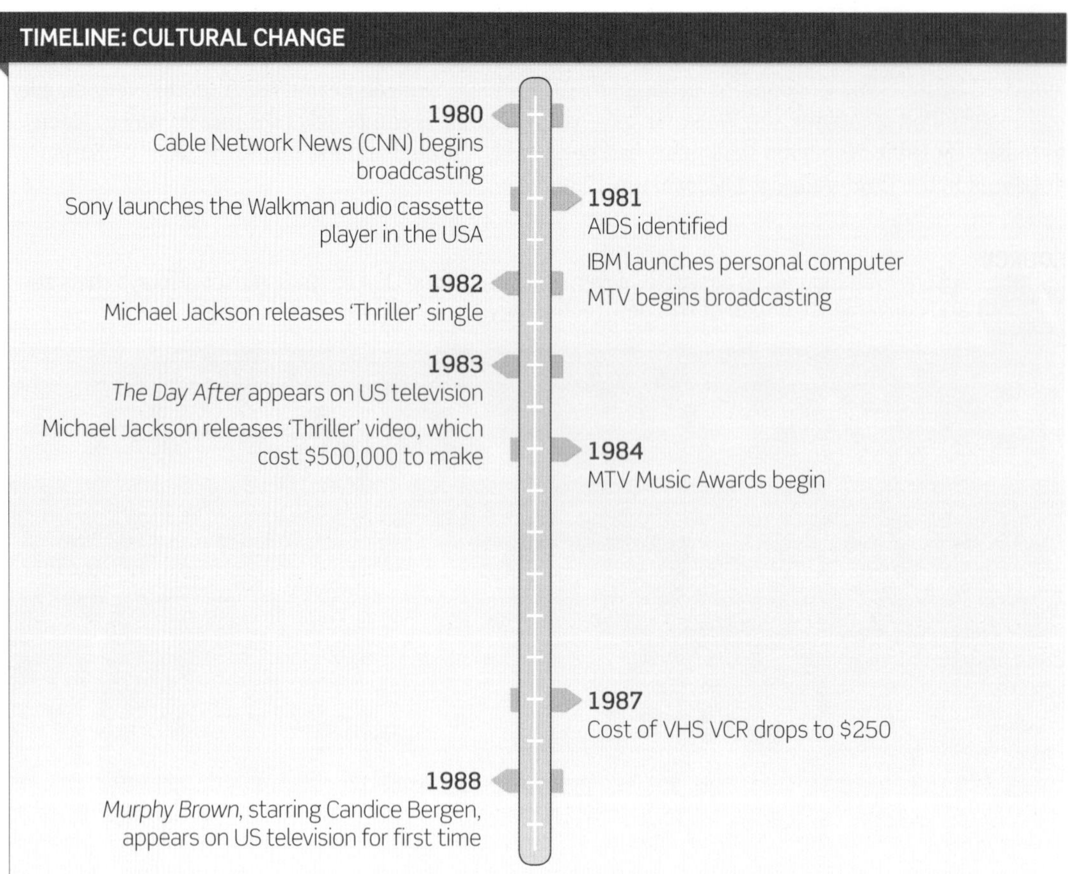


### KEY TERMS

**Cable television**
Television is broadcast via an underground cable. Cable television services are only available to houses that lie close to the cable.

**Satellite television**
Television signals are relayed via satellites and are picked up through a satellite dish on the viewer's house. The signal can be received almost anywhere.

**Terrestrial television**
The earliest form of television broadcast. A large television aerial transmits and relays television signals, which are received through a television aerial on a house or on an individual television.

## The growth of cable television and the influence of MTV

**Cable television** had been a feature of American life since 1972, when Sterling Manhattan Cable launched the first pay-TV network, Home Box Office (HBO). Today HBO is best known for drama series, but it initially showed Hollywood films. However, it wasn't until the 1980s that cable television became a major part of the American television industry. By the 1980s, it was also possible to sign up for **satellite television**. Both developments provided viewers with a choice of dozens of channels, at a time when most viewers in the UK could only access four channels.

The Atlanta businessman R. E. 'Ted' Turner turned these developments to his advantage. Turner established a nationwide network called WTBS, which provided up-to-the-minute sports news and classic movies. In 1980, he set up Cable Network News (CNN), which became a major rival to **terrestrial** networks ABC, CBS and NBC from 1983.

In the 1980s, terrestrial networks' share of the television market fell while viewing figures for cable television rose from nine percent to 26 percent. President Reagan assisted the process by appointing Mark Fowler as Head of the Federal Communications Commission from 1981 to 1987. Fowler was looking for a more competitive television market, and this goal was boosted by the Cable Communications Policy Act of 1984, which provided a favourable regulatory framework for the expansion of cable television. From 1984 to 1992, the cable television industry spent $15 billion on laying cables across the USA, and billions on programme development. By 1990, nearly 53 million households had subscribed to cable television and the number of cable television networks had grown from 28 in 1980 to 79 by 1989. The most important networks were CNN, C-SPAN (Cable Satellite Public Affairs Network), ESPN (Entertainment and Sports Network) and MTV (Music Television).

MTV had a profound impact on popular culture. It began broadcasting 24/7 music video entertainment on 1 August 1981 when Jack Lack, Executive Vice President of Warner-Amex Satellite Entertainment announced, 'Ladies and gentlemen, rock'n'roll.' 'Video Killed the Radio Star', by the Buggles was the first music video shown. MTV played a major part in making stars of Madonna and groups like Duran Duran. The impact on the music industry was immense. To make it, music artists now had to produce a music video as a creative promotional tool for their records.

A major event for MTV came in early December 1983 when it broadcast Michael Jackson's 14-minute video 'Thriller'. The album *Thriller* had been released in November 1982, but after the video for the 'Thriller' single was shown on MTV in 1983 it became a truly global phenomenon. Recognising the growing importance of the music video, Jackson had commissioned Hollywood director John Landis to shoot the video with a budget of $500,000. The rights to show the music video on MTV were sold for $200,000.

## EXTEND YOUR KNOWLEDGE

### Michael Jackson (1958–2009)

Michael Joseph Jackson was born in the steel town of Gary in northern Indiana. His ambitious father, Joseph, who worked as a crane operator, wanted his sons to become pop stars. The Jackson 5's big breakthrough came when they signed with the Motown record label in 1969. Their first album was *Diana Ross presents the Jackson 5*, released in December 1969. At the age of 13 Michael launched his solo career with hits like 'Got to be There'.

In 1975, Jackson broke his links with Motown and signed with Epic Records. His career took off, and by the end of the 1970s he had become one of the USA's best-known recording stars. In 1982, his single 'Thriller' became an international bestseller. The accompanying video, released in 1983, set a new high standard for music videos. Jackson received Grammy awards for writing 'Billie Jean', Best Pop Vocal Performance, and Best Rock Vocal Performance for *Thriller* and shared Grammy Award Album of the Year with producer Quincy Jones. In 1985, he wrote and sang on 'We are the World', a single released to raise charity funds for Africa.

Raised as a Jehovah's Witness, Jackson was shy and retiring off stage. By the late 1980s, he had bought Neverland, his vast estate near Los Angeles where he had amusement rides and pets, including a chimpanzee called Bubbles. In the early 1990s, Jackson was alleged to have committed child abuse. He married twice, once to Lisa Marie Presley, daughter of Elvis, in 1994, and to a nurse, Deborah Rowe, in 1996. He had two children with Rowe before they divorced in 1999 and another child in 2002. Jackson died of cardiac arrest at the age of 50 in 2009.

In 1984, the MTV Music Video Awards were launched, followed in 1992 by the MTV Movie Awards. Also, by the late 1980s MTV started showing non-video programmes geared towards the teenage and young adult market. One was its popular reality series, *The Real World*, launched in 1992. MTV also launched its own animated cartoon programmes such as *Beavis and Butthead*. Eventually MTV would produce documentaries, game shows and public service campaigns on issues such as voting rights and safe sex.

**EXTRACT**

From 'MTV, 30 Years On', by Andy Greene, published on 28 July 2011 in the British magazine *Rolling Stone*. The article describes the experiences of Mark Goodman, one of the first 'video jockeys' on MTV, and about how the channel developed in its early days.

MTV launched on August 1st 1981 at 12.01 a.m. The first images were the launch of the Apollo 11, followed by a video for the Buggles song 'Video Killed the Radio Star'. The network has gone through countless permutations since then, but this weekend VH1 Classic will commemorate MTV's founding with a three-day marathon of footage from the 1980s, including a rebroadcast of the network's first hour, starting Saturday at 6 a.m.

In the earliest days, when MTV was only available in a limited number of cities, the VJs (video jockeys) had to travel to New Jersey to watch it because even New York cable companies didn't offer it. 'Part of the job was to hang out with cable operators and convince them to pick up MTV,' Mark Goodman (early VJ) says. 'Within six months we started getting these stories back from small towns in the Mid West and in the South where people were going into record stores and asking for the Buggles, who had been off the shelves for three years by 1981. I also remember doing an appearance in Cheyenne, Wyoming, at a record store where thousands of people showed up. I said, "What's going on?" They said, "You". I was completely blown away, and I said "Okay, it's working."' The new platform served as a tremendous boost to the record industry. "We sort of propped it up when there was kind of an indulgence in the industry," says Goodman. 'We were coming off "Saturday Night Fever" in 1979 and the industry had this gigantic bubble and then things got awful quiet. We came along just in time and revitalized things, or at least opened people up to more music.'

## The impact of the AIDS crisis

The biggest health scare of the 1980s was the AIDS crisis. The Acquired Immune Deficiency Syndrome (AIDS) was first identified in 1981. It is transmitted through sexual contact or through reuse of contaminated hypodermic needles. As a result, the groups most vulnerable to AIDS infection were people with a variety of sexual partners and those who injected drugs. When it was identified AIDS caused considerable concern because there was no known way of treating the condition successfully. Acquiring AIDS was a virtual death sentence.

By the beginning of 1985, AIDS had been responsible for 5,600 deaths in the USA. By January 1989, the year Ronald Reagan left office, the Centers for Disease Control confirmed 82,764 cases of AIDS, of whom 46,344 had died. This was the biggest medical scare in the USA since the Spanish influenza pandemic of 1918.

The government reaction to AIDS attracted considerable criticism. During his first term in office (1981–85), Reagan did not order a study of AIDS nor make its prevention a high priority. It was only after the death of Rock Hudson, a film-star friend, in late 1985, that Reagan began paying attention to the problem. During Reagan's second term (1985–89) the federal government began devoting more substantial resources to AIDS. The Surgeon General of the USA, C. Everett Koop, said that by 1991 approximately 79,000 Americans would have died from AIDS, and called for widespread sex education in schools.

However, Reagan faced a problem. A high proportion of AIDS sufferers were drug users and gay men. Many of Reagan's supporters from the Moral Majority opposed the idea of helping these groups and the idea of sex education in public schools. Catholic conservatives like Phyllis Schlafly were opposed to the use of condoms as a way of preventing the spread of AIDS. Others termed AIDS a 'gay plague' and reinforced conservative views against homosexuality held by individuals like the Reverend Jerry Falwell. Reagan's problem was further increased by the US Supreme Court's decision in 1986 to uphold a Georgia state law outlawing gay sex in the case *Bowers v Hardwick*. At the time, 24 other states and the District of Columbia had similar laws. These developments limited the ability of the federal government to act decisively in dealing with AIDS.

By 1987, Reagan was willing to state that AIDs was 'public enemy number 1'. He made a speech to the American Foundation for AIDS Research in May 1987, but refused to mention the case of Ryan White, a haemophiliac who had contracted AIDS from an infected blood transfusion. As a result of his infection, White had been ostracised in his hometown of Kokomo, Indiana. Also in 1987, gay organisations staged a parade of 500,000 people in New York City on Columbus Day, demanding better funding for AIDS research.

The debate on AIDS and how to deal with it caused great divisions within US society and highlighted the different social views of Moral Majority conservatives and liberal groups. Even the Reagans were divided. While Nancy Reagan advocated the use of condoms to combat the spread of the condition, the president refused to endorse this approach.

## Controversial social issues in film and television

The most popular television shows of the 1980s were comedies, miniseries and soap operas. Many of the latter included escapist tales of super-rich families, in shows such as *Dallas* and *Dynasty*.

However, a number of socially controversial topics did appear on US television and elicited considerable debate. Perhaps the most significant show to deal with more controversial subject matter appeared on US television on 20 November 1983. The made-for-television movie *The Day After*, directed by Edward Meyer and starring Jason Robards and Steve Guttenberg, dealt with the highly controversial topic of a nuclear holocaust in the USA and included very graphic scenes depicting the USA after a nuclear attack. The movie appeared at the height of the **Second Cold War** and struck a chord with the American public. Reagan had always been appalled by the prospect of nuclear war and *The Day After* was a factor in encouraging Reagan to support the Strategic Defense Initiative, also known as Star Wars. This was a plan to make nuclear war redundant by developing a defensive shield of space-borne missiles.

**KEY TERM**

**Second Cold War**
The First Cold War lasted from 1945 to the period of détente during Nixon's presidency in the early 1970s. The Second Cold War began with the Soviet invasion of Afghanistan in December 1979 and increased in intensity after Reagan's victory in the 1980 elections. This period ended in 1985 when the reformist Mikhail Gorbachev became leader of the Soviet Union.

Ironically, *The Day After* appeared in the same month as Operation Able Archer, a major NATO exercise, which the Soviet leadership perceived as a possible pre-emptive nuclear attack. Tension between the USA and USSR was for a time heightened by Reagan's claim that the Soviet Union was an 'evil empire'.

Another socially important programme was *The Cosby Show*, which appeared between 1984 and 1992 and was one of the most popular series on television. It starred black American actor Bill Cosby and described the life of a middle-class black American doctor and his family. The show mirrored shows about family life from the 1950s and 1960s such as *Father Knows Best* and the *Dick Van Dyke Show*.

A television programme that attracted pronounced political criticism was *Murphy Brown*, starring Candice Bergen. It ran for a decade from 1988 to 1998. The main character was an ambitious single mother, played by Bergen, who worked at a news magazine. Dan Quayle, US vice president from 1989 to 1993, claimed the programme undermined family values by giving the impression that being an ambitious single mother was an acceptable role model for young women.

In American film, blockbuster escapist films like those in the *Indiana Jones* and *Rocky* series were popular but Hollywood did address several important social issues. In 1983, Meryl Streep played Karen Silkwood in the film *Silkwood*, about a worker in a nuclear power plant who gets radiation sickness. In 1988, the film *Rain Man* starring Dustin Hoffman and Tom Cruise dealt with autism. Hoffman went on to win the Best Actor Oscar for his portrayal of an autistic man.

The issue of race relations was dealt with in a number of films. In 1987, British director Richard Attenborough made *Cry Freedom*, about the struggle against apartheid in South Africa. *Mississippi Burning*, starring Gene Hackman and Willem Dafoe, was released the following year and dealt with the murder of white and black civil rights activists during the 'Freedom Summer' of 1964 in Mississippi. The 1991 film *Boyz n the Hood* was set in the gangland of in South Central Los Angeles – the area formerly called Watts, which was the scene of serious race riots in 1965 and again in 1992. In the same year *New Jack City*, starring Wesley Snipes, dealt with drug-taking and drug gangs in New York City. In 1992, the black American director Spike Lee made a film of the life of Malcolm X with the actor Denzel Washington in the title role.

Disability was the focus of the film *My Left Foot*, released in 1989. It told the real life story of Christy Brown, a severely disabled Dublin slum-dweller who went on to be a successful novelist. He was portrayed by Daniel Day-Lewis, who won the Best Actor Oscar that year. *Kiss of the Spider Woman*, released at the height of the AIDS crisis in 1985, portrayed a gay man incarcerated in a Latin-American jail and starred the American actor William Hurt, who also won a Best Actor Oscar for his role.

All these films were popular with American moviegoers and helped bring a wide range of social issues to public attention.

**SOURCE**

From a speech delivered in May 1992 by Republican Vice President Dan Quayle. In this speech he criticised the television series *Murphy Brown*, and in particular the lifestyle of the main character, who is a working, unmarried mother. The speech was made at the start of the 1992 presidential campaign.

Bearing babies irresponsibly is simply wrong. Failing to support children one has fathered is wrong and we must be unequivocal about this. It doesn't help matters when primetime TV has Murphy Brown, a character who supposedly epitomises today's intelligent, highly paid professional woman, mocking the importance of fathers by bearing a child alone and calling it just another lifestyle choice. I know it's not fashionable to talk about moral values, but we need to do it. Even though our cultural leaders in Hollywood, network TV and national newspapers routinely jeer at them, I think most of us in this room know that some things are good and other things are wrong. And now, it's time to make the discussion public. It's time to talk again about the family, hard work, integrity and personal responsibility. We cannot be embarrassed out of our belief that two parents married to each other are better, in most cases, for children than one. That honest work is better than handouts and crime.

ACTIVITY
KNOWLEDGE CHECK

**Cultural change**

1. What impact did new technology have on popular culture in the years 1981 to 1992? How did people's consumption of culture change?
2. What effects did cable television and particularly MTV have on the US television industry?
3. In what ways did the AIDS crisis impact on US society in the years 1981 to 1992?
4. How far did film and television deal with controversial social issues in the years 1981 to 1992?

**AS Level Exam-Style Question Section B**

To what extent was 1981 to 1992 a period of radical change in popular culture? (20 marks)

**Tip**

*This question requires a balanced response. Write about ways in which popular culture changed, as well as ways in which it remained the same, before coming to a balanced conclusion.*

# TO WHAT EXTENT DID THE POSITION OF ETHNIC MINORITIES AND WOMEN IMPROVE IN THE YEARS 1981 TO 1992?

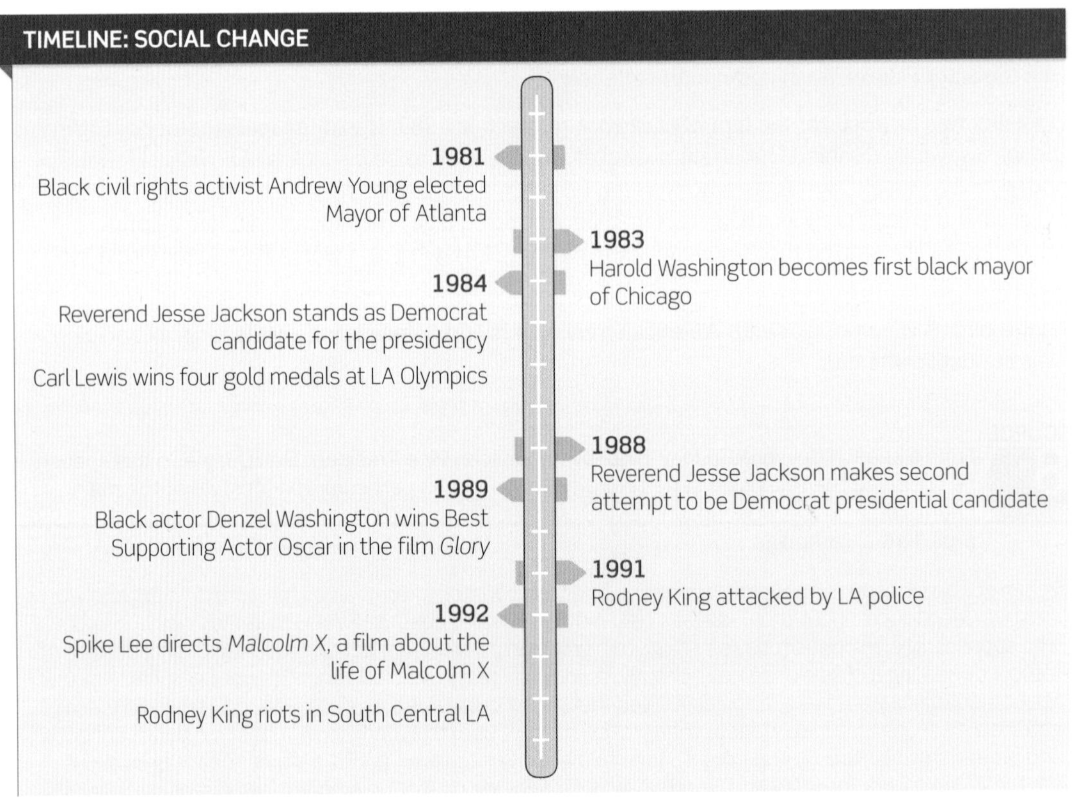


## Ethnic minorities

### The impact of black American success in politics, business, sport and popular culture

At the beginning of the 1980s, black Americans faced many social and economic problems. They made up 11.7 percent of the population, but were 43 percent of those receiving Aid to Families with

Dependent Children and 35.1 percent of people receiving food stamps. However, the decade saw a number of important changes. Symbolically, on 3 November 1983, President Reagan signed a law designating the third Monday in January Martin Luther King Jr Day, a national holiday. The first Martin Luther King Jr Day to be celebrated occurred in 1986.

By the 1980s, black Americans had been elected in such numbers to the House of Representatives that they formed a black **caucus** of 20–25 Congressmen and women, working for black American rights. In Atlanta, Georgia, in the heart of the Old South, one of Martin Luther King's most important colleagues, Andrew Young, was elected mayor in 1981. The growing influence of black Americans in politics is illustrated by the careers of three men: Harold Washington, Jesse Jackson and Clarence Thomas.

KEY TERM

**Caucus**
An informal group created to promote a particular cause or issue.

### Harold Washington

In 1983, Harold Washington became mayor of Chicago. This was a major achievement in a city long-dominated by Irish-American politicians, in particular Richard J. Daley, who was mayor from 1955 to 1976. With black Americans comprising 40 percent of the registered electors, Washington was only able to triumph by attracting white voters. He did this by offering moderate social policies that crossed the racial divide, but the support of black American groups was also important to Washington's success. Washington put together a coalition of black American groups involving the local NAACP, the National Urban League and PUSH (People United to Save Humanity) headed by the Reverend Jesse Jackson and Chicago Black United Communities. These groups helped to add an additional 100,000 new voters to the electoral roll in the period 1982–83. In the mayoral election there was a very high turnout among inner-city blacks of 80 percent, equivalent to the normal voter turnout in white, middle-class suburbs. However, Washington was also aided by a split in the Irish-American city leadership between Jane Byrne, who had been mayor since 1979, and Daley's son, Richard M. Daley. Washington's triumph showed that black Americans could have a major influence on local politics.

### Jesse Jackson

Washington's triumph also aided the most prominent black American politician of the 1980s, the Reverend Jesse Jackson. Like Andrew Young, Jackson had been a close associate of Martin Luther King, and like Washington, he was based in Chicago. In 1984 and 1988, he ran for the Democratic Party nomination for the presidency. In doing so he used a newly formed organisation, the Rainbow Coalition, which grew out of PUSH. In his 1984 bid to become the Democrat presidential candidate, he failed to get the support of some prominent black American leaders, such as Andrew Young, who had been Jackson's rival in Martin Luther King's civil rights campaign. In the nomination race Jackson received 21 percent of the vote in primary election contests and only eight, percent of the delegate votes at the Democratic National Convention. The Democrats chose white politician Walter 'Fritz' Mondale as their candidate. In 1988, Jackson's challenge was much stronger: his campaign was better organised and he won a number of primary elections. Jackson showed that black Americans could become serious contenders for America's highest political office.

EXTEND YOUR KNOWLEDGE

**Reverend Jesse Jackson (1941- )**
Jesse Louis Burns was born in Greenville, South Carolina. He was born out of wedlock and took the surname of Charles Jackson, who married Jesse's mother when Jesse was two years old. He attended Sterling High School, Greenville, the University of Illinois and then North Carolina Agricultural and Technical College, graduating in 1964 with a degree in sociology.

After graduation Jackson went to Chicago to train as a Christian minister and became involved in the civil rights movement. In 1965, he took part in the march from Selma to Montgomery and in 1966 became a full-time member of the Southern Christian Leadership Conference (SCLC). By 1968, he was a close associate of Martin Luther King and was with King when he was assassinated. Jackson left the SCLC to found People United to Save Humanity (PUSH) in Illinois in the 1970s.

In 1984 and 1988 he stood as a possible presidential candidate for the Democratic Party but was defeated both times.

### Clarence Thomas

The appointment of a black American Supreme Court justice in 1991 should have been a cause for celebration among the black community but, in fact, caused controversy. With the retirement of the Supreme Court's first black American justice, Thurgood Marshall, President George Bush Senior nominated black American Clarence Thomas. However, Thomas was a conservative and was opposed to affirmative action. In addition, he had been accused of sexual harassment by a former colleague, black American academic Anita Hill. His nomination was opposed by civil rights and women's groups but it was approved by the Republican-controlled Senate.

**AS Level Exam-Style Question Section A**

***Study Source 9 before you answer this question.***

Why is Source 9 valuable to the historian for an enquiry into why Harold Washington became Chicago's first black American mayor?

Explain your answer using the source, the information about it and your own knowledge of the historical context. (8 marks)

**Tip**

*In your answer you will be expected to refer directly to the provenance of the source and say how this affects its value to the historian. You should use material from within the content of the source to support your argument as well as your own knowledge to place the source in its historical context.*

**SOURCE**

From an election leaflet produced by the campaign to make Harold Washington mayor of Chicago, Illinois, in 1983. Washington was the first black American to hold that office in Chicago.

**The Harold Washington Program for Chicago**

**Harold's First Priority: Jobs**

- Establish a department of employment and economic development that will fulfill the first priority of the Washington administration: the creation and retention of jobs for Chicagoans.
- Work vigorously in Springfield (The Illinois State Capital) and Washington DC for programs that will bring jobs to Chicago.
- Develop a public transportation system that links Chicagoans to the growing suburban jobs market.
- Retain and attract business and industry by using the community colleges, community organizations, and business and labor to develop effective employment and training programs for Chicago's work force.

**Harold's Pledge: Fairness and Justice**

- The Washington administration will demand no more of its employees than a full day's work for a full day's pay.
- Hire, upgrade, and promote city employees on a merit basis.
- Establish a freedom of information ordinance that opens city government files to public examination.
- Conduct city business fairly and equitably.

### Business

The positive effect of civil equality for black Americans, which had been hard won by the civil rights movement in the 1950s and 1960s, began to bear fruit in the 1980s for black Americans in business. By 1992, the number of black-owned businesses in the USA had risen to 621,000 from only a few hundred thousand in the 1960s. This included black businesses in professional areas such as insurance companies and finance.

One of the most high-profile successes in business was the actor and television show host Oprah Winfrey. Beginning in 1986, her chat show became nationally popular. Eventually, *The Oprah Winfrey Show* was distributed to 140 countries. Winfrey created her own television production company and became one of the partners in Oxygen Media Inc., a cable channel and interactive network presenting programming mainly for women. In 1988, she appeared on the front page of *Time* magazine, a clear sign that she had become a national institution in television and business. In 2003, she was listed by *Forbes* magazine as the USA's first female black billionaire.

### Sport

Another area where black Americans achieved considerable success was in sport. The NFL was an area where black sportsmen excelled. In the 1980s, a black American, Randell Cunningham, became the quarterback of the Philadelphia Eagles, a position that had previously been the preserve of whites. In basketball, Earvin 'Magic' Johnson of the Los Angeles Lakers was the star player of the NBA. By 1998, black Americans comprised 80 percent of the players in the NFL, 60 percent of the players in the NBA (basketball) and 25 percent in Major League Baseball (MLB).

Perhaps the greatest achievement for black Americans came in athletics. In the 1984 Los Angeles Olympics, Carl Lewis won four gold medals in the 100 metres, 200 metres, long jump and 4 x 100 metres. In the 1988 Seoul Olympics, he was again awarded the gold medal in the 100 metres following the disqualification of a Canadian, Ben Johnson, for drug-taking. Overall, in the 1984 LA Olympics, black track and field athletes won 40 out of 49 medals awarded to US athletes. In boxing at the same Olympics, black Americans won ten out of the 11 US medals. Comprising only 11.7 percent of the US population in the 1980s, these were remarkable achievements.

### Popular culture

Another area of success for black Americans was popular culture. In film, Denzel Washington won the Best Supporting Actor Oscar for his role in the 1989 picture *Glory*, about the USA's first black regiment in the US Civil War. In 1992, Spike Lee directed and starred in *Malcolm X*, alongside Denzel Washington, who played the title role. On television, Bill Cosby with *The Cosby Show*, his show about the middle-class Huxtable family, and Oprah Winfrey on her chat show, were national celebrities.

However, it was in popular music that black Americans excelled, none more so than Michael Jackson. In 1983, at the 25th anniversary commemoration of the Motown record label, Jackson performed 'Billie Jean' and did his famous moonwalk for the first time on national television. Released in 1982, the single 'Thriller' was in the charts for 80 weeks, 37 as number 1. The video 'Thriller' won 12 Grammy Awards, making it one of the most significant music videos of all time. Other popular black musicians of the 1980s included Prince, Whitney Houston and Tina Turner, and the hip-hop star LL Cool J.

### The extent of racial tolerance by 1992

Unfortunately, racial tension was still a feature of parts of US society in the 1980s. In June 1982, a Chinese American, Vincent Chin, was clubbed to death by two white car-workers in Detroit because they thought he was Japanese, and therefore responsible for lay-offs in the car industry. In 1984, a white man, Bernhard Goetz, was travelling the New York City subway when he was confronted by four aggressive black youths who wanted money. He shot them with a revolver. One youth was brain-damaged. At his trial in 1987 the jury accepted Goetz's plea of self-defence and he received only eight months in prison. In a local poll, 90 percent of whites supported the verdict.

However, the most important incident involving racial intolerance was the Rodney King case of 1991–92. In March 1991, Rodney King, a black American, was stopped in his car by white police in South Central Los Angeles (once known as Watts). He was brutally beaten by them and this was caught on video. On 1 May 1992, the police involved were acquitted in court of wrongdoing, sparking off a major race riot in which 54 people were killed, 2,400 injured and 17,000 arrested. Half those arrested were Hispanic Americans protesting against the police action. 10,000 businesses were destroyed, several owned by Korean Americans, with the loss of 50,000 jobs. The Rodney King case reinforced the popular belief that some police forces were racist and that inner-city areas, like South Central LA were still areas of poverty, high unemployment and crime.

**SOURCE 10** Scene from the Rodney King riots in South Central Los Angeles that erupted following the acquittal of King's police attackers in May 1992. The cost of damage caused by the riots was $1 billion.

## The impact of women in politics and the work place

In 1981, President Reagan nominated the first ever woman to the US Supreme Court, Arizona lawyer, Sandra Day O'Connor. At the 1984 Democratic National Convention, Democrat presidential candidate Walter Mondale caused a sensation by nominating as his vice-presidential running mate a woman, Geraldine Ferraro. Although, Mondale lost, this was an important milestone in US politics.

The press declared the 1992 election year as 'the year of the woman'. Women won several high profile senate races in Illinois and California. Overall, women were returned to Congress in large numbers, partly as a result of 'Emily's List', a programme to put more women into national politics. 1992 also saw the victory of Democrat Bill Clinton in the race to be president. During the campaign his wife Hillary Clinton played a prominent role.

Outside politics many more women were developing careers in white-collar, professional jobs. Women held positions as federal district court judges, law professors and business executives. From 1972 to 1985, the female share of professional jobs increased from 44 to 49 percent and the female share of management jobs nearly doubled, growing from 20 to 36 percent. The sociologist Andrew Hacker reported in the *New York Times Magazine* in 1984 that from 1960 to 1983 the percentage of lawyers who were women had risen from two percent to 15 percent and the percentage of jobs in banking and financial management held by women had risen from nine percent to 39 percent. Half of all 1985 college graduates were women, and women were earning a steadily rising share of all advanced degrees, including close to a third of all degrees in law, business, accounting, and computer and information sciences.

In 1983, Sally Ride became the first US woman in space when she took part in a space shuttle mission on board the *Challenger*. In 1986, the first US teacher in space was Christa McAuliffe, who tragically died when the *Challenger* shuttle exploded just after takeoff, killing the entire crew.

### The changing status of women by 1992

By 1990, the status of women had changed considerably. Women's attitude to marriage and having children had changed: 27 percent of all births in the USA took place outside marriage and 40 percent of marriages ended in divorce. Unmarried, single women were becoming an important sector in American society. The role women played also changed. More and more women were getting involved in politics. Emily's List, first set up in 1984 to get pro-life female candidates into national politics, was regarded as a success. Women's legal rights had also changed. In 1992, the US Supreme Court, in *Planned Parenthood v Casey* upheld its pro-abortion position first put forward in *Roe v Wade* in 1973.

The 1990 census revealed how far the lives of American women had changed. In 1970, 38 percent of the workforce was female. This had risen to 50 percent by 1990, with 58 percent of all women in employment. 33 percent of new doctors in the 1980s were women compared to only four percent in 1970. 40 percent of lawyers were women (only 8.44 percent in 1970). These were major advances.

The status of women in US society had changed considerably during the 1980s but women were still not equal to men in terms of earnings, and although they made up over half the US population and half the college graduates, women had yet to reach full social, economic or political equality. In 2002, women were still earning only 77 percent of the earnings of men for doing a similar job.

In 1992, the social, political and economic role of women was radically different from 1955. In 1955, the traditional role of women was to get married, have children and look after those children while staying at home. By 1992, that model of womanhood had been transformed. Women worked in the professions, politics and business, there had been a female US Supreme Court judge, a vice presidential candidate and female chief executives of large companies: positions unthinkable for women in 1955.

ACTIVITY
KNOWLEDGE CHECK

**Social change**

1 How successful were black Americans in sports, politics, business and popular culture in the years 1981 to 1992? Think about broad developments as well as individual achievements.

2 How far was the USA a racially tolerant society by 1992?

3 Write a short paragraph describing the position of women in US society in 1981 and another describing their position in 1992. What changed during this period? What stayed the same?

ACTIVITY
WRITING

**US words and phrases**

Write a paragraph on how the US political system operates at national level. In your paragraph explain and use all of the following words and phrases:

| Republican | Democrat | presidential candidate | Senate |
|---|---|---|---|
| US Supreme Court | House of Representatives | Constitutional Amendment | |

## Change (6a)

**Separately and together**

Below are some different types of history that historians may identify.

| Political history | Economic history | Social history |
|---|---|---|
| Ethnic minority history | Cultural history | International history |

These are thematic histories, in which a historian focuses on a particular aspect of change. For example, an economic history of the British Empire would focus on trade and the economic reasons for the expansion of the empire, whereas a political history of the empire would focus on governance of the colonies and strategic reasons for its expansion.

Working in groups write a definition for each type of history.

Here are some events in our period:

| **1955–56** Montgomery bus boycott leads to desegregation of public buses in Montgomery | **1964** President Johnson launches his 'Great Society' programme | **1968–72** Rise of the 'Silent Majority' | **1973** *Roe v Wade* decision by US Supreme Court | **1979–80** Iran Hostage Crisis | **1984** President Reagan wins second landslide victory in presidential election |
|---|---|---|---|---|---|

The second and last changes can be classified as 'political' events.

Answer the following:

1 Why was the election of Ronald Reagan so important in US history in the 1980s?

2 What other area of history does this take it into?

3 What social and economic changes came about because of President Johnson's Great Society programme of 1964 to 1969?

4 Was the rise of the 'Silent Majority' political or cultural or both? Explain your answer.

5 What was the social and cultural impact of the *Roe v Wade* Supreme Court decision on the USA after 1973?

6 Did Reagan's victories in the 1980 and 1984 presidential elections occur for just political reasons or were social and economic factors also important?

Working in pairs:

7 Write a statement attacking 'thematic history'.

8 Write three statements defending 'thematic history'.

9 Explain why 'thematic history' is written.

ACTIVITY
SUMMARY

**Republican dominance and its opponents**

1 Think of social, economic and political reasons for the Republican dominance of American politics in the 1980s. Create a spider diagram showing the links between these reasons.

2 Write notes on:

a) Changes in culture and society in the years 1981–92.

b) Changes brought about by Republican governments that affected society and the economy.

3 Using your answers to questions 1 and 2 answer this question, giving reasons for your answer: What do you regard as the most significant change in the USA in the years 1981 to 1992?

## WIDER READING


**Books**

Carson, C. (ed.) *The Eyes on the Prize – Civil Rights Reader: Documents, Speeches and Firsthand Accounts from the Black Freedom Fighters, 1954–1990*, Prentice-Hall (1992)

Cook, R. *Sweet Land of Liberty?: The African-American Struggle for Civil Rights in the Twentieth Century*, Routledge (1997)

de Pennington, J. *Modern America: 1865 to the present*, Hodder (2005)

Farmer, A. *An Introduction to American History, 1860–1990*, Hodder (2002)

Field, R. *Civil Rights in America, 1865–1980*, Cambridge University Press (2002)

Murphy, D. *Flagship History – United States 1776–1992*, Collins Educational (2001)

Paterson, D. *et al. Civil Rights in the USA, 1863–1980*, Heinemann (2001)

Sanders, V. *Politics, Presidency and Society in the USA 1968–2001*, Hodder (2008)

**Web**

Fordham University:

Modern social movements www.fordham.edu/Halsall/mod/modsbook56.asp

Pop culture www.fordham.edu/Halsall/mod/modsbook60.asp

The USA as a world leader www.fordham.edu/Halsall/mod/modsbook48.asp

**Video**

*The Century, America's* Time – documentary

# Preparing for your AS Level Paper 2 exam

### Advance planning

1. Draw up a timetable for your revision and try to keep to it. Spread your timetable over a number of weeks, and aim to cover four or five topics each week.
2. Spend longer on topics that you have found difficult, and revise them several times.
3. Above all, do not try to limit your revision by attempting to 'question spot'. Try to be confident about all aspects of your Paper 2 work, because this will ensure that you have a choice of questions in Section B.

### Paper 2 overview:

| AS Paper 2 | Time: 1 hour 30 minutes | |
|---|---|---|
| Section A | Answer 1 compulsory two-part sources question | 8+12 marks = 20 marks |
| Section B | Answer 1 question from a choice of 3 | 20 marks |
| | Total marks = | 40 marks |

You should familiarise yourself with the layout of the paper by looking at the examples published by Edexcel. The questions for each section are followed by eight pages of lined paper where you should write your answer.

### Section A questions

Each of the two parts of the question will focus on one of the two contemporary sources provided. The sources together will total around 300 words. The (a) question, worth 8 marks, will be in the form of 'Why is Source 1 useful for an enquiry into…?' The (b) question, worth 12 marks, will be in the form of 'How much weight do you give the evidence of Source 2 for an enquiry into…?' In both your answers you should address the value of the content of the source, and then its nature, origin and purpose. Finally, you should use your own knowledge of the context of the source to assess its value.

### Section B questions

These questions ask you to reach a judgement on an aspect of the topic studied. The questions will have the form, for example, of 'How far…', 'To what extent…' or 'How accurate is it to say…'. The questions can deal with historical concepts such as cause, consequence, change, continuity, similarity, difference and significance. You should consider the issue raised in the question, consider other relevant issues, and then conclude with an overall judgement.

The timescale of the questions could be as short as a single year or even a single event (an example from Option 2C.2 could be, 'To what extent was Russia's involvement in the First World War responsible for the fall of the Provisional Government in 1917?'). The timescale could be longer depending on the historical event or process being examined, but questions are likely to be shorter than the those set for Sections A and B in Paper 1.

### Use of time

This is an issue that you should discuss with your teachers and fellow students, but here are some suggestions for you.

1. Do not write solidly for 45 minutes on each question. For Section A it is essential that you have a clear understanding of the content of each source, the points being made, and the nature, origin and purpose of each source. You might decide to spend up to ten minutes reading the sources and drawing up your plan, and 35 minutes writing your answer.
2. For Section B answers you should spend a few minutes working out what the question is asking you to do, and drawing up a plan of your answer before you begin to write your response.

# Preparing for your AS Level exams

## Paper 2: AS Level sample answer with comments

### Section A

Part A requires you to:

- identify key points in the source and explain them
- deploy your own knowledge of the context in which events took place
- make appropriate comments about the author/origin/purpose of the source.

***Study Source 8 (Chapter 1, page 299) before you answer this question.***

*Why is Source 8 valuable to historians for an enquiry about the importance of the issue of black American civil rights in the USA in 1963? Explain your answer, using the source, the information given about it and your own knowledge of the historical context. (8 marks)*

#### Average student answer

The source has value to historians writing about the issue of black American civil rights in the USA in 1963. The source says that black American civil rights are a moral issue. It says that all Americans had been given equal rights and even says that the idea of equality goes back to the time of the Bible, but more importantly the idea of equality is an important part of the US Constitution. It tells us that black Americans face discrimination in a number of areas. They could not go into any restaurant of their choosing because some restaurants discriminated against black Americans. Black Americans also faced discrimination in sending their children to public schools and could not always send their children to the public school of their choice. Perhaps most importantly in a democracy, some black Americans were denied the right to vote.

The opening paragraph links directly to the issue described in the question. It refers to the source's value to historians and selects and summarises information from the source. However, it does not explain why the source might be valuable to historians investigating black American civil rights in 1963.

From my own knowledge I know that black Americans faced legal segregation in many states, most of which were in the Old South, which had fought to preserve slavery in the US Civil War of 1861 to 1865. I also know that by 1963 the black American civil rights movement was very active in the Old South, campaigning for greater equality for black Americans. All these points help explain why the source would be of value to historians writing about the issue of black American civil rights in the USA in 1963. The source is also valuable because it is written by the most important politician in the USA at that time, the president, John F. Kennedy. The source is a televised speech to the American people, which reinforces its value and shows that the issue was so important that the US president felt it necessary to speak about it publicly.

This section answers the question with reference to the provenance of the source, referring to the date of writing and to the position of the author.

The source material provides lots of information about different reasons why the issue of black American civil rights was such an important issue in the USA in 1963. From my own knowledge I know that in 1963 Dr Martin Luther King organised a demonstration against discrimination in the city of Birmingham, Alabama. The demonstrators, many of them schoolchildren, faced violent attacks by the Birmingham police and all this was televised, causing considerable concern across the USA. The president's speech was in response to that event.

The final paragraph makes some additional general comments about the value of the source, linking the timing of the speech to events in Birmingham and explaining those events using own knowledge. The response could be improved by adding more comment on the content of the source, linking this to a direct answer to the question, and by adding a concluding paragraph summing up the points made.

### Verdict

This is an average answer because:

- it demonstrates some understanding of the source material but does not provide sufficient analysis
- it provides some contextual evidence to the source material that helps expand and explain information from the source
- it discusses the usefulness of the source but mainly does this with reference to provenance rather than the content of the source.

Use the feedback on this answer to rewrite it, making as many improvements as you can.

# Paper 2: AS Level sample answer with comments

## Section A

Part B requires you to:

- interrogate the source
- draw reasoned inferences
- deploy your own knowledge to interpret the material in its context
- make a judgement about the value (weight) of the source.

***Study Source 8 (Chapter 3, page 352) before you answer this question.***

*How much weight would you give the evidence of Source 8 in an enquiry into the issue of women's rights in the USA in the 1970s? (12 marks)*

### Average student answer

The source would carry weight and value for any enquiry in the issue of women's rights in the 1970s in the USA. The source states that all Americans had a right to privacy. This was seen as an important part of the US Constitution. Within the right to privacy was the right of women to have, or not to have, the right to terminate a pregnancy. It also states that state governments that deny this right may force upon a woman a distressful life that could involve deterioration of mental or physical health. The source highlights the issue of unwed motherhood where women who become pregnant outside marriage faced possible discrimination by society as a whole. It also refers to the fact that women would make the important decision about a possible termination in consultation with a doctor. The issue of abortion was regarded as an important cause for the development of women's rights in the USA in the 1970s.

The introduction makes reference to weight and value in the opening sentence but goes on to describe rather than evaluate information from the source. The final sentence gives the source some context by referring to abortion within the wider development of women's rights in the 1970s. To improve this paragraph and make it an effective introduction the response should give an initial answer to the question of 'weight' directly linked to the content of the source.

Weight can be placed on the evidence presented in the source because it is written by one of the US Supreme Court's justices, Justice Blackmun. The US Supreme Court had the power to interpret the US Constitution. This shows he was a person of authority and, therefore, considerable weight should be placed on what he said.

In this paragraph the response looks at the provenance of the source, discussing the author's background and position and concluding that these do give the source weight. The paragraph could be improved by looking in more detail at the reasons Blackmun gives for reaching a judgement in favour of a woman's right to abortion and how these add to the weight of the source.

Clearly the source only touches on one of the major issues associated with women's rights in the 1970s and does not discuss other important issues like equal pay for similar work. Even though the author gives the impression that he is a highly educated individual, it is still only one person's point of view and to ascertain the true importance of the source as evidence the historian would need to look at other sources to gauge the true weight of evidence in this source. The source says the extract is a 'majority opinion', so some US Supreme Court justices must have had a different view, which is not mentioned. Finally, the source is from 1973 so it does not provide information about the later part of the 1970s.

The final paragraph gives a number of reasons why the weight of the source is limited. There is no concluding paragraph to give a final judgement on the weight of the source.

### Verdict

This is an average answer because:

- it identifies some key information from the source but says very little about the weight the historian would place on the evidence
- it makes some use of background contextual information about the issue of women's rights in US society in the 1970s
- much of the information in the source is taken at face value and is not questioned or analysed
- it makes a limited judgement about the weight and value of the source, mainly in the conclusion.

Use the feedback on this answer to rewrite it, making as many improvements as you can.

# Paper 2: AS Level sample answer with comments

## Section A

Part A requires you to:

- identify key points in the source and explain them
- deploy your own knowledge of the context in which events took place
- make appropriate comments about the author/origin/purpose of the source.

***Study Source 8 (Chapter 1, page 299) before you answer this question.***

*Why is Source 8 valuable to historians for an enquiry about the importance of the issue of black American civil rights in the USA in 1963? Explain your answer, using the source, the information given about it and your own knowledge of the historical context. (8 marks)*

### Strong student answer

The source is of immense value for an enquiry about the importance of the issue of black American civil rights in 1963. The source is connected with one of the key moments of the civil rights movement: the 1963 riots in Birmingham, Alabama, which followed a peaceful demonstration. It makes direct reference to the importance of black American civil rights because it makes it absolutely clear that one of the key moral issues within the USA, a position supported by the US Constitution, was the right to 'equal rights and opportunities' for all US citizens irrespective of their racial background. The source makes clear that this constitutional right covers such important issues as where an American citizen could eat in public, the public schools children could attend, and perhaps the most important democratic right of all, the right to vote.

This is a very strong opening, which is sharply focused on the question. This is an effective opening because it makes use of the student's own knowledge to place the information in the source in broader historical context.

The importance of the issue of black American civil rights in the USA in 1963 is indicated by the fact that the source is from a nationally televised speech, delivered by President John F. Kennedy. Presidents tended to use such televised speeches to highlight crucial issues in US politics and society. It also shows that the issue was of importance to Kennedy personally. The fact that the president chose to deliver a speech on national television in the immediate aftermath of riots shows that he considered this to be an important issue and an important moment at which to appeal to American citizens' sense of fairness. Kennedy subsequently decided to send a Civil Rights bill to Congress to bring about changes in the law to help enforce black American civil rights.

This section places the value of the source in broader historical context through assessment of the provenance of the source. The author of the speech and the timing and setting in which it was delivered are all considered as indicators of the importance of the issue of black American rights in 1963 and the light this source sheds on this importance.

The nature of the source, its content, authorship and the date it was written makes it of considerable value to the historian in an enquiry into the issue of black American civil rights in 1963. It focuses on an important event and the presidential reaction to that event. However, it does only deal with one person's view of one event. A broader view of the value of this source and the importance of the issue of black American civil rights in 1963 could be gained by looking at, for example, another famous speech delivered in the same year: Dr. Martin Luther King's 'I have a dream' speech at the Civil Rights March on Washington DC.

The concluding paragraph neatly summarises the points made above and adds further context from the student's own knowledge.

### Verdict

This is a strong answer because:

- it has sharp focus on the specific question
- it makes use of both the evidence provided in the introduction to the source and within the source
- it makes good use of wider contextual knowledge
- it deploys appropriate own knowledge accurately and effectively.

# Paper 2: AS Level sample answer with comments

## Section A

Part B requires you to:

- interrogate the source
- draw reasoned inferences
- deploy your own knowledge to interpret the material in its context
- make a judgement about the value (weight) of the source.

***Study Source 8 (Chapter 3, page 352) before you answer this question.***

*How much weight would you give the evidence of Source 8 in an enquiry into the issue of women's rights in the USA in the 1970s? (12 marks)*

### Strong student answer

The source would carry considerable weight and value for any enquiry into the issue of women's rights in the USA in the 1970s. It makes direct reference to one of the most important issues facing women and the campaign for women's rights in the early 1970s, the issue of termination of pregnancy or abortion. The women's movement, including groups such as NOW, the National Organization of Women, claimed it was a woman's right to choose to have an abortion. However, many state governments outlawed the practice and it was these laws that many women wished to see changed. The source states that the right to terminate a pregnancy was an aspect of the right to privacy that was guaranteed by the Constitution.

> This is a very strong opening paragraph, which is sharply focused on the question and makes good use of the student's wider knowledge of the period and issues in question.

The source was written by US Supreme Court justice Blackmun, and explains the majority opinion of the US Supreme Court in the landmark judgement 'Roe versus Wade', which confirmed the constitutional right of women to choose to terminate a pregnancy. It gives an excellent indication of the views of the majority of Supreme Court justices in 1973, but clearly does not offer a wider perspective of the issue of women's rights in the USA over the whole decade.

> This paragraph makes clear links between the author and date of the source and question, which asks about the issue of women's rights throughout the 1970s.

Clearly, the campaign for women's rights was varied and encompassed many different individual issues. The creation of NOW in the 1960s was an organisation that aimed at dealing with what it saw as the inferior position of women in US society. The right to terminate a pregnancy was merely one of the issues on which NOW campaigned. Other issues included the campaign for equal pay for similar work; the right of women to enter all professions; the right of women to live independent lives and the right to possess financial security within marriage. Nevertheless, the issue of abortion was regarded as one of the most important rights in the campaign for equality for women, so a decision in favour of the right to abortion by the US Supreme Court is an indication of progress in women's rights more generally.

> This paragraph gives additional historical context, placing the issue of abortion within the wider campaign for women's rights.

A limitation on the source's value when read in isolation is that it does not give any indication of opposing views and opinions. After 1973 there was a campaign to reverse the 'Roe versus Wade' decision, led by religious and right wing political groups.

The nature of the source, its content, authorship and the date it was written make it of considerable value to the historian and provides evidence that has considerable weight when writing about the issue of women's rights in the USA in the 1970s. However, not all the issues associated with women's rights in the 1970s are mentioned, and the source is limited to one moment in the early 1970s.

> This concluding paragraph offers an effective summary answer to the question.

### Verdict

This is a strong answer because:

- it interrogates the source and selects and comments about key specific points
- it makes effective use of the background information provided
- it brings in some own knowledge and links this source to other events and issues from the time
- it makes an overall judgement about the value of the source.

# Paper 2: AS Level sample answer with comments

## Section B

These questions assess your understanding of the period in some depth. They will ask you about the content you learned about in the four key themes, but may not ask about more than one theme. For these questions remember to:

- give an analytical, not a descriptive response
- support your points with evidence
- cover the whole time period specified in the question
- come to a substantiated judgement.

*How accurate is it to say that Johnson's Great Society programme (1964–68) transformed US society? (20 marks)*

### Average student answer

It is accurate to say that Johnson's Great Society idea was a success in general but he did have some failures.

One way in which the Great Society brought change to the USA was laws to help the poor and the unemployed. In 1964, President Johnson got the Economic Opportunity Act passed. One of the programmes this created was the Jobs Corps, which aimed to give training to people living in inner-city areas. Johnson also set up Community Action Programmes, which set up work clinics and law centres in poor areas. To help children Johnson created the Headstart programme offering pre-school classes to children from poor families. Finally he created VISTA (Volunteers in Service to America), which was a plan for middle-class people to volunteer on community projects. All these projects and programmes showed that Johnson's Great Society planned to transform the USA and help eradicate poverty.

The Great Society also planned to transform the USA with policies on housing and education. In 1965, Congress passed the Omnibus Housing Act, which aimed to provide cheap housing for poor people and rent aid for those who required it because of low incomes. In addition, the Demonstration Cities and Metropolitan Development Act gave over $1 billion dollars for slum clearance and better housing in urban areas like inner cities. As a former teacher Johnson also hoped that reforms in education would help transform the USA. Education reforms formed an important part of the Great Society. In 1965, he got Congress to pass the Elementary and Secondary Education Act. This Act gave $1 billion dollars to help poor students in public schools. A Higher Education Act, passed in the same year, gave over $600 million dollars for scholarships and low-interest loans to poorer students to help them through university and college courses. Therefore, the Great Society greatly helped poor people in housing and education, which helped transform US society.

This is an example of how not to start an answer. A stronger introduction would propose an overall argument and introduce the many different ways in which the Great Society programme attempted to change US society.

This paragraph considers the Great Society programmes aimed at helping the poor and unemployed. The material produced is accurate and detailed but is used descriptively. There is a reference to the idea of 'transforming' US society but it is not explored in detail. To improve this paragraph the student would need to look at the effects of the Great Society on life for the poor and unemployed.

There is a considerable amount of accurate information in this paragraph, however, this information is used in a narrative-descriptive way. The final sentence attempts to offer a brief judgement connected with the question. The paragraph would be improved by splitting it to deal with housing and education separately. It should also discuss clearly how each individual programme impacted on US society.

The Great Society helped those people who needed healthcare support. Up to the 1960s, US citizens did not receive any healthcare support from the federal government. However, in two acts of Congress Johnson transformed healthcare provision. Under the Medicare programme, federal money was used to support medical treatment for the elderly, and under the Medicaid programme a similar scheme was created to help poor people to receive healthcare. These changes involved the expenditure of vast sums of money: $6.5 billion on extra nurses, new hospitals and medical tests. It brought considerable change to important groups within the USA.

This the strongest paragraph in the answer so far, using accurate and detailed factual information linked to an assessment of the importance of these proposals in terms of transforming US society. It could be improved by adding information about how many people were helped.

However, perhaps the most important reforms of the Great Society period involved civil rights. During the early 1960s, the civil rights movement campaigned for equality for black Americans. President J. F. Kennedy had introduced a Civil Rights bill to Congress to bring about greater equality for black Americans and other ethnic minorities. In 1964, Johnson introduced his own Civil Rights bill, which became law. It gave black Americans protection against legal discrimination and brought legal segregation to an end. The following year Congress passed the Voting Rights Act to remove obstacles that prevented many black Americans from registering to vote. These laws made a huge difference to the position of black Americans in US society.

This is a reasonable paragraph that offers balanced coverage of the topic. Although there is some narrative-description there is also an attempt to offer some analysis. To improve the paragraph the analysis of the results of the Great Society programme should be more detailed.

The Great Society programmes of President Johnson were a genuine attempt to help transform US society. Many of these programmes made changes in US society, helping the poor and unemployed and those living in inner cities. The Great Society also attempted to help poor people through better opportunities in education and in help with medical care. Perhaps the most important changes made by Johnson's Great Society were in civil rights, which helped ethnic minorities and in particular the black American population. Overall the Great Society did help transform the USA.

This concluding paragraph sums up the points covered in the answer, but the conclusion is more of a list than a balanced assessment.

## Verdict

This is an average answer because:

- there is some attempt at explanation but there are also descriptive passages
- the material included is accurate but lacks depth
- there is an attempt to reach an overall judgement, but it is not entirely secure
- the answer is organised around answering the question and the general trend of the argument is reasonably clear. However, a couple of paragraphs, though broadly relevant, could be improved with sharper links to the question overall.

Use the feedback on this answer to rewrite it, making as many improvements as you can.

# Paper 2: AS Level sample answer with comments

## Section B

These questions assess your understanding of the period in some depth. They will ask you about the content you learned about in the four key themes, but may not ask about more than one theme. For these questions remember to:

- give an analytical, not a descriptive response
- support your points with evidence
- cover the whole time period specified in the question
- come to a substantiated judgement.

*How accurate is it to say that Johnson's Great Society programme (1964–68) transformed US society? (20 marks)*

### Strong student answer

The Great Society programme of President Johnson planned to engage in a war on poverty and in doing so transform US society. In the period 1964 to 1968, the Johnson administration put forward and passed a set of proposals that affected a wide range of issues. These included programmes aimed at assisting the poor and unemployed; aid for housebuilding and urban development and improvements in education. Also, for the first time, the federal government engaged in providing direct financial help for the healthcare of the elderly and poor. With reference to ethnic minorities, Johnson's civil rights laws brought considerable change and were a landmark in the history of civil rights in the USA. I believe that Lyndon Johnson embarked on one of the most ambitious programmes to bring about social change in the USA since the end of the Second World War. However, how far these proposals transformed US society is a matter for debate.

This is a strong opening paragraph. It clearly links Johnson's Great Society programme to the idea of transformation in US society. It provides a clear introduction to the programmes most closely associated with the Great Society and ends the paragraph with a rhetorical question that sets up a clear framework for the rest of the answer.

Perhaps the most significant area of the Great Society with a profound impact on US society was in the field of civil rights, one of the most divisive issues in US domestic politics in the early 1960s. In the southern states, black Americans faced legal segregation with separate facilities in public schools, transportation, restaurant facilities and toilets racially divided. Johnson's predecessor, J. F. Kennedy, had introduced a Civil Rights bill to help bring to an end legal discrimination and give black Americans greater equality. The Civil Rights Act of 1964 was a landmark in civil rights and helped transform the lives of black Americans. It outlawed legal discrimination on account of race. The Act also aided other under-represented groups such as women: Schedule VII of the Act outlawed discrimination on account of gender. Another significant development in this field was the Voting Rights Act of 1965, which outlawed discriminatory practices against black Americans in voter registration and elections. Taken together these two Acts most certainly helped transform US society, in particular for the 11% of the population who were black Americans.

This is a well-developed paragraph dealing with a significant set of changes in US society. The paragraph contains accurate and detailed factual information that is used to support and sustain a consistent argument leading to a judgement.

The Great Society also introduced a whole range of initiatives and programmes aimed specifically at helping the poor and offering greater job opportunities for the unemployed. The Economic Opportunity Act of 1965 was the cornerstone of these changes. It established the Office of Economic Opportunity, which was responsible for a range of initiatives. These including establishing VISTA (Volunteers in Service to America), a domestic version of J. F. Kennedy's Peace Corps. In addition, the Jobs Corps aimed to provide the unemployed in inner cities with the skills required to gain employment, and Community Action Programmes aimed to empower local residents in deprived areas to develop community job centres and law clinics. Although billions of dollars were spent on these projects, they had a limited impact on inner-city areas. Unemployment did drop during the Great Society years but this was due more to the

This paragraph continues a coherent and consistent argument about the Great Society and comments on the Great Society's limitations. The argument is balanced and is supported and sustained by the inclusion of accurate information.

overall growth of economic activity rather than the result of specific programmes. Even though laws such as the Demonstration Cities and Metropolitan Development Act and Urban Mass Transportation Act did improve life in several inner-city areas, the problems of unemployment, poverty and crime persisted. At the height of the Great Society, in 1965, serious rioting took place in the Watts District of central Los Angeles. Its causes were varied but included issues of poverty, unemployment, crime and racial discrimination. Between 1965 and 1968, inner-city problems were still serious enough to lead to periodic rioting. So the Great Society's attempt to transform US society in this area achieved limited success.

Two areas where the Great Society had an effect across the whole of US society were the fields of education and healthcare. The Johnson administration introduced two important educational reforms: the Elementary and Secondary Education Act and the Higher Education Act, both passed in 1965. These Acts offered billions of dollars in support for scholarships, schools and facilities to aid the poor and disadvantaged. For the first time, large numbers of children and students in poor and deprived areas had the opportunity to have a decent education and the possibility of going to university and college.

In the field of healthcare the changes brought in by the Great Society were even more significant. For the first time, the federal government offered financial support for healthcare. The Medicare and Medicaid Acts offered help to the elderly and poor respectively and helped transform the lives of these two important social groups. The healthcare reforms continued long after Johnson left office.

These two paragraphs show that the Great Society had a very important impact on US society in both education and healthcare. Sound evidence is used to support a clear argument linked to the issue of transforming US society.

The Great Society had the ambitious aim of bringing change to large areas of US society. It transformed the position of black Americans through landmark legislation in the Civil Rights Act of 1964 and the Voting Rights Act of 1965. In addition, reforms in education and healthcare brought the poor and elderly new opportunities. However, not all Great Society programmes were as significant in terms of change. Johnson's war on poverty was perhaps too ambitious. His programmes were expensive to implement and made only a very limited impact on lives in the poor and deprived areas of inner cities.

This is a strong evaluative conclusion. It notes the key areas of change brought about by the Great Society and offers an overall evaluation of the areas in which it was over-ambitious.

### Verdict

This is a strong answer because:

- the key issues relevant to the question are all explored, and individual Great Society programmes are evaluated in relation to transforming US society
- there is a wide range of accurate material deployed to support the points made
- the argument is well-organised, coherent, logical and persuasive throughout.

# Preparing for your A Level Paper 2 exam

## Advance planning

1. Draw up a timetable for your revision and try to keep to it. Spread your timetable over a number of weeks, and aim to cover four or five topics each week.
2. Spend longer on topics that you have found difficult, and revise them several times.
3. Above all, do not try to limit your revision by attempting to 'question spot'. Try to be confident about all aspects of your Paper 2 work, because this will ensure that you have a choice of questions in Section B.

## Paper 2 overview

| AL Paper 2 | Time: 1 hour 30 minutes | |
|---|---|---|
| Section A | Answer 1 compulsory source question | 20 marks |
| Section B | Answer 1 question from a choice of 2 | 20 marks |
| | Total marks = | 40 marks |

You should familiarise yourself with the layout of the paper by looking at the examples published by Edexcel. The questions for each section are followed by eight pages of lined paper where you should write your answer.

## Section A questions

This question asks you to assess two different types of contemporary sources totalling around 400 words, and will be in the form of 'How far could the historian make use of Sources 1 and 2 together to investigate…?' Your answer should evaluate both sources, considering their nature, origin and purpose, and you should use your own knowledge of the context of the sources to consider their value to the specific investigation. Remember, too, that in assessing their value, you must consider the two sources, taken together, as a set.

## Section B questions

These questions ask you to reach a judgement on an aspect of the topic studied. The questions will have the form, for example, of 'How far…', 'To what extent…' or 'How accurate is it to say…'. The questions can deal with historical concepts such as cause, consequence, change, continuity, similarity, difference and significance. You should consider the issue raised in the question, then other relevant issues, and conclude with an overall judgement.

The timescale of the questions could be as short as a single year or even a single event (an example from Option 2C.2 could be, 'To what extent was Russia's involvement in the First World War responsible for the fall of the Romanovs in 1917?'). The timescale could be longer depending on the historical event or process being examined, but questions are likely to be shorter than the those set for Sections A and B in Paper 1.

## Use of time

This is an issue that you should discuss with your teachers and fellow students, but here are some suggestions for you.

1. Do not write solidly for 45 minutes on each question. For Section A it is essential that you have a clear understanding of the content of each source, the points being made, and the nature, origin and purpose of each source. You might decide to spend up to ten minutes reading the sources and drawing up your plan, and 35 minutes writing your answer.
2. For Section B answers you should spend a few minutes working out what the question is asking you to do, and drawing up a plan of your answer before you begin to write your response.

# Preparing for your A Level exams

## Paper 2: A Level sample answer with comments

### Section A

You will need to read and analyse two sources and use them in tandem to assess how useful they are in investigating an issue. For these questions remember to:

- spend time, up to ten minutes, reading and identifying the arguments and evidence present in the sources; then make a plan to ensure that your response will be rooted in these sources
- use specific references from the sources
- deploy your own knowledge to develop points made in the sources and establish appropriate context
- come to a substantiated judgement.

***Study Source 1 and Source 2 (Chapter 4, pages 361 and 362) before you answer this question.***

*How far could the historian make use of Sources 1 and 2 together to investigate the approach of Republican president Ronald Reagan towards economic policy?*

*Explain your answer using both sources, the information given about them and your knowledge of the historical context. (20 marks)*

#### Average student answer

The first source, Source 1, outlines the views of Ronald Reagan, the Republican president who took office in January 1981. He outlines what he thinks should be the role of the federal government within the US political system. He believed that the federal government's growth had led to a diminution of the role of state governments and unbalanced the role of government in the lives of US citizens. He believed the federal government was intervening too much in ordinary people's lives and should be reduced. He says, 'Government can and must provide opportunity, not smother it; foster productivity, not stifle it. It is no coincidence that our present troubles parallel and are proportionate to the intervention and intrusion in our lives that result from unnecessary and excessive growth of government.' As the head of the Republican administration, in his inaugural speech President Reagan was setting out what he thought ought to be an important part of the aims of his Republican administration. He was alluding to the fact that since the 1930s the federal government had grown in importance under successive Democratic and Republican administrations.

The opening paragraph deals only with one source, Source 1. It mostly offers a description of the content of the source but does also provide some contextual evidence in the last sentence. The answer makes a direct reference to the provenance of the source and the date it was delivered but this is not developed. There is no direct answer to the question.

Source 2 also offers valuable information which could be used by the historian for an investigation about Republican president Ronald Reagan's economic policy. The source was written at the end of Reagan's first term as president and states that the policy of Reagan has been very successful in reducing inflation and encouraging jobs growth. The author, Charles Jacobs, even goes so far as describing the changes Reagan has made in economic policy as 'revolutionary'. Reagan's approach was to reduce the role and size of the federal government. He also reduced taxation, particularly on personal income, so the average worker had more money to spend on goods and services. However, the author does mention that Reagan has not cut all areas of public spending, stating that there was a rise in defence expenditure.

The second paragraph also deals with one source, Source 2. The paragraph contains detailed information about what Reagan did in his first term as president and his achievement in economic policy. The information provided is descriptive rather than analytical. The answer does refer to the date the source was written as a way of assessing its value.

I therefore think that both sources offer valuable evidence to the historian writing about President Reagan's approach to economic policy. Source 2 provides evidence from 1985, at the end of Reagan's first term as president. It is important because it is able to draw on concrete achievements made by Reagan as president. Similarly, Source 1, delivered in January 1981, shows how Ronald Reagan viewed economic policy and the role of the federal government in the economy. Taken together the two sources offer coverage of the period 1981 to 1985. However, they do not offer evidence of Reagan's second term as president from 1985 to 1989, when Reagan faced a major deficit in federal spending due to increases in defence spending and tax cuts.

The final, concluding paragraph attempts to bring the information about the sources together as part of an assessment of the value of both sources to an investigation. There is also a brief assessment of their potential limitation as evidence and an attempt to link the source material to the time parameters of the question. The answer also provides some contextual evidence on the post-1985 period.

## Verdict

This is an average response because:

- it is makes direct reference to both sources and selects relevant material from both to illustrate their key features
- it provides some historical context to explain and support inferences in the sources which expands on material in both sources
- it only makes a limited assessment of the provenance of the sources and does not integrate its coverage of the source material until the final paragraph.

Use the feedback on this answer to rewrite it, making as many improvements as you can.

# Paper 2: A Level sample answer with comments

## Section A

You will need to read and analyse two sources and use them in tandem to assess how useful they are in investigating an issue. For these questions remember to:

- spend time, up to ten minutes, reading and identifying the arguments and evidence present in the sources; then make a plan to ensure that your response will be rooted in these sources
- use specific references from the sources
- deploy your own knowledge to develop points made in the sources and establish appropriate context
- come to a substantiated judgement.

---

***Study Source 1 and Source 2 (Chapter 4, pages 361 and 362) before you answer this question.***

*How far could the historian make use of Sources 1 and 2 together to investigate the approach of Republican president Ronald Reagan towards economic policy?*

*Explain your answer using both sources, the information given about them and your knowledge of the historical context. (20 marks)*

### Strong student answer

The two sources certainly provide very different perspectives on Republican president Ronald Reagan's approach to economic policy. In Source 1, Reagan himself is making his inaugural speech, setting out his aims for his first term as US president. Reagan had just defeated the incumbent president, the Democrat Jimmy Carter, and in his campaign he had promised to follow a completely different economic policy. In an inaugural speech presidents attempt to provide the general focus of what they want to achieve, not specific policies. Reagan concentrates on what he regards as the key issue in reviving the economy: the role of the federal government. He makes it clear that he regards federal government's size and role in 1981 as a barrier to economic growth. Charles Jacobs, the author of Source 2, is an academic at a leading US university. He is writing in an academic journal, 'The Law and Contemporary Problems Journal'. As a result, the language and tone of the source are more technical than Source 1. Jacobs makes specific reference to policies introduced by Reagan and their results. He is able to do so because the source was written in 1985, at the end of Reagan's first term of office as president. He clearly regards the policies introduced by Reagan as significant. He even uses the phrase 'a revolution in political economy' in the title. He outlines the achievements of Reagan in his first term and suggests that the president has made a fundamental change in the way federal government works, including its tax policy.

This strong opening paragraph goes into the background of both sources very thoroughly.

The central features of Republican economic policy under Ronald Reagan were to reduce federal government spending and to reduce taxation. The economic problems that plagued the US economy in the 1970s were, according to Reagan, at least partly due to the bloated size of the federal government, which was paid for through taxes and, in Reagan's opinion, stifled economic growth and business enterprise. He says, 'Government can and must provide opportunity, not smother it; foster productivity, not stifle it.' Reagan clearly feels that a completely new approach to economic policy is required. During his first year in office (1981–82), Reagan reduced substantially federal spending on domestic programmes and cut the rate of tax. This was a major departure from the economic policy of his predecessor, Democrat Jimmy Carter. Professor Charles Jacobs, in Source 2, endorses this approach and is able to provide concrete evidence of its results. He points out, using specific examples, how Reagan has

This paragraph maintains the focus on the question and assesses the value and focus of both sources. The content of both sources is discussed in relation to the provenance. To support the argument the paragraph also draws on historical knowledge.

radically changed the role of the federal government. However, Jacob's view is rather one-sided. He is writing shortly after the end of Reagan's first term, when there had been only limited time to assess the true impact of Reagan's policy changes.

Both sources are written in a style appropriate to their viewpoint and audience. Source 1, by Ronald Reagan, begins with a clear direct reference to what he regards as a major obstacle to economic growth when he states, 'It is my intention to curb the size and influence of the federal establishment and to demand recognition of the distinction between the powers granted to the federal government and those reserved to the states or to the people.' The source is a call to action by his Republican administration. The significance of Reagan's changes is also mentioned in Source 2 by Professor Charles Jacobs.

Both sources are valuable to historians investigating Reagan's approach to economic policy. One is by President Reagan setting out his plans for change. The other is by a university professor assessing the impact of Reagan's changes on the federal government. However, the sources only deal with Reagan's first term in office as president and do not provide any information on Reagan's second term of office from 1985 to 1989.

This final paragraph offers a clear summary of what was mentioned in the previous paragraphs and flows logically on from them. It makes an assessment of the value of both sources and finds links between them. It also offers a judgement on the focus and potential bias of the sources in an assessment of their value and weight for an investigation into Reagan's approach to economic policy.

## Verdict

This is a strong answer because:

- it is rooted in the sources and identifies and illustrates their key features
- it deploys a sound range of background knowledge to support the points and provide some context
- it maintains focus and develops a clear and balanced argument.

# Paper 2: A Level sample answer with comments

## Section B

These questions assess your understanding of the period in some depth. They will ask you about the content you learned about in the four key themes, but may not ask about more than one theme. For these questions remember to:

- give an analytical, not a descriptive, response
- support your points with evidence
- cover the whole time period specified in the question
- come to a substantiated judgement.

*To what extent was growth in the ownership and use of cars the most important feature of the US economy and society in the years 1955 to 1963? (20 marks)*

### Average student answer

In many ways, the US economy grew considerably in the years 1955 to 1963. America had the largest economy in the world. It also had the largest car manufacturing industry in the world. Detroit was seen as the centre of car manufacturing and was the headquarters of the three largest car manufacturers: General Motors, Ford and Chrysler. These companies produced hundreds of thousands of cars per year. The vast majority of these cars were sold inside the USA, so car ownership was important and the USA became the world's first car-based economy.

The majority of the opening paragraph is descriptive and makes a very basic attempt to place the issue in historical context. It is linked to the question but does not address it directly. The introduction would be much improved if it looked at other features of the US economy and society and then compared the significance of these with the 'ownership and use of cars', not just the manufacturing industry.

It could be said that the car industry helped drive economic growth in the USA in the year 1955 to 1963. By 1963, the majority of homes possessed at least one car and the car was the most desirable consumer product in the USA. Car production required large amounts of steel, rubber for tyres, electrics and plastics. Therefore, the ownership of cars helped the growth of a whole range of important industries across the USA. The use of cars meant that other industries developed to cater for the car user, including petrol stations, car maintenance companies, drive-in cinemas, drive-in takeaway restaurants and big shopping centres, which were usually built on the edge of towns and cities. Also, to meet the needs of car users thousands of miles of roads had to be built. This helped the growth of the construction industry. Many construction firms were employed building the huge interstate highway network that came about following the passage of the National Interstate and Defense Highways Act of 1956. By 1963, a whole new national network of motorways was in the process of construction and this helped the US economy.

The second paragraph deals directly with the impact of the ownership and use of cars on the US economy and to a much lesser extent the impact on US society. The information is detailed and accurate at times, but is mostly narrative-descriptive and does not directly answer the question. This paragraph would be improved by being split in two, one dealing with the impact of the car on the economy and another with its impact on US society.

Another important development in the USA in the years 1955 to 1963 was the growth of suburbs. These were areas on the edge of towns and cities where new housing developments took place. Perhaps one of the most important developments in bringing about suburbs was the growth of affordable housing, provided by companies such as Levitt, which built suburbs in the north-east USA called Levittowns. The building of affordable housing meant that people could move out of crowded inner-city areas. Levitt houses had modern domestic appliances, a yard and garage. To get to the suburbs the owners of these new houses usually had to use cars as public transport was limited.

The third paragraph highlights the importance of the growth of suburbs. However, the link to the question is weak as cars are only brought in in the final sentence. Again the answer would be much improved if it tackled the impact of car ownership on the economic and social aspects of the suburbs in separate paragraphs.

The US economy and society were also greatly affected by other developments such as the growth of new industries like aeronautics and electrical appliances. Cars were an important consumer product, but so were dishwashers, televisions, refrigerators and record players. The USA went through a consumer boom in the years 1955 to 1963 and the ownership and use of cars was only one part of the changes in the US economy and US society.

This paragraph includes accurate information and for the first time suggests that car ownership was not the only significant feature of the US economy and US society at this time. There is a limited attempt to assess the importance of car ownership against these other developments. The whole answer could be improved by mentioning the other developments earlier and comparing them against the importance of car ownership throughout.

Therefore, the ownership and use of cars had a very significant impact on the US economy and society in the years 1955 to 1963. Cars helped to transform where people lived and helped drive economic growth.

The conclusion is brief and repeats points made above. A stronger conclusion would draw together all the individual points made in the answer to give a final answer to the question.

### Verdict

This is an average answer because:

- it mainly consists of narrative-description rather than attempting any analysis
- the knowledge deployed is adequate and deals directly with the importance of car ownership but makes little attempt to assess this against other important developments in the economy and society
- there is an attempt to reach a judgement, but it is limited in its range and needs more supporting material.

Use the feedback on this answer to rewrite it, making as many improvements as you can.

# Paper 2: A Level sample answer with comments

## Section B

These questions assess your understanding of the period in some depth. They will ask you about the content you learned about in the four key themes, but may not ask about more than one theme. For these questions remember to:

- give an analytical, not a descriptive, response
- support your points with evidence
- cover the whole time period specified in the question
- come to a substantiated judgement.

*To what extent was growth in the ownership and use of cars the most important feature of the US economy and society in the years 1955 to 1963? (20 marks)*

### Strong student answer

The years 1955 to 1963 witnessed considerable change in the US economy. In 1955, the US economy was the largest in the world and the US was the world's first consumer society. The Gross National Product of the USA, the main economic indicator of the size of the US economy, grew by around 25% in the period 1955 to 1963. Major changes took place in the nature and size of US cities and new domestic appliances became more readily available as the average personal income rose. By 1963, all major US cities and towns had expanded and created large suburban areas. These developments took place as the US economy was transformed from one primarily based on agriculture and manufacturing to one that included an important and growing service sector. These substantial changes were brought about by a variety of factors, but how far was this economic change due to the ownership and use of cars?

This is a strong start to the answer. The candidate places the assertion within the context of major changes that took place in the US economy in the years 1955 to 1963. It is focused, covers the period mentioned in the question, and poses a rhetorical question in the last sentence that will offer the opportunity for balanced analysis within the rest of the answer.

Clearly the ownership and use of cars were significant features of the US economy in the years 1955 to 1963. In 1956, there were 56 million cars and trucks on the roads of the USA. By 1960, 75% of Americans owned at least one car and a further 15% owned more than one per family. The US car industry was a key driving force behind the US economy. One in seven of all manufacturing workers was employed in the car industry. The USA's biggest company was General Motors. The car manufacturing industry was backed by hundreds of thousands of jobs in car sales and maintenance. Demand for cars was a major stimulus to the steel and electrics industries. The demand for petrol fuelled the growth of the oil industry. In many ways the engine that drove the US economy in the years 1955 to 1963 was the demand for cars. Cars became the most significant method of transport and were seen as an indispensable consumer item for the majority of American families. By 1963, the USA was a 'car-based culture'.

Linked to the ownership and use of cars came the growth in highway construction. In 1956, Congress passed the National Interstate and Defense Highways Act. This was the most ambitious and significant highway construction programme in US history. In a ten-year programme Congress allocated $25 billion for a national network of four- to eight-lane motorways that would stretch 42,000 miles. The Act was a major boost to the construction and engineering industries and was a major feature of the growth of the US economy in the year 1955 to 1963. The passage of the Act was primarily due to the rise in the ownership and use of cars. The Act also aimed to provide the most effective way of evacuating large urban areas in case of nuclear wars, and the plan to use highways for this purpose reflected the importance of the use of cars in US society.

These two paragraphs are linked directly to the question asked and offer a clear assessment of the impact of the ownership and use of cars on the US economy in the years 1955 to 1963. They make specific reference to the impact of the car industry on the US economy. They also assess the impact of highway construction on US economic development and how this was linked to the ownership and use of cars. These assessments are supported and sustained by detailed information about the period.

Another key feature of the US economy in the years 1955 to 1963 was the growth of suburbia. By 1963, millions of Americans had either moved out of inner cities into suburbs or from country areas into suburbs. The development of these areas was inconceivable without cars. Cars allowed Americans to work in cities and commute home to live in suburbs. But the ownership and use of cars also created a new car-based society in suburban areas. A social development that began in the USA was the drive-in movie theatre, where people could watch films from within their own cars. By the early 1960s, over 3,000 existed across the country. Other car-based retail outlets were also created such as drive-in fast food restaurants. Out-of-town shopping malls were created with large car parks. These retail facilities were designed to exploit the rise in the ownership and use of cars. The widespread availability of cars coupled with the growing affluence of American youth also fuelled the growth of teenage culture. Rock'n'roll went hand in hand with the acquisition of roadster cars. Therefore, much of American urban and suburban society was based on the car, making it a key feature of the US economy and society in the years 1955 to 1963.

This paragraph links the ownership and use of cars to another important feature of the US economy and society: the growth of suburbia. The approach is clear and analytical approach and detailed, accurate historical evidence is used to support and sustain a coherent argument.

However, although the ownership and use of cars was an important feature in the US economy and society in the years 1955 to 1963, there were other very important developments. For instance, as suburbs grew the inner cities lost their middle-class populations. As a result, many inner cities became areas of deprivation, crime and unemployment. Within the inner cities ghettos developed of ethnic minorities, notably black Americans and Hispanic Americans. While much of white America experienced a rise in living standards and greater personal wealth during this period, by 1963 cities such as Philadelphia and Washington DC had whole areas in their inner cities dominated by black Americans living in poverty.

This paragraph offers a balanced approach to the question by identifying another important feature of the US economy and society in the year 1955 to 1963 and highlights the fact that not all Americans benefited from car ownership.

Another important feature of the US economy and society was the increasing availability of credit. Mail-order firms such as Sears Roebuck and new credit card providers helped sustain the boom in the US economy. With easily available credit, US consumers could also purchase new domestic technologies including refrigerators, dishwashers, radios, and televisions. The ownership and use of cars was merely one of a series of important features of the USA's consumer society in the years 1955 to 1963.

This paragraph sustains focus on the question by placing the ownership and use of cars within the wider historical perspective of the growth of a consumer society.

In conclusion, the ownership and use of cars reflected the growing affluence of the US economy and society in the year 1955 to 1963. It would be inconceivable to imagine the need for extensive highway construction and the growth of suburbia without the availability of the car. In addition, car production was a key sector within the US economy and helped drive the economic growth of the USA and changes within US society. However, not all Americans benefited from increased ownership and use of cars. Poor inner-city and rural areas did not experience the same degree of affluence as the rest of the USA. Although the ownership and use of cars was important, even in those areas, it didn't have the same dramatic impact.

A strong answer to this question must consider benefits and costs, and weigh these up before reaching a judgement. This is a good answer; however, there is a slight over-emphasis on the ownership and use of cars to the detriment of discussing other features of the US economy and society, for example the growth in white-collar jobs and service industries, which are mentioned briefly in the introduction.

## Verdict

This is a strong answer because:

- it puts both sides of the case, looking at the importance of the ownership and use of cars against other factors and features of the US economy and society
- it uses a wide range of evidence to support the points made
- it reaches a secure concluding judgement
- it is well organised and communication of material is clear and precise.

# Index

# Acknowledgements


The authors and publisher would like to thank the following individuals and organisations for permission to reproduce photographs and text in this book.

### Photographs

(Key: b-bottom; c-centre; l-left; r-right; t-top)

**Alamy Images:** Brian Harris 124, Jeff Morgan 130, Keystone Pictures USA 84, National Geographic Image Collection 6, The Guardian 101, Trinity Mirror/Mirrorpix 135; **British Cartoon Archive, University of Kent www.cartoons.ac.uk:** John Jensen 72; **Corbis:** Bettmann 169r, 185, 230, 253, 292, 296, 307, 329, 334, 348, 355, 363, Chris Hoffmann 371, ClassicStock 229, ClassicStock/H. Armstrong Roberts 343, Flip Schulke 313, Gary Leonard 359, 379, Henry Diltz 311, 317, Hulton-Deutsch Collection 82; **Daily Express:** 58; **Getty Images:** Express/McCarthy 43, Jimmy Sime 64, Popperfoto 94, The National Archives/SSPL 109; **Image courtesy of The Advertising Archives:** 111, 119; **Mirrorpix:** 41, Trinity Mirror 27; **People's History Museum:** 15; **Press Association Images:** AP/Peter Kemp 22; **Punch Cartoon Library:** 48; **TopFoto:** 169l, 171, 193, 214, 216, 246, ITAR-TASS 286, 301, The Granger Collection 166, 183, 197, 202, 215, 224, 243, 259, 284

**Cover images:** *Front:* **Getty Images:** Peter Skingley/AFP

All other images © Pearson Education

### Figures

Figures 1.2, 1.3, 1.5, 1.7, 1.8 from *The Longman Handbook to Modern British History 1714--2001*, 4th ed. by Chris Cook and John Stevenson, Routledge, 2001, pp. 96ff, 97, 98, 99, 100ff, Copyright © 2001, reproduced by permission of Taylor & Francis Books UK; Figures pp. 24, 26 from Joe Hicks and Grahame Allen, *A Century of Change: Trends in UK Statistics Since 1900*, House of Commons Library Research Paper 99/111 http://www.parliament.uk/briefing-papers/RP99-111/a-century-of-change-trends-in-uk-statistics-since-1900 © Parliamentary Copyright, Contains Parliamentary information licensed under the Open Parliament Licence v3.0; Figure 2.1 from *The Health Services Since the War, II, Government and Health Care, The British National Health Service 1958-1979* by C. Webster, The Stationery Office, 1996, p. 786, Contains public sector information licensed under the Open Government Licence (OGL) v3.0.http://www.nationalarchives.gov.uk/doc/open-government-licence; Figure 2.2 from *The National Health Service, A Political History* by C. Webster, Oxford University Press, 1998, Fig.2, p. 21, reproduced with permission from the author.

### Tables

Tables 'Source 8' p. 31, 'Source 9' p. 31, pp. 55, 56 from *The Longman Handbook to Modern British History 1714-2001*, 4th ed. by Chris Cook and John Stevenson, Routledge, 2001, pp. 223, 203, 161, 160, Copyright © 2001, reproduced by permission of Taylor & Francis Books UK; Tables pp. 32, 94, 100 from *Britain 1914-2000* edited by D. Murphy, Collins Educational, 2000, pp. 334, 350, 360, reprinted by permission of HarperCollins Publishers Ltd. © 2000 D. Murphy; Table p. 50 from *On the State of the Public Health, Annual Reports of the Chief Medical Officer 1967* by George Godber, Table p. 78 based on data from Office for National Statistics, Table p. 83 from *The Ethnic Minority Populations of Britain*, Vol. 2, Ethnicity in the 1991 Census edited by C. Peach, HMSO, 1996, p. 8, Table p. 97 from *Social Trends* 40, ONS, 2010, p. 7 ,www.statistics.gov.uk/socialtrends, Contains public sector information licensed under the Open Government Licence (OGL) v3.0.http://www.nationalarchives.gov.uk/doc/open-government-licence; Table p. 74 based on data from *Women in Britain 1900-2000* by A. Mayer, Hodder & Stoughton, 2002, p. 39; Table p.89 from *The Inter-War Economy: Britain 1919-1939* by D.H. Aldcroft, Batsford, 1973, pp. 352, 364, reproduced with kind permission of B. T. Batsford, part of Pavilion Books Company Limited; Table p. 108 from *Tourism Geography* by S.W. Williams, Routledge, 2002, p. 33 , Copyright © 2002 Routledge, reproduced by permission of Taylor & Francis Books UK; Table p. 191 from *The Longman Companion to America in the Era of the Two World Wars 1910-1945* by Patrick Renshaw, Routledge, 1996, pp.137-139, Copyright © 1996 Routledge, reproduced by permission of Taylor & Francis Books UK; Table p. 289 from 'The consumer society' [% of families owning cars/TVs/fridges/washing machines 1948-55] from *Postwar Economic Trends in the United States* edited by Ralph Freeman, Copyright © 1960 by Massachusetts Institute of Technology. Reprinted by permission of HarperCollins Publishers.

### Text

Quote p. 12 from *The Downfall of the Liberal Party 1914-1935* by T. Wilson, Collins/Cornell University Press, 1966, p. 18; Extract p. 27 from 'Mr Butskell's Dilemma' by Norman Macrae in *The Economist*, 13/02/1954, reproduced with permission; Extract p. 30 from *The Riches Beneath Our Feet: How Mining Shaped Britain* by Geoff Coyle, Oxford University Press, 2010, p. 208 © Geoff Coyle 2010, By permission of Oxford University Press; Extract p. 32 from *Women's Two Roles: Home and Work* by A. Myrdal and V. Klein, Psychology Press, 2003, p. 143, Copyright © 2003 Psychology Press, reproduced by permission of Taylor & Francis Books UK; Extract p. 36 from *The War Cabinet Report for the Year 1917*, HMSO, 1918 , Quote p. 47 from *The Beveridge Report*, November 1942, HMSO CMND 6404, Extract p. 56 from Circular 10/65, Department of Education and Science, HMSO, 1965, Extract p. 57 from *Children and their Primary Schools*, HMSO, 1967, Quote p. 114 from https://www.gov.uk/government/news/death-of-former-prime-minister-lady-thatcher, Contains public sector information licensed under the Open Government Licence (OGL) v3.0.http://www.nationalarchives.gov.uk/doc/open-government-licence; Quote p. 38 from A. J. P. Taylor from *English History 1914-45* by A.J.P. Taylor, Oxford University Press, 1965, p.148, reproduced with permission; Quote p. 38 from Derek Fraser from *The Evolution of the British Welfare State*, 4th ed. by D. Fraser, Palgrave Macmillan, 2009, p. 216, reproduced with permission of Palgrave Macmillan; Quote p. 39 from 'Housing and Town Planning 1900-1939' by Helen Meller in *A Companion to Early Twentieth Century Britain* edited by C. Wrigley, Blackwell Publishing, 2003, p. 399, Copyright ©

2003 by Blackwell Publishers Ltd., republished with permission of John Wiley & Sons, permission conveyed through Copyright Clearance Center, Inc.; Extract 'Source 4' p. 43 from 'This is Your Choice' by Margaret Thatcher in *Signpost Magazine*, 1/09/1959, Copyright © Estate of Lady Thatcher, reproduced with permission from www.margaretthatcher.org, the website of the Margaret Thatcher Foundation; Extract 'Source 5' p. 43 from 'Poverty, Socialism and Labour in Power' by P. Townsend in *Fabian Tract*, Issue 371, p. 28, 1967, Fabian Society, reproduced with permission; Extract p.44 from *Poverty, Social Policy and Welfare* by Mark Walsh, Paul Stephens and Stephen Moore, Stanley Thornes (Publishers) Ltd. , 2000, p. 49, reproduced with permission from the author; Extract p. 52 from 'Health and Healthcare' by Ray Fitzpatrick et al. in *Britain Since 1945* edited by Jonathan Hollowell, Blackwell, 2003, pp. 332-347, reproduced with permission of Blackwell Publishers in the format republish in a book via Copyright Clearance Center; Extract 'Source 2' p. 66 from The Classic Slum by Robert Roberts , Penguin, 1971, p. 199 (Pelican Books 1978, Penguin Books 1991), Copyright © Robert Roberts 1971, reproduced with permission from Penguin Books Ltd.; Extract 'Source 3' p. 66 from *The Road to Wigan Pier* by George Orwell, Victor Gollancz 1937, Martin Secker & Warburg 1959, Penguin Books 1962, 1989, Penguin Classics 2001. Copyright 1937 by Eric Blair. This edition copyright © the Estate of the late Sonia Brownwell Orwell, 1986, Copyright © George Orwell, 1937, Reprinted by permission of Bill Hamilton as the Literary Executor of the Estate of the Late Sonia Brownell Orwell, Copyright © 1997 by the Estate of Sonia B. Orwell. Reprinted by permission of Houghton Mifflin Harcourt Publishing Company. All rights reserved; Extract p. 67 from *Classes and Cultures: England 1918-51* by Ross McKibbin , Oxford University Press, 1998, p. 531 © Ross McKibbin 1998, By permission of Oxford University Press; Extract 'Source 4' p. 68 from *Married Love* by Marie Stopes, Oxford University Press, 2009, 9ff, © The Galton Institute, London; Extract p. 70 from 'Moral Reform and the Law' *Sunday Times*, 28/03/1954, © News UK, reproduced with permission; Extract p. 71 from interview with Margaret Thatcher in *Finchley Press* 02/01/1970, quote p. 71 from Thatcher Archive, CCOPR 883/77 Hosted at http://www.margaretthatcher.org/document/103268, Copyright © Estate of Lady Thatcher, reproduced with permission from www.margaretthatcher.org, the website of the Margaret Thatcher Foundation; Quote from Desmond Morris p. 72 from *The Illustrated Naked Ape* by Desmond Morris, Jonathan Cape, 1986, p. 126, reproduced by permission of The Random House Group Ltd.; Quote p. 72 from *Puzzled People* reproduced with permission of Curtis Brown Group Ltd, London on behalf of The Trustees of the Mass Observation Archive; Extract p.79 from *Making Sense of Television: The Psychology of Audience Interpretation* by Sonia M. Livingstone, Routledge, 1998, p. 63, Copyright © 1998 Routledge, reproduced by permission of Taylor & Francis Books UK; Extract p. 85 from 'Race Relations' by Shamit Saggar in *Britain Since 1945* edited by Jonathan Hollowell, Blackwell, 2003, pp. 326-327, reproduced with permission of Blackwell Publishers in the format republish in a book via Copyright Clearance Center; Quote p. 89 from *The Great War and the British People* by Jay Winter, Harvard University Press, 1985, p.4, reproduced with permission of Palgrave Macmillan; Quote p. 93 from *The Age of Extremes: A History of the World, 1914–1991* by E. Hobsbawm, Vintage, 1996, p.6; Extract p. 89 from 'Consumption and Consumer Behaviour' by Sue Bowden in *A Companion to Early Twentieth-Century Britain* edited by C. Wrigly, Blackwell, 2003, p. 364 © 2003 by Blackwell Publishers Ltd., Extract p.90 from *Twopence to Cross the Mersey* by Helen Forrester, HarperCollins, 1993, p. 20, reprinted by permission of HarperCollins Publishers Ltd. © 1974 Helen Forrester, © Jamunadevi Bhatia 1974, reproduced by permission of Sheil Land Associates Ltd.; Extract 2 p. 92 from 'Great Britain, 1939-45' by Arthur Marwick in *The Twentieth Century* XIV edited by A.J.P. Taylor and J.M. Roberts, Purnell, 1979, p. 1910, reprinted by permission of Peters, Fraser & Dunlop (www.petersfraserdunlop.com) on behalf of The Estate of Arthur Marwick, PFD aka Peters Fraser & Dunlop; Extract 3 p. 92 from *Austerity Britain 1945-51* by David Kynaston, Bloomsbury, 2007, p. 19, Copyright © David Kynaston 2007, with permission from Bloomsbury Publishing Plc; Extract p. 93 from 'Consumption' by James Obelkevich in *Understanding Post-war British Society* edited by Peter Catterall and James Obelkevich, Routledge, 1994, p. 152, Copyright © Routledge, reproduced by permission of Taylor & Francis Books UK; Quote p. 98 from 'Broadcasting and National Unity' in *Impacts and Influences: Media Power in the Twentieth Century* edited by J Curran, A Smith, P Wingate, Routledge, 2013, p. 157ff, Copyright © 2013 Routledge, reproduced by permission of Taylor & Francis Books UK; Extract p. 100 from *Walking in the Shade* by Doris Lessing, Flamingo, 1997, p. 16, reprinted by permission of HarperCollins Publishers Ltd. and Jonathan Clowes Ltd. © Doris Lessing 1997; Quotes p. 102 from *A Companion to Contemporary Britain: 1939-2000* edited by P. Addison and H. Jones, Wiley-Blackwell, 2008, p.129 © 2008 by Blackwell Publishing Ltd.; Extract p. 106 from 'Television and the Transformation of Sport' by Garry Whannel in *Annals of the American Academy of Political and Social Science*, Vol. 625 (1), pp. 205-218, 2009, copyright © 2009 by American Academy of Political and Social Science, reprinted by permission of SAGE Publications; Quote p. 107 from *Modern Britain A Social History 1750-1985* by Edward Royle, Arnold, 1988, p. 265 © Edward Royale 1988, Bloomsbury Academic, an imprint of Bloomsbury Publishing Plc; Extract p. 108 from *British Tourism* by Victor Middleton, Elsevier, 2005, p. 71, Copyright © 2005, reproduced by permission of Taylor & Francis Books UK; Quote p. 108 from *England's Hour* by Vera Brittain, Continuum Publishing, 2005, p. 71, Copyright © Vera Brittain 2005, By permission of Bloomsbury Publishing Plc; Quote p. 112 from *After the Victorians: The World Our Parents Knew* by A.N. Wilson, Hutchinson, 2012, p. 41, reproduced by permission of The Random House Group Ltd. and Farrar, Straus and Giroux; Quote p. 117 from Interview with M. Thatcher, aired 8 June1987, http://www.margaretthatcher.org/document/106647, quotes from M. Thatcher pp. 119, 123, 132 Copyright © Estate of Lady Thatcher, reproduced with permission from www.margaretthatcher.org, the website of the Margaret Thatcher Foundation; Quote p. 119 from http://www.conservative-party.net/manifestos/1987/1987-conservative-manifesto.shtml, reproduced with permission; Extract1 p. 121 and Quote p. 123 from *Finding a Role? Britain 1970-1990* by Brian Harrison, Oxford University Press, 2011, p. 165, By permission of Oxford University Press; Extract 2 p. 121 from 'How the Miners' Strike of 1984-85 Changed Britain Forever' by Donald Macintyre, *New Statesman*, 16/06/2014, first published in *The New Statesman*, reproduced with permission; Extract p. 122 from *Britain Under Thatcher* by Anthony Seldon and Daniel Collings, Routledge, 1999, pp. 93-94, Copyright © 1999 Routledge, reproduced by permission of Taylor & Francis Books UK; Extract 4 p. 126 from *Thatcher & Sons- a Revolution in Three Acts* by Simon Jenkins, Penguin, 2006, p.110, Copyright © Simon Jenkins, 2006, 2007, reproduced with permission from Penguin Books Ltd. and Ed Victor Literary Agency; Extract 5 p. 126 from *The Anatomy of Thatcherism* by Shirley Letwin, 1993, p.310, republished with permission of Transaction Publishers, permission conveyed through Copyright Clearance Center, Inc; Extract p. 129 from 'A Farewell to Alms: Thatcherism's Legacy of Inequality' by Pete Dorey, *British Politics*, Vol. 10, 2015, http://www.palgrave-journals.com/bp/index.html, reprinted by permission from Macmillan Publishers Ltd:, Copyright © 2015, published by Palgrave Macmillan; Extract 7 p. 131 from *Mastering Modern British History* by Norman Lowe, Palgrave, 2009, p. 747, reproduced with permission of Palgrave Macmillan; Extract 8 p. 131 from 'Margaret Thatcher: The Woman Who Made Britain Great Again', *The Daily Telegraph* 08/04/2013 (Telegraph View), copyright © Telegraph Media Group Limited; Quotes pp. 132-133 from http://www.margaretthatcher.org/document/103674 Copyright Estate of Lady Thatcher. Reproduced with permission from www.margaretthatcher.org, the website of the Margaret

Thatcher Foundation; Extract p. 135 from Clause IV of 1918 *Labour Party Constitution* by S. Webb, 1918 , reproduced by permission of The Labour Party; Extract 9 p. 137 from 'Margaret Thatcher and Thatcherism: Dead But Not Buried' by B. Jessop, *British Politics*, Vol. 10, pp. 16-30, 2015, reprinted by permission from Macmillan Publishers Ltd. Copyright © 2015, published by Palgrave Macmillan; Extract 10 p. 137 from 'A New Look at New Labour' by D. Rubinstein, *Politics*, Vol. 20 (3), pp.161-167, 2000, Copyright © Political Studies Association, reproduced with permission from John Wiley & Sons; Extract p. 176 from *Anxious Decades: America in Prosperity and Depression 1920-1941* by Michael Parrish, W.W. Norton, 1994, p.226, Copyright © 1992 by Michael E. Parrish. http://www.amazon.co.uk/Anxious-Decades-Prosperity-Depression-1920-1941/dp/0393311341 Used by permission of W.W. Norton & Company, Inc.; Extract p.180 from 'The Shape of Fear' by W. E. B. Du Bois in *The North American Review*, June 1926, reproduced with permission; Extract p. 184 from *Essays on Art, Race, Politics and World Affairs* (Collected Works of Langston Hughes), Vol. 9 by Langston Hughes, University of Missouri Press, 2002, reproduced with permission; Extract p. 191 adapted from *A Choice of Weapons* by Gordon Parks, Harper & Row, 1966, Copyright © 1965, 1966 by Gordon Parks. Copyright renewed 1994 by Gordon Parks. Reprinted by permission of HarperCollins Publishers; Extract p. 195 from To Louis L. Emmerson, Herbert Hoover, Washington, D.C., 10 July 1931, Courtesy of The Gilder Lehrman Institute of American History, GLC03146, reproduced with permission; Extract p. 196 from *The Presidency of Herbert C. Hoover* by M. F. Fausold, University Press of Kansas, 1985, p. 237, reproduced with permission; Article p. 217 from 'Women in Politics' by E. Roosevelt, *Good Housekeeping*, April 1940, reproduced with permission; Extract p. 220 adapted from 'Segregation' by W. E. B. Du Bois in *Crisis*, 41, January 1934, We wish to thank the Crisis Publishing Co., Inc., the publisher of the magazine of the National Association for the Advancement of Colored People, for the use of this material first published in the January 1934 issue of *Crisis*; Interview p. 225 adapted from Navajo Code Talkers - Peter MacDonald Interview, http://navajocodetalkers.org/peter-macdonald-real-code-talker-interview/ [Interview conducted by Winona University's Oral History Project 23 May 2013; posted online by Navajo Code Talkers Association 7 April 2014; accessed 28 July 2015], with kind permission from Winona University Oral History Project; Extract p. 226 from 'The Courier's Double 'V' For a Double Victory Campaign Gets Country-Wide Support' in *The Pittsburgh Courier* 14/02/1942, reproduced with permission from Pittsburgh Courier Archives; Extract p. 227 from 'Constructing the "People's Music", The Federal Music Project, Nationalism and the New Deal, 1935-1939' by J. A. Gronbeck-Tedesco in *NeoAmericanist*, 1.1, Fall/Winter 2005/06, reproduced with permission; Extract p. 229 from *The Unfinished Journey: America Since World War II* by William H. Chafe, Oxford University Press, 1994, pp.4-5, By permission of Oxford University Press, USA; Extract p. 232 from 'We were Determined to Stay' by Celia Sapersteen Yanish, from the film The Life and Times of Rosie the Riveter, available at www.clarityfilms.org/rosie, reproduced with permission; Article p. 245 from 'How Not to Get Investigated, Ten Commandments for Government Employees' by Thurman Arnold in *Harper's Magazine*, November 1948, Copyright © 1948 Harper's Magazine. All Rights Reserved. Reproduced from the November issue by special permission; Extract p. 253 from *Blacks and White TV: African Americans in Television Since 1948* by J. Fred MacDonald , MacDonald and Associates, 2009, reproduced with permission; Extract p. 254 adapted from *A Cycle of Outrage: America's Reaction to the Juvenile Delinquent in The 1950s* by James Burkhart Gilbert, Oxford University Press, 1986, p.105, By permission of Oxford University Press, USA; Extract p.260 from NAACP in The Atlanta Declaration, 19/05/1954, Harry Ransom Center wishes to thank The National Association for the Advancement of Colored People, for authorizing the use of the excerpt from 'The Atlanta Declaration'; Extract p. 292 from *Daytime to Primetime: The History of American Television Programs* by James Roman, Greenwood Press, 2005, pp. 102-103, republished with permission of Greenwood Press, permission conveyed through Copyright Clearance Center, Inc.; Extract 2 p. 294 from *The Seventh Stream, The Emergence of Rocknroll in American Popular Music* by P. H. Ennis, Wesleyan University Press, 1992, republished with permission of Wesleyan University Press, permission conveyed through Copyright Clearance Center, Inc.; P. 294 'Source 5' From 'Elvis Presley: Tomorrow Night On Television–"The Lord Don't Play Favorites"' by Jack Gould, *New York Times* (1923-Current file) [New York, N.Y.], 16 September 1956, X13, © 1956 The New York Times. All rights reserved. Used by permission and protected by the Copyright Laws of the United States. The printing, copying, redistribution, or retransmission of this Content without express written permission is prohibited; Extract p. 298 from Code of City of Montgomery, Alabama, Charlottesville: Michie City Publishing Company 1952 in the Alabama Dept of Archives and History, Montgomery, Alabama, File Q58427, www.archives.state.Ala.us/teacher/Rights/lesson1/doc1.html Alabama Department of Archives and History, Montgomery, Alabama; Extract p. 306 from *The Peace Corps Volunteer Newsletter*, December 1961, Vol.1 (2), www.peacecorps.gov, Courtesy of the Peace Corps; Extract p. 313 from 'What We Want' by Stokely Carmichael, reproduced with permission from David Grossman Literary Agency Ltd. on behalf of Frances Goldin Literary Agency and the Kwame Ture Foundation; Extract p. 316 from Tom Hayden, 'Two, Three, Many Columbias' in *Ramparts*, 15 June 1968, reproduced with permission from the author; Quote p. 318 from *The Feminine Mystique* by Betty Friedan, W.W. Norton, 1963, p. 425 © Betty Friedan, 1963, reproduced with permission from Orion Publishing Group and W.W. Norton Inc.; Extract p. 318 from *The Redstockings Manifesto*, issued in New York City on 7 July 1969. It first appeared as a mimeographed flyer, designed for distribution at women's liberation events. Further information about the Manifesto and other materials from the 1960's rebirth years of feminism is available from the Redstockings Women's Liberation Archives for Action at www.redstockings.org or PO Box 744 Stuyvesant Station, New York, NY 10009; Extract p. 330 from '4 Kent State Students Killed by Troops: 8 Hurt as Shooting Follows Reported Sniping at Rally 4 Kent State Students, 2 of Them Girls, Killed by Guardsmen' by John Kifner, special to The New York Times, *New York Times* (1923-Current file) [New York, N.Y] 5 May 1970, p. 1© 1970 The New York Times. All rights reserved. Used by permission and protected by the Copyright Laws of the United States. The printing, copying, redistribution, or retransmission of this Content without express written permission is prohibited; Extract p. 350 *From Daytime to Primetime* by James Roman, Greenwood Press, 2005, p. 264, republished with permission of Greenwood Press; permission conveyed through Copyright Clearance Center, Inc.; Extract p. 354 from Harvey Milk speech, GLC 35, Harvey Milk Archives--Scott Smith Collection, San Francisco Public Library, reproduced with permission; Extract p. 362 from 'Reaganomics: The Revolution in American Political Economy' by Charles Jacobs in *Law and Contemporary Problems Journal*, Vol.48 (4), pp. 7-30, Autumn 1985, http://scholarship.law.duke.edu, reproduced with permission; Extract p. 373 from 'MTV 30 Years On' by Andy Greene, *Rolling Stone Magazine*, Copyright © Rolling Stone LLC 2011. All Rights Reserved. Used by Permission; Extract p. 378 from Pamphlet from Committee to Elect Harold Washington as Mayor of the City of Chicago, Courtesy of Harold Washington Collection of Papers [Manuscript] 1980, 1982-83, Box 14, Folder 4, Chicago History Museum, reproduced with permission.

In some instances we have been unable to trace the owners of copyright material, and we would appreciate any information that would enable us to do so.